MEI
Innovators in Mathematics Education

CW01271730

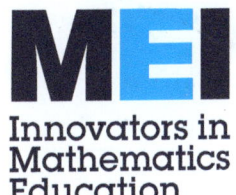

Jean-Paul Muscat

Series editors
Roger Porkess and
Catherine Berry

A LEVEL FURTHER MATHEMATICS

Mechanics

4th Edition

An OCR endorsed textbook

OCR
Oxford Cambridge and RSA

integral

HODDER EDUCATION
LEARN MORE

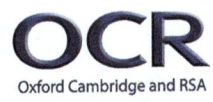

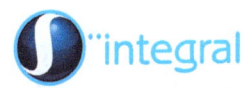

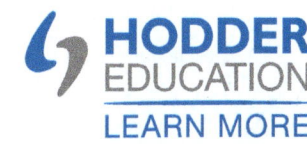

This resource is endorsed by OCR for use with specification H635 OCR AS Level Further Mathematics B (MEI) and with specification H645 OCR A Level Further Mathematics B (MEI). In order to gain OCR endorsement, this resource has undergone an independent quality check. Any references to assessment and/or assessment preparation are the publisher's interpretation of the specification requirements and are not endorsed by OCR. OCR recommends that a range of teaching and learning resources are used in preparing learners for assessment. OCR has not paid for the production of this resource, nor does OCR receive any royalties from its sale. For more information about the endorsement process, please visit the OCR website, www.ocr.org.uk.

Hachette UK's policy is to use papers that are natural, renewable and recyclable products and made from wood grown in well-managed forests and other controlled sources. The logging and manufacturing processes are expected to conform to the environmental regulations of the country of origin.

Orders: please contact Hachette UK Distribution, Hely Hutchinson Centre, Milton Road, Didcot, Oxfordshire, OX11 7HH. Telephone: +44 (0)1235 827827. Email education@hachette.co.uk Lines are open from 9 a.m. to 5 p.m., Monday to Friday. You can also order through our website: www.hoddereducation.co.uk

ISBN: 978 1 4718 5303 6

© Sophie Goldie, Val Hanrahan, Jean-Paul Muscat, Roger Porkess, Susan Whitehouse and MEI 2017

First published in 2017 by

Hodder Education,
An Hachette UK Company
Carmelite House
50 Victoria Embankment
London EC4Y 0DZ

www.hoddereducation.co.uk

Impression number 10 9 8 7 6

Year 2022

All rights reserved. Apart from any use permitted under UK copyright law, no part of this publication may be reproduced or transmitted in any form or by any means, electronic or mechanical, including photocopying and recording, or held within any information storage and retrieval system, without permission in writing from the publisher or under licence from the Copyright Licensing Agency Limited. Further details of such licences (for reprographic reproduction) may be obtained from the Copyright Licensing Agency Limited, www.cla.co.uk

Cover photo © Korovin/iStock/Thinkstock/Getty Images

Typeset in Bembo Std, 11/13 pts. by Aptara®, Inc.

Printed by CPI Group (UK) Ltd, Croydon CR0 4YY

A catalogue record for this title is available from the British Library.

Contents

Getting the most from this book ... v

1 Kinematics ... 1
1.1 The language of motion in one dimension ... 2
1.2 The constant acceleration formulae ... 11
1.3 Variable acceleration ... 17

2 Forces and motion ... 25
2.1 Forces and Newton's laws of motion ... 26
2.2 Working with vectors ... 34
2.3 Forces in equilibrium ... 42
2.4 Finding resultant forces ... 50

3 A model for friction ... 58
3.1 A model for friction ... 59

4 Moments of forces ... 70
4.1 Introduction to moments ... 71
4.2 The moment of a force which acts at an angle ... 83
4.3 Sliding and toppling ... 93

5 Work, energy and power ... 100
5.1 Energy and momentum ... 101
5.2 Gravitational potential energy ... 109
5.3 Power ... 118

6 Impulse and momentum ... 126
6.1 Impulse ... 127
6.2 Conservation of momentum ... 131
6.3 Newton's experimental law ... 138

7 Centre of mass 1 ... 147
7.1 The centre of mass ... 148
7.2 Centre of mass of two- and three-dimensional bodies ... 153

8 Dimensional analysis ... 166
8.1 The dimensions of further quantities ... 168

Practice questions: Set 1 ... 181

9 Motion under a variable force ... 185
9.1 Motion in more than one dimension ... 186
9.2 The equation of a path ... 195
9.3 Path of a projectile ... 199
9.4 Projecting on a uniform slope ... 207
9.5 Motion under variable acceleration ... 214

10 Circular motion ... 226
10.1 Introduction to circular motion ... 227
10.2 Circular motion with constant speed ... 231
10.3 Circular motion with variable speed ... 245

11 Hooke's law ... 267
11.1 Strings and springs ... 268
11.2 Using Hooke's law with more than one spring or string ... 274
11.3 Work and energy ... 282
11.4 Vertical motion involving elastic forces ... 288

12 Modelling oscillations ... 297
12.1 Oscillating motion ... 298
12.2 Simple harmonic motion as a function of time ... 304
12.3 Alternative forms of the equation for SHM ... 312
12.4 Oscillating mechanical systems ... 326

13 Centre of mass 2 ... 341
13.1 Calculating volumes ... 342
13.2 Centres of mass ... 350
13.3 Centres of mass of plane regions ... 361

14 Oblique impact 372

14.1 Impulse and momentum in more than one dimension 373

14.2 Oblique impact of smooth elastic spheres 381

Practice questions: Set 2 389

Answers 392

Index 419

Getting the most from this book

Mathematics is not only a beautiful and exciting subject in its own right but also one that underpins many other branches of learning. It is consequently fundamental to our national wellbeing.

This book covers the Mechanics elements in the MEI AS and A Level Further Mathematics specifications. Students start these courses at a variety of stages. Some embark on AS Further Mathematics in Year 12, straight after GCSE, taking it alongside AS Mathematics, and so have no prior experience of Mechanics. In contrast, others only begin Further Mathematics when they have completed the full A Level Mathematics and so have already met the Mechanics covered in *MEI A Level Mathematics (Year 2)*. Between these two extremes are the many who have covered the Mechanics in AS Mathematics but no more.

This book has been written with all these users in mind. So, it provides a complete course in Mechanics up to the required level. Those who already know some Mechanics will find some revision material in the early chapters.

In the MEI specification, two Mechanics papers are available at AS level, both set at AS standard and both counting for one-third of the AS qualification. Chapters 1 to 8 of this textbook cover the content of Y411 Mechanics a. Chapters 9 to 14 cover the content of Y415 Mechanics b.

At A Level there are two Mechanics papers available, both set at A Level standard. Chapters 1 to 8 of this textbook cover the content of Y431 Mechanics Minor, which counts for one-sixth of the A Level qualification. Chapters 1 to 14 (the whole book) cover the content of Y421 Mechanics Major which counts for one-third of the A Level qualification.

Between 2014 and 2016 A Level Mathematics and Further Mathematics were very substantially revised, for first teaching in 2017. Changes that particularly affect Mechanics include increased emphasis on

- Problem solving
- Mathematical rigour
- Use of ICT
- Modelling.

This book embraces these ideas. A large number of exercise questions involve elements of problem solving and require rigorous logical argument. Mechanics often provides descriptions of real world situations that make them tractable to calculations, and so modelling is key to this branch of mathematics. It pervades the whole of this book.

Throughout the book the emphasis is on understanding and interpretation rather than mere routine calculations, but the various exercises do nonetheless provide plenty of scope for practising basic techniques. The exercise questions are split into three bands. Band 1 questions (indicated by a green bar) are designed to reinforce basic understanding; Band 2 questions (yellow bar) are broadly typical of what might be expected in an examination; Band 3 questions (red bar) explore around the topic and some of them are rather more demanding. In addition, extensive online support, including further questions, is available by subscription to MEI's Integral website, http://integralmaths.org.

In addition to the exercise questions, there are two sets of Practice questions. The first of these covers Chapters 1 to 8 and the second the whole book. These include identified questions requiring problem solving (PS), mathematical proof (MP), use of ICT (T) and modelling (M).

There are places where the work depends on knowledge from earlier in the book or elsewhere and this is flagged up in the Prior knowledge boxes. This should be seen as an invitation to those who have problems with the particular topic to revisit it. At the end of each chapter there is a list of key points covered as well as a summary of the new knowledge (learning outcomes) that readers should have gained.

Those using this book will need a working knowledge of pure mathematics including calculus and trigonometry. So, for example, differentiation and integration are used in kinematics, radians in circular motion and the compound angle formulae in simple harmonic motion.

Two common features of the book are Activities and Discussion points. These serve rather different purposes. The Activities are designed to help readers get into the thought processes of the new work that they are about to meet; having done an Activity, what follows will seem much easier. The Discussion points invite readers to talk about particular points with their fellow students and their teacher and so enhance their understanding. Another feature is a Caution icon ❗, highlighting points where it is easy to go wrong.

Answers to all exercise questions and practice questions are provided at the back of the book, and also online at www.hoddereducation.co.uk/MEIFurtherMathsMechanics

This is a 4th edition MEI textbook so much of the material is well tried and tested. However, as a consequence of the changes to A Level requirements in Further Mathematics, large parts of the book are either new material or have been very substantially rewritten.

Catherine Berry
Roger Porkess

Prior knowledge

No prior knowledge of mechanics is needed for this book. It does however assume that the reader is reasonably fluent in basic algebra and graphs: working with formulae and expressions; solving linear and quadratic equations and inequalities; changing the subject of a formula; working with parametric equations; using logarithms and exponentials.

Basic trigonometry is used throughout, including the identity $\sin^2\theta + \cos^2\theta = 1$. Pythagoras theorem is used to find the resultant of two vectors. A working knowledge of calculus is also required. In the first half of the book polynomial functions are integrated and differentiated with respect to time; calculus is used to find turning points and second derivatives are sometimes used. From Chapter 9 onwards, more advanced calculus is required, including the chain rule and differential equations with separable variables.

- **Chapter 1 Kinematics** introduces the basic ideas and vocabulary associated with motion. It requires basic algebra and calculus.
- **Chapter 2 Forces and motion** introduces Newton's laws of motion. This involves forces and equilibrium. Vectors are introduced and they require the use of elementary trigonometry.
- **Chapter 3 A model for friction** builds on Chapters 1 and 2; the algebra includes inequalities.
- **Chapter 4 Moments of forces** builds on the earlier Chapters, particularly the forces from Chapter 2. There is further use of trigonometry.
- **Chapter 5 Work, energy and power** introduces new concepts based on ideas in Chapters 1 and 2. Algebra is used throughout.
- **Chapter 6 Impulse and momentum** broadens the work in Chapter 5.
- **Chapter 7 Centre of mass 1** extends the use of moments in Chapter 4, and of vectors in Chapter 2. No calculus is used in this chapter; cases that require its use are covered in Chapter 13.
- **Chapter 8 Dimensional analysis** covers the dimensions and units for the quantities that have been introduced in all the early chapters.
- **Chapter 9 Motion under a variable force extends** the use of vectors from Chapter 2 and of variable acceleration from Chapter 1. The calculus required is now more sophisticated and with it comes an increasing demand on algebraic competence.
- **Chapter 10 Circular motion** extends the ideas of variable acceleration, forces and vectors from Chapters 1 and 2. Fluency in basic trigonometry is expected.
- **Chapter 11 Hooke's law** builds on the concepts of force from Chapter 2, work and energy from Chapter 5 and variable acceleration from Chapter 9.
- **Chapter 12 Modelling oscillations** places work in Chapter 12 of *MEI Further Mathematics A Level Year 2 (Core)* in context. It extends some of the ideas covered in Chapters 9 and 10.
- **Chapter 13 Centre of mass 2** extends the work in Chapter 7 to cover shapes requiring the use of calculus to find their centres of mass.
- **Chapter 14 Oblique impact** extends the ideas introduced in Chapter 6 to cases where the impact is not necessarily along the line of motion.

Acknowledgements

The Publishers would like to thank the following for permission to reproduce copyright material.

Practice questions have been provided by David Holland (MEI) (pp. 181–184 and pp. 389–391).

Photo credits

p.1 © goce risteski – Fotolia; **p.25** © bolina – 123RF; **p.58** © andreigilbert – 123RF; **p.70** © Matjoe – Shutterstock; **p.73 (top)** © Evan-Amos – Wikipedia Commons (Public Domain); **p.73 (bottom)** © ConstantinosZ – Shutterstock; **p.79** © MarVil – Shutterstock; **p.93** © Photo courtesy of Millbrook Proving Ground Ltd; **p.100 (top)** © kasiastock – Fotolia.com; **p.100 (bottom)** © All Canada Photos / Alamy Stock Photo; **p.118** © Steve Mann – Fotolia; **p.126** © Blend Images / Alamy Stock PhotoJGI/ Tom Grill; **p.147** © huaxiadragon – Fotolia; **p.166** © Image Source/Alamy Stock Photo; **p.185** © StockTrek/Photodisc/Getty Images/ Science, Technology & Medicine 2 54; **p.226 (left)** © styleuneed – Fotolia; **p.226 (centre)** © Nicholas Piccillo – Fotolia; **p.226 (right)** © NickR – Fotolia; **p.236** © Rick Rudnicki – Getty Images; **p.255** © Colin Anderson – Getty Images; **p.267 (left)** © elina – Shutterstock; **p.267 (centre)** © ChameleonsEye – Shutterstock; **p.267 (right)** © ArtemZ – Shutterstock; **p.279** © Nick Kennedy / Alamy Stock Photo; **p.283 (top)** © Aggie 11 – Shutterstock; **p.283 (bottom)** © Matthew Ashmore / Alamy Stock Photo; **p.297 (left)** © Pavel Vakhrushev – Shutterstock; **p.297 (centre)** © Antonio Gravante – Shutterstock; **p.297 (right)** © Andrii Muzyka – Shutterstock; **p.323** © Mikio Oba – Shutterstock; **p.341 (left)** © Brandon Bourdages – Shutterstock; **p.341 (centre)** © Zoonar GmbH / Alamy Stock Photo; **p.341 (right)** © BasPhoto – Shutterstock; **p.342** © André Karwath aka Aka (https://creativecommons.org/licenses/by-sa/2.5/deed.en); **p.347** © Robert Gendler/ Visuals Unlimited, Inc. via Getty Images; **p.348** © spacekirs – Fotolia; **p.349** © Alex Yeung – Fotolia; **p.350** © domnitsky – Shutterstock; **p.372** © barfisch via Wikipedia Commons https://creativecommons.org/licenses/by-sa/3.0/(https://en.wikipedia.org/wiki/Rules_of_snooker#/media/File:Snooker_Freeball.png).

Every effort has been made to trace all copyright holders, but if any have been inadvertently overlooked, the Publishers will be pleased to make the necessary arrangements at the first opportunity.

Although every effort has been made to ensure that website addresses are correct at time of going to press, Hodder Education cannot be held responsible for the content of any website mentioned in this book. It is sometimes possible to relocate a web page by typing in the address of the home page for a website in the URL window of your browser.

1 Kinematics

The journey of a thousand miles begins with a single step.
Lao Tzu

Discussion point
Describe the motion of the person in this photograph.

1 The language of motion in one dimension

Think of throwing a marble straight up in the air so that it reaches a height of 1.25 m above your hand, before it falls back to the ground 1 m below your hand. The marble moves as it does because of the gravitational pull of the Earth. It is moving vertically up then down. The vertical direction is along the line towards, or away from, the centre of the Earth.

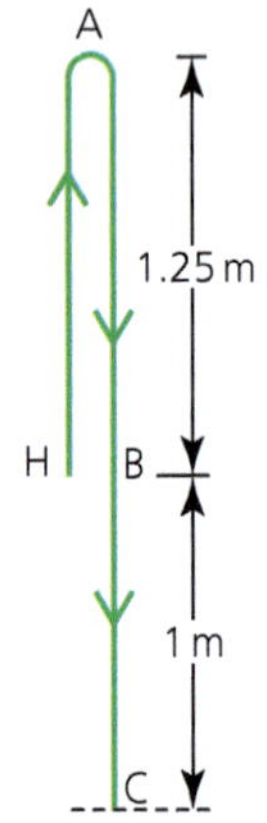

A quantity which has only size, or magnitude, is called a **scalar**. One which has both magnitude and direction is called a **vector**.

- The total **distance travelled** by the marble at any time does not depend on its direction, so it is a scalar quantity. The distance it travels before hitting the ground is 1.25 + 1.25 + 1 = 3.5 m.
- The **position** of the marble is its distance above a fixed origin, for example, the place where it first left your hand. At the top, the position is +1.25 m. When it hits the ground the position is −1 m. Position is a vector quantity.
- A position always refers to a fixed origin but a **displacement** can be measured from any position. When the marble reaches the ground, its displacement is −1 m relative to your hand but −2.25 m relative to the top. Displacement is also a vector.

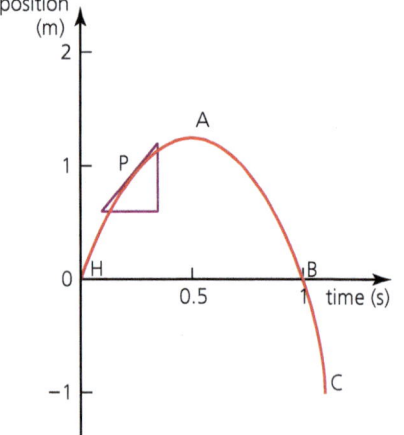

Figure 1.1

Figure 1.1 is a diagram showing the direction of motion of the marble and relevant distances. The direction of motion is indicated by an arrow. Figure 1.2 is a graph showing the position above the level of your hand against the time.

- **Speed** is a scalar quantity and does not involve direction.
- **Velocity** is the vector related to speed; its magnitude is the speed but it also has a direction. The velocity of an object is the rate at which the position changes.

When a position–time graph is curved, as in Figure 1.2, the velocity changes with time. At any instant the velocity is given by the gradient of the tangent to the curve at that point.

Figure 1.2

This means that the velocity, v, can be written as

$$v = \frac{ds}{dt}$$

where s is the position.

Figure 1.3 shows the velocity–time graph for the marble.

- At the point A, the velocity and gradient of the position–time graph are zero. The marble is instantaneously at rest.
- The velocity at H is positive because the marble is moving upwards.
- The velocities at B and C are negative because the marble is moving downwards.
- **Acceleration** is the rate at which the velocity changes. It is a vector quantity and can take different signs in a similar way to velocity.
- The equivalent scalar quantity is **magnitude of acceleration**.

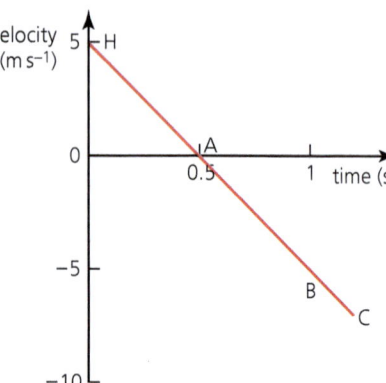

Figure 1.3

This means that acceleration, a, can be written as $a = \frac{dv}{dt}$

Acceleration is given by the gradient of a velocity–time graph.

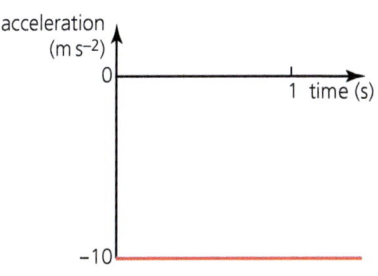

Figure 1.4

The gradient of the line in Figure 1.3 is constant because the line is straight and it is negative because the line is sloping downwards. Using the first 0.5 seconds, its value is found to be

$$\frac{0-5}{0.5-0} = -10.$$

So the acceleration–time graph is as shown in Figure 1.4.

Notation and units

As with most mathematics, you will see in this book that certain letters are commonly used to denote certain quantities. This makes things easier to follow. These are the letters commonly used for motion in one direction:

- s, h, r, x, y and z for position
- t for time measured from a starting instant
- u and v for velocity
- a for acceleration.

Vector quantities are usually printed in bold, for example, **r**, **u**, **v** and **a**, particularly when this work is extended to 2 and 3 dimensions.

The S.I. (Système International d'Unités) unit for **distance** is the metre (m), for **time** is the second (s) and for **mass** is the kilogram (kg). Other units follow from these, so speed is measured in metres per second, written $m\,s^{-1}$.

> **Note**
> You will recognise −10 as an approximation to g, the acceleration due to gravity.

> When an object is slowing down it is often said to be decelerating. Retardation is another word for deceleration.

Next steps

The next example uses and extends the ideas developed so far.

Example 1.1

Tara has a letter to post on her way to college. The post box is 800 m east of her house and the college is 3.2 km to the west. The road is at a slight incline from west to east. Tara cycles at a steady speed of $5\,m\,s^{-1}$ while travelling east to the post box. She takes 40 s at the post box to find her letter and post it. She then cycles at a steady $12.5\,m\,s^{-1}$ while travelling west to college.

(i) Draw a diagram to illustrate Tara's journey to college.

(ii) Find the total distance Tara travels and the time she takes.

(iii) Draw (a) position–time (b) velocity–time (c) distance–time (d) speed–time graphs to illustrate her journey.

(iv) Explain why an acceleration–time graph would not be very interesting.

Solution

(i)

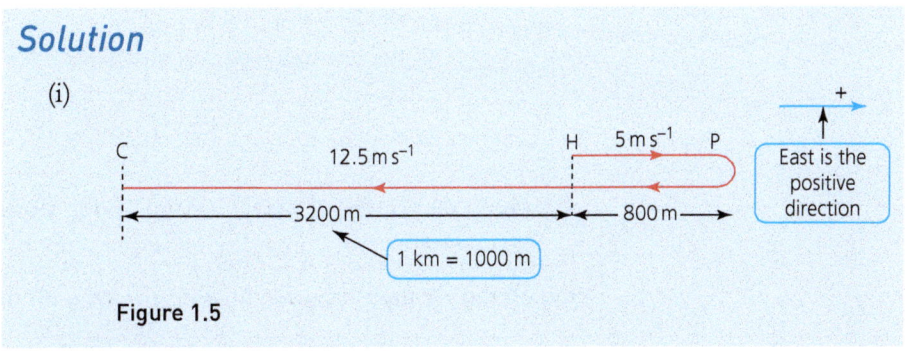

Figure 1.5

The language of motion in one dimension

(ii) The distances and times for the three parts of Tara's journey are:

	Distance	Time
Home to post box	800 m	$\frac{800}{5} = 160$ s
At post box	0 m	40 s
Post box to college	4000 m	$\frac{4000}{12.5} = 320$ s
Total	4800 m	520 s

(iii)

(a) position–time 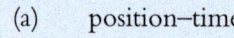 (b) velocity–time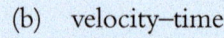

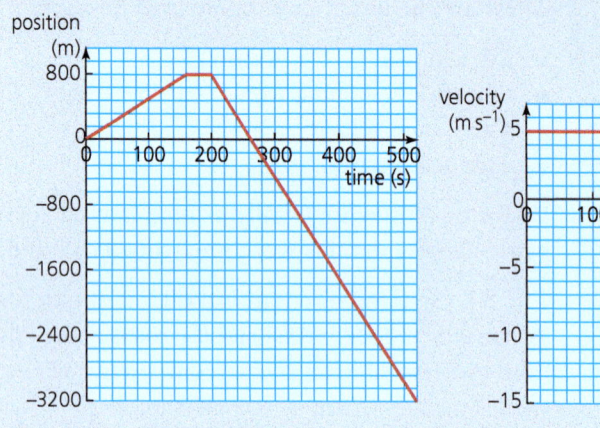

Figure 1.6 Figure 1.7

(c) distance–time (d) speed–time

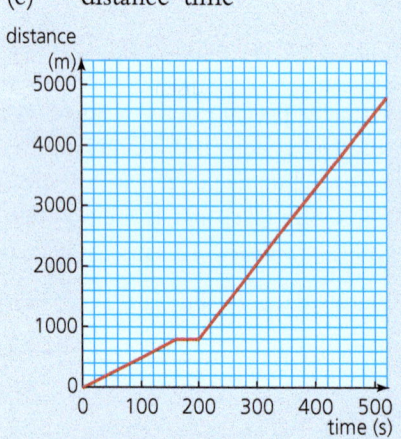 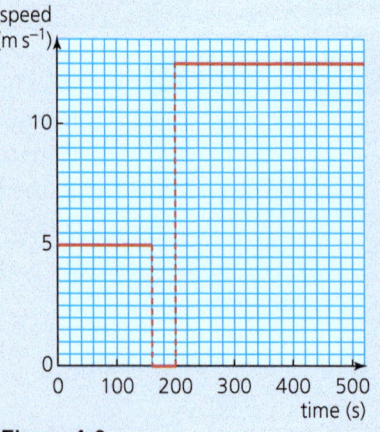

Figure 1.8 Figure 1.9

> **Note**
>
> The distance–time graph of Tara's journey differs from the position–time graph as it shows how far she travels irrespective of her direction. There are no negative values.
>
> The gradient of the distance–time graph represents Tara's speed rather than her velocity so it too has no negative values.

(iv) Tara travels at a steady speed for both parts of her journey so, apart from the short time when she gets up speed, her acceleration is zero. It is also zero when she is posting the letter. So the acceleration–time graph would be almost entirely along the horizontal axis.

Average speed and average velocity

In real world situations it is often the case that you are interested in average values. For example, even on a 'good run' you do not maintain a steady speed

> **Note**
> Notice that the average used here is not the same as that commonly used when finding the mean of a set of numbers. This is not a situation where you add all the numbers together and divide by how many they are.

> In the calculations, the units and direction are included at an early stage for clarity. It is quite usual to leave them out until the final answer.

when driving on the motorway. Instead you are often slowing down and speeding up because of the other traffic.

The definitions of average speed and average velocity are

$$\text{average speed} = \frac{\text{total distance travelled}}{\text{total time taken}}$$

$$\text{average velocity} = \frac{\text{displacement}}{\text{time taken}}$$

In the previous example,

- Tara's average speed is $\frac{\text{total distance travelled}}{\text{time taken}} = \frac{4800 \text{ m}}{520 \text{ s}} = 9.23 \text{ m s}^{-1}$

- Her average velocity is $\frac{\text{displacement}}{\text{time taken}} = \frac{3200 \text{ m west}}{520 \text{ s}} = 6.15 \text{ m s}^{-1}$ west (or -6.15 m s^{-1})

Changing units of speed

Quite often speeds are expressed in terms of km h^{-1} (kilometres per hour). To convert to m s^{-1} you need to multiply by 1000 (1 km = 1000 m) and divide by 3600 (1 hour = 60 × 60 = 3600 s). Or, in other words, you need to divide by 3.6. Conversely, to convert from m s^{-1} to km h^{-1}, you need to multiply by 3.6.

Tara's average speed is thus $9.23 \times 3.6 = 33.23 \text{ km h}^{-1}$. This may also be found from the calculation

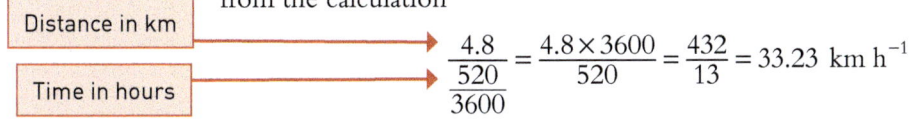

[Distance in km] [Time in hours]

$$\frac{4.8}{\frac{520}{3600}} = \frac{4.8 \times 3600}{520} = \frac{432}{13} = 33.23 \text{ km h}^{-1}$$

Tara's average velocity is $-6.15 \times 3.6 = -22.15 \text{ km h}^{-1}$ which may also be found from the calculation

[Displacement in km] [Time in hours]

$$\frac{-3.2}{\frac{520}{3600}} = \frac{-3.2 \times 90}{13} = \frac{-288}{13} = -22.15 \text{ km h}^{-1}$$

> More strictly, the area under the graph is the area of the region bounded by the lines, or curves, and the horizontal time axis.

Using areas to find distances and displacements

Speed–time and velocity–time graphs give you a lot of information. You have already seen that, as well as the actual values on the graph, the gradient gives you the acceleration. But it doesn't end there. In addition, the area under the graph represents the distance travelled (in the case of a speed–time graph) or the displacement (for a velocity–time graph).

> **Note**
> Since the area under a curve can be found by integration, it follows that $s = \int v \, dt$ and $v = \int a \, dt$

Similarly, the area under an acceleration–time graph represents the change in speed or velocity.

The next two examples illustrate these points.

The language of motion in one dimension

Example 1.2

Tom is cycling home. He turns onto the main road, which is straight, at $5\,\text{m s}^{-1}$ and accelerates uniformly to $8\,\text{m s}^{-1}$ over the next $6\,\text{s}$. He maintains this speed for 20 seconds and then slows down uniformly for 4 seconds to stop outside his home.

(i) Draw a velocity–time graph for Tom's journey and use it to find how far Tom cycles.

(ii) Draw an acceleration–time graph. Explain the significance of the area between this and the time axis.

> **Note**
>
> Many speed–time and velocity–time graphs consists of straight-line sections. The area can easily be found by splitting them up into triangles, rectangles or trapezia.

Solution

(i)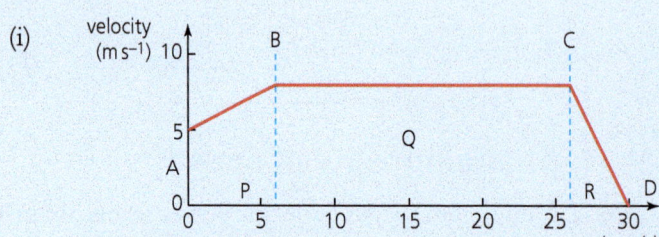

Figure 1.10

The area is split into three regions.

P trapezium: area $= \frac{1}{2}(5+8)\times 6 = 39$ m

Q rectangle: area $= 8\times 20 = 160$ m

R triangle: area $= \frac{1}{2}\times 8\times 4 = 16$ m

total area $= 215$ m

So Tom cycles $215\,\text{m}$.

(ii) The acceleration–time graph is shown in Figure 1.11.

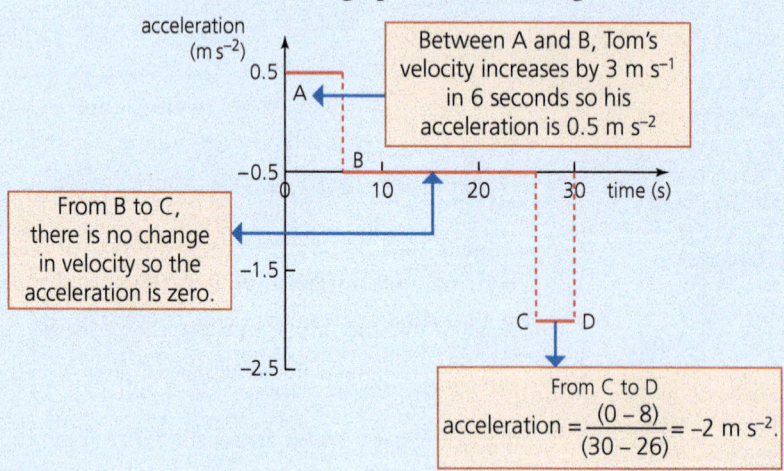

Figure 1.11

From C to D Tom is slowing down while still moving in the positive direction towards home.

The area between the graph and the time axis is
$0.5\times 6 + 0\times 20 + (-2)\times 4 = -5$.

So Tom's velocity decreases by $5\,\text{m s}^{-1}$, from an initial speed of $5\,\text{m s}^{-1}$ to being stationary.

Example 1.3

A car is moving between two sets of traffic lights 1500 m apart on a straight road. Starting from rest at the first traffic light, it accelerates uniformly to a maximum speed, which it maintains for 2 minutes before decelerating uniformly until it stops at the second traffic light. The whole journey takes 2.5 minutes. Find the maximum speed.

Solution

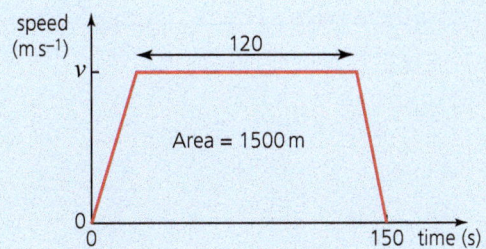

Figure 1.12

The sketch of the speed–time graph of the journey shows the given information, with suitable units. The maximum speed is $v\,\text{m s}^{-1}$.

The area is $\frac{1}{2}(120+150) \times v = 1500$

$$v = \frac{1500}{135} = 11.\dot{1}$$

The maximum speed is $11\,\text{m s}^{-1}$ (to 2 s.f.).

Information given algebraically

So far the information about the motion of an object has been given either in words or in a diagram. However, sometimes you will be given it in algebraic form, as in the next example.

Example 1.4

The position of a particle moving along a straight line is given by $x = t^2 - 8t + 12$ for $0 \leq t \leq 9$ where x is the displacement from a fixed point O in metres and t is the time in seconds.

(i) At what times is the particle at O?

(ii) Draw the position–time graph of the particle for $0 \leq t \leq 9$

(iii) Give the displacement and the distance travelled between $t = 1$ and $t = 9$.

(iv) Give the average velocity and the average speed between $t = 1$ and $t = 9$.

Solution

(i) When the particle is at O, $x = 0$

$\Rightarrow t^2 - 8t + 12 = 0$

$(t-2)(t-6) = 0$

$t = 2$ or $t = 6$

The particle is at the origin at 2 seconds and 6 seconds.

The language of motion in one dimension

(ii)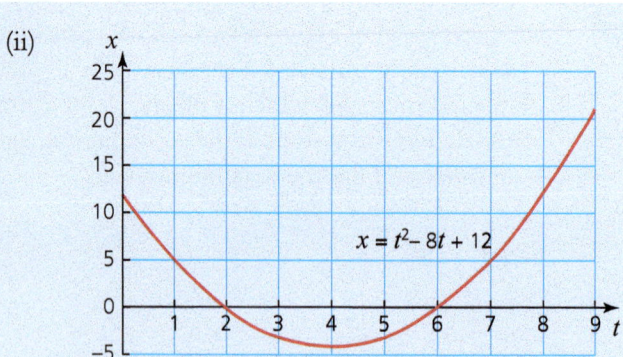

Figure 1.13

(iii) When $t = 1$, $x = 1^2 - 8 \times 1 + 12 = 5$

When $t = 9$, $x = 9^2 - 8 \times 9 + 12 = 21$

The displacement from $t = 1$ to $t = 9$ is $21 - 5 = 16$ m.

When $t = 4$, $x = 4^2 - 8 \times 4 + 12 = -4$

> As you can see from the graph, the particle is at its most negative at time 4 seconds.

From $t = 1$ to $t = 4$ the displacement is $-4 - 5 = -9$; distance travelled $= +9$

From $t = 4$ to $t = 9$ the displacement is $21 - (-4) = 25$; distance travelled $= +25$

Total distance travelled is $9 + 25 = 34$ m

(iv) Average velocity $= \dfrac{\text{displacement}}{\text{time taken}} = \dfrac{16 \text{ m}}{8 \text{ s}} = 2 \text{ m s}^{-1}$

> The time taken is $9 - 1 = 8$ seconds

Average speed $= \dfrac{\text{distance travelled}}{\text{time taken}} = \dfrac{34 \text{ m}}{8 \text{ s}} = 4.25 \text{ m s}^{-1}$

Exercise 1.1

① For the following position–time graphs, calculate the total overall displacement and the total distance travelled.

(i)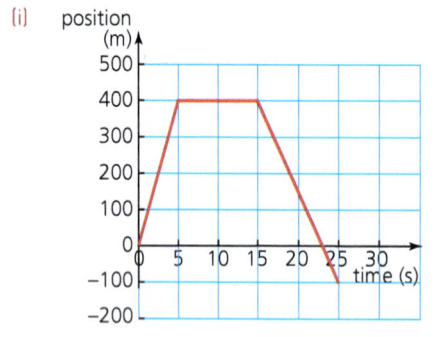

Figure 1.14

(ii)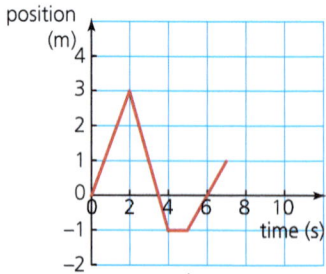

Figure 1.15

② For the following position–time graphs, find
   (i) the initial and final positions
   (ii) the total displacement
   (iii) the total distance travelled

(iv) the velocity and speed for each part of the journey

(v) the average velocity for the whole journey

(vi) the average speed for the whole journey.

(a)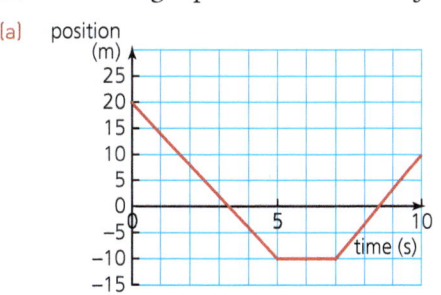

(b)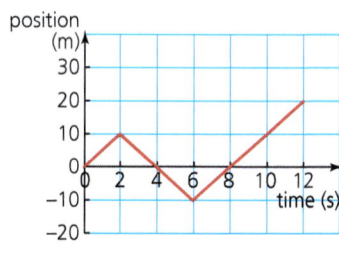

Figure 1.16

Figure 1.17

③ The position of a particle moving along a straight line is $x = 3t^2 - 14t + 11$ where x is in metres and t is in seconds with $0 < t < 5$.

(i) At what time is the particle at O?

(ii) When is the particle furthest from its starting point?

(iii) How far has the particle travelled in the first 5 seconds?

④ A ball is thrown straight up in the air so that its position x m at time t s is given by $x = 2 + 12t - 5t^2$.

(i) Sketch a position–time graph for $0 \leq t \leq 2.5$.

(ii) From what height is the ball thrown?

(iii) Find the ball's displacement relative to its starting position after 2.5 s.

(iv) At what time is the highest point reached and how high does the ball go?

(v) What is the total distance travelled in the 2.5 s?

⑤ A car travels 50 km from A to B at an average speed of 80 km h⁻¹. It stops at B for 30 minutes and then returns to A travelling at an average speed of 60 km h⁻¹.

(i) Find the total time taken for the whole journey.

(ii) Find the average speed for the whole journey.

(iii) Find the car's average velocity.

⑥ The speed of light is 3×10^8 m s⁻¹. The average distance from the Sun to the Earth is 1.5×10^8 km. How long does it take light from the Sun to reach the Earth?

⑦ A cyclist rides uphill a distance of 2.5 km at an average speed of 4.5 m s⁻¹ and returns downhill on the same course with an average speed of 14 m s⁻¹. Find the average speed for the whole trip.

⑧ The velocity–time graph shows the motion of a particle along a straight line.

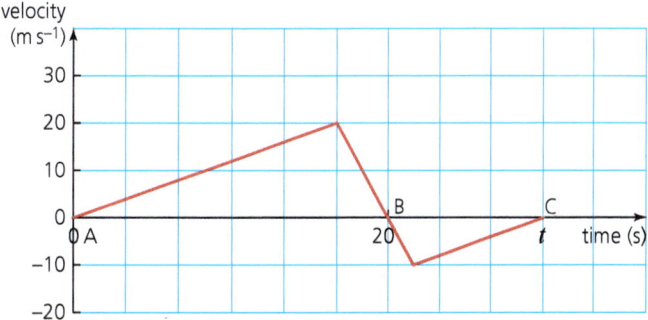

Figure 1.18

(i) The particle starts at A at $t = 0$ and moves to B in the next 20 s. Find the distance AB.

(ii) At a time, T seconds, after leaving A the particle is at C, a distance 50 m from B. Find T.

(iii) Find the displacement of C from A.

⑨ The distance between Victoria and Paddington stations on the London Underground is 3.5 miles. The average speed of the moving tube train is 15 mph and it stops for 2 minutes at each of seven intermediate stations.

(i) Find the average speed for the journey.

(ii) What would the average speed be if the stop at each station was reduced to 45 s?

⑩ A particle starts from rest at time $t = 0$ and moves in a straight line, accelerating as follows:

$a = 2, \quad 0 \leq t \leq 20$

$a = -1, \quad 20 < t \leq 60$

where a is the acceleration in m s^{-2} and t is the time in seconds.

(i) Find the speed of the particle when $t = 10$ and 60.

(ii) Sketch a speed–time graph for the particle in the interval $0 \leq t \leq 60$.

(iii) Find the total distance travelled by the particle in the interval $0 \leq t \leq 60$.

⑪ A particle moves along a straight line. It starts from rest, accelerates at 3 m s^{-2} for 2 seconds and then decelerates uniformly before coming to rest in a further 6 seconds.

(i) Sketch a velocity–time graph.

(ii) Find the total distance travelled.

(iii) Find the deceleration of the particle.

(iv) Find the average speed for the whole journey.

⑫ A train starts from rest and accelerates uniformly for 4 minutes, by which time it has gained a speed of 36 km h^{-1}. It runs at this speed for 5 minutes and then decelerates uniformly, coming to rest in 2 minutes.

(i) Sketch the velocity–time graph.

(ii) Find the total distance travelled.

⑬ The figure shows a velocity–time graph for the motion of a particle in a straight line.

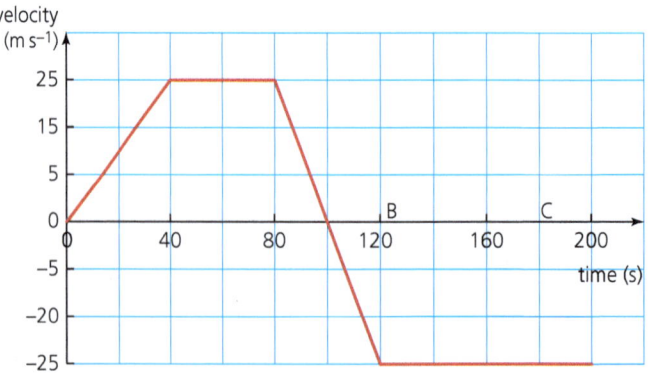

Figure 1.19

(i) Find the displacement of the particle at times $t = 40$, $t = 80$, $t = 120$ and $t = 200$.

(ii) Find the total distance travelled.

(iii) At what time does the particle pass its starting point?

⑭ A tram travels from rest at one station to rest at another station 5 km distant in a time of 10 minutes. The tram gets up to full speed uniformly in the first 250 m and slows down uniformly to rest in the last 125 m. Find the maximum speed of the tram.

⑮ The driver of a train travelling at 90 km h⁻¹ on a straight level track sees a signal to stop at a distance of 500 m and, putting the brakes on, comes to rest at the signal. The train stops for 1 minute and then resumes its journey, attaining the original speed of 90 km h⁻¹ in a distance of 750 m. Assuming that the train accelerates and decelerates at a uniform rate, find the time lost due to the stoppage.

⑯ Two stations A and B are 2 km apart on a straight track. A train starts from rest at A and comes to rest at B. The train accelerates uniformly for $\frac{3}{4}$ of the distance and decelerates uniformly for the remainder. The journey takes 4 minutes. Find

(i) the acceleration

(ii) the deceleration

(iii) the maximum speed of the train.

2 The constant acceleration formulae

In the velocity–time graph shown in Figure 1.20 the initial velocity is u m s⁻¹ and the velocity t s later is v m s⁻¹. The increase in velocity is $(v - u)$ m s⁻¹.

The line is straight and so the acceleration a m s⁻² is constant; it is given by

$$\frac{v - u}{t} = a$$

So

$$v - u = at$$
$$v = u + at \qquad ①$$

The area under the graph represents the displacement, s metres, and is given by the area of the trapezium

$$s = \tfrac{1}{2}(u + v) \times t \qquad ②$$

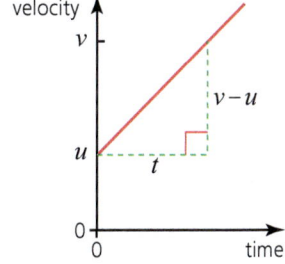

Figure 1.20

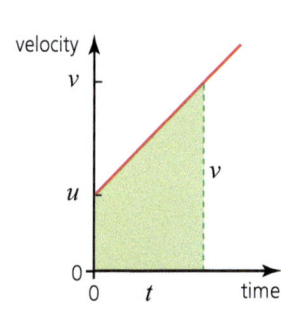

Figure 1.21

The constant acceleration formulae

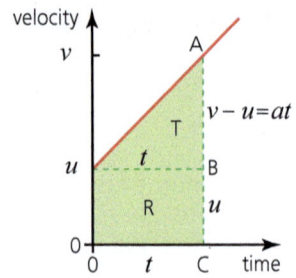

Figure 1.22

The area under the graph may be viewed in a different way, using the rectangle R and the triangle T, as shown in Figure 1.22.

$AC = v$ and $BC = u$

so that $AB = v - u$

$= at$ from equation ①

total area = area of R + area of T

so
$$s = ut + \tfrac{1}{2} \times t \times at$$

giving
$$s = ut + \tfrac{1}{2}at^2 \qquad ③$$

Alternatively, you could write the area as the difference between the larger rectangle of area $v \times t$ and the triangle giving rise to

$$s = vt - \tfrac{1}{2}at^2 \qquad ④$$

To find a formula which does not involve t, you need to eliminate t.

One way to do this is first to rewrite equations ① and ② as

$$v - u = at \text{ and } v + u = \tfrac{2s}{t}$$

And then multiplying these to give

$$(v-u)(v+u) = at \times \tfrac{2s}{t}$$

$$v^2 - u^2 = 2as$$

$$v^2 = u^2 + 2as \qquad ⑤$$

> Equations ①–⑤ are sometimes called the *suvat* equations. Equations ③, ④ and ⑤ can all be derived from ① and ②. Do it for yourself.

Equations ①–⑤ can be used for any motion in a straight line with *constant acceleration*. There are five equations involving 5 variables (s, u, v, a, and t.) Each equation involves 4 variables with the fifth one missing.

① $v = u + at$ has s missing   ② $s = \tfrac{1}{2}(u+v) \times t$ has a missing

③ $s = ut + \tfrac{1}{2}at^2$ has v missing   ④ $s = vt - \tfrac{1}{2}at^2$ has u missing

⑤ $v^2 = u^2 + 2as$ has t missing.

So, in any problem involving linear motion with constant acceleration, if you know three of the variables, then you can obtain the other two.

Example 1.5

A car is travelling at $10\,\text{m s}^{-1}$ and accelerates at $\tfrac{1}{4}\,\text{m s}^{-2}$ for $30\,\text{s}$.

(i) How fast is it travelling at the end of the 30 seconds?

(ii) How far will it have travelled in that time?

Solution

(i) Use the formula $v = u + at$ with $u = 10$, $a = \tfrac{1}{4}$ and $t = 30$.

$$v = 10 + 0.25 \times 30 = 17.5$$

The speed of the car is $17.5\,\text{m s}^{-1}$ after $30\,\text{s}$.

(ii) Use the formula $s = ut + \frac{1}{2}at^2$ with $u = 10$, $a = \frac{1}{4}$ and $t = 30$.

$$s = 10 \times 30 + \frac{1}{2} \times \frac{1}{4} \times 30^2 = 412.5$$

The car has travelled 412.5 m in 30 s.

Example 1.6

A train starts from rest at station A and accelerates uniformly at $0.2\,\text{m s}^{-2}$ for 2 minutes. It then travels at constant speed for 10 minutes, after which it is brought to rest at station B with constant deceleration $1.5\,\text{m s}^{-2}$. Find the distance AB.

Solution

The distance travelled by the train while it is accelerating is found by use of the formula $s = ut + \frac{1}{2}at^2$ with $u = 0$, $a = 0.2$ and $t = 120$.

$$s = \frac{1}{2} \times 0.2 \times 120^2 = 1440\,\text{m}$$

The constant speed of the train is found by using the formula $v = u + at$ with $u = 0$, $a = 0.2$ and $t = 120$.

$$v = 0.2 \times 120 = 24\,\text{m s}^{-1}$$

The distance travelled in 10 minutes at this speed is given by $24 \times 600 = 14\,400\,\text{m}$.

The distance travelled by the train while it is decelerating from $24\,\text{m s}^{-1}$ to 0 is found using the formula $v^2 = u^2 + 2as$ with $u = 24$, $v = 0$ and $a = -1.5$.

$$0 = 24^2 + 2 \times -1.5s$$
$$s = \frac{24^2}{3} = 192\,\text{m}$$

The distance between the stations is AB = 1440 + 14400 + 192 = 16 032 m.

The acceleration due to gravity

When a model ignoring air resistance is used, all objects falling freely under gravity fall with the same acceleration, $g\,\text{m s}^{-2}$. This varies over the surface of the Earth, but it is assumed that all situations encountered here occur in places where $g = 9.8\,\text{m s}^{-2}$.

Example 1.7

A coin is dropped from rest at the top of a building of height 12.25 m and travels in a straight line.

Find the time it takes to reach the ground and the speed of impact.

Solution

Suppose the time taken to reach the ground is t seconds. Use the formula $s = ut + \frac{1}{2}at^2$ with $u = 0$, $a = 9.8$ and $s = 12.25$

The constant acceleration formulae

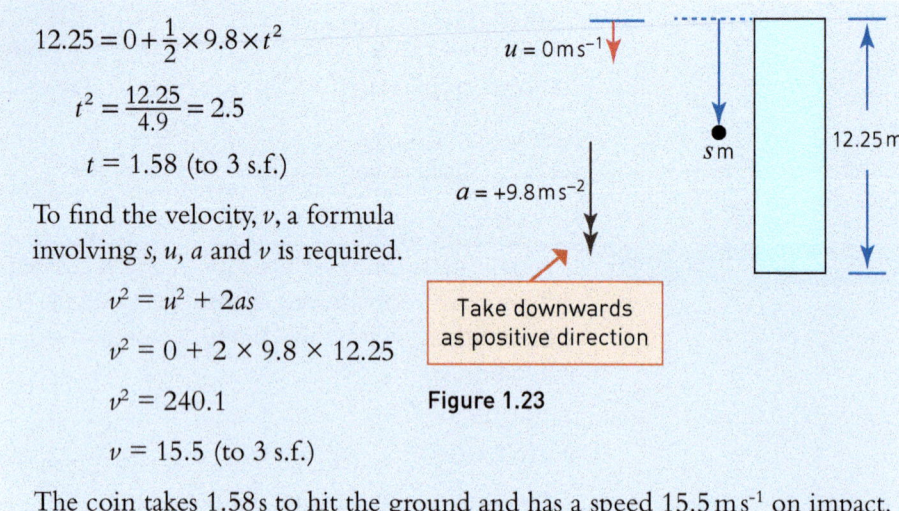

$12.25 = 0 + \frac{1}{2} \times 9.8 \times t^2$

$t^2 = \frac{12.25}{4.9} = 2.5$

$t = 1.58$ (to 3 s.f.)

To find the velocity, v, a formula involving s, u, a and v is required.

$v^2 = u^2 + 2as$

$v^2 = 0 + 2 \times 9.8 \times 12.25$

$v^2 = 240.1$

$v = 15.5$ (to 3 s.f.)

Take downwards as positive direction

Figure 1.23

The coin takes 1.58 s to hit the ground and has a speed 15.5 m s⁻¹ on impact.

The next example illustrates ways of dealing with more complex problems. None of the possible formulae has only one unknown and there are also two situations, so simultaneous equations are used.

Example 1.8

A train decelerating uniformly passes three posts A, B and C spaced at intervals of 100 m. It takes 10 seconds to cover the distance between posts A and B and 15 seconds to cover the distance between posts B and C. Find the deceleration of the train and the distance beyond the third post where the train comes to rest.

Solution

Figure 1.24 shows all the information, taking the acceleration to be a m s⁻² and the speed at A to be u m s⁻¹.

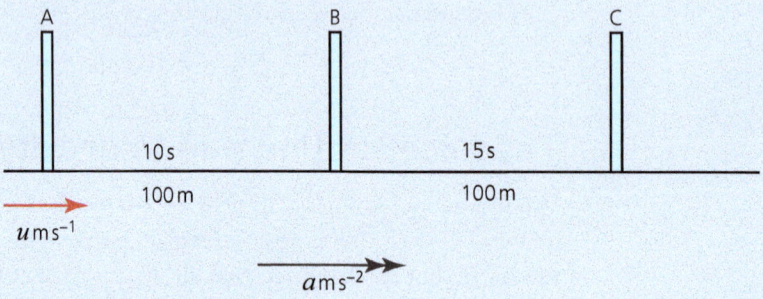

Figure 1.24

Travelling from A to B: You know that $s = 100$ m, $t = 10$ s, the speed at A is u and the acceleration is a, so you use $s = ut + \frac{1}{2}at^2$.

$100 = u \times 10 + \frac{1}{2} \times a \times 10^2$

$100 = 10u + 50a$ ①

To use the same equation for the part from B to C, you would need the velocity at B which brings in another unknown. It is better to consider the whole of the journey from A to C, in which case $s = ut + \frac{1}{2}at^2$ with $s = 200$ m, $t = 25$ s and u and a as before.

$$200 = u \times 25 + \tfrac{1}{2}a \times 25^2$$
$$200 = 25u + 312.5a \qquad ②$$

The two simultaneous equations in u and a can be solved more easily if they are simplified.

① ÷ 5 $\qquad 20 = 2u + 10a \qquad$ ③

② × 0.08 $\qquad 16 = 2u + 25a \qquad$ ④

④ − ③ $\qquad -4 = 15a$

$$a = -\tfrac{4}{15}$$

$$u = 10 - 5 \times \left(-\tfrac{4}{15}\right) = 11\tfrac{1}{3}$$

The train stops at D. To find the distance AD, use the constant acceleration formula $v^2 = u^2 + 2as$ with $v = 0$, $u = 11\tfrac{1}{3}$, and $a = -\tfrac{4}{15}$

$$0 = \left(11\tfrac{1}{3}\right)^2 + 2 \times \left(-\tfrac{4}{15}\right)s$$

$$s = 128\tfrac{4}{9} \times \tfrac{15}{8} = 240\tfrac{5}{6} \text{ m}$$

The distance beyond the third post where the train comes to rest is $40\tfrac{5}{6}$ m.

Exercise 1.2

① The following questions involve motion under constant acceleration.

(i) Find v when $u = 5$, $a = 2.5$ and $t = 2$.

(ii) Find s when $u = 2$, $a = -1.5$ and $t = 4$.

(iii) Find u when $a = -2$, $s = 4$ and $v = 4$.

(iv) Find s when $a = 2$, $v = 5$ and $t = 8$.

(v) Find v when $a = -2$, $s = 100$ and $t = 5$.

② A car travelling at 30 m s⁻¹ decelerates uniformly to rest in 15 s. Find the deceleration and the distance travelled in this time.

③ A stone is dropped down a well. It takes 5 seconds to reach the bottom. How deep is the well?

④ A ball is thrown vertically upwards with a speed of 20 m s⁻¹. One second later another ball is thrown vertically upwards from the same starting height with a speed of 15 m s⁻¹. Find the time when the two balls are at the same height and find the velocity of each ball at this moment.

⑤ A sprinter accelerates uniformly from rest for the first 10 metres of a 100 metre race. He takes 2 seconds to run the first 10 metres.

(i) Find the acceleration in the first 2 seconds of the race.

(ii) Find the speed of the sprinter after 2 s.

(iii) The sprinter completes the 100 m travelling at that speed. Find the total time taken to run the 100 metres.

(iv) Calculate the average speed of the sprinter.

The constant acceleration formulae

6. A particle, X, is projected vertically upwards at $28\,\text{m s}^{-1}$ from a point O on the ground.

    (i) Find the maximum height reached by X.

    When X is at its highest point, a second particle, Y, is projected upwards from O at $20\,\text{m s}^{-1}$.

    (ii) Show that X and Y collide 2 seconds later and determine the height above the ground that this takes place.

7. Two runners are nearing the end of a fun run. Janet is 100 m from the finish line and is running at a constant speed of $5.25\,\text{m s}^{-1}$. Steven, who is 150 m from the finish line and running at $4\,\text{m s}^{-1}$ decides to accelerate to try and beat Janet. He accelerates uniformly to his maximum speed of $8\,\text{m s}^{-1}$ in 4 s and then maintains that speed to the finish line.

    (i) Which of the two runners crosses the finish line first?

    (ii) How far ahead is the winner?

    (iii) What is the time margin between them?

8. Two trains are running on parallel tracks. When they are initially level with each other, one is moving with a uniform speed of $25\,\text{m s}^{-1}$ and the second has a speed of $10\,\text{m s}^{-1}$ but is accelerating at a uniform rate of $0.5\,\text{m s}^{-2}$. How long will it be before they are level again and how far will they have travelled?

9. A stone dropped into a well reaches the water with a velocity of $30\,\text{m s}^{-1}$ and the sound of the splash is heard 3.19 s after it was dropped. From these data, calculate the velocity of sound in air.

10. A train, moving with constant acceleration, is seen to travel 1500 m in one minute and 2500 m in the next.

    (i) Find the speed of the train at the start of the first minute.

    (ii) Find the acceleration.

    (iii) Find the speed of the train at the end of the second minute.

11. A ball is thrown vertically upwards and returns to its point of projection after 4 seconds. Calculate its speed of projection and the maximum height reached.

12. A stone drops from the roof of a building and takes $\frac{1}{8}$ s to pass from the top to the bottom of a window, 1.20 m high. How high is the roof above the top of the window?

13. Which would win a 100 metre race, a sprinter who can cover the distance in 10 s or a motor car which can accelerate to 60 miles per hour from rest in 16 s?

14. Two cars are travelling along a straight road. Car A is moving at $30\,\text{km h}^{-1}$ when it is overtaken by car B travelling at $40\,\text{km h}^{-1}$. A immediately accelerates uniformly and after travelling 500 m overtakes B which has kept its speed constant. Calculate

    (i) the time taken

    (ii) the acceleration of car A

    (iii) the greatest distance between the cars during that time.

⑮ Two trains start together from rest at a station. They travel for 3 minutes and come to rest together at the next station. Train A accelerates uniformly at the rate of 1 m s^{-2} for 30 s, continues at that speed for the next 2 minutes and decelerates uniformly for the last 30 seconds. The other train, B, has a uniform acceleration for 90 seconds and uniform deceleration for the remaining time.

  (i) Draw, on the same diagram, velocity–time graphs for the two train journeys.

  Find

  (ii) the distance between the two stations

  (iii) the acceleration of train B in the first part of its journey

  (iv) the largest distance between the trains.

⑯ Two particles P and Q are moving in the same direction along neighbouring parallel straight lines with constant accelerations of 3 m s^{-2} and 2 m s^{-2}, respectively. At a certain instant, P has velocity 3 m s^{-1} and Q is 30 m behind P and moving at 11.5 m s^{-1}.

  (i) Show that P and Q will be level twice.

  (ii) Find the velocity of P when the particles are level for the first time.

  (iii) Find the maximum distance Q gets ahead of P.

3 Variable acceleration

The equations you have used for constant acceleration do not apply when the acceleration varies. In such cases, you need to go back to first principles.

The velocity of a moving point is the rate at which its position changes with time. When the velocity is not constant, the position–time graph is a curve.

The rate of change of position is the gradient of the tangent to the curve, which can be found by differentiation,

$$v = \frac{ds}{dt} \qquad ①$$

Similarly, the acceleration is the rate at which the velocity changes, so that

$$a = \frac{dv}{dt} = \frac{d^2s}{dt^2} \qquad ②$$

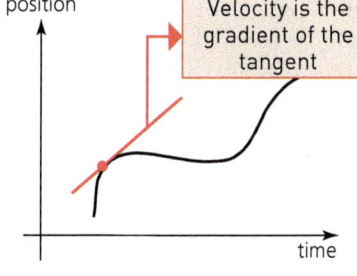

Figure 1.25

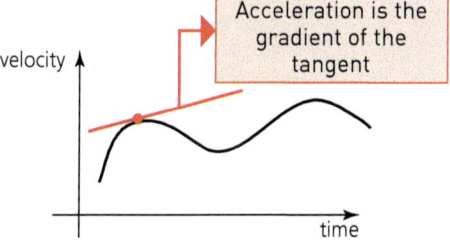

Figure 1.26

Variable acceleration

When you are given the position of a moving point at time t you can use equations ① and ② to solve problems even when the acceleration is not constant.

Example 1.9

A particle is moving in a straight line and its displacement s from a fixed point O is given by the equation

$$s = 18t - 21t^2 + 4t^3$$

(i) Find expressions for the velocity and acceleration of the particle at time t.

(ii) Sketch the graphs of s, v and a against time in the interval $0 \leq t \leq 4$.

(iii) Find the distance travelled between the two times when the velocity is 0.

(iv) Find the distance travelled in the interval $0 \leq t \leq 4$.

Solution

(i) Position $\quad s = 18t - 21t^2 + 4t^3$

Velocity $\quad v = \dfrac{ds}{dt} = 18 - 42t + 12t^2$

Acceleration $\quad a = \dfrac{dv}{dt} = -42 + 24t$

(ii) The three graphs of s, v and a are shown one above the other.

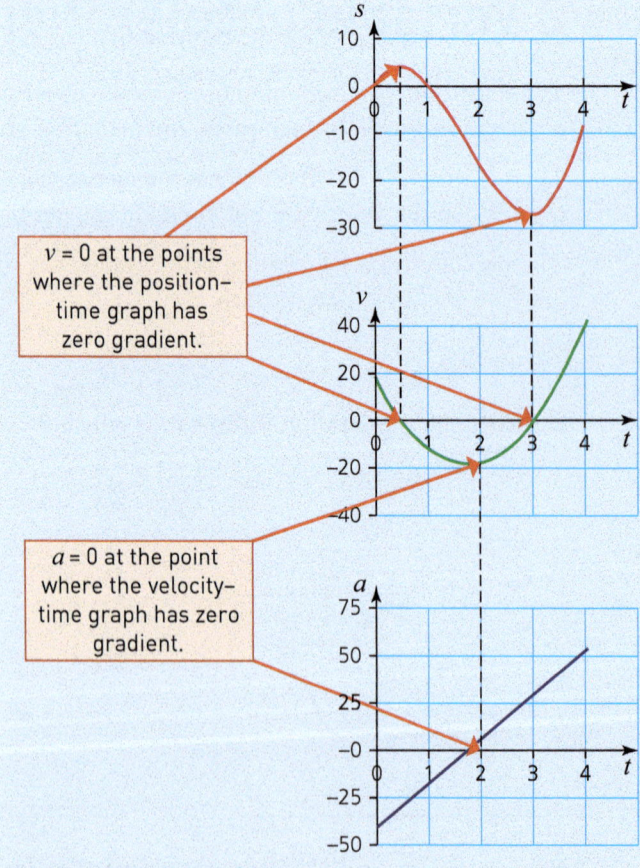

$v = 0$ at the points where the position–time graph has zero gradient.

$a = 0$ at the point where the velocity–time graph has zero gradient.

Figure 1.27

(iii) The velocity is zero when
$$18 - 42t + 12t^2 = 0$$
$$6(2t-1)(t-3) = 0$$
$$t = \tfrac{1}{2} \text{ or } t = 3$$

When $t = \tfrac{1}{2}$, $s = 18 \times \tfrac{1}{2} - 21 \times \tfrac{1}{4} + 4 \times \tfrac{1}{8} = 4\tfrac{1}{4}$

When $t = 3$, $s = 18 \times 3 - 21 \times 9 + 4 \times 27 = -27$

The total distance travelled between $t = \tfrac{1}{2}$ and $t = 3$ is
$27 + 4\tfrac{1}{4} = 31\tfrac{1}{4}$.

(iv) When $t = 4$, $s = 18 \times 4 - 21 \times 16 + 4 \times 64 = -8$

The total distance travelled between $t = 0$ and $t = 4$ is equal to
$4\tfrac{1}{4} + 31\tfrac{1}{4} + 27 - 8 = 54\tfrac{1}{2}$ units

Distance between $t = 0$ and $t = \tfrac{1}{2}$.

Distance between $t = \tfrac{1}{2}$ and $t = 3$.

Distance between $t = 3$ and $t = 4$.

Finding displacement from velocity

> **Note**
> The dt indicates that you must write v in terms of t before integrating.

To find an expression for the position of a particle when the velocity is known you need to integrate with respect to time.

$$v = \frac{ds}{dt} \text{ implies that } s = \int v \, dt$$

Example 1.10

Find the position s of a particle at time t, given that $s = 3$ when $t = 0$ and its velocity is given by $v = 5t - 2$

Solution

The position at time t is given by

$$s = \int (5t - 2) \, dt$$

$$s = \tfrac{5}{2}t^2 - 2t + c$$

Using the initial condition that $s = 3$ when $t = 0$, gives $3 = c$, resulting in

$$s = \tfrac{5}{2}t^2 - 2t + 3$$

Finding velocity from acceleration

You can find the velocity from the acceleration by using integration.

$$a = \frac{dv}{dt} \text{ implies that } v = \int a \, dt$$

Variable acceleration

Example 1.11

The acceleration of a particle (in m s^{-2}) at time t seconds after starting from rest at the origin is given by

$$a = 3t - 2$$

(i) Find expressions for the velocity v and position s at time t.

(ii) Sketch the graphs of a, v and s.

(iii) Show that the particle returns to its starting point after 2 s and find the distance of the particle from the starting point after a further 2 s.

(iv) Find at what time the particle's velocity is 0.

(v) Find the total distance travelled by the particle in the first 4 seconds.

Solution

(i) Acceleration $a = 3t - 2$

Velocity $v = \int (3t - 2) \, dt$

$v = \tfrac{3}{2}t^2 - 2t + c$

> $c = 0$ as the particle starts from rest.

$v = \tfrac{3}{2}t^2 - 2t$

Position $s = \int \left(\tfrac{3}{2}t^2 - 2t\right) dt$

$s = \tfrac{1}{2}t^3 - t^2 + k$

> $k = 0$ as the particle starts from 0.

$s = \tfrac{1}{2}t^3 - t^2$

(ii) The graphs are drawn under each other to show how they relate to one another.

(iii) To show that the particle returns to its starting point after 2 seconds, you need to show that $s = 0$ when $t = 2$.

i.e. $\tfrac{1}{2}2^3 - 2^2 = 4 - 4 = 0$.

The displacement of the particle when $t = 4$, is equal to

$s(4) = \tfrac{1}{2}4^3 - 4^2 = 32 - 16 = 16 \, \text{m}$

(iv) The velocity is zero when

$v(t) = \tfrac{3}{2}t^2 - 2t = 0$

$t\left(\tfrac{3}{2}t - 2\right) = 0$

$t = 0$ or $t = \tfrac{4}{3}$

The velocity is 0 when $t = 0$ or $t = \tfrac{4}{3}$ s.

> The particle starts at 0, goes back at first, stops instantaneously at $t = \tfrac{4}{3}$, then changes direction, returning to 0 at $t = 2$. It then continues moving forwards with increasing speed.

(v) The particle goes backwards in the interval $0 \leq t \leq \tfrac{4}{3}$, turns round at $t = \tfrac{4}{3}$ and then moves forwards in the interval $\tfrac{4}{3} < t \leq 4$.

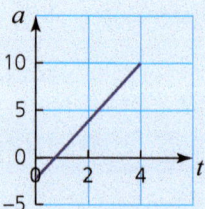
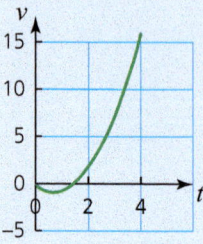
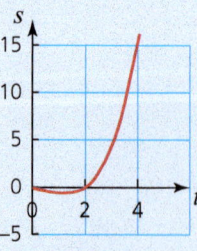

Figure 1.28

The displacement from $t = 0$ to $t = \frac{4}{3}$ is $\left[\frac{1}{2}\left(\frac{4}{3}\right)^3 - \left(\frac{4}{3}\right)^2\right] - [0] = -\frac{16}{27}$

So the distance travelled from $t = 0$ to $t = \frac{4}{3}$ is $+\frac{16}{27}$

The distance travelled in $\frac{4}{3} < t \leq 4$ is equal to $16 - \left(-\frac{16}{27}\right) = 16\frac{16}{27}$.

The total distance travelled in the interval $0 \leq t \leq 4$ is $\frac{16}{27} + 16\frac{16}{27} = 17\frac{5}{27}$.

The particle travels $17\frac{5}{27}$ m in the first 4 seconds.

Exercise 1.3

① In each of the following cases
   (a) $s = 2 + 4t - t^2$
   (b) $s = 5t^2 - t^3$
   (c) $s = t^4 - t^2 + 2$
   (i) Find expressions for the velocity.
   (ii) Use your equations to write down the initial position and velocity.
   (iii) Find the time and position when the velocity is zero.

② The position s of a moving point A at time t seconds is given by
$$s = 2t^3 - 3t^2 + 4t - 10$$
Find the velocity and acceleration of A at the instant $t = 4$.

③ Find the position s m of a particle at time t s if its velocity v m s^{-1} is given by
   (i) $v = 5t - 2$, and $s = 3$ when $t = 0$.
   (ii) $v = 3t^2 + 4t$, and $s = 2$ when $t = 1$.

④ Find the velocity v m s^{-1} and displacement s m of a particle at time t s, if its acceleration is given by
   (i) $a = 12t - 8$ and when $t = 0, s = 5$ and $v = 3$
   (ii) $a = 0.5t^2 - 0.2t + 1$ and when $t = 1, s = 0.5$ and $v = 1$.

⑤

Figure 1.29

A toy car is moving along the straight line Ox, where O is the origin. The time t is in seconds. At time $t = 0$ the car is at A, 5 m from O, as shown in Figure 1.29.

The velocity of the car, v m s^{-1} is given by
$$v = 2 + 9t - 1.5t^2$$
Calculate the distance of the car from O when the acceleration is 0.

⑥ A particle moves along a straight line so that after t seconds, $t \geq 0$, its distance s from the origin O on the line is given by
$$s = (t - 1)^2(t - 2)$$
   (i) Find the velocity and acceleration of the particle on each occasion that it passes the origin.
   (ii) Find the distance of the particle from O each time the velocity is 0.
   (iii) Find the accleration when the velocity is 8 m s^{-1}.

Variable acceleration

⑦ During braking, the speed of a car is given by $v = 12 - 3t^2$ until it stops moving. Find the distance travelled from the time that the braking starts.

⑧ The velocity of a sprinter at the start of a 100 metre race is given as
$$v = 10t - 2.5t^2, \quad 0 \leq t \leq 2$$
$$v = 10, \quad t > 2$$

(i) Find the acceleration of the sprinter at $t = 2$. Hence write down the maximum speed of the sprinter.

(ii) How far does the sprinter run in the first 2 seconds?

(iii) How long does the sprinter take to run 100 metres?

⑨ A particle moves along the x-axis. Its displacement from the origin, O, is given by
$$x = 10 + 36t + 3t^2 - 2t^3$$
where t is the time in seconds and $-4 \leq t \leq 6$.

(i) Write down the displacement of the particle when $t = 0$.

(ii) Find an expression in terms of t for the velocity $v\,\mathrm{m\,s^{-1}}$ of the particle.

(iii) Find the values of t for which $v = 0$ and find the values of x at those times.

(iv) Calculate the distance travelled by the particle from $t = 0$ to $t = 4$.

(v) How many times does the particle go through O in the interval $-4 \leq t \leq 6$?

⑩ A particle P is moving in a straight line. At time t seconds, for small values of t, after starting from the origin, O, its velocity is given by
$$v = t^2(3 - t)$$

(i) Find the values of t when the acceleration is zero.

(ii) After what time, does the particle come to instantaneous rest?

At that time, the particle has reached its furthest point A from O and then reverses back towards O.

(iii) Find the distance OA.

(iv) Find the time taken for the particle to return to O.

⑪ A car moves between two sets of traffic lights, stopping at both. Its speed $v\,\mathrm{m\,s^{-1}}$ at time t s is modelled by
$$v = 6t^2 - t^3$$

(i) Find the times at which the car is stationary.

(ii) Find the maximum speed of the car.

(iii) Find the distance between the two sets of traffic lights.

⑫ A particle is moving in a straight line. The position s of the particle at time t is given by
$$s = 18 - 24t + 9t^2 - t^3, \quad 0 \leq t \leq 5$$

(i) Find the velocity v at time t and the values of t for which $v = 0$.

(ii) Find the position of the particle at those times.

(iii) Find the total distance travelled by the particle in the interval $0 \leq t \leq 5$.

⑬ The distance of a particle from a point O at time t is given by
$$s = 6 \sin 3t + 8 \cos 3t.$$
  (i) Find expressions for the velocity and acceleration in terms of t.
  (ii) Show that the acceleration a and the displacement from O, s, satisfy the equation $a = -9s$.
  (iii) Show that the velocity v and s satisfy the equation $v^2 = 9(100 - s^2)$.

⑭ Two sprinters are having a race over 100 m. They both start from rest. Their accelerations in m s^{-2} are as follows

Sprinter A	Sprinter B
$a = 10 - 5t$, $0 \leq t \leq 2$	$a = 15t - 7.5t^2$, $0 \leq t \leq 2$
$a = 0$, $t > 2$	$a = 0$, $t > 2$

  (i) Find the greatest speed of each sprinter.
  (ii) Find the distance run by each sprinter while reaching greatest speed.
  (iii) How long does each sprinter take to finish the race?
  (iv) Who wins the race, by what time margin and by what distance?

⑮ Two walkers, John and Euan are on a long hike. John walks at a uniform rate of 5.15 km h^{-1} throughout. Euan's speed v_E km h^{-1} is $\dfrac{30}{4.5 + t}$, t hours after he started. How long does it take for John and Euan to finish the 15 km hike? Who gets to the finish line first? How far ahead is the leader at the end of the walk?

KEY POINTS

1

Vectors (with magnitude and direction)	Scalars (magnitude only)
Displacement	Distance
Position: displacement from a fixed origin	
Velocity: rate of change of position	Speed: magnitude of velocity
Acceleration: rate of change of velocity	Magnitude of acceleration
	Time

2 Graphs
  The gradient of a position–time graph is the velocity.
  The gradient of a velocity–time graph is the acceleration.
  The area under a velocity–time graph is the displacement.
  The gradient of a distance–time graph is the speed.
  The gradient of a speed–time graph is the magnitude of the acceleration.
  The area under a speed–time graph is the distance.

3 Averages

  Average speed $= \dfrac{\text{total distance travelled}}{\text{total time taken}}$

  Average velocity $= \dfrac{\text{displacement}}{\text{time taken}}$

  Average acceleration $= \dfrac{\text{change in velocity}}{\text{time taken}}$

Variable acceleration

4 Constant acceleration formulae

$$v = u + at$$

$$s = \frac{1}{2}(u+v)t$$

$$s = ut + \frac{1}{2}at^2$$

$$s = vt - \frac{1}{2}at^2$$

$$v^2 = u^2 + 2as.$$

5 Relationships between variables describing motion

Position	Velocity differentiate →	Acceleration
s	$v = \dfrac{ds}{dt}$	$a = \dfrac{dv}{dt} = \dfrac{d^2s}{dt^2}$

Acceleration	Velocity integrate →	Position
a	$v = \int a \, dt$	$s = \int v \, dt$

> ## LEARNING OUTCOMES
>
> When you have completed this chapter, you should know
> - the difference between position, displacement and distance travelled
> - the difference between speed and velocity and between acceleration and the magnitude of acceleration
> - how to draw and interpret position–time, distance–time, velocity–time, speed–time and acceleration–time graphs and how to use these to solve problems connected with motion in a straight line
> - how to find average speed and average velocity
> - how and when to use the constant acceleration formulae to solve problems involving linear motion
> - how to deal with problems involving motion under gravity
> - how to use calculus to derive expressions for position, velocity and acceleration as functions of time, given suitable information
> - how to solve problems involving linear motion with variable acceleration.

2 Forces and motion

→ This tightrope walker is stationary. There are a number of forces acting on the walker which cancel each other out, resulting in no motion. In order for that to be possible, the cable must make small angles to the horizontal so that the vertical components of the tension can cancel out the weight of the walker. In that case, the tensions in the cable will be greater than the walker's weight.

In the beginning (if there was such a thing) God created Newton's laws of motion together with the necessary masses and forces. This is all; everything beyond this follows from the development of appropriate mathematical methods by means of deduction.
Albert Einstein

1 Forces and Newton's laws of motion

Modelling vocabulary

Mechanics is about modelling the real world. In order to do this, suitable simplifying assumptions are often made so that mathematics can be applied to situations and problems. This process involves identifying factors that can be neglected without losing too much accuracy. Here are some commonly used modelling terms which are used to describe such assumptions.

- negligible: small enough to ignore
- inextensible: for a string with negligible stretch
- light: for an object with negligible mass
- particle: an object with negligible dimensions
- smooth: for a surface with negligible friction
- uniform: the same throughout.

Forces

A force is defined as the physical quantity that causes a change in motion. As it depends on magnitude and direction, it is a vector quantity.

Forces can start motion, stop motion, speed up or slow down objects, or change the direction of their motion. In real situations, several forces usually act on an object. The sum of these forces, known as the resultant force, determines whether or not there is a change of motion.

There are several types of force that you often use.

The force of gravity

Every object on or near the Earth's surface is pulled vertically downwards by the force of gravity. The size of the force on an object of mass M kg is Mg newtons where g is a constant whose value is about $9.8 \,\text{m s}^{-2}$. The force of gravity is also known as the **weight** of the object.

> **Note**
>
> g varies around the world, with $9.8 \,\text{m s}^{-2}$ being a typical value. Singapore, at 9.766, has one of the lowest values, and Helsinki, with 9.825, has one of the highest.

Tension and thrust

When a string is pulled, as in Figure 2.1, it exerts a **tension** force opposite to the pull. The tension acts along the string and is the same throughout the string. A rigid rod can exert a tension force in a similar way to a string when it is used to support or pull an object. It can also exert a **thrust** force when it is in compression, as in Figure 2.2. The thrust acts along the rod and is the same throughout the rod.

The tension on either side of a smooth pulley is the same, as shown in Figure 2.3.

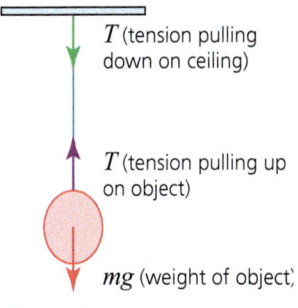

Figure 2.1

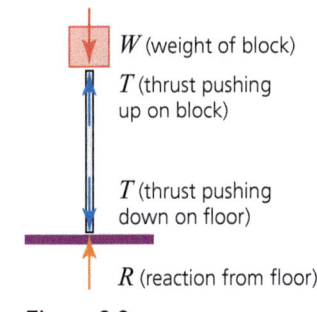

Figure 2.2

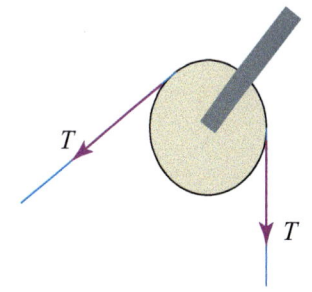

Figure 2.3

Normal reaction

A book resting on a table is subjected to two forces, its weight and the **normal reaction** of the table. It is called normal because its line of action is normal (at right angles) to the surface of the table. Since the book is in equilibrium, the normal reaction is equal and opposite to the weight of the book; it is a positive force.

> **Note**
> In Figure 2.4, the normal reaction is vertical but this is not always the case. For example, the normal reaction on an object on a slope is perpendicular to the slope.

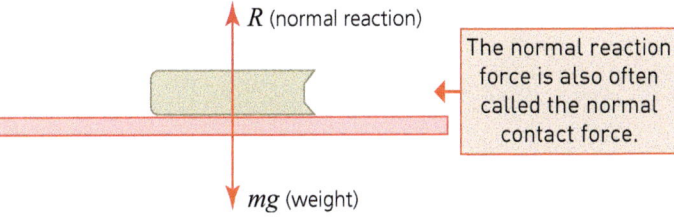

The normal reaction force is also often called the normal contact force.

Figure 2.4

If the book is about to lose contact with the table (which might happen, for instance, if the table is accelerating rapidly downwards), the normal force becomes zero.

Frictional force

In Figure 2.5, the book on the table is being pushed by a force P parallel to the surface. The book remains at rest because P is balanced by a **frictional force**, F, in the opposite direction to P. The magnitude of the frictional force is equal to the pushing force, i.e. $P = F$

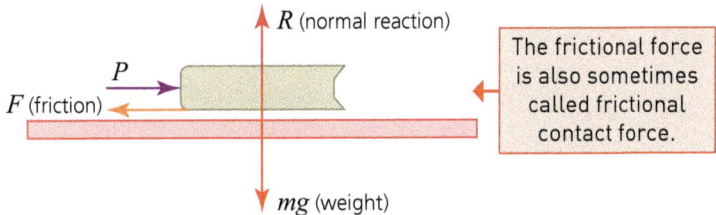

The frictional force is also sometimes called frictional contact force.

Figure 2.5

If P is increased and the book starts to move, F is still present but now $P > F$. Friction always acts in the opposite direction to the motion. Friction may prevent the motion of an object or slow it down if it is moving.

Forces and Newton's laws of motion

Driving force

In problems about moving objects such as cars, all the forces acting along the line of motion can usually be reduced to two or three: the **driving force**, the **resistance** to motion and, possibly, a **braking force**.

Figure 2.6

Example 2.1

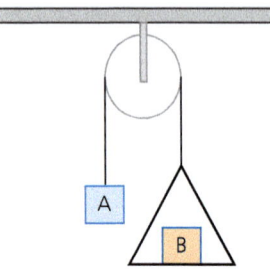

Figure 2.7

Figure 2.7 shows a block A of mass 10 kg connected to a light scale pan by a light inextensible string that passes over a light smooth pulley. The scale pan holds block B, also of mass 10 kg. The system is in equilibrium.

(i) On separate diagrams, show all the forces acting on each of the masses, the scale pan and the pulley.

(ii) Find the value of the tension in the string.

(iii) Find the tension in the rod holding the pulley.

(iv) Find the normal reaction of B on the scale pan.

Solution

(i)

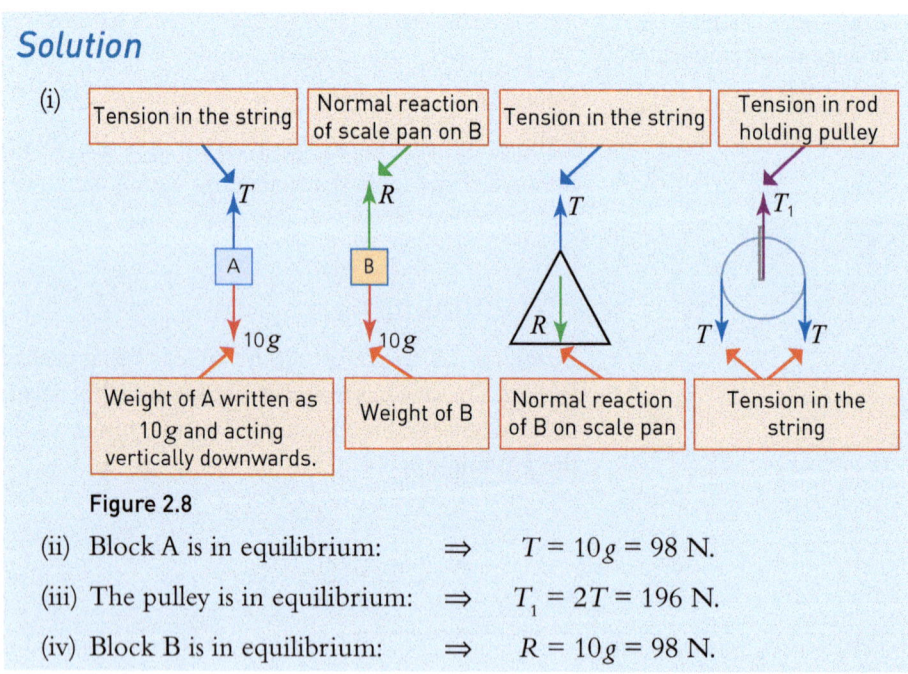

Figure 2.8

(ii) Block A is in equilibrium: $\Rightarrow$ $T = 10g = 98$ N.

(iii) The pulley is in equilibrium: $\Rightarrow$ $T_1 = 2T = 196$ N.

(iv) Block B is in equilibrium: $\Rightarrow$ $R = 10g = 98$ N.

Newton's laws of motion

1 Every object continues in a state of rest or uniform motion in a straight line unless it is acted on by a resultant external force.

2 The acceleration of an object is proportional to, and in the same direction as, the resultant of the forces acting on the object.

$$\mathbf{F} = m\mathbf{a}$$

F is the resultant force.
m is the mass of the object.
a is the acceleration.

> **Historical note**
>
> Isaac Newton was born in Lincolnshire in 1642. He was not an outstanding scholar either as a schoolboy or as a university student, yet later in life he made remarkable contributions in dynamics, optics, astronomy, chemistry, music theory and theology. He became Member of Parliament for Cambridge University and later Warden of the Royal Mint. His tomb in Westminster Abbey reads 'Let mortals rejoice that there existed such and so great an ornament to the Human Race'.

Notice that this is a vector equation, since both the magnitudes and directions of the resultant force and the acceleration are involved. If the motion is along a straight line it is often written in scalar form as $F = ma$.

3   When one object exerts a force on another there is always a reaction, which is equal and opposite in direction to the acting force.

Equation of motion

The equation resulting from Newton's second law is often described as an **equation of motion**, as in the following examples.

Example 2.2

An empty bottle of mass 0.5 kg is released from a submarine and rises with an acceleration of $0.75\,\text{m s}^{-2}$. The water causes a resistance of 1.1 N.

(i)   Draw a diagram showing the forces acting on the bottle and the direction of its acceleration.

(ii) Write down the equation of motion of the bottle.

(iii) Find the size of the buoyancy force.

Solution

(i) The forces acting on the bottle and the acceleration are shown in Figure 2.9.

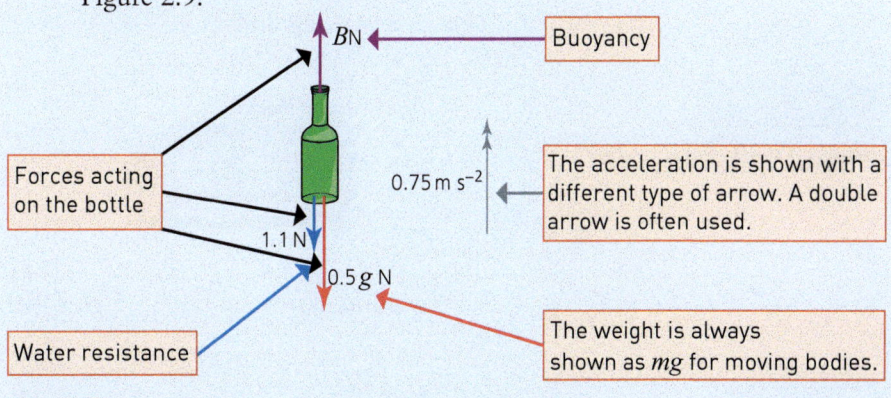

Figure 2.9

(ii) The resultant force acting on the bottle is $(B - 0.5g - 1.1)$ upwards.

The resulting equation

$$B - 0.5g - 1.1 = 0.5a$$

is called the **equation of motion**.

(iii) $B - 4.9 - 1.1 = 0.375$ ← 0.5×0.75

$B = 6.375$

The buoyancy force on the bottle is 6.375 N.

Forces and Newton's laws of motion

Example 2.3

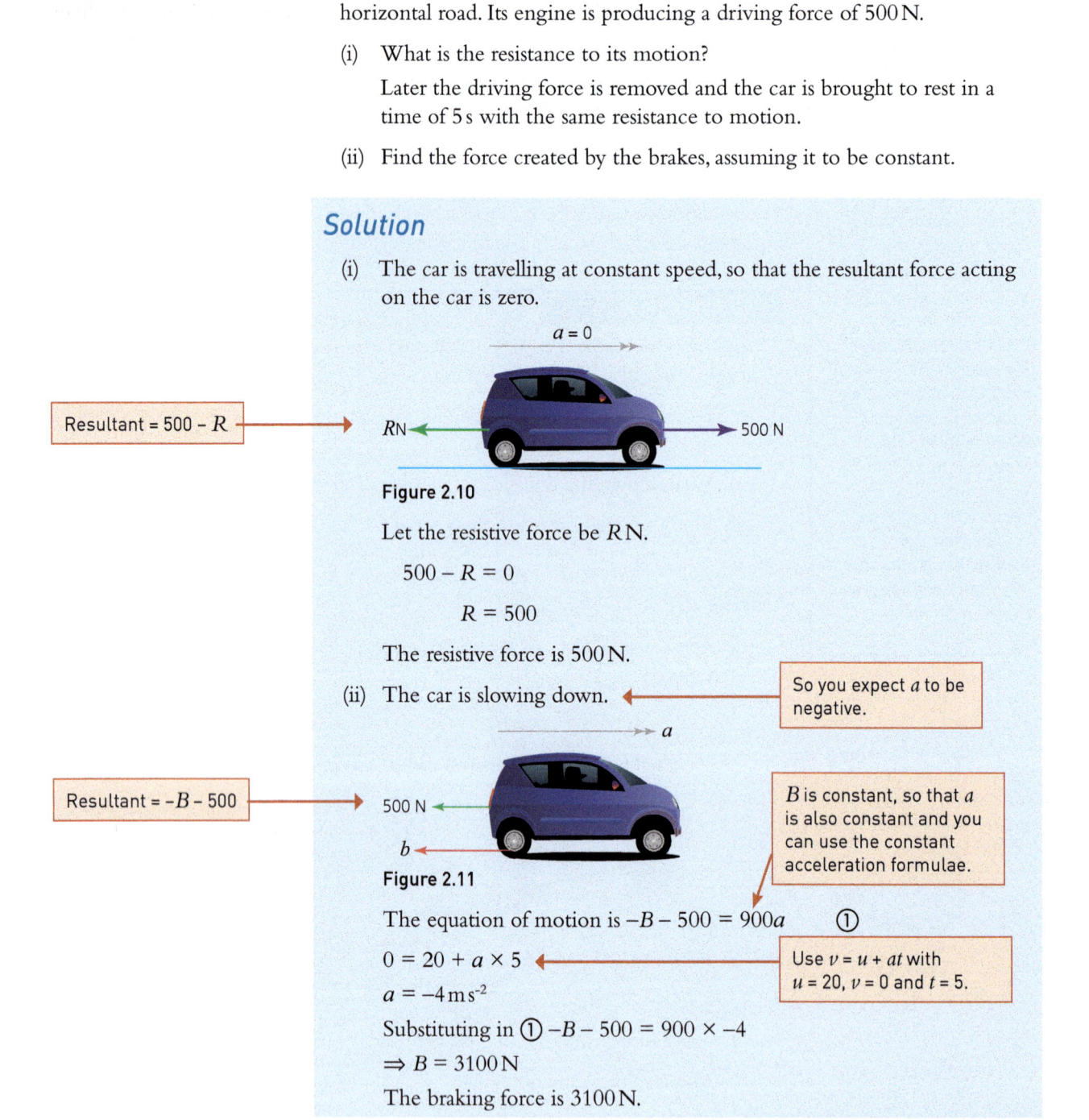

A car of mass 900 kg travels at a constant speed of 20 m s^{-1} along a straight horizontal road. Its engine is producing a driving force of 500 N.

(i) What is the resistance to its motion?

Later the driving force is removed and the car is brought to rest in a time of 5 s with the same resistance to motion.

(ii) Find the force created by the brakes, assuming it to be constant.

Solution

(i) The car is travelling at constant speed, so that the resultant force acting on the car is zero.

Resultant = 500 − R

Figure 2.10

Let the resistive force be R N.

$$500 - R = 0$$
$$R = 500$$

The resistive force is 500 N.

(ii) The car is slowing down. *So you expect a to be negative.*

Resultant = −B − 500

Figure 2.11

The equation of motion is $-B - 500 = 900a$ ①

$0 = 20 + a \times 5$ *Use $v = u + at$ with $u = 20$, $v = 0$ and $t = 5$.*

$a = -4$ m s^{-2}

B is constant, so that a is also constant and you can use the constant acceleration formulae.

Substituting in ① $-B - 500 = 900 \times -4$

$\Rightarrow B = 3100$ N

The braking force is 3100 N.

Example 2.4

Two boxes A and B are descending vertically supported by a parachute. Box A has mass 100 kg. Box B has mass 75 kg and is suspended from box A by a light vertical wire. Both boxes are descending with downwards acceleration $2\,\text{m s}^{-2}$.

(i) Draw a labelled diagram showing all the forces acting on box A and another diagram showing all the forces acting on box B.

(ii) Write down separate equations of motion for box A and for box B.

(iii) Find the tensions in both wires.

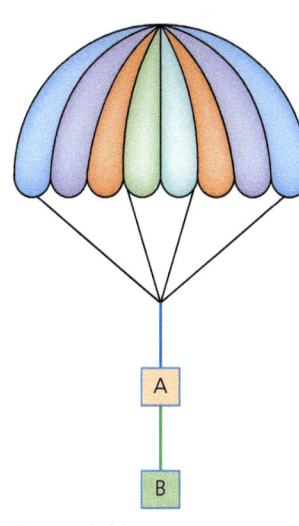

Figure 2.12

Solution

(i)

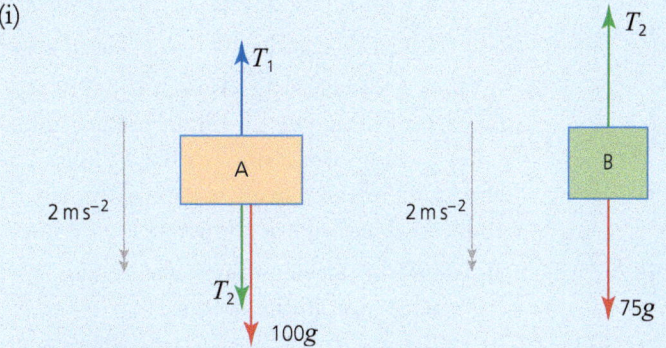

Figure 2.13

(ii) Box A: The resultant downwards force is $T_2 + 100g - T_1$ so the equation of motion is

$$T_2 + 100g - T_1 = 200 \quad \text{①} \quad \text{Since } 100a = 100 \times 2 = 200$$

Box B: The resultant downwards force is $75g - T_2$ so the equation of motion is

$$75g - T_2 = 150 \quad \text{②} \quad \text{Since } 75a = 75 \times 2 = 150$$

(iii) From ②: $\quad T_2 = 75 \times 9.8 - 150$
$\qquad\qquad\qquad\quad = 585\,\text{N}$

Substituting in ①: $\quad T_1 = 585 + 100 \times 9.8 - 200$
$\qquad\qquad\qquad\qquad = 1365\,\text{N}$

The tension in the blue wire linking A to the parachute is 1365 N.
The tension in the green wire linking A to B is 585 N.

> **Note**
>
> T_1 is the tension in the blue wire linking A to the parachute. T_2 is the tension in the green wire linking A to B.
> $T_1 \neq T_2$

Exercise 2.1

① Find the acceleration produced when a force of 100 N acts on an object
   (i) of mass 15 kg
   (ii) of mass 10 g
   (iii) of mass 1 tonne.

② A bullet of mass 20 g is fired into a wall with a velocity of $400\,\text{m s}^{-1}$. The bullet penetrates the wall to a depth of 10 cm. Find the resistance of the wall, assuming it to be uniform.

Forces and Newton's laws of motion

③ A car of mass 1200 kg is travelling along a straight level road.

(i) Calculate the acceleration of the car when a resultant force of 2400 N acts on it in the direction of its motion. How long does it take the car to increase its speed from $4\,\text{m s}^{-1}$ to $12\,\text{m s}^{-1}$?

The car has an acceleration of $1.2\,\text{m s}^{-2}$ when there is a driving force of 2400 N.

(ii) Find the resistance to motion of the car.

④ A load of mass 5 kg is held on the end of a string. Calculate the tension in the string when

(i) the load is raised with an acceleration of $2.5\,\text{m s}^{-2}$

(ii) the load is lowered with an acceleration of $2.5\,\text{m s}^{-2}$

(iii) the load is raised with a constant speed of $2\,\text{m s}^{-1}$

(iv) the load is raised with a deceleration of $2.5\,\text{m s}^{-2}$.

⑤ A block A of mass 10 kg is connected to a block B of mass 5 kg by a light inextensible string passing over a smooth fixed pulley. The blocks are released from rest with A 0.3 m above ground level, as shown in Figure 2.14.

(i) Find the acceleration of the system and the tension in the string.

(ii) Find the speed of the masses when A hits the ground.

(iii) How far does B rise after A hits the floor and the string becomes slack?

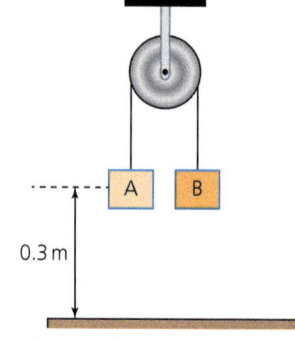

Figure 2.14

⑥ A block A of mass 10 kg is lying on a smooth horizontal table. Light inextensible strings connect A to particle B of mass 6 kg and particle C of mass 4 kg, which hang freely over smooth pulleys at the edge of the table.

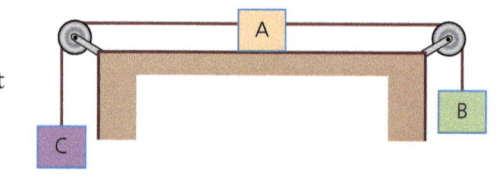

Figure 2.15

(i) Draw force diagrams to show the forces acting on each mass.

(ii) Write down separate equations of motion for A, B and C.

(iii) Find the acceleration of the system and the tensions in the strings.

⑦ A truck of mass 1250 kg is towing a trailer of mass 350 kg along a horizontal straight road. The engine of the truck produces a driving force of 2500 N. The truck is subjected to a resistance of 250 N and the trailer to a resistance of 300 N.

Figure 2.16

(i) Show, in separate diagrams, the horizontal forces acting on the truck and the trailer.

(ii) Find the acceleration of the truck and trailer.

(iii) Find the tension in the coupling between the truck and the trailer.

⑧ A train consists of a locomotive and five trucks with masses and resistances to motion as shown in Figure 2.17. The engine provides a driving force of 29 000 N. All the couplings are light, rigid and horizontal.

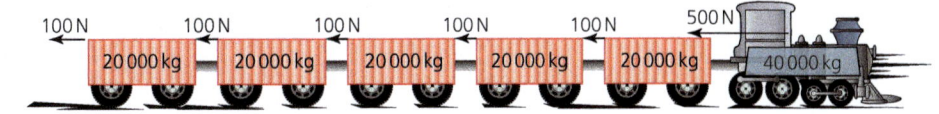

Figure 2.17

(i) Show that the acceleration of the train is $0.2\,\mathrm{m\,s^{-2}}$.

(ii) Find the force in the coupling between the last two trucks.

With the driving force removed, brakes are applied, so adding additional resistances of 3000 N to the locomotive and 2000 N to each truck.

(iii) Find the new acceleration of the train.

(iv) Find the force in the coupling between the last two trucks.

⑨ Block A of mass 2 kg is connected to a light scale pan by a light inextensible string which passes over a smooth fixed pulley.

The scale pan holds two blocks, B and C, of masses 0.5 and 1 kg, as shown in Figure 2.18.

(i) Draw diagrams showing all the forces acting on each of the three particles.

(ii) Write down equations of motion for each of A, B and C.

(iii) Find the acceleration of the system, the tension in the string, the reaction force between B and C and the reaction between C and the scale pan.

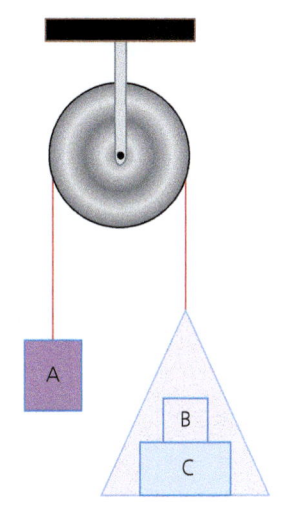

Figure 2.18

⑩ A block A of mass 5 kg is lying on a smooth horizontal table. A light inextensible string connects A to a particle B of mass 1 kg which hangs freely over a smooth pulley at the edge of the table. B is connected to a third particle C of mass 2 kg by another string, as shown in Figure 2.19.

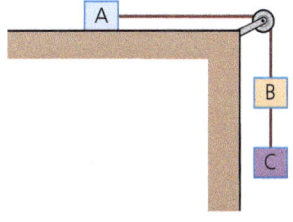

Figure 2.19

(i) Draw diagrams showing all the forces acting on each of the three blocks.

(ii) Write equations of motion for each of A, B and C.

(iii) Find the acceleration of the system and the tension in each string.

2 Working with vectors

A force is a physical quantity that causes a change of motion. A force can start the motion of an object, stop its motion, make it move faster or slower, or change the direction of its motion. By its very nature, a force is a vector quantity just like displacement, velocity or acceleration. It has magnitude and direction, unlike scalar quantities such as distance, speed, mass or time, which have magnitude only.

Notation and representation

A vector can be represented by a directed line segment in a diagram.

In writing, $\overrightarrow{AB}$ represents the vector with magnitude. The magnitude can also be written as $|\overrightarrow{AB}|$. The direction is given by the angle θ which AB makes with a fixed direction, often the horizontal.

In Figure 2.21, **F** is a vector with magnitude $F = |\mathbf{F}|$ and direction ϕ.

Vectors are often written using lowercase letters, like **a**, **b** and **c**. It is common to use **a** for the vector $\overrightarrow{OA}$ where O is the origin.

To determine the direction of a vector in the xy plane, a mathematical convention is used. Starting from the x-axis, angles measured anticlockwise are positive and angles in a clockwise direction are negative.

In the example shown in Figure 2.23, **P** has direction $+75°$ and **Q** has direction $-130°$.

Figure 2.20

Figure 2.21

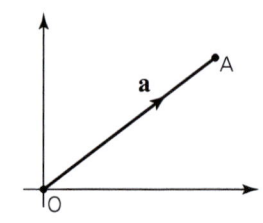

Figure 2.22

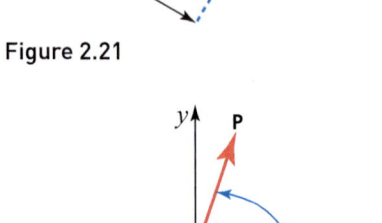

Figure 2.23

Adding vectors

One way to add vectors is to draw them one after another, i.e. where one finishes the next one starts.

$$\overrightarrow{AB} + \overrightarrow{BC} = \overrightarrow{AC}$$

Alternatively, you can make **a** and **b** start at the same place and take the diagonal of the ensuing parallelogram.

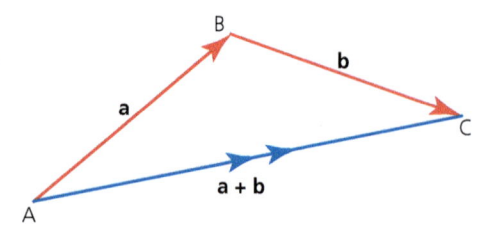

Figure 2.24

This gives the same result, because opposite sides of a parallelogram are equal and in the same direction, so that **b** is repeated at the top right of the parallelogram in Figure 2.25.

Figure 2.25

Resultant forces

The resultant of a number of forces is equal to the sum of these forces. As each force is a vector, the resultant is a vector starting at the start point of the first force and ending at the end point of the last force.

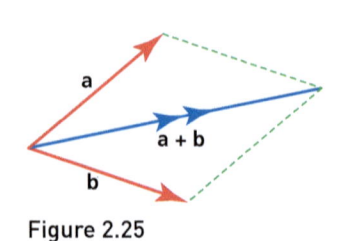

Figure 2.26

$$R = F_1 + F_2 + F_3 + F_4$$

The resultant **R** of the four forces (F_1, F_2, F_3 and F_4) can be found by drawing consecutive lines representing the vectors. The line which completes the polygon is the resultant.

You have met the contact forces of normal reaction force **R** and frictional force **F**. The resultant of them is the total contact force with magnitude $\sqrt{F^2 + R^2}$.

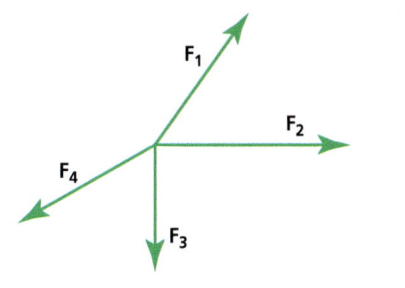

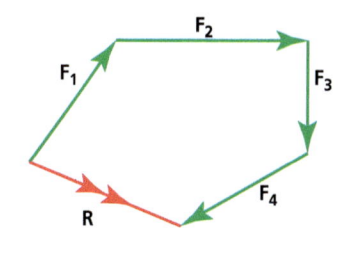

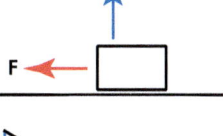

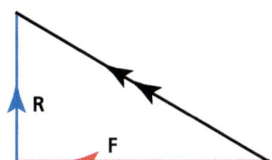

Figure 2.27

Components of a vector

Finding components is the reverse process of adding two vectors. It involves splitting a vector into two perpendicular components.

The result is often described using unit vectors **i** and **j** along the x and y axes, respectively. The vector **a** in Figure 2.28 may be written as $\mathbf{a} = 4\mathbf{i} + 3\mathbf{j}$.

Alternatively, **a** can be written as the *column vector* $\begin{pmatrix} 4 \\ 3 \end{pmatrix}$.

In general,

if **i** and **j** are unit vectors along the x and y direction, respectively, then **a** can be written in terms of components as

$\mathbf{a} = a_x\mathbf{i} + a_y\mathbf{j}$ or in column vector form

$\mathbf{a} = \begin{pmatrix} a_x \\ a_y \end{pmatrix}$ since

$\mathbf{a} = a_x\mathbf{i} + a_y\mathbf{j} = \begin{pmatrix} a_x \\ a_y \end{pmatrix}$

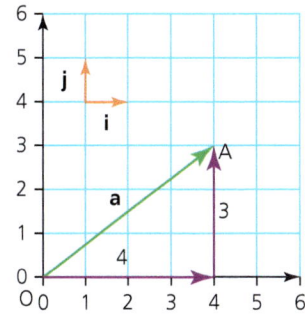

Figure 2.28

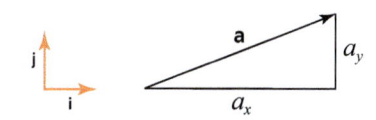

Figure 2.29

Example 2.5

The four vectors **a**, **b**, **c** and **d** are shown in Figure 2.30.

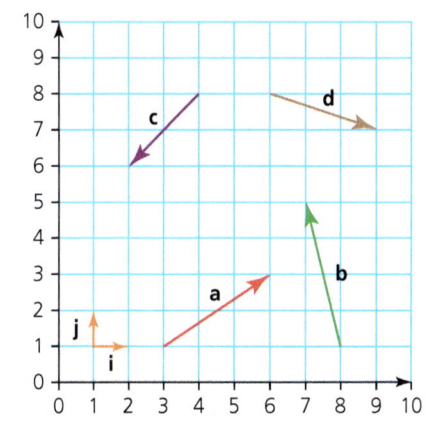

Figure 2.30

Working with vectors

(i) Write them in component form and as column vectors.

(ii) Draw a diagram to show the vectors 2**a**, −**b** and 2**a** − **b** and write these in both forms.

Solution

(i) $\mathbf{a} = 3\mathbf{i} + 2\mathbf{j} = \begin{pmatrix} 3 \\ 2 \end{pmatrix},\qquad \mathbf{b} = -\mathbf{i} + 4\mathbf{j} = \begin{pmatrix} -1 \\ 4 \end{pmatrix},\qquad \mathbf{c} = -2\mathbf{i} - 2\mathbf{j} = \begin{pmatrix} -2 \\ -2 \end{pmatrix},$

$\mathbf{d} = 3\mathbf{i} - \mathbf{j} = \begin{pmatrix} 3 \\ -1 \end{pmatrix}$

(ii)

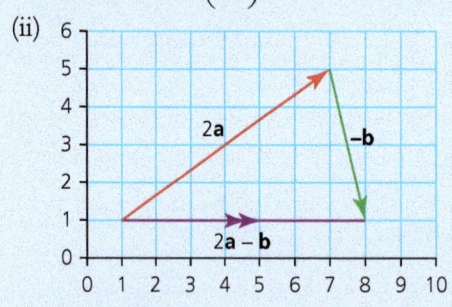

Figure 2.31

$2\mathbf{a} = 2(3\mathbf{i} + 2\mathbf{j}) = 6\mathbf{i} + 4\mathbf{j} = \begin{pmatrix} 6 \\ 4 \end{pmatrix}$

$-\mathbf{b} = -(-\mathbf{i} + 4\mathbf{j}) = \mathbf{i} - 4\mathbf{j} = \begin{pmatrix} 1 \\ -4 \end{pmatrix}$

$2\mathbf{a} - \mathbf{b} = 2\mathbf{a} + (-\mathbf{b}) = 6\mathbf{i} + 4\mathbf{j} + \mathbf{i} - 4\mathbf{j} = 7\mathbf{i} = \begin{pmatrix} 7 \\ 0 \end{pmatrix}$

Position vectors

To specify the position of an object, you define its displacement relative to a fixed origin. **a** and **b** are usually used to define the position vectors of A and B.

The vector between two points

The displacement AB can be replaced by the displacement from A to O followed by that from O to B.

$\mathbf{a} = \overrightarrow{OA},\ \mathbf{b} = \overrightarrow{OB}$
$\overrightarrow{AB} = \overrightarrow{AO} + \overrightarrow{OB}$
$\overrightarrow{AB} = -\mathbf{a} + \mathbf{b}$
$\qquad = \mathbf{b} - \mathbf{a}$

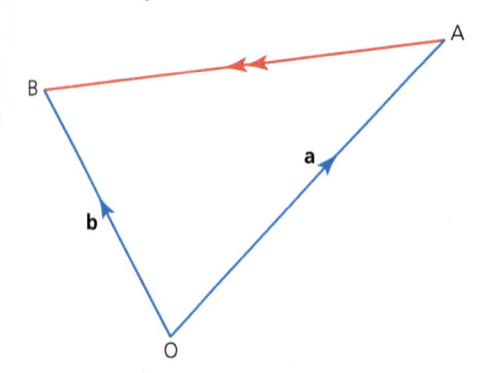

Figure 2.32

Any displacement vector $\overrightarrow{AB}$ can be written in terms of the position vectors of its two end points.

The magnitude and direction of vectors written in component form

The magnitude of a vector is just its length and can be found by using Pythagoras' theorem.

$$a = \sqrt{a_x^2 + a_y^2}$$

The direction is related to the angle the vector makes with the positive x-axis.

$$\theta = \arctan\left(\frac{a_y}{a_x}\right)$$

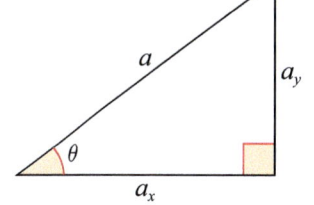

Figure 2.33

or $\theta = \arctan\left(\frac{a_x}{a_y}\right) + 180°$, depending on which quadrant θ is in.

Example 2.6

Find the magnitude and direction of each of the four vectors
$\mathbf{a} = \begin{pmatrix} 3 \\ 2 \end{pmatrix}$, $\mathbf{b} = \begin{pmatrix} -1 \\ 4 \end{pmatrix}$, $\mathbf{c} = -2\mathbf{i} - 2\mathbf{j}$ and $\mathbf{d} = 3\mathbf{i} - \mathbf{j}$.

Solution

$\mathbf{a} = \begin{pmatrix} 3 \\ 2 \end{pmatrix}$

Magnitude $|\mathbf{a}| = \sqrt{3^2 + 2^2} = \sqrt{13} = 3.61$

Direction $\theta = \arctan\left(\frac{2}{3}\right) = 33.7°$

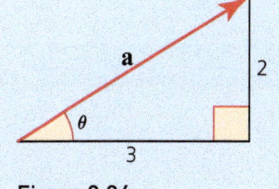

Figure 2.34

$\mathbf{b} = \begin{pmatrix} -1 \\ 4 \end{pmatrix}$

Magnitude $|\mathbf{b}| = \sqrt{(-1)^2 + 4^2} = \sqrt{17} = 4.12$

$\tan\phi = \frac{4}{1} \Rightarrow \phi = \arctan 4 = 76.0°$

Direction $\theta = 180 - \phi = 104°$

$\mathbf{c} = -2\mathbf{i} - 2\mathbf{j}$

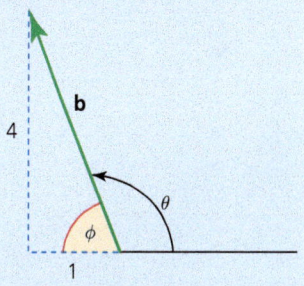

Figure 2.35

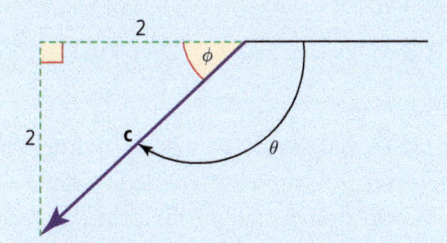

Figure 2.36

Magnitude $|\mathbf{c}| = \sqrt{(-2)^2 + (-2)^2} = \sqrt{8} = 2.83$

$\tan\phi = \frac{2}{2} = 1 \Rightarrow \phi = \arctan 1 = 45°$

Working with vectors

Direction $\theta = -(180° - 45°) = -135°$

$\mathbf{d} = 3\mathbf{i} - \mathbf{j}$

Figure 2.37

Magnitude $|\mathbf{d}| = \sqrt{3^2 + (-1)^2} = \sqrt{10} = 3.16$

Direction $\theta = -\arctan\left(\frac{1}{3}\right) = -18.4°$

Finding unit vectors along given directions

If $\mathbf{a} = a_x\mathbf{i} + a_y\mathbf{j}$, the magnitude of $\mathbf{a}$ is $|\mathbf{a}| = \sqrt{a_x^2 + a_y^2}$. A unit vector along $\mathbf{a}$ (denoted by $\hat{\mathbf{a}}$) has magnitude 1. $\hat{\mathbf{a}}$ is parallel to $\mathbf{a}$ but has a magnitude which is scaled by the factor $\frac{1}{|\mathbf{a}|}$.

$$\hat{\mathbf{a}} = \frac{\mathbf{a}}{|\mathbf{a}|} = \frac{a_x}{\sqrt{a_x^2 + a_y^2}}\mathbf{i} + \frac{a_y}{\sqrt{a_x^2 + a_y^2}}\mathbf{j}$$

Example 2.7

(i) Find a unit vector along $\mathbf{a} = 3.5\mathbf{i} - 12\mathbf{j}$

(ii) Find a vector along $\mathbf{a}$ which is 25 units long.

Solution

(i) The magnitude of $\mathbf{a}$ is $|\mathbf{a}| = \sqrt{3.5^2 + (-12)^2} = \sqrt{12.25 + 144}$
$= \sqrt{156.25} = 12.5$

A unit vector along $\mathbf{a}$ is $\hat{\mathbf{a}} = \frac{3.5}{12.5}\mathbf{i} - \frac{12}{12.5}\mathbf{j} = 0.28\mathbf{i} - 0.96\mathbf{j}$

(ii) $\hat{\mathbf{a}}$ has magnitude 1, so you are looking for a vector along $\mathbf{a}$ which is 25 units long, i.e. $25\hat{\mathbf{a}} = 25(0.28\mathbf{i} - 0.96\mathbf{j}) = 7\mathbf{i} - 24\mathbf{j}$

Resolving a force into components in two perpendicular directions

Draw the vector $\mathbf{F}$, magnitude F, making an angle θ with the x-axis, taken as the $\mathbf{i}$ direction. Make up the right-angled triangle with $\mathbf{F}$ along the hypotenuse and the x and y components along the other two sides. These are then evaluated using trigonometry.

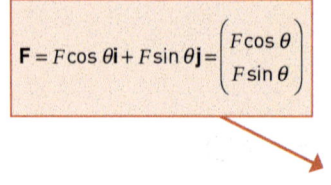

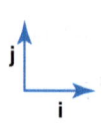

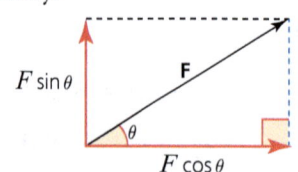

$\mathbf{F} = F\cos\theta\,\mathbf{i} + F\sin\theta\,\mathbf{j} = \begin{pmatrix} F\cos\theta \\ F\sin\theta \end{pmatrix}$

Figure 2.38

Example 2.8

Resolve a weight W N in two directions which are along and at right angles to a slope making an angle θ with the horizontal.

Solution

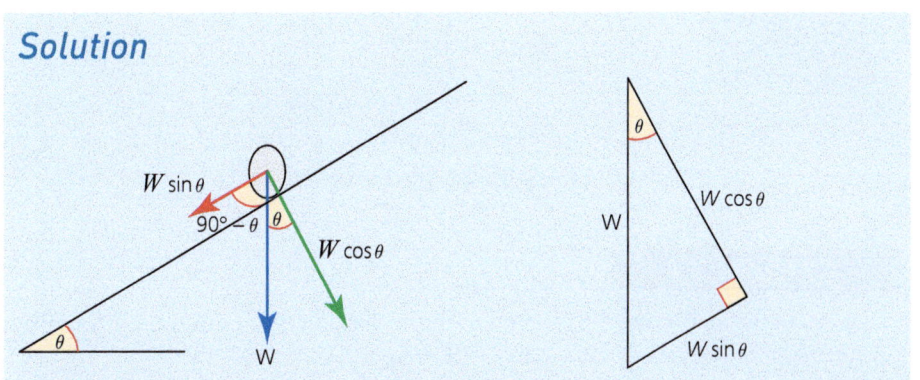

Figure 2.39

W is the hypotenuse of the right-angled triangle. The components are along the other two sides. The component parallel to the slope is $W \cos(90° - \theta) = W \sin \theta$.

The component perpendicular to the slope is $W \cos \theta$.

Example 2.9

Two forces **P** and **Q** have magnitudes 10 N and 15 N in the directions shown in Figure 2.40.

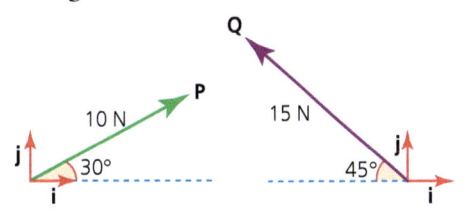

Figure 2.40

Find the magnitude and direction of the resultant force **P** + **Q**.

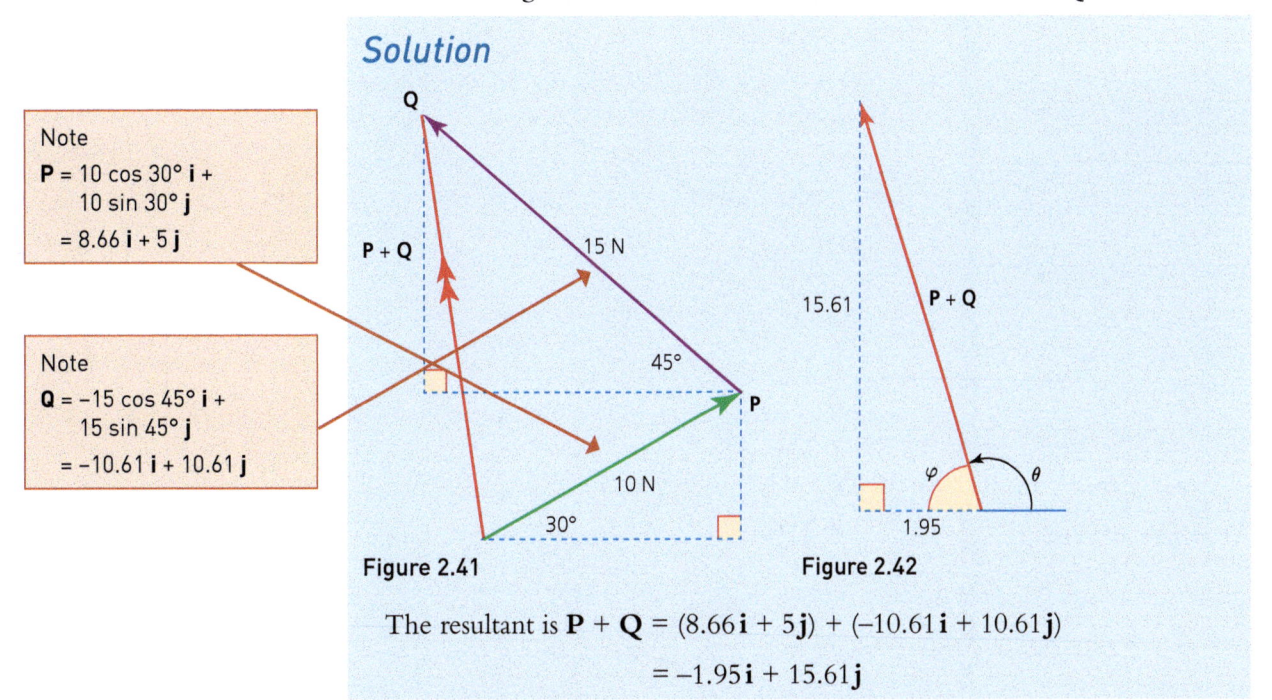

Solution

Note
$\mathbf{P} = 10 \cos 30°\, \mathbf{i} + 10 \sin 30°\, \mathbf{j}$
$= 8.66\, \mathbf{i} + 5\, \mathbf{j}$

Note
$\mathbf{Q} = -15 \cos 45°\, \mathbf{i} + 15 \sin 45°\, \mathbf{j}$
$= -10.61\, \mathbf{i} + 10.61\, \mathbf{j}$

Figure 2.41   **Figure 2.42**

The resultant is $\mathbf{P} + \mathbf{Q} = (8.66\, \mathbf{i} + 5\, \mathbf{j}) + (-10.61\, \mathbf{i} + 10.61\, \mathbf{j})$

$= -1.95\, \mathbf{i} + 15.61\, \mathbf{j}$

It is shown in Figure 2.42.

The magnitude of the resultant is $|P+Q| = \sqrt{(-1.95)^2 + 15.61^2} = 15.73$

The direction of the resultant:

$\tan \varphi = \frac{15.61}{1.95} \Rightarrow \varphi = \arctan(8.01) = 82.9°$

$\theta = 180° - 82.9° = 97.1°$

The resultant force **P + Q** has magnitude 15.73 and direction 97.1° relative to the positive *x*-axis.

Exercise 2.2

① Four vectors are given in component form by **a** = 3**i** + 4**j**, **b** = 6**i** – 7**j**, **c** = –2**i** + 5**j** and **d** = –5**i** – 3**j**.

Find the vectors

(i) **a** + **b** (ii) **b** + **c** (iii) **c** + **d**
(iv) **a** + **b** + **d** (v) **a** – **b** (vi) **d** – **b** + **c**

② A, B, C are the points (1, 2), (5, 1) and (7, 8).

(i) Write down in terms of **i** and **j** the position vectors of these three points.

(ii) Find the component form of the displacements $\overrightarrow{AB}$, $\overrightarrow{BC}$ and $\overrightarrow{CA}$.

(iii) Draw a diagram to show the position vectors of A, B and C and your answers to part (ii).

③ Three vectors **a**, **b** and **c** are given by $\mathbf{a} = \begin{pmatrix} 1 \\ 1 \end{pmatrix}$, $\mathbf{b} = \begin{pmatrix} -1 \\ 2 \end{pmatrix}$ and $\mathbf{c} = \begin{pmatrix} 3 \\ -4 \end{pmatrix}$.

R is the endpoint of the displacement 2**a** – 3**b** + **c** and (1, –2) is the starting point. What is the position vector of R?

④ Find the magnitude and direction of the following vectors

(i) 12**i** – 5**j** (ii) 7**i** + 24**j** (iii) –**i** + **j**
(iv) 3**i** + 4**j** (v) 2**i** – 3**j** (vi) –**i** – 2**j**

⑤ Write down the following vectors in component form in terms of **i** and **j**

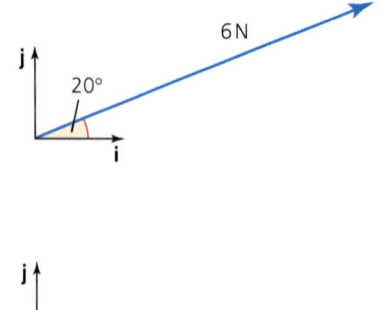

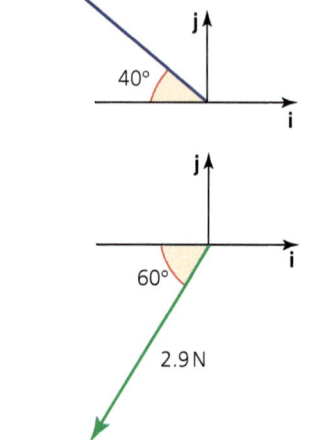

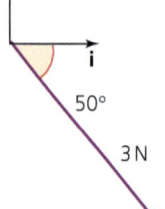

Figure 2.43

⑥ (i) Find a unit vector in the direction of $\begin{pmatrix} 10 \\ 24 \end{pmatrix}$.

A force **F** acts in the direction of $\begin{pmatrix} 10 \\ 24 \end{pmatrix}$ and has magnitude 39 N.

(ii) Use your answer to part (i) to write **F** in component form.

⑦ Find the vector with magnitude 8.2 that is parallel to the vector $40\mathbf{i} - 9\mathbf{j}$.

⑧ Write down each of the following vectors in terms of **i** and **j**. Find the resultant of each set of vectors in terms of **i** and **j**.

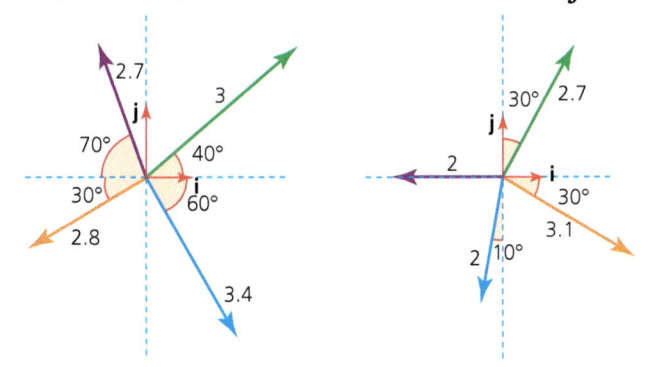

Figure 2.44

⑨ The displacement of B from A is $\begin{pmatrix} 4 \\ 1 \end{pmatrix}$. The displacement of C from A is $\begin{pmatrix} -2 \\ 3 \end{pmatrix}$. The displacement of D from A is $\begin{pmatrix} 0 \\ -4 \end{pmatrix}$.

Draw a diagram showing the relative position of A, B, C and D. Find

(i) $\overrightarrow{DB}$ (ii) $\overrightarrow{DC}$ (iii) $\overrightarrow{CB}$ (iv) $\overrightarrow{BC}$

⑩ Three vectors **a**, **b** and **c** are represented by the sides of a triangle ABC, as shown in Figure 2.45.

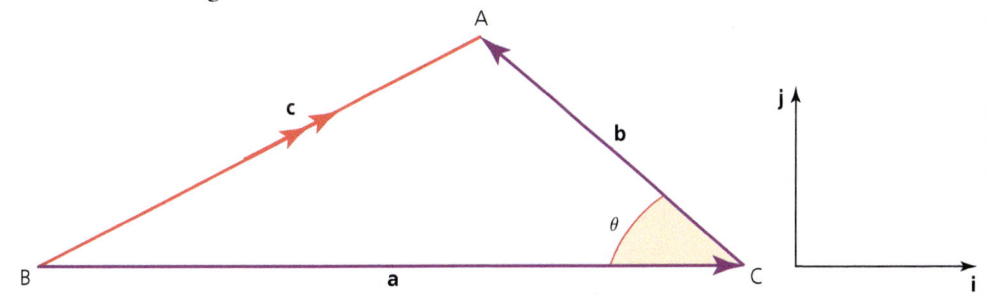

Figure 2.45

The angle C is θ and $|\mathbf{a}|$, $|\mathbf{b}|$ and $|\mathbf{c}|$ are a, b and c. Answer each part in terms of θ, a, b and c.

(i) Write **a** and **b** in terms of **i** and **j**.

(ii) Find $\mathbf{a} + \mathbf{b}$ and hence $|\mathbf{a} + \mathbf{b}|^2$.

(iii) Use your answer to part (ii) to express c^2 in terms of a, b and θ.

3 Forces in equilibrium

When forces are in equilibrium their vector sum is zero and the sum of the resolved parts in **any** direction is zero.

Example 2.10

A brick of mass 5 kg is at rest on a rough plane inclined at an angle of 35° to the horizontal. Find the frictional force F N, and the normal reaction R N of the plane on the brick.

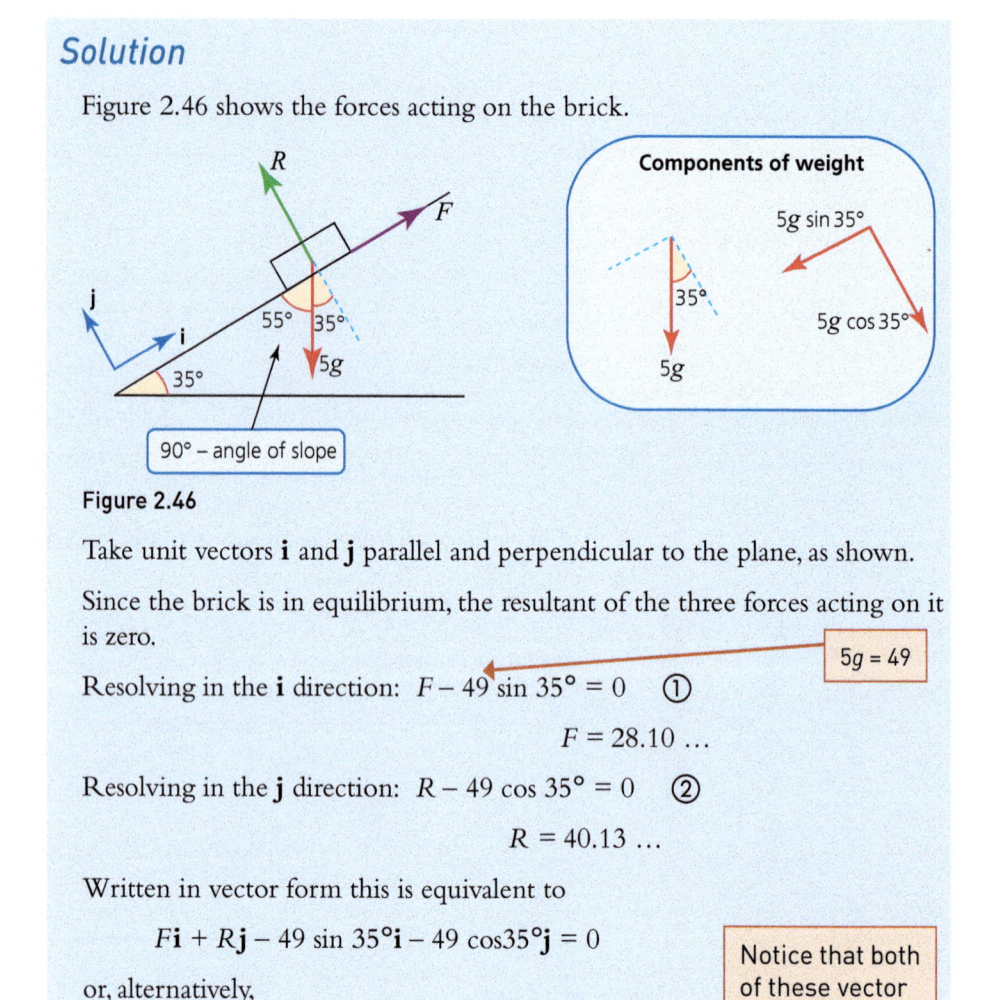

Solution

Figure 2.46 shows the forces acting on the brick.

Figure 2.46

Take unit vectors **i** and **j** parallel and perpendicular to the plane, as shown.

Since the brick is in equilibrium, the resultant of the three forces acting on it is zero.

Resolving in the **i** direction: $F - 49 \sin 35° = 0$ ①

$$F = 28.10 \ldots$$

Resolving in the **j** direction: $R - 49 \cos 35° = 0$ ②

$$R = 40.13 \ldots$$

Written in vector form this is equivalent to

$$F\mathbf{i} + R\mathbf{j} - 49 \sin 35°\mathbf{i} - 49 \cos 35°\mathbf{j} = 0$$

or, alternatively,

$$\begin{pmatrix} F \\ 0 \end{pmatrix} + \begin{pmatrix} 0 \\ R \end{pmatrix} + \begin{pmatrix} -49 \sin 35° \\ -49 \cos 35° \end{pmatrix} = \begin{pmatrix} 0 \\ 0 \end{pmatrix}$$

Notice that both of these vector equations lead to the equations ① and ② above.

$5g = 49$

The triangle of forces

When there are only three (non-parallel) forces acting and they are in equilibrium, the polygon of forces becomes a closed triangle, as shown for the brick on the plane.

Note

The triangle is closed because the resultant is zero.

When a body is in equilibrium under the action of three non-parallel forces, then:

(i) the forces can be represented in magnitude and direction by the sides of a triangle

(ii) the lines of action of the forces pass through the same point. They are concurrent.

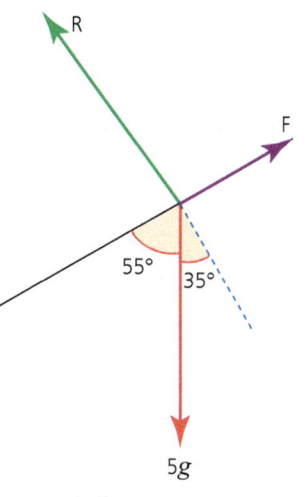

Figure 2.47

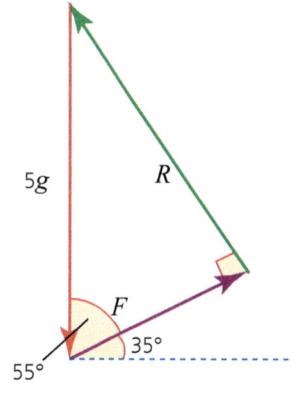

Figure 2.48

Then
$$\frac{F}{5g} = \cos 55°$$
$$F = 49 \cos 55° = 28.1 \, \text{N}$$

And similarly
$$R = 49 \sin 55° = 40.1 \, \text{N}$$

This is an example of the theorem known as the *triangle of forces*.

When more than three forces are in equilibrium, the first statement still holds but the triangle is then a polygon. The second statement is not necessarily true.

The next example illustrates two methods for solving problems involving forces in equilibrium. With experience, you will find it easier to judge which method is more suitable for a particular problem.

Example 2.11

A sign of mass 10 kg is to be suspended by two strings arranged as shown in Figure 2.49. Find the tension in each string.

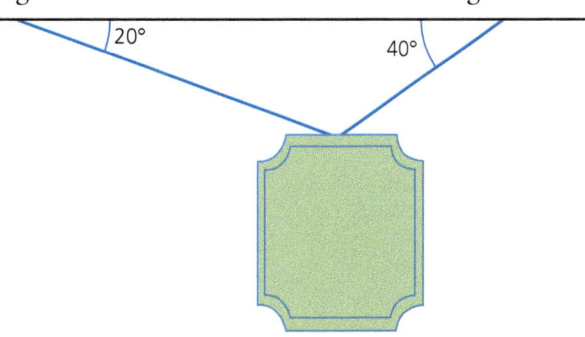

Figure 2.49

Solution

The force diagram for this situation is given in Figure 2.50.

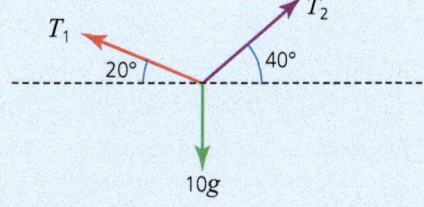

Figure 2.50

Forces in equilibrium

Method 1: Resolving forces

Vertically (↑): $T_1 \sin 20° + T_2 \sin 40° - 10g = 0$ ①

$$0.342\ldots T_1 + 0.642\ldots T_2 = 98$$

Horizontally (→): $-T_1 \cos 20° + T_2 \cos 40° = 0$ ②

$$-0.939\ldots T_1 + 0.766\ldots T_2 = 0$$

The set of simultaneous equations is solved in the usual way. Whether you are using the equation solver on your calculator or working it out on paper, it is important that you keep as much accuracy as possible by substituting for the different sines and cosines only at the very end of the calculation.

Multiply ① by $\cos 20°$ and then add ② × $\sin 20°$ to give

> You may recognise that this is the compound angle form for $\sin(40° + 20°)$ and so is the same as $\sin 60°$.

$$T_2(\sin 40° \cos 20° + \cos 40° \sin 20°) = 98 \cos 20°$$

$$T_2 = \frac{98 \cos 20°}{\sin 40° \cos 20° + \cos 40° \sin 20°}$$

$$T_2 = 106.33\ldots$$

Substituting back in ② now gives

$$T_1 = \frac{T_2 \cos 40°}{\cos 20°} = 86.68\ldots$$

The tensions in the strings are 86.7 N and 106.3 N.

Method 2: Triangle of forces

Since the three forces are in equilibrium they can be represented by the sides of a triangle taken in order.

> **Discussion point**
> In what order would you draw the three lines in Figure 2.51?

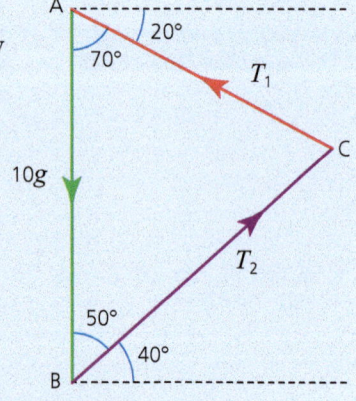

Figure 2.51

You can estimate the tensions by measurements. This will tell you that $T_1 \approx 87$ and $T_2 \approx 106$ in newtons.

Alternatively, you can use the sine rule to calculate T_1 and T_2 accurately.

In triangle ABC, $\widehat{CAB} = 70°$ and $\widehat{ABC} = 50°$, so $\widehat{BCA} = 60°$.

So

$$\frac{T_1}{\sin 50°} = \frac{T_2}{\sin 70°} = \frac{98}{\sin 60°}$$

> $180° - 70° - 50° = 60°$

giving $T_1 = \dfrac{98 \sin 50°}{\sin 60°}$ and $T_2 = \dfrac{98 \sin 70°}{\sin 60°}$

As before, the tensions are found to be 86.7 N and 106.3 N.

> **Discussion point**
>
> Lami's theorem states that when three forces acting at a point, as shown in Figure 2.52, are in equilibrium
>
> $$\frac{F_1}{\sin\alpha} = \frac{F_2}{\sin\beta} = \frac{F_3}{\sin\gamma}.$$
>
> Sketch a triangle of forces and say how the angles in the triangle are related to α, β and γ. Hence explain why Lami's theorem is true.
>
> **Figure 2.52**

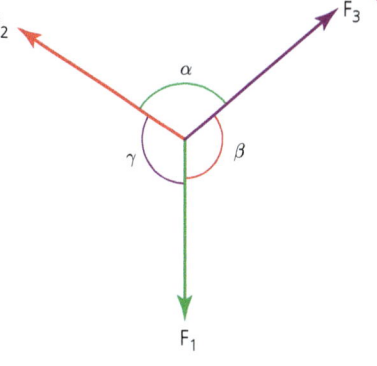

Example 2.12

Two husky dogs are pulling a sledge. They both exert forces of 60 N but at different angles to the line of the sledge, as shown in Figure 2.53. The sledge is moving straight forwards.

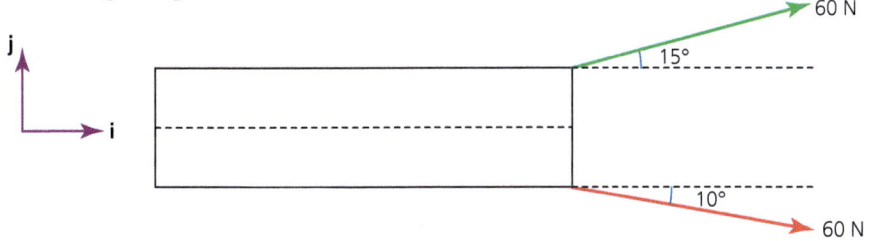

Figure 2.53

(i) Resolve the two forces into components parallel and perpendicular to the line of the sledge.

(ii) Find the overall forward force from the dogs and the overall sideways force.

The resistance to motion is 20 N along the line of the sledge and up to 400 N perpendicular to it.

(iii) Find the magnitude and direction of the overall horizontal force on the sledge.

(iv) How much force is lost due to the dogs not pulling straight forwards?

Solution

(i) Taking unit vectors $\mathbf{i}$ along the line of the sledge and $\mathbf{j}$ perpendicular to the line of the sledge.

The forces exerted by the two dogs are

$$60\cos 15°\,\mathbf{i} + 60\sin 15°\,\mathbf{j}$$

$$= 57.95\ldots\mathbf{i} + 15.52\ldots\mathbf{j}$$

and $\quad 60\cos 10°\,\mathbf{i} - 60\sin 10°\,\mathbf{j}$

$$= 59.08\ldots\mathbf{i} - 10.41\ldots\mathbf{j}$$

Forces in equilibrium

(ii) The overall forward force is equal to
$$60\cos 15° + 60\cos 10° = 117.04\ldots$$

The overall sideways force is equal to
$$60\sin 15° - 60\sin 10° = 5.11\ldots$$

(iii) The sideways force is cancelled by the resistance force opposing it.

The forward force is reduced by an amount 20 N from the resistance to motion.

So that the overall forward force is 97 N and the overall sideways force is 0.

The magnitude of the overall force on the sledge is thus 97 N in the direction of motion.

(iv) If the dogs were pulling straight, the overall force on the sledge would be 100 N, so the amount of force lost due to the dogs not pulling straight is thus 3 N.

[100 − 97.04…]

[60 + 60 − 20 (60 N from each dog less 20 N from the resistance)]

Exercise 2.3

① The following sets of forces are in equilibrium. Find the value of p and q in each case.

(i) $\begin{pmatrix} 24 \\ 18 \end{pmatrix}$ N, $\begin{pmatrix} 25 \\ 60 \end{pmatrix}$ N and $\begin{pmatrix} p \\ q \end{pmatrix}$ N

(ii) $\begin{pmatrix} p \\ -2 \end{pmatrix}$ N, $\begin{pmatrix} -3 \\ 4 \end{pmatrix}$ N and $\begin{pmatrix} 2 \\ -q \end{pmatrix}$ N

(iii) $\begin{pmatrix} 2p \\ 5 \end{pmatrix}$ N, $\begin{pmatrix} q \\ 4p \end{pmatrix}$ N, $\begin{pmatrix} p \\ -3 \end{pmatrix}$ N and $\begin{pmatrix} 5 \\ -q \end{pmatrix}$ N.

② A brick of mass 2 kg is resting on a rough plane inclined at 40° to the horizontal.

(i) Draw a diagram showing all the forces acting on the brick.

(ii) Find the normal reaction of the plane on the brick.

(iii) Find the frictional force acting on the brick.

③ A particle is in equilibrium under the three forces shown in Figure 2.54. Find the magnitude of the force F and the angle θ.

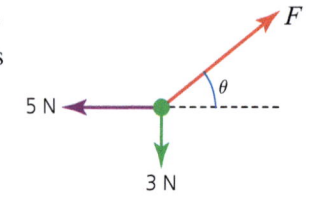

Figure 2.54

④ A box of mass 10 kg is at rest on a horizontal floor.

(i) Find the value of the normal reaction of the floor on the box.

The box remains at rest on the floor when a force of 30 N is applied to it at an angle of 25° to the upward vertical, as shown in Figure 2.55.

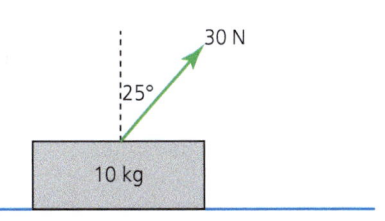

Figure 2.55

(i) Draw a diagram showing all the forces acting on the box.

(ii) Calculate the new value of the normal reaction of the floor on the box and also the frictional force.

⑤ A block of weight 100 N is on a rough plane that is inclined at 30° to the horizontal. The block is in equilibrium with a force of 35 N acting on it in the direction of the plane, as shown in Figure 2.56.

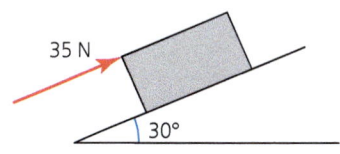

Figure 2.56

Calculate the frictional force acting on the block.

⑥ A crate of mass 10 kg is being pulled across rough horizontal ground by a rope making an angle θ with the horizontal. The tension in the rope is 60 N and the frictional force between the crate and the ground is 35 N. The crate is in equilibrium.

(i) Draw a labelled diagram showing all the forces acting on the crate.

(ii) Find the angle θ.

(iii) Find the normal reaction between the floor and the crate.

⑦ Each of three light strings has a block attached to one of its ends. The other ends of the strings are tied together at a point A. The strings are in equilibrium with two of them passing over fixed smooth pulleys and with the blocks hanging freely.

The weights of the blocks, and the angles between the sloping parts of the strings and the vertical, are as shown in the diagram. Find the values of W_1 and W_2.

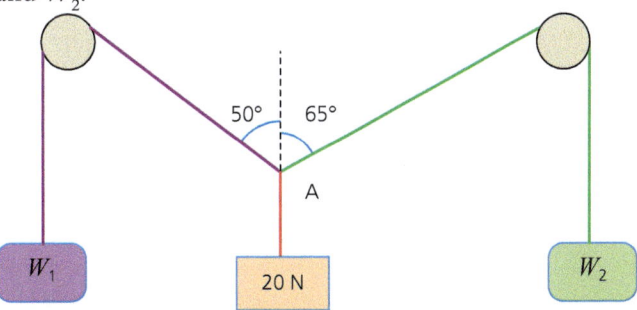

Figure 2.57

⑧ A block of mass 10 kg rests in equilibrium on a smooth plane inclined at 30° to the horizontal. It is held by a light string making an angle of 15° with the line of greatest slope of the plane.

(i) Draw a labelled diagram showing all the forces acting on the block.

(ii) Find the tension in the string and the normal reaction of the plane on the block.

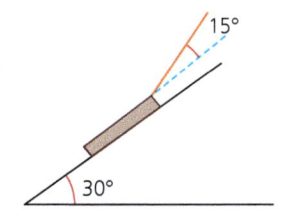

Figure 2.58

Forces in equilibrium

⑨ A particle A of mass 3 kg is at rest in equilibrium on horizontal rough ground. A is attached to two light, inextensible strings making angles of 20° and 50° with the vertical. The tensions in the two strings are 10 N and 20 N, as shown in Figure 2.59.

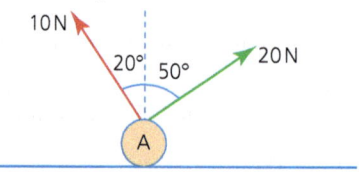

Figure 2.59

(i) Draw a diagram showing all the forces acting on A.
(ii) Find the normal reaction between the ground and A.
(iii) Find the magnitude of the frictional force, indicating the direction in which it is acting.

⑩ Four wires, all of them horizontal, are attached to the top of a telegraph pole as shown in this plan view. There is no overall force on the pole and tensions in the wires are as shown.

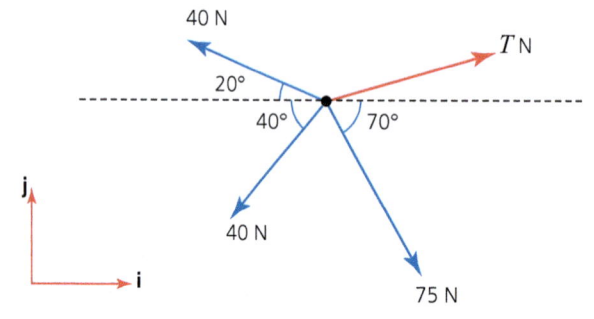

Figure 2.60

(i) Using perpendicular directions as shown in Figure 2.60, show that the force of 75 N may be written as $(25.7\mathbf{i} - 70.5\mathbf{j})$ N (to 3 significant figures).
(ii) Find T in both component form and magnitude and direction form.
(iii) The force T is changed to $(40\mathbf{i} + 50\mathbf{j})$ N. Show that there is now a resultant force on the pole and find its magnitude and direction.

⑪ A ship is being towed by two tugs. They exert forces on the ship as indicated.

There is also a drag force on the ship.

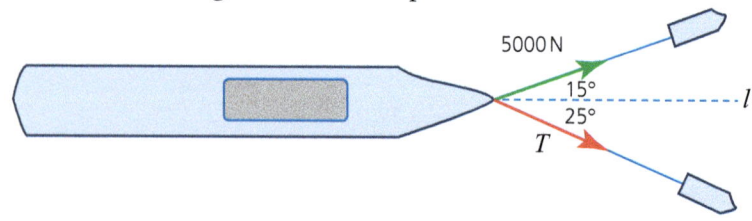

Figure 2.61

(i) Write down the components of the tensions in the towing cables along and perpendicular to the line of motion, l, of the ship.
(ii) Show that there is no resultant force perpendicular to the line l. Find T.
(iii) The ship is travelling with constant velocity along the line l. Find the magnitude of the drag force acting on it.

⑫ A skier of mass 60 kg is skiing down a slope inclined at 20° to the horizontal.
  (i) Draw a diagram showing the forces acting on the skier.
  (ii) Resolve these forces into components parallel and perpendicular to the slope.
  (iii) The skier is travelling at constant speed. Find the normal reaction of the slope on the skier and the resistive force on her.
  (iv) The skier later returns to the top of the slope by being pulled up it at constant speed by a rope parallel to the slope. Assuming the resistance on the skier is the same as before, calculate the tension in the rope.

⑬ Figure 2.62 shows a block of mass 10 kg on a rough inclined plane. The block is attached to a 7 kg weight by a light string which passes over a smooth pulley; it is on the point of sliding up the slope.
  (i) Draw a diagram showing the forces acting on the block.

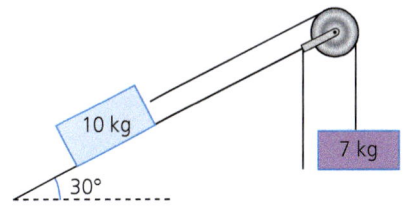

Figure 2.62

  (ii) Resolve these forces into components parallel and perpendicular to the slope.
  (iii) Find the force of resistance to the block's motion.

The 7 kg mass is replaced by one of mass m kg.

  (iv) Find the value of m for which the block is on the point of sliding down the slope, assuming the resistance to motion is the same as before.

⑭ Figure 2.63 shows a sign attached to a point A by a light rigid rod AB. It is supported by two light rigid rods AC and AD. AC is horizontal and AD makes an angle θ with the horizontal with $\tan \theta = 0.75$. The mass of the sign is 20 kg.

Find the forces in the rods AB, AC and AD, stating whether they are in tension or compression.

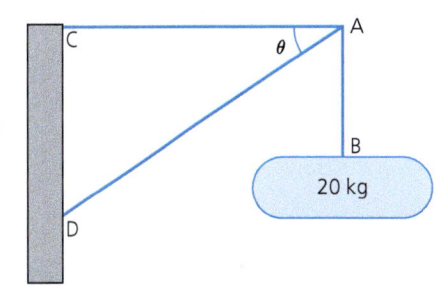

Figure 2.63

⑮ A block of mass 75 kg is in equilibrium on smooth horizontal ground with one end of a light string attached to its upper edge. The string passes over a smooth pulley, with a block of mass m kg attached at the other end.

The part of the string between the pulley and the block makes an angle of 65° with the horizontal. A horizontal force F is also acting on the block.

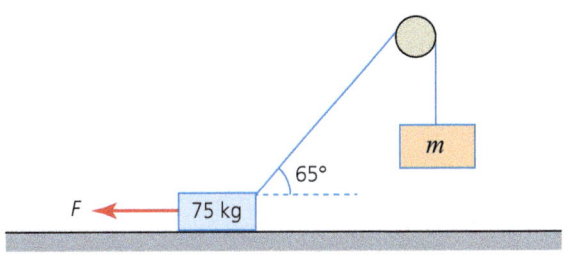

Figure 2.64

  (i) Find a relationship between T, the tension in the string, and R, the normal reaction between the block and the ground.

The block is on the point of lifting off the ground.

  (ii) Find T and m.
  (iii) Find F.

Finding resultant forces

⑯ Two boxes of masses 15 kg and 12 kg are held by light strings AB, BC and CD. As shown in the figure, AB makes an angle α with the horizontal and is fixed at A.

Angle α is such that $\sin \alpha = 0.28$. BC is horizontal and CD makes an angle β with the horizontal.

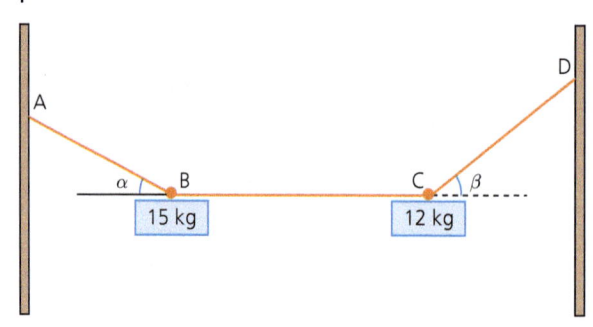

Figure 2.65

(i) By considering the equilibrium of point B, find the tension in string AB and show that the tension in string BC is 504 N.

(ii) Find β and the tension in CD.

4 Finding resultant forces

When forces are in equilibrium, their resultant is zero. However, forces are not always in equilibrium. The next example shows you how to find the resultant of forces that are not in equilibrium. You know from Newton's second law that the acceleration of the body will be in the same direction as the resultant force; remember that force and acceleration are both vector quantities.

Example 2.13

A sledge is being pulled up a smooth slope inclined at an angle of 15° to the horizontal by a rope which makes an angle of 30° with the slope. The mass of the sledge is 5 kg and the tension in the rope is 40 N.

(i) Draw a diagram to show the forces acting on the sledge.

(ii) Find the resultant of these forces.

(iii) Find the acceleration of the sledge.

Solution

(i) Figure 2.66 is the force diagram.

(ii) **Method 1**

Resolve the forces into components parallel and perpendicular to the slope.

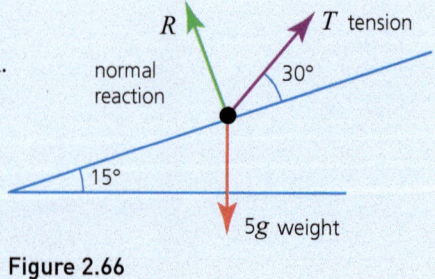

Figure 2.66

> **Note**
>
> When the sledge is modelled as a particle, all the forces can be assumed to be acting at a point.

> **Note**
> There is no frictional force because the slope is smooth.

> **Hint**
> Notice that although the sledge is moving up the slope this does not mean that the resultant force is up the slope. Its direction depends on the acceleration of the sledge which may be up or down the slope, or zero if the sledge is moving at constant speed.

Components of the weight

Components of the tension

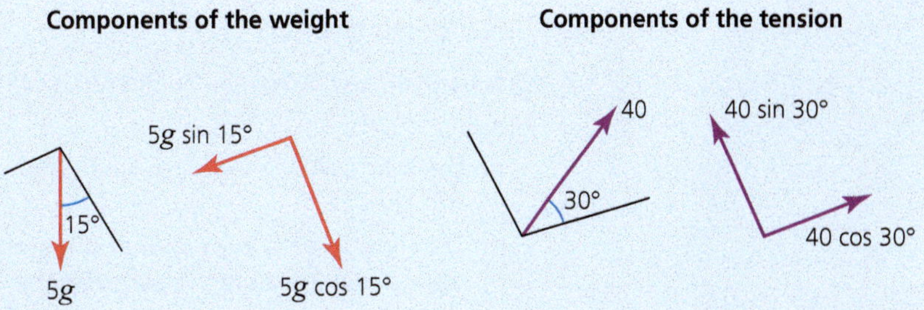

Figure 2.67

Resolve parallel to the slope: →

The resultant is $F = 40\cos 30° - 5g\sin 15°$
$= 21.959...$

*The force **R** is perpendicular to the slope so it has no component in this direction*

Resolve perpendicular to the slope: →

$R + 40\sin 30° - 5g\cos 15° = 0$
$R = 5g\cos 15° - 40\sin 30° = 27.33$

There is no resultant force in this direction because the motion is parallel to the slope

To 3 significant figures, the normal reaction is 27.3 N and the resultant force is 22.0 N up the slope.

Method 2

Alternatively, you could have worked in column vectors as follows.

$$\begin{pmatrix} 0 \\ R \end{pmatrix} + \begin{pmatrix} 40\cos 30° \\ 40\sin 30° \end{pmatrix} + \begin{pmatrix} -5g\sin 15° \\ -5g\cos 15° \end{pmatrix} = \begin{pmatrix} F \\ 0 \end{pmatrix}$$

Parallel to slope

Perpendicular to slope

normal reaction + tension + weight = resultant force

(iii) Once you know the resultant force you can work out the acceleration of the sledge using Newton's second law.

$F = ma$
$21.959... = 5a$
$a = \dfrac{21.959...}{5} = 4.392...$

The acceleration is $4.4\,\text{m s}^{-2}$ (correct to 1 d.p.)

> **Discussion point**
> Try resolving horizontally and vertically. You will obtain 2 equations in the two unknowns F and R. It is perfectly possible to solve these equations, but is quite a lot of work. How can you decide which directions will be easiest to work with?

The resultant force is in the direction of motion and so must be parallel to the slope

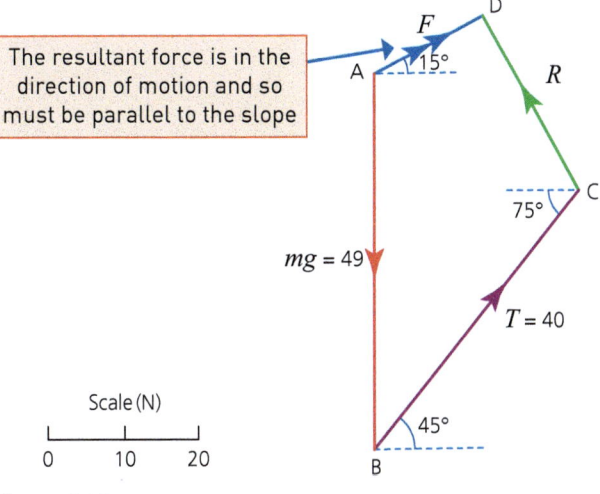

An alternative way of approaching the previous example is to draw a scale diagram with the three forces represented by three of the sides of a quadrilateral taken in order (with the arrows following each other, $\overrightarrow{AB}, \overrightarrow{BC}$ and $\overrightarrow{CD}$), as shown in Figure 2.68. The resultant is represented by the fourth side AD.

From the diagram, you can estimate the normal reaction to be about 30 N and the resultant 20 N.

> **Discussion point**
> In what order would you draw the lines in the diagram?

Figure 2.68

Finding resultant forces

> **Discussion point**
>
> What can you say about the acceleration of the sledge in the cases when:
>
> (i) the length AD in Figure 2.68 on the previous page is not zero?
>
> (ii) the length AD is zero so that the starting point on the quadrilateral is the same as the finishing point?
>
> (iii) BC is so short that the point D is to the left of A as shown in Figure 2.69?
>
> Figure 2.69

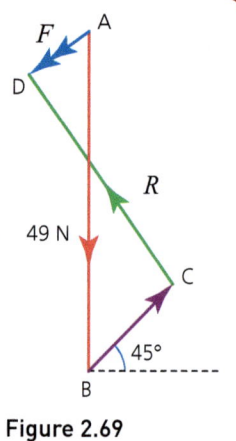

Example 2.14

Two forces **P** and **Q** act at a point O on a particle of mass 2 kg. Force **P** has magnitude 50 N and acts along a bearing of 030°. Force **Q** has magnitude of 30 N and acts along a bearing of 315°.

(i) Find the magnitude and bearing of the resultant force **P** + **Q**.

(ii) Find the acceleration of the particle.

Solution

(i) Forces **P** and **Q** are illustrated below.

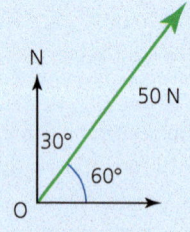

Figure 2.70

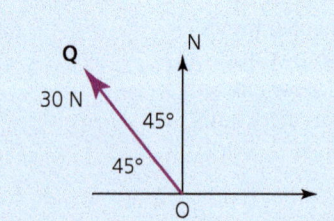

$$\mathbf{P} = \begin{pmatrix} 50\cos 60° \\ 50\sin 60° \end{pmatrix}$$

$$= \begin{pmatrix} 25 \\ 43.30... \end{pmatrix}$$

$$\mathbf{Q} = \begin{pmatrix} -30\cos 45° \\ 30\sin 45° \end{pmatrix}$$

$$= \begin{pmatrix} -21.21... \\ 21.21... \end{pmatrix}$$

$$\mathbf{P} + \mathbf{Q} = \begin{pmatrix} 25 \\ 43.30... \end{pmatrix} + \begin{pmatrix} -21.21... \\ 21.21... \end{pmatrix}$$

$$= \begin{pmatrix} 3.78... \\ 64.51... \end{pmatrix}$$

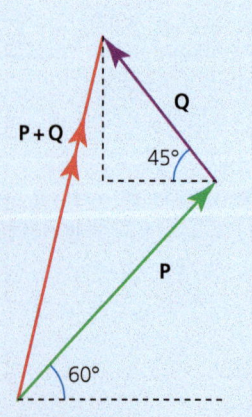

Figure 2.71

> **Note**
>
> Notice that **P** and **Q** are written as vectors.

The resultant is shown in Figure 2.72.

Magnitude $|\mathbf{P}+\mathbf{Q}| = \sqrt{3.78...^2 + 64.51...^2}$
$= 64.62$

Direction $\tan\theta = \dfrac{64.51...}{3.78...}$
$\theta = 86.64...°$

The bearing is $90° - 86.64...° = 3.36...°$

The force $\mathbf{P} + \mathbf{Q}$ has magnitude 65 N and bearing 003°.

(ii) The acceleration of the particle is given by

$$\mathbf{a} = \tfrac{1}{2}(\mathbf{P}+\mathbf{Q}) = \tfrac{1}{2}\begin{pmatrix}3.78...\\64.51...\end{pmatrix} = \begin{pmatrix}1.89\\32.3\end{pmatrix}$$

The magnitude of the acceleration is $= \sqrt{1.89^2 + 32.3^2} = 32.4$.

The bearing is $\arctan\left(\dfrac{1.89}{32.3}\right) = 3.35°$.

$\mathbf{P}$ and $\mathbf{Q}$ give the particle an acceleration of $32.3\,\text{m s}^{-2}$ on a bearing of 003°.

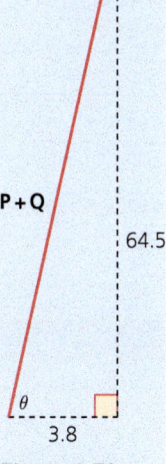

Figure 2.72

Sometimes, as in the next example, it is just as easy to work with the trigonometry of the diagram as with the components of the forces.

Example 2.15

The angle between the lines of action of two forces $\mathbf{X}$ and $\mathbf{Y}$ is θ. Find the magnitude and direction of the resultant.

Solution

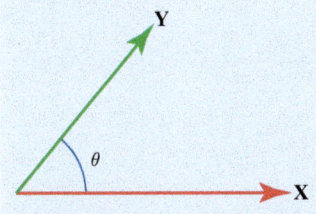

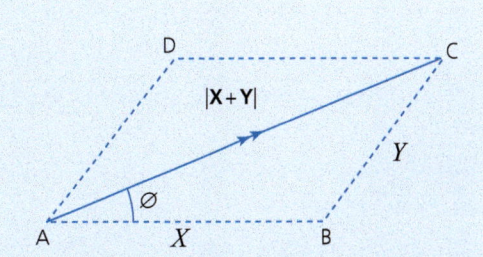

Figure 2.73

Use the cosine rule in triangle ABC. The magnitude of the resultant is F.

$$F = |\mathbf{X}+\mathbf{Y}| = \sqrt{AB^2 + BC^2 - 2AB \times BC \times \cos(\widehat{ABC})}$$
$$= \sqrt{X^2 + Y^2 - 2XY\cos(180° - \theta)}$$
$$= \sqrt{X^2 + Y^2 + 2XY\cos\theta}$$

Use the sine rule in triangle ABC. The resultant makes an angle $\varnothing$ with the $\mathbf{X}$ force.

Finding resultant forces

$$\frac{\sin \widehat{CAB}}{BC} = \frac{\sin \widehat{ABC}}{AC}$$

$$\frac{\sin \emptyset}{Y} = \frac{\sin(180° - \theta)}{F}$$

$$\sin \emptyset = \frac{Y}{F} \sin \theta$$

$$\emptyset = \arcsin\left(\frac{Y}{F} \sin \theta\right)$$

The resultant of the two forces **X** and **Y** inclined at θ has magnitude $F = \sqrt{X^2 + Y^2 + 2XY \cos \theta}$ and makes an angle $\arcsin\left(\frac{Y}{F} \sin \theta\right)$ with the **X** force.

Exercise 2.4

For questions 1–6, carry out the following steps. All forces are in newtons.

(i) Draw a scale diagram to show the forces and their resultant.

(ii) State whether you think the forces are in equilibrium and, if not, estimate the magnitude and direction of the resultant.

(iii) Write the forces in component form, using the directions indicated and so obtain the components of the resultant. Hence find the magnitude and direction of the resultant.

(iv) Compare your answers to parts (ii) and (iii).

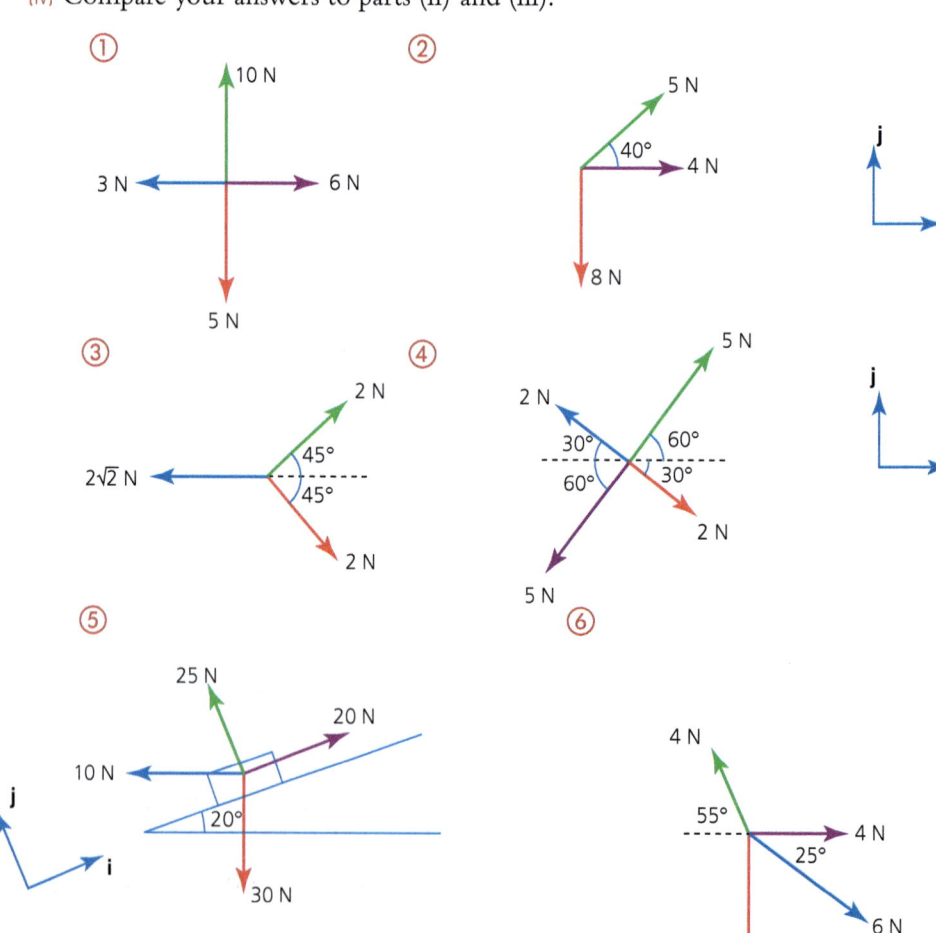

Figure 2.74

⑦ Four horizontal wires are attached to a telephone post and exert the following tensions on it: 25 N in the north direction, 30 N in the east direction, 45 N in the north-west direction and 50 N in the south-west direction. Calculate the resultant tension on the post and find its direction.

⑧ Forces of magnitude 7 N, 10 N and 15 N act on a particle of mass 1.5 kg in the directions shown in Figure 2.75.

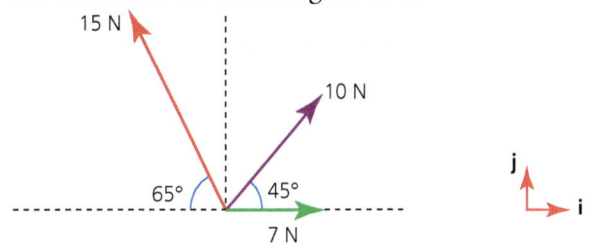

Figure 2.75

(i) Find the components of the resultant of the three forces in the **i** and **j** directions.

(ii) Find the magnitude and direction of the resultant.

(iii) Find the acceleration of the particle.

⑨ (i) Find the resultant of the set of 6 forces whose magnitudes and directions are shown in Figure 2.76.

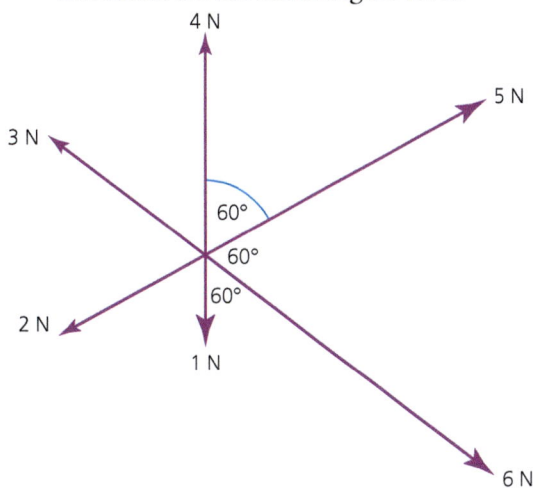

Figure 2.76

The forces are acting on a particle P of mass 5 kg which is initially at rest at O.

(ii) How fast is P moving after 3 s and how far from O is it now?

⑩ A force **P** of magnitude 5 N makes an angle of 60° with a force **Q** of magnitude 4 N. Find the magnitude of the resultant force and the angle it makes with the **P** force.

⑪ Two forces **P** and **Q** are at right angles to each other. The resultant has magnitude 20 N and makes an angle 60° with **P**. Find the magnitude of **P** and **Q**.

⑫ The resultant of two forces **P** and **Q** acting on a particle has magnitude $P = |\mathbf{P}|$. The resultant of the two forces 3**P** and 2**Q** acting in the same directions as before has magnitude 2P. Find the magnitude of **Q** and the angle between **P** and **Q**.

Finding resultant forces

KEY POINTS

1. **Newton's laws of motion**
   - Every object continues in a state of rest or uniform motion in a straight line unless it is acted on by an external force.
   - Resultant force = mass × acceleration or **F** = m**a**
   - When one object exerts a force on another there is always a reaction force which is equal and opposite in direction to the acting force.

2. Force is a vector. It may be represented in either magnitude–direction form or in component form

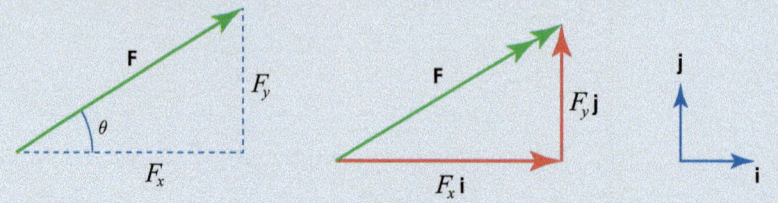

Figure 2.77

Magnitude of $\mathbf{F} = |\mathbf{F}| = \sqrt{F_x^2 + F_y^2}$ $\mathbf{F} = F_x\mathbf{i} + F_y\mathbf{j} = \begin{pmatrix} F_x \\ F_y \end{pmatrix}$

Direction of **F** $\theta = \arctan\left(\dfrac{F_y}{F_x}\right)$

3. **Resolving forces**

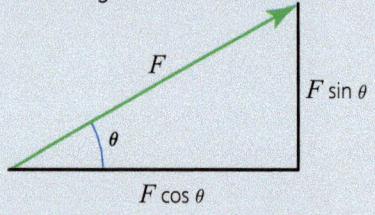

Figure 2.78

$\mathbf{F} = F\cos\theta\,\mathbf{i} + F\sin\theta\,\mathbf{j} = \begin{pmatrix} F\cos\theta \\ F\sin\theta \end{pmatrix}$

4. **Resultant forces**

$\mathbf{R} = \mathbf{F} + \mathbf{G} + \mathbf{H} = \begin{pmatrix} F_x \\ F_y \end{pmatrix} + \begin{pmatrix} G_x \\ G_y \end{pmatrix} + \begin{pmatrix} H_x \\ H_y \end{pmatrix}$

$\mathbf{R} = \begin{pmatrix} X \\ Y \end{pmatrix}$, $X = F_x + G_x + H_x$, $Y = F_y + G_y + H_y$

Figure 2.79

Magnitude of $\mathbf{R} = \sqrt{X^2 + Y^2}$ Direction of **R** $\theta = \arctan\left(\dfrac{Y}{X}\right)$

5. **Equilibrium**
   When the resultant is zero, the forces are in equilibrium.

6. **Triangle of forces**
   If an object is in equilibrium under three non-parallel forces, their lines of action are concurrent and they can be represented by a triangle.

LEARNING OUTCOMES

When you have finished this chapter, you should be able to

- draw a diagram showing the forces acting on a body
- apply Newton's laws of motion to problems in one or more dimensions
- resolve a force into components having selected suitable directions for resolution
- find the resultant of several concurrent forces
- realise that a particle is in equilibrium under a set of concurrent forces if and only if the resultant force is zero
- know that a closed polygon may be drawn to represent the forces acting on a particle in equilibrium
- formulate equations for equilibrium by resolving forces in suitable directions
- formulate the equation of motion of a particle which is being acted on by several forces
- know that contact between two surfaces is lost when the normal reaction force becomes zero.

3 A model for friction

A gem cannot be polished without friction, nor a man perfected without trials
— Lucius Annaeus Seneca

Figure 3.1 When an accident involving a collision happens, skid marks are sometimes left on the roadway by a vehicle that has locked its brakes. By measuring the skid marks and applying mechanics, it is possible to estimate the speed of the vehicle, prior to collision.

Discussion point

In the situation illustrated here, the red car left a 10 metre skid mark on the road. The driver of the car claimed that this showed he was driving within the speed limit of 30 mph.

It is the duty of a court to decide whether the driver of the red car was innocent or guilty. Is it possible to deduce his speed from the skid mark? Draw a sketch and make a list of the important factors that you would need to consider when modelling this situation.

1 A model for friction

Clearly, the key information about the accident involving the red car is provided by the skid marks. To interpret it, you need a model for how friction works; in this case, between the car's tyres and the road.

As a result of experimental work, Coulomb formulated a model for friction between two surfaces. The following laws are usually attributed to him.

1. Friction always opposes relative motion between two surfaces in contact.
2. Friction is independent of the relative speed of the surfaces.
3. The magnitude of the frictional force has a maximum which depends on the normal reaction between the surfaces and on the roughness of the surfaces in contact.
4. If there is no sliding between the surfaces

    $F \leq \mu R$

    where F is the force due to friction and R is the normal reaction. μ is called the **coefficient of friction**.
5. When sliding is just about to occur, friction is said to be **limiting** and $F = \mu R$.
6. When sliding occurs $F = \mu R$.

According to Coulomb's model, μ is a constant for any pair of surfaces. Typical values and ranges of values for the coefficient of friction μ are given in the table.

Surfaces in contact	μ
Wood sliding on wood	0.2–0.6
Metal sliding on metal	0.15–0.3
Normal tyres on dry road	0.8
Racing tyres on dry road	1.0
Sandpaper on sandpaper	2.0
Skis on snow	0.02

> **Discussion point**
> How good is this model and would you be confident in offering the answer as evidence in your defence in court? Look carefully at the three assumptions. What effect do they have on the estimate of the initial speed?

How fast was the driver of the red car going?

You can proceed with the problem. As an initial model, the driver of the red car made the following assumptions:

1. that the road was level
2. that his car was travelling at $2\,\text{m s}^{-1}$ when it hit the orange car (this was consistent with the damage to the cars)
3. that the car and driver could be treated as a particle, subject to Coulomb's laws of friction with $\mu = 0.8$ (i.e. dry road conditions).

Taking the direction of travel as positive, let the car and driver have acceleration $a\,\text{m s}^{-2}$ and mass $m\,\text{kg}$. You have probably realised that the acceleration will be negative. The forces (in N) and acceleration are shown in Figure 3.2.

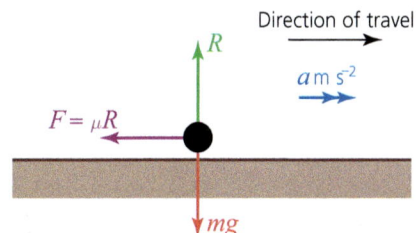

Figure 3.2

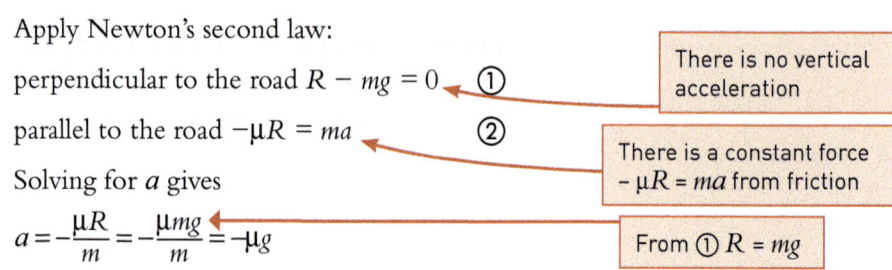

A model for friction

Apply Newton's second law:

perpendicular to the road $R - mg = 0$ ① *(There is no vertical acceleration)*

parallel to the road $-\mu R = ma$ ② *(There is a constant force $-\mu R = ma$ from friction)*

Solving for a gives

$$a = -\frac{\mu R}{m} = -\frac{\mu mg}{m} = -\mu g$$

(From ① $R = mg$)

Taking $\mu = 0.8$ and $g = 9.8\,\text{m s}^{-2}$ gives $a = -7.84\,\text{m s}^{-2}$.

The constant acceleration formula

$$v^2 = u^2 + 2as$$

can be used to calculate the initial speed of the red car. Substituting $s = 10$, $v = 2$ and $a = -7.84$ gives

$$u = \sqrt{2^2 + 2 \times 7.84 \times 10} = 12.68\,\text{m s}^{-1}$$

Convert this figure to miles per hour.

$$\text{Speed} = \frac{12.68 \times 3600}{1600}$$

$$= 28.5\,\text{mph}$$

(1 hour is 60×60 seconds)

(1 mile is approx. 1600 m)

So the model suggests that the red car was travelling at a speed of just under 30 mph before skidding began.

> **Discussion point**
> In this example the brakes were locked. What happens when you slow down in normal driving? Where does friction act?

Modelling with friction

While there is always some frictional force between two sliding surfaces, its magnitude is often so small as to be negligible. In such cases, the surfaces are described as **smooth**.

In situations where frictional forces cannot be ignored, the surface(s) are described as **rough**. Coulomb's law is the standard model for dealing with such cases.

Frictional forces are essential in many ways. For example, a ladder leaning against a wall would always slide if there were no friction between the foot of the ladder and the ground. The absence of friction in icy conditions causes difficulties for road users: pedestrians slip over, cars and motorcycles skid.

Remember that friction always opposes sliding motion.

> **Discussion point**
> In what direction is the frictional force between the back wheel of a cycle and the road?

Example 3.1

A stone slides in a straight line across a frozen pond. It starts to move with a speed of $8\,\text{m s}^{-1}$ and slides for 40 m before coming to rest. Calculate the coefficient of friction between the stone and the pond.

Solution

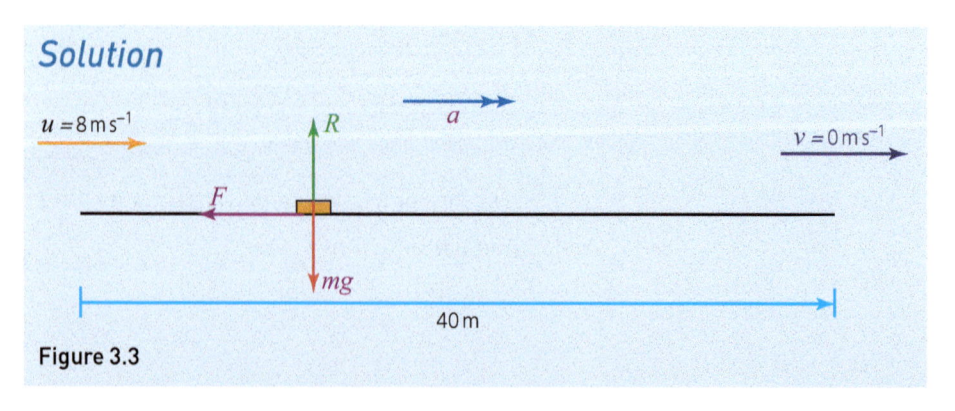

Figure 3.3

The only force acting on the stone in the direction of motion is the frictional force F, which is uniform, which thus gives rise to a constant acceleration a. In order to find a, use the constant acceleration formula

$v^2 = u^2 + 2as$

$0 = 8^2 + 2 \times 40 \times a$

$a = -\dfrac{64}{80} = -0.8$

Use Newton's second law to give   [Since the stone is in motion: $F = \mu R$]

$-F = -0.8m$ [Vertical equilibrium means $R = mg$]

$-\mu mg = -0.8m$

$\mu = \dfrac{0.8}{9.8} = 0.0816...$

The coefficient of friction between the stone and the pond is 0.082.

Example 3.2

A box of mass 2 kg rests on rough horizontal ground. The coefficient of friction between the box and the ground is 0.4. A light inextensible string is attached to the box in order to pull it along. If the tension in the string is T N, find the value that T must exceed if the box is to accelerate when the string is

(i) horizontal

(ii) 30° above the horizontal

(iii) 30° below the horizontal.

Solution

(i) The forces acting on the box are shown in Figure 3.4.

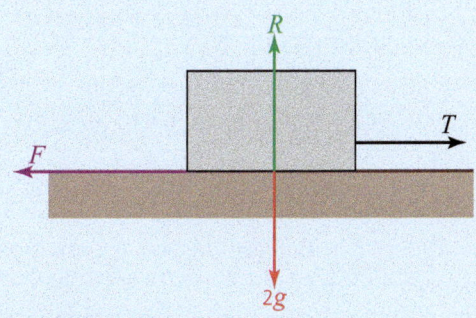

Figure 3.4

Horizontal forces: $T > F$ [This is the condition for the box to accelerate]

Vertical forces: $R = 2g$

$R = 2 \times 9.8 = 19.6$

The law of friction states that for a moving object

$F = \mu R$

So in this case

A model for friction

$F = 0.4 \times 19.6$

$F = 7.84\,\text{N}$

T must exceed $7.84\,\text{N}$ for the box to accelerate.

(ii) The forces acting on the box are shown in Figure 3.5.

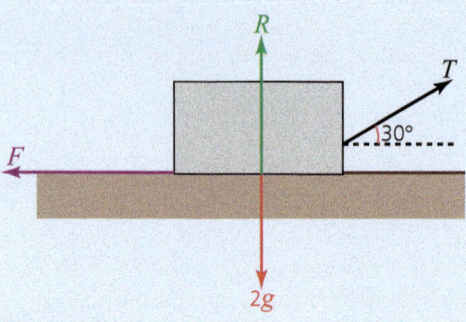

Figure 3.5

Resolving horizontally: $T\cos 30° > F$ ① ← *This is the condition for the box to accelerate*

vertically: $R + T\sin 30° = 2g$

So that $R = 2g - T\sin 30°$ ← *This equation shows that in this situation the magnitude of R is less than $2g$*

When motion occurs: $F = \mu R = 0.4(2g - T\sin 30°)$

Substituting in ①: $T\cos 30° > 0.4(2g - T\sin 30°)$

Rearranging: $T(\cos 30° + 0.4\sin 30°) > 0.8g$

$$T > \frac{0.8 \times 9.8}{(\cos 30° + 0.4\sin 30°)} = \frac{7.84}{1.066} = 7.35\ldots$$

T must exceed $7.35\,\text{N}$ for the box to accelerate.

(iii) The forces acting on the box are shown in Figure 3.6.

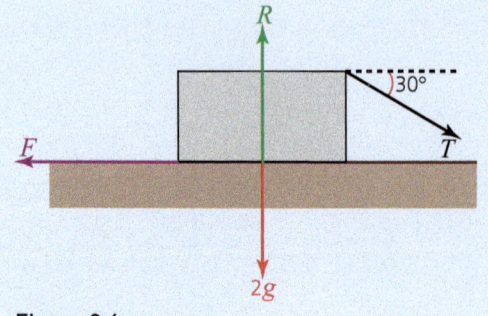

Figure 3.6

Resolving horizontally: $T\cos 30° > F$

vertically: $R = T\sin 30° + 2g$

When motion occurs: $F = 0.4R = 0.4(T\sin 30° + 2g)$

So that $T\cos 30° > 0.4(T\sin 30° + 2g)$

$$T > \frac{7.84}{(\cos 30° - 0.4\sin 30°)} = \frac{7.84}{0.666}$$

$T > 11.77\ldots$

T must exceed $11.8\,\text{N}$ for the box to accelerate.

> **Note**
>
> It is clear from the example that the force required to move the box is largest when the force from the string is pointing downwards. The component of the force in the downward direction increases the normal reaction, which in turn increases the frictional force.

Example 3.3

Figure 3.7 shows a block of mass 5 kg resting on a rough table and connected by a light inextensible string passing over a smooth pulley to a block of mass 4 kg. The coefficient of friction between the 5 kg block and the table is 0.4.

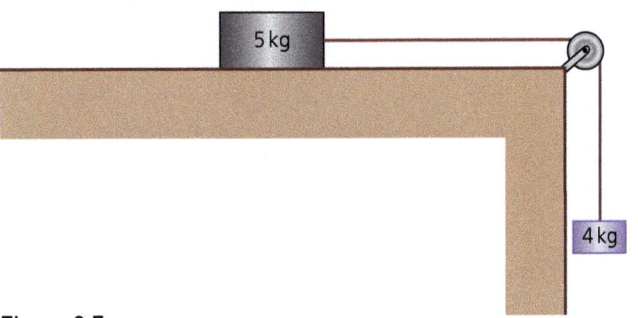

Figure 3.7

(i) Draw diagrams showing the forces acting on each block and the direction of the system's acceleration.
(ii) Show that acceleration does take place.
(iii) Find the acceleration of the system and the tension in the string.

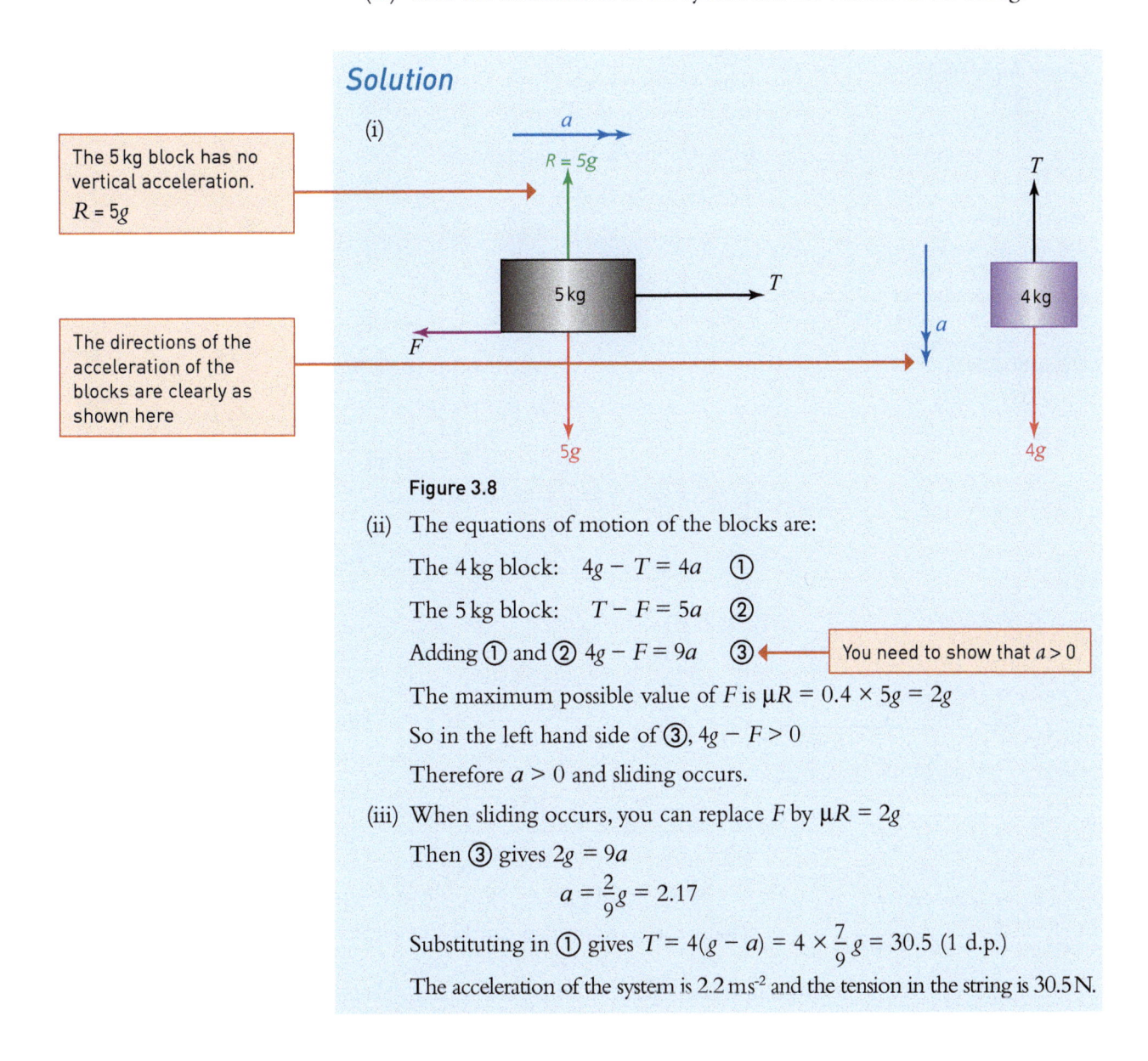

Solution

(i)

> The 5 kg block has no vertical acceleration.
> $R = 5g$

> The directions of the acceleration of the blocks are clearly as shown here

Figure 3.8

(ii) The equations of motion of the blocks are:

The 4 kg block: $4g - T = 4a$ ①

The 5 kg block: $T - F = 5a$ ②

Adding ① and ② $4g - F = 9a$ ③ ← You need to show that $a > 0$

The maximum possible value of F is $\mu R = 0.4 \times 5g = 2g$

So in the left hand side of ③, $4g - F > 0$

Therefore $a > 0$ and sliding occurs.

(iii) When sliding occurs, you can replace F by $\mu R = 2g$

Then ③ gives $2g = 9a$

$$a = \frac{2}{9}g = 2.17$$

Substituting in ① gives $T = 4(g - a) = 4 \times \frac{7}{9}g = 30.5$ (1 d.p.)

The acceleration of the system is 2.2 ms⁻² and the tension in the string is 30.5 N.

A model for friction

Example 3.4

A block of mass m kg is placed on a slope inclined at an angle θ to the horizontal. The coefficient of friction between the block and the slope is 0.4.

(i) Find the values of θ for which the block would be at rest.

The angle of the slope is actually 30°.

(ii) Find the time taken for the block to slide a distance of 1.5 m down the slope, assuming it starts at rest.

Solution

(i) The forces acting on the block are shown in Figure 3.9.

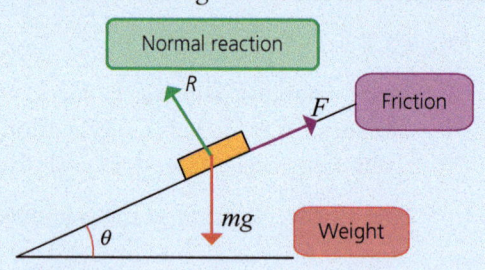

Figure 3.9

The weight mg can be resolved into components $mg\cos\theta$ perpendicular to the slope and $mg\sin\theta$ parallel to the slope.

Since the block is in equilibrium

Parallel to the slope: $\quad F = mg\sin\theta \quad$ ①

Perpendicular to the slope: $R = mg\cos\theta \quad$ ②

Since the block is at rest: $\quad F \leq \mu R$

$$mg\sin\theta \leq \mu mg\cos\theta$$
$$\Rightarrow \sin\theta \leq \mu\cos\theta$$
$$\Rightarrow \tan\theta \leq \mu$$
$$\theta \leq \arctan\mu$$

In this case $\mu = 0.4$, so $\tan\theta \leq 0.4$ and $\theta \leq 21.8°$.

The block is at rest for values of θ less than 21.8°.

(ii)

Figure 3.11

The block is now sliding down the plane. It has an acceleration, a.

The equation of motion for the block is

$$ma = mg\sin 30° - F \quad ③$$

> **Note**
> In a situation like this where an object is on a slope, it is almost always easier to work with directions perpendicular and parallel to the slope rather than vertical and horizontal.

> **Note**
> You can think of the weight mg as the resultant of two resolved components.

Substituting for F and R from ① and ②

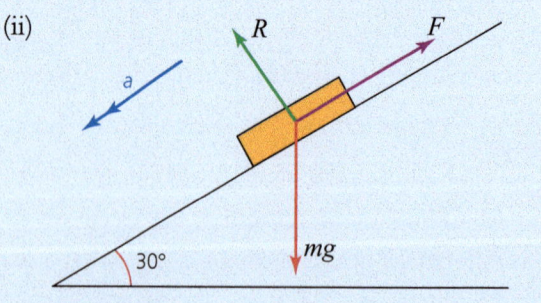

Figure 3.10

Since the block is moving

$$F = \mu R = 0.4mg \cos 30° \quad \text{④}$$

Substituting ④ into ③

$$ma = mg \sin 30° - 0.4mg \cos 30°$$

Dividing through by m

$$a = g(\sin 30° - 0.4 \cos 30°)$$
$$= 9.8 \times (0.5 - 0.4 \times 0.866 \ldots)$$
$$= 1.505 \ldots$$

Using the constant acceleration formula $s = ut + \frac{1}{2}at^2$ with $u = 0$, $s = 1.5$ and $a = 1.505..$

$$1.5 = 0.5 \times 1.505 \ldots \times t^2$$
$$\Rightarrow t = \sqrt{\frac{1.5}{0.5 \times 1.505\ldots}} = 1.41\ldots$$

The block takes 1.4 s to slide down the slope.

Historical note

Charles Augustin de Coulomb was born in Angoulême in France in 1736 and is best remembered for his work on electricity rather than that on friction. Coulomb's law concerns the forces on charged particles and was determined using a torsion balance. The unit for electric charge is named after him. Coulomb worked in many fields, including the elasticity of metal, silk fibres and the design of windmills. He died in Paris in 1806.

Note

1 The result is independent of the mass of the block. This is often found when simple models are applied to mechanics problems. For example, two objects of different mass fall to the ground with the same acceleration. However when such models are refined, for example, to take account of air resistance, mass is often found to have some effect on the result.

2 The angle for which the block is about to slide down the slope is called the *angle of friction*. The angle of friction is often denoted by λ (lambda) and is defined by tan λ = μ.
When the angle of the slope is equal to the angle of the friction, it is just possible for the block to stay on the slope without sliding. If the slope is slightly steeper, the block will start to slide.

Exercise 3.1

① A block of mass 25 kg is resting on a horizontal surface. It is being pulled by a horizontal force T N, and is on the point of sliding. Draw a diagram showing the forces acting and find the coefficient of friction when

(i) $T = 20$

(ii) $T = 5$.

② A box of mass 25 kg is resting on rough horizontal ground. The box can just be moved by a horizontal force of 60 N. Find the coefficient of friction between the box and the floor.

③ A stone is sliding across a frozen pond. It travels a distance of 12 m before coming to rest from an initial speed of 4 m s^{-1}.

Find the coefficient of friction between the stone and the pond.

④ A parcel drops out of a van travelling at 20 m s^{-1}. The parcel slides a distance of 30 m before coming to rest. Calculate the coefficient of friction between the parcel and the road.

A model for friction

⑤ In each of the following situations find, in any order, the acceleration of the system, the tension(s) in the string(s) and the magnitude of the frictional force.

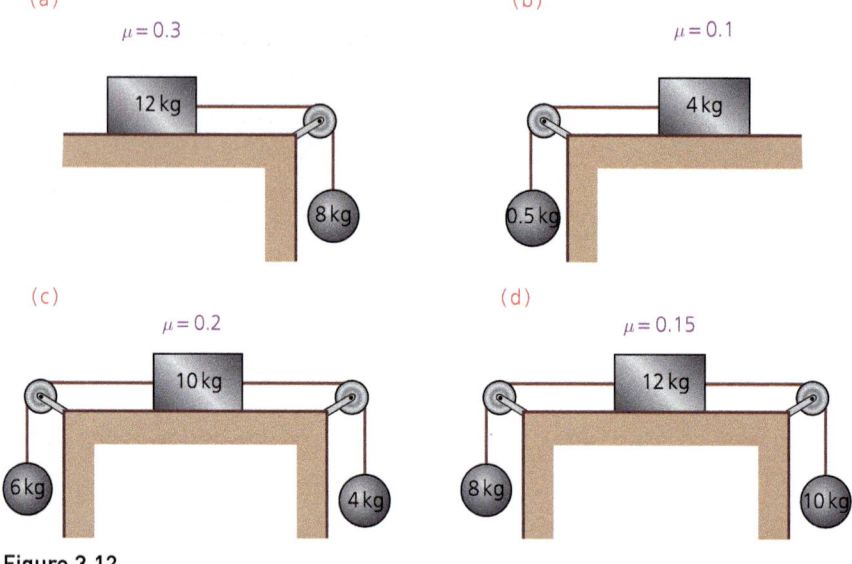

(a) $\mu = 0.3$, 12 kg on table, 8 kg hanging

(b) $\mu = 0.1$, 4 kg on table, 0.5 kg hanging

(c) $\mu = 0.2$, 10 kg on table, 6 kg and 4 kg hanging on each side

(d) $\mu = 0.15$, 12 kg on table, 8 kg and 10 kg hanging on each side

Figure 3.12

⑥ A block of mass 5 kg is about to move up a rough plane inclined at 30° to the horizontal, under the application of a force of 50 N parallel to the slope, as shown in Figure 3.13.

Find the value of the coefficient of friction between the block and the plane.

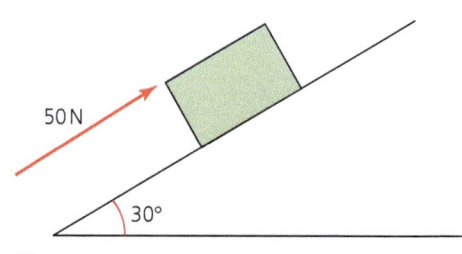

Figure 3.13

⑦ An ice hockey player is sliding a puck of mass 50 g across the ice rink. The initial speed of the puck is $8\,\text{m s}^{-1}$ and it takes it 40 m to come to rest.

  (i) Find the deceleration of the puck.
  (ii) Find the frictional force acting on the puck.
  (iii) Find the coefficient of friction between the puck and the ice rink.
  (iv) How far will a 60 g puck travel if it, too, is given an initial speed of $8\,\text{m s}^{-1}$?

⑧ A car of mass 1200 kg is travelling at $30\,\text{m s}^{-1}$ when it is forced to perform an emergency stop. Its wheels lock as soon as the brakes are applied so that they slide along the road without rotating. For the first 40 m the coefficient of friction between the wheels and the road is 0.75, but then the road surface changes and the coefficient of friction becomes 0.8.

  (i) Find the deceleration of the car immediately after the brakes are applied.
  (ii) Find the speed of the car when it comes to the change of road surface.
  (iii) Find the total distance the car travels before it comes to rest.

⑨ A girl, whose mass is 25 kg, is sitting on a sledge of mass 10 kg which is being pulled at constant speed along horizontal ground by her brother. The coefficient of friction between the sledge and the snow-covered ground is 0.1. Find the tension in the rope from the boy's hand to the sledge when

  (i) the rope is horizontal
  (ii) the rope makes an angle of 20° with the horizontal.

⑩ A particle of mass 5 kg is projected upwards along a plane that is inclined at an angle of 25° to the horizontal, with a speed of 10 m s⁻¹. The particle comes to rest after 10 m.

(i) Find the deceleration of the particle.

(ii) Find the frictional force F and the normal reaction R, and hence deduce the coefficient of friction between the particle and the plane.

The particle then starts to move down the plane with acceleration a m s⁻².

(iii) Find a and the speed of the particle as it passes its starting point.

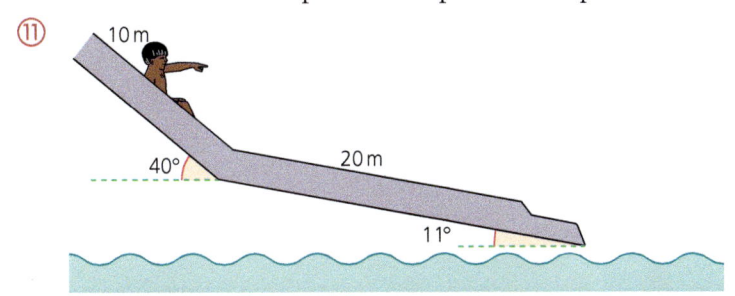

⑪

Figure 3.14

A chute at a water sports centre has been designed so that swimmers first slide down a steep part which is 10 m long and at an angle of 40° to the horizontal. They then come to a 20 m section with a gentler slope, at 11° to the horizontal, where they travel at constant speed.

(i) Find the coefficient of friction between a swimmer and the chute.

(ii) Find the acceleration of a swimmer on the steeper part.

(iii) Find the speed of a swimmer at the end of the chute. (You may assume that no speed is lost at the point where the slope changes.)

An alternative design of chute is made out of the same material. It has the same starting and finishing points but has a constant gradient.

(iv) With what speed do swimmers arrive at the end of this chute?

⑫ A 10 kg block lies on a rough horizontal table. The coefficient of friction between the block and the table is 0.15. The block is attached by a light inextensible string which passes over a smooth pulley to a mass of 2 kg hanging freely. The 10 kg block is 1.2 m from the pulley and the 2 kg mass is 1 m from the floor. The system is released from rest. Find

(i) the acceleration of the system

(ii) the time taken for the 2 kg mass to reach the floor

(iii) the velocity with which the 10 kg mass hits the pulley.

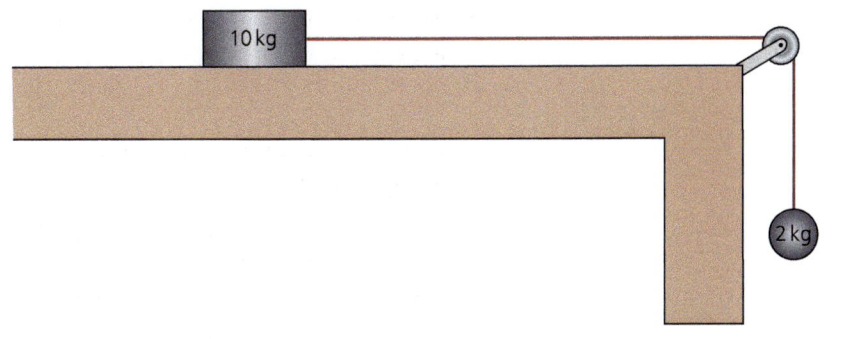

Figure 3.15

A model for friction

⑬ A box of mass 250 kg is placed on a rough inclined plane of slope $\arcsin\left(\frac{7}{25}\right)$ and coefficient of friction $\frac{1}{4}$. A rope is attached to the box and the direction of the rope makes an angle $\arcsin\left(\frac{3}{5}\right)$ with the upper surface of the plane. If the tension in the rope is T N, find the limiting values of T for which the box remains in equilibrium.

⑭ A box of weight 200 N is pulled at a steady speed across a rough horizontal surface by a rope which makes an angle α with the horizontal. The coefficient of friction between the box and the surface is 0.5. Assume that the box slides on its underside and does not tip up.

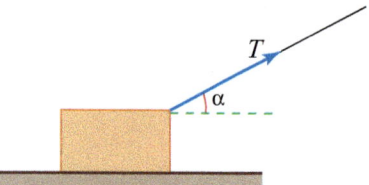

Figure 3.16

(i) Find an expression for the value of T for any angle α.

(ii) For what value of α is T a minimum and what is the value of that minimum?

⑮ A block of mass 10 kg is lying on a rough plane inclined at 30° to the horizontal. A horizontal force P is applied to the block, as shown in Figure 3.17. The coefficient of friction between the block and the plane is 0.5.

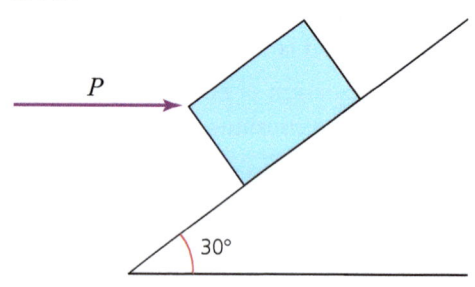

Figure 3.17

(i) Find the least force, P, necessary to start the block sliding up the plane.

(ii) Find the least force, P, necessary to stop the block from sliding down the plane.

⑯ A block of mass m is on the point of slipping down a plane inclined at an angle α to the horizontal. The same plane is now raised so that it is inclined at an angle β to the horizontal, with $\beta > \alpha$. Show that the least force, P, parallel to the plane which is required to keep the block in equilibrium is

$$mg \sin(\beta - \alpha) \sec \alpha$$

KEY POINTS

1 The total contact force between two surfaces may be expressed in terms of a frictional force and a normal reaction.
2 The frictional force, F, between two surfaces is given by:
   $F < \mu R$ when there is no sliding and not in limiting equilibrium
   $F = \mu R$ in limiting equilibrium
   $F = \mu R$ when sliding occurs
   where R is the normal reaction of one surface on the other and μ is the coefficient of friction between the surfaces.
3 The frictional force always acts in the direction to oppose sliding.
4 The magnitude of the normal reaction is affected by any force which has a component perpendicular to the direction of sliding.

LEARNING OUTCOMES

When you have completed this chapter, you should

- understand that the total contact force between surfaces may be expressed in terms of a frictional force and a normal reaction
- be able to draw a force diagram to represent a situation involving friction
- understand that a frictional force may be modelled by $F \leq \mu R$
- know that a frictional force acts in the direction to oppose sliding
- be able to model friction using $F = \mu R$ when sliding occurs
- know how to apply Newton's laws of motion to situations involving friction
- be able to derive and use the result that a body on a rough slope inclined at angle α to the horizontal is on the point of slipping if $\mu = \tan \alpha$.

4 Moments of forces

A system is in equilibrium when the forces constituting it are arranged in such a way as to compensate each other, like two weights pulling at the arms of a pair of scales.

Rudolf Arnheim

→ The photograph shows a mobile tower crane, consisting of the main vertical section housing the engine, winding gear and controls and the boom which supports the load and the counterweight. The counterweight is at a fixed distance from the centre line and the load is at a variable distance from the centre line. Why is the counterweight needed?

1 Introduction to moments

The operation of the crane depends on turning effects or *moments* of forces. To understand these you might find it helpful to look at a simpler situation.

Two children sit on a simple see-saw, made of a plank balanced on a fulcrum as in Figure 4.1. Will the see-saw balance?

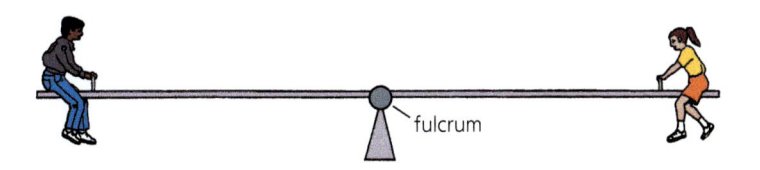

Figure 4.1

If both children have the same mass and sit the same distance from the fulcrum, then you expect to see the see-saw balance.

Now consider possible changes to this situation:

(i) If one child is heavier than the other, then you expect the heavier one to go down.

(ii) If one child moves nearer to the centre, you expect that child to go up.

You can see that both the weights of the children and their distances from the fulcrum are important.

What about this case? Both children now sit on one side of the seesaw and their father is on the other side. The father has a mass of 84 kg and sits 1.25 m from the fulcrum. The children of mass 25 kg and 35 kg sit 2.1 m and 1.5 m from the fulcrum on the other side.

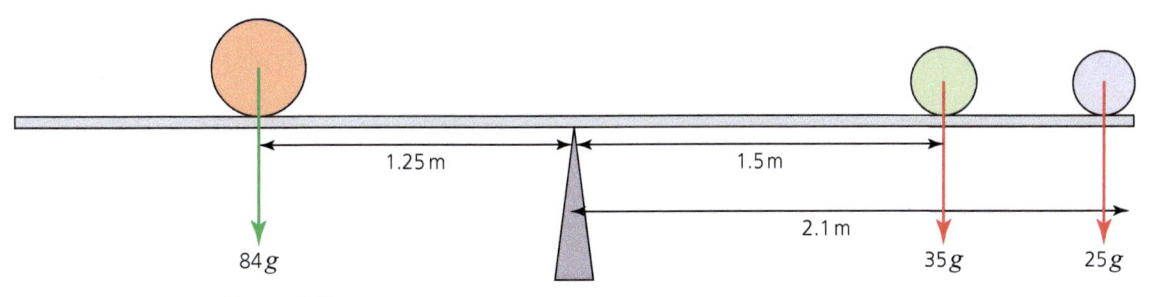

Figure 4.2

Taking the products of their weights and their distances from the fulcrum, gives

Father: $84g \times 1.25 = 105g$

Child A: $25g \times 2.1 = 52.5g$

Child B: $35g \times 1.5 = 52.5g$

Both children: $52.5g + 52.5g = 105g$

So you might expect the see-saw to balance, and this indeed is what would happen.

Introduction to moments

Rigid bodies

Until now the particle model has provided a reasonable basis for the analysis of the situations you have met. In an example like the see-saw, however, where turning is important, this model is inadequate because the forces do not all act through the same point.

In such cases you need the *rigid body model* in which an object, or *body*, is recognised as having size and shape, but is assumed not to be deformed when forces act on it.

Suppose that you push a tray lying on a smooth table with one finger so that the force acts parallel to one edge and through the centre of mass (Figure 4.3).

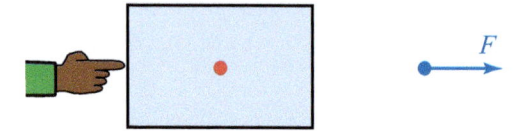

Figure 4.3

The particle model is adequate here: the tray travels in a straight line in the direction of the applied force.

If you push the tray equally hard with two fingers, as in Figure 4.4, symmetrically either side of the centre of mass, the particle model is still adequate.

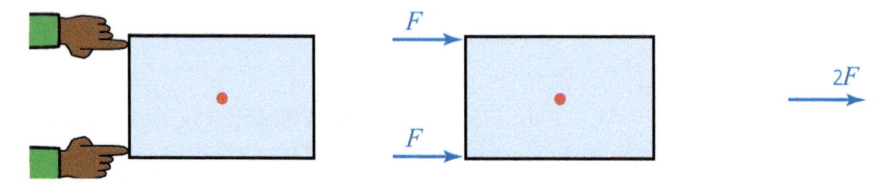

Figure 4.4

However, if the two forces are not equal or are not symmetrically placed, or, as in Figure 4.5, are in different directions, the particle model cannot be used.

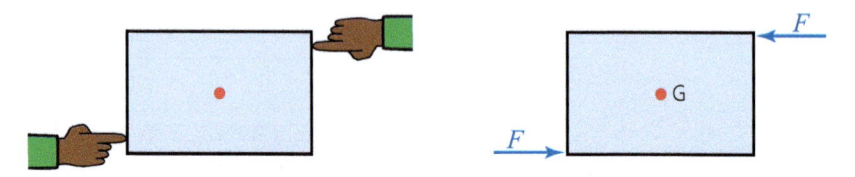

Figure 4.5

The resultant force in Figure 4.5 is zero, since the individual forces are equal in magnitude but opposite in direction. What happens to the tray? Experience tells you that it starts to rotate about G. How fast it starts to rotate depends, among other things, on the magnitude of the forces and the width of the tray. The rigid body model allows you to analyse the situation.

Moments

The example of the see-saw involved the product of each force and its distance from a fixed point. This product is called the *moment* of the force about the point.

The see-saw balances because the moments of the forces on either side of the fulcrum are of the same magnitude and act in opposite directions. One would tend to make the see-saw turn clockwise, the other anticlockwise. By contrast, the moments about G of the forces on the tray in the last situation do not balance. They both tend to turn it anticlockwise, so rotation occurs.

Conventions and units

The moment of a force F about a point O is defined by

$$\text{moment} = Fd$$

where d is the perpendicular distance from the point O to the line of action of the force (Figure 4.6).

In two dimensions, the sense of a moment is described as either positive (anticlockwise) or negative (clockwise), as shown in Figure 4.7.

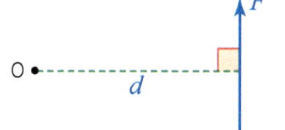

Figure 4.6

> **Hint**
> The line of the force and its perpendicular make a T (for 'turning')

(i) clockwise movement (negative)

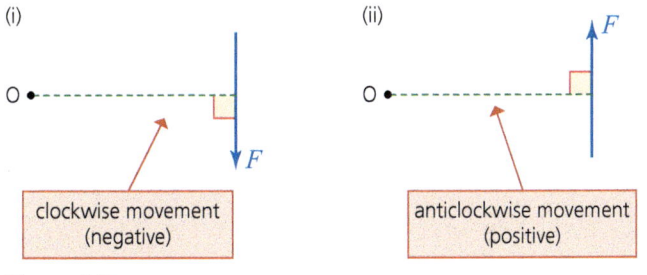

(ii) anticlockwise movement (positive)

Figure 4.7

If you imagine putting a pin at O and pushing along the line of F, your page would turn clockwise for (i) and anticlockwise for (ii).

In the S.I. system, the unit for moment is the newton metre (N m), because a moment is the product of a force, the unit of which is the newton, and distance, the unit of which is the metre. Remember that moments are always taken about a point and you must always specify which point. A force acting through the point will have no moment about that point because in that case $d = 0$.

Couples

Whenever two forces of the same magnitude act in opposite directions along different lines, they have a zero resultant force, but do have a turning effect. In fact, the moment will be Fd about any point, where d is the perpendicular distance between the forces. This is demonstrated in Figure 4.9.

> **Discussion point**
> Figure 4.8 shows two tools used for tightening nuts. Discuss the advantages and disadvantages of each.
>
> **Figure 4.8**

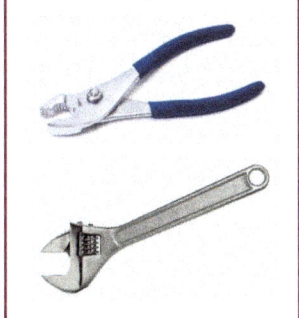

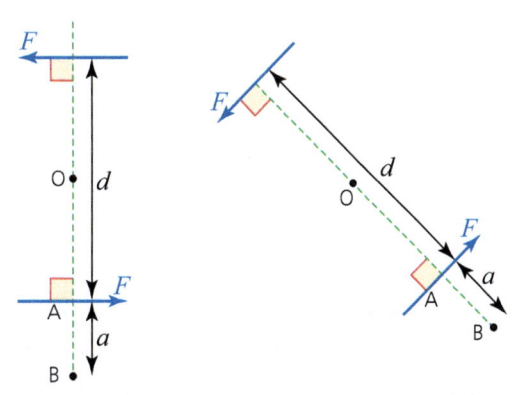

Figure 4.9

Introduction to moments

In each of these situations:

Moment about O $\quad F\dfrac{d}{2} + F\dfrac{d}{2} = Fd \quad$ ← Anticlockwise is positive

Moment about A $\quad 0 + Fd = Fd$

Moment about B $\quad -aF + (a+d)F = Fd$

Any set of forces like these with a zero resultant force but a non-zero total moment is known as a *couple*. The effect of a couple on a rigid body is to cause rotation.

Equilibrium revisited

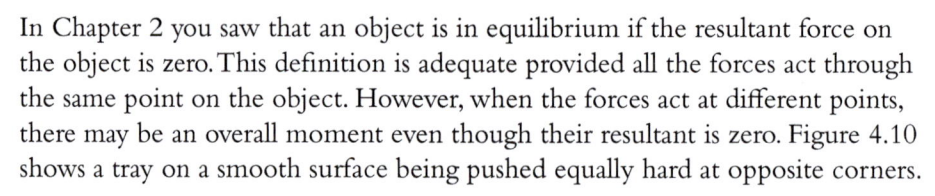

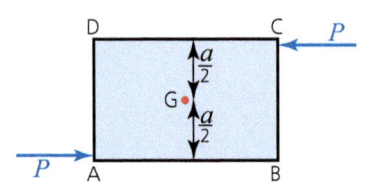

In Chapter 2 you saw that an object is in equilibrium if the resultant force on the object is zero. This definition is adequate provided all the forces act through the same point on the object. However, when the forces act at different points, there may be an overall moment even though their resultant is zero. Figure 4.10 shows a tray on a smooth surface being pushed equally hard at opposite corners.

Figure 4.10

The resultant force on the tray is clearly zero, but the resultant moment about its centre point, G, is

$$P \times \dfrac{a}{2} + P \times \dfrac{a}{2} = Pa.$$

The tray will start to rotate about its centre and so it is clearly not in equilibrium.

So you now need to tighten the mathematical definition of equilibrium to include moments. For an object to remain at rest (or moving at constant velocity) when a system of forces is applied, both the resultant force and the total moment must be zero.

To check that an object is in equilibrium under the action of a system of forces, you need to check two things:

(i) that the resultant force is zero

(ii) that the resultant moment about any point is zero. (You only need to check one point.)

> **Note**
> You could have taken moments about any of the corners, A, B, C or D, or any other point in the plane of the paper and the answer would have been the same, Pa anticlockwise.

Another way of saying the resultant moment is zero is
clockwise moments = anticlockwise moments

Example 4.1

A three metre uniform rod AB of mass 10 kg is hinged at one end to a vertical wall. The other end is attached to a vertical cable so that the rod is horizontal. A block of mass 15 kg is resting on the rod 2 m from the wall.

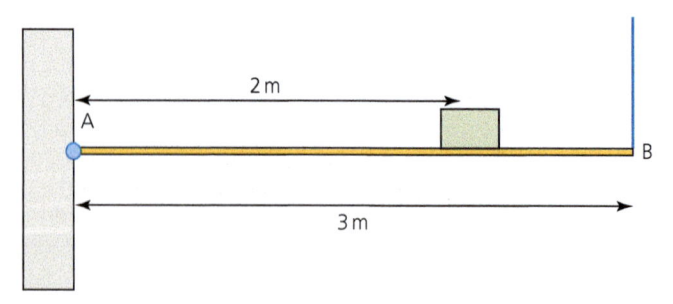

Figure 4.11

(i) Find the tension in the cable.

(ii) Find the magnitude and direction of the force exerted by the hinge on the rod.

Solution

(i) The forces acting on the rod are shown in Figure 4.12.

[Force exerted by the hinge; could be in any direction] → F

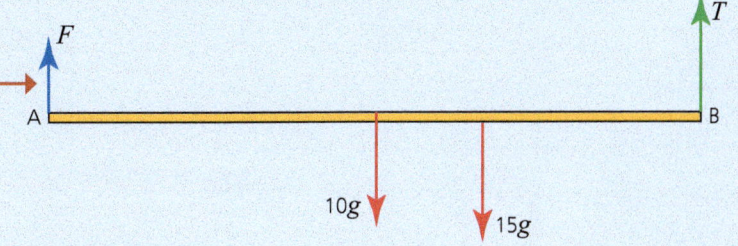

Figure 4.12

The rod is in equilibrium, so the total moment about any point is zero.

[Choose A to eliminate F from the moment equation.] → Take moments about A.

$$F \times 0 + 10g \times 1.5 + 15g \times 2 - T \times 3 = 0$$

[As F goes through A]

[The rod is uniform so the mass is at the centre of the rod]

This gives

$$15g + 30g - 3T = 0$$

$$\Rightarrow \qquad T = 15g = 147\,\text{N}$$

The tension in the cable is 147 N.

(ii) The rod is in equilibrium so the resultant of the forces acting on it is zero. This means that the force exerted by the hinge must be vertically upwards.

$$F + T - 10g - 15g = 0$$

$$F = 25g - T$$

Substituting for T now gives

$$F = 25g - 15g = 10g$$

$$= 98\,\text{N}$$

The force at the hinge has magnitude 98 N and is in same direction as T.

Note

The reaction force at a hinge may act in any direction, according to the forces elsewhere in the system. A hinge can be visualised in cross-section, as shown in Figure 4.13. If the hinge is well oiled, and the friction between the inner and outer parts is negligible, the hinge cannot exert any moment. In this situation the door is said to be 'freely hinged'.

[Contact may occur anywhere inside this circle]

Figure 4.13

Introduction to moments

Example 4.2

A uniform plank AB of length 1.2 m and mass 5 kg carries 2 particles. One is of mass 2 kg and lies at C, 40 cm from A. The other is at B and is of mass 1 kg.

The plank is supported at A and at a point D, 20 cm from B so that it rests horizontally.

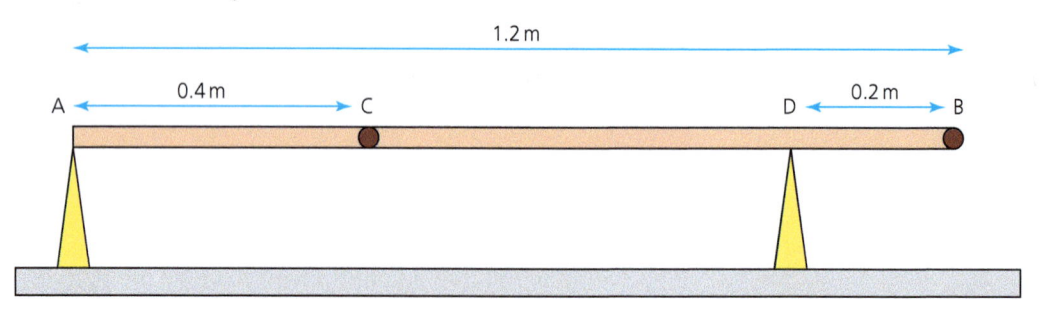

Figure 4.14

Find the reaction forces acting on the plank.

Solution

Figure 4.15 shows the forces acting on the plank.

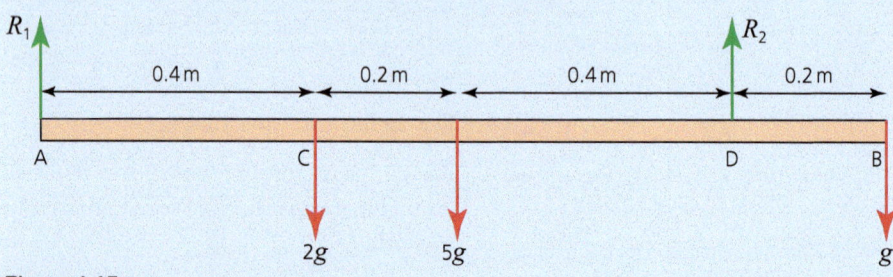

Figure 4.15

For the plank to be in equilibrium, both the resultant force and the total moment about any point must be zero.

All the forces act vertically.

$$R_1 + R_2 - 8g = 0 \quad \text{①}$$

(= $2g + 5g + g$)

A is chosen so that the number of unknowns in the equation is minimised.

Taking moments about the point A gives (R_1 passes through A)

$$R_1 \times 0 + 2g \times 0.4 + 5g \times 0.6 - R_2 \times 1 + g \times 1.2 = 0 \quad \text{②}$$

The plank is uniform so the mass is at its centre.

② reduces to $\quad 0.8g + 3g - R_2 + 1.2g = 0$

$$\Rightarrow \quad R_2 = 5g = 49\,\text{N}$$

Substitute in ① to give

$$R_1 = 8g - R_2 = 3g$$
$$= 29.4\,\text{N}$$

The reaction forces on the plank at A and D are 29.4 N and 49 N.

> **Note**
> 1. You cannot solve this problem without taking moments.
> 2. You can take moments about any point and can, for example, show that by taking moments about B you get the same answer.
> 3. The whole weight of the plank is being considered to act at its centre.
> 4. When a force acts through the point about which moments are being taken, its moment about that point is zero.

Levers

A lever can be used to lift or move a heavy object using a relatively small force. Levers depend on moments for their action.

Two common lever configurations are shown in Figures 4.16 and 4.17. In both cases, a load W is being lifted by an applied force F, using a lever of length l. The calculations assume equilibrium.

Case 1

The fulcrum is within the lever, Figure 4.16.

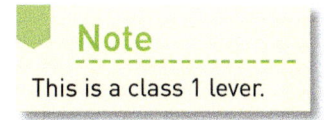

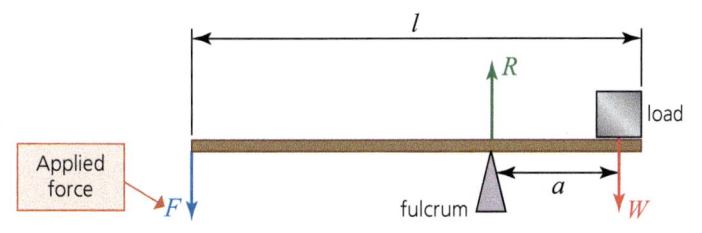

> **Note**
> This is a class 1 lever.

Figure 4.16

Taking moments about the fulcrum:
$$F \times (l-a) - W \times a = 0$$
$$F = W \times \frac{a}{l-a}$$

Provided that the fulcrum is nearer the end with the load, the applied force is less than the load.

Examples of class 1 levers are seesaws, crowbars and scissors.

Case 2

The fulcrum is at one end of the lever, Figure 4.17.

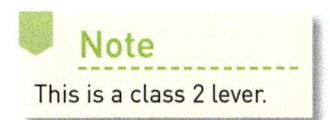

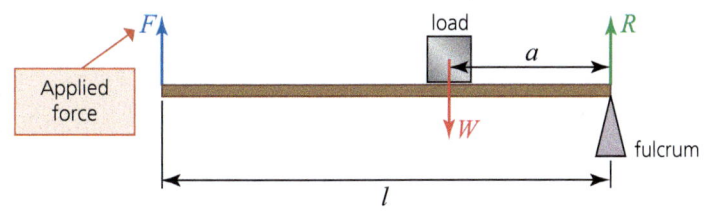

> **Note**
> This is a class 2 lever.

Figure 4.17

Taking moments about the fulcrum:
$$F \times l - W \times a = 0$$
$$F = W \times \frac{a}{l}$$

Since a is much smaller than l, the applied force F is much smaller than the load W.

Examples of class 2 levers include wheelbarrows, nutcrackers or bottle openers.

These examples also indicate how to find a single force equivalent to two parallel forces. The force equivalent to F and W should be equal and opposite to R and with the same line of action.

Introduction to moments

Example 4.3

Describe the single force equivalent to P and Q in each of these cases.

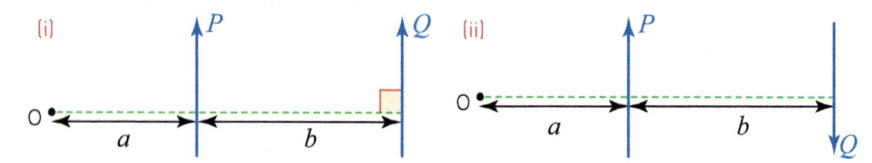

Figure 4.18

In each case state its magnitude and line of action.

Solution

(i)

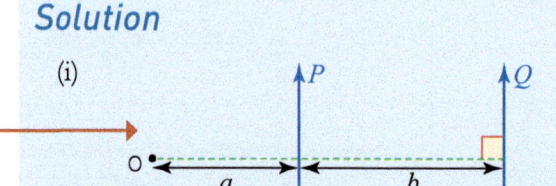

Figure 4.19

The single force equivalent to P and Q is shown in Figure 4.20.

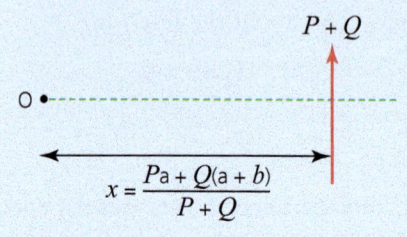

$$x = \frac{Pa + Q(a+b)}{P+Q}$$

Figure 4.20

The resultant of the two forces P and Q is a force of magnitude $P+Q$ pointing upwards.

The total moment about O of P and Q is equal to $P \times a + Q \times (a+b)$

Replacing P and Q by a single force $(P+Q)$ requires placing it at a distance x from O, such that $(P+Q)x = Pa + Q(a+b)$

leading to $x = \frac{Pa + Q(a+b)}{P+Q}$

(ii)

Figure 4.21

The single force equivalent to P and Q is the force $P - Q$ pointing upwards and distant $\frac{Pa - Q(a+b)}{P - Q}$ from O

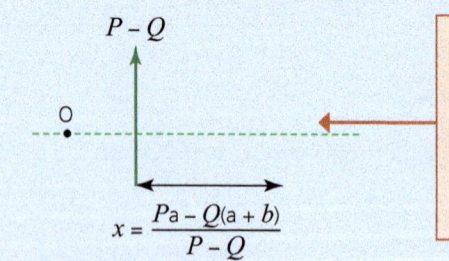

$$x = \frac{Pa - Q(a+b)}{P - Q}$$

Figure 4.22

The resultant of the two forces P and Q; $(P > Q)$ is the force of magnitude $(P - Q)$ pointing upwards.

The total moment of the forces P and Q is $P \times a - Q \times (a+b)$

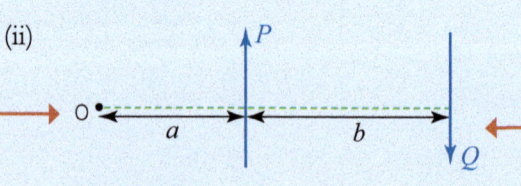

Replacing P and Q by a single force $P - Q$ requires placing it at distance y from O such that $(P-Q)y = Pa - Q(a+b)$

Notice that in Figure 4.22 if $P < Q$, the single force $P - Q$ is negative and so acts downwards. Notice also that in this case $y > 0$; if $y < 0$, the line of action of the single force is to the left of O.

> **Discussion point**
> The stays on a sailing boat are taut wires fastened to the top of the mast(s) and the hull of the boat. Why are they needed?
>
> **Figure 4.23**

Chapter 4 Moments of forces

Exercise 4.1

1. In each of the situations shown here, find the moment of the force about the point and state whether it is positive (anticlockwise) or negative (clockwise).

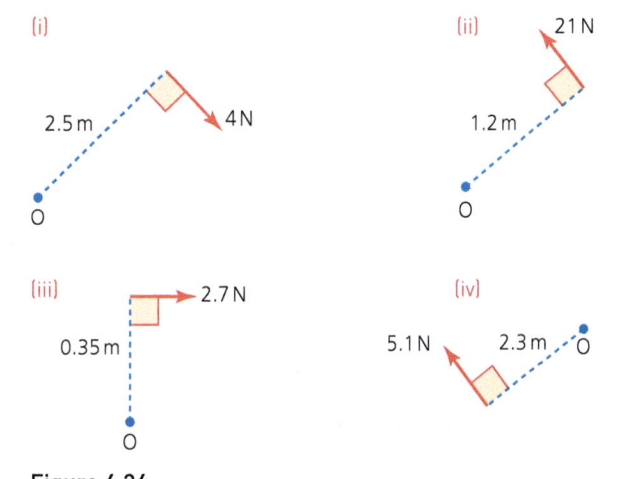

   (i) 2.5 m, 4 N

   (ii) 1.2 m, 21 N

   (iii) 0.35 m, 2.7 N

   (iv) 5.1 N, 2.3 m

   Figure 4.24

Introduction to moments

② The situations below involve several forces acting on each object. For each one, find the total moment.

(i)

3 N
1.2 N
0.4 m
O 1.4 m

(ii)

0.8 N
2.1 m
O
1 m
1.2 N

(iii)

2 N
2 N
0.5 m
O 0.8 m
1.2 m
3 N

(iv)

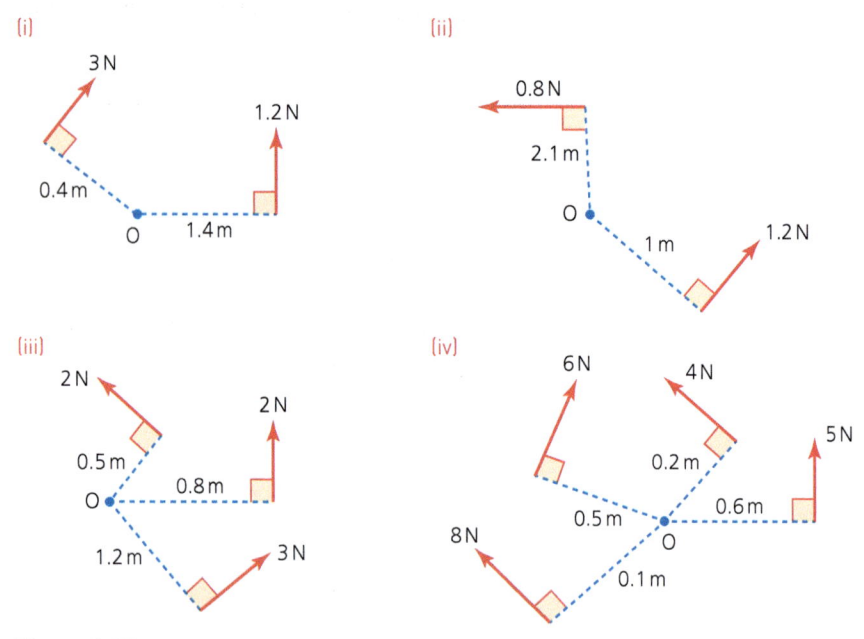

6 N
4 N
0.2 m
5 N
0.5 m
0.6 m
8 N
O
0.1 m

Figure 4.25

③ Each situation shows a uniform beam, of weight 50 N and length 4 m, held horizontally in equilibrium by two light inextensible strings. Find the tension in each string.

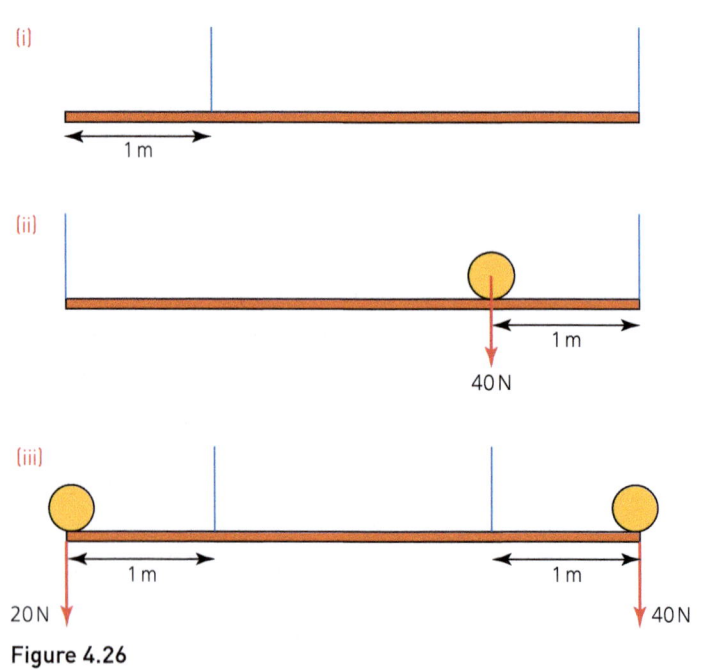

(i)

1 m

(ii)

1 m
40 N

(iii)

1 m   1 m
20 N   40 N

Figure 4.26

④ A uniform plank has length 6 m and mass 40 kg. It is placed on horizontal ground at the edge of a vertical river bank, so that 1.5 m of the plank is projecting over the edge, as shown in Figure 4.27.

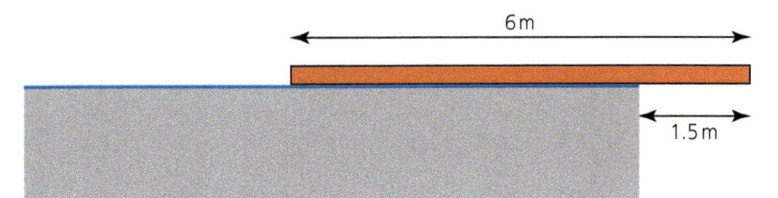

Figure 4.27

How far can a man of mass 70 kg walk along the plank without tipping it?

⑤ Two young children of mass 30 kg and 35 kg sit at the ends of a see-saw. Each child is 2.5 m from the fulcrum. Their father whose mass is 75 kg joins them. Where must he sit in order for the see-saw to balance?

⑥ A light rod, 2 m long is hanging horizontally supported by vertical strings at each end. The maximum tension which the strings can exert is 80 N.

Along what range of positions on the rod is it safe to hang a 10 kg mass.

⑦ A sign consists of a uniform rectangular lamina of weight 50 N. It is suspended in equilibrium in a vertical plane by vertical light chains attached to the sign at the points A and B so that AB is horizontal, as shown in Figure 4.28.

> A lamina is a flat object that has negligible thickness compared with its length and width.

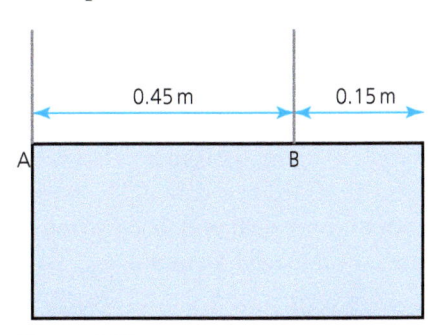

Figure 4.28

(i) Draw a diagram showing all the forces acting on the sign.
(ii) Find the tensions in the chains.

⑧ AB represents a uniform shelf of weight 30 N which is supported at X and Y so that it is horizontal. Blocks are placed along the shelf, as shown in Figure 4.29.

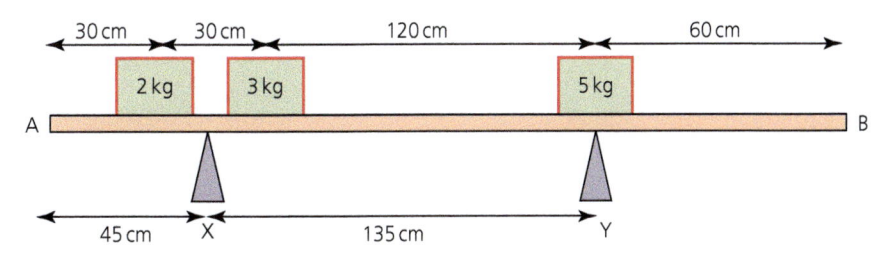

Figure 4.29

(i) Find the reaction forces of the supports on the shelf at X and Y.
(ii) What is the greatest mass of an object which can be placed at B without the shelf tipping?

Introduction to moments

9. A uniform plank 9 m long of mass 80 kg is horizontal. It is supported by vertical strings attached at 1 m and 8 m from one end.
   What is the mass of an object which should be placed on one end, so that
   (i) the tension in one string just vanishes
   (ii) the tension in one string is double the tension in the other.

10. Figure 4.30 shows a rigid, horizontal rod PQ. Y is the resultant of the two forces X N and 4 N acting at P and Q, respectively. Find X and Y.

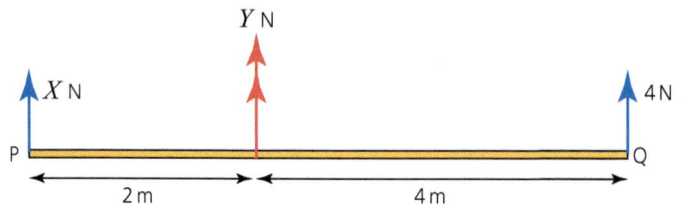

   Figure 4.30

11. Figure 4.31 shows a rigid, horizontal rod AB. Find the magnitude, direction and line of action of the resultant of this system of forces acting on AB.

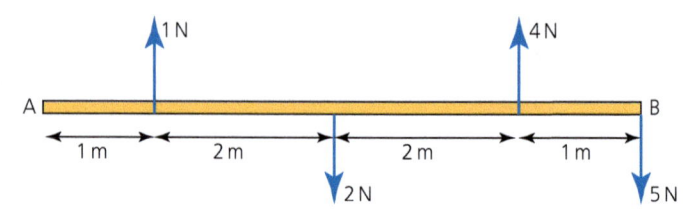

   Figure 4.31

12. A rigid rod AB, of mass 10 kg and length 3 m, whose centre of mass is 125 cm from A, is suspended horizontally by two vertical strings attached to points C and D, 50 cm from each end. Each string could just support the weight of the rod. Particles of mass m_1 kg and m_2 kg are placed at A and B, respectively.
   (i) Show that the tension in one of the strings is
   $(15 - m_1 + 5m_2)\frac{g}{4}$ and find the tension in the other string.
   (ii) Find the values of m_1 and m_2 when both the strings are on the point of breaking.

EXPERIMENT

Set up the apparatus shown in Figure 4.32 and experiment with two or more weights in different positions.

Figure 4.32

Record your results in a table showing weights, distances from O and moments about O.

Two masses are suspended from the rule in such a way that the rule balances in a horizontal position. What happens when the rule is then moved to an incline position and released?

Now attach a pulley, as in Figure 4.33. Start with equal weights and measure d and l. Then try different weights and pulley positions.

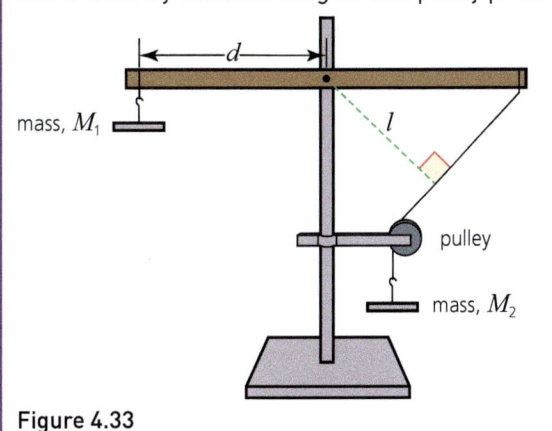

Figure 4.33

2 The moment of a force which acts at an angle

From the experiment, you will have seen that the moment of a force about the pivot depends on the *perpendicular distance* from the pivot to the line of the force.

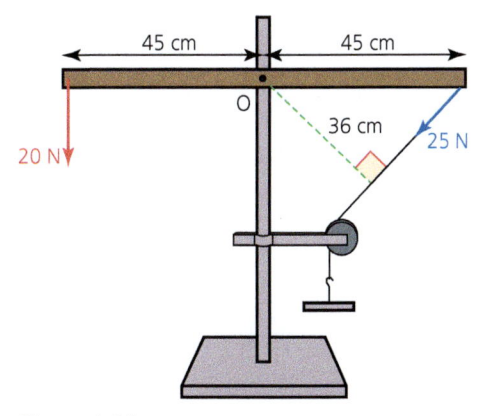

Figure 4.34

In Figure 4.34, where the system remains at rest, the moment about O of the 20 N force is $20 \times 0.45 = 9$ N m. The moment about O of the 25 N force is $-25 \times 0.36 = -9$ N m. The system is in equilibrium even though unequal forces act at equal distances from the pivot.

The magnitude of the moment of the force F about O in Figure 4.35 is given by

$$F \times l = F d \sin \alpha$$

The moment of a force which acts at an angle

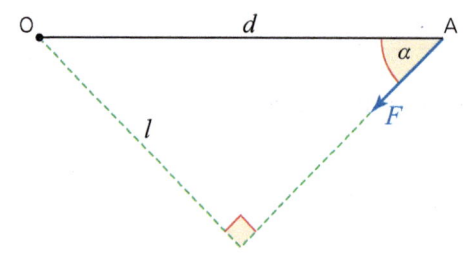

Figure 4.35

Alternatively, the moment can be found by noting that the force F can be resolved into components $F\cos\alpha$ parallel to AO and $F\sin\alpha$ perpendicular to AO, both acting through A (Figure 4.36). The moment of each component can be found and then summed to give the total moment.

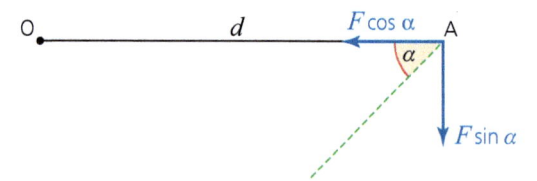

Figure 4.36

The moment of the component along AO is zero because it acts through O. The magnitude of the moment of the perpendicular component is $F\sin\alpha \times d$ so the total moment is $Fd\sin\alpha$, as expected.

Example 4.4

A force of 40 N is exerted on a rod as shown. Find the moment of the force about the point marked O.

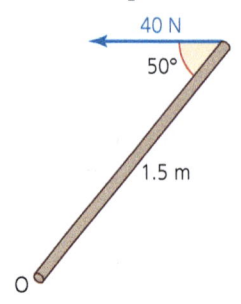

Figure 4.37

Solution

In order to calculate the moment, the perpendicular distance between O and the line of action of the force must be found. This is shown in Figure 4.38.

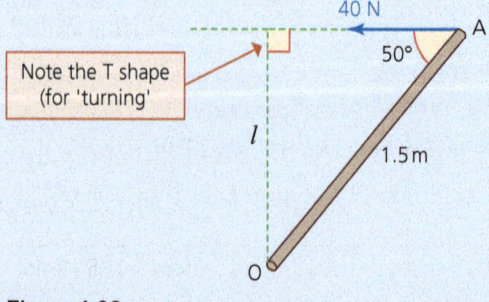

Note the T shape (for 'turning')

Figure 4.38

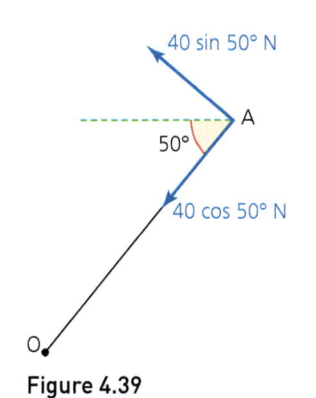

Here $l = 1.5 \times \sin 50°$.

So the moment about O is

$$F \times l = 40 \times (1.5 \times \sin 50°)$$
$$= 46.0 \, \text{N m}$$

Alternatively, you can resolve the 40 N force into components as in Figure 4.39.

The component of the force parallel to AO is $40 \cos 50°$ N. The component perpendicular to AO is $40 \sin 50°$ (or) $40 \cos 40°$ N.

So the moment about O is

$$40 \sin 50° \times 1.5 = 60 \sin 50°$$
$$= 46.0 \, \text{N m}$$

Figure 4.39

Example 4.5

A sign is attached to a light, horizontal rod of length 1 m which is freely hinged to the wall and supported in a vertical plane by a light string, as in Figure 4.40.

The sign is assumed to be a uniform rectangle of mass 10 kg. The angle of the string to the horizontal is 25°.

(i) Find the tension in the string.

(ii) Find the magnitude and direction of the reaction force of the hinge on the sign.

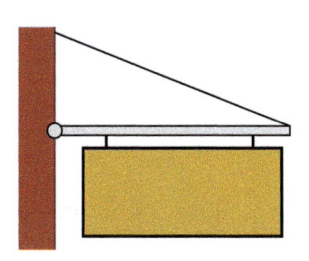

Figure 4.40

Solution

(i) Figure 4.41 shows the forces acting on the rod OA, where R_H and R_V are the magnitudes of the horizontal and vertical components of the reaction R on the rod at the wall.

Taking moments about O:

$$0 \times R_V + 0 \times R_H - 10g \times 0.5 + T \sin 25° \times 1 = 0$$

$$\Rightarrow \qquad T \sin 25° = 5g$$

$$T = 116 \text{ (to 3 s.f.)}$$

The tension is 116 N.

(ii) You can resolve to find the reaction at the wall.

Horizontally: $\qquad R_H = T \cos 25°$

$$\Rightarrow \qquad R_H = 105$$

Vertically: $R_V + T \sin 25° = 10g$

$$\Rightarrow \qquad R_V = 10g - 5g = 49$$

$$R = \sqrt{105^2 + 49^2}$$
$$= 116$$

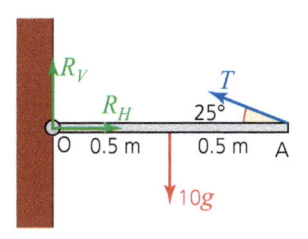

Figure 4.41

> **Discussion point**
> In Figure 4.41 the vertical component of the force at O has been marked as upwards. Why has this been done?

The moment of a force which acts at an angle

> **Discussion point**
> Is it by chance that R and T have the same magnitude and act at the same angle to the horizontal?

$\tan \theta = \dfrac{49}{105}$

$\theta = 25°$ (to the nearest degree)

The reaction at the hinge has magnitude 116 N and acts at 25° above the horizontal.

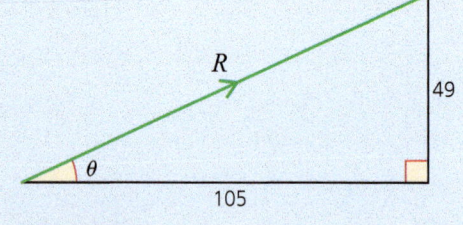

Figure 4.42

Example 4.6

A uniform ladder is standing on rough horizontal ground and leaning against a smooth vertical wall at an angle of 60° to the ground. The ladder has length 4 m and mass 15 kg. Find the normal reaction forces at the wall and ground and the frictional force at the ground.

Solution

Figure 4.43 shows the forces acting on the ladder. The forces are in newtons.

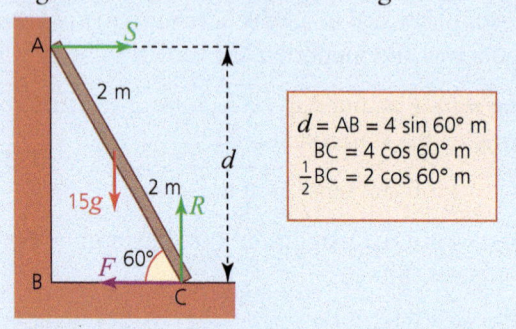

$d = AB = 4 \sin 60°$ m
$BC = 4 \cos 60°$ m
$\frac{1}{2} BC = 2 \cos 60°$ m

Figure 4.43

The diagram shows that there are three unknown forces S, R and F so you need three equations from which to find them. If the ladder remains at rest (in equilibrium), then the resultant force is zero and the resultant moment is zero.

These two conditions provide the three necessary equations.

Equilibrium of horizontal components: $\quad S - F = 0 \quad$ ①

Equilibrium of vertical components: $\quad R - 15g = 0 \quad$ ②

Moments about the foot of the ladder:

> Taking moments about the foot of the ladder means that there are only two moments to consider because the forces F and R both act through the foot of the ladder and so have zero moment.

$R \times 0 + F \times 0 + 15g \times 2 \cos 60° - S \times 4 \sin 60° = 0$

$\Rightarrow \qquad\qquad\qquad 147 - 4S \sin 60° = 0$

$\Rightarrow \qquad\qquad S = \dfrac{147}{4 \sin 60°} = 42.4$ (to 3 s.f.)

From ① $\quad F = S = 42.4$

From ② $\quad R = 147$

The force at the wall is 42.4 N, and those at the ground are 42.4 N horizontally and 147 N vertically.

Exercise 4.2

① Find the moment about O of each of the forces illustrated in Figure 4.44.

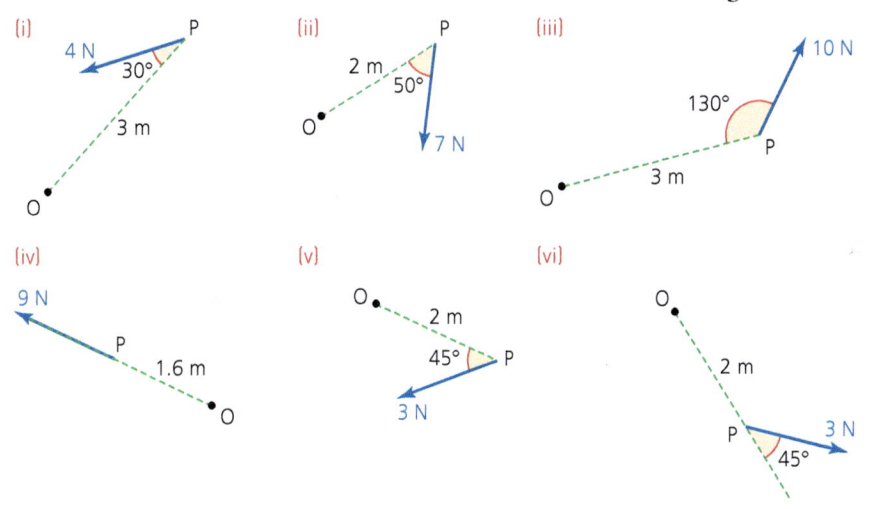

Figure 4.44

② Figure 4.45 shows three children pushing a horizontal playground roundabout. Hannah and David want it to go one way but Rabina wants it to go the other way. Who wins?

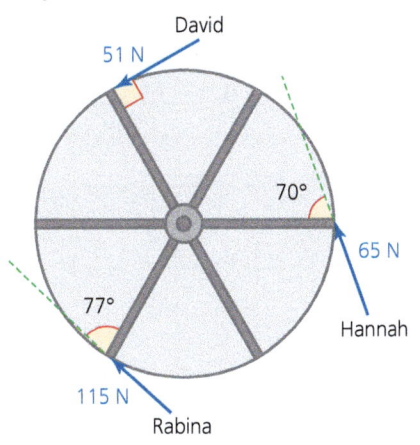

Figure 4.45

③ The operating instructions for a small crane specify that when the jib is at an angle of 25° above the horizontal, the maximum safe load for the crane is 5000 kg. Assuming that this maximum load is determined by the maximum moment that the pivot can support, what is the maximum safe load when the angle between the jib and the horizontal is

(i) 40°

(ii) an angle θ?

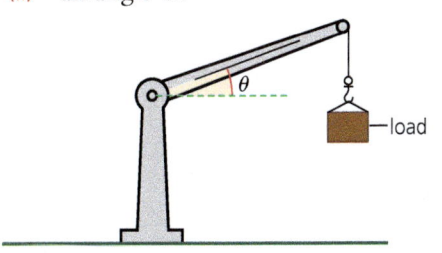

Figure 4.46

The moment of a force which acts at an angle

④ In each of these diagrams in Figure 4.47, a uniform beam of mass 5 kg and length 4 m, freely hinged at one end, A, is in equilibrium. Find the magnitude of the force T in each case.

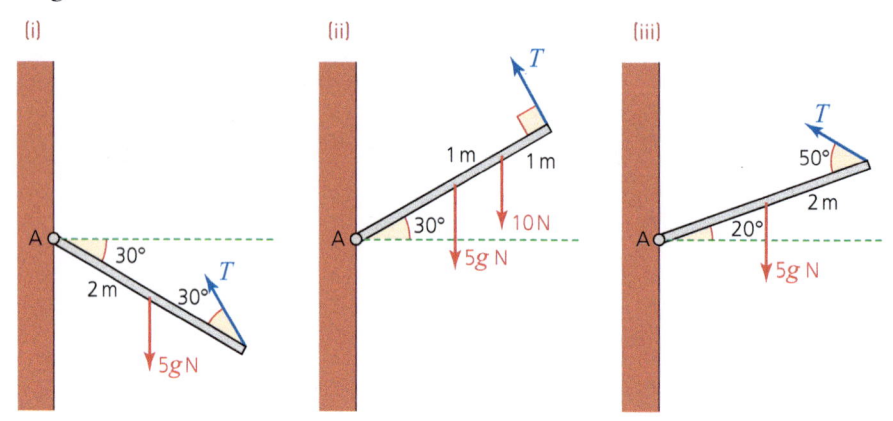

(i) (ii) (iii)

Figure 4.47

⑤ Figure 4.48 shows a uniform rectangular sign ABCD, 3 m × 2 m, of weight 20 N. It is freely hinged at A and supported by the string CE, which makes an angle of 30° with the horizontal. The sign is vertical and CD is horizontal. The tension in the string is T (in N).

(i) Resolve the tension T into horizontal and vertical components.

(ii) Hence show that the moment of the tension in the string about A is given by $2T \cos 30° + 3T \sin 30°$.

(iii) Write down the moment of the sign's weight about A.

(iv) Hence show that $T = 9.28$.

(v) Hence find the horizontal and vertical components of the reaction on the sign at the hinge, A.

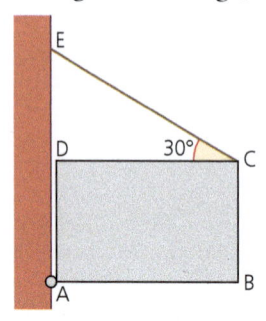

Figure 4.48

You can also find the moment of the tension in the string about A as $d \times T$, where d is the length of AF as shown in Figure 4.49.

(vi) Find

(a) the angle ACD

(b) the length d.

(vii) Show that you get the same value for T when it is calculated in this way.

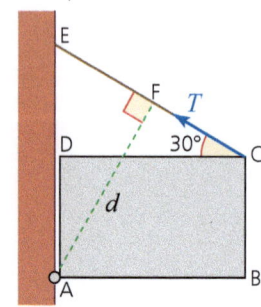

Figure 4.49

⑥ Figure 4.50 shows a simple crane supporting a 50 kg mass. The weight of the jib (AB) may be ignored. The crane is in equilibrium in the position shown.

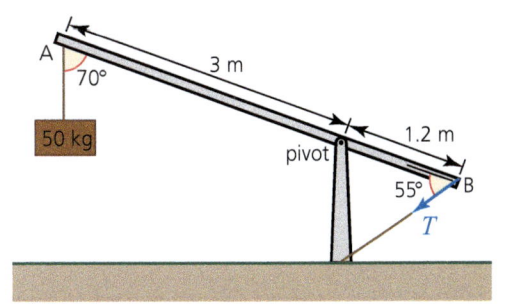

Figure 4.50

(i) By taking moments about the pivot, find the magnitude of the tension T (in N).

(ii) Find the reaction of the pivot on the jib in the form of components parallel and perpendicular to the jib.

(iii) Show that the total moment about the end A of the forces acting on the jib is zero.

(iv) What would happen if
  (a) the rope holding the 50 kg mass snapped?
  (b) the rope with tension T snapped?

⑦ A uniform plank, AB, of mass 50 kg and length 6 m is in equilibrium leaning against a smooth wall at an angle of 60° to the horizontal. The lower end, A, is on rough horizontal ground.

(i) Draw a diagram showing all the forces acting on the plank.

(ii) Write down the total moment about A of all the forces acting on the plank.

(iii) Find the normal reaction of the wall on the plank at point B.

(iv) Find the frictional force on the foot of the plank. What can you deduce about the coefficient of friction between the ground and the plank?

(v) Show that the total moment about B of all the forces acting on the plank is zero.

⑧ A uniform ladder of mass 20 kg and length $2l$ rests in equilibrium with its upper end against a smooth vertical wall and its lower end on a rough horizontal floor. The coefficient of friction between the ladder and the floor is μ. The normal reaction at the wall is S, the frictional force at the ground is F and the normal reaction at the ground is R. The ladder makes an angle α with the horizontal.

(i) Draw a diagram showing the forces acting on the ladder.

For each of the cases
  (a) $\alpha = 60°$,
  (b) $\alpha = 45°$

(ii) Find the magnitudes of S, F and R.

(iii) Find the least possible value of μ.

The moment of a force which acts at an angle

⑨ Figure 4.51 shows a car's handbrake. The force F is exerted by the hand in operating the brake, and this creates a tension T in the brake cable. The hand brake is freely pivoted at point B and is assumed to be light.

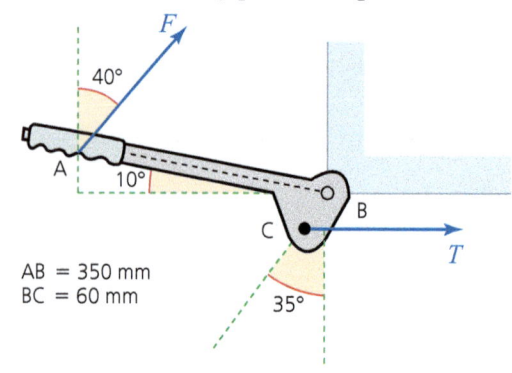

AB = 350 mm
BC = 60 mm

Figure 4.51

(i) Draw a diagram showing all the forces acting on the handbrake.

(ii) What is the required magnitude of force F if the tension in the brake cable is to be 1000 N?

(iii) A child applies the handbrake with a force of 10 N. What is the tension in the brake cable?

⑩ Figure 4.52 shows four tugs manoeuvring a ship. A and C are pushing it, B and D are pulling it.

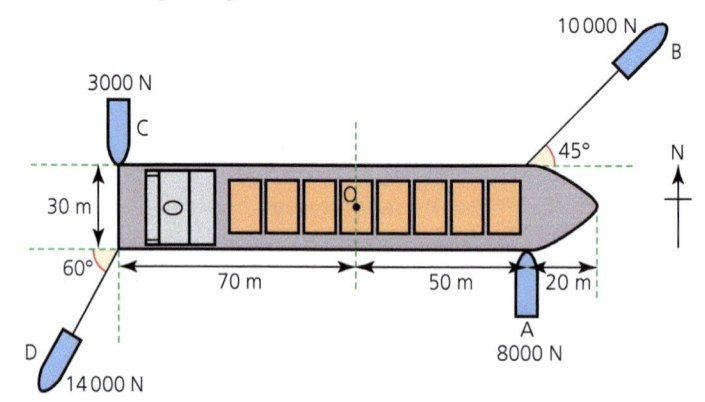

Figure 4.52

(i) Show that the resultant force on the ship is less than 100 N.

(ii) Find the overall turning moment on the ship about its centre point, O.

A breeze starts to blow from the south, causing a total force of 2000 N to act uniformly along the length of the ship, at right angles to it.

(iii) How (assuming B and D continue to apply the same forces) can tugs A and C, counteract the sideways force on the ship by altering the forces with which they are pushing, while maintaining the same overall moment about the centre of the ship?

⑪ Jules is cleaning windows. Her ladder is uniform and stands on rough ground at an angle of 60° to the horizontal and with the top resting on the edge of a smooth window sill. The ladder has a mass 12 kg and length 2.8 m and Jules has mass 56 kg.

(i) Draw a diagram to show the forces on the ladder when nobody is standing on it. Show that the reaction at the sill is then $3g$ N.

(ii) Find the friction and normal reaction forces at the foot of the ladder.

Jules needs to be sure that the ladder will not slip however high she climbs.

(iii) Find the least possible value of μ for the ladder to be safe at 60° to the horizontal.

(iv) The value of μ is in fact 0.4. How far up the ladder can Jules stand before it begins to slip?

⑫ Overhead cables for a tramway are supported by uniform, rigid, horizontal beams of weight 1500 N and length 5 m. Each beam, AB, is freely pivoted at one end A and supports two cables which may be modelled by vertical loads, each of 1000 N, one 1.5 m from A and the other at 1 m from B.

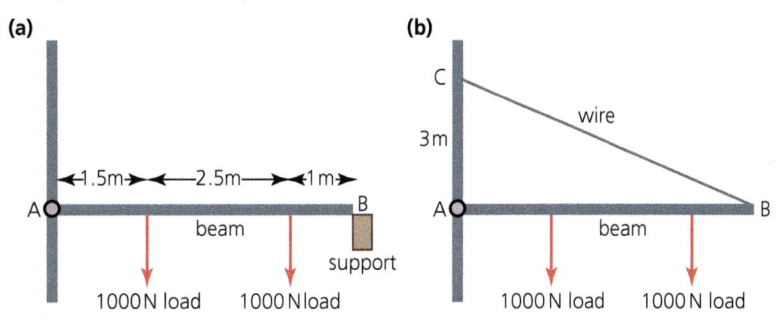

Figure 4.53

In one situation, the beam is held in equilibrium by resting on a small horizontal support at B, as shown in Figure 4.53 (a).

(i) Draw a diagram showing all the forces acting on the beam AB. Show that the vertical force acting on the beam at B is 1850 N.

In another situation, the beam is supported by a wire, *instead of the support at B*. The wire is light, attached at one end to the beam at B and at the other to the point at C which is 3 m vertically above A, as shown in Figure 4.53 (b).

(ii) Calculate the tension in the wire.

(iii) Find the magnitude and direction of the force on the beam at A.

⑬ A uniform rod AB of length 6 m and weight 2000 N is hung from a point O by two light wires, each of length 5 m, attached to each end of the rod. A weight of 500 N is placed at a point C, 2 m from B. The tension in wire AO is T_1 and that in wire BO is T_2. The rod rests in equilibrium at an angle θ to the horizontal. The point X is directly below O and M is the midpoint of the rod.

The moment of a force which acts at an angle

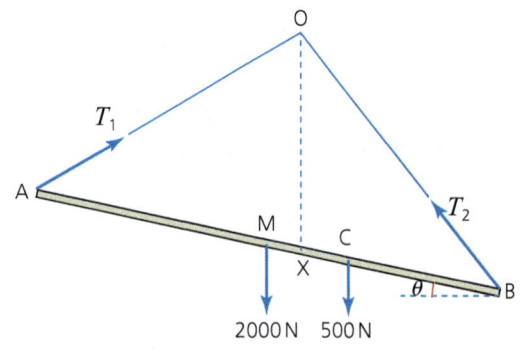

Figure 4.54

(i) By taking moments about O, find the distances MX and XC.

(ii) Find the angle θ.

(iii) By taking moments about each end of the rod, show that the ratio of the tensions in the wires is $T_1:T_2 = 7:8$ and use this to find T_1 and T_2.

⑭ Figure 4.55 shows a uniform ladder AB of mass m and length $2l$ resting in equilibrium with its upper end A against a smooth vertical wall and its lower end B on a smooth inclined plane. The inclined plane makes an angle θ with the horizontal and the ladder makes an angle ϕ with the wall. What is the relationship between θ and ϕ?

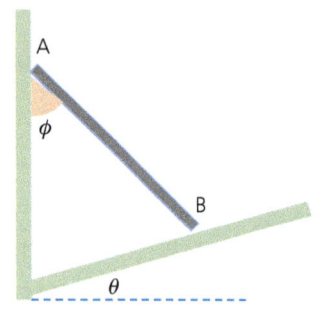

Figure 4.55

⑮ A uniform ladder of length 8 m and weight 180 N rests against a smooth, vertical wall and stands on a rough, horizontal surface. A woman of weight 720 N stands on the ladder so that her weight acts at a distance x m from its lower end, as shown in Figure 4.56. The system is in equilibrium with the ladder at 20° to the vertical.

(i) Show that the frictional force between the ladder and the horizontal surface is F N, where
$$F = 90(1+x)\tan 20°$$

(ii) Deduce that F increases as x increases and hence find the values of the coefficient of friction between the ladder and the surface for which the woman can stand anywhere on the ladder without it slipping.

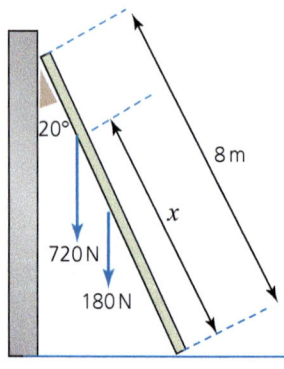

Figure 4.56

3 Sliding and toppling

Figure 4.57 shows a double decker bus on a test ramp. The angle of the ramp to the horizontal is slowly increased.

Discussion point
What happens to the bus? Would a loaded bus behave differently from the empty bus in the photograph?

Figure 4.57

EXPERIMENT

The diagrams show a force being applied to a cereal packet in different positions

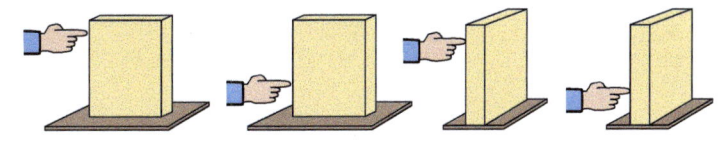

Figure 4.58

In which case do you think the packet is most likely to fall over? In which case is it most likely to slide? Investigate your answers practically, using boxes of different shapes.

Discussion point
Figure 4.59 shows the cereal packet placed on a slope. Is the box more likely to topple or slide as the angle of the slope to the horizontal increases?

Figure 4.59

To what extent is this situation comparable to that of the bus on the test ramp?

Two critical cases

When an object stands on a surface, the only forces acting on it are its weight W and the *resultant* of all the contact forces between the surfaces, which must act through a point on both surfaces. This resultant contact force is often resolved into two components: the friction, F, parallel to any possible sliding and the normal reaction, R, perpendicular to F, as in Figures 4.60–4.62.

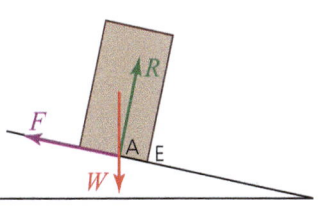

In equilibrium or sliding $F \leq \mu R$

Figure 4.60

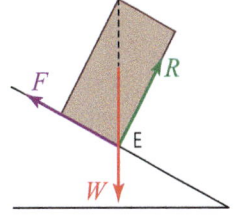

About to topple about the pivot edge E

Figure 4.61

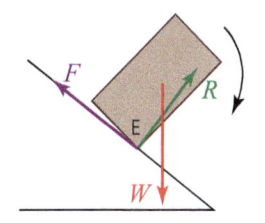

Toppling about the pivot edge E

Figure 4.62

Sliding and toppling

> **Discussion point**
> Why does the object topple in Figure 4.62?

Equilibrium can be broken in two ways.

(i) **The object is on the point of sliding.** Then $F = \mu R$ according to the model.

(ii) **The object is on the point of toppling.** The pivot is at the lowest point of contact which is the point E in Figure 4.62. In this critical case:
 - the centre of mass is directly above E so the weight acts vertically downwards through E
 - the resultant reaction of the plane on the object acts through E, vertically upwards. This is the resultant of F and R.

When three non-parallel forces are in equilibrium, their lines of action must be concurrent (they must all pass through one point). Otherwise there is a resultant moment about the point where two of them meet, as in Figure 4.62.

Example 4.7

An increasing force P newtons is applied to a block, as shown in Figure 4.63, until the block moves. The coefficient of friction between the block and the plane is 0.4.

Does it slide or topple?

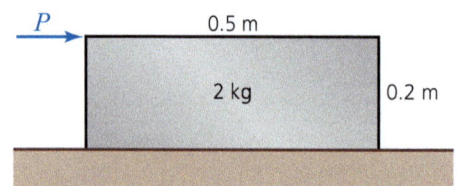

Figure 4.63

Solution

The forces acting are shown in Figure 4.64. The normal reaction may be thought of as a single force acting somewhere within the area of contact. When toppling occurs (or is about to occur), the line of action is through the edge about which it topples.

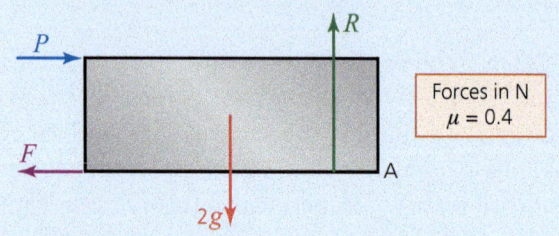

Figure 4.64

Until the block moves, it is in equilibrium.

Horizontally: $\qquad P = F$ ①

Vertically: $\qquad R = 2g$ ②

If *sliding* is about to occur, $\quad F = \mu R$

From ① $\quad P = \mu R = 0.4 \times 2g$

$\qquad\qquad = 7.84$

> **Hint**
> R acts through A

If the block is about to topple, then A is the pivot point and the reaction of the plane on the block acts at A. Taking moments about A gives

[anticlockwise] $2g \times 0.25 - P \times 0.2 = 0$

$$P = 24.5$$

So in order to slide P needs to exceed 7.84 N but to topple it needs to exceed 24.5 N: the block will slide before it topples.

Example 4.8

A rectangular block of mass 3 kg is placed on a slope as shown. The angle α is gradually increased.
What happens to the block given that the coefficient of friction between the block and the slope is 0.6?

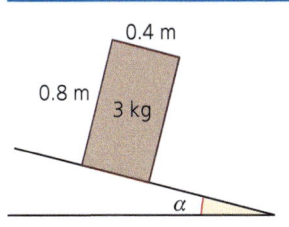

Figure 4.65

Solution

Check for possible sliding

Figure 4.66 shows the forces acting when the block is in equilibrium.

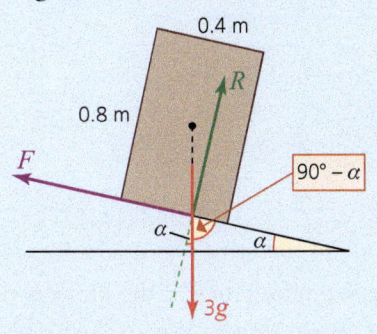

Figure 4.66

Resolve parallel to the slope: $F = 3g \sin\alpha$

Perpendicular to the slope: $R = 3g \cos\alpha$

When the block is on the point of sliding, $F = \mu R$ so

$$3g \sin\alpha = \mu \times 3g \cos\alpha$$

$\Rightarrow \quad \tan\alpha = \mu = 0.6$

$\Rightarrow \quad \alpha = 31.0°$

The block is on the point of sliding when $\alpha = 31°$

Check for possible toppling.

When the block is on the point of toppling about the edge E the centre of mass is vertically above E, as shown in Figure 4.67.

Then the angle α is given by

$$\tan\alpha = \frac{0.4}{0.8}$$

$$\alpha = \arctan(0.5) = 26.6°$$

Sliding and toppling

The block topples when $\alpha = 26.6°$.

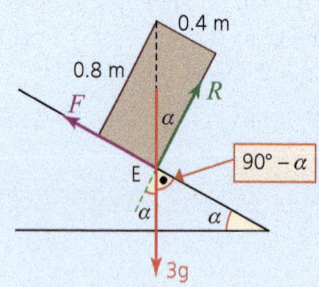

Figure 4.67

Discussion point
Is it possible for sliding and toppling to occur for the same angle?

The angle for sliding (31°) is greater than the angle for toppling (26.6°), so the block topples without sliding when $\alpha = 26.6°$.

Exercise 4.3

① A force of magnitude P newtons acts as shown on a block resting on a horizontal plane. The coefficient of friction between the block and the plane is 0.7.

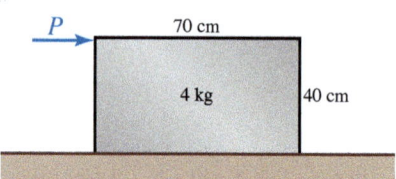

Figure 4.68

The magnitude of the force P is gradually increased from zero.

(i) Find the magnitude of P if the block is on the point of sliding, assuming it does not topple.

(ii) Find the magnitude of P if the block is on the point of toppling, assuming it does not slide.

(iii) Does the block slide or topple?

② A solid uniform cuboid is placed on a horizontal surface. A force is P is applied, as shown in Figure 4.69.

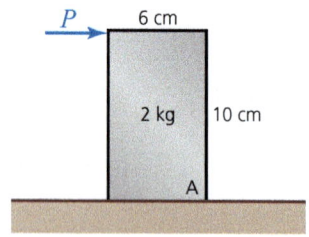

Figure 4.69

(i) If the block is on the point of sliding, express P in terms of μ, the coefficient of friction between the block and the plane.

(ii) Find the magnitude of P if the block is on the point of toppling.

(iii) For what values of μ will the block slide before it topples?

(iv) For what values of μ will the block topple before it slides?

③ A uniform rectangular block of height 30 cm and width 10 cm is placed on a rough plane inclined at an angle α to the horizontal. The block lies with its shorter side parallel to the slope of the plane. The coefficient of friction between the block and the plane is 0.25.

  (i) Assuming that it does not topple, for what value of α does the block just slide?

  (ii) Assuming that it does not slide, for what value of α does the block just topple?

  (iii) The angle α is increased slowly from 0°. Which happens first, sliding or toppling?

④ A horizontal force of increasing magnitude is applied to the middle of the face of a 50 cm uniform cube, at right angles to the face. The coefficient of friction between the cube and the surface is 0.4 and the cube is on a level surface. What happens to the cube?

⑤ A solid uniform cube of side 4 cm and weight 60 N is situated on a rough horizontal plane. The coefficient of friction between the cube and the plane is 0.4. A force P acts in the middle of one of the edges of the top of the cube, as shown in Figure 4.70.

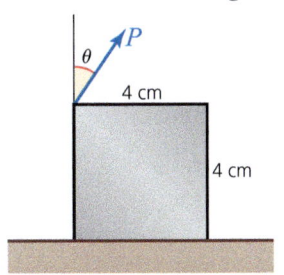

Figure 4.70

In the cases when the value of θ is (a) 60°, (b) 80°, find

  (i) the force P needed to make the cube slide, assuming it does not topple;

  (ii) the force P needed to make the cube topple, assuming it does not slide;

  (iii) whether it first slides or topples as the force P is increased.

For what value of θ do toppling and sliding occur for the same value of P, and what is that value of P?

⑥ A solid uniform cuboid, 10 cm × 20 cm × 50 cm, is to stand on an inclined plane, which makes an angle α with the horizontal. One edge of the cuboid is to be parallel to the line of the slope. The coefficient of friction between the cuboid and the plane is μ.

  (i) Which face of the cuboid should be placed on the slope to make it

    (a) least likely and (b) most likely to topple?

  (ii) How does the cuboid's orientation influence the likelihood of it sliding?

  (iii) Find the range of possible values of μ in the situations where:

    (a) it will slide whatever its orientation

    (b) it will topple whatever its orientation.

Sliding and toppling

7. A man is trying to move a uniform scaffold plank of length 3 m and weight 150 N which is resting on horizontal ground. You may assume that he exerts a slowly increasing force of magnitude PN at a constant angle θ to the vertical and at right angles to the edge CD as shown in Figure 4.71.

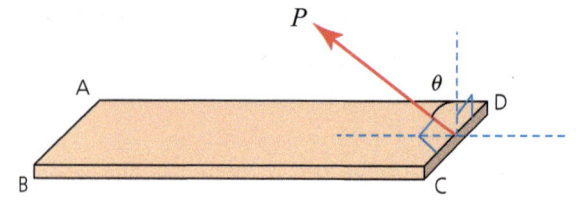

Figure 4.71

As P increases the plank will either slide or start to turn about the end AB depending on the values of θ and the coefficient of friction μ between the plank and the ground.

Assume that the plank slides before it turns and is on the point of sliding.

(i) Show that the normal reaction of the ground on the plank is
$$(150 - P\cos\theta)\,\text{N}.$$

(ii) Obtain two expressions involving the frictional force acting on the plank and deduce that
$$P = \frac{150\mu}{\sin\theta + \mu\cos\theta}$$

Assume now that the plank starts to turn about the edge AB before it slides and is on the point of turning.

(iii) Where is the line of action of the normal reaction of the ground on the plank?

(iv) Show that $P = \dfrac{75}{\cos\theta}$

Given that the plank slides before it turns about AB as the force P is gradually increased,

(v) find the relationship between μ and θ. Simplify your answer. [MEI]

8. A cube of side 4 cm and mass 100 g is acted on by a force as shown in Figure 4.72.

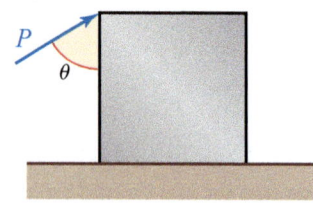

Figure 4.72

The coefficient of friction between the cube and the plane is 0.3. What happens to the cube if

(i) $\theta = 45°$ and $P = 0.3\,\text{N}$?

(ii) $\theta = 15°$ and $P = 0.45\,\text{N}$?

⑨ A cube of side l and weight W is resting on a rough horizontal plane. A force of magnitude T is applied to a point P on the top edge of the cube. This force makes an angle θ with the horizontal such that $\tan\theta = \frac{3}{4}$ and the force is in the vertical plane containing P and the centre of the cube. The cube does not slip and is on the point of tipping.

Show that $T = 2.5W$.

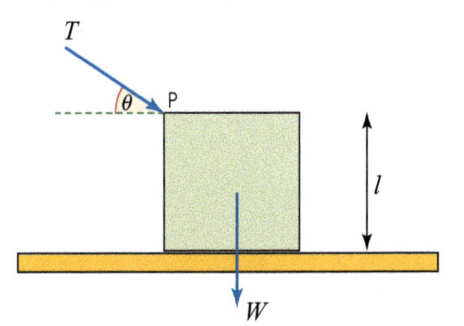

Figure 4.73

KEY POINTS

1. The moment of a force F about a point O is given by the product Fd where d is the perpendicular distance from O to the line of action of the force.

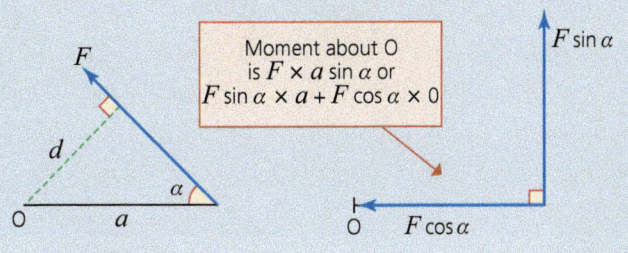

   Moment about O is $F \times a \sin\alpha$ or $F\sin\alpha \times a + F\cos\alpha \times 0$

   Figure 4.74

2. The S.I. unit for moment is the newton metre (N m)
3. Anticlockwise moments are usually called positive, clockwise negative.
4. If a body is in equilibrium the resultant force is zero and the sum of the moments of the forces acting on it, about any point, is zero.

LEARNING OUTCOMES

When you have completed this chapter, you should

▶ be able to calculate the moment about a fixed point O of a force acting on a body as the product of the force and the perpendicular distance of O from the line of action of the force or by first resolving the force into components and then finding the product of that component which does not go through O and its distance from O

▶ be able to find the resultant of a set of parallel forces

▶ know how different types of lever work

▶ know the meaning of the word couple

▶ know that an object is in equilibrium if the resultant of all the applied forces acting on it is zero and the sum of their moments about any point is also zero

▶ be able to identify how equilibrium can be broken by sliding or toppling.

5 Work, energy and power

I like work: it fascinates me. I can sit and look at it for hours.

Jerome K. Jerome

> **Discussion point**
> This photograph shows the tidal power station at Annapolis in Nova Scotia, Canada. Where does the energy it produces come from?

Figure 5.1

1 Energy and momentum

When describing the motion of objects in everyday language the words **energy** and **momentum** are often used quite loosely and sometimes no distinction is made between them. In mechanics they must be defined precisely.

For an object of mass m moving with velocity **v**:

- Kinetic energy = $\frac{1}{2}mv^2$ (this is the energy it has due to its motion)
- Momentum = $m\mathbf{v}$

> v is the speed, the magnitude of the velocity $v = |\mathbf{v}|$.

Notice that kinetic energy is a scalar quantity with magnitude only, but momentum is a vector in the same direction as the velocity.

Both the kinetic energy and the momentum are liable to change when a force acts on a body and you will learn more about how the energy is changed in this chapter. You will meet momentum again in Chapter 6.

Work and energy

In everyday life you encounter many forms of energy such as heat, light, electricity and sound. You are familiar with the conversion of one form of energy to another: from chemical energy stored in wood to heat energy when you burn it; from electrical energy to the energy of a train's motion, and so on. The S.I. unit for energy is the joule, J.

Mechanical energy and work

In mechanics, two forms of energy are particularly important.

- **Kinetic energy** is the energy which a body possesses because of its motion.
- The kinetic energy of a moving object = $\frac{1}{2} \times$ mass $\times$ (speed)^2.
- **Potential energy** is the energy which a body possesses because of its position. It may be thought of as stored energy which can be converted into kinetic energy or other forms of energy. You will meet this again later in this chapter.
- The energy of an object is usually changed when it is acted on by a force. When a force is applied to an object which moves in the direction of its line of action, the force is said to do *work*.
  The work done by a constant force = force × distance moved in the direction of the force.

The following examples illustrate how to use these ideas.

Example 5.1

A brick, initially at rest, is raised by a force averaging 40 N to a height of 5 m above the ground, where it is left stationary. How much work is done by the force?

Solution

The work done by the force in raising the brick is given by

work done = force × distance
         = 40 × 5
         = 200 J

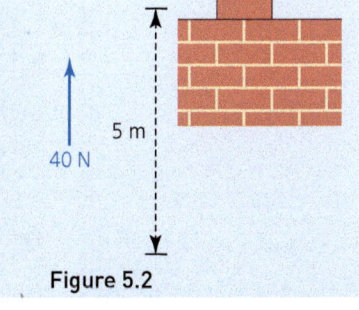

Figure 5.2

Energy and momentum

Examples 5.2 and 5.3 show how the work done by a force can be related to the change in kinetic energy of an object.

Example 5.2

A train travelling on level ground is subject to a resistive force (from the brakes and air resistance) of 250 kN for a distance of 5 km. How much kinetic energy does the train lose?

> **Note**
> Work and energy have the same units.

Solution

The forward force is $-250\,000$ N.

The work done by it is $-250\,000 \times 5000 = -1\,250\,000\,000$ J.

So $-1\,250\,000\,000$ J of kinetic energy are gained by the train. In other words, $+1\,250\,000\,000$ J of kinetic energy are lost and the train slows down. This energy is converted to other forms such as heat and perhaps a little sound.

Example 5.3

A car of mass m kg is travelling at $u\,\text{m s}^{-1}$ when the driver applies a constant driving force F N. The ground is level and the road is straight and resistance to motion can be ignored. The speed of the car increases to $v\,\text{m s}^{-1}$ in a period of t s over a distance of s m. Show that the change in kinetic energy of the car is equal to the work done by the driving force.

Solution

Treating the car as a particle and applying Newton's second law:

$$F = ma$$
$$a = \frac{F}{m}$$

Since F is assumed constant, the acceleration is constant also, so using the constant acceleration equation $v^2 = u^2 + 2as$

$$v^2 = u^2 + \frac{2Fs}{m}$$

$$\Rightarrow \tfrac{1}{2}mv^2 = \tfrac{1}{2}mu^2 + Fs$$

$$Fs = \tfrac{1}{2}mv^2 - \tfrac{1}{2}mu^2 \quad \text{change in kinetic energy}$$

$\Rightarrow$ work done by force = final kinetic energy − initial kinetic energy of the car.

> **Note**
> This is an important result given in symbols and in words.

The work–energy principle

Examples 5.4 and 5.5 illustrate the **work–energy principle** which states that:

> ❗ The total work done by the forces acting on a body is equal to the increase in the kinetic energy of the body.

Example 5.4

A sledge of total mass 30 kg, initially moving at $2\,\text{m s}^{-1}$, is pulled 14 m across smooth horizontal ice by a horizontal rope in which there is a constant tension of 45 N. Find its final velocity.

This is the horizontal force on the sledge.

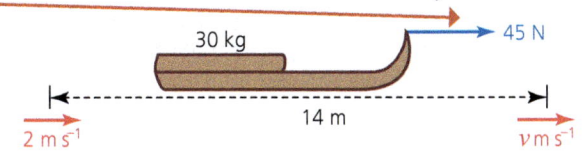

Figure 5.3

Solution

Since the ice is smooth, the work done by the force is all converted into kinetic energy and the final velocity can be found by using

work done by force = final kinetic energy − initial kinetic energy

$$45 \times 14 = \tfrac{1}{2} \times 30 \times v^2 - \tfrac{1}{2} \times 30 \times 2^2$$

So $v^2 = 46$ and the final velocity of the sledge is $6.8\,\text{m s}^{-1}$ (to 2 s.f.).

Example 5.5

The combined mass of a cyclist and her bicycle is 65 kg. She accelerates from rest to $8\,\text{m s}^{-1}$ in 80 m along a horizontal road.

(i) Calculate the work done by the net force in accelerating the cyclist and her bicycle.

(ii) Hence calculate the net forward force (assuming the force to be constant).

Solution

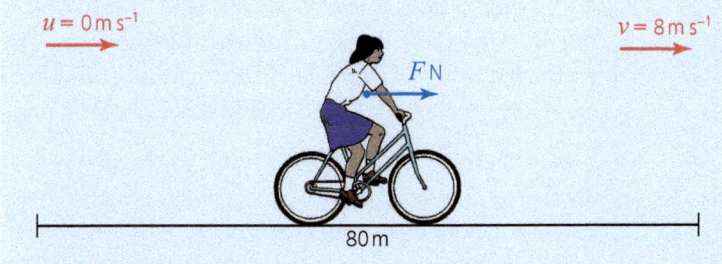

Figure 5.4

(i) The work done by the net force F is given by

$$\text{work} = \text{final K.E.} - \text{initial K.E.}$$
$$= \tfrac{1}{2}mv^2 - \tfrac{1}{2}mu^2$$
$$= \tfrac{1}{2} \times 65 \times 8^2 - 0$$
$$= 2080\,\text{J}$$

The work done is 2080 J.

(ii) Work done = Fs
$$= F \times 80$$

So $80F = 2080$

$F = 26$

The net forward force is 26 N.

Energy and momentum

Work

It is important to realise that:

- work is done by a force
- work is only done when there is movement
- a force only does work on an object when it has a component in the direction of motion of the object.

Notice that if you stand holding a brick stationary above your head, painful though it may be, the force you are exerting on it is doing no work. Nor is the vertical force doing any work if you walk round the room holding the brick at the same height. However, once you start climbing the stairs, a component of the brick's movement is in the direction of the upward force that you are exerting on it, so the force is now doing some work.

When applying the work–energy principle, you have to be careful to include all the forces acting on the body. In the example of a brick of weight 40 N being raised 5 m vertically, starting and ending at rest, the change in kinetic energy is clearly 0.

This seems paradoxical when it is clear that the force which raised the brick has done $40 \times 5 = 200$ J of work. However, the brick was subject to another force, namely, its weight, which did $-40 \times 5 = -200$ J of work on it, giving a total of $200 + (-200) = 0$ J.

Conservation of mechanical energy

The net forward force on the cyclist in Example 5.5 is her driving force minus resistive forces such as air resistance and friction in the bearings. In the absence of such resistive forces, she would gain more kinetic energy. Also the work she does against them is lost; it is dissipated as heat and sound. Contrast this with the work a cyclist does against gravity when going uphill. This work can be recovered as kinetic energy on a downhill run. The work done against the force of gravity is conserved and gives the cyclist potential energy (see page 109).

Forces such as friction which result in the dissipation of mechanical energy are called *dissipative forces*. Forces which conserve mechanical energy are called *conservative forces*. The force of gravity is a conservative force and so is the tension in an elastic string; you can test this using an elastic band.

The mechanical energy of a system is the sum of its potential energy and its kinetic energy. If there are no dissipative forces, the mechanical energy of the system is conserved.

Example 5.6

A bullet of mass 25 g is fired at a wooden barrier 3 cm thick. When it hits the barrier it is travelling at 200 m s^{-1}. The barrier exerts a constant resistive force of 5000 N on the bullet.

(i) Does the bullet pass through the barrier and, if so, with what speed does it emerge?

(ii) Is energy conserved in this situation?

Solution

(i) The work done *by* the force is defined as the product of the force and the distance moved **in the direction of the force**. Since the bullet is moving in the direction opposite to the net resistive force, the work done by this force is negative.

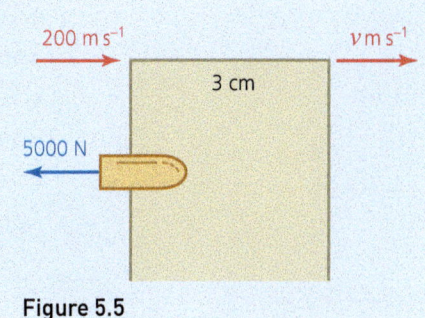

Figure 5.5

Work done = -5000×0.03 *(3 cm = 0.03 m)*

$\qquad\qquad = -150\,\text{J}$

The initial kinetic energy of the bullet is

Initial K. E. $= \frac{1}{2}mu^2$

$= \frac{1}{2} \times 0.025 \times 200^2$ *(25 g = 0.025 kg)*

$= 500\,\text{J}$

A loss in energy of 150 J will not reduce kinetic energy to zero, so the bullet will still be moving on exit.

Since the work done is equal to the change in kinetic energy,

$$-150 = \frac{1}{2}mv^2 - 500$$

Solving for v

$$\frac{1}{2}mv^2 = 500 - 150$$

$$v^2 = \frac{2 \times (500 - 150)}{0.025}$$

$$v = 167 \text{ (to nearest whole number)}$$

So the bullet emerges from the barrier with a speed of $167\,\text{m s}^{-1}$.

(ii) Total energy is conserved but there is a loss of mechanical energy of $\frac{1}{2}mu^2 - \frac{1}{2}mv^2 = 150\,\text{J}$. This energy is converted into non-mechanical forms such as heat and sound.

Example 5.7

An aircraft of mass m kg is flying at a constant velocity $v\,\text{m s}^{-1}$ horizontally. Its engines are providing a horizontal driving force F N.

(i) (a) Draw a diagram showing the driving force, the lift force L N, the air resistance (drag force) R N and the weight of the aircraft.

(b) State which of these forces are equal in magnitude.

(c) State which of the forces are doing no work.

(ii) In the case when $m = 100\,000$, $v = 270$ and $F = 350\,000$ find the work done in a 10-second period by those forces which are doing work, and show that the work–energy principle holds in this case.

Energy and momentum

At a later time the pilot increases the thrust of the aircraft's engines to 400 000 N. When the aircraft has travelled a distance of 30 km, its speed has increased to 300 m s^{-1}.

(iii) Find the work done against air resistance during this period, and the average resistance force.

Solution

(i) (a)

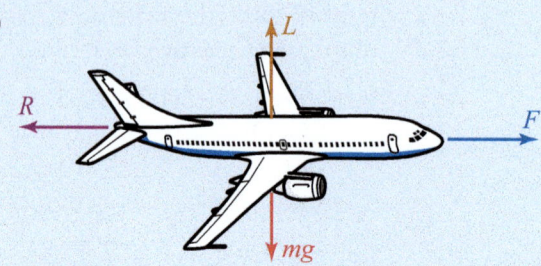

Figure 5.6

(b) Since the aircraft is travelling at constant velocity it is in equilibrium.

Horizontal forces: $F = R$

Vertical forces: $L = mg$

(c) Since the aircraft's velocity has no vertical component, the vertical forces, L and mg, are doing no work.

(ii) In 10 s at 270 m s^{-1} the aircraft travels 2700 m.

Work done by driving force $F = 350\,000 \times 2700 = 945\,000\,000$ J

Work done by resistance force $R = 350\,000 \times -2700 = -945\,000\,000$ J

The work–energy principle states that in this situation

work done by F + work done by R = change in kinetic energy.

Now work done by F + work done by R = (945 000 000 − 945 000 000) = 0 J, and change in kinetic energy = 0 (since velocity is constant), so the work–energy principle does indeed hold in this case.

(iii) Final K.E. − initial K.E. $= \frac{1}{2}mv^2 - \frac{1}{2}mu^2$

$= \frac{1}{2} \times 100\,000 \times 300^2 - \frac{1}{2} \times 100\,000 \times 270^2$

$= 855 \times 10^6$ J

Work done by driving force $= 400\,000 \times 30\,000$

$= 12\,000 \times 10^6$ J

Total work done = K.E. gained

Work done by resistance force $+ 12\,000 \times 10^6 = 855 \times 10^6$

Work done by resistance force $= -11\,145 \times 10^6$ J

Average force × distance = work done by force

Average force $\times 30\,000 = 11\,145 \times 10^6$

⇒ The average resistance force is 371 500 N (in the negative direction).

> **Note**
>
> When an aircraft is in flight, most of the work done by the resistance force results in air currents and the generation of heat. A typical large jet cruising at 35 000 feet has a body temperature about 30°C above the surrounding air temperature. For supersonic flight the temperature difference is much greater. Concorde used to fly with a skin temperature more than 200°C above that of the surrounding air.

Exercise 5.1

① Find the kinetic energy of the following objects.
  (i) An ice skater of mass 50 kg travelling with speed 10 m s^{-1}.
  (ii) An elephant of mass 5 tonnes moving with speed 4 m s^{-1}.
  (iii) A train of mass 7000 tonnes travelling with speed 40 m s^{-1}.
  (iv) The Moon of mass 7.4×10^{22} kg, travelling at 1000 m s^{-1} in its orbit around the Earth.
  (v) A bacterium of mass 2×10^{-16} g which has a speed of 1 mm s^{-1}.

② Find the work done by a man in the following situations.
  (i) He pushes a packing case of mass 35 kg a distance of 5 m across a rough floor against a resistance of 200 N. The case starts and finishes at rest.
  (ii) He pushes a packing case of mass 35 kg a distance of 5 m across a rough floor against a resistance of 200 N. The case starts at rest and finishes with a speed of 2 m s^{-1}.
  (iii) He pushes a packing case of mass 35 kg a distance of 5 m across a rough floor against a resistance of 200 N. Initially the case has speed 2 m s^{-1} but it ends at rest.
  (iv) He is handed a packing case of mass 35 kg. He holds it stationary, at the same height, for 20 s and then someone else takes it away from him.

③ A sprinter of mass 60 kg is at rest at the beginning of a race and accelerates to 12 m s^{-1} in a distance of 30 m. Assume air resistance is negligible.
  (i) Calculate the kinetic energy of the sprinter at the end of the 30 m.
  (ii) Write down the work done by the sprinter over this distance.
  (iii) Calculate the forward force exerted by the sprinter, assuming it to be constant, using work = force × distance.
  (iv) Using force = mass × acceleration and the constant acceleration formulae, show that this force is consistent with the sprinter having a speed of 12 m s^{-1} after 30 m.

④ A sports car of mass 1.2 tonnes accelerates from rest to 30 m s^{-1} in a distance of 150 m. Assume air resistance to be negligible.
  (i) Calculate the work done in accelerating the car. Does your answer depend on an assumption that the driving force is constant?
  (ii) If the driving force is, in fact, constant, what is its magnitude?
  (iii) Is it reasonable to assume that air resistance is negligible?

⑤ A car of mass 1600 kg is travelling at a speed of 25 m s^{-1} when the brakes are applied so that it stops after moving a further 75 m. Assuming that other resistive forces can be neglected, find
  (i) the work done by the brakes.
  (ii) the retarding force from the brakes, assuming that it is constant.

⑥ The forces acting on a hot air balloon of mass 500 kg are its weight and the total uplift force.
  (i) Find the total work done when the vertical speed of the balloon changes from
    (a) 2 m s^{-1} to 5 m s^{-1}
    (b) 8 m s^{-1} to 3 m s^{-1}.
  (ii) If the balloon rises 100 m vertically while its speed changes, calculate, in each case, the work done by the uplift force.

Energy and momentum

7. A bullet of mass 20 g, found at the scene of a police investigation, had penetrated 16 cm into a wooden post. The speed for that type of bullet is known to be 80 m s^{-1}.
   (i) Find the kinetic energy of the bullet before it entered the post.
   (ii) What happened to this energy when the bullet entered the wooden post?
   (iii) Write down the work done in stopping the bullet,
   (iv) Calculate the resistive force on the bullet, assuming it to be constant.

   Another bullet of the same mass and shape had clearly been fired from a different and unknown type of gun. This bullet had penetrated 20 cm into the post.
   (v) Estimate the speed of this bullet before it hit the post.

8. The highway code gives the braking distance for a car travelling at 22 m s^{-1} (50 mph) to be 38 m (125 ft). A car of mass 1300 kg is brought to rest in just this distance. It may be assumed that the only resistance forces come from the car's brakes.
   (i) Find the work done by the brakes.
   (ii) Find the average force exerted by the brakes.
   (iii) What happened to the kinetic energy of the car?
   (iv) What happens when you drive a car with the handbrake on?

9. A car of mass 1200 kg experiences a constant resistance force of 600 N. The driving force from the engine depends upon the gear, as shown in the table.

Gear	1	2	3	4
Force (N)	2800	2100	1400	1000

   Starting from rest, the car is driven 20 m in first gear, 40 m in second, 80 m in third and 100 m in fourth. How fast is the car travelling at the end?

10. In this question take g to be 10 m s^{-2}. A chest of mass 60 kg is resting on a rough horizontal floor. The coefficient of friction between the floor and the chest is 0.4. A woman pushes the chest in such a way that its speed–time graph is as shown below.

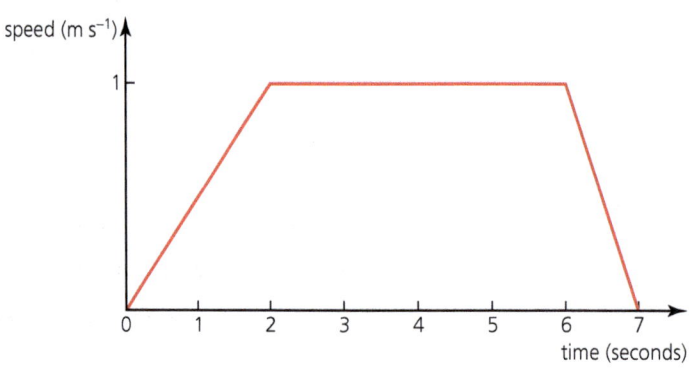

    Figure 5.7

    (i) Find the force of frictional resistance acting on the chest when it moves.
    (ii) Use the speed–time graph to find the total distance travelled by the chest.
    (iii) Find the total work done by the woman.

(iv) Find the acceleration of the chest in the first 2 seconds of its motion and hence the force exerted by the woman during this time, and the work done.

(v) In the same way find the work done by the woman during the time intervals 2 to 6 seconds, and 6 to 7 seconds.

(vi) Show that your answers to parts (iv) and (v) are consistent with your answer to part (iii).

2 Gravitational potential energy

As you have seen, kinetic energy (K.E.) is the energy that an object has because of its motion. Potential energy (P.E.) is the energy an object has because of its position. The units of potential energy are the same as those of kinetic energy or any other form of energy, namely, joules.

One form of potential energy is **gravitational potential energy**. The gravitational potential energy of the object in Figure 5.8 of mass m kg at height h m above a particular reference level, 0, is mgh J. If it falls to the reference level, the force of gravity does mgh J of work and the body loses mgh J of potential energy.

A loss in gravitational potential energy is an alternative way of accounting for the work done by the force of gravity.

If a mass m kg is **raised** through a distance h m, the gravitational potential energy **increases** by mgh J. If a mass m kg is **lowered** through a distance h m the gravitational potential energy **decreases** by mgh J.

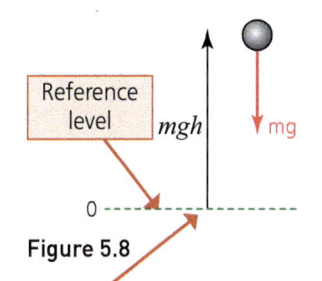

Figure 5.8

You will often have to choose the reference level for a particular situation. It could be ground level, the top of a building or the height of an aircraft. There is no right answer but choosing a suitable level can make your calculations easier.

Example 5.8

Calculate the gravitational potential energy, relative to the ground, of a ball of mass 0.15 kg at a height of 2 m above the ground.

Solution

Mass $m = 0.15$, height $h = 2$.

Gravitational potential energy $= mgh$

$= 0.15 \times 9.8 \times 2$

$= 2.94$ J

> **Note**
>
> Assuming no other forces, the gain in K.E. is 2.94 J so that the maximum theoretical speed of the ball when it hits the ground is $\sqrt{\frac{2 \times 2.94}{0.15}} = 6.26 \text{ m s}^{-1}$.
> In reality, there would be air resistance, so the ball's speed would be less than this.

> **Note**
>
> If the ball falls:
>
> loss in P.E. = work done by gravity
> = gain in K.E.
>
> There is no change in the total energy (P.E. + K.E.) of the ball assuming there are no other forces acting on the ball.

Gravitational potential energy

Using conservation of mechanical energy

When gravity is the only force which does work on a body, mechanical energy is conserved. When this is the case, many problems are easily solved using energy. This is possible even when the acceleration is not constant.

Example 5.9

A skier starts from rest and slides down a ski slope 400 m long which is at an angle of 30° to the horizontal. The slope is smooth and air resistance can be neglected.

(i) Find the speed of the skier when he reaches the bottom of the slope.

At the foot of the slope the ground becomes horizontal and is made rough in order to help skiers stop. The coefficient of friction between the skis and the ground is $\frac{1}{4}$.

(ii) Find how far the skier travels before coming to rest.

(iii) In what way is your model unrealistic?

Solution

(i) The skier is modelled as a particle.

The slope is smooth so the frictional force is zero.

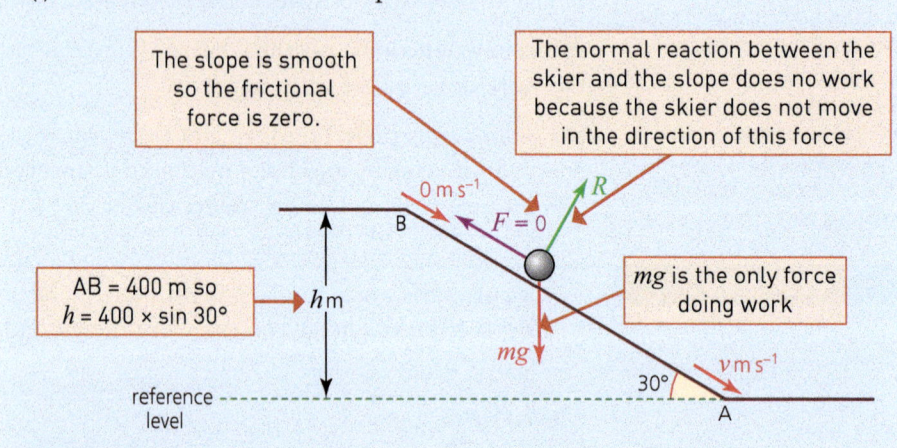

The normal reaction between the skier and the slope does no work because the skier does not move in the direction of this force

AB = 400 m so $h = 400 \times \sin 30°$

mg is the only force doing work

Figure 5.9

Mechanical energy is conserved.

Total mechanical energy at B $= mgh + \frac{1}{2}mu^2$

$= m \times 9.8 \times 400 \sin 30° + 0$

$= 1960 m$ J

Total mechanical energy at A $= \left(0 + \frac{1}{2}mv^2\right)$ J

Since mechanical energy is conserved.

$\frac{1}{2}mv^2 = 1960m$

$v^2 = 3920$

$v = 62.6 \ldots$

Notice that the mass of the skier cancels out. In this model all skiers should arrive at the bottom of the slope with the same speed.

The slope could be curved and the model would give the same speed as long as the total height lost is the same.

The skier's speed at the bottom of the slope is 62.6 m s^{-1} (to 3 s.f.).

(ii) For the horizontal part there is some friction. Suppose the skier travels a further distance s m before stopping.

Note

An alternative approach to this problem is to use the constant acceleration formulae. Make sure you are comfortable with both approaches.

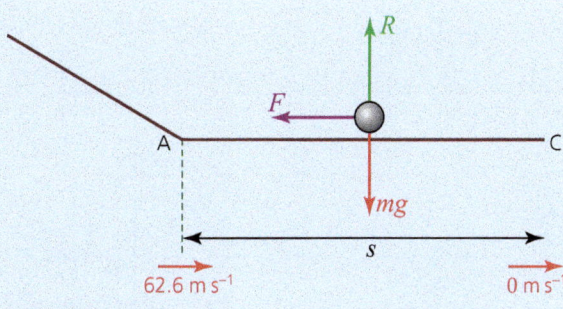

Figure 5.10

The frictional force is $F = \mu R = \frac{1}{4}R$.

There is no vertical acceleration, so $R = mg$

and so $F = \frac{1}{4}mg$.

> Negative because the force is in the opposite direction to the motion.

Work done by the friction force $= -F \times s = -\frac{1}{4}mgs$

The increase in kinetic energy between A and C $= \left(0 - \frac{1}{2}mv^2\right)$ J.

$$-\frac{1}{4}mgs = -\frac{1}{2}mv^2 = -1960m \text{ from } ①$$

Solving for s gives $s = 800$.

> The increase in kinetic energy $0 - \frac{1}{2}mv^2$ = work done

So the distance the skier travels before stopping is 800 m.

(iii) The assumptions made in solving this problem are that friction on the slope and air resistance are negligible, and that the slope ends in a smooth curve at A. Clearly the speed of 62.6 m s^{-1} is very high, so the assumption that air resistance is negligible must be suspect.

Example 5.10

Ama, whose mass is 40 kg, is taking part in an assault course. The obstacle shown in Figure 5.11 is a river at the bottom of a ravine that is 8 m wide. She has to cross the ravine by swinging on an inextensible rope 5 m long secured to a point on the branch of a tree, immediately above the centre of the ravine.

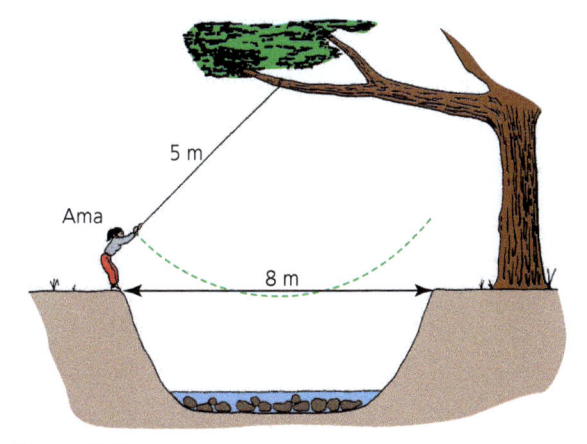

Figure 5.11

(i) Find how fast Ama is travelling at the lowest point of her crossing
  (a) if she starts from rest
  (b) if she launches herself off at a speed of 1 m s^{-1}.
(ii) Will her speed be 1 m s^{-1} faster throughout her crossing?

Gravitational potential energy

Solution

(i) (a) The vertical height Ama loses is HB in Figure 5.12.

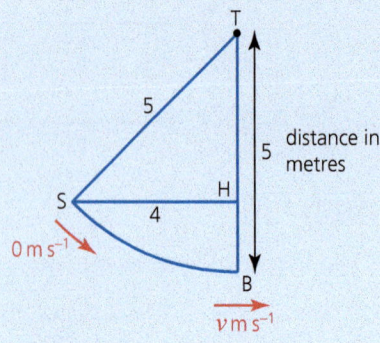

Figure 5.12

[Using Pythagoras' theorem in triangle TSH.]

$TH = \sqrt{5^2 - 4^2} = 3$

$HB = 5 - 3 = 2$

P.E. lost $= mgh$

$\phantom{\text{P.E. lost }}= 40 \times 9.8 \times 2 = 784$

K.E. gained $= \frac{1}{2}mv^2 - 0$

$\phantom{\text{K.E. gained }}= \frac{1}{2} \times 40 \times v^2 = 20v^2$

Conservation of mechanical energy, K.E. gained = P.E. lost

$20v^2 = 784$

$v = \sqrt{39.2} = 6.26$

Ama is travelling at $6.26\,\text{m s}^{-1}$.

(b) If she has initial speed $1\,\text{m s}^{-1}$ at S and speed $v\,\text{m s}^{-1}$ at B, her initial K.E. is $\frac{1}{2} \times 40 \times 1^2$ and her K.E. at B is $\frac{1}{2} \times 40 \times v^2$.

Using conservation of mechanical energy,

$\frac{1}{2} \times 40 \times v^2 - \frac{1}{2} \times 40 \times 1^2 = 40 \times 9.8 \times 2$

$20v^2 - 20 = 784$

$v = 6.34$

Ama is travelling at $6.34\,\text{m s}^{-1}$.

(ii) Ama's speed at the lowest point is only $0.08\,\text{m s}^{-1}$ faster in part (i) (b) compared with that in part (i) (a), so she clearly will not travel $1\,\text{m s}^{-1}$ faster throughout the crossing in part (i) (b).

Historical note

James Joule was born in Salford in Lancashire on Christmas Eve 1818. He studied at Manchester University at the same time as the famous chemist, John Dalton.

Joule spent much of his life conducting experiments to measure the equivalence of heat and mechanical forms of energy to ever increasing degrees of accuracy. Working with Thompson, he also made the discovery that when a gas is allowed to expand without doing work against external forces it cools. It was this discovery that paved the way for the development of refrigerators. Joule died in 1889; his contribution to science is remembered with the S.I. unit for energy named after him.

Work and kinetic energy for two-dimensional motion

Discussion point

Imagine that you are cycling along a level winding road in a strong wind. Suppose that the strength and direction of the wind are constant, but, because the road is winding, sometimes the wind is directly against you but at other times it is from your side or even behind you.

How does the work you do in travelling a certain distance, say 1 m, change with your direction?

Work done by a force at an angle to the direction of motion

You have probably decided that as a cyclist you would do work against the component of the wind force that is directly against you. The sideways component does not resist your forward progress.

Suppose you are cycling along the straight bit of the horizontal road OP shown (seen from above) in Figure 5.13. The force of the wind on you is F N. In a certain time you travel a distance s m along the road. The component of this distance in the direction of F is d m, as shown in the diagram.

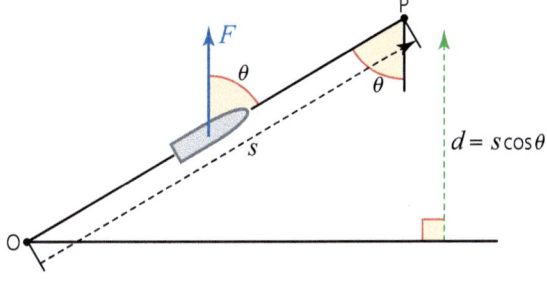

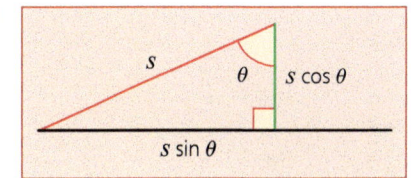

Figure 5.13

Work done by $F = Fd$

The work done by the force F is $Fs \cos\theta$. This can also be written as the product of the component of F along OP, $F \cos\theta$, and the distance moved along OP, s.

$$F \times s \cos\theta = F \cos\theta \times s$$

Example 5.11

A car of mass m kg drives up a slope inclined at an angle α to the horizontal, along a line of greatest slope. It experiences a constant resistive force F N and a driving force D N.

(i) Draw a diagram showing the forces acting on the car.

(ii) State what can be said about the work done by each of the forces as the car moves a distance d up the slope.

(iii) What can be deduced about the work done by the force D when

    (a) the car moves at constant speed?

    (b) the car slows down?

    (c) the car gains speed?

The initial and final speeds of the car are denoted by u ms^{-1} and v ms^{-1}, respectively.

(iv) Write v^2 in terms of the other variables.

Gravitational potential energy

Solution

(i)

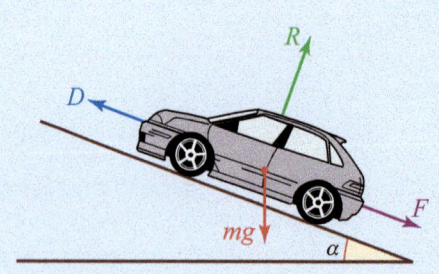

Figure 5.14

(ii)
Force	Work done
Resistance F	$-Fd$
Normal reaction	0
Force of gravity mg	$-mgd \sin \alpha$
Driving force D	Dd
Total work done	$Dd - Fd - mgd \sin \alpha$

(iii) (a) If the car moves at a constant speed, there is no change in kinetic energy so the total work done is zero, giving

work done by D is
$$Dd = Fd + mgd \sin \alpha$$

(b) If the car slows down, the total work done by the forces is negative, and hence work done by D is
$$Dd < Fd + mgd \sin \alpha$$

(c) If the car gains speed, the total work done by the forces is positive so work done by D is
$$Dd > Fd + mgd \sin \alpha.$$

(iv) Total work done = Final K.E. − initial K.E.
$$\Rightarrow \quad Dd - Fd - mgd \sin \alpha = \tfrac{1}{2}mv^2 - \tfrac{1}{2}mu^2$$

Multiplying by $\tfrac{2}{m}$
$$\Rightarrow \quad v^2 = u^2 + \tfrac{2d}{m}(D - F) - 2gd \sin \alpha$$

Exercise 5.2

① Calculate the gravitational potential energy, relative to the reference level OA, for each of the objects shown.

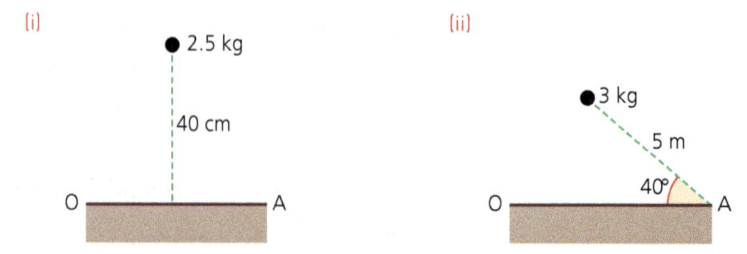

(i) 2.5 kg, 40 cm

(ii) 3 kg, 5 m, 40°

(iii) [pendulum: O to A, 3 m down to 2 kg mass]

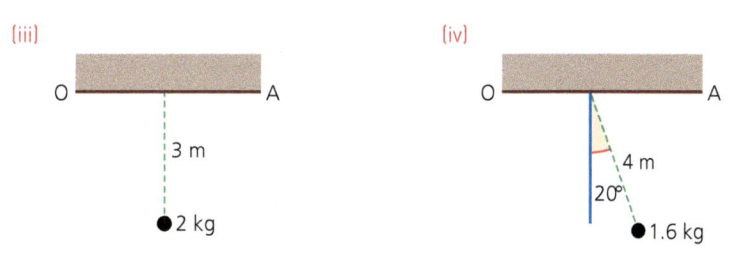

(iv) [pendulum: O to A, 4 m at 20° from vertical, 1.6 kg mass]

Figure 5.15

② Calculate the change in gravitational potential energy when each object moves from A to B in the situation shown below. State whether the change is an increase or a decrease.

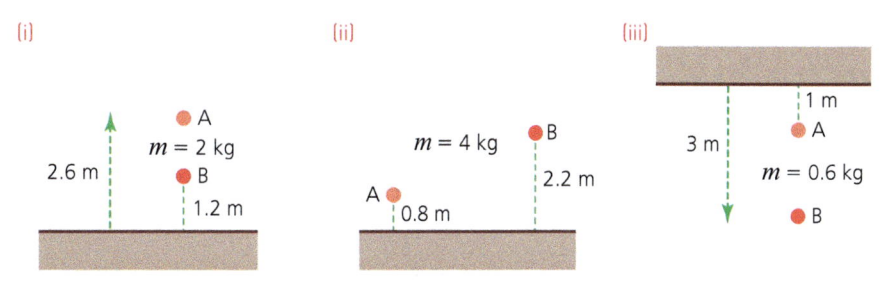

(i) A at 2.6 m, B at 1.2 m, $m = 2$ kg (moving upward)

(ii) B at 2.2 m, A at 0.8 m, $m = 4$ kg

(iii) A at 1 m below shelf, B at 3 m below A, $m = 0.6$ kg

Figure 5.16

③ A vase of mass 1.2 kg is lifted from ground level and placed on a shelf at a height of 1.5 m. Find the work done against the force of gravity.

④ Find the increase in gravitational potential energy of a woman of mass 60 kg who climbs to the twelfth floor of a block of flats. The distance between the floors is 3.3 m.

⑤ A sledge of mass 10 kg is being pulled across level ground by a rope which makes an angle of 20° with the horizontal. The tension in the rope is 80 N and there is a resistance force of 14 N.

(i) Find the work done while the sledge moves a distance of 20 m by
  (a) the tension in the rope
  (b) the resistance force.

(ii) Find the speed of the sledge after it has moved 20 m
  (a) if it starts at rest
  (b) if it starts at 4 m s^{-1}.

⑥ A bricklayer carries a hod of bricks of mass 25 kg up a ladder of length 10 m inclined at an angle of 60° to the horizontal.

(i) Calculate the increase in the gravitational potential energy of the bricks.

(ii) If instead he had raised the bricks vertically to the same height, using a rope and pulleys, would the increase in potential energy be less, the same, or more than in part (i)?

⑦ A girl of mass 45 kg slides down a smooth water chute of length 6 m inclined at an angle of 40° to the horizontal.

(i) Find
  (a) the decrease in her potential energy
  (b) her speed at the bottom.

(ii) How are answers to part (i) affected if the slide is not smooth?

Gravitational potential energy

8. A gymnast of mass 50 kg swings on a rope of length 10 m. Initially the rope makes an angle of 50° with the vertical.
   (i) Find the decrease in her potential energy when the rope has reached the vertical.
   (ii) Find her kinetic energy and hence her speed when the rope is vertical, assuming that air resistance may be neglected.
   (iii) The gymnast continues to swing. What angle will the rope make with the vertical when she is next temporarily at rest?
   (iv) Explain why the tension in the rope does no work.

9. A car of mass 0.9 tonnes is driven 200 m up a slope inclined at 5° to the horizontal. There is a resistive force of 100 N.
   (i) Find the work done by the car against gravity.
   (ii) Find the work done against the resistance.
   (iii) When asked to work out the total work done by the car, a student replied '$(900g + 100) \times 200$ J'. Explain the error in this answer.
   (iv) If the car slows down from 12 m s^{-1} to 8 m s^{-1}, what is the total work done by the engine?

10. A stone of mass 0.2 kg is dropped from the top of a building 80 m high. After t s it has fallen a distance x m and has speed v m s^{-1}. Air resistance may be neglected.
    (i) What is the gravitational potential energy of the stone relative to ground level when it is at the top of the building?
    (ii) What is the potential energy of the stone t s later?
    (iii) Show that, for certain values of t, $v^2 = 19.6x$ and state the range of values of t for which it is true.
    (iv) Find the speed of the stone when its kinetic energy is 10 J.
    (v) Find the kinetic energy of the stone when its gravitational potential energy relative to the ground is 66.8 J.

11. Wesley, whose mass is 70 kg, inadvertently steps off a bridge 50 m above water. When he hits the water, Wesley is travelling at 25 m s^{-1}.
    (i) Calculate the potential energy Wesley has lost and the kinetic energy he has gained.
    (ii) Find the size of the resistive force acting on Wesley while he is in the air, assuming it to be constant.

    Wesley descends to a depth of 5 m below the water surface, then returns to the surface.
    (iii) Find the total upthrust (assumed constant) acting on him while he is moving downwards in the water.

12. A hockey ball of mass 0.15 kg is hit from the centre of the pitch. Its position vector (in m), t s later is modelled by
    $$\mathbf{r} = 10t\mathbf{i} + (10t - 4.9t^2)\mathbf{j}$$
    where the unit vectors $\mathbf{i}$ and $\mathbf{j}$ are in the directions along the line of the pitch and vertically upwards.
    (i) What value of g is used in this model?
    (ii) Find an expression for the gravitational potential energy of the ball at time t. For what values of t is your answer valid?

(iii) What is the maximum height of the ball? What is its velocity at that instant?

(iv) Find the initial velocity, speed and kinetic energy of the ball.

(v) Show that, according to this model, mechanical energy is conserved and state what modelling assumption is implied by this. Is it reasonable in this context?

⑬ A ski-run starts at altitude 2471 m and ends at 1863 m.

(i) If all resistive forces could be ignored, what would the speed of a skier be at the end of the run?

A particular skier of mass 70 kg actually attains a speed of 42 m s^{-1}. The length of the run is 3.1 km.

(ii) Find the average force of resistance acting on a skier.

Two skiers are equally skilful.

(iii) Which would you expect to be travelling faster by the end of the run, the heavier or the lighter?

⑭ A tennis ball of mass 0.06 kg is hit vertically upwards with speed 20 m s^{-1} from a point 1.1 m above the ground. It reaches a height of 16 m.

(i) Find the initial kinetic energy of the ball, and its potential energy when it is at its highest point.

(ii) Calculate the loss of mechanical energy due to air resistance.

(iii) Find the magnitude of the air resistance on the ball, assuming it to be constant while the ball is moving.

(iv) With what speed does the ball land?

⑮ Akosua draws water from a well 12 m below the ground. Her bucket holds 5 kg of water and by the time she has pulled it to the top of the well it is travelling at 1.2 m s^{-1}.

(i) How much work does Akosua do in drawing the bucket of water?

On an average day, 150 people in the village each draw 6 such buckets of water. One day, a new electric pump is installed that takes water from the well and fills an overhead tank 5 m above ground level every morning. The flow rate through the pump is such that the water has speed 2 m s^{-1} on arriving in the tank.

(ii) Assuming that the villagers' demand for water remains unaltered, how much work does the pump do in one day?

⑯ A block of mass 20 kg is pulled up a slope passing through points A and B with speeds 10 m s^{-1} and 2 m s^{-1}, respectively. The distance between A and B is 100 m and B is 12 m higher than A. For the motion of the block from A to B, find

(i) the loss in kinetic energy of the block

(ii) the gain in potential energy of the block.

The resistance to motion of the block has magnitude 10 N.

(iii) Find the work done by the pulling force acting on the block.

The pulling force acting on the block has constant magnitude 25 N and acts at an angle α upwards from the slope.

(iv) Find the value of α.

Power

3 Power

Figure 5.17

It is claimed that a motorcycle engine can develop a maximum **power** of 26.5 kW at a top **speed** of 165 km h^{-1}. This suggests that power is related to speed and this is indeed the case.

Power is the rate at which work is being done. A powerful car does work at a greater rate than a less powerful one.

Think of a force, F, acting for a very short time t over a small distance s. Assume F to be constant over this short time.

Power is the rate of working so

$$\text{power} = \frac{\text{work}}{\text{time}}$$
$$= \frac{Fs}{t}$$
$$= Fv$$

> **Note**
> This gives you the power at an *instant* of time. The result is true whether or not F is constant.

The power of a vehicle moving at speed v under a driving force F is given by Fv.

For a motor vehicle the power is produced by the engine, whereas for a bicycle it is produced by the cyclist. They both make the wheels turn, and the friction between the rotating wheels and the ground produces a forward force on the machine.

The unit of power is the watt (W), named after James Watt. The power produced by a force of 1 N acting on an object that is moving at 1 m s^{-1} is 1 W. Because the watt is such a small unit, you will probably use kilowatts more often (1 kW = 1000 W).

> This is the case for any moving vehicle, so applies to a train, a ship, a bicycle and so on.

You will meet two ways of describing the power of a vehicle: 'the power developed by a car' and 'the power developed by the engine'. These are not quite the same as some of the engine's power is lost in the system. In this book a modelling assumption is made

- that the power lost in the system is negligible.

Under this assumption the two forms of wording are equivalent and they are used interchangeably here.

Example 5.12

A car of mass 1000 kg can produce a maximum power of 45 kW. Its driver wishes to overtake another vehicle. Ignoring air resistance, find the maximum acceleration of the car when it is travelling at

(i) $12\,\text{m}\,\text{s}^{-1}$

(ii) $28\,\text{m}\,\text{s}^{-1}$.

Solution

(i) Power = force × velocity

The driving force at $12\,\text{m}\,\text{s}^{-1}$ is F_1 N, where

$$45\,000 = F_1 \times 12$$

$$\Rightarrow \qquad F_1 = 3750$$

By Newton's second law, $F = ma$

$$\Rightarrow \qquad \text{acceleration} = \frac{3750}{1000} = 3.75\,\text{m}\,\text{s}^{-2}$$

(ii) Now the driving force F_2 is given by

$$45\,000 = F_2 \times 28$$

$$\Rightarrow \qquad F_2 = 1607$$

$$\Rightarrow \qquad \text{acceleration} = \frac{1607}{1000} = 1.61\,\text{m}\,\text{s}^{-2}.$$

This example shows why it is easier to overtake a slow moving vehicle.

Example 5.13

A car of mass 900 kg produces a power of 45 kW when moving at a constant speed. It experiences a resistance of 1700 N.

(i) What is its speed?

(ii) The car comes to a downhill stretch inclined at 2° to the horizontal. What is its maximum speed downhill if the power and resistance remain unchanged?

Solution

(i) As the car is travelling at a constant speed, there is no resultant force on the car. In this case, the forward force of the engine must have the same magnitude as the resistance forces, i.e. 1700 N.

Denoting the speed of the car by $v\,\text{m}\,\text{s}^{-1}$, $P = Fv$ gives

$$v = \frac{P}{F} = \frac{45\,000}{1700} = 26.5$$

The speed of the car is $26.5\,\text{m}\,\text{s}^{-1}$ (which is approximately 60 mph).

Power

(ii) Figure 5.18 shows the forces acting.

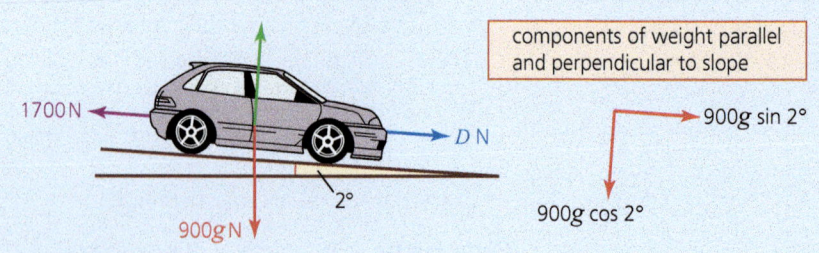

Figure 5.18

At maximum speed there is no acceleration so the resultant force down the slope is zero.

When the driving force is D N

$$D + 900g \sin 2° - 1700 = 0$$

$$\Rightarrow \qquad D = 1392$$

But power is Dv so $45\,000 = 1392v$

$$\Rightarrow \qquad v = \frac{45\,000}{1392}$$

The maximum speed is $32.3\,\text{m}\,\text{s}^{-1}$ (about 73 mph).

Historical note

James Watt was born in 1736 in Greenock in Scotland, the son of a house- and ship-builder. As a boy, James was frail and he was taught by his mother rather than going to school. This allowed him to spend time in his father's workshop where he developed practical and inventive skills.

As a young man, he manufactured mathematical instruments: quadrants, scales, compasses and so on. One day, he was repairing a model steam engine for a friend and noticed that its design was very wasteful of steam. He proposed an alternative arrangement, which was to become standard on later steam engines.

This was the first of many engineering inventions which made possible the subsequent industrial revolution. James Watt died in 1819, a well-known and highly respected man. His name lives on as the S.I. unit for power.

Example 5.14

A car of mass 1000 kg travels along a horizontal straight road. The power provided by the car's engine is constant and equal to 20 kW. The resistance to the car's motion is constant and equal to 800 N. The car passes two points A and B with speeds 15 m s^{-1} and 25 m s^{-1}, respectively, and takes 40 seconds to travel from A to B. Find the distance AB.

Solution

The work done by the engine in travelling from A to B is

$$20\,000 \times 40 = 800\,000\,\text{J}$$

The work done against the resistance is
$$800 \times AB \text{ J}$$
The increase in the kinetic energy of the car is
$$\tfrac{1}{2} \times 1000 \times 25^2 - \tfrac{1}{2} \times 1000 \times 15^2 = 200\,000 \text{ J}$$
Using the work–energy principle:
$$800\,000 - 800AB = 200\,000$$
$$AB = \frac{600\,000}{800} = 750 \text{ m}$$

The distance AB is 750 m.

Example 5.15

A car of mass 1200 kg is travelling at a constant speed of 15 m s^{-1}, while climbing for 30 s along a uniform slope of elevation arcsin (0.05) against a constant resistance of 900 N.

Calculate the power generated by the driving force.

Solution

The distance travelled by the car along the slope is 15 × 30 = 450 m

The work done against the resistance force is thus 900 × 450 = 405 000 J

The vertical height gained by the car is 450 × 0.05 = 22.5 m

The gravitational potential energy gained by the car is therefore
$$1200 \times 9.8 \times 22.5 = 264\,600 \text{ J}$$
The total work done by the driving force is
$$405\,000 + 264\,600 = 669\,600 \text{ J}$$
This work is produced in 30 s, and thus the rate of doing work is equal to
$$669\,600 \div 30 = 22\,320 \text{ W}$$
The power generated by the driving force is 22 320 W.

Exercise 5.3

① A builder hoists bricks up to the top of the house he is building. Each brick weighs 3.5 kg and the house is 9 m high. In the course of one hour, the builder raises 120 bricks from ground level to the top of the house, where they are unloaded by his assistant.

(i) Find the increase in gravitational potential energy of one brick when it is raised in this way.

(ii) Find the total work done by the builder in one hour of raising bricks.

(iii) Find the average power with which he is working.

Power

② A weightlifter takes 2 seconds to lift 120 kg from the floor to a position 2 m above it, where the weight has to be held stationary.
   (i) Calculate the work done by the weightlifter.
   (ii) Calculate the average power developed by the weightlifter.

   The weightlifter is using the 'clean and press' technique. This means that in the first stage of the lift he raises the weight 0.8 m from the floor in 0.5 s. He then holds it stationary for 1 s before lifting it up to the final position in another 0.5 s.

   (iii) Find the average power developed by the weightlifter during each of the stages of the lift.

③ A winch is used to pull a crate of mass 180 kg up a rough slope of angle 30° to the horizontal against a frictional force of 450 N. The crate moves at a steady speed of $1.2\,\text{m}\,\text{s}^{-1}$.
   (i) Calculate the gravitational potential energy given to the crate during 30 s.
   (ii) Calculate the work done against friction during this time.
   (iii) Calculate the total work done per second by the winch.

   The cable from the winch to the crate runs parallel to the slope.

   (iv) Calculate the tension, T, in the cable.
   (v) What information is given by the product of T and the speed of the crate?

④ The power output from the engine of a car of mass 50 kg which is travelling along level ground at a constant speed of $33\,\text{m}\,\text{s}^{-1}$ is 23 200 W.
   (i) Find the total resistance on the car under these conditions.
   (ii) You were given one piece of unnecessary information. Which is it?

⑤ A motorcycle has a maximum power output of 26.5 kW and a top speed of 103 mph (about $46\,\text{m}\,\text{s}^{-1}$). Find the force exerted by the motorcycle engine when the motorcycle is travelling at top speed.

⑥ A crane is raising a load of 500 tonnes at a steady rate of $5\,\text{cm}\,\text{s}^{-1}$. What power is the engine of the crane producing? (Assume that there are no forces from friction or air resistance.)

⑦ A cyclist, travelling at a constant speed of $8\,\text{m}\,\text{s}^{-1}$ along a level road, experiences a total resistance of 70 N.
   (i) Find the power which the cyclist is producing.
   (ii) Find the work done by the cyclist in 5 minutes under these conditions.

⑧ A mouse of mass 15 g is stationary 2 m below its hole when it sees a cat. It runs to its hole, arriving 1.5 seconds later with a speed of $3\,\text{m}\,\text{s}^{-1}$.
   (i) Show that the acceleration of the mouse is not constant.
   (ii) Calculate the average power of the mouse.

⑨ A train consists of a diesel shunter of mass 100 tonnes pulling a truck of mass 25 tonnes along a level track. The engine is working at a rate of 125 kW. The resistance to motion of the truck and shunter is 50 N per tonne.
   (i) Calculate the constant speed of the train.

   While travelling at this constant speed, the truck becomes uncoupled. The shunter engine continues to produce the same power.

(ii) Find the acceleration of the shunter immediately after this happens.

(iii) Find the greatest speed the shunter can now reach.

⑩ A supertanker of mass 4×10^8 kg is steaming at a constant speed of $8\,\text{m s}^{-1}$. The resistance force is 2×10^6 N.

(i) What power is being produced by the ship's engines?

One of the ship's two engines suddenly fails but the other continues to work at the same rate.

(ii) Find the deceleration of the ship immediately after the failure.

The resistance force is directly proportional to the speed of the ship.

(iii) Find the eventual steady speed of the ship under one engine only, assuming that the single engine maintains constant power output.

⑪ A car of mass 850 kg has a maximum speed of $50\,\text{m s}^{-1}$ and a maximum power output of 40 kW. The resistance force, R N, at speed $v\,\text{m s}^{-1}$ is modelled by $R = kv$

(i) Find the value of k.

(ii) Find the resistance force when the car's speed is $20\,\text{m s}^{-1}$.

(iii) Find the power needed to travel at a constant speed of $20\,\text{m s}^{-1}$ along a level road.

(iv) Find the maximum acceleration of the car when it is travelling at $20\,\text{m s}^{-1}$

(a) along a level road

(b) up a hill at 5° to the horizontal.

⑫ A car of mass 1 tonne is moving at a constant velocity of $60\,\text{km h}^{-1}$ up an inclined plane which makes an angle of 6° with the horizontal.

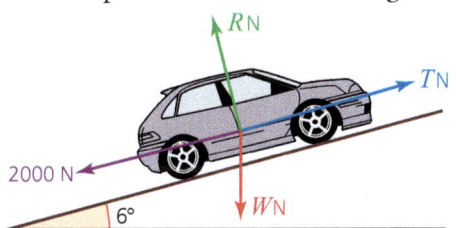

Figure 5.19

(i) Calculate the weight W of the car and the normal reaction R between the car and the road.

Given that the non-gravitational resistance down the slope is 2000 N, find

(ii) the tractive force T which is propelling the car up the slope

(iii) the rate at which T is doing work.

The engine has a maximum power output of 80 kW.

(iv) Assuming the resistances stay the same as before, calculate the maximum speed of the car up the slope.

[MEI]

Power

⑬ A boat of mass 1200 kg is winched a distance 30 m up a flat beach inclined at 10° to the horizontal.

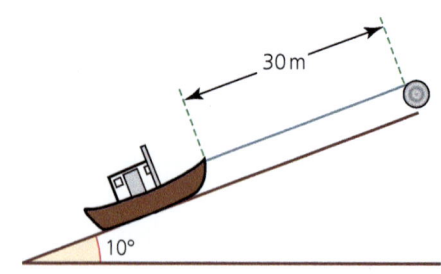

Figure 5.20

Initially a very approximate model is used in which all resistances are neglected.

(i) Calculate the work done.

(ii) Given that the process takes 2 minutes and that the boat moves at a constant speed, calculate the power of the winch motor.

A better model takes account of the resistance of the beach to the motion.

Assuming that the winch motor develops a constant 4.5 kW, the resistance of the beach on the boat is a constant 5 kN and the boat moves at a constant speed.

(iii) Calculate how long the winching will take.

(iv) Show that if the winch cable suddenly broke off at the boat whilst the winching was in progress, the boat would come to rest in about 35 mm. [MEI]

⑭ A tractor and its plough have a combined mass of 6000 kg. When developing a power of 5 kW, the tractor is travelling at a steady speed of 2.5 m s⁻¹ along a horizontal field.

(i) Calculate the resistance to the motion.

The tractor comes to a patch of wet ground where the resistance to motion is different. The power developed by the tractor during the next 10 seconds has an average value of 8 kW over this time. During this time, the tractor accelerates uniformly from 2.5 m s⁻¹ to 3 m s⁻¹.

(ii) Show that the work done against the resistance to motion during the 10 seconds is 71 750 J. Assuming that the resistance to the motion is constant, calculate its value.

The tractor now comes to a slope at $\arcsin\left(\frac{1}{20}\right)$ to the horizontal. The non-gravitational resistance to motion on this slope is 2000 N. The tractor accelerates uniformly from 3 m s⁻¹ to 3.25 m s⁻¹ over a distance of 100 m while climbing the slope.

(iii) Calculate the time taken to travel this distance of 100 m and the average power required over this time period.

⑮ A car of mass 1250 kg has a maximum power of 50 kW. Resistive forces have a constant magnitude of 1500 N.

(i) Find the maximum speed of the car on level ground.

The car is now ascending a hill with inclination θ and $\sin\theta = 0.1$.

(ii) Calculate the maximum steady speed of the car when ascending the hill.

(iii) Calculate the acceleration of the car when it is descending the hill at 20 m s⁻¹ working at half the maximum power.

⑯ A car of mass 1000 kg travels along a horizontal straight road. The power provided by the car's engine is a constant 15 kW. The resistance to the car's motion is a constant 400 N. The car passes through two points A and B with speeds 10 m s^{-1} and 20 m s^{-1}, respectively. The car takes 30 seconds to travel from A to B.

(i) Find the acceleration at A.

(ii) Find the distance AB.

KEY POINTS

1. The work done by a constant force F is given by Fs where s is the distance moved in the direction of the force.
2. The kinetic energy (K.E.) of a body of mass m moving with speed v is given by $\frac{1}{2}mv^2$. Kinetic energy is the energy a body possesses on account of its motion.
3. The work–energy principle states that the total work done by all the forces acting on a body is equal to the increase in the kinetic energy of the body.
4. The gravitational potential energy of a body of mass m at a height h above a given reference level is given by mgh. It is the work done against the force of gravity in raising the body.
5. Mechanical energy (kinetic energy + gravitational potential energy) is conserved when no forces other than gravity do work.
6. Power is the rate of doing work, and is given by Fv.
7. Average power = total work done ÷ total time taken
8. The S.I. unit for energy is the joule and for power is the watt.

LEARNING OUTCOMES

When you have completed this chapter, you should be able to

▶ understand the language relating to work, energy and power
▶ calculate the work done by a force which moves either along its line of action or at an angle to it
▶ calculate kinetic energy and gravitational potential energy
▶ understand and use the principle of conservation of energy
▶ understand and use the work–energy principle
▶ understand and use the concept of power.

6 Impulse and momentum

I collided with a stationary truck coming the other way.

Statement on an insurance form reported in the Toronto News

→ The karate expert in the photograph has just broken a pile of wooden planks with a single blow from his hand. Forces in excess of 3000 N have been measured during karate chops. How is this possible?

1 Impulse

Although the karate expert produces a very large force, it acts for only a short time. This is often the case in situations where impacts occur, as in the following example involving a tennis player.

Example 6.1

A tennis player hits the ball as it is travelling towards her at $10\,\text{m}\,\text{s}^{-1}$ horizontally. Immediately after she hits it, the ball is travelling away from her at $20\,\text{m}\,\text{s}^{-1}$ horizontally. The mass of the ball is $0.06\,\text{kg}$. What force does the tennis player apply to the ball?

Solution

You cannot tell unless you know how long the impact lasts, and that will vary from one shot to another.

> **Discussion point**
> Show that the average force she applies to the ball in the cases where the impact lasts 0.1 s and 0.015 s are 18 N and 120 N, respectively. What does 'average' mean in this context?

Although you cannot calculate the force unless you know the time for which it acts, you can work out the product force × time. This is called the **impulse**. An impulse is usually denoted by **J** and its magnitude by J.

When a constant force acts for a time t the impulse of the force is defined as

$$\text{impulse} = \text{force} \times \text{time}.$$

The impulse is a vector in the direction of the force. Impulse is often used when force and time cannot be known separately but their combined effect is known, as in the case of the tennis ball. The S.I. unit for impulse is the newton second (N s).

Impulse and momentum

When the motion is in one dimension and the velocity of an object of mass m is changed from u to v by a constant force F, you can use Newton's second law and the equations for motion with constant acceleration.

$$F = ma$$
$$\text{and} \quad v = u + at$$
$$\Rightarrow \quad mv = mu + mat$$
$$\text{Substituting } F \text{ for } ma \text{ gives} \quad mv = mu + Ft$$
$$\Rightarrow \quad Ft = mv - mu \quad \text{①}$$

> **Discussion point**
> The magnitude of the momentum of an object is often thought of as its resistance to being stopped. Compare the momentum and kinetic energy of a cricket ball of mass 0.15 kg bowled very fast at $40\,\text{m}\,\text{s}^{-1}$ and a 20 tonne railway truck moving at the very slow speed of 1 cm per second.
> Which would you rather be hit by, an object with high momentum and low energy, or one with high energy and low momentum?

The quantity 'mass × velocity' is defined as the **momentum** of the moving object.

The equation ① can be written as

$$\text{impulse of force} = \text{final momentum} - \text{initial momentum} \quad \text{②}$$

This equation also holds for any large force acting for a short time even when it cannot be assumed to be constant. The force on the tennis ball will increase as it embeds itself into the strings and then decrease as it is catapulted away, but you can calculate the impulse of the tennis racket on the ball as

$$0.06 \times 20 - 0.06 \times (-10) = 1.8\,\text{N}\,\text{s}$$

- So impulse = change in momentum
- final momentum
- initial momentum
- the −10 takes account of the change in direction
- impulse

Equation ② is also true for a variable force. It is also true, but less often used, when a longer time is involved.

Impulse

Example 6.2

A ball of mass 50 g hits the ground with a speed of 4 m s⁻¹ and rebounds with an initial speed of 3 m s⁻¹. The situation is modelled by assuming that the ball is in contact with the ground for 0.01 s and that during this time the reaction force on it is constant.

(i) Find the average force exerted on the ball.

(ii) Find the loss in kinetic energy during the impact.

(iii) Which of the answers to parts (i) and (ii) would be affected by a change in the modelling assumption that the ball is only in contact with the ground for 0.01 s?

!> Be careful not to confuse J as a symbol for impulse and as the short form of joule, the unit for energy.

Solution

(i) The impulse is given by:

$$J = mv - mu$$
$$= 0.05 \times 3 - 0.05 \times (-4)$$
$$= 0.35$$

The impulse is also given by

$$J = Ft$$

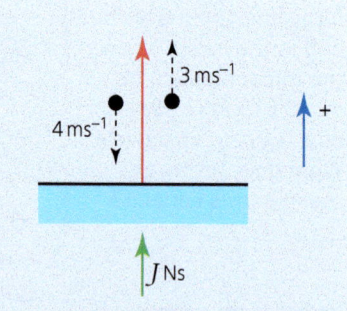

Figure 6.1

where F is the average force, i.e. the constant force which, acting for the same time interval, would have the same effect as the variable force which actually acted.

$$\therefore \quad 0.35 = F \times 0.01$$
$$F = 35$$

So the ground exerts an average upward force of 35 N.

(ii) Initial K.E. $= \frac{1}{2} \times 0.05 \times 4^2$
$$= 0.400 \text{ joules}$$

Final K.E. $= \frac{1}{2} \times 0.05 \times 3^2$
$$= 0.225 \text{ joules}$$

Loss in K.E. $= 0.175$ joules

(This is converted into heat and sound.)

(iii) A change in the model will affect the answer to part (i), but not part (ii).

> **Note**
>
> Example 6.2 demonstrates the important point that mechanical energy is not conserved during an impact.
>
> Although the force of gravity acts during the impact, its impulse is negligible over such a short time.

Example 6.3

A car of mass 800 kg is pushed with a constant force of magnitude 200 N for 10 s. The car starts from rest. Resistance to motion may be ignored.

(i) Find its speed at the end of the ten-second interval by using

(a) the impulse on the car (b) Newton's second law.

(ii) Comment on your answers to part (i).

Solution

(i) (a) The force of 200 N acts for 10 s, so the impulse on the car is

$$J = 200 \times 10 = 2000 \, \text{N s}$$

> The impulse is in the direction of the force.

Hence the change in momentum (in N s) is

$$mv = 2000$$

$$\therefore \quad v = \frac{2000}{800} = 2.5$$

The speed at the end of the time interval is $2.5 \, \text{m s}^{-1}$.

(b) Newton's second law

$$F = ma$$
$$200 = 800a$$
$$a = 0.25 \, \text{m s}^{-2}$$
$$v = u + at$$
$$v = 0 + 0.25 \times 10 = 2.5 \, \text{m s}^{-1}$$

> Since the force is assumed to be constant, so is the acceleration and so you can use the constant acceleration formulae.

(ii) Both methods give the same answer but the method based on Newton's second law and the constant acceleration formulae only works because the force is constant.

Consider a variable force $F(t)$ acting on an object which changes its velocity from U to V in the interval of time $0 \leq t \leq T$.

At any instant, Newton's second law gives

$$F = ma = m\frac{dv}{dt}$$

and so the overall effect is given by

$$\int_0^T F \, dt = m \int_{v=U}^{v=V} \frac{dv}{dt} dt = m \int_U^V dv$$

$$= mV - mU$$

This is the impulse–momentum equation.

Exercise 6.1

① Find the momentum of the following objects, assuming each of them to be travelling in a straight line.
   (i) An ice skater of mass 50 kg travelling with speed $10 \, \text{m s}^{-1}$.
   (ii) An elephant of mass 5 tonnes moving at $4 \, \text{m s}^{-1}$.
   (iii) A train of mass 7000 tonnes travelling at $40 \, \text{m s}^{-1}$.
   (iv) A bacterium of mass 2×10^{-16} g moving with speed $1 \, \text{mm s}^{-1}$.

② Calculate the impulse required in each of these situations:
   (i) to stop a car of mass 1.3 tonnes travelling at $14 \, \text{m s}^{-1}$
   (ii) to putt a golf ball of mass 1.5 g with speed $1.5 \, \text{m s}^{-1}$
   (iii) to stop a cricket ball of mass 0.15 kg travelling at $20 \, \text{m s}^{-1}$
   (iv) to fire a bullet of mass 25 g with speed $400 \, \text{m s}^{-1}$.

Impulse

③ A stone of mass 1.5 kg is dropped from rest. After a time interval t s, it has fallen a distance s m and has velocity v m s⁻¹.

Take g to be 10 m s⁻² and neglect air resistance.

(i) Write down the force F (in N) acting on the stone.

(ii) Find s when $t = 2$.

(iii) Find v when $t = 2$.

(iv) Write down the value, units and meaning of Fs and explain why this has the same value as $\frac{1}{2} \times 1.5 v^2$.

(v) Write down the value, units and meaning of Ft and explain why this has the same value as $1.5v$.

④ A ball of mass 200 g is moving in a straight line with a speed of 5 m s⁻¹ when a force of 20 N is applied to it for 0.1 s in the direction of motion. Find the final speed of the ball

(i) using the impulse–momentum equation

(ii) using Newton's second law and the constant acceleration formulae.

(iii) Compare the methods.

⑤ A girl throws a ball of mass 0.06 kg vertically upwards with initial speed 20 m s⁻¹.

Take g to be 10 m s⁻² and neglect air resistance.

(i) What is the initial momentum of the ball?

(ii) How long does it take for the ball to reach the top of its flight?

(iii) What is the momentum of the ball when it is at the top of its flight?

(iv) What impulse acted on the ball over the period between its being thrown and its reaching maximum height?

⑥ A netball of mass 425 g is moving horizontally with speed 5 m s⁻¹ when it is caught.

(i) Find the impulse needed to stop the ball.

(ii) Find the average force needed to stop the ball if it takes

　(a) 0.1 s　　(b) 0.05 s.

(iii) Why does the action of taking a ball into your body make it easier to catch?

⑦ A car of mass 0.9 tonnes is travelling at 13.2 m s⁻¹ when it crashes head-on into a wall. The car is brought to rest in a time of 0.12 s.

Taking g to be 10 m s⁻², find

(i) the impulse acting on the car

(ii) the average force acting on the car

(iii) the average deceleration of the car in terms of g.

(iv) Explain why many cars are designed with crumple zones rather than with completely rigid construction.

⑧ Boris is sleeping on a bunk-bed at a height of 1.5 m when he rolls over and falls out. His mass is 20 kg.

(i) Find the speed with which he hits the floor.

(ii) Find the impulse that the floor has exerted on him when he has come to rest.

(iii) Find the impulse he has exerted on the floor.

It takes Boris 0.2 s to come to rest.

(iv) Find the average force acting on him during this time.

⑨ A railway truck of mass 10 tonnes is travelling at $3\,\text{m s}^{-1}$ along a siding when it hits some buffers. After the impact it is travelling at $1.5\,\text{m s}^{-1}$ in the opposite direction.

(i) Find the initial momentum of the truck.

(ii) Find the momentum of the truck after it has left the buffers.

(iii) Find the impulse that has acted on the truck.

During the impact the force $F\,\text{N}$ that the buffers exert on the truck varies as shown in this graph.

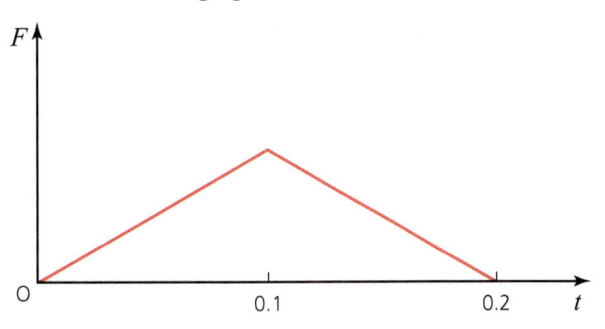

Figure 6.2

(iv) State what information is given by the area under the graph.

(v) What is the greatest value of the force F.

⑩ A van of mass $2500\,\text{kg}$ starts from rest. In the first 4 seconds after starting, the driving force on its engine follows the relationship $F(t) = 2400t - 300t^2$.

(i) Find the total impulse on the van over the 4 seconds.

(ii) Find the speed of the van, ignoring the effect of air resistance.

2 Conservation of momentum

Collisions

In an experiment to investigate car design, two vehicles were made to collide head-on. How would you investigate this situation? What is the relationship between the change in momentum of the van and that of the car?

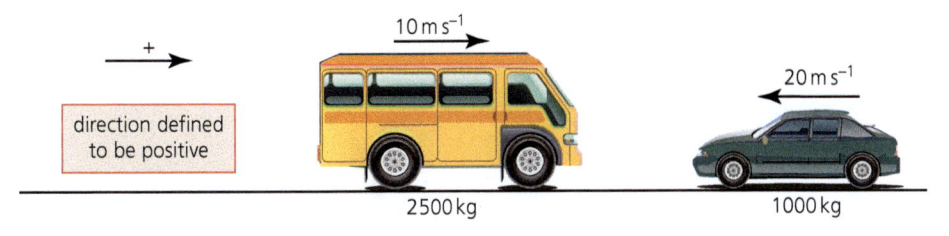

Figure 6.3

Remember Newton's third law. The force that body A exerts on body B is equal to the force that B exerts on A, but in the opposite direction.

Suppose that once the van is in contact with the car, it exerts a force F on the car for a time t. Newton's third law tells us that the car also exerts a force F on the van for a time t. (This applies whether F is constant or variable.) So both vehicles receive equal impulses, but in opposite directions. Consequently, the

Conservation of momentum

increase in momentum of the car in the positive direction is exactly equal to the increase in momentum of the van in the negative direction. For the two vehicles together, the total change in momentum is zero.

This example illustrates the **law of conservation of momentum**.

> The law of conservation of momentum states that when there are no external influences on a system, the total momentum of the system is constant.

Since momentum is a vector quantity, this applies to the magnitude of the momentum in any direction.

For a collision you can say

$$\text{total momentum before collision} = \text{total momentum after collision}$$

> It is important to remember that although momentum is conserved in a collision, mechanical energy is not conserved. Some of the work done by the forces is converted into heat and sound.

Example 6.4

The two vehicles in the previous discussion collide head-on, and, as a result, the van comes to rest.

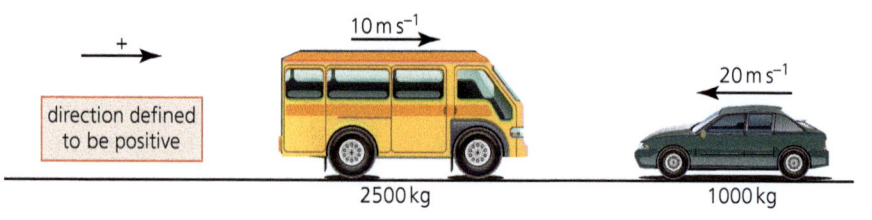

Figure 6.4

(i) Draw diagrams showing the situation before and after the collision.

(ii) Find the final velocity of the car, $v\,\text{m s}^{-1}$

(iii) Find the impulse on each vehicle

(iv) Find the kinetic energy lost.

(v) In modelling the collision, it is assumed that the impact lasts for one-twentieth of a second. Find the average force on each vehicle and the acceleration of each vehicle.

Solution

(i) The vehicles are modelled as particles.

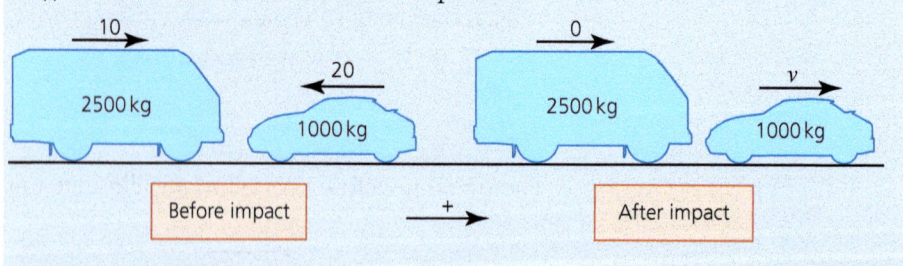

Figure 6.5

> **Note**
>
> When you are solving an impact problem, always draw a 'before' and 'after' diagram like Figure 6.5.
> All relevant information on the masses and velocities of the two vehicles is given on it.

(ii) Using conservation of momentum, and taking the positive direction as being to the right:

$$2500 \times 10 + 1000 \times (-20) = 2500 \times 0 + 1000 \times v$$

$$5000 = 1000\,v$$

$$v = 5$$

> **Note**
>
> The vehicles experience equal and opposite impulses.

The final velocity of the car is 5 m s⁻¹ in the positive direction (i.e. the car travels backwards).

(iii)   Impulse = final momentum − initial momentum

For the van, impulse = $2500 \times 0 - 2500 \times 10$

$$= -25\,000 \text{ N s}$$

For the car, impulse = $1000 \times 5 - 1000 \times (-20)$

$$= +25\,000 \text{ N s}$$

The van experiences an impulse of 25 000 N s in the negative direction; the car 25 000 N s in the positive direction.

(iv) Total initial K.E. = $\frac{1}{2} \times 2500 \times 10^2 + \frac{1}{2} \times 1000 \times 20^2$

$$= 325\,000 \text{ joules}$$

Total final K.E. = $\frac{1}{2} \times 2500 \times 0^2 + \frac{1}{2} \times 1000 \times 5^2$

$$= 12\,500 \text{ joules}$$

Loss in K.E. = 312 500 joules

(v) The impulse is equal to the average force × time. If F is the average force, then

$$25\,000 = F \times \frac{1}{20}$$

$$F = 500\,000 \text{ N}$$

The average force on the car is 500 000 N to the right and that on the van is 500 000 N to the left.

Using $F = ma$ on each vehicle gives an average acceleration of 500 m s⁻² for the car and −200 m s⁻² for the van.

This is over 50g and most people black out at less than 10g.

> **Discussion point**
>
> These accelerations (500 m s⁻² and −200 m s⁻²) seem very high. Are they realistic for a head-on collision?
>
> Work out the distance each vehicle travels during the time interval of one-twentieth of a second between impact and separation. This will give you an idea of the amount of damage there would be.
>
> Is it better for cars to be made strong so that there is little damage, or to be designed to crumple under impact?

Example 6.5

In an experiment on lorry bumper design, the Transport Research Laboratory arranged for a car and a lorry, of masses 1 and 3.5 tonnes to travel towards each other, both with speed 9 m s⁻¹.

After colliding, both vehicles moved together. What was their combined velocity after the collision?

Solution

The situation before the collision is illustrated in Figure 6.6.

The vehicles are treated as particles and all relevant information is in the diagram.

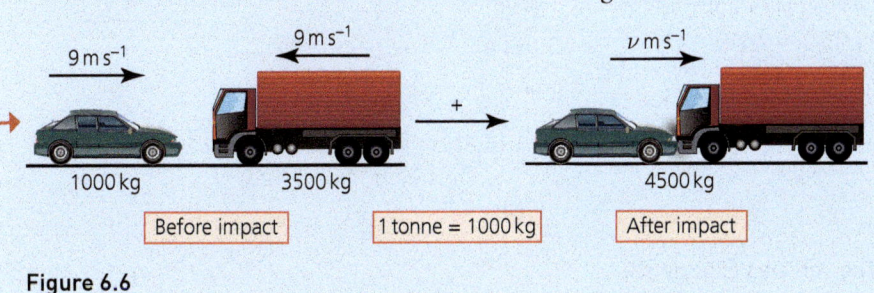

Before impact: car 1000 kg at 9 m s⁻¹ → , lorry 3500 kg at 9 m s⁻¹ ←

After impact: combined 4500 kg at v m s⁻¹ →

1 tonne = 1000 kg

Figure 6.6

Conservation of momentum

Taking the positive direction to be to the right, before the collision

momentum of the car in N s: $1000 \times 9 = 9000$

momentum of the lorry in N s: $3500 \times (-9) = -31\,500$

total momentum in N s: $9000 - 31\,500 = -22\,500$

After the collision, assume that they move as a single object of mass 4.5 tonnes with velocity $v\,\text{m s}^{-1}$ in the positive direction so that the total momentum is now $4500v\,\text{N s}$.

Momentum is conserved so $4500v = -22\,500$

$v = -5$

The car and lorry move at $5\,\text{m s}^{-1}$ in the direction in which the lorry was moving.

Example 6.6

A child of mass 30 kg running through a supermarket at $4\,\text{m s}^{-1}$ leaps on to a stationary shopping trolley of mass 15 kg. Find the speed of the child and trolley together, assuming that the trolley is free to move easily.

Solution

Figure 6.7 shows the situation before the child hits the trolley.

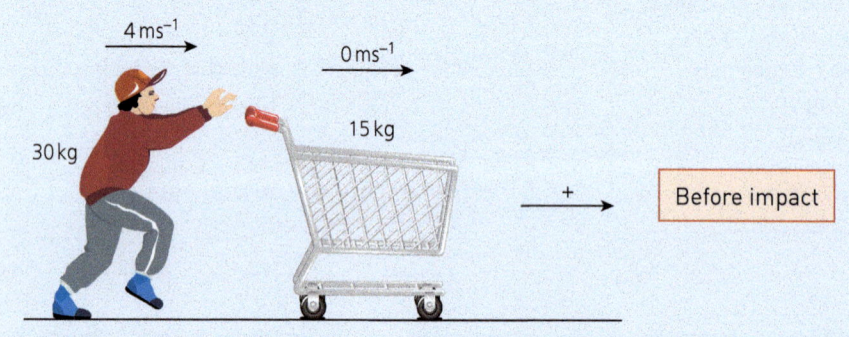

Figure 6.7

Taking the direction of the child's velocity as positive, the total momentum before impact is equal to $4 \times 30 + 0 \times 15 = 120\,\text{N s}$.

The situation after impact is shown in Figure 6.8.

Figure 6.8

The total mass of child and trolley is 45 kg, so the total momentum after is $45v$ Ns.

Conservation of momentum gives:

$45v = 120$

$v = 2\frac{2}{3}$

The child and the trolley together move at $2\frac{2}{3}$ m s^{-1}.

Explosions

Conservation of momentum also applies when explosions take place provided there are no external forces. For example when a bullet is fired from a rifle, or a rocket is launched.

Example 6.7

A rifle of mass 8 kg is used to fire a bullet of mass 80 g at a speed of 200 m s^{-1}. Calculate the initial recoil speed of the rifle.

Solution

Before the bullet is fired, the total momentum of the system is zero.

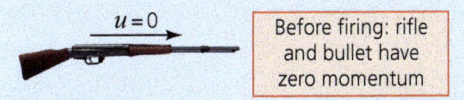

Before firing: rifle and bullet have zero momentum

Before explosion

Figure 6.9

After firing, the situation is as illustrated below.

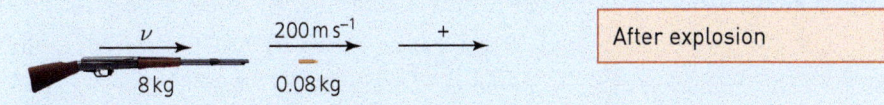

After explosion

Figure 6.10

The total momentum in the positive direction after the firing is $8v + 0.08 \times 200$.

For momentum to be conserved,

$$8v + 0.08 \times 200 = 0$$

so that

$$v = \frac{-0.08 \times 200}{8} = -2$$

You probably realised that v would turn out to be negative.

The recoil speed of the rifle is 2 m s^{-1}.

Conservation of momentum

Exercise 6.2

1. A spaceship of mass 50 000 kg travelling with speed 200 m s^{-1} docks with a space station of mass 500 000 kg travelling in the same direction with speed 195 m s^{-1}. What is their speed after the docking is completed?

2. A railway truck of mass 20 tonnes is shunted with speed 3 m s^{-1} towards a stationary truck of mass 10 tonnes. What is the speed after impact
   (i) if the two trucks remain in contact?
   (ii) if the second truck now moves at 3 m s^{-1}?

3. The driver of a car of mass 1000 kg falls asleep while it is travelling at 30 m s^{-1}. The car runs into the back of the car in front which has mass 800 kg and is travelling in the same direction at 20 m s^{-1}. The bumpers of the two cars become locked together and they continue as one vehicle.
   (i) What is the speed of the cars immediately after impact?
   (ii) What impulse does the larger car give to the smaller one?
   (iii) What impulse does the smaller car give to the larger one?

4. A lorry of mass 5 tonnes is about to tow a car of mass 1 tonne. Initially the tow rope is slack and the car stationary. As the rope becomes taut the lorry is travelling at 2 m s^{-1}.
   (i) Find the speed of the car once it is being towed.
   (ii) Find the magnitude of the impulse transmitted by the tow rope and state the direction of the impulse on each vehicle.

5. A bullet of mass 50 g is moving horizontally at 200 m s^{-1} when it becomes embedded in a stationary block of mass 16 kg which is free to slide on a smooth horizontal table.
   (i) Calculate the speed of the bullet and the block after the impact.
   (ii) Find the impulse from the bullet on the block.
   The bullet takes 0.01 s to come to rest relative to the block.
   (iii) What is the average force acting on the bullet while it is decelerating?

6. A spaceship of mass 50 000 kg is travelling through space with speed 5000 m s^{-1} when a crew member throws a box of mass 5 kg out of the back with speed 10 m s^{-1} relative to the spaceship.
   (i) What is the absolute speed of the box?
   (ii) What is the speed of the spaceship after the box has been thrown out?

7. A gun of mass 500 kg fires a shell of mass 5 kg horizontally with muzzle speed 300 m s^{-1}.
   (i) Calculate the recoil speed of the gun.
   An army commander would like soldiers to be able to fire such a shell from a rifle held against their shoulders (so they can attack armoured vehicles).
   (ii) Explain why such an idea has no hope of success.

8. Manoj (mass 70 kg) and Alka (mass 50 kg) are standing stationary facing each other on a smooth ice rink. They then push against each other with a force of 35 N for 1.5 s. The direction in which Manoj faces is taken as positive.
   (i) What is their total momentum before they start pushing?
   (ii) Find the velocity of each of them after they have finished pushing.
   (iii) Find the momentum of each of them after they have finished pushing.
   (iv) What is their total momentum after they have finished pushing?

⑨ A truck P of mass 2000 kg starts from rest and moves down an incline from A to B as illustrated in Figure 6.11. The distance from A to B is 50 m and $\sin \alpha = 0.05$. CBDE is horizontal.

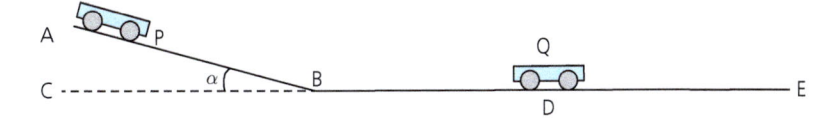

Figure 6.11

Neglecting resistance to motion, calculate

(i) the potential energy lost by the truck P as it moves from A to B

(ii) the speed of the truck P at B.

Truck P then continues from B without loss of speed towards a second truck Q of mass 1500 kg at rest at D. The two trucks collide and move on towards E together. Still neglecting resistances to motion, calculate

(iii) the common speed of the two trucks just after they become coupled together

(iv) the percentage loss of kinetic energy in the collision.

⑩ A pile-driver has a block of mass 2 tonnes which is dropped from a height of 5 m on to a pile of mass 600 kg which it is driving vertically into the ground. The block rebounds with a speed of $2 \, \text{m s}^{-1}$ immediately after the impact. Taking g to be $10 \, \text{m s}^{-2}$, find

(i) the speed of the block immediately before the impact

(ii) the impulse acting on the block

(iii) the impulse acting on the pile.

From the moment of impact the pile takes 0.025 s to come to rest.

(iv) Calculate the force of resistance on the pile, assuming it to be constant.

(v) How far does the pile move?

⑪ Katherine (mass 40 kg) and Elizabeth (mass 30 kg) are on a sledge (mass 10 kg) which is travelling across smooth horizontal ice at $5 \, \text{m s}^{-1}$. Katherine jumps off the back of the sledge with speed $4 \, \text{m s}^{-1}$ backwards relative to the sledge.

(i) What is Katherine's absolute speed when she jumps off?

(ii) With what speed does Elizabeth, still on the sledge, then go?

Elizabeth then jumps off in the same manner, also with speed $4 \, \text{m s}^{-1}$ relative to the sledge.

(iii) What is the speed of the sledge now?

(iv) What would the final speed of the sledge have been if Katherine and Elizabeth had both jumped off at the same time, with speed $4 \, \text{m s}^{-1}$ backwards relative to the sledge?

⑫ A sledge of mass 5 kg is initially at rest on a smooth, horizontal surface. All resistances to motion may be neglected. Give all answers correct to three significant figures.

(i) A snowball of mass 0.1 kg is thrown at the sledge, strikes it horizontally at $10 \, \text{m s}^{-1}$ and coalesces with it. At what speed does the sledge move off?

(ii) If a second identical snowball is thrown in the same way, what will the new speed of the sledge be?

(iii) After n identical snowballs have been thrown in the same way show that the speed of the sledge, $v\,\text{m s}^{-1}$ is given by $v = \dfrac{n}{5 + 0.1n}$.

(iv) Show that the expression in (iii) may be written as $v = 10 - \dfrac{50}{5 + 0.1n}$ and hence sketch a graph of the relationship between v and n. How does the velocity of the sledge change as n increases?

(v) If the snowball were replaced by a rubber ball of the same mass as in (i), so that it bounced back off the sledge, would the speed of the sledge be greater, the same or less? Give brief reasons for your answer.

⑬ Ben, whose mass is 80 kg, is standing at the front of a sledge of length 5 m and mass 40 kg. The sledge is initially stationary and on smooth ice. Ben then walks towards the back with speed $1\,\text{m s}^{-1}$ relative to the sledge.

(i) Find the velocity of the sledge while Ben is walking towards the back of it.

(ii) Show that, throughout his walk, the combined centre of mass of Ben and the sledge does not move.

(iii) Investigate whether the result of part (ii) is true in general for this type of situation, or just a fluke depending on the particular values of the variables involved.

3 Newton's experimental law

> **Discussion point**
> If you drop two different balls, say a tennis ball and a cricket ball, from the same height, will they both rebound to the same height? How will the height of the second bounce of each ball compare with the height of the first?

Your own experience probably tells you that different balls will rebound to different heights.

For example, a tennis ball will rebound to a greater height than a cricket ball. Furthermore, the surface on which the ball is dropped will affect the bounce. A tennis ball dropped onto a concrete floor will rebound higher than if dropped onto a carpeted floor. The following experiment allows you to look at this situation more closely.

> **EXPERIMENT**
> The aim of this experiment is to investigate what happens when balls bounce. Make a table to record your results.
> 1 Drop a ball from a variety of heights and record the heights of release h_a and rebound h_s. Repeat several times for each height.
> 2 Use your values of h_a and h_s to calculate h_a and h_s, the speeds on impact and rebound. Enter your results in your table.
> 3 Calculate the ratio $\dfrac{v_s}{v_a}$ for each pair of readings of h_a and h_s and enter the results in your table.
> 4 What do you notice about these ratios?
> 5 Repeat the experiment with different types of ball.

Coefficient of restitution

Newton's experiments on collisions led him to formulate a simple law relating the speeds before and after a direct collision between two bodies. This is **Newton's experimental law.**

$$\dfrac{\text{speed of separation}}{\text{speed of approach}} = \text{constant}$$

> This can be written as
>
> speed of separation = constant × speed of approach

This constant is called the **coefficient of restitution** and is conventionally denoted by the letter e. For two particular surfaces, e is a constant between 0 and 1. It does not have any units, being the ratio of two speeds.

For very bouncy balls, e is close to 1, and for balls that do not bounce, e is close to 0. A collision for which $e = 1$ is called perfectly elastic, and a collision for which $e = 0$ is called perfectly inelastic.

For perfectly elastic collisions there is no energy loss. For perfectly inelastic collisions the objects coalesce and the energy loss is the largest it can be.

Direct impact with a fixed surface

The value of e for the ball you used in the experiment is given by $\dfrac{v_s}{v_a}$, and you should have found that this had approximately the same value each time for any particular ball. When a moving object hits a fixed surface which is perpendicular to its motion, it rebounds in the opposite direction. If the speed of approach is v_a and the speed of separation is v_s,

Newton's experimental law gives

$$\frac{v_s}{v_a} = e$$

$$\Rightarrow \quad v_s = ev_a$$

Figure 6.12

Collisions between bodies moving in the same straight line

Figure 6.13 shows two objects that collide while moving along a straight line. Object A is catching up with B, and after the collision either B moves away from A or they continue together.

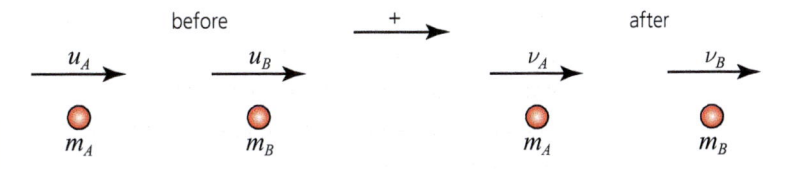

Figure 6.13

$u_A > u_B$ for the collision to occur

$v_B \geq v_A$ as B moves away from A

If the particles coalesce then $v_A = v_B$

Speed of approach: $u_A - u_B$

Speed of separation: $v_B - v_A$

By Newton's law

$$\text{speed of separation} = e \times \text{speed of approach}$$

$$\Rightarrow \quad v_B - v_A = e(u_A - u_B) \qquad \text{①}$$

Newton's experimental law

The law of conservation of momentum gives a second equation relating the velocities before and after impact.

momentum after collision = momentum before collision

$$m_A v_A + m_B v_B = m_A u_A + m_B u_B \qquad ②$$

These two equations ① and ②, allow you to calculate the final velocities, v_A and v_B, after any collision, as shown in the next two examples.

Example 6.8

A direct collision takes place between two smooth snooker balls with the same radius. The white cue ball travelling at $2\,\text{m}\,\text{s}^{-1}$ hits a stationary red ball. After the collision, the red ball moves in the direction in which the cue ball was moving before the collision. The balls have equal mass and the coefficient of restitution between the two balls is 0.6. Predict the velocities of the two balls after the collision.

Solution

Let the mass of each ball be m. Before the collision, their velocities are u_W and u_R. After the collision, their velocities are v_W and v_R.

The situation is summarised in Figure 6.14.

$u_R = 0$ since the red ball is stationary

Before impact: $u_W = 2$, $u_R = 0$
After impact: v_W, v_R

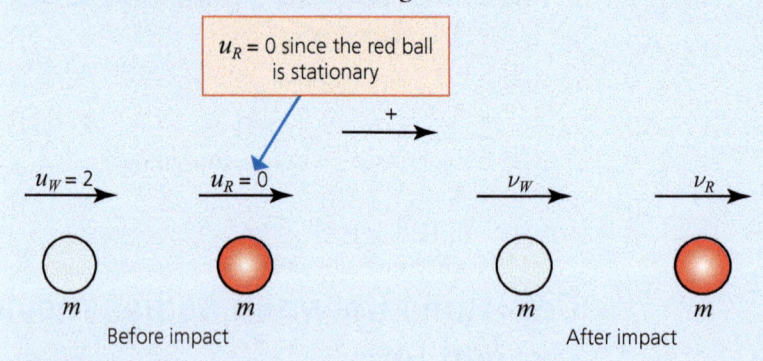

Figure 6.14

Speed of approach = $2 - 0 = 2$

Speed of separation = $v_R - v_W$

By Newton's law of impact

Speed of separation = $e \times$ Speed of approach

$\Rightarrow \quad v_R - v_W = 0.6 \times 2$

$\Rightarrow \quad v_R - v_W = 1.2 \qquad ①$

Conservation of momentum

$$mv_W + mv_R = mu_W + mu_R$$

Dividing through by m, and substituting $u_W = 2$, $u_R = 0$, this becomes

$$v_W + v_R = 2 \qquad ②$$

Adding ① + ② gives $2v_R = 3.2$

so $v_R = 1.6$, and from equation ②, $v_W = 0.4$.

After the collision both balls move in the original direction of the white cue ball, the red ball at a speed of $1.6\,\text{m}\,\text{s}^{-1}$ and the cue ball at a speed of $0.4\,\text{m}\,\text{s}^{-1}$.

Example 6.9

An object A of mass m moving with speed $2u$ hits an object B of mass $2m$ moving with speed u in the opposite direction to A. The coefficient of restitution is e.

(i) Show that the ratio of speeds remains unchanged whatever the value of e.

(ii) Find the loss of kinetic energy in terms of m, u and e.

Solution

(i) Let the velocities of A and B after the collision be v_A and v_B, respectively.

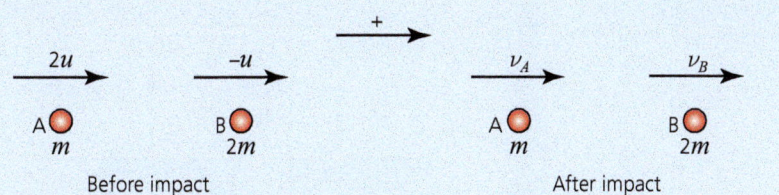

Figure 6.15

Speed of approach = $2u - (-u) = 3u$

Speed of separation = $v_B - v_A$

Using Newton's law of impact

speed of separation = $e \times$ speed of approach

$$v_B - v_A = e \times 3u \quad \text{①}$$

Conservation of momentum gives

$$mv_A + 2mv_B = m(2u) + 2m(-u)$$

Dividing by m gives

$$v_A + 2v_B = 0 \quad \text{②}$$

Equation ① is $\quad v_B - v_A = 3eu$

Adding ① + ② $\quad 3v_B = 3eu$

$$v_B = eu$$

From ②, $\quad v_A = -2eu$

The ratio of speeds was initially $2u:u$ and finally $2eu:eu$ so the ratio of speeds is unchanged at $2:1$ (providing $e \neq 0$).

(ii)

Initial K.E. of A	$\frac{1}{2}m \times (2u)^2$	$= 2mu^2$
Initial K.E. of B	$\frac{1}{2}(2m) \times u^2$	$= mu^2$
Total K.E before impact		$= 3mu^2$
Final K.E. of A	$\frac{1}{2}m \times 4e^2u^2$	$= 2me^2u^2$
Final K.E. of B	$\frac{1}{2}(2m) \times e^2u^2$	$= me^2u^2$
Total K.E. after impact		$= 3me^2u^2$
Loss of K.E.		$= 3mu^2(1 - e^2)$

> **Note**
>
> In this case, A and B lose *all* their energy when $e = 0$, but this is not true in general. Only when $e = 1$ is there no loss in K.E. Kinetic energy is lost in any collision in which the coefficient of restitution is not equal to 1.

Newton's experimental law

Exercise 6.3

You will find it helpful to draw diagrams when answering these questions.

1. In each of the situations shown in Figure 6.16, find the unknown quantity, either the initial speed u, the final speed v or the coefficient of restitution e.

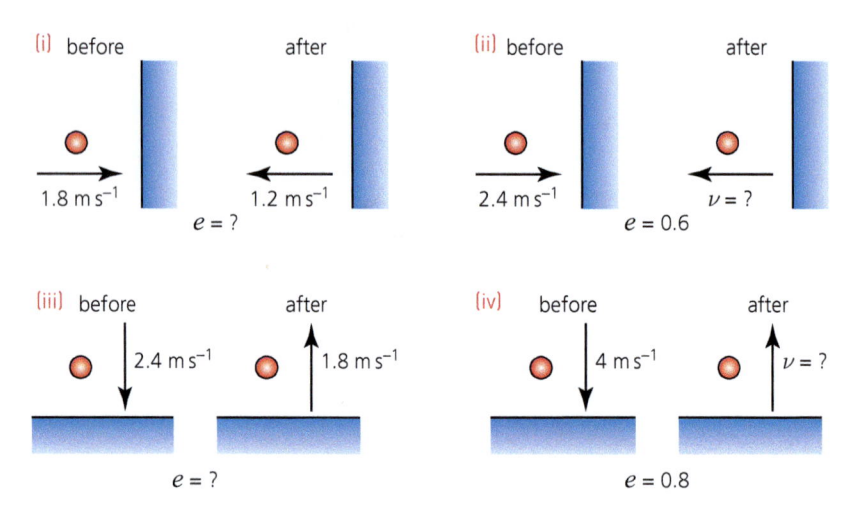

   (i) before: $1.8\,\text{m s}^{-1}$ → after: ← $1.2\,\text{m s}^{-1}$; $e = ?$

   (ii) before: $2.4\,\text{m s}^{-1}$ → after: ← $v = ?$; $e = 0.6$

   (iii) before: ↓ $2.4\,\text{m s}^{-1}$ after: ↑ $1.8\,\text{m s}^{-1}$; $e = ?$

   (iv) before: ↓ $4\,\text{m s}^{-1}$ after: ↑ $v = ?$; $e = 0.8$

   Figure 6.16

2. Find the coefficient of restitution in the following situations.
   (i) A football hits the goalpost at $10\,\text{m s}^{-1}$ and rebounds in the opposite direction with speed $3\,\text{m s}^{-1}$.
   (ii) A beanbag is thrown against a wall with speed $5\,\text{m s}^{-1}$ and falls straight down to the ground.
   (iii) A superball is dropped onto the ground, landing with speed $8\,\text{m s}^{-1}$ and rebounds with speed $7.6\,\text{m s}^{-1}$.
   (iv) A photon approaches a mirror along a line normal to its surface with speed $3 \times 10^8\,\text{m s}^{-1}$ and leaves it along the same line with speed $3 \times 10^8\,\text{m s}^{-1}$.

3. A tennis ball of mass $60\,\text{g}$ is hit against a practice wall. At the moment of impact it is travelling horizontally with speed $15\,\text{m s}^{-1}$. Just after the impact its speed is $12\,\text{m s}^{-1}$, also horizontally. Find
   (i) the coefficient of restitution between the ball and the wall
   (ii) the impulse acting on the ball
   (iii) the loss of kinetic energy during the impact.

4. A ball of mass $80\,\text{g}$ is dropped from a height of $1\,\text{m}$ onto a level floor and bounces back to a height of $0.81\,\text{m}$. Find
   (i) the speed of the ball just before it hits the floor
   (ii) the speed of the ball just after it has hit the floor
   (iii) the coefficient of restitution
   (iv) the change in the kinetic energy of the ball from just before it hits the floor to just after it leaves the floor
   (v) the change in the potential energy of the ball from the moment when it was dropped to the moment when it reaches the top of its first bounce
   (vi) the height of the ball's next bounce.

⑤ In each of the situations below, a collision is about to occur. Masses are given in kilograms, speeds are in metres per second. In each case
   (i) draw diagrams showing the situation before and after impact, including known velocities and the symbols you are using for velocities that are not yet known.
   (ii) Use the equations corresponding to the law of conservation of momentum and to Newton's law of impact to find the final velocities.
   (iii) Find the loss of kinetic energy during the collision.

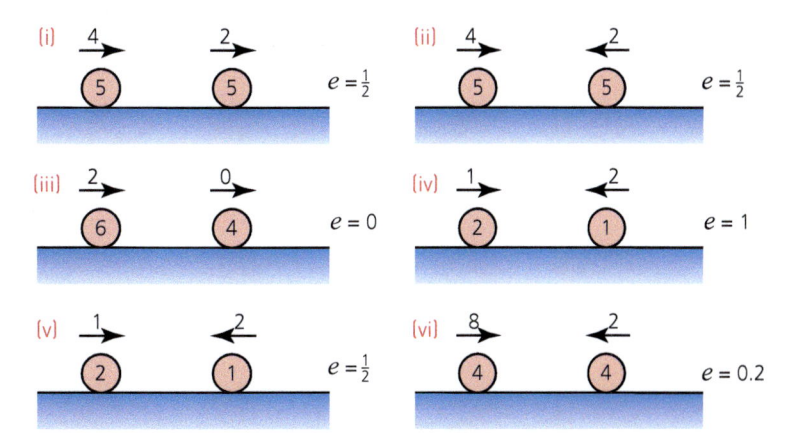

(i) 5 kg (4) → , 5 kg (2) → , $e = \tfrac{1}{2}$
(ii) 5 kg (4) → , 5 kg (2) ← , $e = \tfrac{1}{2}$
(iii) 6 kg (2) → , 4 kg (0) → , $e = 0$
(iv) 2 kg (1) → , 1 kg (2) ← , $e = 1$
(v) 2 kg (1) → , 1 kg (2) ← , $e = \tfrac{1}{2}$
(vi) 4 kg (8) → , 4 kg (2) ← , $e = 0.2$

Figure 6.17

⑥ Two children drive dodgems straight at each other, and collide head-on. Both dodgems have the same mass (including their drivers) of 150 kg. Isobel is driving at 3 m s⁻¹, Stuart at 2 m s⁻¹. After the collision Isobel is stationary. Find
   (i) Stuart's velocity after the collision
   (ii) the coefficient of restitution between the cars
   (iii) the impulse acting on Stuart's car
   (iv) the kinetic energy lost in the collision.

⑦ A trapeze artist of mass 50 kg falls from a height of 20 m into a safety net.
   (i) Find the speed with which she hits the net. (You may ignore air resistance.)

   Her speed on leaving the net is 15 m s⁻¹.

   (ii) What is the coefficient of restitution between her and the net?
   (iii) What impulse does the trapeze artist receive?
   (iv) How much mechanical energy is absorbed in the impact?
   (v) If you were a trapeze artist, would you prefer a safety net with a high coefficient of restitution or a low one?

⑧ Two spheres of equal mass, m, are travelling towards each other along the same straight line when they collide. Both have speed v just before the collision and the coefficient of restitution between them is e. Your answers should be given in terms of m, v and e.
   (i) Draw diagrams to show the situation before and after the collision.
   (ii) Find the velocities of the spheres after the collision.
   (iii) Show that the kinetic energy lost in the collision is given by $mv^2(1 - e^2)$.
   (iv) Explain why the result in part (iii) shows that e cannot have a value greater than 1.

Newton's experimental law

⑨ Three identical spheres are lying in the same straight line. The coefficient of restitution between any pair of spheres is $\frac{1}{2}$. Initially the left-hand sphere has a velocity of $2\,\text{m s}^{-1}$ towards the other two which are both stationary. What are the final velocities of all three, when no more collisions can occur?

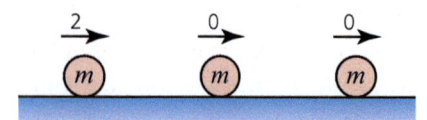

Figure 6.18

⑩ Figure 6.19 shows two snooker balls and one edge cushion. The coefficient of restitution between the balls and the cushion is 0.5 and that between the balls is 0.75. Ball A (the cue ball) is hit directly towards the stationary ball B with speed $8\,\text{m s}^{-1}$. Find the speed and directions of the two balls after their second impact with each other.

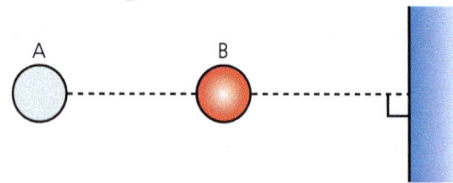

Figure 6.19

⑪ A spacecraft has two parts which may separate in flight, the body with mass $15\,000\,\text{kg}$ and the nose-cone with mass $5000\,\text{kg}$. They rejoin by means of a 'docking' procedure which requires the nose-cone and body to approach along the axis shown in Figure 6.20 with a speed of approach of no more than $3\,\text{m s}^{-1}$. If the speed of approach is too great, the linking mechanism will not engage and the two parts will bounce off each other with a speed of separation which is $\frac{1}{4}$ of the speed of approach (i.e. a coefficient of restitution of 0.25). At all times both parts may be taken as travelling in a straight line.

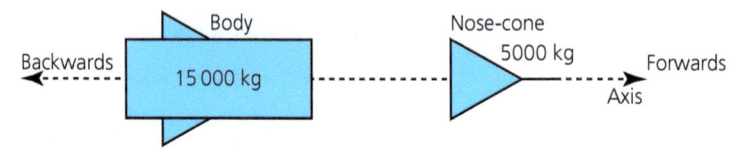

Figure 6.20

On one occasion the body is travelling forwards at $105\,\text{m s}^{-1}$ and the nose-cone at $103\,\text{m s}^{-1}$.

(i) Draw diagrams showing the velocities of the parts before and after docking.

(ii) Calculate the final velocity of the spacecraft.

On another occasion the nose-cone is moving backwards at $5.5\,\text{m s}^{-1}$ and the body forwards at $2.5\,\text{m s}^{-1}$.

(iii) Show that the body comes to rest and find the direction and speed of the nose-cone.

After this has happened, before a further attempt to dock is made, the speed of the body is changed in its line of motion by expelling a mass $m\,\text{kg}$ of fuel. The fuel is expelled at a speed of $2000\,\text{m s}^{-1}$ and you may assume that all the fuel is expelled instantaneously (i.e. before the body changes speed).

(iv) What value of m would cause the body to have a forward speed of $2.5\,\text{m s}^{-1}$ after the fuel is expelled?

12. Two particles A and B, of masses 20 kg and m kg, respectively, are initially at rest. A force of 15 N acts for 12 s on particle A.

    (i) Calculate the magnitude of the impulse given to particle A. Show that the speed of the particle at the end of the 12 s is $9\,\text{m s}^{-1}$.

    Particle A now collides with particle B. Except during the collision, the forces acting on the particles are negligible.

    (ii) Explain why the linear momentum of the pair of particles is conserved in the collision but the linear momentum of each individual particle is not.

    Immediately after the collision, particles A and B have speeds of $3\,\text{m s}^{-1}$ and $5\,\text{m s}^{-1}$, respectively, in the original direction of motion of particle A.

    (iii) Find the coefficient of restitution between the particles in the collision.

    (iv) Calculate the value of m. Calculate also the impulse given to particle A in the collision.

    Figure 6.21 shows a new situation in which particle C collides with particle D. Particle C has mass 20 kg and speed $8\,\text{m s}^{-1}$. Particle D has mass M kg and speed $13\,\text{m s}^{-1}$. The coefficient of restitution is $\frac{1}{3}$.

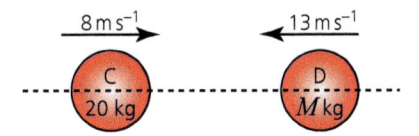

    Figure 6.21

    (v) If particle C is brought to rest in the collision, find M. What would happen to particle C after the collision if the mass of particle D were greater than this value.

13. A disc A of mass 2 kg is sliding with speed $u\,\text{m s}^{-1}$ over a smooth horizontal table when it makes direct contact with disc B of mass 3 kg which is initially at rest. The coefficient of restitution in the collision is e.

    (i) Draw a diagram indicating the velocities of the discs before and after the collision.

    (ii) Write down two equations involving the velocities of the discs before and after the collision. Solve the equations to show that after the collision disc A has a speed of $\frac{u}{5}(2-3e)$ in the original direction of its motion, and find the velocity of disc B.

    (iii) For what values of e will the direction of the motion of disc A change in the collision?

    (iv) Find the value of e for which disc A moves off after the collision with speed $\frac{u}{10}$ in the opposite direction to its original motion. Find an expression for the kinetic energy lost in the collision in this case.

14. The coefficient of restitution between a ball and the floor is e. The ball is dropped from a height h. Air resistance may be neglected, and your answers should be given in terms of e, h, g and n, the number of bounces.

    (i) Find the time it takes the ball to reach the ground and its speed when it arrives there.

    (ii) Find the ball's height at the top of its first bounce.

    (iii) Find the height of the ball at the top of its nth bounce.

Newton's experimental law

(iv) Find the time that has elapsed when the ball hits the ground for the second time, and for the nth time.

(v) Show that according to this model the ball comes to rest within a finite time having completed an infinite number of bounces.

(vi) What distance does the ball travel before coming to rest?

⑮ Two spheres which are travelling at the same speed in opposite directions collide directly. Immediately after the collision they move in the same direction with equal momenta. If the coefficient of restitution between the spheres is $\frac{1}{2}$, show that the ratio of the masses of the spheres is $(2+\sqrt{3}):1$.

⑯ Three identical smooth spheres A, B and C lie at rest on a smooth horizontal table with their centres in a straight line and B lying between A and C. A is projected towards B with speed u. If the coefficient of restitution at each collision is e, where $0 < e < 1$, find the velocity of each of the spheres just after C is set in motion. Show that A strikes B a second time whatever the value of e and that B strikes C a second time if e is less than $3 - 2\sqrt{2}$.

KEY POINTS

1. The impulse from a force **F** is given by **F**t where t is the time for which the force acts.
2. Impulse is conventionally denoted by **J**. It is a vector quantity.
3. The momentum of a body of mass m travelling with velocity **v** is given by m**v**. Momentum is a vector quantity.
4. The S.I. unit of impulse and momentum is the newton second (N s)
5. The impulse–momentum equation is

$$\text{impulse} = \text{final momentum} - \text{initial momentum}$$

6. The law of conservation of momentum states that when no external forces are acting on a system, the total momentum of the system is constant. Since momentum is a vector quantity this applies to the magnitude of the momentum in any direction.
7. Newton's law of impact:

Coefficient of restitution $e = \dfrac{\text{speed of separation}}{\text{speed of approach}}$

speed of separation = $e \times$ speed of approach

LEARNING OUTCOMES

When you have completed this chapter, you should

▶ know how to apply the principle of conservation of momentum to direct impacts
▶ understand Newton's law of impact and know the meaning of coefficient of restitution
▶ know and use the fact that $0 \leq e \leq 1$
▶ understand the implications of values of 0 and 1 for the coefficient of restitution
▶ understand that when the coefficient of restitution is less than 1, energy is not conserved during an impact
▶ be able to find the loss of kinetic energy during a direct impact
▶ know that for perfectly elastic collisions there is no energy loss
▶ know that for perfectly inelastic collisions the energy loss is the largest it can be.

7 Centre of mass 1

Let man then contemplate the whole of nature in her full and grand mystery.... It is an infinite sphere, the centre of which is everywhere, the circumference nowhere.

Blaise Pascal

Discussion point
Figure 7.1, which is drawn to scale, shows a mobile suspended from the point P. The horizontal rods and the strings are light but the geometrically shaped pieces are made of uniform heavy card. Does the mobile balance? If it does, what can you say about the position of its centre of mass?

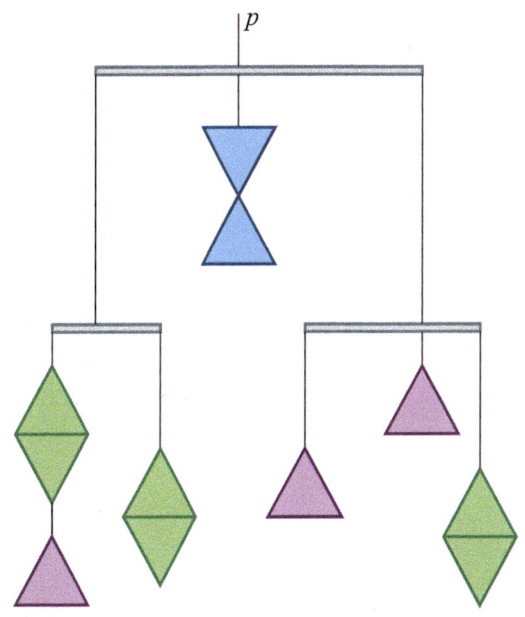

Figure 7.1

The centre of mass

1 The centre of mass

In this chapter, you meet the concept of centre of mass in the context of two general models.

The particle model
The centre of mass is the single point at which the whole mass of the body may be taken to be situated.

The rigid body model
The centre of mass is the balance point of a body with size and shape.

The following examples show how to calculate the position of the centre of mass of a body.

Centre of mass of one-dimensional bodies

Example 7.1

An object consists of three point masses 8 kg, 5 kg and 4 kg attached to a rigid, horizontal light rod, as shown.

Figure 7.2

Calculate the distance of the centre of mass of the object from O. (Ignore the mass of the rod.)

Solution

Suppose the centre of mass C is $\bar{x}$ m from O.

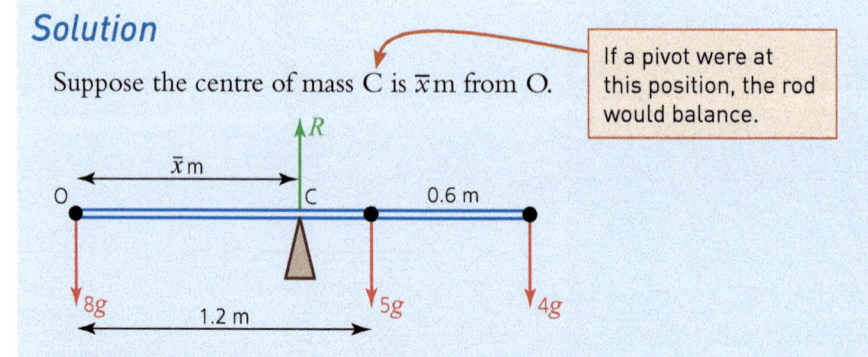

If a pivot were at this position, the rod would balance.

Figure 7.3

For equilibrium $\quad R = 8g + 5g + 4g = 17g$

Taking moments of the forces about O gives:

Total clockwise moment $= (8g \times 0) + (5g \times 1.2) + (4g \times 1.8)$
$= 13.2g \, \text{N m}$

Total anticlockwise moment $= R\bar{x}$
$= 17g\bar{x} \, \text{N m}$

The overall moment must be zero for the rod to be in balance, so
$$17g\bar{x} - 13.2g = 0$$
$$\Rightarrow \quad 17\bar{x} = 13.2$$
$$\Rightarrow \quad \bar{x} = \frac{13.2}{17} = 0.776 \text{ (to 3 s.f.)}$$

The centre of mass is 0.776 m from the end O of the rod.

Note

Although g was included in the calculation, it cancelled out. The answer depends only on the masses and their distances from the origin and not on the value of g.

This example can be generalised to give a method for finding the position of a centre of mass. In the first place, consider a set of n point masses $m_1, m_2, \ldots, m_n$ attached to a rigid light rod (whose mass is neglected) at positions $x_1, x_2, \ldots, x_n$ from one end O. The situation is shown in Figure 7.4.

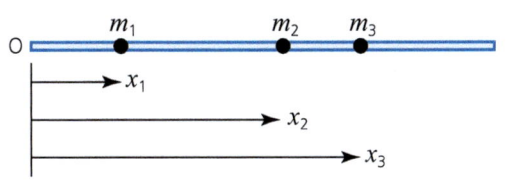

Figure 7.4

The position, $\bar{x}$, of the centre of mass relative to O is defined by the equation

moment of whole mass at centre of mass = sum of moments of individual masses

$$(m_1 + m_2 + m_3 + \cdots)\bar{x} = m_1 x_1 + m_2 x_2 + m_3 x_3 + \cdots$$

or

$$M\bar{x} = \sum_{i=1}^{n} m_i x_i$$

where M is the total mass (or Σm_i).

The symbol Σ (sigma) means 'the sum of'.

Example 7.2

A uniform, horizontal rod of length 2 m has mass 5 kg. Masses of 4 kg and 6 kg are fixed at each end of the rod. Find the centre of mass of the rod.

Solution

Since the rod is uniform, it can be treated as a point mass at its centre. Figure 7.5 illustrates this situation.

Figure 7.5

Discussion point

Check that the rod would balance about a pivot $1\frac{2}{15}$ m from A.

Taking the end A as the origin

$$M\bar{x} = \sum m_i x_i$$
$$(4 + 5 + 6)\bar{x} = 4 \times 0 + 5 \times 1 + 6 \times 2$$
$$15\bar{x} = 17$$
$$\bar{x} = \frac{17}{15} = 1\frac{2}{15}$$

So the centre of mass is 1.133 m from the 4 kg point mass.

Example 7.3

A horizontal rod of mass 1.1 kg and length 1.2 m has its centre of mass 0.48 m from the end A. What mass should be attached to the end B to ensure that the centre of mass is at the midpoint of the rod?

The centre of mass

Solution

Let the extra mass be m kg.

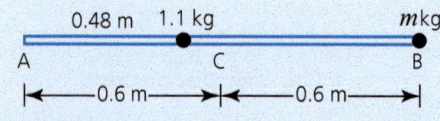

Figure 7.6

Method 1

Refer to the midpoint, C, as origin, so $\bar{x} = 0$. Then

$$(1.1 + m) \times 0 = 1.1 \times (-0.12) + m \times 0.6$$
$$\Rightarrow \quad 0.6m = 1.1 \times 0.12$$
$$\Rightarrow \quad m = 0.22$$

The 1.1 kg mass has negative x referred to C.

A mass of 220 grams should be attached to B.

Method 2

Refer to the end A, as origin, so $\bar{x} = 0.6$. Then

$$(1.1 + m) \times 0.6 = 1.1 \times 0.48 + m \times 1.2$$
$$\Rightarrow \quad 0.66 + 0.6m = 0.528 + 1.2m$$
$$\Rightarrow \quad 0.132 = 0.6m$$
$$m = 0.22 \text{ as before.}$$

Composite bodies

The position of the centre of mass of a composite body such as a cricket bat, tennis racquet or golf club is important to sports people who like to feel its balance. If the body is symmetrical, then the centre of mass will be on the axis of symmetry. The next example shows how to model a composite body as a system of point masses so that the methods of the previous section can be used to find the centre of mass.

Example 7.4

A squash racquet of mass 200 g and total length 70 cm consists of a handle of mass 150 g whose centre of mass is 20 cm from the end, and a frame of mass 50 g, whose centre of mass is 55 cm from the end of the handle.

Find the distance of the centre of mass from the end of the handle.

Solution

Figure 7.7 shows the squash racquet and its dimensions.

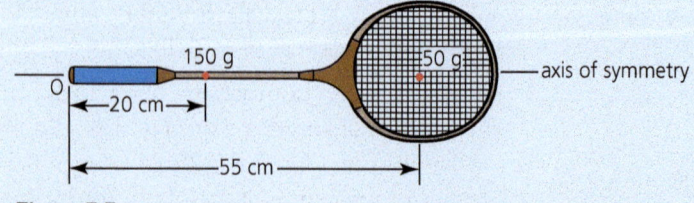

Figure 7.7

The centre of mass lies on the axis of symmetry. Model the handle as a point mass of 0.15 kg at a distance 0.2 m from O and the frame as a point mass of 0.05 kg a distance 0.55 m from the end O.

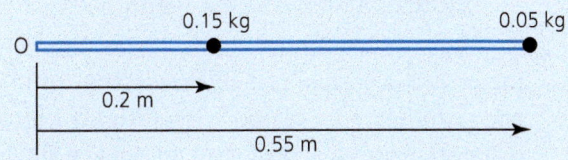

Figure 7.8

The distance $\bar{x}$ of the centre of mass from O is given by

$$(0.15 + 0.05)\bar{x} = (0.15 \times 0.2) + (0.05 \times 0.55)$$
$$\bar{x} = 0.2875$$

The centre of mass of the squash racquet is 28.75 cm from the end of the handle.

Exercise 7.1

① The diagrams show point masses attached to rigid light rods. In each case calculate the position of the centre of mass relative to the point O.

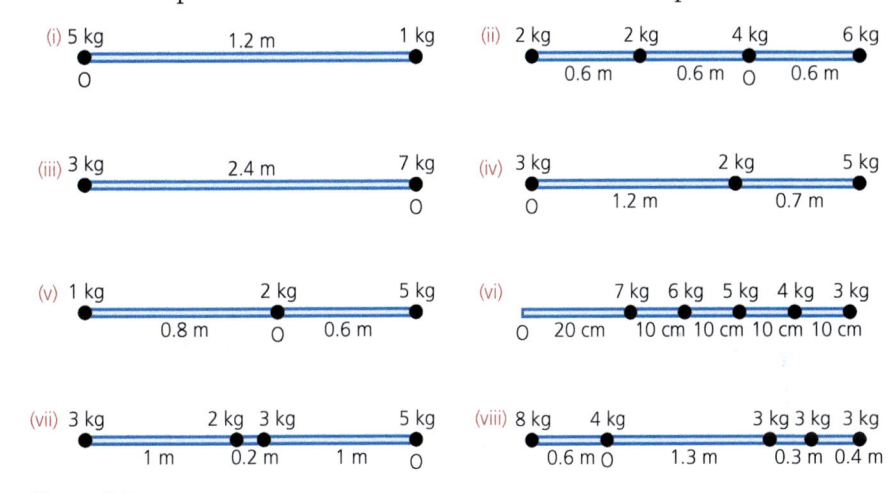

(i) 5 kg — 1.2 m — 1 kg, O at left end

(ii) 2 kg, 2 kg, 4 kg, 6 kg; 0.6 m, 0.6 m, O, 0.6 m

(iii) 3 kg — 2.4 m — 7 kg, O at right end

(iv) 3 kg, 2 kg, 5 kg; O, 1.2 m, 0.7 m

(v) 1 kg, 2 kg, 5 kg; 0.8 m, O, 0.6 m

(vi) 7 kg, 6 kg, 5 kg, 4 kg, 3 kg; O, 20 cm, 10 cm, 10 cm, 10 cm, 10 cm

(vii) 3 kg, 2 kg, 3 kg, 5 kg; 1 m, 0.2 m, 1 m, O

(viii) 8 kg, 4 kg, 3 kg, 3 kg, 3 kg; 0.6 m, O, 1.3 m, 0.3 m, 0.4 m

Figure 7.9

② A see-saw consists of a uniform plank 4 m long of mass 10 kg. Calculate the centre of mass when two children, of masses 20 kg and 25 kg, sit, one on each end.

③ A weightlifter's bar in a competition has mass 10 kg and length 1 m. By mistake, 50 kg is placed on one end and 60 kg on the other end. How far is the centre of mass of the bar from the centre of the bar itself?

④ The masses of the Earth and the Moon are 5.98×10^{24} kg and 7.38×10^{22} kg, and the distance between their centres is 3.84×10^5 km. How far from the centre of the Earth is the centre of mass of the Earth–Moon system?

⑤ A crossing supervisor carries a sign which consists of a uniform rod of length 1.5 m, and mass 1 kg, on top of which is a circular disc of radius 0.25 m and mass 0.2 kg. Find the distance of the centre of mass from the free end of the stick.

Figure 7.10

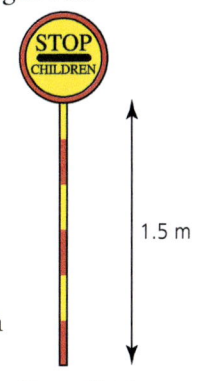

The centre of mass

6. A rod has length 2 m and mass 3 kg. The centre of mass should be in the middle but due to a fault in the manufacturing process it is not. This error is corrected by placing a 200 g mass 5 cm from the centre of the rod. Where is the centre of mass of the rod itself?

7. A child's toy consists of four uniform discs, all made out of the same material. They each have thickness 2 cm and their radii are 6 cm, 5 cm, 4 cm and 3 cm. They are placed symmetrically on top of each other to form a tower. How high is the centre of mass of the tower?

8. A standard lamp consists of a uniform heavy metal base of thickness 4 cm, attached to which is a uniform metal rod of length 1.75 m and mass 0.25 kg.

   What is the minimum mass for the base if the centre of mass of the lamp is no more than 12 cm from the ground?

9. A uniform scaffold pole of length 5 m has brackets bolted to it, as shown in Figure 7.11. The mass of each bracket is 1 kg.

   0.5 m 0.5 m 0.5 m 0.5 m   1 m   1 m   1 m

   Figure 7.11

   The centre of mass is 2.44 m from the left-hand end. What is the mass of the pole?

10. An object of mass m_1 is placed at one end of a light rod of length l. An object of mass m_2 is placed at the other end. Find the position of the centre of mass.

11. The diagram illustrates a mobile tower crane. It consists of the main vertical section (mass M tonnes), housing the engine, winding gears and controls, and the boom which is horizontal. The centre of mass of the main section is on its centre line. The boom, which has negligible mass, supports the load (L tonnes) and the counterweight (C tonnes). The main section stands on supports at P and Q, distance $2d$ m apart. The counterweight is held at a fixed distance a m from the centre line of the main section and the load at a variable distance l m.

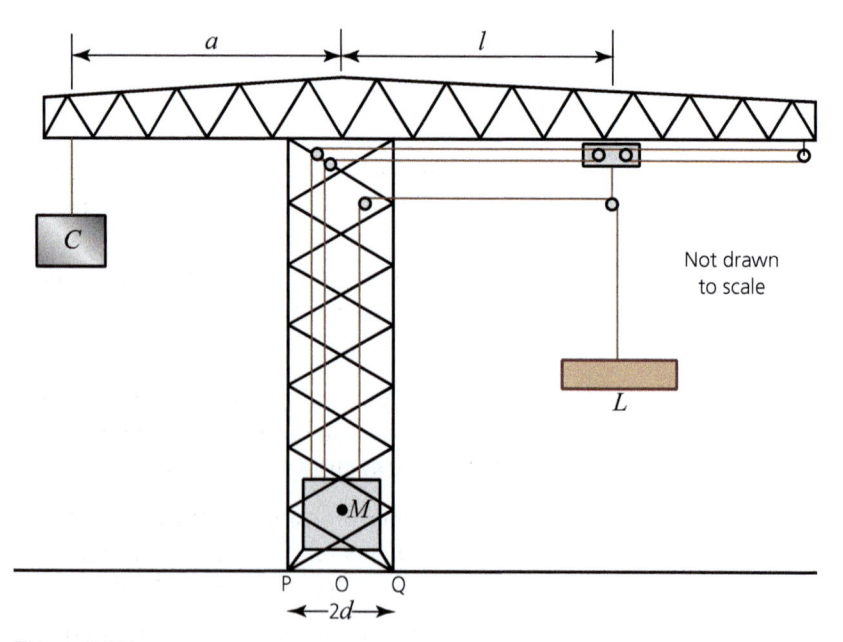

Figure 7.12

(i) In the case when $C = 3, M = 10, L = 7, a = 8, d = 2$ and $l = 13$, find the horizontal position of the centre of mass and say what happens to the crane.

(ii) Show that for these values of C, M, a, d and l the crane will not fall over when it has no load, and find the maximum safe load that it can carry.

(iii) Formulate two inequalities in terms of C, M, L, a, d and l that must hold if the crane is to be safe loaded or unloaded.

(iv) Find, in terms of M, a, d and l, the maximum load that the crane can carry.

2 Centre of mass of two- and three-dimensional bodies

The techniques developed for finding the centre of mass using moments can be extended to two and three dimensions.

If a two-dimensional body consists of a set of n point masses $m_1, m_2, \ldots, m_n$ located at positions $(x_1, y_1), (x_2, y_2), \ldots, (x_n, y_n)$, as in Figure 7.13, then the position of the centre of mass of the body $(\bar{x}, \bar{y})$ is given by

$$M\bar{x} = \sum m_i x_i \text{ and } M\bar{y} = \sum m_i y_i$$

where $M\left(= \sum m_i\right)$ is the total mass of the body.

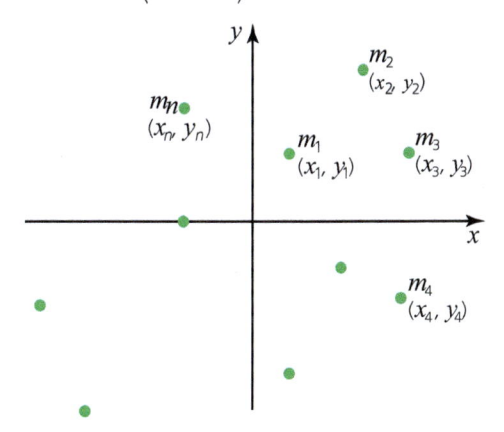

Figure 7.13

In three dimensions, the z coordinates are also included; to find $\bar{z}$ use

$$M\bar{z} = \sum m_i z_i$$

The centre of mass of any composite body in two or three dimensions can be found by replacing each component by a point mass at its centre of mass.

Example 7.5

Joanna makes herself a pendant in the shape of a letter J made up of uniform rectangular shapes, as shown in Figure 7.14.

(i) Find the position of the centre of mass of the pendant relative to the coordinate system shown in Figure 7.14.

(ii) Find the angle that AB makes with the horizontal if she hangs the pendant from a point M in the middle of AB.

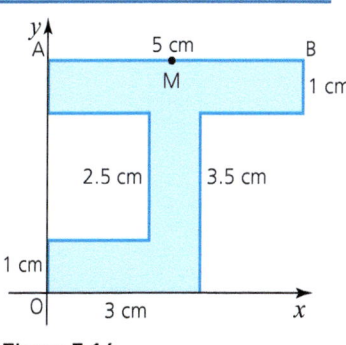

Figure 7.14

Centre of mass of two- and three-dimensional bodies

She wishes to hang the pendant so that AB is horizontal.

(iii) How far along AB should she place the ring that the suspending chain will pass through?

Solution

(i) The first step is to split the pendant into three rectangles.

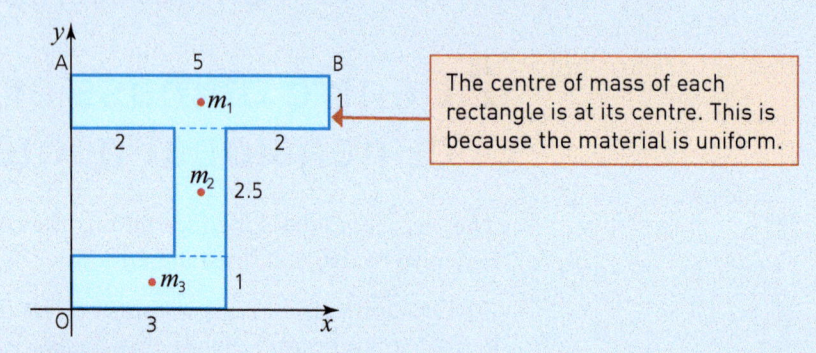

Figure 7.15

The centre of mass of each rectangle is at its centre. This is because the material is uniform.

You can model the pendant as three point masses m_1, m_2 and m_3, which are proportional to the areas of the rectangular shapes. Since the areas are $5\,\text{cm}^2$, $2.5\,\text{cm}^2$ and $3\,\text{cm}^2$, the masses in suitable units are 5, 2.5 and 3, and the total mass is $5 + 2.5 + 3 = 10.5$ (in the same units).

The table below gives the mass and position of m_1, m_2 and m_3.

Mass		m_1	m_2	m_3	M
Mass units		5	2.5	3	10.5
Position of centre of mass	x	2.5	2.5	1.5	$\bar{x}$
	y	4	2.25	0.5	$\bar{y}$

Now it is possible to find $\bar{x}$:

$$M\bar{x} = \sum m_i x_i$$

$$10.5\bar{x} = 5 \times 2.5 + 2.5 \times 2.5 + 3 \times 1.5$$

$$\bar{x} = \frac{23.25}{10.5} = 2.2\,\text{cm}$$

Similarly for $\bar{y}$:

$$M\bar{y} = \sum m_i y_i$$

$$10.5\bar{y} = 5 \times 4 + 2.5 \times 2.25 + 3 \times 0.5$$

$$\bar{y} = \frac{27.125}{10.5} = 2.6\,\text{cm}$$

The centre of mass is at (2.2, 2.6)

(ii) When the pendant is suspended from M, the centre of mass, G, is vertically below M, as shown in Figure 7.16.

The pendant hangs like in Figure 7.15 but you might find it easier to draw your own diagram like Figure 7.16.

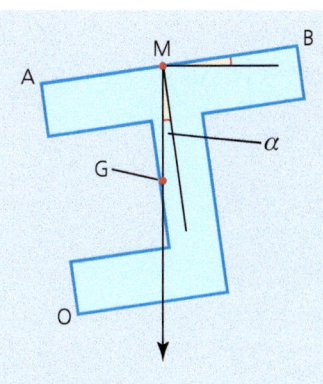

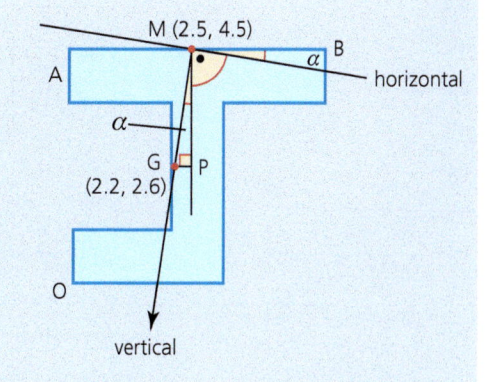

Figure 7.16

$$GP = 2.5 - 2.2 = 0.3$$
$$MP = 4.5 - 2.6 = 1.9$$
$$\therefore \quad \tan \alpha = \frac{0.3}{1.9} \Rightarrow \alpha = 9°$$

AB makes an angle of 9° with the horizontal (or 8.5° working with unrounded figures).

(iii) For AB to be horizontal the point of suspension must be directly above the centre of mass, and so it is 2.2 cm from A.

Example 7.6

Find the centre of mass of a body consisting of a uniform square plate of mass 3 kg and side length 2 m, with small objects of mass 1 kg, 2 kg, 4 kg and 5 kg at the corners of the square.

Solution

Figure 7.17 shows the square plate, with the origin taken at the corner at which the 1 kg mass is located. The mass of the plate is represented by a 3 kg point mass at its centre.

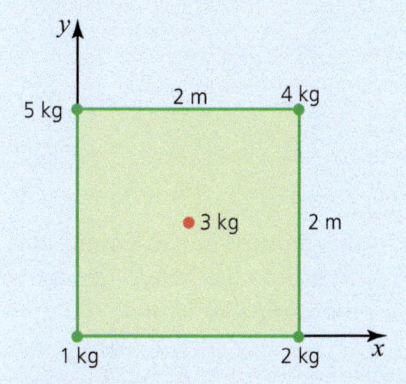

Figure 7.17

In this example, the total mass M (in kilograms) is $1 + 2 + 4 + 5 + 3 = 15$.

The two formulae for $\bar{x}$ and $\bar{y}$ can be combined into one using column vector notation:

Centre of mass of two- and three-dimensional bodies

$$\begin{pmatrix} M\bar{x} \\ M\bar{y} \end{pmatrix} = \begin{pmatrix} \sum m_i x_i \\ \sum m_i y_i \end{pmatrix}$$

which is equivalent to

$$M \begin{pmatrix} \bar{x} \\ \bar{y} \end{pmatrix} = \sum m_i \begin{pmatrix} x_i \\ y_i \end{pmatrix}$$

Substituting our values for M and m_i and x_i and y_i

$$15 \begin{pmatrix} \bar{x} \\ \bar{y} \end{pmatrix} = 1\begin{pmatrix} 0 \\ 0 \end{pmatrix} + 2\begin{pmatrix} 2 \\ 0 \end{pmatrix} + 4\begin{pmatrix} 2 \\ 2 \end{pmatrix} + 5\begin{pmatrix} 0 \\ 2 \end{pmatrix} + 3\begin{pmatrix} 1 \\ 1 \end{pmatrix}$$

$$15 \begin{pmatrix} \bar{x} \\ \bar{y} \end{pmatrix} = \begin{pmatrix} 15 \\ 21 \end{pmatrix}$$

$$\begin{pmatrix} \bar{x} \\ \bar{y} \end{pmatrix} = \begin{pmatrix} 1 \\ 1.4 \end{pmatrix}$$

The centre of mass is the point (1, 1.4).

Example 7.7

A metal disc of radius 15 cm has a hole of radius 5 cm cut in it, as shown in Figure 7.18. Find the centre of mass of the disc. Coordinate axes are defined with origin O, as shown in Figure 7.18.

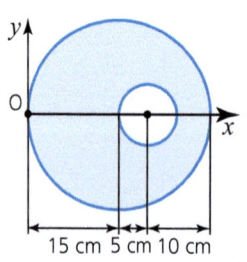

Figure 7.18

Solution

The disc is symmetrical about the x axis. The centre of mass must therefore be on the x axis.

Think of the original uncut disc as a composite body made up of the final body and a disc to fit into the hole. Since the material is uniform, the mass of each part is proportional to its area.

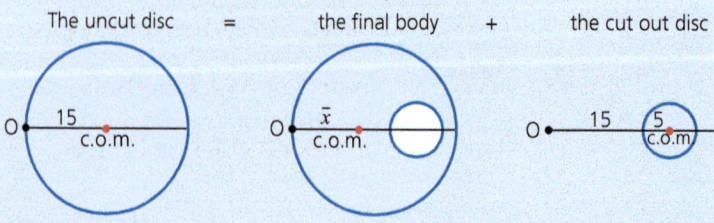

The uncut disc = the final body + the cut out disc

Figure 7.19

	Uncut disc	Final body	Cut out disc
Area	$15^2\pi = 225\pi$	$15^2\pi - 5^2\pi = 200\pi$	$5^2\pi = 25\pi$
Distance from O To centre of mass	15 cm	$\bar{x}$ cm	20 cm

Taking moments about O:

$225\pi \times 15 = 200\pi \times \bar{x} + 25\pi \times 20$ ← Divide by π

$$\Rightarrow \quad \bar{x} = \frac{225 \times 15 - 25 \times 20}{200}$$

$$= 14.375$$

The centre of mass is 14.4 cm from O; that is, 0.6 cm to the left of the centre of the disc.

Centre of mass of a triangle

The triangle in Figure 7.20 is divided up into thin strips parallel to the side AB.

The centre of mass of each strip lies in the middle of the strip, at the points $C_1, C_2, C_3, \ldots$

When these points are joined they form the median of the triangle drawn from C. Similarly, the centre of mass also lies on the medians from A and B. Therefore, the centre of mass lies at the intersection of the three medians; this is the *centroid* of the triangle. This point is $\frac{2}{3}$ of the distance along the median from each vertex.

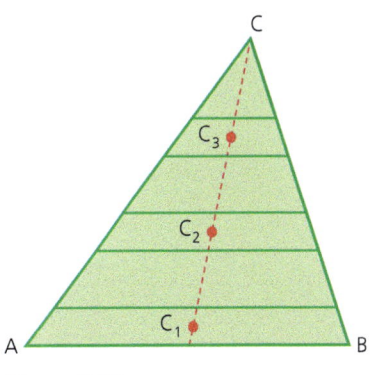

Figure 7.20

> **Note**
> The median of a triangle joins a vertex to the midpoint of the opposite side.

Example 7.8

Find the coordinates of the centre of mass of a uniform triangular lamina with vertices at A(4, 4), B(1, 1) and C(5, 1).

If the lamina is suspended from A, find the angle that the line BC makes with the horizontal.

Solution

The midpoint of BC is at M with coordinates (3, 1). The centre of mass G is $\frac{2}{3}$ of the way down the median AM.

G has x coordinate: $4 - \frac{2}{3} \times (4-3) = 3\frac{1}{3}$

and y coordinate: $4 - \frac{2}{3} \times (4-1) = 2$

The centre of mass G of the lamina is at $\left(3\frac{1}{3}, 2\right)$

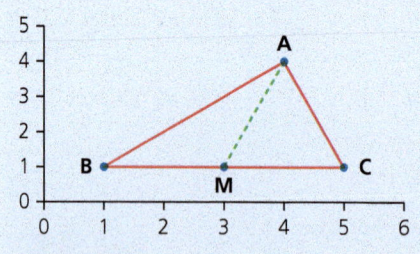

Centre of mass of two- and three-dimensional bodies

Figure 7.21

The lamina is suspended from A. G will be directly below A. The line AG and also the median AM will be along the vertical. The horizontal through M makes an angle θ with BC. The same angle θ is shown in the triangle AMH from which you can derive

$$\tan\theta = \frac{MH}{AH} = \frac{4-3}{4-1} = \frac{1}{3} \Rightarrow \theta = 18.4°.$$

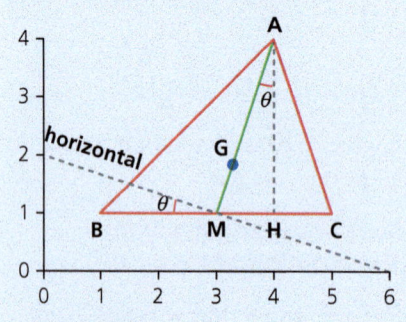

Figure 7.22

The line BC makes an angle 18.4° with the horizontal when the lamina is suspended from A.

Centres of mass of other shapes

The table below gives the position of the centre of mass of some uniform objects which you may encounter or wish to include within models of composite bodies.

The centre of mass for each of these shapes lies on its line of symmetry.

These standard results may be obtained using calculus methods which are introduced in Chapter 13.

Body	Position of centre of mass	Diagram
Solid cone or pyramid	$\frac{1}{4}h$ from base	
Hollow cone or pyramid	$\frac{1}{3}h$ from base	
Solid hemisphere	$\frac{3}{8}r$ from base	

Body	Position of centre of mass	Diagram
Hollow hemisphere	$\frac{1}{2}r$ from base	
Semicircular lamina	$\frac{4r}{3\pi}$ from base	

Example 7.9

Find the centre of mass of the uniform lamina illustrated in Figure 7.23.

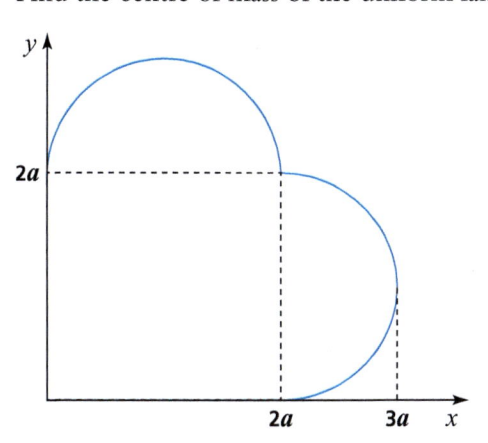

Remember that a lamina is a flat object that has negligible thickness compared with its length and width

Figure 7.23

Solution

The shape is symmetrical about the line $y = x$. It thus follows that the centre of mass lies on that line. In other words, you need only find one of the coordinates. The shape is made up of a square of side $2a$ with two semicircles of radius a added on at the edges. The square has centre of mass at (a, a). The semicircles have centre of mass at $\left(a, 2a + \frac{4a}{3\pi}\right)$ and $\left(2a + \frac{4a}{3\pi}, a\right)$.

The mass of each shape is proportional to its area: $4a^2$ for the square and $\frac{1}{2}\pi a^2$ for the semicircles. This gives rise to the moments equation

$$(4a^2 + \tfrac{1}{2}\pi a^2 + \tfrac{1}{2}\pi a^2)\bar{x} = 4a^2 \times a + \tfrac{1}{2}\pi a^2 \times a + \tfrac{1}{2}\pi a^2 \times \left(2a + \frac{4a}{3\pi}\right)$$

$$\bar{x}(4a^2 + \pi a^2) = \frac{14}{3}a^3 + \frac{3\pi}{2}a^3$$

$$\Rightarrow \quad \bar{x} = \frac{a}{6}\left(\frac{28 + 9\pi}{4 + \pi}\right) = 1.313\ldots a$$

The centre of mass is at $(1.31a, 1.31a)$.

Centre of mass of two- and three-dimensional bodies

Exercise 7.2

1. Find the centre of mass of the following sets of point masses.

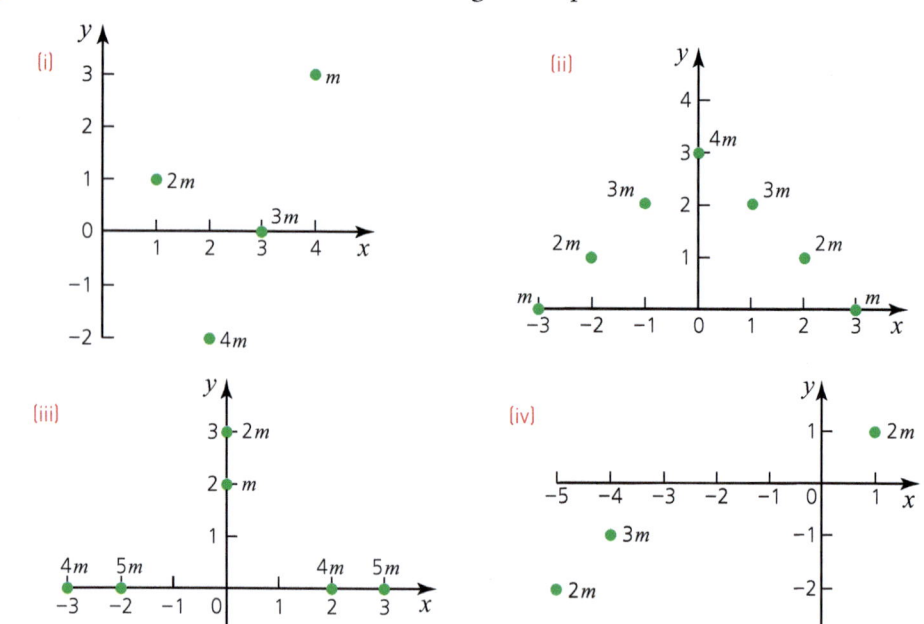

Figure 7.24

2. Masses of 1, 2, 3 and 4 grams are placed at the corners A, B, C and D of a square piece of uniform cardboard of side 10 cm and mass 5 g. Find the position of the centre of mass relative to axes through AB and AD.

3. As part of an illuminated display, letters are produced by mounting bulbs in holders 30 cm apart on light wire frames. The combined mass of a bulb and its holder is 200 g. Find the position of the centre of mass for each of the letters shown below, in terms of its horizontal and vertical displacement from the bottom left-hand corner of the letter.

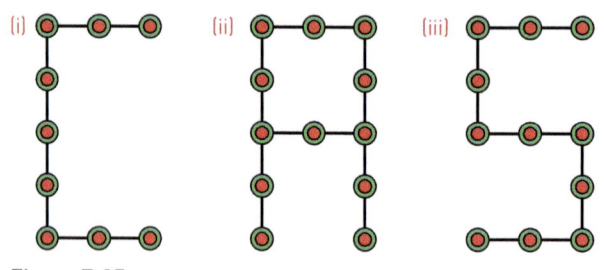

Figure 7.25

4. Four people of masses 60 kg, 65 kg, 62 kg and 75 kg sit on the four seats of the fairground ride shown below. The seat and the connecting arms are light. Find the radius of the circle described by the centre of mass when the ride rotates about O.

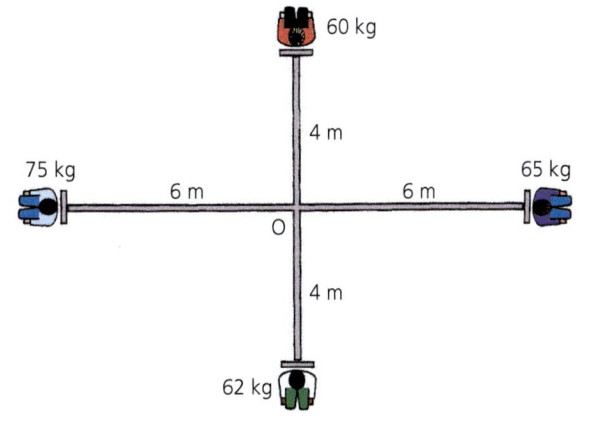

Figure 7.26

⑤ Find the coordinates of the centre of mass of each of these uniform laminae.

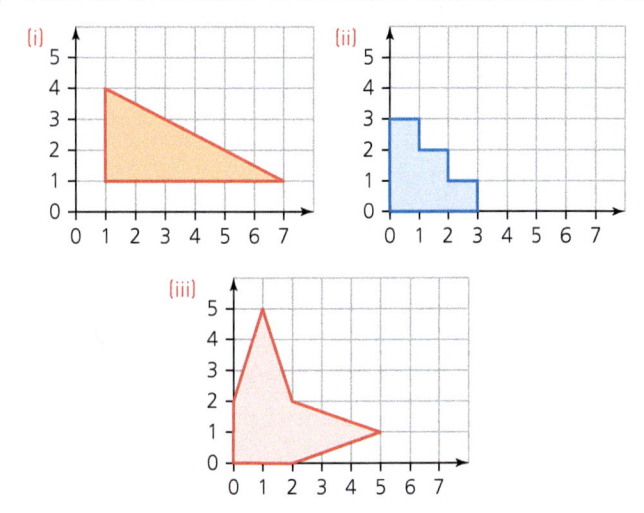

(i), (ii), (iii)

Figure 7.27

⑥ The following shapes are made of uniform card.

For each shape find the coordinates of the centre of mass relative to O.

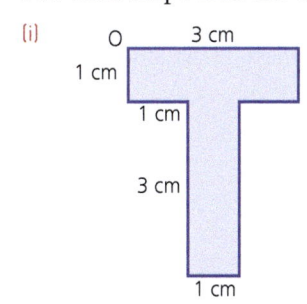

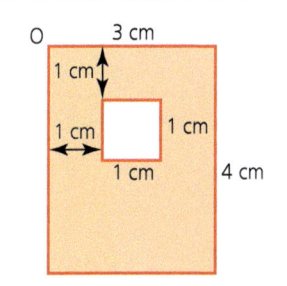

(i) and (ii)

Figure 7.28

⑦ A pendant is made from a uniform circular disc of mass $4m$ and radius 2 cm with a decorative edging of mass m, as shown. The centre of mass of the decoration is 1 cm below the centre, O, of the disc. The pendant is symmetrical about the diameter AB.

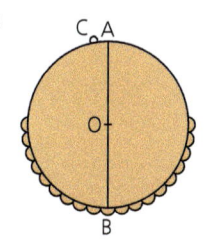

(i) Find the position of the centre of mass of the pendant.

The pendant should be hung from A but the light ring for hanging it is attached at C, where angle AOC is 10°.

Figure 7.29

(ii) Find the angle between AB and the vertical when the pendant is hung from C.

⑧ ABCD is a rectangular plate, with AB = 5 cm and AD = 8 cm. E is the midpoint of BC. The triangular portion ABE is removed and the remainder is suspended from A.

Find the angle that AD makes with the vertical.

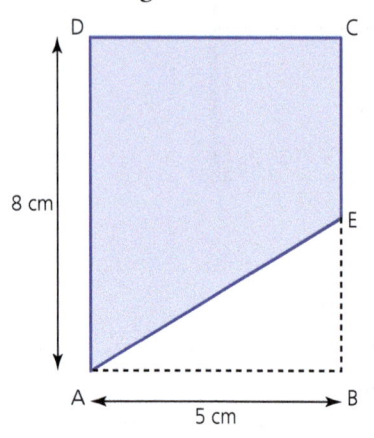

Figure 7.30

⑨ A uniform rectangular lamina, ABCD, where AB is of length a and BC of length $2a$, has a mass $10m$. Further point masses m, $2m$, $3m$ and $4m$ are fixed to the points A, B, C and D, respectively.

(i) Find the centre of mass of the system relative to x and y axes along AB and AD, respectively.

(ii) If the lamina is suspended from the point A find the angle that the diagonal AC makes with the vertical.

(iii) To what must the mass at the point D be altered if this diagonal is to hang vertically? [MEI]

⑩ A vase is made from a uniform solid cylinder of height 25 cm and radius 10 cm by removing a smaller cylinder of height 22 cm and radius 9 cm from it so that there is an axis of symmetry vertically through the centre of the base.

Find the centre of mass of the vase.

Figure 7.31

⑪ A filing cabinet has the dimensions shown in Figure 7.32. The body of the cabinet has mass 20 kg and its construction is such that its centre of mass is at a height of 60 cm, and is 25 cm from the back of the cabinet. The mass of a drawer and its contents may be taken to be 10 kg and its centre of mass to be 10 cm above its base and 30 cm from its front face.

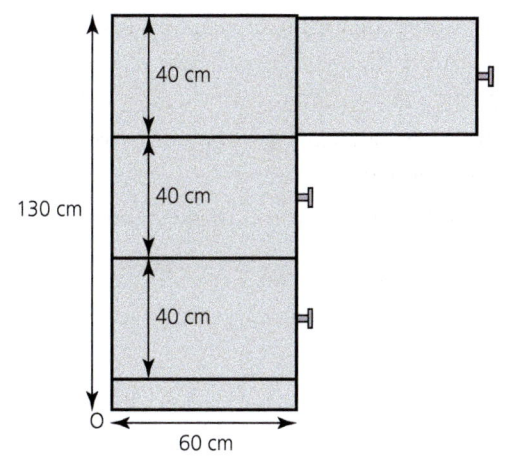

Figure 7.32

(i) Find the position of the centre of mass when all the drawers are closed.

(ii) Find the position of the centre of mass when the two top drawers are fully open.

(iii) Show that when all three drawers are fully opened the filing cabinet will tip over.

(iv) Two drawers are fully open. How far can the third drawer be opened without the cabinet tipping over?

12 Uniform wooden bricks have length 20 cm and height 5 cm. They are glued together as shown in Figure 7.33 with each brick 5 cm to the right of the one below it. The origin is taken to be at O.

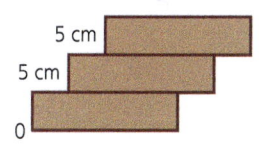

Figure 7.33

(i) Find the coordinates of the centre of mass for

    (a) 1   (b) 2   (c) 3   (d) 4   (e) 5 bricks.

(ii) How many bricks is it possible to assemble in this way without them tipping over?

(iii) If the displacement were changed from 5 cm to 2 cm, find the coordinates of the centre of mass for n bricks. How many bricks can now be assembled without them tipping over?

(iv) If the displacement is $\frac{1}{2}$ cm, what is the maximum height possible for the centre of mass of such an assembly of bricks without them tipping over?

13 Figure 7.34 gives the dimensions of the design of a uniform metal plate.

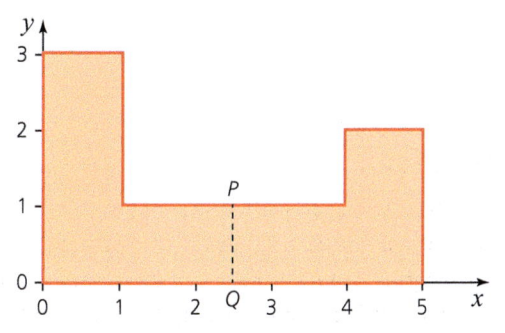

Figure 7.34

(i) Using a coordinate system with O as origin, the *x* and *y* axes as shown and 1 metre as 1 unit show that the centre of mass has *y* coordinate 1 and find its *x* coordinate.

The design requires the plate to have its centre of mass half way across (i.e. on the line *PQ* in Figure 7.34) and in order to achieve this a circular hole centred on $\left(\frac{1}{2}, \frac{1}{2}\right)$ is considered.

(ii) Find the appropriate radius for such a hole and explain why this idea is not feasible.

It is then decided to cut out two holes of radius *r*, both centred on the line $x = \frac{1}{2}$. The first hole is centred at $\left(\frac{1}{2}, \frac{1}{2}\right)$ and the centre of mass of the plate is to be at P.

(iii) Find the value of *r* and the coordinates of the centre of the second hole.   [MEI]

⑭ A toy consists of a solid hemisphere of radius *R* joined to a solid right cone of radius *R* and height *H*. The hemispherical base is made of a material which is twice as dense as the conical top.

Show that the centre of mass of the toy lies at a distance

$$\frac{H^2 - 6R^2}{4(H + 4R)}$$

from the common face of the two solids.

⑮ Find the centre of mass of the following uniform lamina in Figure 7.35.

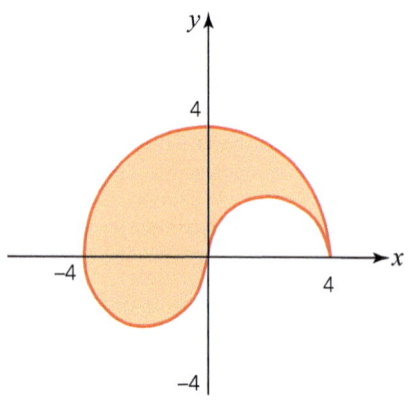

Figure 7.35

⑯ A drink can is symmetrical, with height *h* cm, and when empty its mass is *m* g. The drink that fills it has mass *M* g and can be taken to fill the can completely.

(i) Find the height of the centre of mass when the can is standing on a level table and

   (a) it is half full

   (b) a proportion, α, of the drink remains.

When the can is full, the centre of mass is clearly half way up it, at a height of $\frac{1}{2}h$. The same is true when it is completely empty. In between these two extremes, the centre of mass is below the middle.

(ii) Show that when the centre of mass is at its minimum height, α satisfies the equation $M\alpha^2 + 2\alpha m - m = 0$ and that the centre of mass lies on the surface of the drink.

KEY POINTS

1. The centre of mass of a body has the property that the moment, about any point, of the whole mass of the body taken at the centre of mass is equal to the sum of moments of the various particles comprising the body.

   $M\bar{\mathbf{r}} = \sum m_i \mathbf{r}_i$ where $M = \sum m_i$

2. In one dimension

   $M\bar{x} = \sum m_i x_i$

3. In two dimensions

   $M \begin{pmatrix} \bar{x} \\ \bar{y} \end{pmatrix} = \sum m_i \begin{pmatrix} x_i \\ y_i \end{pmatrix}$

4. In three dimensions

   $M \begin{pmatrix} \bar{x} \\ \bar{y} \\ \bar{z} \end{pmatrix} = \sum m_i \begin{pmatrix} x_i \\ y_i \\ z_i \end{pmatrix}$

LEARNING OUTCOMES

When you have finished this chapter, you should
- be able to find the centre of mass of a system of particles of given position and mass
- be able to find the centre of mass of a simple shape
- know how to use symmetry when finding a centre of mass
- know the positions of the centres of mass of simple shapes
- be able to find the centre of mass of a composite body
- be able to use centres of mass in problems involving the equilibrium of a rigid body.

8 Dimensional analysis

But whatever his weight in pounds, shillings and ounces,

He always seems bigger because of his bounces.

The house at Pooh Corner,
A.A. Milne

→ What makes the rhyme on the left about Tigger sound so ridiculous? Look at the units in the line of the rhyme. Pounds can be units of either money or mass, shillings are units of money and ounces are units of mass. You can see at once that not only is there a mixture of units, but also of the underlying quantities which they are measuring.

Introduction to dimensional analysis

In this chapter, you will look at the quantities that you will meet in mechanics and classify them according to their **dimensions**. The dimensions of a quantity are closely related to the units in which it is measured.

All of the quantities you will meet in this book can be described in terms of three fundamental quantities, Mass, Length and Time. Take, for example, the quantity *area;* there are many familiar ways of finding area, depending on the shape involved (see Figure 8.1).

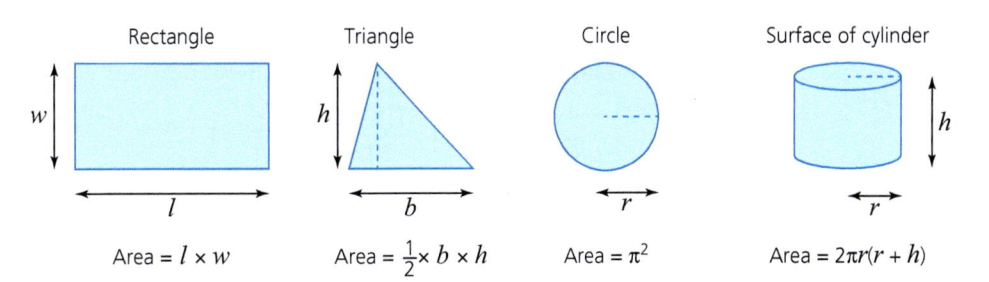

Rectangle	Triangle	Circle	Surface of cylinder
Area = $l \times w$	Area = $\frac{1}{2} \times b \times h$	Area = πr^2	Area = $2\pi r(r + h)$

Figure 8.1

All of these formulae have essentially the same form

$$\text{area} = \text{number} \times \text{length} \times \text{length}$$

In the case of the rectangle, the 'number' is 1 and the two 'lengths' are the length and breadth of the shape. For the circle, the two 'lengths' are the same, namely, the radius and the 'number' is π. For the surface area of the cylinder, one of the 'lengths' is a sum of 2 lengths: the radius of the base and the height of the cylinder. However, the structure of the formula is the same for all four shapes, and, indeed, for any other area formula you can think of (for example, the area of a trapezium or the surface area of a cone).

The dimensions of the quantity Area can therefore be summarised using the formula

$$[\text{Area}] = L^2$$

The square brackets [ ] mean the *dimensions of,* and the letter L represents the quantity Length. So the whole statement reads

The dimensions of area are Length squared.

There are two important points to notice about this.

1. The numbers at the start of the formulae (in the four cases above, they are 1, $\frac{1}{2}$, π and 2π) do not feature in the dimensions of the quantity because they are dimensionless.
2. The units in which a quantity is measured are derived directly from its dimensions. In the S.I. system, the unit of length is 1 metre. Since the dimensions of area are L^2, it follows that the S.I. unit for area is 1 metre squared, usually written m².

> **Note**
> The area under a curve is often found by calculus methods, using the formula
> Area = $\int y \, dx$
> In this case, both y and the infinitesimal quantity dx represent lengths and so the integral has dimensions L^2, as must be the case since it represents an area.

The dimensions of further quantities

> **Discussion point**
> How many formulae can you find for the volumes of objects?
> Show that all your formulae for volume involve multiplying three lengths together so that
> [Volume] = L^3

1 The dimensions of further quantities

So far the quantities discussed, area and volume, have only involved lengths. What are the dimensions of speed (or velocity) and of acceleration?

To find the dimensions of any quantity, start by writing down a simple formula which you might use to calculate it. For example, to calculate speed you might use

$$\text{Speed} = \frac{\text{Distance}}{\text{Time}}$$

The dimensions follow immediately from this. A distance is clearly a length, so

$$[\text{Speed}] = \frac{[\text{Distance}]}{[\text{Time}]} = \frac{L}{T} = LT^{-1}$$

It follows that the S.I. unit for speed is 1 metre per second, written ms^{-1}. Notice that a second fundamental dimension, T (Time), is now involved.

Similarly $\quad\text{Acceleration} = \frac{\text{Change in velocity}}{\text{Time taken}}$

and so $\quad [\text{Acceleration}] = \frac{[\text{Speed}]}{[\text{Time}]}$

$$= \frac{LT^{-1}}{T}$$

$$= LT^{-2}$$

The corresponding S.I. unit is therefore $1\,ms^{-2}$.

Exactly the same procedure allows you to find the dimensions of force.

Force = Mass × Acceleration

[Force] = [Mass] × [Acceleration]

$\quad\quad\quad = M \times LT^{-2}$

$\quad\quad\quad = MLT^{-2}$

Therefore the S.I. unit for force is 1 kilogram metre per second squared. Because force is an important concept, and this unit would be such a mouthful, it is given a name of its own, the newton (N).

$1\,N = 1\,kg\,m\,s^{-2}$

Notice that now all three of the basic dimensions, M, L and T are being used.

Example 8.1

(i) Find the dimensions of

    (a) kinetic energy

    (b) gravitational potential energy

    (c) work.

(ii) Comment on the significance of your answers.

Solution

(i) (a) Kinetic energy $= \frac{1}{2}mv^2$

$$[\text{K.E.}] = M \times (LT^{-1})^2$$
$$= ML^2T^{-2}$$

(b) Gravitational potential energy $= mgh$ ← *g is an acceleration so it has dimensions LT^{-2}.*

$$[\text{G.P.E}] = M \times LT^{-2} \times L$$
$$= ML^2T^{-2}$$

(c) Work = Force × Distance

$$= MLT^{-2} \times L$$
$$= ML^2T^{-2}$$

(ii) All three have the same dimensions because they are examples of the same underlying quantity, energy. The S.I. unit could be written as $1\,\text{kg}\,\text{m}^2\,\text{s}^{-2}$ but is actually given the special name of 1 joule (J).

Dimensionless quantities

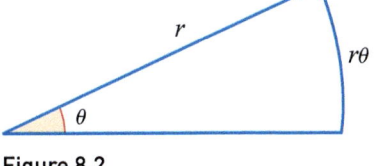

Some quantities have no dimensions. For example, angles are dimensionless. The angle θ in radians in Figure 8.2 is defined as

$$\theta = \frac{\text{arc length}}{\text{radius}}$$

Consequently, $[\theta] = \frac{L}{L}$ and θ is dimensionless.

Figure 8.2

Notice that although, in this case, the formula used gave θ in radians, the same result would have been obtained for θ in degrees, using

$$\theta = 360 \times \frac{\text{arc length}}{2\pi \times \text{radius}}$$

The dimensions of a quantity cannot be altered by changing the units in which it is measured.

All numbers are dimensionless, including the trigonometrical ratios, for example $\sin\theta, \cos\theta, \tan\theta$ and irrational numbers such as π and e. This is the reason why you ignore any numbers in a formula when considering its dimensions: numbers, being dimensionless, cannot be included in this analysis.

Dimensionless quantities may be ratios of two lengths, such as $\pi = \frac{\text{circumference}}{\text{diameter}}$ or the golden ratio $\phi = \frac{1+\sqrt{5}}{2}$, or ratios of two forces, such as the coefficient of friction between two surfaces in contact $\mu = \frac{F}{R}$, or even ratios of two speeds such as the coefficient of restitution, $e = \frac{\text{speed of separation}}{\text{speed of approach}}$.

Other systems of units

The units used in this book are almost entirely S.I. units. There are other self-consistent sets of units, such as the 'cgs' system (centimetre, gram, second) or the Imperial system (foot, pound, second). Knowing the dimensions of a quantity allows you to find the appropriate unit within any system.

The dimensions of further quantities

The set of dimensions may also be extended to include quantities that arise in electricity and magnetism. For example, Q represents the dimension of electrical charge.

Change of units

It is helpful to know the dimensions of a quantity when you are changing the units in which it is to be measured, as in the following example.

Example 8.2

The energy of a body is 5000 foot poundals (imperial units based on feet, pounds and seconds). Write this in S.I. units, i.e. joules.

(To 3 s.f. 1 pound (lb) = 0.454 kg and 1 foot = 0.305 m)

Solution

The dimensions of energy are $ML^2T^{-2} = \dfrac{ML^2}{T^2}$

So
$$1 \text{ foot poundal} = \dfrac{1 \text{ lb} \times (1 \text{ foot})^2}{(1 \text{ second})^2}$$
$$= \dfrac{0.454 \text{ kg} \times (0.305 \text{ m})^2}{(1 \text{ second})^2}$$
$$= 0.0422 \text{ J}$$

and
$$5000 \text{ foot poundals} = 5000 \times 0.0422 \text{ J}$$
$$= 211 \text{ J (to 3 s.f.)}$$

ACTIVITY 8.1

Draw up a table like this one and, having copied the first two lines, extend it to cover the other quantities.

Quantity	Formula	Dimensions	S.I. unit
Area	$l \times w$	L^2	m^2
Volume	$l \times w \times h$	L^3	m^3
Speed			
Acceleration			
g			
Force (= mass × acceleration)			
Weight			
Kinetic energy			
Gravitational potential energy			
Work			

Quantity	Formula	Dimensions	S.I. unit
Power			
Impulse			
Momentum			
Pressure (= force/area)			
Density			
Moment			
Angle			
Gravitational constant (G)			
Coefficient of friction			
Coefficient of restitution			

> Use these blank lines for other quantities as you come across them.
>
> You may find it helpful to keep the completed table somewhere handy for reference.

Dimensional consistency

In any equation or formula, all the terms must have the same dimensions. If that is the case, the equation is said to be **dimensionally consistent**. If not, for example, if force and area are being added or subtracted, or if a mass is being equated to a velocity, the equation is said to be dimensionally inconsistent.

Any statement that is dimensionally inconsistent **must** be wrong. In the quotation at the start of this chapter, the phrase '*his weight in pounds, shillings and ounces*' is nonsense because it is dimensionally inconsistent.

Example 8.3

Show that the formula

$$s = ut + \frac{1}{2}at^2$$

is dimensionally consistent.

Solution

There are three terms, with dimensions as follows:

$$[s] = L$$
$$[ut] = LT^{-1} \times T = L$$
$$\left[\frac{1}{2}at^2\right] = LT^{-2} \times T^2 = L$$

All three terms have the same dimensions, and so the formula is dimensionally consistent.

The dimensions of further quantities

The fact that a formula is dimensionally consistent does not mean it is necessarily right, but if it is dimensionally inconsistent it is certainly wrong.

Good mathematicians develop the habit of automatically checking the dimensional consistency of anything they write. A consequence of this is that they tend to leave everything written in symbols until the final calculation. You know, for example, that g has dimensions LT^{-2} but if it is replaced by an approximate value, e.g. 10, its dimensions are no longer evident: $h = \frac{1}{2}gt^2$ is dimensionally correct but $h = 5t^2$ seems not to be.

Example 8.4

A mathematician writes down the equation

$$\tfrac{1}{2}m_1v_1^2 = m_2gh + m_2v_2$$

Show that it must be wrong.

Solution

Checking for dimensional consistency:

$$\left[\tfrac{1}{2}m_1v_1^2\right] = M \times \left(LT^{-1}\right)^2 = ML^2T^{-2}$$

$$[m_2gh] = M \times LT^{-2} \times L = ML^2T^{-2}$$

$$[m_2v_2] = M \times LT^{-1} = MLT^{-1}$$

The third term is dimensionally different from the other two and so the equation is incorrect.

Finding the form of a relationship

It is sometimes possible to determine the form of a relationship just by looking at the dimensions of the quantities likely to be involved. Consider this example.

A pendulum consists of a light string of length l with a bob of mass m attached to the end. You would expect that the period, t, might depend in some way on the variables l and m and also on the value of g.

This can be expressed in the form

$$t = kl^\alpha m^\beta g^\gamma$$

where k is dimensionless and the powers α, β and γ are to be found.

Writing down the dimensions of each side gives

$$T = L^\alpha \times M^\beta \times \left(LT^{-2}\right)^\gamma$$

$$T = L^{\alpha+\gamma} M^\beta T^{-2\gamma}$$

The left-hand side of the equation, T, may be written as $L^0 M^0 T^1$ and so

$$L^0 M^0 T^1 = L^{\alpha+\gamma} M^\beta T^{-2\gamma}$$

Equating the powers of L, M and T gives:

L: $\quad 0 = \alpha + \gamma$

M: $\quad 0 = \beta$

T: $\quad 1 = -2\gamma$

Solving these gives $\alpha = \frac{1}{2}$, $\beta = 0$ and $\gamma = -\frac{1}{2}$ and so the relationship is

$$t = k\sqrt{\frac{l}{g}}$$

In Chapter 12 you will meet simple harmonic motion and you will then be equipped to find that the value of k is 2π, so the complete formula is

$$t = 2\pi\sqrt{\frac{l}{g}}$$

In the method used here, all you had to do was to think about the dimensions, a very beautiful piece of mathematics. Of course, the dimensions method does not tell you that the value of k is 2π, but it does provide the correct form of the relationship.

Notice that the mass of the pendulum bob, m, does not feature in the formula for the period. This is found to be the case in practice: a heavier bob makes no difference to the period.

What about the angle of swing of the pendulum, θ? Since angles are dimensionless it cannot feature in this argument. You may like to think of its effect as being included within the dimensionless k. In fact, the value of k is approximately constant (equal to 2π) for small values of θ, but it does vary with θ for larger swings.

In the next example, the work is taken a step further. First, the form of a relationship is proposed, then data are used to determine the constant involved. The resulting formula is used to predict the outcome of a future experiment. Notice that the units look after themselves providing you are consistent with their use; in this case, they happen to be in the cgs system.

Example 8.5

In an experiment, small spheres are dropped into a container of liquid which is sufficiently deep for them to attain terminal velocity. For any sphere, the terminal velocity, V, is thought to depend on its radius, r, its weight mg and the viscosity of the liquid, η (the Greek letter 'eta'). (Viscosity is a measure of the 'stickiness' of a liquid and has dimensions $ML^{-1}T^{-1}$.)

Note

At terminal velocity the force of resistance is equal to the weight of the sphere, so its acceleration is zero and it does not go any faster.

(i) Write down a formula for V as the product of unknown powers of r, mg, η and a dimensionless constant k.

(ii) Find the powers of and r, mg, and η and write down the formula for V with these values substituted in.

In a particular liquid it is found that a sphere of mass $0.02\,g$ and radius $0.1\,cm$ has a terminal velocity $5\,cm\,s^{-1}$.

(iii) Find the value of $\frac{k}{\eta}$ taking g to be $1000\,cm\,s^{-2}$.

(iv) Find, using these values, the terminal velocity of a sphere of mass $0.03\,g$ and radius $0.2\,cm$.

The dimensions of further quantities

Solution

(i) $V = kr^\alpha (mg)^\beta \eta^\gamma$

(ii) Taking dimensions of both sides of the equation gives

$$LT^{-1} = L^\alpha \times (MLT^{-2})^\beta \times (ML^{-1}T^{-1})^\gamma$$

$$M^0 L^1 T^{-1} = M^{\beta+\gamma} L^{\alpha+\beta-\gamma} T^{-2\beta-\gamma}$$

Equating powers: M: $\quad 0 = \beta + \gamma$
 L: $\quad 1 = \alpha + \beta - \gamma$
 T: $\quad -1 = -2\beta - \gamma$

Solving these gives $\alpha = -1$, $\beta = 1$ and $\gamma = -1$ and so the formula is

$$V = \frac{kmg}{r\eta} \qquad ①$$

(iii) Substituting $m = 0.02$, $r = 0.1$, $g = 1000$ and $V = 5$ gives

$$5 = \frac{k \times 0.02 \times 1000}{0.1 \times \eta}$$

$$\frac{k}{\eta} = 0.025 \quad \text{(in cgs units)}$$

(iv) Substituting $m = 0.03$, $r = 0.2$, $g = 1000$ and $\frac{k}{\eta} = 0.025$ in ① gives

$$V = \frac{0.025 \times 0.03 \times 1000}{0.2}$$

$$= 3.75$$

The terminal velocity of this sphere is $3.75\,\text{cm s}^{-1}$.

The method of dimensions

This method for finding the form of a proposed formula is sometimes called **the method of dimensions**; at other times it is simply referred to as **dimensional analysis**. There are a number of points which you should realise when using it.

1. In mechanics, relationships are based on three fundamental quantities, Mass, Length and Time, and so the right-hand side of the formula can involve no more than three independent quantities. Otherwise you will end up with three equations to find four or more unknown powers. (The last example actually involved four quantities, m, g, r and η, but the first two of these were tied together as the weight, mg, and were not therefore independent.)
2. The method requires you to make modelling assumptions about which quantities are going to be important and which can be ignored. You must always be prepared to review these assumptions.
3. This method can only be used when a quantity can be written as a product of powers of other quantities. There are many situations which cannot be modelled by this type of formula and for these situations this method is not appropriate. For example, the formula $s = ut + \frac{1}{2}at^2$ has two separate terms which are added together on the right-hand side. The form of this relationship could not be predicted using the method of dimensions.

Exercise 8.1

① Check the dimensional consistency of each of the formulae below and hence state whether it could be correct or is definitely wrong. You may assume that all letters have their conventional meanings.

(i) $v^2 - u^2 = 2as$

(ii) $x = \dfrac{(m_1 x_1 + m_2 x_2)}{m_1 + m_2}$

(iii) $F - mg = ma$

(iv) $T_1 - T_2 = \dfrac{1}{2}mv^2$ (T_1 and T_2 are tensions)

(v) $Fs = mv - mu$

(vi) $mg \sin \alpha - \mu mg \cos \alpha = ma$

(vii) $m_1 g d_1 - m_2 g d_2 = (m_1 + m_2)a$

(viii) $\dfrac{1}{2}mv^2 = \dfrac{1}{2}mu^2 + mgh \sin \theta$

(ix) $\dfrac{1}{2}F(u+v) = \dfrac{(v^2 - u^2)}{2t}$

② A scientist thinks that the speed, v, of a wave travelling along the surface of an ocean depends on the depth of the ocean, h, the density of the water in the ocean, ρ (the Greek letter 'rho'), and g.

(i) Write down the dimensions of each of the quantities v, h, ρ and g.

The scientist expresses his idea using the formula

$v = kh^\alpha \rho^\beta g^\gamma$ where k is dimensionless.

(ii) Use dimensional analysis to find the values of α, β and γ and write out the formula with these values substituted in.

(iii) Do waves travel faster in deep water or shallow water?

(iv) Do waves travel faster in winter (when the water density is greater) or in summer?

③ A water container has a hole in the bottom. When it is filled to a depth d it takes time t for the water to run out. The time t may be modelled as the product of powers of d and g and a dimensionless constant k.

(i) Write down a formula for t.

(ii) Use dimensional analysis to find the powers of d and g in the formula.

When the container is filled to a depth of 0.4 m it takes 30 s to empty.

(iii) Taking g to be $10\,\text{m}\,\text{s}^{-2}$, find the value of k.

(iv) How long does it take the container to empty when it is filled to a depth of 60 cm?

④ A plane uniform circular disc of radius a and mass m hangs at rest in a vertical plane from a pivot at a point on its circumference about which it can freely rotate. It is believed that the periodic time T of small oscillations of the disc about its rest position might depend upon a, m and the local gravitational acceleration g through a relationship of the form

$T = km^\alpha a^\beta g^\gamma$

where k is a dimensionless constant.

The dimensions of further quantities

(i) Use a dimensional argument to show that T does not depend on m.

(ii) Find an expression for T in terms of a and g.

A number of careful observations of the small oscillations of a disc of radius 0.50 m in a local gravitational acceleration of 9.8 m s^{-2} shows that they have a period of 1.74 s.

(iii) Determine the numerical value of the dimensionless constant k suggested by these observations.

5. A ball of mass m travelling with velocity v vertically downwards hits a horizontal surface and bounces back up, rising to a height h. The coefficient of restitution between the ball and the surface is e.

(i) Use the definition of coefficient of restitution to show that e is dimensionless.

It is believed that h depends on a product of powers of v, m, g and a dimensionless constant, so a formula is proposed of the form

$$h = kv^\alpha m^\beta g^\gamma$$

where k is dimensionless.

(ii) Use dimensional analysis to find the values of α, β and γ, and write down the formula with these values substituted in.

(iii) Two balls, identical in all respects except that one is heavier than the other, fall with equal speeds. Explain how your answer to part (ii) allows you to decide which (if either) bounces higher.

(iv) The height h clearly does also depend on e. Why was it not considered useful to include it in the formula?

(v) Use your knowledge of mechanics to find a formula for h in terms of v, m, g and e.

(vi) Explain the relationship between k in the answer to part (ii) and e.

6. The volume rate of flow R (in m^3 s^{-1}) of a liquid with a viscosity η, (in kg m^{-1} s^{-1}) through a cylindrical pipe of length a (in m) and an internal radius r (in m) is believed to be of the form

$$R = k\eta^w a^x r^y p^z,$$

where k is a non-dimensional constant and p (in N m^{-2}) is the pressure difference between the ends of the pipe.

Using dimensional considerations

(i) show that $w = -1$ and $z = 1$

(ii) find the relationship between x and y.

Observations of a water supply provided at constant pressure and viscosity produced the following recordings:

Pipe length, a (m)	100	200
Internal radius, r (m)	0.050	0.050
Flow rate, R (m^3 s^{-1})	0.420	0.210

(iii) Derive a formula for R in terms of a and r for such a supply.

(iv) Find the rate of flow of water through 1000 m of pipe with an internal radius of 0.075 m under the same pressure and with the same viscosity.

7. In an investigation into viscosity, small spheres are allowed to fall from rest through a column of viscous liquid and their terminal speeds are measured.

It is believed that the terminal speed V of a sphere depends upon a product of powers of its weight mg, its radius r and the viscosity η of the liquid and a dimensionless constant.

(i) Given that the dimensions of viscosity are $ML^{-1}T^{-1}$ use the method of dimensions to establish the form of the relationship for V in terms of m, r, η and g.

(ii) The mass m of the sphere may be written in terms of its radius r and its density ρ. Write down this relationship.

(iii) Using (i) and (ii) write down a relationship for V in terms of ρ, r, η and g.

(iv) A steel sphere of radius $0.15\,\text{cm}$ and density $7.8\,\text{g cm}^{-1}$ falls through a column of a viscous liquid and is found to have a terminal speed of $6.0\,\text{cm s}^{-1}$. A lead sphere of density $11.4\,\text{g cm}^{-3}$ falling through the same liquid is found to have a terminal speed of $5.0\,\text{cm s}^{-1}$. Determine the radius of the lead sphere.

8. (i) Define π and hence find its dimensions.

(ii) Newton's law of universal gravitation states that the magnitude of the force F on a point mass m_1 due to the presence of a point mass m_2 at a distance r is given by
$$F = \frac{Gm_1m_2}{r^2}$$
Find the dimensions of G.

(iii) The constant G has a value 6.67×10^{-11} in S.I. units. An astronomer proposes a system of units based upon the mass of the Earth, M_e, its radius, R_e, and the time it takes for one revolution about the Sun, T_e. Given that $M_e = 5.98 \times 10^{24}\,\text{kg}$, $R_e = 6.37 \times 10^6\,\text{m}$ and $T_e = 3.16 \times 10^7\,\text{s}$, find the value of G in terms of these Earth units.

(iv) Comment briefly upon the different natures of the constants π and G.

9. Newton's law of universal gravitation states that the magnitude of the force F on a point mass m_1 due to the presence of a point mass m_2 at a distance r is given by
$$F = \frac{Gm_1m_2}{r^2}$$

(i) Find the dimensions of G.

Consider the case of a point mass (m) at the surface of a much larger spherical mass (M) of radius (R). The acceleration due to gravity of the mass m is thus given by
$$g = \frac{GM}{R^2}$$

(ii) The universal constant G has a value of 6.674×10^{-11} in S.I. units. An astronomer proposes a system of units based upon the mass of the Earth ($M_E = 5.976 \times 10^{24}\,\text{kg}$), the radius of the Earth ($R_E = 6.371 \times 10^6\,\text{m}$) and the acceleration due to gravity at the surface of the Earth ($g_E = 9.807\,\text{m s}^{-2}$). Find the value of G in these Earth units.

(iii) The mass of the Moon is $7.346 \times 10^{22}\,\text{kg}$ and the mean radius is $1.738 \times 10^6\,\text{m}$. Express these in terms of Earth units and use your results to find the acceleration due to gravity on the Moon's surface.

The dimensions of further quantities

    (iv) The corresponding data for Mars are $M = 6.417 \times 10^{23}$ kg and $R = 3.396 \times 10^6$ m. Find g for Mars, in terms of g_E.

10. For a wave travelling with speed c, the wavelength is denoted by λ and the frequency, which is the number of complete oscillations per second, by f

    (i) Verify that the relation $c = \lambda f$ is dimensionally consistent.

For a sound wave travelling in either air or water, the frequency, f, depends on the wavelength, λ, the density, ρ, and the pressure, P. [Pressure is force per unit area.]

    (ii) State the dimensions of P and ρ.

    (iii) Assuming a relation of the form $f = K\lambda^\alpha P^\beta \rho^\gamma$, find the value of α, β and γ given that K is a dimensionless constant with a different value for air and water. How can the value of K be found?

The speed of propagation, c, of a sound wave is known to be given by

$$c = \sqrt{\frac{AP}{\rho}}$$ where $A = 1.4$ for air.

    (iv) By using this expression for c and the equation in (i), find the value of K for sound waves in air.

    (v) It is observed that the density of water is much greater than the density of air and that the speed of sound in water is much greater than in air. What does this imply about the value of A for water? Explain your answer.

11. The magnitude of the force of gravitational attraction, F, between two objects of mass m_1 and m_2 at a distance d apart is given by

$$F = \frac{Gm_1 m_2}{d^2}$$

where G is the universal constant of gravitation.

    (i) Find the dimensions of G.

An astronomer proposes a model in which the lifetime, t of a star depends on a product of powers of its mass, m, its initial radius r_0, G and a dimensionless constant.

    (ii) Use the method of dimensions to find the resulting formula for t.

Observation shows that the larger the initial radius, the longer the lifetime of the star, but that the larger the mass, the shorter the lifetime of the star.

    (iii) Is the model consistent with these observations?

    (iv) Show that the model can be expressed more simply if the initial density, ρ_0, of the star is used as one of the variables.

12. In the early seventeenth century, Mersenne (1588–1648) conducted experiments with long lengths of rope and so obtained the law for the frequency of transverse vibrations of strings.

Assuming that the frequency depends on products of powers of T, the tension in the rope, l, the length of the rope, and m, the mass per unit length of the rope,

    (i) Find, by dimensional analysis, the form of the relationship.

A rope of length 24 m and mass 0.5 kg m^{-1} under tension of 72 N is found to vibrate with a frequency of $\frac{1}{4}$ of a cycle per second.

    (ii) State the exact relationship between the frequency, T, l and m.

(iii) Find the frequency of vibration of a string of length 20 cm and mass 0.005 g cm^{-1} under a tension of 8×10^5 dynes. (The dyne is the cgs unit of force: 1 dyne is the force required to give a mass of 1 g an acceleration of 1 cm s^{-2}.)

⑬ An artillery officer is conducting a series of experiments to find the maximum range, R, of a gun which fires shells from ground level across level ground.

(i) Show, by considering the shell as a projectile with initial velocity u at an angle α to the horizontal and ignoring air resistance, that

$$R = \frac{u^2}{g}\sin 2\alpha$$

and that this has a maximum value, R_M, when α is 45°.

(ii) Show that the expression for R in part (i) is dimensionally consistent.

The officer finds that the shells fall some distance short of their predicted range. Deciding that this must be due to air resistance, he proposes a model in which the magnitude of the force of resistance, F, is proportional to the speed of the shell, v,

$$F = cv$$

(iii) Show that the constant c is not dimensionless and write down its dimensions.

The officer then suggests that a better model for the range of the shell, when fired at 45° to the horizontal, is given by:

$$R = R_M(1 - \varepsilon)$$

where ε (epsilon) is a number less than 1 representing the proportion of the range which is lost.

(iv) State the dimensions of ε.

The officer believes that ε depends on a product of powers of the speed of projection, u, the constant c, g and the mass m of the shell.

(v) Use dimensional analysis to find an expression for ε in which the power of u is 1. Express the improved model as a formula for R.

It is suggested that a more accurate and more general model still would have the form

$$R = R_M\left(1 + a_1\varepsilon + a_2\varepsilon^2 + a_3\varepsilon^3 + \cdots\right)$$

Where $a_1, a_2, a_3, \ldots$ are dimensionless coefficients, taking into account (among other things) the angle of projection. (Clearly, a_1 would be negative.)

(vi) Show that such a model is dimensionally consistent.

⑭ Kepler's third law of planetary motion compares the orbital period and the radius of the orbit of a planet around the Sun. The comparison being made is that the ratio of the square of the periods to the cube of the average distances from the Sun is the same for every one of the planets. If T is the period of the planet and R is the average distance from the Sun then

$$T^2 = KR^3$$

(i) Find the dimension of K.

The dimensions of further quantities

The average distance of the Earth from the Sun is 1.4957×10^{11} m. This is known as an astronomical unit (1 a.u.)

The orbital period of the Earth around the Sun is one year or 3.156×10^7 s.

(ii) Find the value of K in S.I. units.

The distances of the planets from the Sun are given in the table below.

Planet	Mercury	Venus	Earth	Mars	Jupiter	Saturn	Uranus	Neptune
Distance (a.u.)	0.387	0.723	1	1.52	5.21	9.55	19.2	30.1
Period (year)			1					

(iii) Find the periods of the planets.

KEY POINTS

1. Any quantity in mechanics may be expressed in terms of the three fundamental dimensions: mass, M; length, L; time, T.
2. The dimension of a quantity d is denoted by $[d]$.
3. The unit for any quantity is derived from the three fundamental dimensions.
4. Numbers are dimensionless.
5. All formulae and equations must be dimensionally consistent.
6. Using dimensional analysis you can sometimes find the form of a relationship as the product of powers of the quantities involved and a dimensionless constant.

LEARNING OUTCOMES

When you have completed this chapter, you should be able to
- find the dimensions of a quantity in terms of M, L and T
- use the dimensions of a quantity to determine its units
- change the units in which a quantity is given
- understand that some quantities are dimensionless
- use dimensional analysis to check a relationship for consistency
- use dimensional analysis to determine unknown indices in a proposed formula
- use a model based on dimensional analysis.

PRACTICE QUESTIONS: SET 1

① Most of the world outside of the UK expresses the fuel consumption of cars in litres per 100 kilometres.

What are the dimensions of this measure of fuel consumption?

Express 1 litre per 100 kilometres in SI base units. [3 marks]

② Three small circular discs are on a smooth horizontal surface. The centres of the discs initially lie on a straight line and all the motion takes place on this line. Discs A, B and C have masses $2m$, m and m. Initially, B is at rest. A is travelling towards B with speed $U\,\text{m}\,\text{s}^{-1}$ and C is travelling towards B from the other side with speed $kU\,\text{m}\,\text{s}^{-1}$, where $k > 0$. This situation is shown in Figure 1 below.

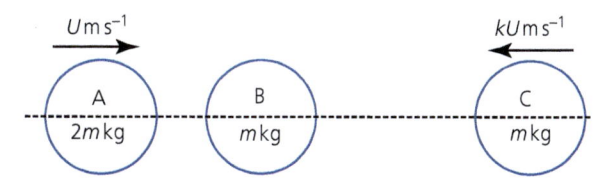

Figure 1

The first collision is between A and B. The coefficient of restitution is e.

(i) Find an expression in terms of U and e for the speed of B after the collision. Show that the speed of A is $\dfrac{U}{3}(2-e)$. [6 marks]

B now collides with C and the discs coalesce to form the body D.

(ii) Find an expression in terms of k, U and e for the speed of D. [3 marks]

(iii) Show that A will collide with D if $k > \dfrac{2}{3}(2e-1)$. [3 marks]

Suppose A collides with D and they coalesce to form the body E.

(iv) Show that the speed of E is independent of e.

Find the speed of E in terms of U in the case $k = \dfrac{4}{9}$. [4 marks]

③ A car of mass $1200\,\text{kg}$ is travelling at $15\,\text{m}\,\text{s}^{-1}$ with acceleration $0.7\,\text{m}\,\text{s}^{-2}$ up a uniform slope at an angle α with the horizontal, where $\sin\alpha = 0.1$. At this speed, the air resistance to its motion is $250\,\text{N}$. Other resistances to the motion of the car are negligible.

(i) Calculate the power of the driving force of the car. [5 marks]

The driver of the car sees an obstruction, removes the driving force and presses the brake pedal so hard that the wheels stop rotating and the car slides until it comes to rest.

You are given the following information:

- the car starts sliding when its speed is $12\,\text{m}\,\text{s}^{-1}$
- the coefficient of friction between the car's tyres and the road is 0.4
- the total work done against air resistance while the car is sliding is $1500\,\text{J}$.

(ii) Using an energy method, calculate the distance the car travels while it is sliding. [5 marks]

Practice Questions: Set 1

(iii) State a modelling assumption that is necessary in order to calculate the frictional force between the road and the sliding car. [1 mark]

④ A thin rigid uniform rectangular plank AB has weight W N and length 5 m. End A of the plank rests on a rough horizontal floor; a light string is attached to end B.

In one situation, the plank is in equilibrium at an angle α with the floor with the string horizontal and in tension. Figure 2 shows this information and the forces acting: W N is the weight of the plank; T N is the tension in the string; R N is the normal reaction of the floor on the plank; F N is the frictional force between the plank and the floor. The plank is on the point of slipping.

Figure 2

(i) Show that the coefficient of friction between the plank and the floor is $\dfrac{1}{2\tan\alpha}$. [5 marks]

In another situation, shown in Figure 3, the plank is in equilibrium with $\cos\alpha = \dfrac{3}{5}$ and the string at an angle β to the horizontal, where $\alpha + \beta = 90°$.

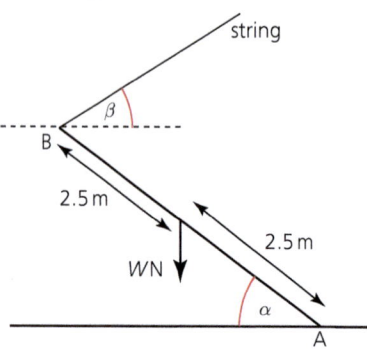

Figure 3

(ii) Draw a diagram showing the forces acting and find an expression for the range of values of the coefficient of friction between the plank and the floor. [9 marks]

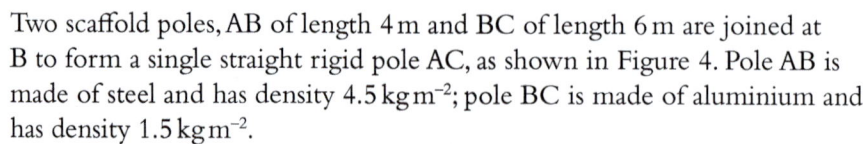

⑤ Two scaffold poles, AB of length 4 m and BC of length 6 m are joined at B to form a single straight rigid pole AC, as shown in Figure 4. Pole AB is made of steel and has density $4.5\,\text{kg}\,\text{m}^{-2}$; pole BC is made of aluminium and has density $1.5\,\text{kg}\,\text{m}^{-2}$.

Figure 4

(i) Show that the centre of mass of AC is $\dfrac{11}{3}$ m from A. [3 marks]

Pole OP is a copy of pole AC (so O is at the steel end).

These poles are joined so they are perpendicular with O at the centre of AC, as shown in Figure 5, to form the structure S. Figure 5 also shows the coordinate axes Ox and Oy.

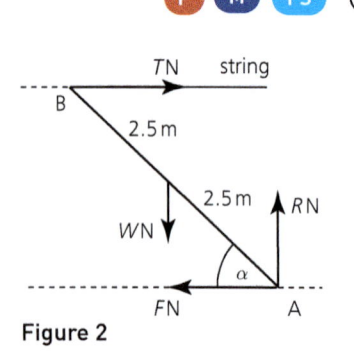

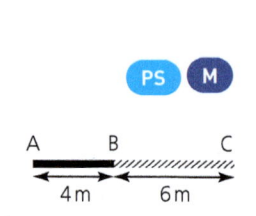

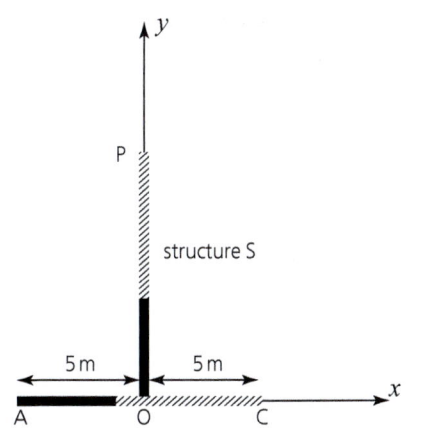

Figure 5

(ii) Find the coordinates of the centre of mass of S, referred to the axes shown in Figure 5. [4 marks]

S is freely suspended from P and hangs in equilibrium.

(iii) Calculate the angle of AC to the horizontal. [4 marks]

6. Figure 6 shows a rod OA of length 2 m and mass 0.25 kg with its centre of mass at G which is 1.6 m from O. The rod is attached to a hinge at O and moves only in a vertical plane. One end of a string is attached to end A of the rod. This string passes over a pulley at B and an object of mass m kg hangs from the other end of the string. OB is vertical and the distance OB is 2 m.

The angle AOB is θ and the angle OAB is ϕ.

Table 1

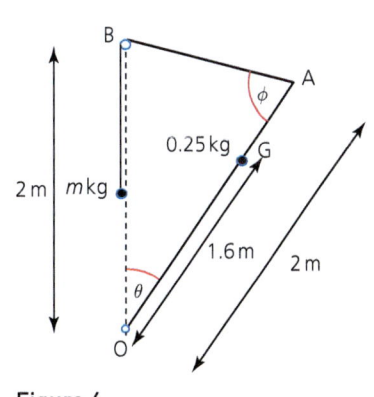

θ rad	c.w. moment	a.c. moment
1.1	3.493 532 851	4.177 370 158
1.15	3.578 034 646	4.112 042 282
1.2	3.653 593 217	4.044 144 513
1.25	3.720 019 708	3.973 719 286
1.3	3.777 148 087	3.900 810 613
1.35	3.824 835 563	3.825 464 061
1.4	3.862 962 942	3.747 726 718
1.45	3.891 434 925	3.667 647 168
1.5	3.910 180 347	3.585 275 457
1.55	3.919 152 356	3.500 663 067
1.6	3.918 328 524	3.413 862 876

Figure 6

A number of modelling assumptions are made: the rod is thin and rigid; the rod moves freely about the hinge; the string is light; the pulley is small and smooth; the object is a particle and hangs freely.

(i) Show that, for all θ such that $0 \leq \theta < \pi$, the clockwise (c.w.) moment about O is $0.4g\sin\theta$ and the anti-clockwise (a.c.) moment is $2mg\sin\phi$. [2 marks]

Practice Questions: Set 1

The system is set up with $m = 0.25$.

The values of the clockwise and anticlockwise moments of the forces acting on the rod predicted by the model for some values of θ are shown in Table 1.

(ii) Estimate the value of θ predicted by the model for which the system is in equilibrium. [1 mark]

The system is to be released from rest with $\theta = 1.3$.

(iii) Using the values in the table, state what the model predicts will happen. [1 mark]

When the experiment is carried out it is found that the system does not move.

(iv) What does this tell you about the model? [1 mark]

9 Motion under a variable force

→ The Hubble space telescope floats against a background of Earth in this photograph from the service module used to repair it. How would you describe its motion?

Evolution has ensured that our brains just aren't equipped to visualise 11 dimensions directly. However, from a purely mathematical point of view it is just as easy to think in 11 dimensions as it is to think in 3 or 4.
Steven Hawking

1 Motion in more than one dimension

The first chapter of this book covers motion along a straight line. This is now extended to cover motion in 2 and 3 dimensions. The first step is to establish the notation and vocabulary.

Notation and vocabulary

Position

In 2 dimensions the **position** of a point is usually defined using standard x-y axes. Figure 9.1 shows a general point A with position (x, y).

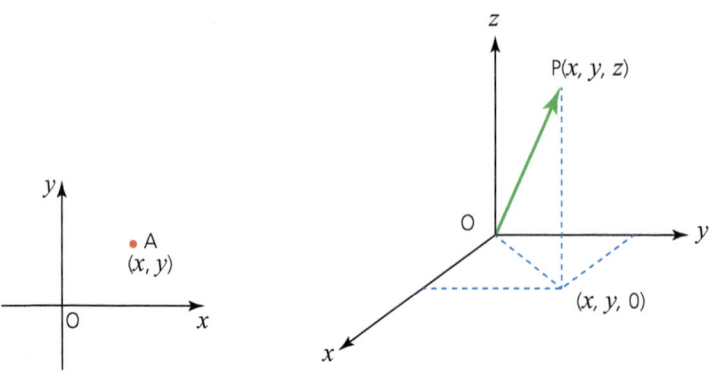

Figure 9.1

Figure 9.2

The equivalent in 3 dimensions is the general point P in Figure 9.2 with coordinates (x, y, z).

Position vector

The displacement of a point from the origin, in this case $\overrightarrow{OA}$ or $\overrightarrow{OP}$, is called its **position vector**. A position vector is often denoted by **r**.

In 2 dimensions, this can be given in terms of unit vectors **i** and **j** parallel to the x and y axes, or as a column vector.

Thus $\overrightarrow{OA} = \mathbf{r} = x\mathbf{i} + y\mathbf{j} = \begin{pmatrix} x \\ y \end{pmatrix}$.

In 3 dimensions, the unit vectors are **i**, **j** and **k**.

$\overrightarrow{OP} = \mathbf{r} = x\mathbf{i} + y\mathbf{j} + z\mathbf{k} = \begin{pmatrix} x \\ y \\ z \end{pmatrix}$.

In 2 dimensions

Figure 9.3

In 3 dimensions

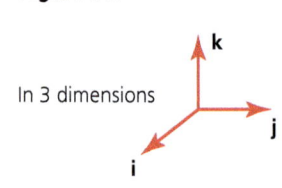

Figure 9.4

> **Note**
> Notice that vector quantities are always shown in bold type.

Displacement

The displacement of a point T from a point S is the vector $\overrightarrow{ST}$. The term can be used whatever the number of dimensions.

Distance

Distance is the length of the displacement. It is a scalar quantity. Thus the distance of the point A from the origin is $\sqrt{x^2 + y^2}$. The 3-dimensional equivalent for P is $\sqrt{x^2 + y^2 + z^2}$. This distance is denoted by r or $|\mathbf{r}|$.

Velocity

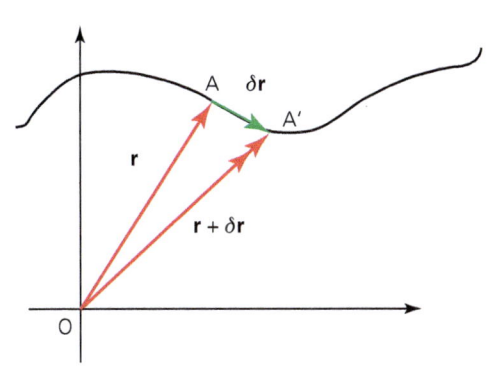

Figure 9.5

Figure 9.5 shows a particle moving in 2 dimensions from A at time t to A′ at time $t + \delta t$.

The displacement is $\overrightarrow{AA'} = \delta\mathbf{r}$, where $\delta\mathbf{r}$ is the vector $\delta x \mathbf{i} + \delta y \mathbf{j}$; δx and δy are small increments in the direction of the x and y axes.

The average **velocity** during the time interval δt is given by
$$\frac{\delta r}{\delta t} = \frac{\delta x}{\delta t}\mathbf{i} + \frac{\delta y}{\delta t}\mathbf{j}.$$

As $\delta t \to 0$ and A approaches A′, $\frac{\delta r}{\delta t}$ tends to the limiting vector $\frac{d\mathbf{r}}{dt}$, the derivative of $\mathbf{r}$ with respect to t.

The **velocity** of P is given by

$$\mathbf{v} = \frac{d\mathbf{r}}{dt} = \frac{dx}{dt}\mathbf{i} + \frac{dy}{dt}\mathbf{j}$$

This can also be written as $\mathbf{v} = \dot{x}\mathbf{i} + \dot{y}\mathbf{j} = \begin{pmatrix} \dot{x} \\ \dot{y} \end{pmatrix}$.

> **Note**
> A dot placed above the variable means differentiation with respect to time.

The equivalent ways of writing velocity in 3 dimensions are

$$\mathbf{v} = \frac{d\mathbf{r}}{dt} = \frac{dx}{dt}\mathbf{i} + \frac{dy}{dt}\mathbf{j} + \frac{dz}{dt}\mathbf{k} = \dot{x}\mathbf{i} + \dot{y}\mathbf{j} + \dot{z}\mathbf{k} = \begin{pmatrix} \dot{x} \\ \dot{y} \\ \dot{z} \end{pmatrix}.$$

Speed

Speed is a the magnitude of velocity, written v or $|\mathbf{v}|$ and so it is a scalar quantity. In 2 dimensions it is given by $\sqrt{\dot{x}^2 + \dot{y}^2}$ (and equivalent forms) and in 3 dimensions by $\sqrt{\dot{x}^2 + \dot{y}^2 + \dot{z}^2}$

The speed of P is then given by $|\mathbf{v}| = \sqrt{\dot{x}^2 + \dot{y}^2 + \dot{z}^2}$.

Motion in more than one dimension

Acceleration

Acceleration is the rate of change of velocity. It is a vector quantity. So its derivation from velocity is similar to that of velocity from displacement and it is given by

$$\mathbf{a} = \frac{d\mathbf{v}}{dt} = \frac{d^2\mathbf{r}}{dt^2}.$$

There are several equivalent ways of writing acceleration including the following.

2 dimensions

$$\mathbf{a} = \ddot{x}\mathbf{i} + \ddot{y}\mathbf{j} = \begin{pmatrix} \ddot{x} \\ \ddot{y} \end{pmatrix}$$

3 dimensions

$$\mathbf{a} = \ddot{x}\mathbf{i} + \ddot{y}\mathbf{j} + \ddot{z}\mathbf{k} = \begin{pmatrix} \ddot{x} \\ \ddot{y} \\ \ddot{z} \end{pmatrix}$$

Magnitude of acceleration

Magnitude of acceleration, denoted by a or $|\mathbf{a}|$, is given by $\sqrt{\ddot{x}^2 + \ddot{y}^2}$ or equivalent forms in 2 dimensions and by $\sqrt{\ddot{x}^2 + \ddot{y}^2 + \ddot{z}^2}$ in 3 dimensions. It is a scalar quantity.

Example 9.1

The position vector of a particle at time t seconds is given in metres by

$$\mathbf{r} = t^2\mathbf{i} - 5t\mathbf{j} + (t^2 - 1)\mathbf{k}$$

(i) Find expressions for its velocity $\mathbf{v}$ and acceleration $\mathbf{a}$.

(ii) Calculate the distance of the particle from the origin, its speed and the magnitude of its acceleration when $t = 2$.

Solution

(i) The velocity is the rate of change of the position vector.

$$\mathbf{v} = \frac{d\mathbf{r}}{dt} = 2t\mathbf{i} - 5\mathbf{j} + 2t\mathbf{k}$$

The acceleration is the rate of change of the velocity.

$$\mathbf{a} = \frac{d\mathbf{v}}{dt} = \frac{d^2\mathbf{r}}{dt^2} = 2\mathbf{i} + 2\mathbf{k}$$

(ii) When $t = 2$, $\mathbf{r} = \begin{pmatrix} 4 \\ -10 \\ 3 \end{pmatrix}$

So the distance of the particle from the origin is

$$\sqrt{4^2 + (-10)^2 + 3^2} = \sqrt{125} = 11.18\ldots \text{ m}$$

It is moving with velocity $\begin{pmatrix} 4 \\ -5 \\ 4 \end{pmatrix}$.

So its speed is $\sqrt{4^2 + (-5)^2 + 4^2} = \sqrt{57} = 7.54\ldots$ ms^{-1}

Its acceleration is $\begin{pmatrix} 2 \\ 0 \\ 2 \end{pmatrix}$.

So the magnitude of its acceleration is $\sqrt{2^2 + 2^2} = 2.82\ldots$ ms^{-2}

You have seen how successive differentiation allows you to use an expression for a position vector in terms of time to find expressions for velocity and acceleration. Similarly, you may use the same process in reverse and use integration with respect to time to find the velocity and position vector of a point from its acceleration.

$$\mathbf{v} = \int \mathbf{a}\, dt \text{ and } \mathbf{r} = \int \mathbf{v}\, dt$$

These results are summarised in the table below.

Position	→ differentiate ← integrate	Velocity	→ differentiate ← integrate	Acceleration

The next example illustrates the use of integration in this way.

Example 9.2

A particle of mass 5 kg is initially at rest at a point (2, 3). It is acted on by a force

$\mathbf{F} = 20t\mathbf{i} + (30 - 10t)\mathbf{j}$ N

where t is the time in seconds.

Find, when $t = 5$,

(i) the magnitude of the acceleration

(ii) the speed

(iii) the distance of the particle from the origin.

Solution

(i) By Newton's second law, $\mathbf{F} = m\mathbf{a}$

So $\mathbf{a} = \dfrac{\mathbf{F}}{m} = \dfrac{(20t\mathbf{i} + (30 - 10t)\mathbf{j})}{5}$

$= 4t\mathbf{i} + (6 - 2t)\mathbf{j}$

When $t = 5$, $\mathbf{a} = 20\mathbf{i} - 4\mathbf{j}$

and $a = |\mathbf{a}| = \sqrt{20^2 + (-4)^2} = 20.4$, in ms^{-2}.

Motion in more than one dimension

> c_1 and c_2 are constants of integration, one for each component.

(ii) Integrating **a** with respect to t gives
$$\mathbf{v} = \left(2t^2 + c_1\right)\mathbf{i} + \left(6t - t^2 + c_2\right)\mathbf{j}$$

Initially, the particle is at rest, so $\mathbf{v} = \mathbf{0}$ at $t = 0$

> Both components of **v** must be zero if **v** = **0**.

$\Rightarrow c_1 = c_2 = 0$.

$$\mathbf{v} = 2t^2\mathbf{i} + \left(6t - t^2\right)\mathbf{j}$$

When $t = 5$, $\mathbf{v} = 50\mathbf{i} + 5\mathbf{j}$ and $v = |\mathbf{v}| = \sqrt{50^2 + 5^2} = 50.2$, in ms^{-1}.

(iii) Integrating again gives
$$\mathbf{r} = \left(\tfrac{2}{3}t^3 + k_1\right)\mathbf{i} + \left(3t^2 - \tfrac{1}{3}t^3 + k_2\right)\mathbf{j}$$

> This comes from using $\mathbf{r} = \int \mathbf{v}\, dt$

Substituting the initial condition, that $\mathbf{r} = 2\mathbf{i} + 3\mathbf{j}$ when $t = 0$, gives $k_1 = 2$ and $k_2 = 3$.

Therefore $\mathbf{r} = \left(\tfrac{2}{3}t^3 + 2\right)\mathbf{i} + \left(3t^2 - \tfrac{1}{3}t^3 + 3\right)\mathbf{j}$

When $t = 5$, $\mathbf{r} = \tfrac{256}{3}\mathbf{i} + \tfrac{109}{3}\mathbf{j}$ and $r = |\mathbf{r}| = 92.7$, in m.

The constant acceleration formulae

You can use integration to obtain the constant acceleration formulae.

When the acceleration **a** is a constant vector, $\mathbf{v} = \int \mathbf{a}\, dt = \mathbf{a}t + \mathbf{c}$

If the initial velocity is **u**, then $\mathbf{v} = \mathbf{u}$ when $t = 0$, leading to $\mathbf{c} = \mathbf{u}$ and

$$\mathbf{v} = \mathbf{u} + \mathbf{a}t \qquad \text{①}$$

Integrating again gives $\mathbf{r} = \int \mathbf{v}\, dt = \int (\mathbf{u} + \mathbf{a}t)\, dt$

$$\mathbf{r} = \mathbf{u}t + \tfrac{1}{2}\mathbf{a}t^2 + \mathbf{n}$$

Initially $\mathbf{r} = \mathbf{r}_0$, so $\mathbf{r}_0 = \mathbf{k}$ and $\mathbf{r} = \mathbf{u}t + \tfrac{1}{2}\mathbf{a}t^2 + \mathbf{r}_0 \qquad \text{②}$

Rearrange ① to give $\mathbf{a}t = \mathbf{v} - \mathbf{u}$, which is substituted in ② to give

$$\mathbf{r} = \mathbf{u}t + \tfrac{1}{2}(\mathbf{v} - \mathbf{u})t + \mathbf{r}_0$$

$$\mathbf{r} = \tfrac{1}{2}(\mathbf{u} + \mathbf{v})t + \mathbf{r}_0 \qquad \text{③}$$

Rearrange ① to give $\mathbf{u} = \mathbf{v} - \mathbf{a}t$, and substitute in ② to give

$$\mathbf{r} = (\mathbf{v} - \mathbf{a}t)t + \tfrac{1}{2}\mathbf{a}t^2 + \mathbf{r}_0$$

$$\mathbf{r} = \mathbf{v}t - \tfrac{1}{2}\mathbf{a}t^2 + \mathbf{r}_0 \qquad \text{④}$$

Equations ①–④ are the vector equivalent of the constant acceleration formulae used for motion in one dimension found in Chapter 1.

Motion in one dimension	Vector form
$v = u + at$	$\mathbf{v} = \mathbf{u} + \mathbf{a}t$
$s = ut + \frac{1}{2}at^2 + s_0$	$\mathbf{r} = \mathbf{u}t + \frac{1}{2}\mathbf{a}t^2 + \mathbf{r}_0$
$s = \frac{1}{2}(u+v)t + s_0$	$\mathbf{r} = \frac{1}{2}(\mathbf{u}+\mathbf{v})t + \mathbf{r}_0$
$s = vt - \frac{1}{2}at^2 + s_0$	$\mathbf{r} = \mathbf{v}t - \frac{1}{2}\mathbf{a}t^2 + \mathbf{r}_0$

In the case of one dimension, there is a fifth equation $[v^2 = u^2 + 2a(s - s_0)]$. There is a vector form of this equation which can be found by use of the scalar product between two vectors.

The scalar product between two vectors **A** and **B** is defined as

$$\mathbf{A}.\mathbf{B} = \begin{pmatrix} A_x \\ A_y \\ A_z \end{pmatrix} . \begin{pmatrix} B_x \\ B_y \\ B_z \end{pmatrix} = A_x B_x + A_y B_y + A_z B_z$$

From equation ③: $\mathbf{r} - \mathbf{r}_0 = \frac{1}{2}(\mathbf{u}+\mathbf{v})t$

From equation ①: $\mathbf{a} = \dfrac{\mathbf{v} - \mathbf{u}}{t}$

$$\Rightarrow \quad 2\mathbf{a}.(\mathbf{r} - \mathbf{r}_0) = 2\left(\dfrac{\mathbf{v} - \mathbf{u}}{t}\right).\dfrac{1}{2}(\mathbf{u}+\mathbf{v})t$$

$$= (\mathbf{v} - \mathbf{u}).(\mathbf{u} + \mathbf{v})$$

$$= \mathbf{v}.\mathbf{v} - \mathbf{u}.\mathbf{u} = v^2 - u^2$$

$$\Rightarrow \quad 2\mathbf{a}.(\mathbf{r} - \mathbf{r}_0) = v^2 - u^2 \qquad ⑤$$

> The magnitude of any vector, say **p**, is denoted by p or $|\mathbf{p}|$. This is given by
> $p = \sqrt{p_x^2 + p_y^2 + p_z^2}$ and so
> $p^2 = p_x^2 + p_y^2 + p_z^2 = \mathbf{p}.\mathbf{p}$.
> In this case $\mathbf{v}.\mathbf{v} = v^2$ and $\mathbf{u}.\mathbf{u} = u^2$.

This is the vector form of the fifth constant acceleration equation.

Example 9.3

A particle is moving with constant acceleration $\mathbf{a} = \begin{pmatrix} 3 \\ -5 \end{pmatrix}$. It passes O at $t = 0$ with initial velocity.

$\mathbf{u} = \begin{pmatrix} -1 \\ 3 \end{pmatrix}$. The unit vectors $\begin{pmatrix} 1 \\ 0 \end{pmatrix}$ and $\begin{pmatrix} 0 \\ 1 \end{pmatrix}$ are in the directions due east and due north, respectively.

(i) Show that after 1 s the particle is moving south-east and find its speed.

(ii) Calculate the bearing of the particle from O after it has been moving for 2.5 s.

Motion in more than one dimension

Solution

(i) Use the formula $\mathbf{v} = \mathbf{u} + \mathbf{a}t$

[a is constant so you can use the constant acceleration formulae]

$$\mathbf{v} = \begin{pmatrix} -1 \\ 3 \end{pmatrix} + \begin{pmatrix} 3 \\ -5 \end{pmatrix} t$$

$$= \begin{pmatrix} -1 + 3t \\ 3 - 5t \end{pmatrix}$$

After 1 s $\quad \mathbf{v} = \begin{pmatrix} 2 \\ -2 \end{pmatrix}$

The bearing of the motion is $(90° + \theta)$

$$\theta = \arctan 1 = 45°$$

So that the bearing is $90° + 45° = 135°$.

[The angle θ is shown in Figure 9.6]

The speed of the particle is
$\sqrt{2^2 + 2^2} = \sqrt{8} = 2.82 \text{ m s}^{-1}$.

The particle is moving south-east with speed 2.82 m s^{-1}.

[The direction of motion is the direction of v]

Figure 9.6

(ii) Use the formula $\mathbf{r} = \mathbf{u}t + \frac{1}{2}\mathbf{a}t^2$

Substituting $t = 2.5$ gives:

$$\mathbf{r} = \begin{pmatrix} -1 \\ 3 \end{pmatrix} \times 2.5 + 0.5 \times \begin{pmatrix} 3 \\ -5 \end{pmatrix} \times 6.25$$

$$= \begin{pmatrix} -2.5 \\ 7.5 \end{pmatrix} + \begin{pmatrix} 9.375 \\ -15.625 \end{pmatrix}$$

$$= \begin{pmatrix} 6.875 \\ -8.125 \end{pmatrix}$$

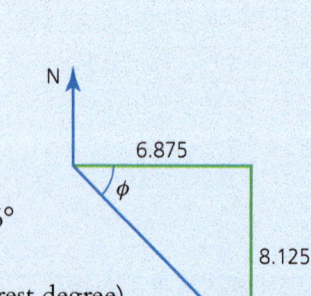

$$\phi = \arctan\left(\frac{8.125}{6.875}\right) = 49.76°$$

[The position of the particle r determines its bearing.]

So the bearing is $90° + 49.46° = 140°$ (nearest degree)

The bearing of the particle from O after 2.5 s is $140°$.

Figure 9.7

Exercise 9.1

① The position vector of a moving point P at time t seconds is given by
$$\mathbf{r} = 4t\mathbf{i} + 3t^2\mathbf{j}$$
Find the speed of P at time $t = 2$

② At time t seconds a particle has position vector
$$\mathbf{r} = 2t^3\mathbf{i} + (t^2 - 5)\mathbf{j}$$
$\mathbf{i}$ and $\mathbf{j}$ are unit vectors in the directions east and north.
Find the speed of the particle and its direction of motion when $t = 1$.

③ A particle P of mass m kg is at the point with position vector

$$\mathbf{r} = \begin{pmatrix} 2t^3 + t \\ 3t \\ 5t^2 - 2 \end{pmatrix}$$

at time t. Find the acceleration of P at time t and the force required to produce this acceleration.

④ A particle P of mass 2 kg is acted on by a force $\mathbf{F}(t) = \begin{pmatrix} 5t \\ 2t \\ 3 \end{pmatrix}$. Initially P is at a point $(0, 1, 3)$ and is moving with velocity $\begin{pmatrix} 2 \\ 0 \\ 5 \end{pmatrix}$. Find the position vector of P at time t.

⑤ A particle moves with constant acceleration so that its velocity at time t is given by $\mathbf{v} = (5 - 0.1t)\mathbf{i} + (3 + 0.2t)\mathbf{j}$, where $\mathbf{i}$ and $\mathbf{j}$, are unit vectors in directions east and north.

(i) Write down $\mathbf{a}$ and $\mathbf{u}$.

(ii) Find the time t when the particle is travelling in the direction NE and find its speed.

(iii) Find the distance and bearing of the particle from its starting point at that time.

⑥ A particle has position vector $\mathbf{r} = 3t^2\mathbf{i} - 4t\mathbf{j}$ at time t. Find the angle between its position vector and its direction of motion at time $t = 2$.

⑦ Two forces $\mathbf{F}_1 = \begin{pmatrix} 5 \\ -8 \\ 6 \end{pmatrix}$ and $\mathbf{F}_2 = \begin{pmatrix} 3 \\ 2 \\ -2 \end{pmatrix}$ are acting on a particle of mass 2 kg.

(i) Find the resultant force acting on the particle and hence the acceleration of the particle.

(ii) When $t = 10$ seconds, the velocity of the particle is given by $\mathbf{v} = \begin{pmatrix} 10 \\ -15 \\ 30 \end{pmatrix}$. Find the initial velocity $\mathbf{u}$.

(iii) Find when the speed of the particle is $10\sqrt{5}$.

⑧ Calculate the magnitude and direction of the acceleration of a particle that moves so that its position vector in metres is given by

$$\mathbf{r} = (3 + 5t - 6t^2)\mathbf{i} + (8 - 3t - 2.5t^2)\mathbf{j}$$

where t is the time in seconds and $\mathbf{i}$ and $\mathbf{j}$ are unit vectors in the directions east and north.

⑨ A particle is initially at rest at the origin. It experiences an acceleration given by $\mathbf{a} = 4t\mathbf{i} + (6 - 2t)\mathbf{j}$, where $\mathbf{i}$ and $\mathbf{j}$ are unit vectors in the directions east and north.

(i) Find expressions for the velocity and position of the particle at time t.

(ii) At what time is the particle moving north-east and what is its speed?

(iii) How far is the particle from O, when $t = 2$. What is its bearing from O?

⑩ A speed boat is initially moving at 5 m s^{-1} on a bearing of 120°.

(i) Express the initial velocity as a vector in terms of $\mathbf{i}$ and $\mathbf{j}$, which are unit vectors east and north, respectively.

The boat then begins to accelerate with an acceleration modelled by $\mathbf{a} = 0.2t\mathbf{i} + 0.1t\mathbf{j}$ in m s^{-2}.

Motion in more than one dimension

(ii) Find the velocity of the boat 10 seconds after it begins to accelerate and its displacement over the 10 second period.

⑪ At time t, a particle has position vector with respect to an origin O given by $\mathbf{r} = \begin{pmatrix} 20t+12 \\ 15t^2 - t^3 \end{pmatrix}$, and $\begin{pmatrix} 1 \\ 0 \end{pmatrix}$ and $\begin{pmatrix} 0 \\ 1 \end{pmatrix}$ are unit vectors in the east and north directions, respectively.

(i) When $t = 2$ the particle is at P. Find the distance and bearing of P from O.
(ii) Find the velocity of the particle at time t and show that it is never 0.
(iii) Determine the value of t when the acceleration is zero.
(iv) Find the maximum speed of the particle.

⑫ A rock of mass 6 kg is acted on by forces $-60\mathbf{k}$ N and $(-\mathbf{i} + 12\mathbf{j} + 54\mathbf{k})$ N, where $\mathbf{i}$ and $\mathbf{j}$ are perpendicular unit vectors in a horizontal plane and $\mathbf{k}$ is a unit vector vertically upward.

(i) Show that the acceleration of the rock is $-\frac{1}{6}\mathbf{i} + 2\mathbf{j} - \mathbf{k}$ m s⁻²

The rock passes through the origin O, with velocity $(\mathbf{i} - 6\mathbf{j} + 4\mathbf{k})$ m s⁻¹ and 6 seconds later passes through A.

(ii) Find the position vector of A.
(iii) Find the distance OA.
(iv) Find the angle that OA makes with the horizontal.

⑬ A force $\mathbf{F} = (9\mathbf{i} + 12\mathbf{j})$ N acts on a particle P of mass 5 kg which is free to move in a horizontal plane.

(i) Calculate the magnitude of the acceleration of P.

Initially the particle passes through a fixed point A with speed 2 m s⁻¹ in the same direction as $\mathbf{F}$.

(ii) Show that the velocity of the particle at time t is $\mathbf{v} = \left(\frac{2}{3} + t\right)(1.8\mathbf{i} + 2.4\mathbf{j})$.
(iii) Find the vector $\overrightarrow{AP}$ at time t.
(iv) A is the point (30, 25). Find the vector $\overrightarrow{OP}$ at time $= 5$.

⑭ At time t s, a particle of mass m kg has a position vector $\mathbf{r}$ relative to a fixed origin, where $\mathbf{r} = \cos(\lambda t^2)\mathbf{i} + \sin(\lambda t^2)\mathbf{j} + \lambda t^2 \mathbf{k}$

(i) Find expressions for the velocity and acceleration of the particle at time t.
(ii) Show that the particle is initially at rest and that the acceleration has magnitude $2\sqrt{2}\lambda$.
(iii) Find in terms of m, λ and t, an expression for the kinetic energy T of the particle.
(iv) Show that $T = c\mathbf{k}.\mathbf{r}$ where c is a constant to be found.

2 The equation of a path

Once you know the position vector **r** of a moving point in terms of t, you can trace the path followed by the point. This is shown in the following example.

Example 9.4

A ball is hit into the air across level horizontal ground. Its position vector in metres at time t seconds is modelled by the equation

$$\mathbf{r} = \begin{pmatrix} x \\ y \end{pmatrix} = \begin{pmatrix} 60t \\ 11t - 5t^2 \end{pmatrix}$$

This is the position vector of a particle projected with initial velocity $\begin{pmatrix} 60 \\ 11 \end{pmatrix}$ and acceleration $\begin{pmatrix} 0 \\ -10 \end{pmatrix}$.

(i) Plot the path of the ball while it is in the air
(ii) Find the equation of the trajectory of the ball.
(iii) Comment on the shape of the trajectory.

Solution

According to the equation
$$x = 60t$$
$$y = 11t - 5t^2$$

The table below gives the values of the vector **r** at intervals of 0.5 seconds and also for $t = 2.2$, incorporating the values of x and y.

At $t = 2.2$ the ball hits the ground and so the motion is over. It is the time when $y = 0$.

t	0	0.5	1	1.5	2	2.2
r	$\begin{pmatrix} 0 \\ 0 \end{pmatrix}$	$\begin{pmatrix} 30 \\ 4.25 \end{pmatrix}$	$\begin{pmatrix} 60 \\ 6 \end{pmatrix}$	$\begin{pmatrix} 90 \\ 5.25 \end{pmatrix}$	$\begin{pmatrix} 120 \\ 2 \end{pmatrix}$	$\begin{pmatrix} 132 \\ 0 \end{pmatrix}$

(i) The figures are plotted on the graph.

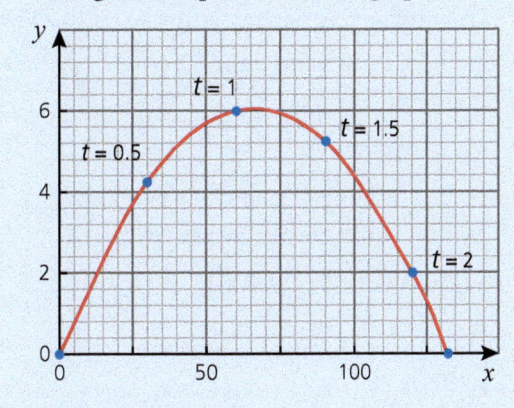

Figure 9.8

The equation of a path

(ii) The Cartesian equation of the path can be found by eliminating t between the two variables x and y.

$$x = 60t \quad \Rightarrow \quad t = \frac{x}{60}$$

$$y = 11 \times \frac{x}{60} - 5 \times \left(\frac{x}{60}\right)^2$$

$$y = \frac{11x}{60} - \frac{x^2}{720}$$

$y = 0 \Rightarrow$
$\frac{x}{720}(11 \times 12 - x) = 0$
i.e. $x = 0$ or $x = 132$.

(iii)
- The curve in the graph looks like a parabola. This is consistent with the quadratic form of its equation.
- Substituting $y = 0$ into the equation $y = \frac{11x}{60} - \frac{x^2}{720}$ gives $x = 0$ or 132 and this is shown by the graph.
- Putting $\frac{dy}{dx} = 0$ indicates a maximum value of 6.05 when $x = 66$ and this too appears to be consistent with the graph.

$\frac{dy}{dx} = \frac{11}{60} - \frac{x}{360} = \frac{1}{360}(66-x)$
$= 0$ when $x = 66 \Rightarrow$
$y_m = \frac{11}{60} \times 66 - \frac{66^2}{720}$
$= 12.1 - 6.05 = 6.05$

When the position vector $\mathbf{r}$ is given as a function of t, both x and y are expressed in terms of a third variable t, i.e $x = f(t)$ and $y = g(t)$

The variable t is known as the **parameter**, and the equations are described as parametric equations of the curve.

The Cartesian equation of the curve links y and x directly and, as seen in the previous example, can then be found by eliminating the parameter from the parametric equations. The dependence of y on x may not always be explicit; you may not always be able to write y as a function of x, but there will be an implicit dependence which may be written as $F(x, y) = 0$ where F is a function of both x and y.

Example 9.5

A particle P is initially at the origin and moving with velocity $\begin{pmatrix} 5 \\ 0 \end{pmatrix}$. It is subject to an acceleration $\mathbf{a} = \begin{pmatrix} 0 \\ 2 - 3t \end{pmatrix}$.

(i) Find expressions for (a) the velocity and (b) the position vector of P at time t.

(ii) Eliminate t between the 2 variables x and y to find the Cartesian equation of the path of P.

(iii) Plot the path of P.

Solution

(i) (a) $\mathbf{v} = \int \mathbf{a}\, dt$

So $\mathbf{v} = \int \begin{pmatrix} 0 \\ 2 - 3t \end{pmatrix} dt = \begin{pmatrix} c_1 \\ 2t - 1.5t^2 + c_2 \end{pmatrix}$

Using the initial condition $\mathbf{v} = \begin{pmatrix} 5 \\ 0 \end{pmatrix}$ at $t = 0$ gives $c_1 = 5$ and $c_2 = 0$

So the velocity is given by
$$\mathbf{v} = \begin{pmatrix} 5 \\ 2t - 1.5t^2 \end{pmatrix}$$

(b) Integrating again gives
$$\mathbf{r} = \begin{pmatrix} 5t + k_1 \\ t^2 - 0.5t^3 + k_2 \end{pmatrix}$$

Using the initial condition $\mathbf{r} = 0$ at $t = 0$ gives $k_1 = k_2 = 0$.
So the position vector is
$$\mathbf{r} = \begin{pmatrix} x \\ y \end{pmatrix} = \begin{pmatrix} 5t \\ t^2 - 0.5t^3 \end{pmatrix}$$

(ii) The position vector gives equations for x and y with parameter t

$$x = 5t \qquad \text{①}$$
and $\qquad y = t^2 - 0.5t^3 \qquad \text{②}$

To eliminate the parameter, rearrange ① to give $t = \dfrac{x}{5}$.
Substituting for t in ② to give

$$y = \left(\dfrac{x}{5}\right)^2 - 0.5\left(\dfrac{x}{5}\right)^3$$
$$y = 0.04x^2 - 0.004x^3$$

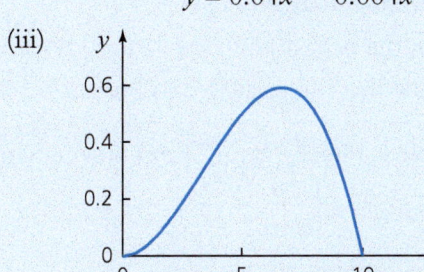

$\dfrac{dy}{dx} = 0.08x - 0.012x^2$

$= 0.004x(20 - 3x)$

$\dfrac{dy}{dx} = 0$ when $x = 0$ or

$x = \dfrac{20}{3} = 6\dfrac{2}{3}$ and $y = 0$ or

$y = 0.04 \times 6.6^2 - 0.004 \times 6.6^3 = 0.59$.
The curve has a minimum at $(0,0)$ and a maximum at $(6.6, 0.59)$.

(iii)

Figure 9.9

$y = 0.004x^2(10 - x) = 0$ when $x = 0$ or $x = 10$.

The curve goes through the points $(0, 0)$, $(10, 0)$ and $(6.6, 0.59)$

Exercise 9.2

① In each of the following cases, find the Cartesian equation of the path of the particle with position vector given by

(i) $\mathbf{r} = 5t\mathbf{i} + (12t - 5t^2)\mathbf{j}$

(ii) $\mathbf{r} = \begin{pmatrix} 2t^2 \\ 8t \end{pmatrix}$

(iii) $\mathbf{r} = (4t - 3)\mathbf{i} + (2 + 3t - 5t^2)\mathbf{j}$

(iv) $\mathbf{r} = \begin{pmatrix} 5t^2 \\ 4 - t^2 \end{pmatrix}$

The equation of a path

    (v) $\mathbf{r} = (t^3 + t)\mathbf{i} + (5t^3 + 1)\mathbf{j}$

    (vi) $\mathbf{r} = \begin{pmatrix} e^t \\ t^2 \end{pmatrix}$

    (vii) $\mathbf{r} = 2t\mathbf{i} + \dfrac{5}{t}\mathbf{j}$

2. In each of the following cases, plot the path of the moving point with position vector

    (i) $\mathbf{r} = 2t^2\mathbf{i} + (4t - t^2)\mathbf{j};\ 0 \leq t \leq 4$

    (ii) $\mathbf{r} = \begin{pmatrix} t^2(6-t) \\ 12.5 + 4.5t^2 - t^3 \end{pmatrix};\ 0 \leq t \leq 5$

    (iii) $\mathbf{r} = 3\cos t\,\mathbf{i} + 4\sin 2t\,\mathbf{j};\ 0 \leq t \leq 2\pi$

3. In each of the following cases, the velocity $\mathbf{v}$ of a particle is given in terms of t, as

    (A) $\mathbf{v} = 4\mathbf{i} + (3 - 10t)\mathbf{j}$

    (B) $\mathbf{v} = 3\mathbf{i} + (6t - t^2)\mathbf{j}$

    (i) Find the displacement vector.

    (ii) Find the Cartesian equation of the path.

4. The velocity $\mathbf{v}$ of a particle is given in terms of t as

$$\mathbf{v} = (2 + t)\mathbf{i} + (5 - 2t)\mathbf{j}$$

    (i)   Find the displacement vector.

    (ii) Plot the path of the particle for $0 \leq t \leq 5$.

    (iii) Show that the particle has constant acceleration and state its magnitude.

5. A particle is initially at $\begin{pmatrix} 0 \\ 80 \end{pmatrix}$ and moving with initial velocity $\mathbf{u} = \begin{pmatrix} 30 \\ 0 \end{pmatrix}$ and acceleration $\mathbf{a} = \begin{pmatrix} -2 \\ -10 \end{pmatrix}$.

    (i)   Find the velocity at time t.

    (ii) Find the position vector at time t.

    (iii) Plot the path of the particle for $0 \leq t \leq 4$.

6. A particle initially at O is moving with initial velocity $\mathbf{u} = \begin{pmatrix} 10 \\ 20 \end{pmatrix}$ under the acceleration $\mathbf{a} = \begin{pmatrix} 0 \\ 3 - 12t \end{pmatrix}$.

    (i)   Find the velocity $\mathbf{v}$ at time t.

    (ii) Find the position vector at time t.

    (iii) Find the Cartesian equation of the path.

    (iv) Sketch the graph of the path followed by the particle.

7. The position vector of a particle at time t s is given by $\mathbf{r} = \begin{pmatrix} 3\cos t \\ 3\sin t \end{pmatrix}$. Distances are in metres.

    (i)   Show that the equation of the path of the particle is $x^2 + y^2 = 9$. Describe this path.

    (ii) Find the velocity and acceleration of the particle at time t, giving your answers as column vectors.

    (iii) Show that both the speed and the magnitude of the acceleration of the particle are constant.

    (iv) Show that, at all times, $\ddot{\mathbf{r}} = -\mathbf{r}$.

⑧ The position vector, in metres, of a particle at time t s is given by
$$\mathbf{r} = \begin{pmatrix} 1 + 2\cos 3t \\ -1 + 2\sin 3t \end{pmatrix}.$$

(i) Find the equation of the path of the particle and describe it.

(ii) Find the velocity and acceleration of the particle at time t, giving your answers as column vectors.

(iii) Show that at all times $\ddot{\mathbf{r}} = -\omega^2(\mathbf{r} + \mathbf{c})$ where ω and $\mathbf{c}$ are to be determined.

⑨ A force of $\begin{pmatrix} -8\cos 2t \\ 8\sin 2t \end{pmatrix}$ acts on particle of mass 2 kg.

Initially the particle has position vector $\begin{pmatrix} 3 \\ 4 \end{pmatrix}$ m and velocity $\begin{pmatrix} 0 \\ -2 \end{pmatrix}$ m s⁻¹.

Find the Cartesian equation of the path of the particle.

⑩ The graph shows the path of a particle.
The position vector of the particle at time t is given by $\mathbf{r} = \begin{pmatrix} \sin t \\ \cos 2t \end{pmatrix}$.

You may find it helpful to obtain this curve on a graphical calculator or other graph drawing software.

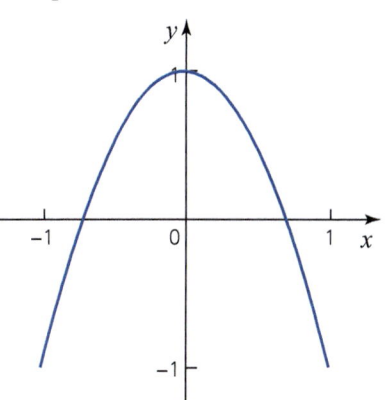

(i) Find the Cartesian equation of the curve and the coordinates of the points where it crosses the x- and y-axes.

(ii) The graph is drawn for $0 \leq t \leq T$. Find the least value of T for which the curve goes through one complete cycle.

Figure 9.10

(iii) Find the values of t when the particle is instantaneously stationary.

(iv) Describe the motion of the particle as it goes through one cycle and explain how you would use suitable software to show it.

(v) Using a spreadsheet or otherwise, determine the first time when the force acting on the particle has its minimum value. Give your answer to 2 decimal places.

3 Path of a projectile

Projectile motion is often described using the standard model. This requires a number of assumptions.

- The projectile is a particle.
- The acceleration due to gravity, g, is constant in magnitude and direction (towards the centre of the earth).
- Air resistance is neglected.

Note

The value of g varies slightly from one place to another and it decreases with height. A typical value at the earth's surface is 9.8 m s⁻² and this value is usually used in this book; however in places the value of 10 m s⁻² is used to simplify calculations.

Path of a projectile

In the following two examples, two further assumptions are made: that the projectile starts at ground level and that the ground is a horizontal plane.

Example 9.6

A projectile starts at ground level with initial speed u m s^{-1} at an angle α to the horizontal.

(i) Write its initial velocity and acceleration as vectors with horizontal and vertical components.

(ii) Write down equations for its velocity, $\mathbf{v}$ m s^{-1}, and position vector $\mathbf{r}$ m at time t s.

(iii) Obtain the Cartesian equation of its trajectory.

(iv) Draw the graph of its trajectory.

Solution

(i) Initial velocity $\mathbf{u} = \begin{pmatrix} u\cos\alpha \\ u\sin\alpha \end{pmatrix}$

Acceleration $\mathbf{a} = \begin{pmatrix} 0 \\ -g \end{pmatrix}$

> **Note**
> Another notation for the initial velocity is
> $\mathbf{u} = \begin{pmatrix} u_x \\ u_y \end{pmatrix}$

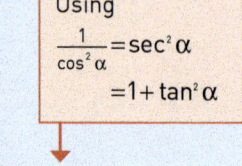

Using the constant acceleration formulae.

(ii) Velocity $\mathbf{v} = \begin{pmatrix} u\cos\alpha \\ u\sin\alpha \end{pmatrix} + \begin{pmatrix} 0 \\ -g \end{pmatrix} t$ or $\begin{pmatrix} v_x \\ v_y \end{pmatrix} = \begin{pmatrix} u\cos\alpha \\ u\sin\alpha - gt \end{pmatrix}$

Position vector $\mathbf{r} = \begin{pmatrix} u\cos\alpha \\ u\sin\alpha \end{pmatrix} t + \frac{1}{2}\begin{pmatrix} 0 \\ -g \end{pmatrix} t^2$ or $\begin{pmatrix} x \\ y \end{pmatrix} = \begin{pmatrix} ut\cos\alpha \\ ut\sin\alpha - \frac{1}{2}gt^2 \end{pmatrix}$

(iii) The equation of the trajectory $x = ut\cos\alpha \Rightarrow t = \dfrac{x}{u\cos\alpha}$

Substituting for t in the equation for
$y \Rightarrow y = u\sin\alpha \times \dfrac{x}{u\cos\alpha} - \dfrac{1}{2}g \times \left(\dfrac{x}{u\cos\alpha}\right)^2$

Using
$\dfrac{1}{\cos^2\alpha} = \sec^2\alpha$
$= 1 + \tan^2\alpha$

Tidying up gives: $y = x\tan\alpha - \dfrac{gx^2}{2u^2\cos^2\alpha}$

This can also be written as: $y = x\tan\alpha - \dfrac{gx^2(1+\tan^2\alpha)}{2u^2}$

(iv)

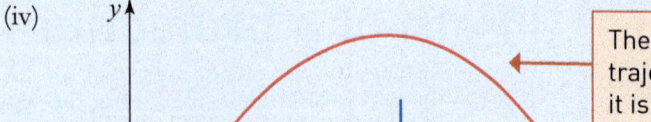

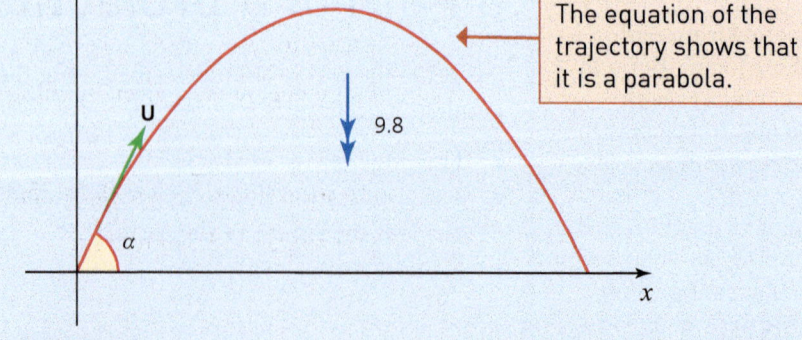

The equation of the trajectory shows that it is a parabola.

Figure 9.11

Example 9.7

A projectile starts at ground level with initial speed $20\,\text{ms}^{-1}$ at an angle $30°$ to the horizontal.

The ground is horizontal.

(i) Write down equations for its velocity and position vector at time t s.

(ii) Find its maximum height.

(iii) Find its range.

Solution

(i) Velocity $\mathbf{v} = \begin{pmatrix} 20\cos 30° \\ 20\sin 30° \end{pmatrix} + \begin{pmatrix} 0 \\ -g \end{pmatrix} t$

or $\begin{pmatrix} v_x \\ v_y \end{pmatrix} = \begin{pmatrix} 20 \times \dfrac{\sqrt{3}}{2} \\ 20 \times \dfrac{1}{2} - 9.8t \end{pmatrix} = \begin{pmatrix} 10\sqrt{3} \\ 10 - 9.8t \end{pmatrix}$

Position vector $\mathbf{r} = \begin{pmatrix} 20\cos 30° \\ 20\sin 30° \end{pmatrix} t + \dfrac{1}{2}\begin{pmatrix} 0 \\ -9.8 \end{pmatrix} t^2$

or $\begin{pmatrix} x \\ y \end{pmatrix} = \begin{pmatrix} 10\sqrt{3}\, t \\ 10t - 4.9t^2 \end{pmatrix}$

(ii) The projectile reaches the highest point when $v_y = 0$

So $t = \dfrac{10}{9.8} = 1.020\ldots$

The height at that time is given by

$y = 10 \times 1.020\ldots - 4.9 \times (1.020\ldots)^2 = 5.102\ldots$

So the maximum height is $5.10\,\text{m}$ to 3 s.f.

(iii) The range is the horizontal distance the projectile has travelled when it returns to the ground and so $y = 0$.

Substituting $y = 0$ in $y = 10t - 4.9t^2$ gives $4.9t^2 - 10t = 0$

and so $t = 0$ or $t = \dfrac{10}{4.9} = 2.040\ldots$

> The time $t = 0$ is the starting time.

The time $t = 2.040\ldots$ is the flight time. Notice that it is twice the time it took to reach maximum height.

The range, R m, is given by substituting for t in the horizontal equation

and so $R = 10\sqrt{3} \times 2.040\ldots = 35.347\ldots$

The range is $35.3\,\text{m}$ to 3 s.f.

Path of a projectile

Finding the angle of projection

The equation of the trajectory allows you to find the angle of projection needed for a projectile to hit a particular target. This is shown in the next example.

Example 9.8

A projectile starts at ground level with initial speed $20\,\text{ms}^{-1}$ at an angle α to the horizontal.

(i) A target is situated at the point $(20, 6)$; the units are metres. Find the values of α for the projectile to hit the target.

(ii) Another target is at the point $(20, 18)$. Can the projectile hit this target?

(iii) A third target is at a horizontal distance of $20\,\text{m}$ from the starting point of the projectile. Find the height at which it can just be hit.

Solution

(i) The equation of the trajectory of a projectile is
$$y = x\tan\alpha - \frac{gx^2(1+\tan^2\alpha)}{2u^2}.$$
In this case $u = 20$ and $g = 9.8$.

The target is at $(20, 6)$ and so when the projectile hits it $x = 20$ and $y = 6$. Substituting all these values gives an equation for $\tan\alpha$. It can be written
$$6 = 20\tan\alpha - 4.9(1+\tan^2\alpha)$$
or as $4.9\tan^2\alpha - 20\tan\alpha + 10.9 = 0$

Solving this with the quadratic formula gives

either $\tan\alpha = 3.433\ldots \Rightarrow \alpha = 73.8°$

or $\tan\alpha = 0.647\ldots \Rightarrow \alpha = 32.9°$: both angles to 3 s.f.

Note

If a target is within range there are two possible angles of projection. The lower one is usually the more accurate.

(ii) In this case, the target is at $(20, 18)$.

The equation for $\tan\alpha$ is derived in the same way but, in this case, $y = 18$. It is
$$4.9\tan^2\alpha - 20\tan\alpha + 22.9 = 0$$

This equation has no real roots because the discriminant is less than zero. So there is no suitable angle of projection. The target cannot be hit.

> Remember that in the standard quadratic equation $ax^2+bx+c=0$

(iii) In part (i) there were 2 possible values of α. In part (ii) there were none.

with solution $x = \dfrac{-b \pm \sqrt{b^2-4ac}}{2a}$, there are no real roots if the discriminant $b^2 - 4ac$ is negative.

The limiting case is when there is one repeated root.

Note

If a target is on the limit of the range there is just one possible angle of projection.

Suppose the target is at position $(20, h)$ so that its height is $h\,\text{m}$.

> The quadratic equation for $\tan\alpha$ is now
>
> $$4.9\tan^2\alpha - 20\tan\alpha + (h+4.9) = 0$$
>
> Setting the discriminant of this equation equal to 0 gives
>
> $$20^2 - 4 \times 4.9 \times (h+4.9) = 0$$
>
> This gives $h = 15.508...$ so, to 3 s.f., the height at which it can just be hit is 15.8 m.

The bounding parabola

In the previous example you saw that if a target is within range of a projectile there are two possible angles of projection and if it is out of range there are no possible angles. Between these two situations there is the limiting case where the target can just be reached. This corresponds to a repeated root for $\tan\alpha$ in the equation of the trajectory.

The blue curves on Figure 9.12 show the trajectories of a projectile for angles of projection at 5° intervals, from 5° through to 175°. In each case the initial speed is the same and the point of projection is O. The red curve is the locus of all the limiting points that can just be reached. You will see that its shape looks like a parabola and that indeed is the case. It is called the **bounding parabola**. In some contexts the region outside the bounding parabola can be thought of a zone of safety.

> **Note**
>
> Notice how two curves intersect at every point inside the bounding parabola in Figure 9.12. That is because there are two possible angles of projection for each such point.

> **Note**
>
> In Figure 9.12 the point O is on level horizontal ground. That doesn't have to be the case. O could be up in the air and in that case all the trajectories and the bounding parabola would go further down.

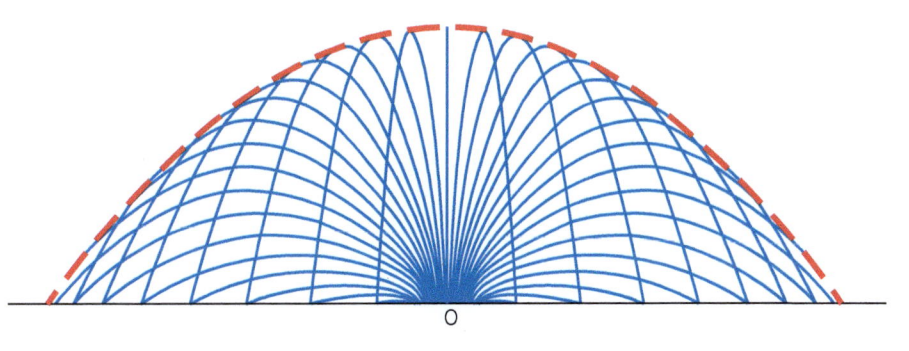

Figure 9.12

To find the equation of the bounding parabola start with the equation of the trajectory

$$y = x\tan\alpha - \frac{gx^2(1+\tan^2\alpha)}{2u^2}$$

and write it as a quadratic equation in $\tan\alpha$.

$$\frac{gx^2}{2u^2}\tan^2\alpha - x\tan\alpha + \left(y + \frac{gx^2}{2u^2}\right) = 0$$

Now set the discriminant equal to zero, as in part (iii) of Example 9.8.

$$(-x)^2 - 4 \times \frac{gx^2}{2u^2} \times \left(y + \frac{gx^2}{2u^2}\right) = 0$$

Path of a projectile

Making y the subject of this equation gives:

$$y = \frac{u^2}{2g} - \frac{gx^2}{2u^2}$$

> **Note**
> Notice that this has involved dividing through by x^2.

This is the equation of the bounding parabola.

Notes
- Substituting $x = 0$ gives $y = \frac{u^2}{2g}$; this is the greatest height the projectile can attain and occurs when its initial velocity is vertically upwards.
- Substituting $y = 0$ gives $x = \pm\frac{u^2}{g}$; this is the greatest possible range (in either the positive or negative direction) for a projectile and is attained when the angle of projection is 45°.

Exercise 9.3

① A particle is projected from a point on level horizontal ground with initial velocity $35\,\text{m s}^{-1}$ at an angle of α to the horizontal where $\sin\alpha = \frac{4}{5}$.
  (i) Write the initial velocity as a vector with horizontal and vertical components.
  (ii) Write down vector equations for the particle's velocity and position vector.
  (iii) Find the particle's maximum height.
  (iv) Find the range of the particle.

② Mr McGregor is a keen vegetable gardener. A pigeon that eats his vegetables is his great enemy.

One day he sees the pigeon sitting on a small branch of a tree. He takes a stone from the ground and throws it. The trajectory of the stone is in a vertical plane that contains the pigeon. The same vertical plane intersects the window of his house. Figure 9.13 illustrates this situation.

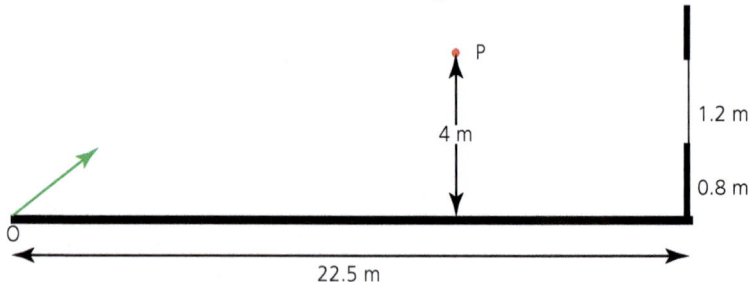

Figure 9.13

- The stone is thrown from point O on level ground. Its initial velocity is $15\,\text{m s}^{-1}$ in the horizontal direction and $8\,\text{m s}^{-1}$ in the vertical direction.
- The pigeon is at point P. Its horizontal distance from O is 12 m and its height is 4 m.
- The house is 22.5 m from O.
- The bottom of the window is 0.8 m above the ground and the top of the window is 1.2 m high.

Show that the stone does not reach the height of the pigeon.

Determine whether the stone hits the window. [MEI]

③ A golf ball is hit at an angle of 60° to the horizontal from a point, O, on level horizontal ground. Its initial speed is 20 m s⁻¹. The standard projectile model, in which air resistance is neglected, is used to describe the subsequent motion of the golf ball. At time t s the horizontal and vertical components of its displacement from O are denoted by x m and y m.

(i) Write down equations for x and y in terms of t.

(ii) Hence show that the equation of the trajectory is $y = \sqrt{3}x - 0.049x^2$.

(iii) Find the range of the golf ball.

(iv) A bird is hovering at position (20, 16).
Find whether the golf ball passes above it, passes below it or hits it.
[MEI]

④ The equation of the trajectory of a projectile is $y = 2x - \dfrac{x^2}{50}$.

(i) Find the initial velocity of the projectile.

(ii) Find the range of the projectile:
 (A) using the initial velocity
 (B) using the equation of the trajectory.

⑤ (i) The equation of a projectile's trajectory is $y = x\tan\alpha - \dfrac{gx^2}{2u^2}(1+\tan^2\alpha)$.
Show that this equation is dimensionally consistent.

(ii) The equation of a projectile's bounding parabola is $y = \dfrac{u^2}{2g} - \dfrac{gx^2}{2u^2}$.
Show that this equation too is dimensionally consistent.

⑥ A particle is projected from a point on level horizontal ground at an angle α to the horizontal; its initial speed is u m s⁻¹.

(i) Show that its range is $\dfrac{u^2 \sin 2\alpha}{g}$.

(ii) Hence show that the maximum range occurs when $\alpha = 45°$, and state the value of the maximum range.

⑦ A ball is thrown from a point O on level horizontal ground. It passes through the point P with position vector $60\mathbf{i} + 73.5\mathbf{j}$, where the directions $\mathbf{i}$ and $\mathbf{j}$ are horizontal and vertical and O is the origin. 2 seconds later the ball is at Q with position vector $100\mathbf{i} + 73.5\mathbf{j}$.

(i) Find the initial speed of the ball and its angle of projection.

Another ball is thrown from O and also passes through P. It has the same initial speed as the first ball but a different angle of projection.

(ii) Find the angle of projection of the second ball.

⑧ At time $t = 0$, a particle is projected from a point O with speed u at an angle of elevation α. At time t, the horizontal and vertical distances of the particle from O are x and y respectively.

(i) Express x and y in terms of u, α, t and g.

(ii) Show that

$$y = x\tan\alpha - \dfrac{gx^2}{2u^2}(1+\tan^2\alpha)$$

Path of a projectile

A golf ball is struck from a point A, leaving A with speed 30 m s⁻¹ at an angle of elevation θ and lands without bouncing in a bunker at a point B, which is at the same horizontal level as A. Before landing in the bunker, the ball just clears the top of a tree which is at a horizontal distance of 72 m from A, the top of the tree being 9 m above the level of AB.

(iii) Find the two possible values of θ.

(iv) Find the distance AB in each case.

⑨ The components of the initial velocity of a particle, projected under gravity from the origin O, are u_x and u_y referred to horizontal and vertical axes Ox and Oy, respectively.

(i) Show that the equation of its path is
$$2u_x^2 y = 2u_x u_y x - 9.8x^2$$

A particle is projected from a point on a horizontal plane so that it just clears a vertical wall of height 0.5 m at a horizontal distance of 1 m from the point of projection and strikes the plane at a horizontal distance 3 m beyond the wall.

(ii) Find the angle of projection with the horizontal.

(iii) Find the speed at which the particle is projected.

⑩ Two particles, A and B, are projected from the same point at the same time across level horizontal ground. The point of projection is on the ground.

A has initial speed 25 m s⁻¹ at 30° to the horizontal.

B has initial speed 25 m s⁻¹ at 60° to the horizontal.

(i) Show that A and B land at the same place.

(ii) State a conjecture generalising this result and prove that it is true.

Find an expression for the difference in the flight times in the general case. Your answer should not contain unnecessary variables.

⑪ A particle is projected from the origin with initial speed 35 m s⁻¹.

(i) Find the equation of its trajectory when the angle of projection is α.

(ii) Use your answer to part (i) to show that the equation of the bounding parabola for its flight is
$$y = 62.5 - \frac{x^2}{250}$$

A long time ago the inhabitants of a village believed they were in danger of attack by a flying dragon. To defend themselves they developed a catapult which launched stones with initial speed 35 m s⁻¹. They situated this on top of a narrow tower 40 m high. They then practised projecting stones at different angles. The villagers who were not involved stood and watched. The ground was level and horizontal.

(iii) Using the equation of the bounding parabola, find the area around the tower where it would be unsafe for the watching villagers to stand. Give your answer to 3 significant figures.

(iv) Show that the dragon cannot get closer to the point of projection than 62.5 metres without risk of being hit by a stone.

⑫ Figure 9.14 shows two balls, P and Q, which are about to be projected in 3 dimensions.

Their initial positions are $(0, 0, 0)$ and $(a, 0, 0)$ as shown.

Their initial velocities are $\begin{pmatrix} p_1 \\ p_2 \\ p_3 \end{pmatrix}$ and $\begin{pmatrix} q_1 \\ q_2 \\ q_3 \end{pmatrix}$ in the x-, y- and z-directions.

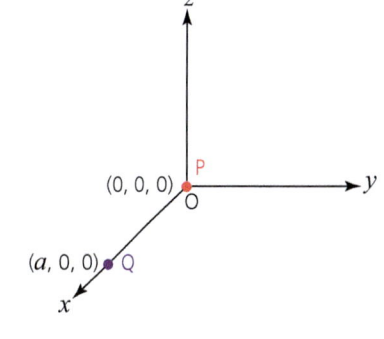

Figure 9.14

While they are still in the air they collide.

Write down 4 conditions involving the variables given in the question, and possibly g, for this to be possible and give an expression for the height at which the collision occurs.

4 Projecting on a uniform slope

When considering the motion of a projectile on an inclined plane, it is usual to use directions along and perpendicular to the line of greatest slope of the plane. So different notation is needed.

> A line of greatest slope goes straight up the plane so it makes the same angle as the plane with the horizontal.

Notation

- The plane is taken to be at an angle θ to the horizontal.
- The angle of projection is taken to be at an angle α to the sloping plane.
- The point of projection is at an origin O on the plane.
- Distances from O are denoted by
  ➤ X in the upwards direction parallel to the plane
  ➤ Y in the upwards perpendicular direction.
- Unit vectors **i** and **j** are parallel and perpendicular to the plane.

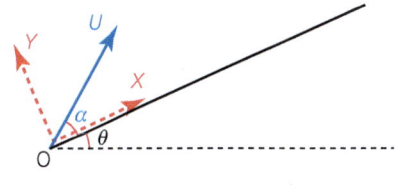

Figure 9.15

Figure 9.16

Using this notation, the acceleration due to gravity is $\mathbf{a} = -g\sin\theta\,\mathbf{i} - g\cos\theta\,\mathbf{j} = \begin{pmatrix} -g\sin\theta \\ -g\cos\theta \end{pmatrix}$ (see Figure 9.17)

the initial velocity vector is $\mathbf{u} = u\cos\alpha\,\mathbf{i} + u\sin\alpha\,\mathbf{j} = \begin{pmatrix} u\cos\alpha \\ u\sin\alpha \end{pmatrix}$ (see Figure 9.18).

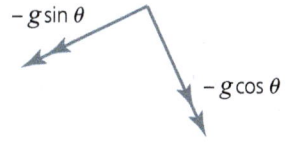

Figure 9.17

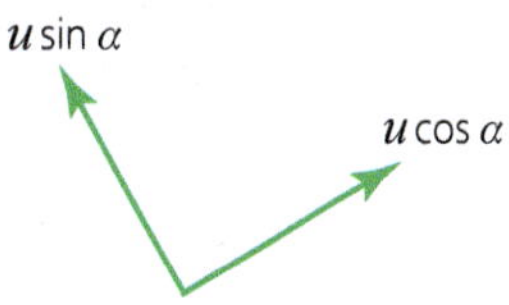

Figure 9.18

Projecting on a uniform slope

Example 9.9

A stone is projected up a slope inclined at 15° to the horizontal with an initial velocity of 40 m s⁻¹ at 30° to the slope.

(i) Write down expressions for the stone's velocity and position vector at time t s.

(ii) Find the range of the stone up the slope.

Solution

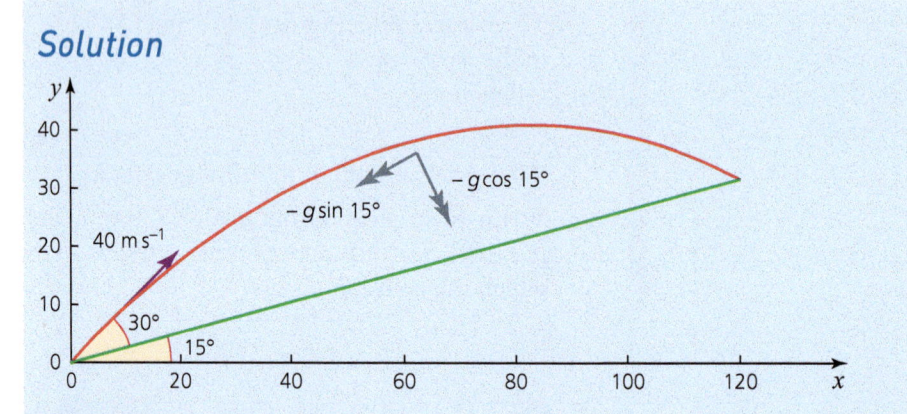

Figure 9.19

Method 1 (Using components parallel and perpendicular to the slope)

(i) Acceleration $\mathbf{a} = \begin{pmatrix} -9.8\sin 15° \\ -9.8\cos 15° \end{pmatrix} = \begin{pmatrix} -2.54 \\ -9.47 \end{pmatrix}$

Initial velocity $\mathbf{u} = \begin{pmatrix} 40\cos 30° \\ 40\sin 30° \end{pmatrix} = \begin{pmatrix} 34.64 \\ 20 \end{pmatrix}$

> **Note**
> These can also be written as
> $\mathbf{a} = -9.8\sin 15° \, \mathbf{i} - 9.8\cos 15° \, \mathbf{j}$
> $\mathbf{u} = 40\cos 30° \, \mathbf{i} + 40\sin 30° \, \mathbf{j}$

The velocity at time t is given by:

$$\mathbf{v} = \mathbf{u} + \mathbf{a}t$$

$$\mathbf{v} = \begin{pmatrix} 34.64 - 2.54t \\ 20 - 9.47t \end{pmatrix}$$

The position vector at time t is given by:

$$\mathbf{r} = \mathbf{u}t + \tfrac{1}{2}\mathbf{a}t^2$$

$$\mathbf{r} = \begin{pmatrix} X \\ Y \end{pmatrix} = \begin{pmatrix} 34.64t - 1.27t^2 \\ 20t - 4.73t^2 \end{pmatrix}$$

(ii) The stone hits the slope when $y = 0$

i.e. $20t - 4.73t^2 = 0$

$t(20 - 4.73t) = 0$

$t = 0$ or $t = \dfrac{20}{4.73} = 4.2256\ldots$

The time of flight is: $T = 4.23$ s to 3 s.f.

The range is the value of X when $t = T$

$R = 34.64 \times 4.23 - 1.27 \times 4.23^2 = 123.73$ m

The range up the slope is 124 metres to 3 s.f.

Method 2 (Using horizontal and vertical components)

(ii) The equation of the trajectory $y = x\tan\alpha - \dfrac{gx^2}{2u^2}(1+\tan^2\alpha)$

In this equation α is the angle of projection to the horizontal:
$\alpha = 15° + 30° = 45°$

> Using $\tan 45° = 1$

So the trajectory is:
$$y = x - \dfrac{gy^2}{u^2}$$

Substituting for u and g gives:
$$y = x - 0.006125x^2$$

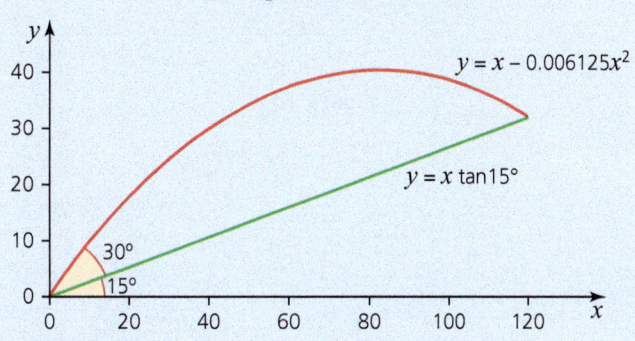

Figure 9.20

The line of the slope is $y = x\tan 15°$ or $y = 0.268x$

> The line of greatest slope has equation $y = x \tan 15°$ or $y = 0.268x$

The stone lands at the point of intersection of the trajectory and the line of the slope.

$$x - 0.006125x^2 = 0.268x$$
$$0.732x - 0.006125x^2 = 0$$
$$x(0.732 - 0.006125x) = 0$$
$\Rightarrow \quad x = 0$ or $x = \dfrac{0.732}{0.006125} = 119.52$
$\Rightarrow \quad y = 0$ or $y = 32.02$

The points of intersection are $(0, 0)$ and $(119.52, 32.02)$

The range of the stone along the plane is then equal to:
$$R = \sqrt{119.52^2 + 32.02^2} = 123.73\,\text{m} \text{ or } 124 \text{ to 3 s.f.}$$

> **Discussion point**
> As you would expect, the two methods used in this example gave the same answer.
> Which do you prefer, and why?

Example 9.10

An archer fires an arrow up a slope inclined at 30° to the horizontal with an initial velocity of $60\,\text{m s}^{-1}$ at an angle of 45° to the slope.

(i) Find the range of the arrow up the slope.

The archer decides to retrieve the arrow and to fire it downhill at the same angle to the slope.

(ii) What speed must he give the arrow for it to land at the same spot at the bottom of the hill?

Projecting on a uniform slope

Solution

(i)

$\mathbf{u} = \begin{pmatrix} 60\cos 45° \\ 60\sin 45° \end{pmatrix} = \begin{pmatrix} 42.43 \\ 42.43 \end{pmatrix}$

$\mathbf{a} = \begin{pmatrix} -9.8\sin 30° \\ -9.8\cos 30° \end{pmatrix} = \begin{pmatrix} -4.9 \\ -8.49 \end{pmatrix}$

Figure 9.21

Along the slope:
$$X = 60t\cos 45° - \frac{9.8}{2}\sin 30° \, t^2$$
$$= 42.43t - 2.45t^2$$

Perpendicular to the slope:
$$Y = 60t\sin 45° - \frac{9.8}{2}\cos 30° \, t^2$$
$$= 42.43t - 4.24t^2$$

Time of flight: $Y = 0 \Rightarrow 42.43t - 4.24t^2 = 0$

$\Rightarrow t = 0$ or $t = T = \dfrac{42.43}{4.24} = 9.9979\ldots = 10\,\text{s}$

Range:
$$X = 42.43 \times T - 2.45T^2$$
$$= 179.3\,\text{m}$$

The range of the arrow up the slope is 179 m.

$\mathbf{u} = \begin{pmatrix} -9.8\sin 30° \\ -9.8\cos 30° \end{pmatrix} = \begin{pmatrix} -4.9 \\ -8.49 \end{pmatrix}$

(ii) Down the slope.

$\mathbf{u} = \begin{pmatrix} -u\cos 45° \\ u\sin 45° \end{pmatrix}$

Figure 9.22

In this case the motion is down the slope so you will expect X to be negative.

Component up the slope: $X = -ut\cos 45° - 2.45\,t^2$

Component perpendicular to the slope: $Y = ut\sin 45° - 4.24\,t^2$

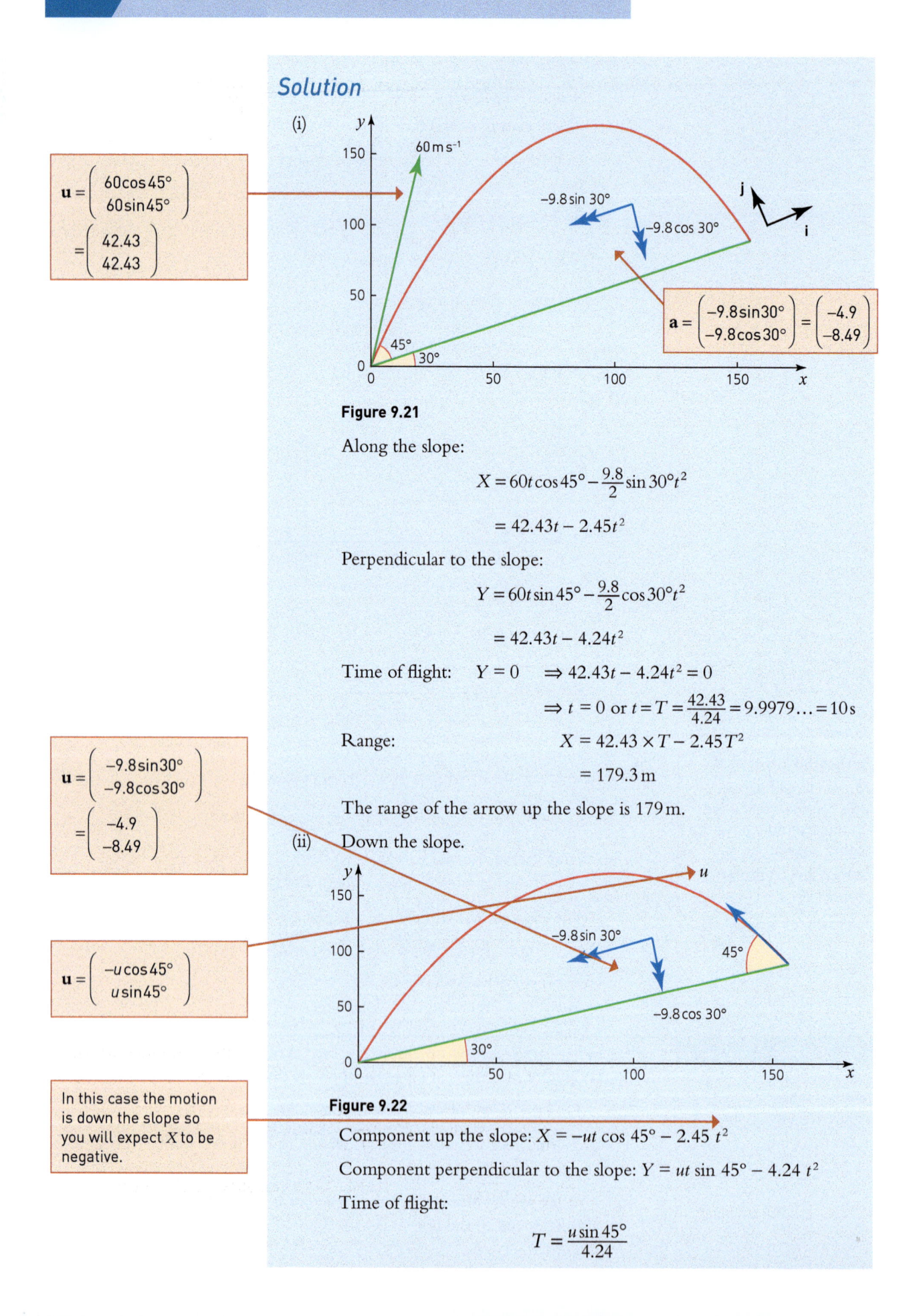

Time of flight:
$$T = \frac{u\sin 45°}{4.24}$$

Range: $R = -\dfrac{u^2 \sin 45° \cos 45°}{4.24} - \dfrac{2.45 \times u^2 \times \sin^2 45°}{4.24^2}$

$= -u^2 (0.1178 + 0.0680)$

$= -0.1858 \, u^2 = -179.3$ ← The range must be 179.3 m, the same as in part (i) but this time down the slope.

$\Rightarrow u = \sqrt{\dfrac{179.3}{0.1858}} = 31 \text{ m s}^{-1}$

The initial speed of the arrow is 31 m s⁻¹.

Example 9.11

A particle is projected up a slope inclined at 30° to the horizontal, with initial velocity 10 m s⁻¹ at an angle α to the slope. Find the maximum range and the associated angle of projection.

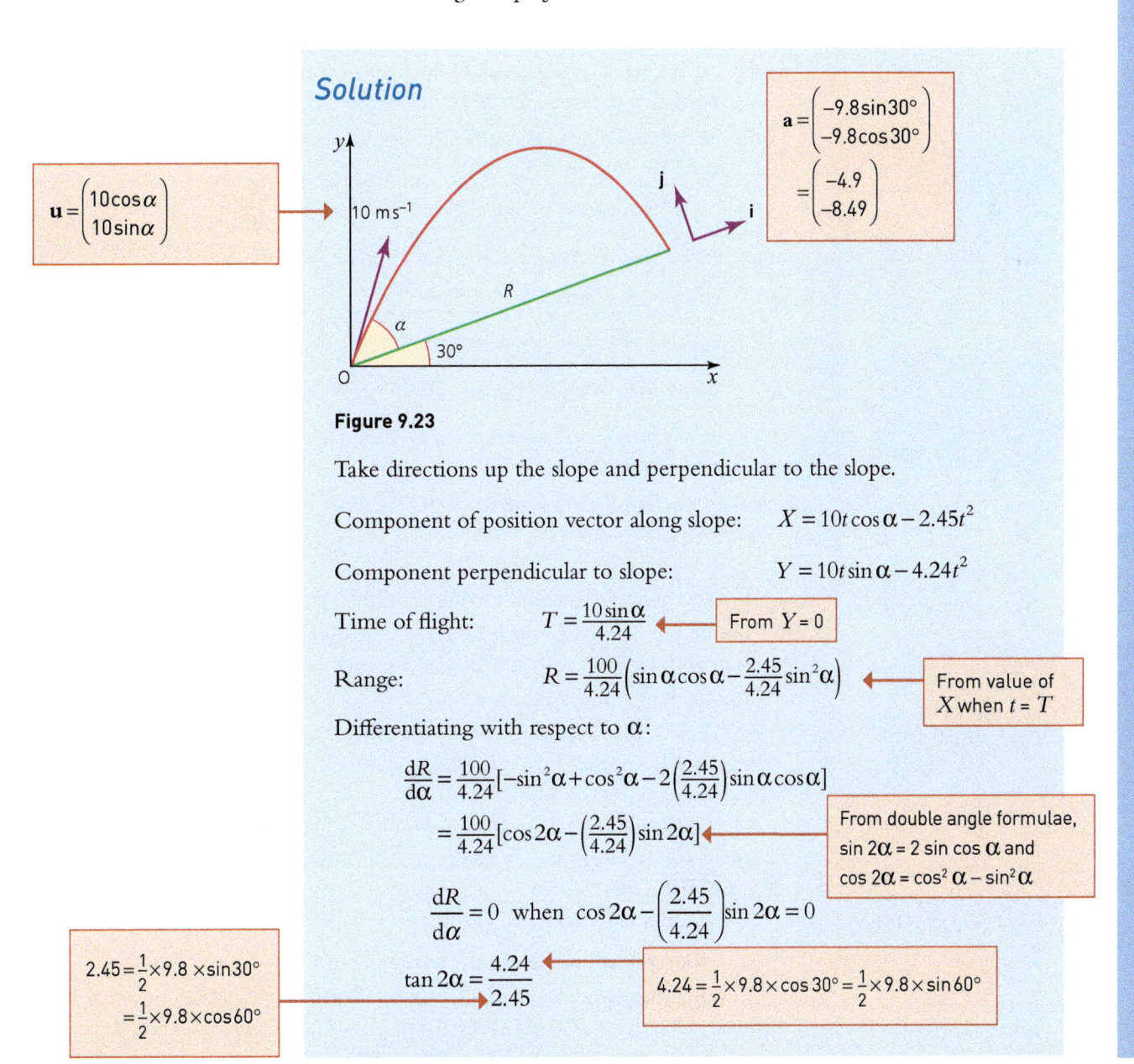

Solution

$\mathbf{u} = \begin{pmatrix} 10\cos\alpha \\ 10\sin\alpha \end{pmatrix}$

$\mathbf{a} = \begin{pmatrix} -9.8\sin 30° \\ -9.8\cos 30° \end{pmatrix} = \begin{pmatrix} -4.9 \\ -8.49 \end{pmatrix}$

Figure 9.23

Take directions up the slope and perpendicular to the slope.

Component of position vector along slope: $X = 10t\cos\alpha - 2.45t^2$

Component perpendicular to slope: $Y = 10t\sin\alpha - 4.24t^2$

Time of flight: $T = \dfrac{10\sin\alpha}{4.24}$ ← From $Y = 0$

Range: $R = \dfrac{100}{4.24}\left(\sin\alpha\cos\alpha - \dfrac{2.45}{4.24}\sin^2\alpha\right)$ ← From value of X when $t = T$

Differentiating with respect to α:

$\dfrac{dR}{d\alpha} = \dfrac{100}{4.24}\left[-\sin^2\alpha + \cos^2\alpha - 2\left(\dfrac{2.45}{4.24}\right)\sin\alpha\cos\alpha\right]$

$= \dfrac{100}{4.24}\left[\cos 2\alpha - \left(\dfrac{2.45}{4.24}\right)\sin 2\alpha\right]$ ← From double angle formulae, $\sin 2\alpha = 2\sin\cos\alpha$ and $\cos 2\alpha = \cos^2\alpha - \sin^2\alpha$

$\dfrac{dR}{d\alpha} = 0$ when $\cos 2\alpha - \left(\dfrac{2.45}{4.24}\right)\sin 2\alpha = 0$

$2.45 = \tfrac{1}{2} \times 9.8 \times \sin 30°$
$= \tfrac{1}{2} \times 9.8 \times \cos 60°$

$\tan 2\alpha = \dfrac{4.24}{2.45}$

$4.24 = \tfrac{1}{2} \times 9.8 \times \cos 30° = \tfrac{1}{2} \times 9.8 \times \sin 60°$

Projecting on a uniform slope

> **Note**
> The result from this example illustrates the result that for a projectile on a slope the maximum range occurs when the line of projection bisects the angle between the slope and the vertical. This result is proved in question 12 of the following exercise.

$\Rightarrow 2\alpha = 60°$

$\alpha = 30°$

The maximum range is obtained for $\alpha = 30°$.

$R_m = \dfrac{100}{4.24}\left[\dfrac{1}{2} \times \dfrac{\sqrt{3}}{2} - \dfrac{1}{\sqrt{3}} \times \dfrac{1}{4}\right]$

From $\sin 30° = \dfrac{1}{2}$, $\cos 30° = \dfrac{\sqrt{3}}{2}$ and $\tan 60° = \sqrt{3}$

$R_m = \dfrac{25}{4.24}\left[\sqrt{3} - \dfrac{1}{\sqrt{3}}\right] = 6.81$ m

The maximum range is 6.81 m when $\theta = 30°$.

Exercise 9.4

1. A uniform slope makes an angle θ with the horizontal. A stone is projected up the slope at an angle α to a line of greatest slope with initial speed u.

   (i) Write the acceleration and initial velocity as vectors with components parallel and perpendicular to the slope.

   (ii) Write down expressions for the stone's velocity and position vector at time t.

   (iii) Show that the stone hits the slope at time $\dfrac{2u \sin \alpha}{g \cos \theta}$

   (iv) Show that the range up the slope is given by
   $$R = \dfrac{2u^2 \sin \alpha}{g \cos^2 \theta}(\cos \theta \cos \alpha - \sin \theta \sin \alpha)$$

   (v) Show that when $\theta = 0$, $R = \dfrac{2u^2 \sin \alpha \cos \alpha}{g}$ and interpret this result.

In the remaining questions you are expected to obtain the answers from first principles and not to quote standard formulae.

2. A particle is projected from the foot of a plane inclined at 30° to the horizontal. It is given an initial velocity of 20 m s⁻¹ at an angle of 30° to the slope.

   Find the time of flight and the range up the plane.

3. A stone is projected down a slope inclined at 45° to the horizontal. It is given an initial velocity of 10 m s⁻¹ at an angle of 15° to the slope.

   Find the range down the plane.

4. A particle is projected up a slope inclined at 30° to the horizontal. It is given a velocity of 50 m s⁻¹ at 30° to the slope. Show that it strikes the slope at an angle of 60° to the slope.

5. A ball is thrown with a velocity of 20 m s⁻¹ at an angle of 45° to the horizontal. How far does it go along a slope inclined at 30° to the horizontal if it is thrown

   (a) up

   (b) down the plane.

6. A stone is thrown from a point O on a uniform sloping plane. Its initial speed is 39.2 m s⁻¹ in an upwards direction. It hits the plane 2 seconds later and at that instant it is travelling horizontally.

(i) Find the angle between the plane and the initial direction of the stone's motion.

The stone is then thrown back from the point at which it landed. Its initial direction is horizontal and its speed is that with which it landed.

(ii) Find whether it land beyond, at, or before O.

⑦ A particle is projected from a point on a plane sloping at 30° to the horizontal. Referred to directions parallel to the slope and perpendicular to it, the initial velocity of the particle is $\begin{pmatrix} 24.5 \\ 12.25\sqrt{3} \end{pmatrix}$ in m s^{-1}.

(i) Find the angle that the line of the particle's motion makes with the plane at the instant when it is projected.

(ii) Find the angle that the line of the particle's motion makes with the plane at the instant when it is lands.

(iii) Find the range of the particle up the plane.

(iv) State, with justification, whether the particle will travel any further up the plane after it lands.

⑧ A plane inclined at an angle θ to the horizontal. A particle is projected with velocity u at an angle β to the horizontal.

(i) Show that the time of flight is $\dfrac{2u\sin(\beta-\theta)}{g\cos\theta}$.

The particle strikes the inclined plane horizontally. Show that

(ii) $\tan\beta = 2\tan\theta$

(iii) the range is $\dfrac{2u^2 \sin(\beta-\theta)\cos(\beta)}{g\cos^2\theta}$

⑨ A particle P is projected horizontally, with speed V, from a point O on a plane which is inclined at an angle β to the horizontal. The particle hits the plane at a point A which is on the line of greatest slope through O.

(i) Show that the time of flight is $\dfrac{2V}{g}\tan\beta$.

(ii) Find OA.

(iii) Find the tangent of the acute angle between the horizontal and the direction of motion of P when P reaches A.

⑩ A particle P is projected, from a point O on a plane inclined at an angle θ to the horizontal with speed u in a direction perpendicular to the plane.

(i) Find the time taken for P to return to the plane.

P returns to the plane at a point A.

(ii) Find OA.

(iii) Find the tangent of the acute angle between the plane and the direction of motion of P when it reaches A.

⑪ A particle is projected with speed u from a point O.

(i) Write down the equation of the bounding parabola for the particle's motion, using O as the origin.

O is a point on a uniform sloping plane. The gradient of a line of maximum slope is m.

The maximum possible range of the particle down the plane is 4 times that up the plane.

(ii) Find the equation of the line of greatest slope that passes through O.

(iii) Hence find the value of m and the angle the slope makes with the horizontal.

⑫ A uniform slope is at an angle θ to the horizontal. A particle is projected up the slope at an angle α to the line of greatest slope.

(i) Show that the range of the particle is $R = \dfrac{2u^2 \sin\alpha \cos(\alpha+\theta)}{g \cos^2\theta}$.

(ii) Show that R has its maximum value when $2\alpha + \theta = 90°$.

(iii) Explain how this shows that for maximum range the initial velocity bisects the angle between the plane and the vertical.

Confirm this result in the case when the slope angle θ is zero.

(iv) Show that the greatest value of range of R is $\dfrac{u^2}{g(1+\sin\theta)}$.

5 Motion under variable acceleration

Acceleration dependent on velocity

The main assumption used in formulating the theory of projectiles is the neglect of air resistance.

It is well known that air resistance is by no means negligible, especially for fast moving objects. It is thus often important to incorporate an element of velocity dependence for the air resistance term.

To see the effect of building air resistance into a model, the motion of a projectile is considered first without it and then with it. In order to simplify the working, the value of g is taken to be $10\,\text{m s}^{-2}$.

> **Note**
> Another assumption is that g is constant, and for short trajectories near to the Earth's surface this is entirely reasonable.

Referred to the origin O, the projectile moves with initial velocity $\mathbf{u} = \begin{pmatrix} 24 \\ 7 \end{pmatrix}$ under the acceleration $\mathbf{a} = \begin{pmatrix} 0 \\ -10 \end{pmatrix}$. The position vector $\mathbf{r}$ is given by:

$$\mathbf{r} = \begin{pmatrix} 24t \\ 7t - 5t^2 \end{pmatrix}$$

> Note that $g = 10\,\text{m s}^{-2}$

> Using $\mathbf{r} = \mathbf{u}t + \tfrac{1}{2}\mathbf{a}t^2$ with $\mathbf{u} = \begin{pmatrix} 24 \\ 7 \end{pmatrix}$ and $\mathbf{a} = \begin{pmatrix} 0 \\ -10 \end{pmatrix}$

Speed of projection $= \sqrt{24^2 + 7^2} = 25$. Angle of projection is $\arctan \dfrac{7}{24} = 16.26°$.

The Cartesian equation is

$$y = \tfrac{7}{24}x - 5\left(\tfrac{x}{24}\right)^2$$

> Eliminating t between $x = 24t$ and $y = 7t - 5t^2$

The time of flight is $T = 1.4\,\text{s}$ and the range is $R = 33.6\,\text{m}$.

> Using $y = 7t - 5t^2 = 0$

> Using $R = 24T = 24 \times 1.4$

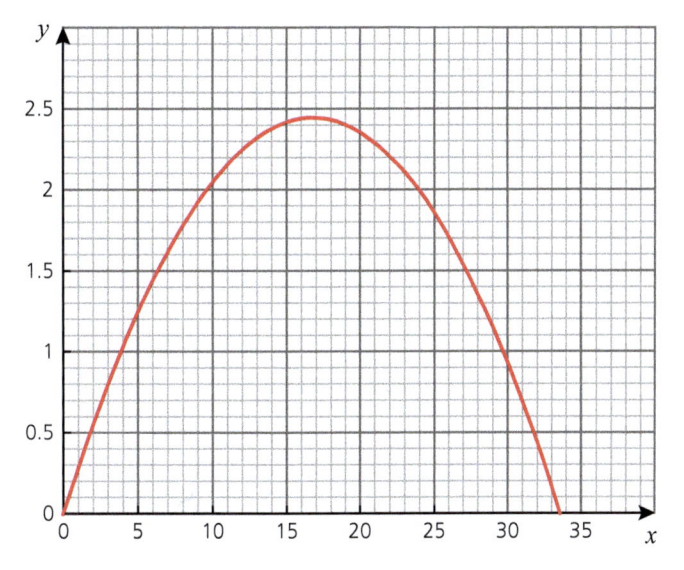

Figure 9.24

This is to be the reference case. The results are to be compared with those from a model that includes air resistance.

In the new model, it is assumed that air resistance is directly proportional to the velocity at that instant. Consequently, the acceleration is given by:

$$\mathbf{a} = \mathbf{a}_0 - k\mathbf{v} = \begin{pmatrix} 0 \\ -10 \end{pmatrix} - k\begin{pmatrix} v_x \\ v_y \end{pmatrix}, \text{ where } k \text{ is a constant.}$$

This means that each component of the acceleration varies with the same component of the velocity.

This defines a differential equation for each component of the velocity.

$$\frac{dv_x}{dt} = -kv_x$$

and

$$\frac{dv_y}{dt} = -10 - kv_y$$

The next example shows how these differential equations can be solved.

> **Note**
>
> It is often easiest to solve the differential equations for the different components separately. So much of this work is effectively carried out in one dimension.

Example 9.12

A particle is initially at the origin. It moves with initial velocity $\mathbf{u} = \begin{pmatrix} 24 \\ 7 \end{pmatrix}$ with acceleration $\mathbf{a} = \begin{pmatrix} -v_x \\ -10 - v_y \end{pmatrix}$.

(i) Find an expression for the velocity $\mathbf{v}$ at time t.

(ii) Find an expression for the position vector $\mathbf{r}$ at time t.

(iii) Find the Cartesian equation of the path.

(iv) Find the time of flight and the range of the particle.

Motion under variable acceleration

> **Note**
> The variables v_x and t can be separated, $\dfrac{dv_x}{v_x} = -dt$, and then integrated.

Solution

(i) Starting from the acceleration, $\mathbf{a} = \dfrac{d\mathbf{v}}{dt} = \begin{pmatrix} \dfrac{dv_x}{dt} \\ \dfrac{dv_y}{dt} \end{pmatrix} = \begin{pmatrix} -v_x \\ -10 - v_y \end{pmatrix}$.

These are two first-order separable differential equations for v_x and v_y.

$$\frac{dv_x}{dt} = -v_x \quad \text{①}$$

$$\frac{dv_y}{dt} = -10 - v_y \quad \text{②}$$

$$\text{①} \Rightarrow \int \frac{dv_x}{v_x} = \int -dt$$

$$\ln v_x = -t + c$$

Or in exponential form: $v_x = Ae^{-t}$

The initial condition is $v_x = 24$, when $t = 0$.

This leads to $A = 24$ and so the solution of the differential equation ① is:

$$v_x = 24e^{-t}$$

> *v is a constant of integration.*

$$\text{②} \Rightarrow \int \frac{dv_y}{10 + v_y} = \int -dt$$

> Separating the variables $\dfrac{dv_y}{10+v_y} = -dt$.

$$\ln(10 + v_y) = -t + c$$

> $A = v^c$

$$10 + v_y = Ae^{-t}$$

> $10 + 7 = A \times v^0$

Now using the initial condition $v_y = 7$ when $t = 0$ leads to $A = 17$ and the solution to ② is

$$v_y = -10 + 17e^{-t}$$

At time t the velocity is $\mathbf{v} = \begin{pmatrix} 24e^{-t} \\ -10 + 17e^{-t} \end{pmatrix}$

(ii) The position vector $\mathbf{r}$ is obtained from the velocity vector $\mathbf{v}$ by integrating with respect to t.

$$\mathbf{r} = \begin{pmatrix} x \\ y \end{pmatrix} = \begin{pmatrix} \int 24e^{-t} dt \\ \int (-10 + 17e^{-t}) dt \end{pmatrix}$$

Starting with x: $\quad x = \int 24e^{-t} dt$

$$x = -24e^{-t} + c_1$$

> c_1 is a constant of integration

Applying the initial condition $x = 0$ when $t = 0$ gives $c_1 = 24$ and thus

$$x = 24(1 - e^{-t})$$

> $0 = -24 \times e^0 + c_1$

216

Now, looking at y: $y = \int (-10 + 17e^{-t})dt$

$y = -10t - 17e^{-t} + c_2$

[$0 = -10 \times 0 - 17 \times e^0 + c_2$]

Using the initial condition $y = 0$ when $t = 0$ leads to $c_2 = 17$ and thus

$$y = -10t + 17(1 - e^{-t})$$

At time t, the position vector is $\mathbf{r} = \begin{pmatrix} 24(1 - e^{-t}) \\ -10t + 17(1 - e^{-t}) \end{pmatrix}$

(iii) To obtain the Cartesian equation, t needs to be eliminated from the two equations:

$$x = 24(1 - e^{-t}) \quad \text{③}$$

and

$$y = -10t + 17(1 - e^{-t}) \quad \text{④}$$

Rearranging ③: $(1 - e^{-t}) = \frac{x}{24}$

[$e^{-t} = 1 - \frac{x}{24}$]

$\Rightarrow \quad -t = \ln\left(1 - \frac{x}{24}\right)$

Substituting in ④ yields $y = 10\ln\left(1 - \frac{x}{24}\right) + \frac{17}{24}x$

This is the Cartesian equation of the path. It is sketched below and compared with the path followed by the particle when the air resistance is neglected.

> **Note**
> This example involved a particular model for the form of air resistance. It was assumed to have the form $k\mathbf{v}$ and then the value of k was taken to be 1. A smaller value of k would often be realistic. Furthermore, depending on the conditions, the resistance might well depend on a power of v, for example on v^2.
>
> So, while the model in the example is a step forward on the standard projectile model, it is not the final answer.

> **Note**
> Define $f(t) = 17(1 - e^{-t}) - 10t$, then $f'(t) = 17e^{-t} - 10$ and the iteration formula is
> $$T_{n+1} = T_n - \frac{17(1 - e^{-T_n}) - 10T_n}{17e^{-T_n} - 10}.$$
> Starting with $T_0 = 0$ results in a value for $T = 1.175\,016\,283$ after 4 iterations.

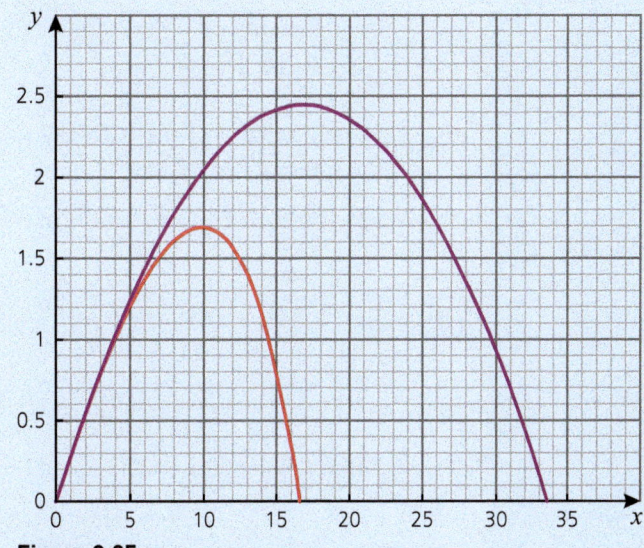

Figure 9.25

(iv) To find the time of flight, you have to find the value of t for which $y = 0$, i.e. you need to solve the equation $17(1 - e^{-t}) - 10t = 0$. This can only be done numerically using, for example, the Newton–Raphson method.

The time of flight is equal to 1.175 s.

This compares with 1.4 s from the reference model in which it was assumed that air resistance was negligible. The range is equal to the value of x when $t = T$: i.e. R $= 24(1 - e^{-1.175}) = 16.588$ m.

This is very different from the value of 33.6 m given by the reference model.

Motion under variable acceleration

Acceleration dependent on position

In the next example, the acceleration is dependent on the position. This is a situation that you will meet later in this book, in Chapter 11 on elastic strings and springs and in Chapter 12 on simple harmonic motion.

For this form of dependence there are two different sorts of differential equations that you may need to use.

- Connecting s (or x or y) and t. Acceleration is written in the form:

$$a = \frac{d^2s}{dt^2} \left(\text{or } \frac{d^2x}{dt^2} \text{ or } \frac{d^2y}{dt^2}\right).$$

- Connecting v and s (or x or y). Acceleration is written in the form $a = v\frac{dv}{ds}$.

The first of these is the subject of the next example.

> This form for acceleration is based on the chain rule.
> $v\frac{dv}{ds} = \frac{ds}{dt} \times \frac{dv}{ds}$
> $= \frac{dv}{dt}$
> $= a$

Example 9.13

A particle is initially at the origin and moving with initial velocity $\begin{pmatrix} 6 \\ 8 \end{pmatrix}$ under the acceleration $\mathbf{a} = \begin{pmatrix} -4x \\ -y \end{pmatrix}$.

(i) Verify that the position vector of the particle at time t is given by

$$\mathbf{r} = \begin{pmatrix} 3\sin 2t \\ 8\sin t \end{pmatrix}$$

(ii) Sketch a graph of the path followed by the particle for values of t in the interval $0 \leq t \leq 2\pi$.

(iii) Find the Cartesian equation of the path followed by the particle.

> **Note**
> These are the equations for simple harmonic motion which is covered in detail in Chapter 12.

Solution

(i) $\mathbf{a} = \begin{pmatrix} -4x \\ -y \end{pmatrix}$ may be written in terms of differential equations for x and for y.

$$\frac{d^2x}{dt^2} = -4x \quad \text{(A)}$$

and

$$\frac{d^2y}{dt^2} = -y \quad \text{(B)}$$

In this example, you were asked to verify the solution. This means that you must do two things for each equation:

- show that the proposed solution is indeed a solution of the differential equation: in the case of equation (A), the function $x = 3\sin 2t$ satisfies $\frac{d^2x}{dt^2} = -4x$
- show that it obeys any boundary or initial conditions: in the case of equation (A), that $x = 0$ and $\frac{dx}{dt} = 6$ when $t = 0$.

> **Equation (A)**
> $x = 3\sin 2t \Rightarrow \frac{dx}{dt} = 6\cos 2t$
> $\Rightarrow \frac{d^2x}{dt^2} = -12\sin 2t$
> $= -4(3\sin 2t) = -4x$
> when $t = 0$, $\frac{dx}{dt} = 6 \times 1 = 6$ and $x = 0$.
> So that $x = 3\sin 2t$ is the solution of (A) subject to the initial conditions $x = 0$ and $\frac{dx}{dt} = 6$ when $t = 0$.

> **Equation (B)**
> $y = 8\sin t \Rightarrow \frac{dy}{dt} = 8\cos t$
> $\Rightarrow \frac{d^2y}{dt^2} = -8\sin t = -y$
> when $t = 0$, $\frac{dy}{dt} = 8$ and $y = 0$
> so that $y = 8\sin t$ is the solution of (B), subject to the initial conditions $y = 0$ and $\frac{dy}{dt} = 8$ when $t = 0$.

(ii) For each value of t you can find values for x and y.

t	0	$\frac{1}{4}\pi$	$\frac{1}{2}\pi$	$\frac{3}{4}\pi$	π	$\frac{5}{4}\pi$	$\frac{3}{2}\pi$	$\frac{7}{4}\pi$	2π
x	0	3	0	-3	0	3	0	-3	0
y	0	5.66	8	5.66	0	-5.66	-8	-5.66	0

These are shown in the graph.

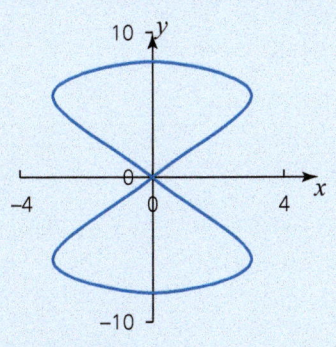

Figure 9.26

(iii) To find the Cartesian equation of the path, you need to eliminate t from the equations for x and y.

This can be done as follows:

> From the identity $\sin^2 t + \cos^2 t = 1$

$y = 8 \sin t \Rightarrow y^2 = 64 \sin^2 t \Rightarrow \sin^2 t = \dfrac{y^2}{64} \Rightarrow \cos^2 t = 1 - \dfrac{y^2}{64}$

$x = 3 \sin 2t = 6 \sin t \cos t$

> From the double angle formula $\sin 2t = 2 \sin t \cos t$

$x^2 = 36 \sin^2 t \cos^2 t = 36 \dfrac{y^2}{64}\left(1 - \dfrac{y^2}{64}\right)$

Rearranging gives:

$$1024 x^2 = 9y^2(64 - y^2)$$

The next example uses the form $a = v\dfrac{dv}{dx}$ for resisted motion in the x direction.

Example 9.14

A particle moves along the x-axis. It is initially at the origin and moving with speed $6\,\text{m s}^{-1}$ in the positive direction. When its displacement is x its acceleration is given by $a = -4x$ in m s^{-2}.

(i) Write down a differential equation connecting the velocity $v\,\text{m s}^{-1}$ of the particle with x.

(ii) Solve the differential equation subject to the initial conditions to give v as a function of x.

(iii) Write your answer to part (ii) as a differential equation connecting x and t.

(iv) Solve this equation.

Motion under variable acceleration

Solution

(i) The differential equation is $v\dfrac{dv}{dx} = -4x$

(ii) Separating variables gives
$$\int v\,dv = -4\int x\,dx$$
$$\dfrac{v^2}{2} = -2x^2 + c$$

Initial conditions, $v = 6$ when $x = 0 \Rightarrow c = 18$
$$\Rightarrow v = \pm\sqrt{36 - 4x^2}$$

(iii) $\dfrac{dx}{dt} = \pm 2\sqrt{9 - x^2}$

(iv) Separating variables
$$\int \dfrac{dx}{\sqrt{9 - x^2}} = 2\int dt$$

The left-hand side is a standard integral:
$$\arcsin\left(\dfrac{x}{3}\right) + c = 2t$$

Initial conditions, $x = 0$ when $t = 0 \Rightarrow x = 3\sin 2t$

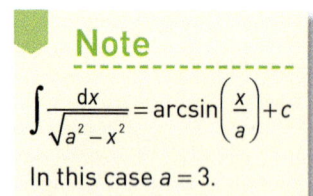

> **Note**
> $\int \dfrac{dx}{\sqrt{a^2 - x^2}} = \arcsin\left(\dfrac{x}{a}\right) + c$
> In this case $a = 3$.

You may have noticed that the last example involved the same acceleration as the x-component of the one before. In the x-direction, the acceleration was given by $a = -4x$ and the initial conditions were the same.

However, the approach to solving it was quite different.

Using $a = v\dfrac{dv}{dx}$ is particularly helpful when you are dealing with stretched strings. In the simplest cases, Newton's second law and Hooke's law (which you will meet in Chapter 11) leads to the relationship $ma = -kx$ and to the differential equation $mv\dfrac{dv}{dx} = -kx$.

The solution of this is $\tfrac{1}{2}mv^2 = -\tfrac{1}{2}kx^2 + c$ and this is a very useful energy equation. Parts (iii) and (iv) went a stage further, providing the solution for x in terms of t.

However, to find x in terms of t, it would be more usual to use $\dfrac{d^2x}{dt^2}$ for the acceleration and solve the resulting second-order differential equation using the auxiliary equation method. An example of this is given on page 321 in Chapter 12.

Exercise 9.5

① In each of the following cases a particle of mass 1 kg is under the influence of a single force F N in a constant direction, but with a variable magnitude given as a function of
  - either velocity v m s^{-1}
  - or displacement x m
  - or time t s.

The particle is initially at rest at the origin.

In each case, write down the equation of motion and solve it to supply the required information.

(i) $F = 5t + 1$; find v when $t = 2$.

(ii) $F = \dfrac{2}{5+x}$; find v when $x = 5$.

(iii) $F = \dfrac{2}{(1+x)^2}$; find v when $x = 1$.

(iv) $F = 9 - v^2$; find t when $v = 1$.

(v) $F = 1 + v^2$; find x when $v = 1$.

(vi) $F = 1 + v^2$; find t when $v = 1$.

(vii) $F = \dfrac{2}{(2+x)^3}$; find v when $x = 1$.

(viii) $F = 2\sin 3t$; find v when $t = \dfrac{\pi}{2}$.

② A particle moves with initial velocity $\begin{pmatrix} 10 \\ 20 \end{pmatrix}$ under the acceleration $\begin{pmatrix} -2 \\ -10 \end{pmatrix}$.

(i) Give expressions for the velocity and position vectors of the moving point.

(ii) Sketch the curve of the path followed by the particle.

(iii) Find the coordinates of the highest point of the path.

③ A ball P of mass 0.25 kg is projected vertically upwards from ground level with an initial speed of 20 m s⁻¹. A resisting force of magnitude $0.05v$ N acts on P during its ascent, where v m s⁻¹ is the speed and x m is the displacement of the ball at time t s after it starts to move.

(i) Show that $\dfrac{dv}{dt} = -0.2(49 + v)$.

(ii) Find an expression for v as a function of t.

(iii) Find the displacement x as a function of t.

(iv) Find the greatest height reached by the ball.

④ A particle starts from O and moves in a straight line. When the displacement is x m its velocity is v m s⁻¹ and its acceleration is $\dfrac{2}{x+1}$.

(i) Given that $v = 3$ when $x = 0$ show that $v^2 = 4\ln|x+1| + 9$.

(ii) Find the value of v when the acceleration is $\dfrac{2}{5}$.

⑤ A particle moves with initial velocity $\begin{pmatrix} 15 \\ 20 \end{pmatrix}$ under the acceleration
$\mathbf{a} = \begin{pmatrix} -0.5v_x \\ -10 - 0.5v_y \end{pmatrix}$

(i) Find an expression for the velocity $\mathbf{v}$ at time t.

(ii) Find an expression for the position vector $\mathbf{r}$ at time t.

(iii) Find the Cartesian equation of the path

(iv) Sketch the path followed by the particle.

⑥ A rocket of mass 1000 kg is launched from rest at ground level and travels vertically upwards. The mass of the rocket is constant and the only forces acting on it are its weight, a driving force of 20 000 N and a resistance force $5v$.

(i) Show that $\dfrac{dv}{dt} = 10.2 - 0.005v$.

(ii) Find v in terms of t.

(iii) Find the distance travelled by the rocket in the first 5 seconds of its motion.

⑦ A cyclist and her bicycle have a combined mass of 64 kg. She starts from rest and rides in a straight line, exerting a constant force of 128 N. The motion is opposed by a resistance of magnitude $8v$ N, where v is the cyclist speed at time t s after starting.

Motion under variable acceleration

(i) Show that $\dfrac{8}{16-v}\dfrac{dv}{dt}=1$.

(ii) Express v in terms of t.

(iii) Find the distance travelled by the cyclist in the first 8 seconds of the motion.

⑧ (i) Show that the equation of the path for a particle moving with initial velocity $\begin{pmatrix}4\\3\end{pmatrix}$ and acceleration $\begin{pmatrix}0\\-10\end{pmatrix}$ is $y=\dfrac{3}{4}x-\dfrac{5}{16}x^2$. Find the range of the particle.

A particle moves with initial velocity $\begin{pmatrix}4\\3\end{pmatrix}$ with acceleration $\mathbf{a}=\begin{pmatrix}-v_x^2\\-10\end{pmatrix}$.

(ii) Find an expression for the velocity at time t.

(iii) Find an expression for the position vector at time t.

(iv) Find the Cartesian equation of the path. Sketch the path and compare it with the path found in part (i).

(v) Find the range of the particle and compare it with that found in part (i).

⑨ A particle is projected with speed U at time $t=0$ and moves in a straight line. At time t, its velocity is v and the distance travelled is x. The acceleration of the particle is $-k\sqrt{v}$, where k is a constant.

(i) Show that the particle will come to rest when $t=\dfrac{2\sqrt{U}}{k}$.

(ii) Find in terms of k and U the distance travelled while the particle comes to rest.

⑩ Take $g=10\,\text{m s}^{-2}$ in this question.

A particle of mass $0.4\,\text{kg}$ is projected vertically upwards with a speed of $20\,\text{m s}^{-1}$. The particle experiences a resistance of $0.5v$, where v is the velocity of the particle.

(i) Find the time taken for the particle to come to instantaneous rest.

(ii) Find the greatest height attained by the particle.

Having reached its highest point, the particle then drops down against a resistance of $0.5v$.

(iii) Show that $\dfrac{dv}{dt}=1.25(8-v)$ and use it to find an expression for v as a function of t.

(iv) Find the distance travelled as a function of t and hence show that the time taken for the particle to drop down to ground level is greater than the time taken to reach its highest point.

⑪ Starting from the point $(0, 3)$, a particle is moving with initial velocity $\begin{pmatrix}12\\0\end{pmatrix}$ under the acceleration $\mathbf{a}=-9\mathbf{r}=\begin{pmatrix}-9x\\-9y\end{pmatrix}$.

(i) Show that the position vector $\mathbf{r}$ is given by $\mathbf{r}=\begin{pmatrix}x\\y\end{pmatrix}=\begin{pmatrix}4\sin 3t\\3\cos 3t\end{pmatrix}$.

(ii) Sketch a graph of the path followed by the particle for values of t in the range $0\leq t\leq \dfrac{2\pi}{3}$.

(iii) Eliminate t between the equations for x and y to reveal the Cartesian equation of the curve.

⑫ A particle of mass 0.5 kg moves in a straight line on a smooth horizontal surface. A variable resisting force acts on the particle. At time t s, the displacement of the particle from a point O on the line is x m and its velocity is $(4 - x^2)$ m s^{-1}. It is given that $x = 0$ when $t = 0$.

(i) Find the acceleration of the particle in terms of x and hence find the magnitude of the resisting force when $x = 1.5$ m.

(ii) Find an expression for x in terms of t.

(iii) How far from O can the particle ever get?

⑬ A space probe of mass m enters a large cloud of gas with speed u. The gas provides a resistance force to the probe's motion; there is no other force acting on it.

When it has travelled a distance s in the cloud the probe's speed is $\frac{u}{2}$.

The distance across the gas cloud is $3s$.

Three models are considered for the resistance force, R, in terms of the probe's speed v.

In each case find

(i) the value of k in terms of m, u and s

(ii) the dimensions of k

(iii) the speed with which the probe leaves the gas cloud

(iv) the distance the probe travels inside the gas cloud.

(A) Model A, $R = k$

(B) Model B, $R = kv$

(C) Model C, $R = kv^2$

KEY POINTS

1 Relationships between the variables describing motion

Position	Velocity	Acceleration
→	differentiate	→
$\mathbf{r} = x\mathbf{i} + y\mathbf{j} + z\mathbf{k}$	$\mathbf{v} = \dfrac{d\mathbf{r}}{dt} = v_x\mathbf{i} + v_y\mathbf{j} + v_z\mathbf{k}$	$\mathbf{a} = \dfrac{d\mathbf{v}}{dt} = \dfrac{d^2\mathbf{r}}{dt^2} = a_x\mathbf{i} + a_y\mathbf{j} + a_y\mathbf{k}$
$\mathbf{r} = \begin{pmatrix} x \\ y \\ z \end{pmatrix}$	$\mathbf{v} = \begin{pmatrix} v_x \\ v_y \\ v_z \end{pmatrix} = \begin{pmatrix} \dot{x} \\ \dot{y} \\ \dot{z} \end{pmatrix}$	$\mathbf{a} = \begin{pmatrix} \dfrac{dv_x}{dt} \\ \dfrac{dv_y}{dt} \\ \dfrac{dv_z}{dt} \end{pmatrix} = \begin{pmatrix} \ddot{x} \\ \ddot{y} \\ \ddot{z} \end{pmatrix}$
Distance from O $\sqrt{\dot{x}^2 + \dot{y}^2 + \dot{z}^2}$	**Speed** $\sqrt{x^2 + y^2 + z^2}$	**Magnitude of acceleration** $\sqrt{\ddot{x}^2 + \ddot{y}^2 + \ddot{z}^2}$

Motion under variable acceleration

Acceleration	Velocity	Position
$\longrightarrow$	integrate $\longrightarrow$	
$\mathbf{a} = \begin{pmatrix} a_x \\ a_y \\ a_z \end{pmatrix}$	$\mathbf{v} = \int \mathbf{a}\,dt$	$\mathbf{r} = \int \mathbf{v}\,dt$
	$\mathbf{v} = \int \begin{pmatrix} a_x \\ a_y \\ a_z \end{pmatrix} dt$	$\mathbf{r} = \int \begin{pmatrix} v_x \\ v_y \\ v_z \end{pmatrix} dt$

2 Acceleration may be due to a change in direction.

3 For constant acceleration

$$\mathbf{v} = \mathbf{u} + \mathbf{a}t \qquad \mathbf{r} = \mathbf{r}_0 + \mathbf{u}t + \tfrac{1}{2}\mathbf{a}t^2$$

$$\mathbf{r} = \mathbf{r}_0 + \tfrac{1}{2}(\mathbf{u}+\mathbf{v})t \qquad \mathbf{r} = \mathbf{r}_0 + \mathbf{v}t - \tfrac{1}{2}\mathbf{a}t^2$$

4 Newton's second law, using vectors

$$\mathbf{F} = m\mathbf{a}$$

5 Elimination of t between x and y components of $\mathbf{r}$, for motion in 2 dimensions leads to the equation of the path.

6 The equation of a projectile's trajectory is $y = x\tan\alpha - \dfrac{gx^2}{2u^2}(1+\tan^2\alpha)$.

7 The equation of a projectile's bounding parabola is $y = \dfrac{u^2}{2g} - \dfrac{gx^2}{2u^2}$.

8 To find the range of a projectile up or down a slope, resolve the initial velocity $\mathbf{u}$ and the acceleration $\mathbf{a}$, in directions along and perpendicular to the slope.

9 Differential equations may be used to model resisted motion. Acceleration may be expressed in a number of different ways and these give rise to different types of differential equations.
- Connecting v and t: $\quad a = \dfrac{dv}{dt}$
- Connecting s and t: $\quad a = \dfrac{d^2s}{dt^2}$
- Connecting v and s: $\quad a = v\dfrac{dv}{ds}$

10 To verify the solution of a differential equation you must
- check that the function satisfies the differential equation
- check that it is consistent with the initial or boundary conditions.

LEARNING OUTCOMES

When you have completed this chapter, you should

- be able to extend the scope of techniques from motion in one dimension to that in two and three dimensions by using vectors
- be able to find the acceleration, velocity and position vector subject to a constant or varying force in one, two or three dimensions
- be able to use acceleration, velocity and position vectors of a particle to solve problems
- be able to eliminate a parameter from expressions for the position vector of a moving particle in two dimensions
- derive the Cartesian equation of the path of a particle in two dimensions from the expression for its position vector
- be able to work with the trajectory of a projectile
- know the meaning of a projectile's bounding parabola
- be able to find the range of a projectile up or down a slope
- be able to find the maximum range of a projectile up or down a slope and the associated angle of projection
- be able to formulate differential equations for motion under variable acceleration in one and two dimensions
- know the different ways in which acceleration may be expressed
- be able to verify the solution of a differential equation.

10 Circular motion

Whirlpools and storms his circling arm invest; With all the might of gravitation blest.
            Alexander Pope

Discussion point

→ These photographs show some objects that move in circular paths. What other examples can you think of?
→ What makes objects move in circles?
→ Why does the Moon circle the Earth?
→ What happens to the hammer when the athlete lets it go?
→ Do the pilots of the planes need to be strapped into their seats at the top of a loop in order not to fall out?

1 Introduction to circular motion

The answers to the questions on the previous page lie in the nature of circular motion. Even if an object is moving at constant speed in a circle, its velocity keeps changing because its direction of motion keeps changing. Consequently, the object is accelerating and so, according to Newton's first law, there must be a force acting on it. The force required to keep an object moving in a circle can be provided in many ways.

Without the Earth's gravitational force, the Moon would move off at constant speed in a straight line into space. The wire attached to the athlete's hammer provides a tension force which keeps the ball moving in a circle. When the athlete lets go, the ball flies off at a tangent because the tension has disappeared.

Although it would be sensible for the pilot to be strapped in, no upward force is necessary to stop him falling out of the plane because his weight contributes to the force required for motion in a circle.

In this chapter, these effects are explained.

Notation

To describe circular motion (or indeed any other topic) mathematically you need a suitable notation. It will be helpful in this chapter to use the notation (attributed to Newton) for differentiation with respect to time in which, for example, $\frac{ds}{dt}$ is written as $\dot{s}$, and $\frac{d^2\theta}{dt^2}$ as $\ddot{\theta}$.

Figure 10.1 shows a particle P moving round the circumference of a circle of radius r, centre O. At time t, the position vector OP of the particle makes an angle θ (in radians) with the fixed direction OA. The arc length AP is denoted by s.

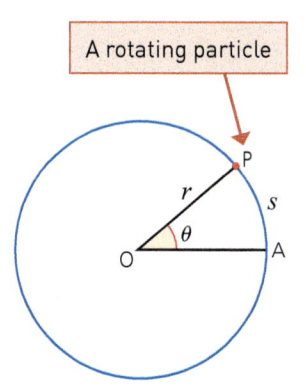

Figure 10.1

Angular speed

Using this notation,

$$s = r\theta$$

Differentiating with respect to time using the product rule gives

$$\frac{ds}{dt} = r\frac{d\theta}{dt} + \theta\frac{dr}{dt}.$$

Since r is constant for a circle, $\frac{dr}{dt} = 0$, so the rate at which the arc length increases is

$$\frac{ds}{dt} = r\frac{d\theta}{dt} \quad \text{or} \quad \dot{s} = r\dot{\theta}.$$

In this equation, $\dot{s}$ is the speed at which P is moving round the circle (often denoted by v), and $\dot{\theta}$ is the rate at which the angle θ is increasing, i.e. the rate at which the position vector $\overline{OP}$ is rotating.

The quantity $\frac{d\theta}{dt}$, or $\dot{\theta}$, can be called the **angular velocity** or the **angular speed** of P.

In more advanced work, angular velocity is treated as a vector, whose direction is taken to be that of the axis of rotation. In this book, $\frac{d\theta}{dt}$ is often referred to as angular speed, but is given a sign: positive for an anticlockwise rotation and negative for a clockwise rotation.

Introduction to circular motion

Note

It is common practice to give angular speed as multiples of π

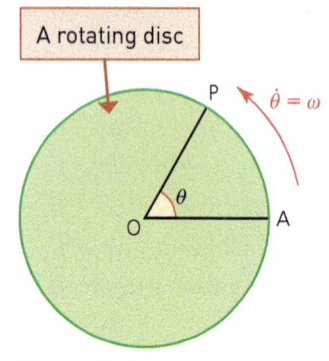

Angular speed is often denoted by ω, the Greek letter omega. So the equation $\dot{s} = r\dot{\theta}$ may be written as

$$v = r\omega$$

Notice that for this equation to hold, θ must be measured in radians, so the angular speed is measured in radians per second or $\text{rad}\,\text{s}^{-1}$.

Figure 10.2 shows a disc rotating about its centre, O, with angular speed ω. The line OP represents any radius.

Every point on the disc describes a circular path, and all the points have the same angular speed. However, the actual speed of any point depends on its distance from the centre: increasing r in the equation $v = r\omega$ increases v. You will appreciate this if you have ever been at the end of a rotating line of people in a dance or watched a body of marching soldiers wheeling round a corner.

Angular speeds are sometimes measured in revolutions per second or revolutions per minute (rpm) where one revolution is equal to 2π radians. For example, a computer hard disc might spin at 7200 rpm or more; at cruising speeds, crankshafts in car engines typically rotate at 3000 to 4000 rpm.

Figure 10.2 A rotating disc

Example 10.1

A police car drives at 40 mph around a circular bend of radius 16 m. A second car moves so that it has the same angular speed as the police car but in a circle of radius 12 m. Is the second car breaking the 30 mph speed limit? (Use the approximation 1 mile = $\frac{8}{5}$ km.)

Notes

1. Notice that working in fractions gives an exact answer.
2. A quicker way to do this question would be to notice that, because the cars have the same angular speed, the actual speeds of the cars are proportional to the radii of the circles in which they are moving. Using this method it is possible to stay in mph. The ratio of the two radii is $\frac{12}{16}$ so the speed of the second car is $\frac{12}{16} \times 40$ mph = 30 mph.

Solution

Converting miles per hour to metres per second gives:

$$40 \text{ mph} = 40 \times \frac{8}{5} \text{ km}\,\text{h}^{-1}$$

$$= \frac{40 \times 8 \times 1000}{5 \times 3600} \text{ m}\,\text{s}^{-1}$$

$$= \frac{160}{9} \text{ m}\,\text{s}^{-1}$$

Using $v = r\omega$

$$\omega = \frac{160}{9 \times 16} \text{ rad}\,\text{s}^{-1}$$

$$= \frac{10}{9} \text{ rad}\,\text{s}^{-1}$$

The speed of the second car is:

$$v = 12\omega$$

$$= \frac{10}{9} \times 12 \text{ m}\,\text{s}^{-1}$$

$$= \frac{120 \times 5 \times 3600}{9 \times 8 \times 1000} \text{ mph}$$

$$= 30 \text{ mph}$$

The second car is just on the speed limit.

Exercise 10.1

① Find the angular speed in radians per second to one decimal place, of antique records rotating at

   (i) 78 rpm   (ii) 45 rpm   (iii) $33\frac{1}{3}$ rpm.

② A flywheel is rotating at $300\,\text{rad}\,\text{s}^{-1}$. Express this angular speed in rpm, correct to the nearest whole number.

③ The London Eye observation wheel has a diameter of 135 m and completes one revolution in 30 minutes.

   (i) Calculate its angular speed in

   (a) rpm   (b) radians per second.

   (ii) Calculate the speed of the point on the circumference where passengers board the moving wheel.

④ A lawnmower engine is started by pulling a rope that has been wound round a cylinder of radius 4 cm. Find the angular speed of the cylinder at a moment when the rope is being pulled with a speed of $1.3\,\text{m}\,\text{s}^{-1}$. Give your answer in radians per second, correct to one decimal place.

⑤ The wheels of a car have radius 20 cm. What is the angular speed, in radians per second, correct to one decimal place, of a wheel when the car is travelling at

   (i) $10\,\text{m}\,\text{s}^{-1}$ (ii) $30\,\text{m}\,\text{s}^{-1}$?

⑥ The angular speed of an audio CD changes continuously so that a laser can read the data at a constant speed of $12\,\text{m}\,\text{s}^{-1}$. Find the angular speed (in rpm) when the distance of the laser from the centre is

   (i) 30 mm   (ii) 55 mm.

⑦ What is the average angular speed of the Earth in radians per second as it

   (i) orbits the Sun?

   (ii) rotates about its own axis?

   The radius of the Earth is 6400 km.

   (iii) At what speed is someone on the equator travelling relative to the centre of the Earth?

   (iv) At what speed are you travelling relative to the centre of the Earth?

⑧ A tractor has front wheels of diameter 70 cm and back wheels of diameter 1.6 m.

   What is the ratio of their angular speeds when the tractor is being driven along a straight road?

⑨ (i) Find the kinetic energy of a 50 kg person riding a big wheel with radius 5 m when the ride is rotating at 3 rpm. You should assume that the person can be modelled as a particle.

   (ii) Explain why this modelling assumption is necessary.

⑩ The minute hand of a clock is 1.2 m long and the hour hand is 0.8 m long.

   (i) Find the speeds of the tips of the hands.

   (ii) Find the ratio of the speeds of the tips of the hands and explain why this is not the same as the ratio of the angular speeds of the hands.

⑪ Figure 10.3 represents a 'Chairoplane' ride at a fair. It completes one revolution every 2.5 seconds.

   (i) Find the radius of the circular path which a rider follows.

   (ii) Find the speed of a rider.

Introduction to circular motion

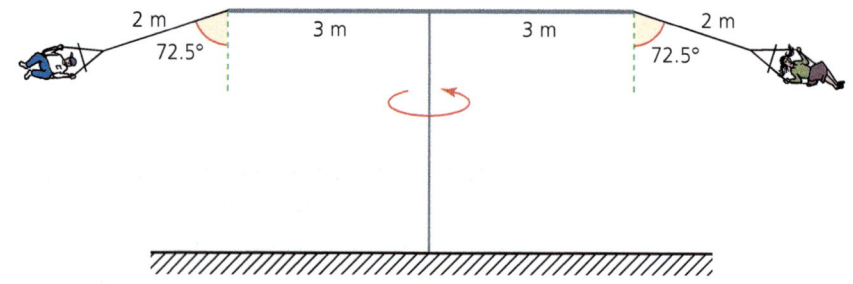

Figure 10.3

⑫ The position vector of a rider on a helter-skelter is given by

$$\mathbf{r} = 2\sin t\, \mathbf{i} + 2\cos t\, \mathbf{j} + \left(8 - \tfrac{1}{2}t\right)\mathbf{k}$$

where the units are in metres and seconds. The unit vector $\mathbf{k}$ is vertically upwards.

(i) Find an expression for the velocity of the rider at time t.

(ii) Find the speed of the rider at time $t = \tfrac{\pi}{4}$.

(iii) Find the magnitude and direction of the rider's acceleration when $t = \tfrac{\pi}{4}$.

Velocity and acceleration

Velocity and acceleration are both vector quantities. They can be expressed either in magnitude–direction form, or in components. When describing circular motion or other orbits, it is most convenient to take components in directions along the radius (**radial** direction) and at right angles to it (**transverse** direction).

For a particle moving round a circle of radius r, the velocity has:

radial component: $\quad 0$

transverse component: $\quad r\dot{\theta}$ or $r\omega$.

The acceleration of a particle moving round a circle of radius r has:

radial component: $\quad -r\dot{\theta}^2$ or $-r\omega^2$

transverse component: $\quad r\ddot{\theta}$ or $r\dot{\omega}$.

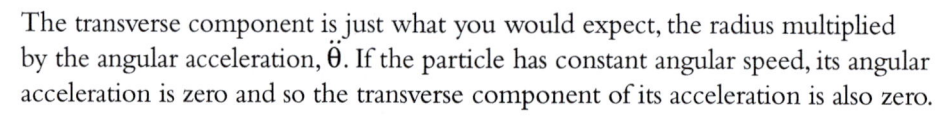

The transverse component is just what you would expect, the radius multiplied by the angular acceleration, $\ddot{\theta}$. If the particle has constant angular speed, its angular acceleration is zero and so the transverse component of its acceleration is also zero.

In contrast, the radial component of the acceleration, $-r\omega^2$, is almost certainly not a result you would have expected intuitively. It tells you that a particle travelling in a circle is always accelerating towards the centre of the circle, but without getting any closer to the centre. If this seems a strange idea, you may find it helpful to remember that circular motion is not a natural state; left to itself a particle will travel in a straight line. To keep a particle in the unatural state of circular motion it must be given an acceleration at right angles to its motion, i.e. towards the centre of the circle.

The derivation of these expressions for the acceleration of a particle in a circular motion is complicated by the fact that the radial and transverse directions are themselves changing as the particle moves round the circle, in contrast to the fixed x and y directions in the Cartesian system. The derivation is given in a mathematical note on page 264. At first reading you may prefer to accept the results, but make sure that at a later stage you work through and understand the derivation.

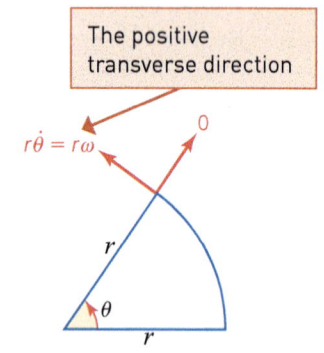

Figure 10.4 Velocity — The positive transverse direction; $r\dot{\theta} = r\omega$

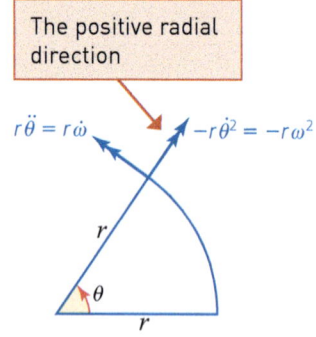

Figure 10.5 Acceleration — The positive radial direction; $r\ddot{\theta} = r\dot{\omega}$; $-r\dot{\theta}^2 = -r\omega^2$

2 Circular motion with constant speed

In this section, the circular motion is assumed to be uniform and so have no transverse component of acceleration. Later in the chapter, situations are considered in which the angular speed varies.

Problems involving circular motion often refer to the actual speed of the object, rather than its angular speed. It is easy to convert one into the other using the relationship $v = r\omega$. The relationship can also be used to express the magnitude of the acceleration in terms of v and r.

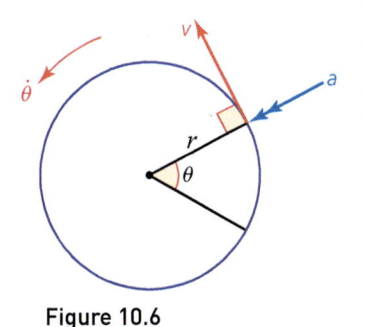

$$\omega = \frac{v}{r}$$

$$a = r\omega^2 = r\left(\frac{v}{r}\right)^2$$

$$\Rightarrow a = \frac{v^2}{r} \text{ towards the centre}$$

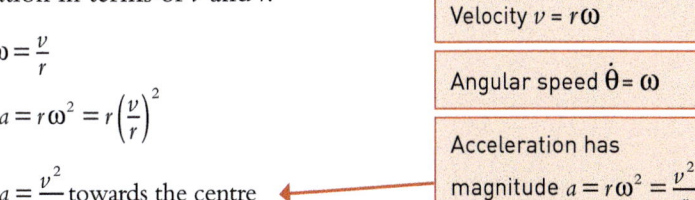

Velocity $v = r\omega$

Angular speed $\dot{\theta} = \omega$

Acceleration has magnitude $a = r\omega^2 = \frac{v^2}{r}$ and is directed towards the centre

Figure 10.6

Example 10.2

A turntable is rotating at 45 rpm. A fly is standing on it, 8 cm from its centre.

Find

(i) the angular speed of the fly in radians per second

(ii) the speed of the fly in metres per second

(iii) the acceleration of the fly.

Hint

One revolution is 2π radians.

Solution

(i) $45 \text{ rpm} = 45 \times 2\pi \text{ rad min}^{-1}$

$= \frac{45 \times 2\pi}{60} \text{ rad s}^{-1}$

$= \frac{3\pi}{2} \text{ rad s}^{-1}$.

(ii) v can be found using

$v = r\omega$

$= 0.08 \times \frac{3\pi}{2}$

$= 0.376...$

So the speed of the fly is 0.38 m s^{-1} (to 2 dp).

(iii) The acceleration of the fly is given by

$r\omega^2 = 0.08 \times \left(\frac{3\pi}{2}\right)^2 \text{ m s}^{-2}$

$= 1.78 \text{ m s}^{-2}$

It is directed towards the centre of the record.

Circular motion with constant speed

The forces required for circular motion

Newton's first law of motion states that a body will continue in a state of rest or uniform motion in a straight line unless acted upon by an external force. Any object moving in a circle, such as the police car and the fly in Examples 10.1 and 10.2, must therefore be acted upon by a resultant force in order to produce the required acceleration towards the centre.

A force towards the centre is called a **centripetal** (centre-seeking) force. A resultant centripetal force is necessary for a particle to move in a circular path.

Examples of circular motion

You are now in a position to use Newton's second law to determine theoretical answers to some of the questions which were posed at the beginning of this chapter. These will, as usual, be obtained using models of the true motion which will be based on simplifying assumptions, for example zero air resistance.

Example 10.3

A coin is placed on a rotating horizontal turntable, 5 cm from the centre of rotation. The coefficient of friction between the coin and the turntable is 0.5.

(i) The speed of rotation of the turntable is gradually increased. At what angular speed will the coin begin to slide?

(ii) What happens next?

Solution

(i) Because the speed of the turntable is increased only gradually, the coin will not slip tangentially.

Figure 10.7 shows the forces acting on the coin, and its acceleration.

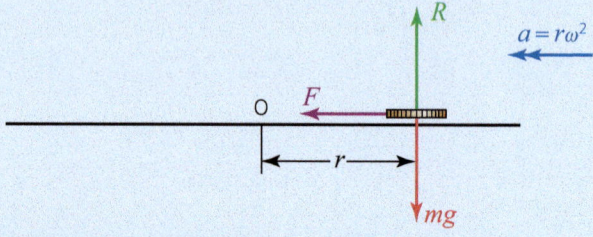

Figure 10.7

The acceleration is towards the centre of the circular path, O, so there must be a frictional force F in that direction.

There is no vertical component of acceleration, so the resultant force acting on the coin has no vertical component.

Therefore

$$R - mg = 0$$

$$R = mg \qquad \text{①}$$

By Newton's second law towards the centre of the circle:

$$\text{Force } F = ma = mr\omega^2$$

The coin will not slide so long as $F \leq \mu R$. ②

Substituting from ① and ② this gives

$$mr\omega^2 \leq \mu mg$$
$$\Rightarrow \quad r\omega^2 \leq \mu g$$

> Notice that the mass, m, has been eliminated at this stage, so the answer does not depend upon it.

Taking g in m s^{-2} as 9.8 and substituting $r = 0.05$ and $\mu = 0.5$

$$\omega^2 \leq 98$$
$$\omega \leq \sqrt{98}$$
$$\omega \leq 9.89...$$

The coin will move in a circle provided the angular speed is less than about $10 \, \text{rad s}^{-1}$ and the speed is independent of the mass of the coin.

(ii) When the angular speed increases beyond this, the coin slips to a new position. If the angular speed continues to increase, it will slip off the turntable. When it reaches the edge, it will fly off in the direction of the tangent.

The conical pendulum

A conical pendulum consists of a small bob tied to one end of a string. The other end of the string is fixed and the bob is made to rotate in a horizontal circle below the fixed point so that the string describes a cone, as in Figure 10.8.

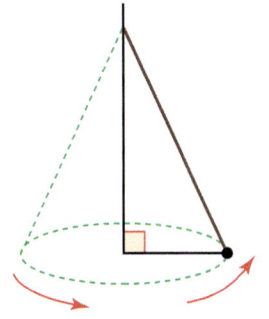

Figure 10.8

EXPERIMENT

1. Draw a diagram showing the magnitude and direction of the acceleration of the bob and the forces acting on it.
2. In the case that the radius of the circle remains constant, try to predict the effect of the angular speed when the length of the string is increased or when the mass of the bob is increased. What might happen when the angular speed increases?

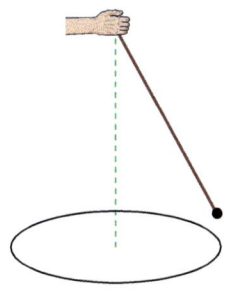

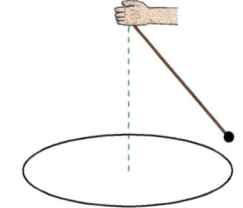

Figure 10.9

3. Draw two circles of equal diameter on horizontal surfaces so that two people can make the bobs of two conical pendulums rotate in circles of the same radius.
   (i) Compare pendulums of different lengths with bobs of equal mass.
   (ii) Compare pendulums of the same length but with bobs of different masses.
   Does the angular speed depend on the length of the pendulum or the mass of the bob?
4. What happens when somebody makes the speed of the bob increase?
5. Can the bob be made to rotate with the string horizontal?

Circular motion with constant speed

Theoretical model for the conical pendulum

A conical pendulum may be modelled as a particle of mass m attached to a light, inextensible string of length l. The mass is rotating in a horizontal circle with angular speed ω and the string makes an angle α with the downward vertical. The radius of the circle is r and the tension in the string is T, all in consistent units (e.g. S.I. units). The situation is shown in Figure 10.10.

The magnitude of the acceleration is $r\omega^2$. The acceleration acts in a horizontal direction towards the centre of the circle. This means that there must be a resultant force acting towards the centre of the circle.

There are two forces acting on this particle, its weight mg and the tension T in the string.

As the acceleration of the particle has no vertical component, the resultant force has no vertical component, so

$$T \cos \alpha - mg = 0 \qquad \text{①}$$

Using Newton's second law towards the centre, O, of the circle

$$T \sin \alpha = ma = mr\omega^2 \qquad \text{②}$$

In triangle AOP $\qquad r = l \sin \alpha$

Substituting for r in ② gives $\quad T \sin \alpha = m(l \sin \alpha) \omega^2$

$$\Rightarrow \qquad T = ml\omega^2$$

Substituting this in ① gives

$$ml\omega^2 \cos \alpha - mg = 0$$

$$\Rightarrow \qquad l \cos \alpha = \frac{g}{\omega^2} \qquad \text{③}$$

This equation provides sufficient information to give theoretical answers to the questions in the experiment.

- When r is kept constant and the length of the string is increased, the length $AO = l \cos \alpha$ increases. Equation ③ indicates that the value of $\frac{g}{\omega^2}$ increases and so the angular speed ω decreases. Conversely, the angular speed increases when the string is shortened.
- The mass of the particle does not appear in equation ③, so it has no effect on the angular speed, ω.
- When the length of the pendulum is unchanged, but the angular speed is increased, $\cos \alpha$ decreases, leading to an increase in the angle α and hence in r.
- If $\alpha \geq 90°$, $\cos \alpha \leq 0$, so $\frac{g}{\omega^2} \leq 0$, which is impossible. You can see from Figure 10.10 that the tension in the string must have a vertical component to balance the weight of the particle.

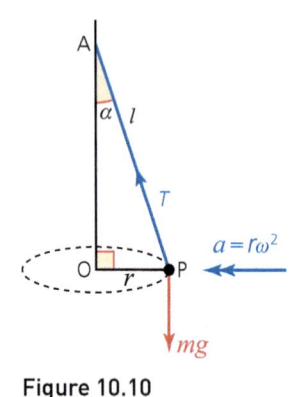

Figure 10.10

Example 10.4

The diagram of Figure 10.11 on the right represents one of several arms of a fairground ride shown on the left. The arms rotate about an axis and riders sit in chairs linked to the arms by chains.

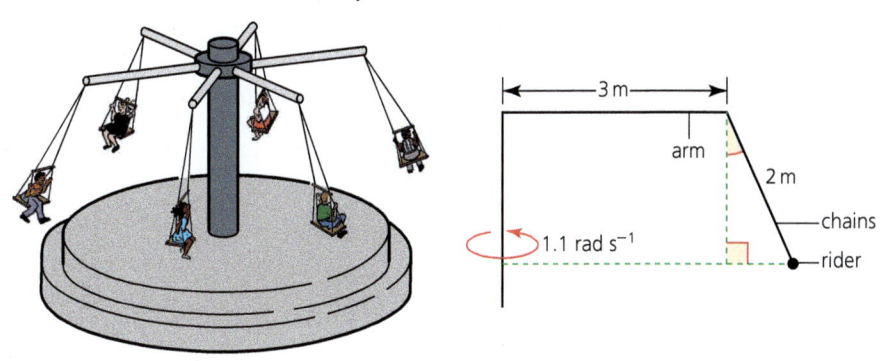

Figure 10.11

The chains are 2 m long and the arms are 3 m long. Find the angle that the chains make with the vertical when the rider rotates at 1.1 rad s⁻¹.

Solution

Let T be the resultant tension in the chains holding a chair and let m kg be the mass of the chair and rider.

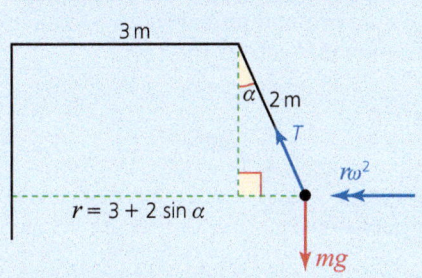

Figure 10.12

If the chains make an angle α with the vertical, the motion is in a horizontal circle with radius given by

$r = 3 + 2 \sin \alpha$.

The magnitude of the acceleration is given by

$r\omega^2 = (3 + 2 \sin \alpha) 1.1^2$

It is in a horizontal direction towards the centre of the circle. Using Newton's second law in this direction gives

$$\text{Force} = mr\omega^2$$

$\Rightarrow \quad T \sin \alpha = m(3 + 2\sin\alpha)1.1^2$ ①

$\qquad\qquad\quad = 1.21\, m(3 + 2\sin\alpha)$

Vertically $\quad T \cos \alpha - mg = 0$

$\Rightarrow \qquad\qquad T = \dfrac{mg}{\cos\alpha}$

Circular motion with constant speed

> **Note**
> Since the answer does not depend on the mass of the rider and chair, when riders of different masses, or even no riders, are on the equipment all the chains should make the same angle with the vertical.

Substituting for T in equation ①:

$$\frac{mg}{\cos\alpha}\sin\alpha = 1.21\,m(3+2\sin\alpha)$$

$$\Rightarrow \quad 9.8\tan\alpha = 3.63 + 2.42\sin\alpha$$

> Since m cancels out at this stage, the angle does not depend on the mass of the rider.

This equation cannot be solved directly, but a numerical method will give you the solution 25.5° correct to three significant figures. You might like to solve the equation yourself or check that this solution does in fact satisfy the equation.

Banked tracks

ACTIVITY 10.1

Place a coin on a piece of stiff A4 card and hold it horizontally at arm's length with the coin near your hand.

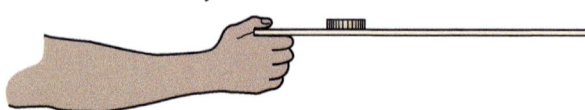

Figure 10.13

Turn round slowly so that your hand moves in a horizontal circle. Now gradually speed up. The outcome will probably not surprise you.
What happens though if you tilt the card?

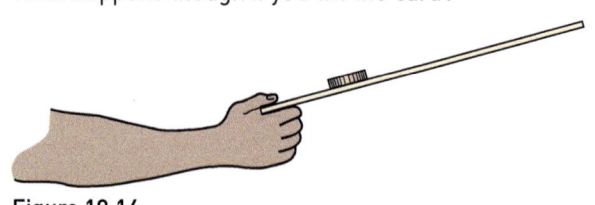

Figure 10.14

> **Note**
> Keep away from other people and breakable objects when carrying out this activity.

Figure 10.15

You may have noticed that when they curve round bends, most roads are banked so that the edge at the outside of the bend is slightly higher than that at the inside. For the same reason, the outer rail of a railway track is slightly higher than the inner rail when it goes round the bend. On bobsleigh tracks the bends are almost bowl shaped, with a much greater gradient on the outside.

Figure 10.16 shows a car rounding a bend on a road which is banked so that the cross-section makes an angle α with the horizontal.

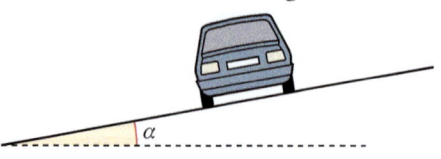

Figure 10.16

In modelling such situations, it is usual to treat the bend as part of a horizontal circle whose radius is large compared to the width of the car. In this case, the radius of the circle is taken to be r metres, and the speed of the car constant at v metres per second.

Discussion point

The direction of the frictional force F will be up or down the slope depending on whether the car has a tendency to slip sideways towards the inside or outside of the bend.

Under what conditions do you think each of these will occur?

The car is modelled as a particle which has an acceleration of $\frac{v^2}{r}$ m s^{-2} in a horizontal direction towards the centre of the circle. The forces and acceleration are shown in Figure 10.17.

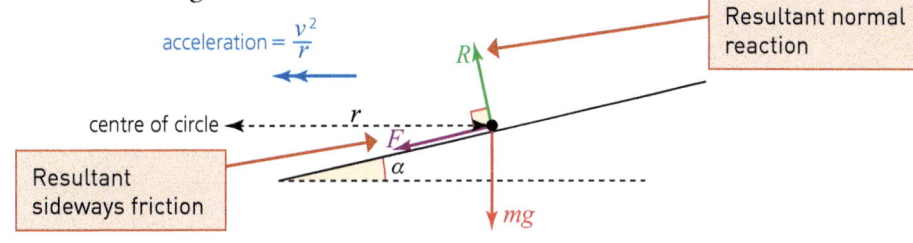

Figure 10.17

Example 10.5

A car is rounding a bend of radius 100 m which is banked at an angle of 10° to the horizontal. At what speed must the car travel to ensure that it has no tendency to slip sideways?

Solution

When there is no tendency to slip there is no frictional force, so, in the plane perpendicular to the direction of motion of the car, the forces and acceleration are as shown in Figure 10.18. The only horizontal force is provided by the horizontal component of the normal reaction of the road on the car.

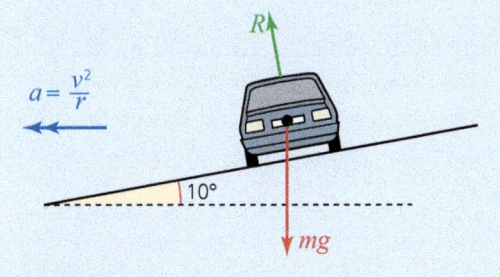

Figure 10.18

Note

The normal reaction R is resolved into components
$R \sin 10°$ horizontally ←
$R \cos 10°$ vertically ↑

Vertically there is no acceleration so there is no resultant force

$$R \cos 10° - mg = 0$$

$$\Rightarrow \quad R = \frac{mg}{\cos 10°} \quad ①$$

By Newton's second law, in the horizontal direction towards the centre of the circle

$$R \sin 10° = ma = \frac{mv^2}{r}$$

$$= \frac{mv^2}{100}$$

Circular motion with constant speed

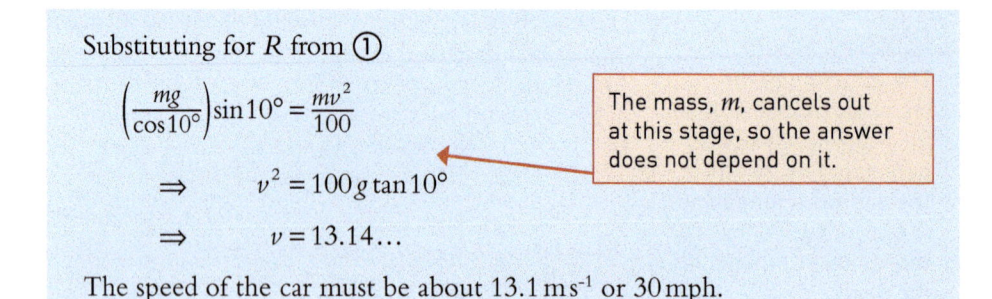

> Substituting for R from ①
>
> $$\left(\frac{mg}{\cos 10°}\right)\sin 10° = \frac{mv^2}{100}$$
>
> $$\Rightarrow \quad v^2 = 100g\tan 10°$$
>
> $$\Rightarrow \quad v = 13.14\ldots$$
>
> The speed of the car must be about $13.1\,\text{m s}^{-1}$ or $30\,\text{mph}$.

[The mass, m, cancels out at this stage, so the answer does not depend on it.]

There are two important points to notice in this example.

- The speed is the same whatever the mass of the car.
- The example looks at the situation when the car does not tend to slide and finds the speed at which this is the case. At this speed, the car does not depend on friction to keep it from sliding and, indeed, it could travel safely round the bend at this speed even in very icy conditions. However, at other speeds there is a tendency to slide, and friction actually helps the car to follow its intended path.

Safe speeds on a bend

What would happen in the previous example if the car travelled either more slowly than $13.1\,\text{m s}^{-1}$ or more quickly?

The answer is that there would be a frictional force acting so as to prevent the car from sliding across the road.

There are two possible directions for the frictional force. When the vehicle is stationary or travelling slowly, there is a tendency to slide down the slope and the friction acts up the slope to prevent this. When it is travelling quickly round the bend, the car is more likely to slide up the slope, so the friction acts down the slope.

Fortunately, under most road conditions, the coefficient of friction between tyres and the road is large, typically about 0.8. This means that there is a range of speeds that are safe for negotiating any particular bend.

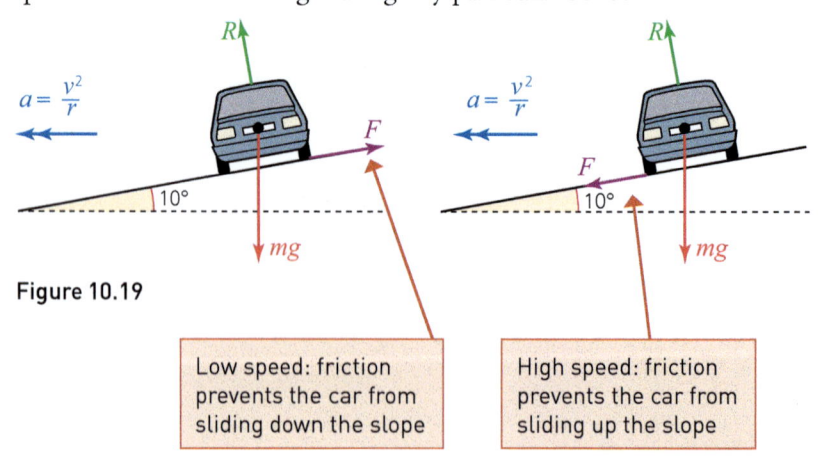

Figure 10.19

Low speed: friction prevents the car from sliding down the slope

High speed: friction prevents the car from sliding up the slope

> **Discussion points**
>
> 1. Using a particle model for the car, show that it will not slide up or down the slope provided
>
> $$\sqrt{rg\frac{(\sin\alpha - \mu\cos\alpha)}{(\cos\alpha + \mu\sin\alpha)}} < v < \sqrt{rg\frac{(\sin\alpha + \mu\cos\alpha)}{(\cos\alpha - \mu\sin\alpha)}}$$
>
> If $r = 100$ and $\alpha = 10°$ (so that $\tan\alpha = 0.176$) the minimum and maximum safe speeds (in mph) for different values of μ are given in the following table.
>
> | μ | 0 | 0.1 | 0.2 | 0.3 | 0.4 | 0.5 | 0.6 | 0.7 | 0.8 | 0.9 | 1.0 | 1.1 | 1.2 |
> |---|---|---|---|---|---|---|---|---|---|---|---|---|---|
> | Minimum safe speed | 30 | 19 | 0 | 0 | 0 | 0 | 0 | 0 | 0 | 0 | 0 | 0 | 0 |
> | Maximum safe speed | 30 | 37 | 44 | 50 | 55 | 61 | 66 | 70 | 75 | 80 | 84 | 89 | 93 |
>
> 2. Would you regard this bend as safe? How, by changing the values of r and α, could you make it safer?

Example 10.6

A bend on a railway track has a radius of 500 m and is to be banked so that a train can negotiate it at 60 mph without the need for a lateral force between its wheels and the rail. The distance between the rails is 1.43 m.

How much higher should the outside rail be than the inside one?

Solution

There is very little friction between the track and the wheels of a train. Any sideways force required is provided by the 'lateral thrust' between the wheels and the rail. The ideal speed for the bend is such that the lateral thrust is zero.

Figure 10.20 shows the forces acting on the train and its acceleration when the track is banked at an angle α to the horizontal.

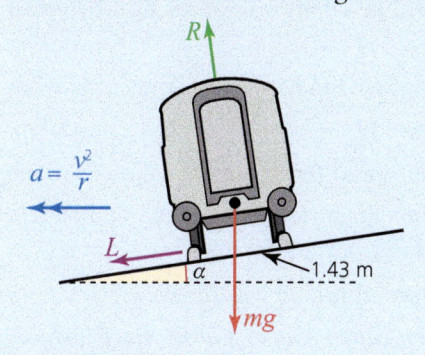

Figure 10.20

Circular motion with constant speed

When there is no lateral thrust, $L = 0$.

Horizontally: $\quad R \sin \alpha = \dfrac{mv^2}{r}$ ①

Vertically: $\quad R \cos \alpha = mg$ ②

Dividing ① by ② gives $\quad \tan \alpha = \dfrac{v^2}{rg}$

Using the fact that 60 mph = 26.8 m s⁻¹ this becomes

$$\tan \alpha = 0.147$$
$$\Rightarrow \quad \alpha = 8.4° \text{ (to 2 sf)}$$

The outside rail should be raised by $1.43 \sin \alpha$ metres, i.e. about 21 cm.

Exercise 10.2

① Figure 10.21 shows two cars A and B, travelling at constant speeds in different lanes (radii 24 m and 20 m) round a circular traffic island. Car A has speed 18 m s⁻¹ and car B has speed 15 m s⁻¹.

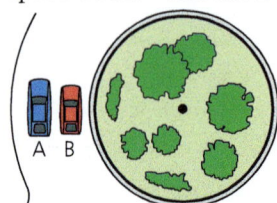

Figure 10.21

Answer the following questions, giving reasons for your answers.
- (i) Which car has the greater angular speed?
- (ii) Is one car overtaking the other?
- (iii) Find the magnitude of the acceleration of each car.
- (iv) In which direction is the resultant force on each car acting?

② Two coins are placed on a horizontal turntable. Coin A has mass 15 g and is placed 5 cm from the centre; coin B has mass 10 g and is placed 7.5 cm from the centre. The coefficient of friction between each coin and the turntable is 0.4.
- (i) Describe what happens to the coins when the turntable turns at
  - (a) 6 rad s⁻¹
  - (b) 8 rad s⁻¹
  - (c) 10 rad s⁻¹.
- (ii) What would happen if the coins were interchanged?

③ A car is travelling at a steady speed of 15 m s⁻¹ round a roundabout of radius 20 m on a flat horizontal road.
- (i) Criticise this false argument:

  The car is travelling at a steady speed and so its speed is neither increasing nor decreasing and therefore the car has no acceleration.

- (ii) Calculate the magnitude of the acceleration of the car.
- (iii) The car has mass 800 kg. Calculate the sideways force on each wheel assuming it to be the same for all four wheels.
- (iv) Is the assumption in part (iii) realistic?

④ A fairground ride has seats at 3 m and at 4.5 m from the centre of rotation. Each rider travels in a horizontal circle. Say whether each of the following statements is TRUE or FALSE, giving your reasons.

(i) Riders in the two positions have the same angular speed at any time.

(ii) Riders in the two positions have the same speed at any time.

(iii) Riders in the two positions have the same magnitude of acceleration at any time.

⑤ A skater of mass 60 kg follows a circular path of radius 4 m, moving at 2 m s⁻¹.

(i) Calculate

(a) the angular speed of the skater

(b) the magnitude of the acceleration of the skater

(c) the resultant force acting on the skater.

(ii) What modelling assumptions have you made?

⑥ Two spin driers, both of which rotate about a vertical axis, have different specifications as given in the table below.

Model	Rate of rotation	Drum diameter
A	600 rpm	60 cm
B	800 rpm	40 cm

State with reasons, which model you would expect to be the more effective.

⑦ A satellite of mass M_s is in a circular orbit around the Earth, with a radius of r metres. The force of attraction between the Earth and the satellite is given by

$$F = \frac{GM_e M_s}{r^2}$$

where $G = 6.67 \times 10^{-11}$ in S.I. units. The mass of the earth M_e is 5.97×10^{24} kg.

(i) Find in terms of r, expressions for

(a) the speed of the satellite, v m s⁻¹

(b) the time T s, it takes to complete one revolution.

(ii) Hence show that, for all satellites, T^2 is proportional to r^3.

A geostationary satellite orbits the Earth so that it is always above the same place on the equator.

(iii) How far is it from the centre of the Earth?

> **Note**
> The law found in part (ii) was discovered experimentally by Johannes Kepler (1571–1630) to hold true for the planets as they orbit the Sun, and is commonly known as Kepler's third law.

⑧ A rotary lawn mower uses a piece of light nylon string with a small metal sphere on the end to cut the grass. The string is 20 cm in length and the mass of the sphere is 30 g.

(i) Find the tension in the string when the sphere is rotating at 2000 rpm assuming that the string is horizontal.

(ii) Explain why it is reasonable to assume that the string is horizontal.

(iii) Find the speed of the sphere when the tension in the string is 80 N.

⑨ In this question, you should assume that the orbit of the Earth around the Sun is circular, with radius 1.44×10^{11} m, and that the Sun is fixed.

(i) Find the magnitude of the acceleration of the Earth as it orbits the Sun.

Circular motion with constant speed

The force of attraction between the Earth and the Sun is given by

$$F = \frac{GM_e M_s}{r^2}$$

where M_e is the mass of the Earth, M_s is the mass of the Sun, r is the radius of the Earth's orbit and G the universal constant of gravitation (6.67×10^{-11} S.I. units).

(ii) Calculate the mass of the Sun.

(iii) Comment on the significance of the fact that you cannot calculate the mass of the Earth from the radius of its orbit.

⑩ Sarah ties a model aeroplane of mass 180 g to the end of a piece of string 80 cm long and then swings it round so that the plane travels in a horizontal circle.

The aeroplane is not designed to fly and there is no lift force acting on its wings.

(i) Explain why it is not possible for the string to be horizontal.

Sarah gives the aeroplane an angular speed of 120 rpm.

(ii) What is the angular speed in radians per second?

(iii) Copy Figure 10.22 below and mark the tension in the string, the weight of the aeroplane and the direction of the acceleration.

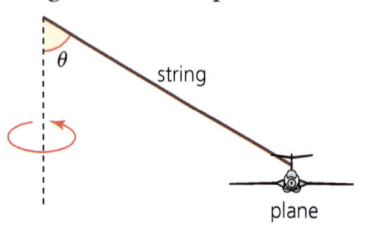

Figure 10.22

(iv) Write down the horizontal radial equation of motion for the aeroplane and the vertical equilibrium equation in terms of the angle θ.

(v) Show that, under these conditions, θ has a value between 85° and 86°.

(vi) Find the tension in the string.

⑪ Experiments carried out by the police accident investigation department suggest that a typical value for a coefficient of friction between the tyres of a car and a road surface is 0.8.

(i) Using this information, find the maximum safe speed on a level circular motorway slip road of radius 50 m.

(ii) How much faster could cars travel if the road were banked at an angle of 5° to the horizontal?

⑫ The coefficient of friction between the tyres of a car and the road is 0.8. The mass of the car and its passengers is 800 kg. Model the car as a particle.

(i) Find the maximum frictional force that the road can exert on the car and describe what might be happening when this maximum force is acting

(a) at right angles to the line of motion

(b) along the line of motion.

(ii) What is the maximum speed that the car can travel without skidding on level ground round a circular bend of radius 120 m?

Figure 10.23 shows the car now travelling around a bend of radius 120 m on a road banked at an angle α to the horizontal. The car's speed is such that there is no sideways force (up or down the slope) exerted on its tyres by the road.

Figure 10.23

(iii) Draw a diagram showing the weight of the car, the normal reaction of the road on it and the direction of its acceleration.

(iv) Resolve the forces in the horizontal radial and vertical directions and write down the horizontal equation of motion and the vertical equilibrium equation.

(v) Show that $\tan\alpha = \dfrac{v^2}{120\,g}$ where v is the speed of the car in metres per second.

(vi) On this particular bend, vehicles are expected to travel at $15\,\text{m s}^{-1}$. At what angle, α, should the road be banked?

⑬ A big wheel at a fair ground is rotating in a vertical circle at a constant rate of one revolution per minute.

(i) Calculate the angular speed of the wheel in radians per second.

(ii) Calculate the linear speed of a point 10 m from the axis of rotation.

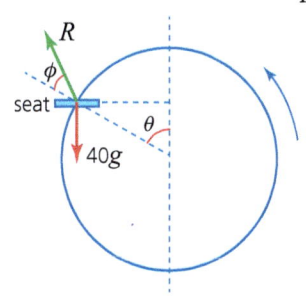

Figure 10.24

A child of mass 40 kg is sitting 10 m from the axis of rotation on a seat on the wheel.

The situation may be modelled by assuming that there is negligible distance between the seat and the child's centre of mass and that the seat remains horizontal at all times. When the radius joining the seat to the axis is inclined at θ to the upward vertical, the reaction R of the seat on the child is inclined at φ to that radius, as shown in Figure 10.24.

(iii) By resolving the forces acting on the child in a direction perpendicular to the radius, explain why

$R\sin\phi = 40g\sin\theta.$

(iv) Write down the equation of motion of the child in the radial direction.

(v) Given that $\theta = \dfrac{\pi}{6}$, find R and φ.

Circular motion with constant speed

14. A light inextensible string of length 0.8 m is threaded through a smooth ring and carries a particle at each end. Particle A of mass m kg is at rest at a distance of 0.3 m below the ring. The other particle, B, of mass M kg is rotating in a horizontal circle whose centre is A.

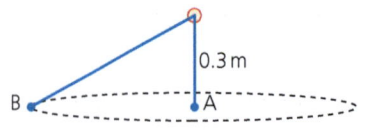

    Figure 10.25

    (i) Express M in terms of m.
    (ii) Find the angular velocity of B.

15. A particle of mass 0.2 kg is moving on the smooth inside surface of a fixed hollow sphere of radius 0.75 m. The particle moves in a horizontal circle whose centre is 0.45 m below the centre of the sphere (see Figure 10.26).

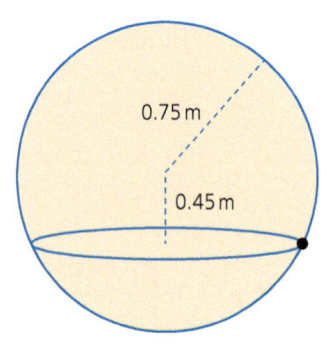

    Figure 10.26

    (i) Show that the force exerted by the sphere on the particle has magnitude $\frac{1}{3}g$.
    (ii) Find the speed of the particle.
    (iii) Find the time taken for the particle to complete one revolution.

16. A particle P of mass 0.25 kg is attached to one end of each of two inextensible strings which are both taut. The other end of the longer string is attached to a fixed point A, and the other end of the shorter string is attached to a fixed point B, which is vertically below A.

    String AP is 0.2 m long and string BP is 0.15 m long. P moves in a horizontal circle of radius 0.12 m with constant angular speed $10\,\text{rad}\,\text{s}^{-1}$. Both strings are taut: T_1 is the tension in AP and T_2 is the tension in BP.

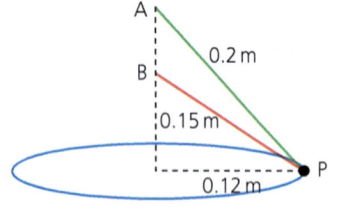

    Figure 10.27

    (i) Resolve vertically to show that $8T_1 + 6T_2 = 2.5g$.
    (ii) Find another equation connecting T_1 and T_2 and hence calculate T_1 and T_2.

3 Circular motion with variable speed

You have already met the general expressions for the acceleration of a particle in circular motion:

- the **transverse component of acceleration** is $r\dot{\omega}$ or $r\ddot{\theta}$ along the tangent
- the **radial component of acceleration** is $-r\omega^2$ or $-r\dot{\theta}^2$ along the radius.

For circular motion with variable speed, the radial component, $-r\dot{\theta}^2$, is the same as that for circular motion with constant speed. The effect of the varying speed appears in the transverse component, $r\ddot{\theta}$.

You may remember that the speed was found by differentiating $s = r\theta$ with respect to time to give $\dot{s} = r\dot{\theta}$. The transverse component of acceleration for circular motion is found by differentiating again: $\ddot{s} = r\ddot{\theta}$.

The symbols $\ddot{\theta}$ and $\dot{\omega}$ denote the rate of change of angular velocity, or the **angular acceleration**. This quantity is measured in radians per second squared ($\text{rad}\,\text{s}^{-2}$).

In the next two sections, you will be studying two types of circular motion with variable speed:

1. motion with constant angular acceleration
2. unforced motion in a vertical circle.

Circular motion with constant acceleration

When the angular acceleration of an object moving in a circle is constant, it is convenient to use the standard notation

$$\ddot{\theta} = \alpha$$

You can find the angular speed and the angular displacement by integrating this with respect to time:

$$\dot{\theta} = \alpha t + c \text{ for some constant } c.$$

It is usual to call the initial angular speed ω_0. In this case, $\dot{\theta} = \omega_0$ when $t = 0$, so $c = \omega_0$.

This gives

$$\dot{\theta} = \omega_0 + \alpha t \text{ or } \omega = \omega_0 + \alpha t.$$

Integrating again and assuming that $\theta = 0$ when $t = 0$:

$$\theta = \omega_0 t + \frac{1}{2}\alpha t^2$$

These two equations may look familiar to you. They are very much like the equations for motion in a straight line with constant acceleration:

$$v = u + at$$

and

$$s = ut + \frac{1}{2}at^2.$$

Circular motion with variable speed

There is a direct correspondence between the variables.

Motion in a straight line with constant acceleration	s	u	v	a
Circular motion with constant angular acceleration	θ	ω_0	$\omega \ (= \dot\theta)$	α

In fact, it can be shown that each equation for motion in a straight line with constant acceleration corresponds to an equation for circular motion with constant angular acceleration.

$$v = u + at \quad \leftrightarrow \quad \omega = \omega_0 + \alpha t$$

$$s = ut + \tfrac{1}{2}at^2 \quad \leftrightarrow \quad \theta = \omega_0 t + \tfrac{1}{2}\alpha t^2$$

$$s = \tfrac{1}{2}(u+v)t \quad \leftrightarrow \quad \theta = \tfrac{1}{2}(\omega_0 + \omega)t$$

$$s = vt - \tfrac{1}{2}at^2 \quad \leftrightarrow \quad \theta = \omega t - \tfrac{1}{2}\alpha t^2$$

$$v^2 = u^2 + 2as \quad \leftrightarrow \quad \omega^2 = \omega_0^2 + 2\alpha\theta$$

Example 10.7

Oliver is standing on a horizontal playground roundabout at a distance of 2 m from the centre.

Imogen pushes the roundabout with constant angular acceleration for 2 s and in this time the angular speed increases from $0.3\,\text{rad}\,\text{s}^{-1}$ to $1.5\,\text{rad}\,\text{s}^{-1}$. Find

(i) the angular acceleration of the roundabout

(ii) the magnitude and direction of the resultant horizontal force acting on Oliver just before Imogen stops pushing the roundabout. (Oliver's mass is 40 kg.)

Solution

(i) Using standard notation: $\omega_0 = 0.3$, $\omega = 1.5$, $t = 2$. To find α the required equation is:

$$\omega = \omega_0 + \alpha t$$

$$\Rightarrow 1.5 = 0.3 + 2\alpha$$

$$\Rightarrow \alpha = 0.6$$

The angular acceleration is $0.6\,\text{rad}\,\text{s}^{-2}$

(ii)

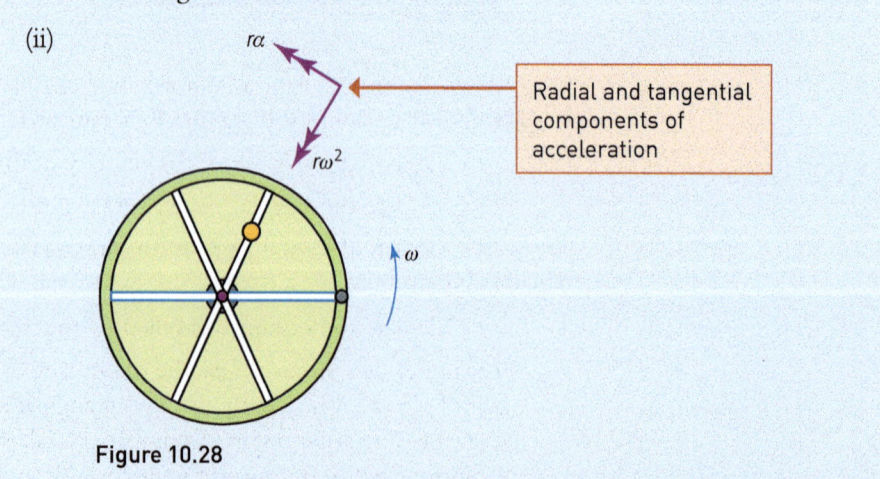

Radial and tangential components of acceleration

Figure 10.28

Just before Imogen stops pushing, Oliver's acceleration has two horizontal components.

Transverse motion: $r\ddot{\theta} = r\alpha$

$= 2 \times 0.6$

$= 1.2 \, \text{m s}^{-2}$

Radial motion towards the centre: $r\dot{\theta}^2 = r\omega^2$

$= 2 \times 1.5^2$

$= 4.5 \, \text{m s}^{-2}$

The resultant acceleration has two perpendicular components $1.2 \, \text{m s}^{-2}$ and $4.5 \, \text{m s}^{-2}$. Its magnitude is $\sqrt{1.2^2 + 4.5^2} = 4.657\ldots$ or $4.66 \, \text{m s}^{-2}$ (3 s.f.) and it makes an angle $\arctan\left(\dfrac{4.5}{1.2}\right) = 75.068\ldots$ or $75°$ (to the nearest degree) with the transverse direction shown.

By Newton's second law, the resultant horizontal force is given by

$F = ma$

$= 40 \times 4.657\ldots$

So the resultant force is $186 \, \text{N}$ (to 3 s.f.) at $75°$ to the transverse direction.

Exercise 10.3

① A flywheel is initially rotating at $6 \, \text{rad s}^{-1}$. After 5 minutes it comes to rest. Find

(i) the angular deceleration of the flywheel (assumed constant)

(ii) the total angle through which it turns before coming to rest.

② A skater spins at 1 revolution per second with her arms out sideways horizontally. She then takes 2 s to lower her arms and increases her angular speed to 3 revolutions per second. Find

(i) the angular acceleration in rad s^{-2} (assumed constant)

(ii) the number of complete revolutions she makes during the 2 s while she is lowering her arms.

③ A small stone slides round a horizontal circular track of radius 2 m. Its initial speed is $8 \, \text{m s}^{-1}$ and it has a constant transverse deceleration of $0.001 \, \text{m s}^{-2}$.

(i) Calculate the initial angular velocity of the stone.

(ii) Calculate the angular deceleration of the stone.

(iii) Calculate the total angle through which the stone travels before coming to rest.

(iv) Calculate the distance travelled by the stone before it comes to rest.

④ In a model of a discus throw, the discus is rotated in a horizontal circle of radius 0.75 m with steadily increasing angular speed up to the moment of release. The athlete starts from rest and takes 1.5 seconds to do 1.5 revolutions before releasing the discus. With what speed is it thrown?

Motion in a vertical circle

5. Figure 10.29 shows the big wheel at a fairground. It has a radius of 3 m. Once it is loaded with passengers, it is given a uniform angular acceleration for 20 s and then runs at uniform angular speed for 2 minutes. It then slows down at a uniform rate over a further 10 s. During the main part of the ride, the wheel completes 1 revolution every 10 s.

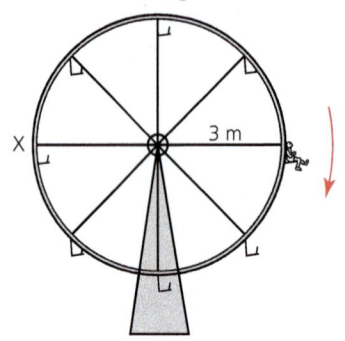

Figure 10.29

(i) Draw a graph showing the angular speed of the wheel against time and state what information is given by the area under the graph.

(ii) Find the total angle through which a passenger moves and the distance the passenger travels.

(iii) Find the magnitude of the acceleration of a passenger at the top of the ride when it is travelling at maximum speed. Draw a force diagram to show the forces on a passenger of mass 20 kg at the highest point of the ride.

(iv) Describe the acceleration vector of a passenger who is at point X where the wheel is half-way through its acceleration phase.

4 Motion in a vertical circle

Figure 10.30 shows the forces acting on a particle of mass m undergoing free circular motion in a vertical plane. For free motion it is assumed that there is no transverse force.

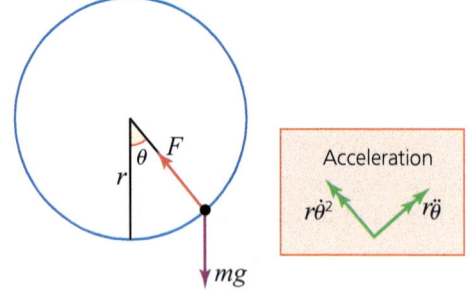

Figure 10.30

> **Note**
>
> The weight, mg, is resolved into components
>
> Radial $mg\cos\theta$
>
> Transverse $mg\sin\theta$

For circular motion to take place, there must be a resultant force acting on the particle towards the centre of the circle, as you have seen. This is denoted by F.

When the circle is vertical, the force of gravity also acts in this plane, and is therefore relevant to the motion. When the particle is in the position shown in Figure 10.30, Newton's second law gives the following equations.

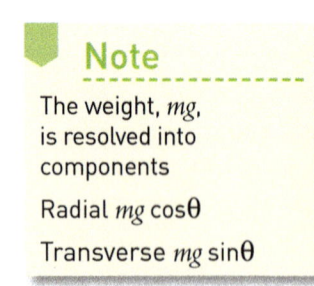

Towards the centre $\qquad F - mg\cos\theta = mr\dot\theta^2 \qquad$ ①

Transverse motion $\qquad -mg\sin\theta = mr\ddot\theta \qquad$ ②

The force, F, in the first equation might be the tension in a string or the normal reaction from a surface. This force will vary with θ and so equation ① is not helpful in describing how θ varies with time. The second equation, however, does not involve F and may be written as

$$\frac{d^2\theta}{dt^2} = -\frac{g}{r}\sin\theta$$

This differential equation can be solved, using suitable calculus techniques, to obtain an expression for θ in terms of t. The work is beyond the scope of this book.

Using conservation of energy

A different (and at this stage more profitable) approach is to consider the energy of the particle. Since there is no motion in the radial direction, and no force in the transverse direction, the principle of conservation of mechanical energy can be applied.

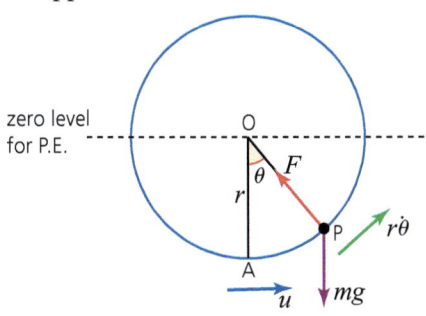

Figure 10.31

Take u to be the speed of the particle at A, the lowest point of the circle, and take the zero level of gravitational potential energy to be that through the centre of the circle, O, as shown in Figure 10.31.

The total energy at A is $\quad \frac{1}{2}mu^2 - mgr$
$\qquad\qquad\qquad\qquad\quad$ (K.E.) (P.E.)

The total energy at P is $\quad \frac{1}{2}m(r\dot\theta)^2 - mgr\cos\theta$
$\qquad\qquad\qquad\qquad\quad$ (K.E.) $\quad$ (P.E.)

By the principle of conservation of energy

$$\tfrac{1}{2}m(r\dot\theta)^2 - mgr\cos\theta = \tfrac{1}{2}mu^2 - mgr$$

$$\Rightarrow \qquad r\dot\theta^2 = \frac{u^2}{r} - 2g(1-\cos\theta)$$

This tells you the angular speed, $\dot\theta$, of the particle when OP is at an angle θ to OA.

The next two examples show how conservation of energy may be applied to theoretical models of problems involving motion in a vertical circle.

Motion in a vertical circle

Example 10.8

A particle of mass 0.03 kg is attached to the end, P, of a light rod OP of length 0.5 m which is free to rotate in a vertical circle with centre O. The particle is set in motion starting at the lowest point of the circle.

The initial speed of the particle is $2\,\text{m s}^{-1}$.

(i) Find the initial kinetic energy of the particle.

(ii) Find an expression for the potential energy gained when the rod has turned through an angle θ.

(iii) Find the value of θ when the particle first comes to rest.

(iv) Find the stress in the rod at this point, stating whether it is a tension or a thrust.

(v) Repeat parts (i) to (iv) using an initial speed of $4\,\text{m s}^{-1}$.

(vi) Why is it possible for the first motion (when $v_0 = 2$) to take place if the rod is replaced by a string, but not in the second (when $v_0 = 4$)?

Solution

(i) Kinetic energy $= \tfrac{1}{2}mv^2$

$= \tfrac{1}{2} \times 0.03 \times 2^2$

$= 0.06$

The initial kinetic energy is $0.06\,\text{J}$.

(ii) Figure 10.32 shows the position of the particle when the rod has rotated through an angle θ.

It has risen a distance AN, where

AN = OA − ON

$= 0.5 - 0.5\cos\theta$

$= 0.5\,(1 - \cos\theta)$

The gain in potential energy at P is therefore

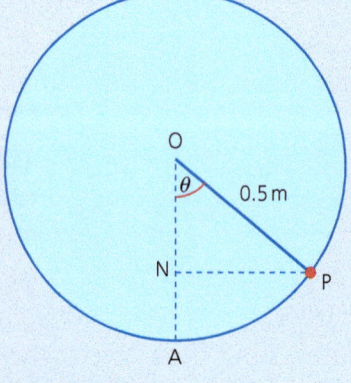

$0.03g \times 0.5(1 - \cos\theta) = 0.015g(1 - \cos\theta)\,\text{J}$

Figure 10.32

(iii) When the particle first comes to rest, the kinetic energy is zero, so by the principle of conservation of energy,

$0.015g(1 - \cos\theta) = 0.06$

$1 - \cos\theta = \dfrac{0.06}{0.015g}$

$= 0.408\ldots$

$\Rightarrow \quad \cos\theta = 0.591\ldots$

$\Rightarrow \quad \theta = 53.7°.$

(iv) The forces acting on the particle and its acceleration are as shown in Figure 10.33.

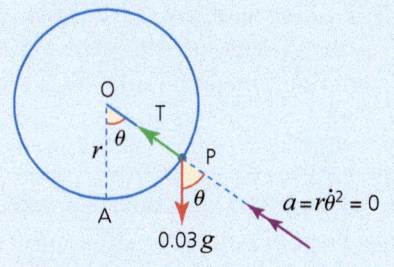

Figure 10.33

The component of the acceleration towards the centre of the circle is $r\dot{\theta}^2$ which equals zero when the angular speed is zero. Resolving towards the centre,

$$T - 0.03g \cos\theta = 0 \qquad \qquad ①$$

$$T = 0.03 \times 9.8 \times \cos 53.7° = 0.174.$$

Since this is positive, the stress in the rod is a tension. Its magnitude is $0.174\,\text{N}$.

(v) When the initial speed is $4\,\text{m s}^{-1}$, the initial kinetic energy is

$$\tfrac{1}{2} \times 0.03 \times 4^2 = 0.24\,\text{J}.$$

The gain in potential energy at P, as shown in part (ii),

$$= 0.015g(1 - \cos\theta)\,\text{J}.$$

When the particle first comes to rest, the kinetic energy is zero, so by the principle of conservation of energy,

$$0.015g(1 - \cos\theta) = 0.24$$

$$\cos\theta = 1 - \frac{0.24}{0.015 \times 9.8} = -0.632\ldots$$

$$\theta = 129°.$$

Now equation ① gives the tension in the rod as

$$T = 0.03g \cos\theta = -0.186.$$

The negative tension means that the stress is in fact a thrust of magnitude $0.186\,\text{N}$.

Figure 10.34 illustrates the forces acting in this position.

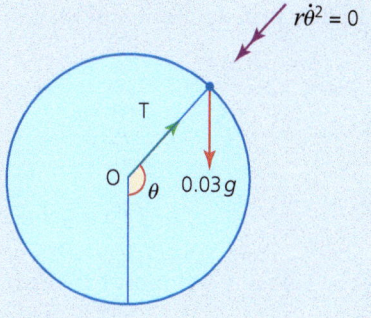

Figure 10.34

Motion in a vertical circle

(vi) A string cannot exert a thrust so, although the rod could be replaced by a string in the first case, it would be impossible in the second. In the absence of any radial thrust, the particle would leave its circular path at the point where the tension is zero and before reaching the position where the velocity is zero.

Example 10.9

Hint

When a bead is threaded on a wire it can't fall off.

A bead of mass 0.01 kg is threaded onto a smooth circular wire of radius 0.6 m and is set in motion with a speed of u m s^{-1} at the bottom of the circle. This just enables the bead to reach the top of the wire.

(i) Find the value of u.

(ii) What is the direction of the reaction of the wire on the bead when the bead is at the top of the circle?

Solution

(i) The initial kinetic energy is

$$\tfrac{1}{2} \times 0.01\, u^2 = 0.005\, u^2$$

If the bead just reaches the top, the speed there is zero. If this is the case, the kinetic energy at the top will also be zero.

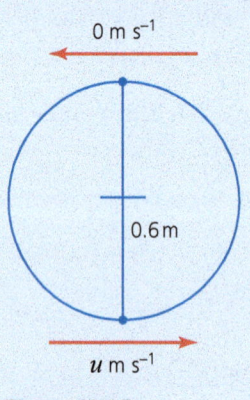

Figure 10.35

It has then risen a height of $2 \times 0.6 = 1.2$ m, so its gain in potential energy is

$$0.01g \times 1.2 = 0.012g$$

By the principle of conservation of energy,

loss in K.E. = gain in P.E.

$$0.005\, u^2 = 0.012g$$
$$u^2 = 2.4g$$
$$u = \sqrt{2.4 \times 9.8} = 4.849\ldots$$

The initial speed must be 4.85 m s^{-1} (to 2 d.p.).

(ii) The reaction of the wire on the bead could be directed either towards the centre of the circle or away from it. The bead has zero angular speed at the top, so the component of its acceleration, and therefore the resultant force towards the centre, is zero. The reaction must be outwards, as shown in Figure 10.36, and equal to $0.01g$ N.

The mass of the bead is 0.01 kg.

Discussion point
Would this motion be possible if the bead were tied to the end of a string instead of being threaded on a wire?

Figure 10.36

The breakdown of circular motion

ACTIVITY 10.2

Tie a small object to the end of a piece of strong thread and tie the other end loosely (to minimise friction) round a smooth knitting needle (or a smooth rod with a cork on one end).
Hold the pointed end of the needle and make the object move in a vertical circle, as shown in Figure 10.37.

Note
When carrying out this activity, keep well away from other people and breakable objects.

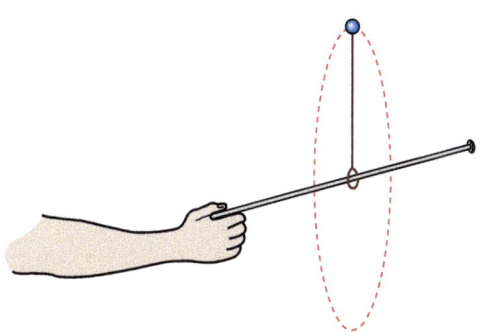

Figure 10.37

Demonstrate these three types of motion.
1 The object travels in complete circles.
2 The object swings like a pendulum.
3 The object rises above the level of the needle but then fails to complete a full circle.
What would happen if the string broke?
What would happen if a rod were used rather than a string?

Motion in a vertical circle

The three different types of motion mentioned in the Activity, and the case in which the string breaks, are illustrated in the following diagrams in Figure 10.38.

(a) Object oscillates in complete circles.

(b) Object oscillates backwards and forwards.

(c) Object leaves circle at some point and falls inwards.

(d) String breaks and object starts to move away along a tangent.

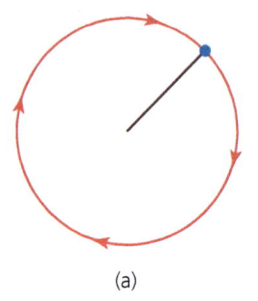

Figure 10.38

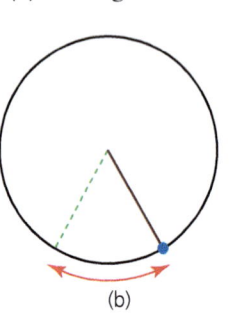

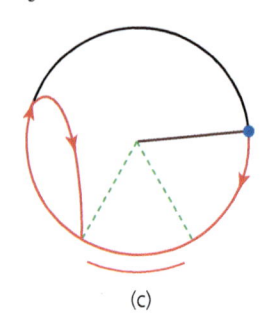

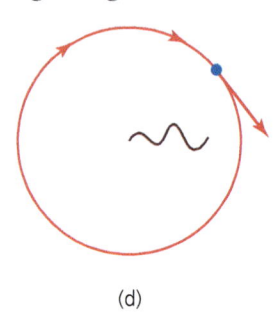

Modelling the breakdown of circular motion

For what reasons might something depart from motion in a circle? For example, under what conditions will a particle attached to a string and moving in a vertical circle fall out of the circle? Under what conditions will a bicycle travelling over a speed bump with circular cross-section leave the road?

A particle on a string

Figure 10.39 shows a particle P of mass m attached to a string of length r, rotating with angular speed ω in a vertical circle, centre O.

There are two forces acting on the particle, its weight, mg, and the tension, T, in the string. The acceleration of the particle is $r\omega^2$ towards the centre of the circle.

Applying Newton's second law towards the centre gives

$$T + mg\cos\alpha = mr\omega^2 \qquad \text{①}$$

where α is the angle shown in Figure 10.39.

While the particle is in circular motion, the string is taut and so $T > 0$. At the instant it starts to leave the circle, the string goes slack and $T = 0$.

Substituting $T = 0$ in ① gives $\quad mg\cos\alpha = mr\omega^2$

$$\Rightarrow \qquad \cos\alpha = \frac{r\omega^2}{g}$$

The equation $\cos\alpha = \dfrac{r\omega^2}{g}$ allows you to find the angle α at which the particle leaves the circle, if it does.

The greatest possible value for $\cos\alpha$ is 1, so if $\dfrac{r\omega^2}{g}$ is greater than 1 throughout the motion, the equation has no solution and this means that the particle never leaves the circle. Thus the condition for the particle to stay in circular motion is that $\omega^2 \geq \dfrac{g}{r}$ throughout.

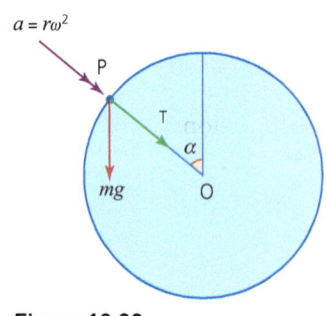

Figure 10.39

In this example of a particle on a string, ω varies throughout the motion. As you saw earlier, the value of ω at any instant is given by the energy equation which in this case is

$$\tfrac{1}{2}mr^2\omega^2 + mgr(1+\cos\alpha) = \tfrac{1}{2}mu^2$$

where u is the speed of the particle at the lowest point.

A particle moving on the inside of a vertical circle

The same analysis applies to a particle sliding around the inside of a smooth circle. The only difference is that, in this case, the tension, T, is replaced by the normal reaction, R, of the surface on the particle (see Figure 10.41). When $R = 0$, the particle leaves the surface.

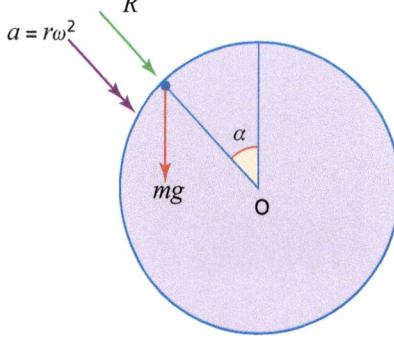

Figure 10.40

Figure 10.41

A particle moving on the outside of a vertical circle

The forces acting on a particle moving on the outside of a vertical circle, such as a car going over a hump-backed bridge, are the normal reaction, R, acting outwards and the weight of the particle, as shown in Figure 10.42.

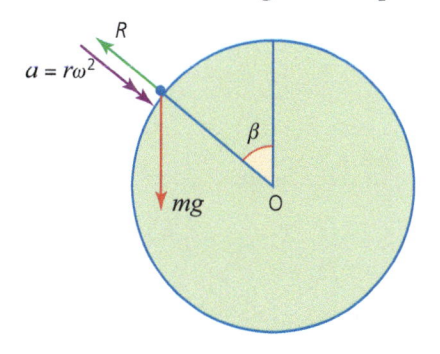

Figure 10.42

Applying Newton's second law towards the centre gives

$$mg\cos\beta - R = mr\omega^2 \qquad ②$$

where β is the angle shown.

If the normal reaction is zero, it means there is no force between the particle and the surface and so the particle is leaving the surface.

Substituting $R = 0$ in ② gives $\quad mg\cos\beta = mr\omega^2$

$$\Rightarrow \qquad \cos\beta = \frac{r\omega^2}{g}$$

> **Discussion point**
>
> The conditions for the breakdown of circular motion seem to be the same in the cases of a particle on the end of a string and a particle on the outside of a circle.
>
> However, everyday experience tells you that circular motion on the end of a string is only possible if the angular speed is large enough whereas a particle will only stay on the outside of a circle if the angular speed is small enough.
>
> How do the conditions $T > 0$ and $R > 0$ explain this difference?

Motion in a vertical circle

Example 10.10

Determine whether it is possible for a particle, P, of mass m kg to be in the position shown in Figure 10.43 moving round a vertical circle of radius 0.5 m with an angular speed of $4\,\text{rad}\,\text{s}^{-1}$ when it is

(i) sliding on the outside of a smooth surface

(ii) sliding on the inside of a smooth surface

(iii) attached to the end of a string OP

(iv) threaded on a smooth vertical ring.

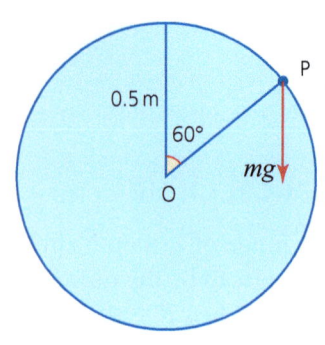

Figure 10.43

Solution

(i) On the outside of a smooth surface:

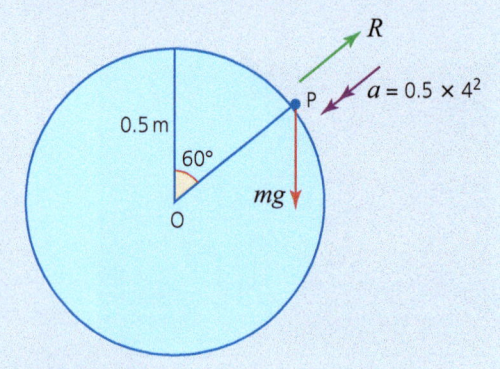

Figure 10.44

The normal reaction R N of the surface on the particle must be acting outwards, so Newton's second law towards the centre gives

$$mg\cos 60° - R = m \times 0.5 \times 4^2$$

$$\Rightarrow \qquad R = mg\cos 60° - 8m$$

$$= -3.1m$$

Whatever the mass, m, this negative value of R is impossible, so the motion is impossible. The particle will already have left the surface.

(ii) On the inside of a smooth surface:

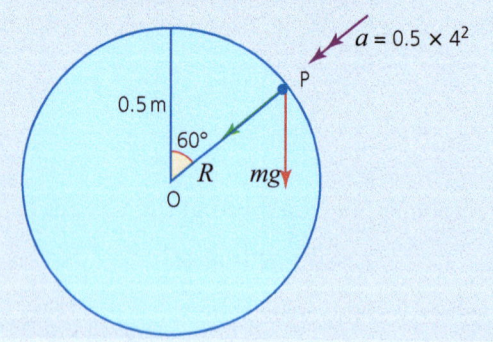

Figure 10.45

The normal reaction of the surface on the particle will now be acting towards the centre and so

$$R + mg\cos 60° = m \times 0.5 \times 4^2$$
$$\Rightarrow \quad R = +3.1m$$

This is possible.

(iii) Attached to the end of a string:

This situation is like that in part (ii) since the tension acts towards the centre, so the motion is possible.

(iv) Threaded on a smooth ring:

If the particle is threaded on a ring, the normal reaction can act inwards or outwards so the motion can take place whatever the angular speed. This is also the case when a particle is attached to the centre by a light rod. The rod will exert a tension or a thrust as required.

> **Discussion point**
> Which of the situations in Example 10.10 are possible when the angular speed is $3\,\text{m s}^{-1}$?

Example 10.11

Eddie, a skier of mass m kg, is skiing down a hillside when he reaches a smooth hump in the form of an arc AB of a circle with centre O and radius 8 m, as shown in Figure 10.46. O, A and B lie in a vertical plane and OA and OB make angles of 20° and 40° with the vertical, respectively. Eddie's speed at A is $7\,\text{m s}^{-1}$. Determine whether Eddie will lose contact with the ground before reaching the point B.

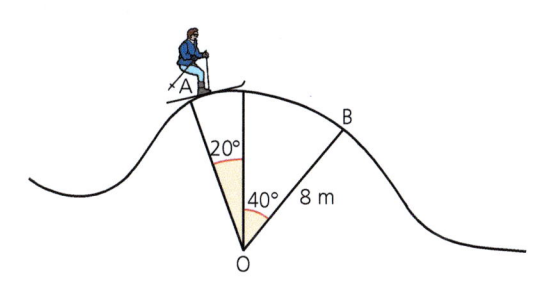

Figure 10.46

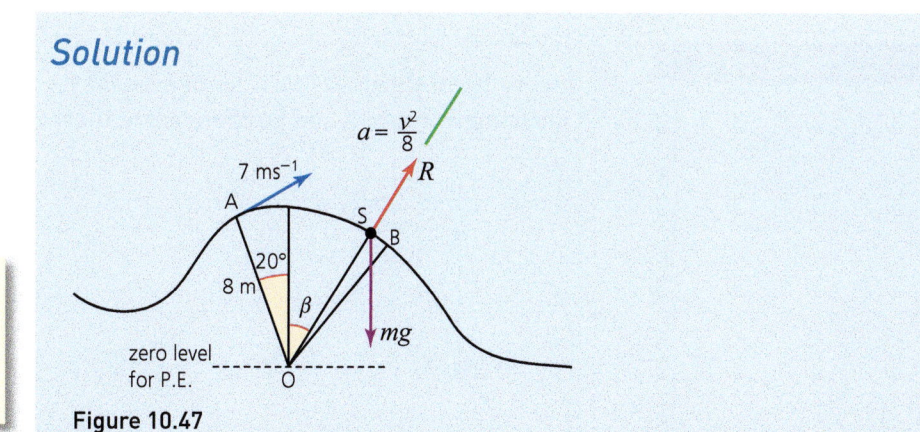

Solution

Figure 10.47

> **Note**
> S is a general point on the surface of the arc of the circle.

Motion in a vertical circle

Taking the zero level for potential energy to be a horizontal line through O, the initial energy at A is

$$\tfrac{1}{2} m \times 7^2 + mg \times 8 \cos 20°$$

The energy at point S is

$$\tfrac{1}{2} mv^2 + mg \times 8 \cos \beta$$

By the principle of conservation of energy these are equal.

$$\tfrac{1}{2} mv^2 + mg \times 8 \cos \beta = \tfrac{1}{2} m \times 7^2 + mg \times 8 \cos 20°$$

$$\Rightarrow \quad v^2 + 16g \cos \beta = 49 + 147.34\ldots$$

$$\Rightarrow \quad v^2 = 196.34\ldots - 16g \cos \beta \qquad ①$$

Using Newton's second law towards the centre of the circle

$$mg \cos \beta - R = m \frac{v^2}{8}$$

$$\Rightarrow \quad R = m \left(g \cos \beta - \frac{v^2}{8} \right)$$

If Eddie leaves the circle at point S, then $R = 0$

$$\Rightarrow \quad v^2 = 8g \cos \beta$$

Substituting in ①

$$8g \cos \beta = 196.34\ldots - 16g \cos \beta$$

$$\Rightarrow \quad 24g \cos \beta = 196.34\ldots$$

$$\Rightarrow \quad \cos \beta = \frac{196.34\ldots}{24 \times 9.8} = 0.834\ldots$$

$$\Rightarrow \quad \beta = 33.4°$$

This gives $\beta = 33.4°$, which is less than 40°, so Eddie will lose contact with the ground before he reaches the point B.

Exercise 10.4

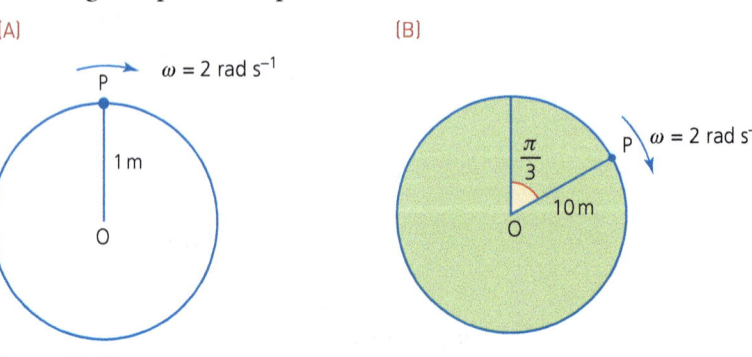

① Figure 10.48 show two particles of mass m kg moving in vertical circles. Their angular speeds and positions are as shown.

(A) P, $\omega = 2$ rad s^{-1}, 1 m, O

(B) $\frac{\pi}{3}$, P, $\omega = 2$ rad s^{-1}, 10 m, O

Figure 10.48

(i) Write down the components of their acceleration along PO.

(ii) By considering the forces acting on the particle, determine, in each case, whether it is possible for it to be moving with this speed in this position when it is:

(a) sliding on the outside of a smooth surface

(b) sliding on the inside of a smooth surface

(c) attached to the end of a string OP

(d) threaded on a smooth ring in a vertical plane.

② Each of the following diagrams in Figure 10.49 shows a particle of mass m which is constrained to move in a vertical circle. Initially, it is in the position shown and moving with the given speed.

(A)

(B)

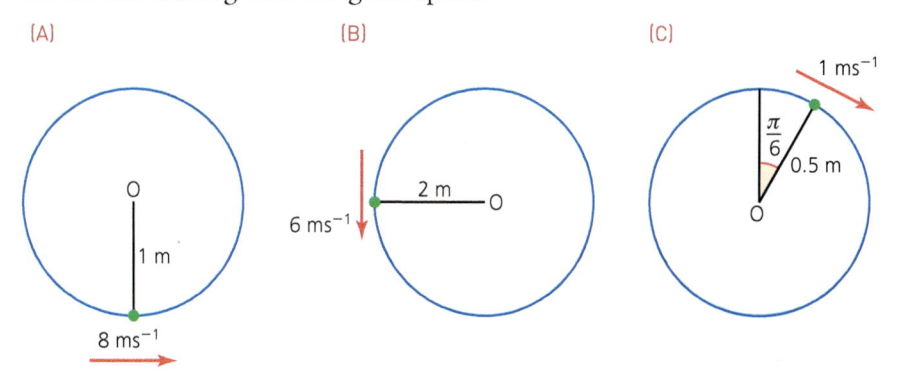

(C) 1 ms^{-1}, $\frac{\pi}{6}$, 0.5 m

2 m, 6 ms^{-1}

1 m, 8 ms^{-1}

Figure 10.49

In each case:

(i) Using the horizontal through the centre of the circle as the zero level for potential energy, write down the total initial mechanical energy of the particle.

(ii) Decide whether the particle will make complete revolutions or whether it will come to rest below the highest point. If it makes complete revolutions, determine the speed at the top. Otherwise find the height above the centre when it comes to rest.

(iii) Assuming that the particle is moving under the action of its weight and a radial force only, find the magnitude and direction of the radial force

(a) initially

(b) when it reaches the top or comes to rest.

③ A smooth hemispherical bowl of radius r, with lowest point A, is fixed with its rim uppermost and horizontal. A particle of mass m is projected along the inner surface of the bowl with a speed $\sqrt{gr}$ towards A, from a point at a vertical height $\frac{1}{2}r$ above A, so that its motion is in a vertical plane through A.

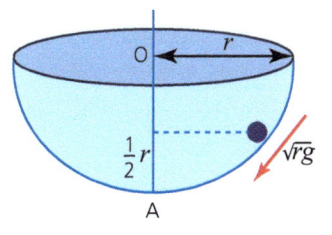

Figure 10.50

Motion in a vertical circle

   (i) Show that the particle will just reach the top of the bowl.

   (ii) Find the reaction between the particle and the bowl when it is at a height $\frac{1}{3}r$ above A.

④ A bead B of mass m is threaded onto a fixed smooth circular wire, with centre O and radius a, whose plane is vertical. When the bead is at the lowest point of the wire, it is projected horizontally with velocity u and, in the subsequent motion, B reaches a maximum vertical height of $\frac{1}{2}a$ above O.

   (i) Show that $u^2 = 3ga$.

   (ii) If θ is the angle which OB makes with the downward vertical, prove that the reaction R of B on the wire is given by

   $R = mg(1 + 3\cos\theta)$.

⑤ Figure 10.51 shows a model car track. You may assume that all parts of the track lie in the same vertical plane.

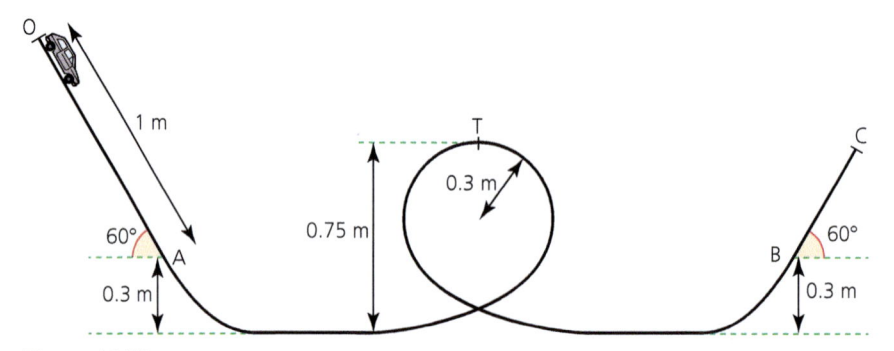

Figure 10.51

Between A and B the track is symmetrical about a vertical line through T; its length from A to T is 2.1 m. OA and BC are straight and the top of the loop is an arc of a circle of radius 0.3 m. For a car of mass m kg there is a frictional resistance of $0.06mg$ N.

The car starts from rest at the point O.

   (i) Find the work done against friction between O and T.

   (ii) Use the work–energy principle to show that the kinetic energy at T is $0.230mg$ J.

   (iii) By considering circular motion at T, show that the car will move right round the loop in contact with the track.

   (iv) The car stops at C before returning. Find the length BC.

   (v) Will the car reach T on the return journey?

⑥ A particle of mass m hangs by a string of length a from a fixed point. The particle is given a horizontal velocity of $\sqrt{\frac{7}{2}ga}$.

   (i) Show that the string will be about to become slack when it makes an angle of 60° with the upward vertical.

   (ii) Find the tension in the string when it makes an angle of 60° with the downward vertical.

⑦ A metal sphere of mass 0.5 kg is moving in a vertical circle of radius 0.8 m at the end of a light, inelastic string. At the top of the circle the sphere has speed $3\,\text{m s}^{-1}$.

   (i) Calculate the gravitational potential energy lost by the sphere when it reaches the bottom of the circle and hence calculate its speed at this point.

(ii) Find an expression for the speed of the sphere when the string makes an angle, θ, with the upward vertical.

(iii) Find the tension in the string when the sphere is
   (a) at the top of the circle
   (b) at the bottom of the circle.

(iv) Draw a diagram showing the forces acting on the sphere when the string makes an angle θ with the upward vertical. Find expressions for the tension in the string and the transverse component of the sphere's acceleration at this instant.

⑧ A glider is travelling horizontally until the pilot executes a loop-the-loop manoeuvre, as shown in Figure 10.52. The loop may be modelled as a vertical circle. The glider is initially at a height of 700 m, travelling at 30 m s^{-1}. The bottom of the loop is at a height 400 m and the radius of the loop is 100 m.

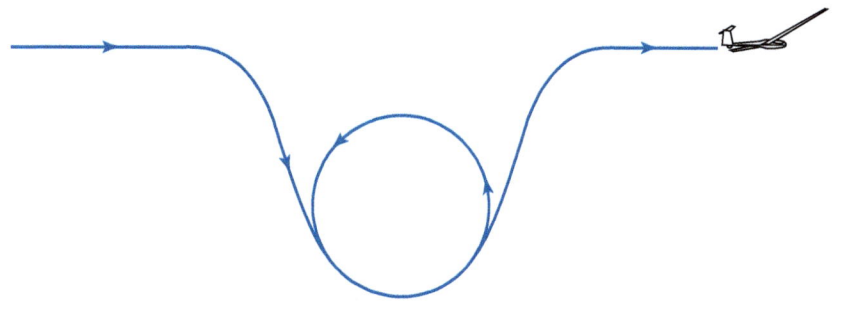

Figure 10.52

Assuming that the mechanical energy is conserved, calculate

(i) the speed of the glider at the lowest and highest points of the loop

(ii) the magnitude of the acceleration of the glider at the lowest and highest points of the loop.

The mass of the pilot is 70 kg.

(iii) Draw diagrams to show the reaction forces acting on him at the lowest and highest points of the loop and state their magnitudes.

(iv) What would happen if he attempted a loop of radius 150 m, starting from the same lowest point?

(v) What is the maximum radius for a successful loop from this point?

⑨ As a challenge, a girl is required to swing a bucket of water in a vertical circular arc above her head. If the bucket is not moving fast enough, she will get wet. This may be modelled by taking the girl's arm to be 55 cm long and the bucket 35 cm from base to handle. The handle is taken to be rigidly attached to the bucket and is held firmly so that her arm is always in line with the centre of the base. Assume that the water behaves as a solid block.

The girl considers three possible depths of water in the bucket: 5 cm, 10 cm and 15 cm.

(i) For which depth does she need to give the bucket the highest angular speed?

In the event, she is forced to have 15 cm of water in the bucket.

(ii) Find the minimum angular speed at the top of the arc for the water to stay in the bucket.

Motion in a vertical circle

(iii) Deduce the average angular acceleration the girl must give the bucket, assuming that it is at rest at the lowest point.

One girl, doing this for real, ended with the bucket as well as the water hitting her head.

(iv) How could you model this situation?

⑩ Figure 10.53 shows a ride at an amusement park. The loop is, to a good approximation, a circle of radius 8 m, in a vertical plane.

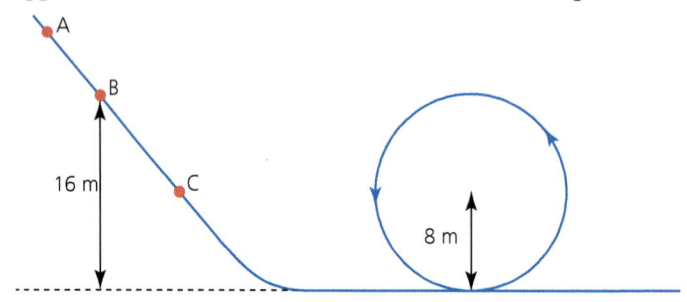

Figure 10.53

In answering the following questions, you should assume that no energy is lost to forces such as friction and air resistance, and that the car starts from rest.

(i) Explain why a car which starts just above point B, 16 m above ground level, will not complete the loop.

(ii) For a car to complete the loop successfully, it must start at or above point A. What is the height of A?

(iii) On 'Kiddie days' the organisers start the car below point C. Describe what happens to the car and state the maximum height of point C for it to be safe.

⑪ Figure 10.54 illustrates an old road bridge over a river. The road surface follows an approximately circular arc with radius 15 m.

A car is being driven across the bridge and you should model it as a particle.

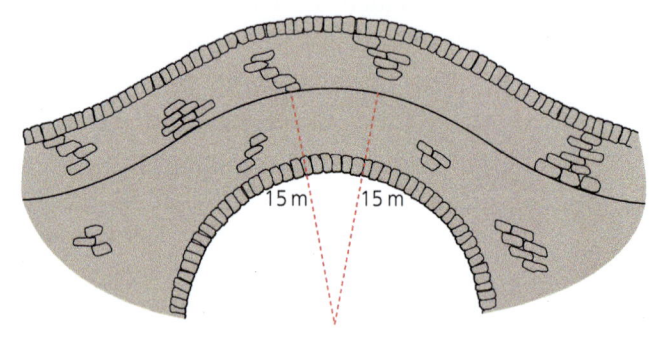

Figure 10.54

(i) Calculate the greatest constant speed at which it is possible to drive the car across the bridge without it leaving the road, giving your answer both in ms^{-1} and in mph.

(ii) Comment on the fact that the bridge is old.

(iii) How is it possible to improve the design of the bridge?

⑫ A car of mass 200 kg travels along the track of a roller-coaster. In one section of the track, the car travels around the inside of a vertical circle of radius 10 m, as shown in Figure 10.55.

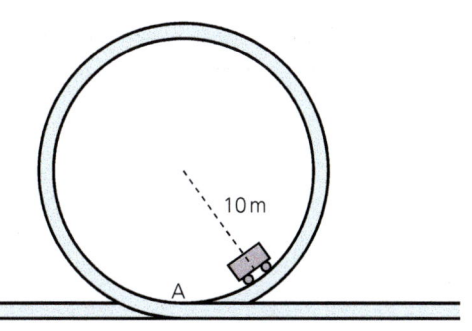

Figure 10.55

The car is attached to the track so that it can move freely along it, but cannot leave the circular path. While the car is travelling around the circle, there is no driving force present. Friction and air resistance may be neglected.

The car enters the circle at its lowest point, A, with a speed of $21\,\text{m s}^{-1}$.

(i) Show that the speed of the car at the highest point is $7\,\text{m s}^{-1}$.

(ii) Find the radial acceleration at the highest point. Hence calculate the force that the track exerts on the car at this point. Could the roller-coaster operate if the car was not attached to the track?

Explain your answer briefly.

(iii) Calculate the radial and tangential components of acceleration when the car has travelled through $120°$ round the circle from A. Show that the resultant acceleration at this point is directed towards A.   [MEI]

⑬ A particle of mass m is attached to one end, A, of a light, inelastic string of length l. The other end, B, of the string is attached to a ceiling so that the particle is free to swing in a vertical plane; the angle between the string and the downward vertical is θ radians. You may assume that the air resistance on the particle is negligible.

Initially, $\theta = \frac{\pi}{3}$ and the particle is released from rest.

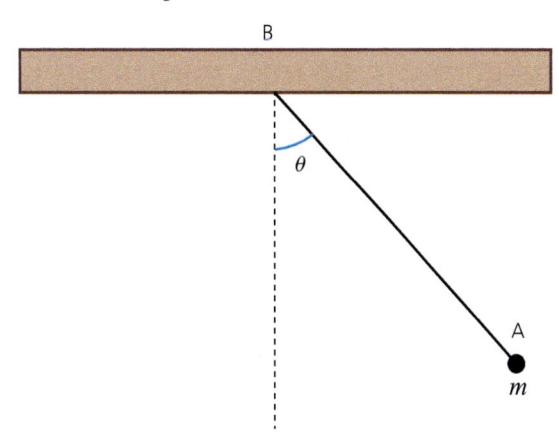

Figure 10.56

(i) Show that the potential energy lost by the particle since leaving its initial position is $\frac{mgl}{2}(2\cos\theta - 1)$. Hence find an expression for v^2, where v is the linear speed of the particle, in terms of l, g and θ.

(ii) Show that the tension in the string at any point of the motion is $mg(3\cos\theta - 1)$.

(iii) Find the greatest tension in the string. What is the position of the particle when the tension in the string is greatest?

Before its release with $\theta = \frac{\pi}{3}$, the particle is held in position by means of a second light string inclined at an acute angle, α, to the downward vertical, as shown in Figure 10.57. The second string is cut to allow the particle to swing.

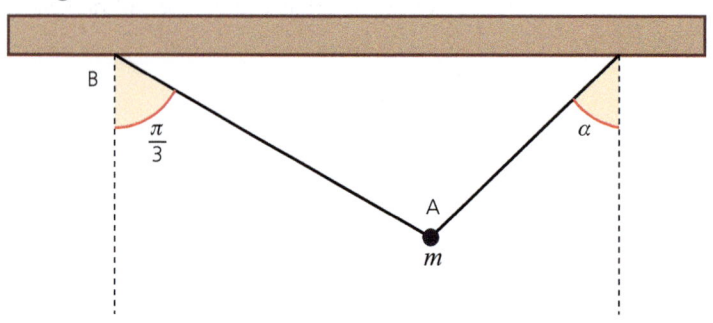

Figure 10.57

(iv) What is the direction of the acceleration of the particle just after the string is cut?

You are given that the tension in the string AB when the particle is being supported is

$$\frac{2mg}{1+\sqrt{3}\cot\alpha}$$

(v) Calculate the value of α for which the tension in AB remains unchanged when the string is cut. [MEI]

Velocity and acceleration for motion in a circle

When a particle moves in a circle, it is convenient for the velocity and acceleration to be expressed in the radial and transverse directions. For this reason, unit vectors **r** and **θ** are defined in these two directions. However, unlike the unit vectors **i** and **j**, these vectors are not constant. Their magnitudes are constant and equal to 1 but their directions change as the particle moves round the circle.

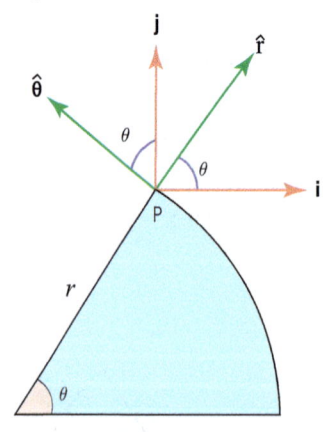

Figure 10.58

When the particle P is at a general position, as shown in Figure 10.58, **r** and **θ** are given by the following expressions:

$$\mathbf{r} = \cos\theta\,\mathbf{i} + \sin\theta\,\mathbf{j}$$

and

$$\boldsymbol{\theta} = -\sin\theta\,\mathbf{i} + \cos\theta\,\mathbf{j}$$

Differentiating **r** with respect to time,

$$\frac{d\mathbf{r}}{dt} = \frac{d}{dt}(\cos\theta)\mathbf{i} + \frac{d}{dt}(\sin\theta)\mathbf{j}$$

$$= -\sin\theta\frac{d\theta}{dt}\mathbf{i} + \cos\theta\frac{d\theta}{dt}\mathbf{j}$$

$$= (-\sin\theta\mathbf{i} + \cos\theta\mathbf{j})\dot\theta \quad \text{where } \dot\theta = \frac{d\theta}{dt}.$$

You will recognise that the vector in brackets $(-\sin\theta\mathbf{i} + \cos\theta\mathbf{j})$ is the same as $\hat{\boldsymbol{\theta}}$, the unit vector in the transverse direction. Consequently,

$$\frac{d\mathbf{r}}{dt} = \dot\theta\boldsymbol{\theta}$$

Similarly,

$$\frac{d\boldsymbol{\theta}}{dt} = -\cos\theta\,\dot\theta\mathbf{i} - \sin\theta\,\dot\theta\mathbf{j}$$

$$= -(\cos\theta\mathbf{i} + \sin\theta\mathbf{j})\dot\theta$$

i.e. $\quad \frac{d\boldsymbol{\theta}}{dt} = -\dot\theta\mathbf{r}.$

> **Note**
> These two results $\frac{d\mathbf{r}}{dt} = \dot\theta\boldsymbol{\theta}$ and $\frac{d\boldsymbol{\theta}}{dt} = -\dot\theta\mathbf{r}$ apply to all motion described in polar coordinates, not just circular motion.

In the case of circular motion with radius r, the displacement from the centre at any time is given by

$$\text{displacement} = r\mathbf{r} \qquad \text{(the displacement is in the radial direction)}$$

Differentiating this with respect to time, you obtain

$$\text{velocity} = \frac{dr}{dt}\mathbf{r} + r\frac{d\mathbf{r}}{dt}$$

$$= 0 + r\dot\theta\boldsymbol{\theta} \qquad \text{(since } r \text{ is constant)}$$

$$= r\dot\theta\boldsymbol{\theta} \qquad \text{(the velocity is in the transverse direction).}$$

Differentiating again you obtain

$$\text{acceleration} = \frac{dr}{dt}\dot\theta\boldsymbol{\theta} + r\frac{d\dot\theta}{dt}\boldsymbol{\theta} + r\dot\theta\frac{d\boldsymbol{\theta}}{dt}$$

$$= 0 + r\ddot\theta\boldsymbol{\theta} - r\dot\theta^2\mathbf{r}$$

$$= r\ddot\theta\boldsymbol{\theta} - r\dot\theta^2\mathbf{r}$$

Thus the acceleration has two components:

a transverse component: $\quad r\ddot\theta$

and a radial component: $\quad -r\dot\theta^2$.

KEY POINTS

1 Position, velocity and acceleration of a particle moving on a circle of radius r.

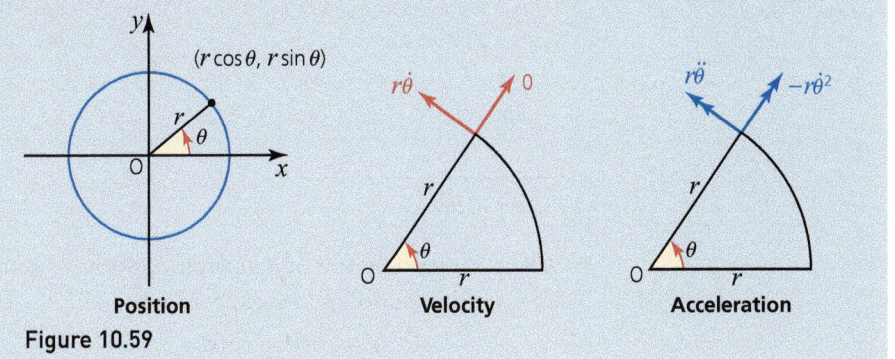

Figure 10.59

Position: $(r\cos\theta, r\sin\theta)$

Velocity: $r\dot\theta$

Acceleration: $r\ddot\theta$, $-r\dot\theta^2$

Motion in a vertical circle

- position $(r\cos\theta, r\sin\theta)$
- velocity   transverse component: $v = r\dot\theta = r\omega$
  radial component: 0
  where $\dot\theta$ or ω is the angular velocity of the particle
- acceleration   transverse component: $r\ddot\theta = r\dot\omega$
  radial component: $-r\dot\theta^2 = -r\omega^2 = -\dfrac{v^2}{r}$
  where $\ddot\theta$ or $\dot\omega$ is the angular acceleration of the particle.

2. By Newton's second law, the forces acting on a particle of mass m in circular motion are equal to
   - transverse component
   - radial component

   $mr\dot\theta^2 = mr\omega = m\dfrac{v^2}{r} = v\omega$ towards the centre

   $-mr\dot\theta^2 = -mr\omega^2 = -m\dfrac{v^2}{r} = -v\omega$ away from the centre

3. Problems involving free motion in a vertical circle can be solved using the conservation of energy principle

   P. E. + K.E. = constant

   in conjunction with Newton's second law.

4. Circular motion breaks down when the available force towards the centre is $< mr\omega^2$.

5. The equations for circular motion with constant acceleration α are
   - $\omega = \omega_0 + \alpha t$
   - $\theta = \frac{1}{2}(\omega_0 + \omega)t$
   - $\theta = \omega_0 t + \frac{1}{2}\alpha t^2$
   - $\theta = \omega t - \frac{1}{2}\alpha t^2$
   - $\omega^2 = \omega_0^2 + 2\alpha\theta$

   where ω_0 is the initial angular speed.

LEARNING OUTCOMES

When you have finished this chapter, you should be able to

- understand the language and notation associated with circular motion
- identify the forces acting on a body in circular motion
- calculate acceleration towards the centre of circular motion
- model situations involving circular motion with uniform speed in a horizontal plane
- model situations involving circular motion with non-uniform speed in a horizontal plane
- model situations involving motion in a vertical circle
- identify the conditions under which a particle departs from circular motion.

11 Hooke's law

The only way of finding the limits of the possible is by going beyond them into the impossible.

Arthur C. Clarke

→ The photographs show people bungee jumping.

→ Bungee jumping is a dangerous sport which originated in the South Sea Islands where creepers were used instead of ropes. In the more modern version, a person jumps off a high bridge or crane to which they are attached by an elastic rope around their ankles or with a harness.

Discussion point

If somebody bungee jumping from a bridge wants the excitement of just reaching the surface of the water below, how would you calculate the length of rope required?

Strings and springs

The answer to this question clearly depends on the height of the bridge, the mass of the person jumping and the elasticity of the rope. All ropes are elastic to some extent, but it would be extremely dangerous to use an ordinary rope for this sport because the impulse necessary to stop somebody falling would involve a very large tension acting in the rope for a short time and this would provide too great a shock to the system. A bungee is a strong elastic rope, similar to those used to secure loads on cycles, cars or lorries, with the essential property for this sport that it allows the impulse to act over a much longer time so that the rope exerts a smaller force on the jumper.

Generally in mechanics, the word **string** is used to represent such things as ropes which can be in tension but not in compression. In this chapter, you will be studying some of the properties of elastic strings and springs and will return to the problem of the bungee jumper as a final investigation.

In contrast, a **spring** can be compressed as well as stretched. So a spring can be in compression or in tension. In this book, it is assumed that springs are open coiled.

1 Strings and springs

So far, in situations involving strings, it has been assumed that they do not stretch when they are under tension. Such strings are called **inextensible**. For some materials this is a good assumption, but for others the length of the string increases significantly under tension. Strings and springs which stretch are said to be **elastic**.

The length of a string or spring when there is no force applied to it is called its **natural length**. If it is stretched, the increase in length is called its **extension**, and if a spring is compressed, it is said to have a **negative extension** or **compression**.

When stretched, a spring exerts an inward force, or **tension**, on whatever is attached to its ends (Figure 11.1(b)). When compressed, it exerts an outward force, or **thrust,** on its ends (Figure 11.1 (c)). An elastic string exerts a tension when stretched, but when slack exerts no force.

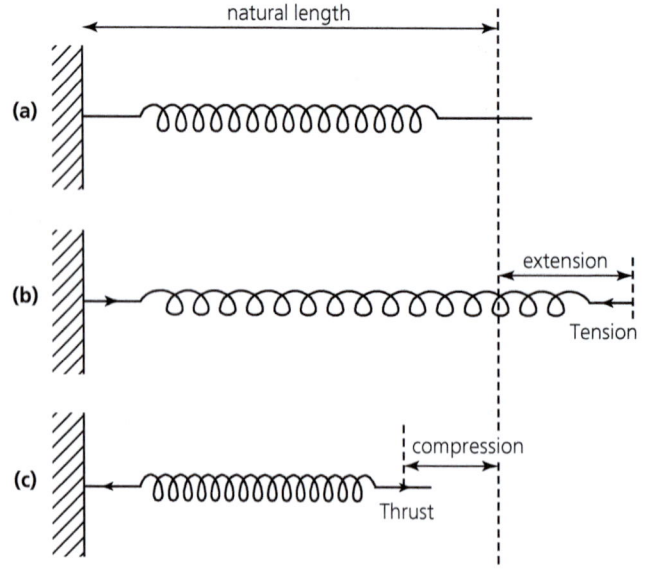

Figure 11.1

Here are some questions for you to think about.

1 How are the extension of a string and the weight of an object hung from it related?
2 If a string of the same material but twice the natural length has the same weight attached, how does the extension change?
3 Does the string return to its original length when unloaded
   (i) if the weight of the object is small?
   (ii) if the weight of the object is large?

You may choose to carry out experiments to help you answer these questions. If you do you will need some elastic strings, some open coiled springs, some weights and a support stand. Set up the apparatus as shown in Figure 11.2.

Now, for each string, plot a graph of tension, i.e. the weight of the object (vertical axis) against the extension (horizontal axis) to help you to answer these questions.

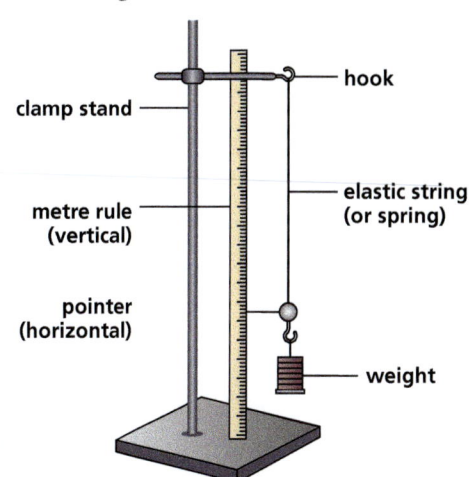

Figure 11.2

> You can use the same equipment to find the period of oscillation of an object hanging on an elastic string or spring. This is described on page 329.

Design and carry out an experiment which will investigate the relationship between the thrust in an open coiled spring and the decrease in its length.

If you carry out these experiments, you should make the following observations:

- Each string or spring returns to its original length once the object is removed, up to a certain limit.
- The graph of tension or thrust against extension for each string or spring is a straight line for all or part of the data.
- The gradient of the linear part of the graph is roughly halved when the string is doubled in length.
- If you keep increasing the weight, the string or spring may stop stretching or may stretch without returning to its original length. In this case, the graph is no longer a straight line: the material has passed its **elastic limit**.
- During your experiment using an open coiled spring you may have found it necessary to prevent the spring from buckling. You may also have found that there comes a point when the coils are completely closed and a further decrease in length is impossible.

> Strings or springs which exhibit this linear behaviour are said to be *perfectly elastic*.

Hooke's law

In 1678, Robert Hooke formulated a **rule or law of nature in every springing body** which, for small extensions relative to the length of the string or spring, can be stated as follows:

Strings and springs

Note

The tension in an elastic spring or string is proportional to the extension. If a spring is compressed, the thrust is proportional to the decrease in length of the spring.

When a string or spring is described as elastic, it means that it is reasonable to apply the modelling assumption that it obeys Hooke's law. A further assumption, that it is light (i.e. has zero mass) is usual and is made in this book.

There are three ways in which Hooke's law is commonly expressed for a string. Which one you use depends on the extent to which you are interested in the string itself rather than just its overall properties. Denoting the natural length of the string by l_0 and its area of cross-section by A, the different forms are as follows.

- $T = \dfrac{EA}{l_0} x$ In this form, E is called **Young's modulus** and is a property of the material out of which the string is formed. This form is commonly used in physics and engineering, subjects in which properties of materials are studied. It is rarely used in mathematics. The S.I. unit for Young's modulus is Nm^{-2}.

- $T = \dfrac{\lambda}{l_0} x$ The constant λ is called the **modulus of elasticity** of the string and will be the same for any string of a given cross-section made out of the same material. Many situations require knowledge of the natural length of a string and this form may well be the most appropriate in such cases. The S.I. unit for the modulus of elasticity is N.

- $T = kx$ In this simplest form, k is called the **stiffness** of the string. It is a property of the string as a whole. You may choose to use this form if neither the natural length nor the cross-sectional area of the string is relevant to the situation. The S.I. unit for stiffness is Nm^{-1}.

Notice that $k = \dfrac{\lambda}{l_0} = \dfrac{EA}{l_0}$

In this book, only the forms using the modulus of elasticity and stiffness are used, and these can be applied to springs as well as strings.

Example 11.1

A light elastic string of natural length 0.7 m and modulus of elasticity 50 N has one end fixed and a particle of mass 1.4 kg attached to the other. The system hangs vertically in equilibrium. Find the extension of the string.

Solution

The forces acting on the particle are the tension, T N, upwards and the weight, $1.4g$ N downwards.

Since the particle is in equilibrium
$$T = 1.4g$$

Using Hooke's law: $T = \dfrac{\lambda}{l_0} x$

$\Rightarrow$ $1.4g = \dfrac{50}{0.7} x$

$\Rightarrow$ $x = \dfrac{0.7 \times 1.4g}{50}$

     $= 0.192$

The extension in the string is 0.19 m (to 2 s. f.)

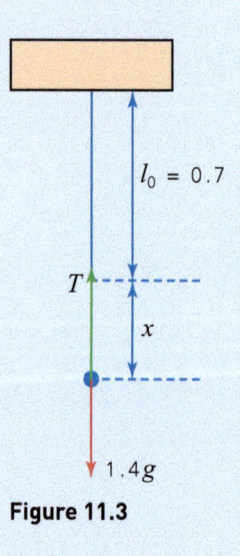

Figure 11.3

Example 11.2

The mechanism of a set of kitchen scales consists of a light scale pan supported on a spring. When measuring 1.5 kg of flour, the spring is compressed by 7 mm. Find

(i) the stiffness of the spring
(ii) the mass of the heaviest object that can be measured if it is impossible to compress the spring by more than 15 mm.

Solution

(i) The forces on the scale pan with its load of flour are the weight, $1.5g$ N, downwards, and the thrust of the spring, T N, upwards.

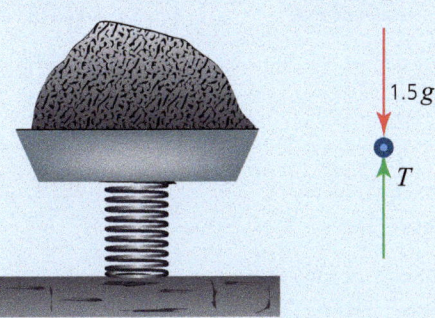

Figure 11.4

Since it is in equilibrium

$$T = 1.5g$$

Applying Hooke's law with stiffness k N m^{-1}.

$$T = k \times 0.007$$

$$\Rightarrow \quad 1.5g = 0.007k$$

$$\Rightarrow \quad k = 2100$$

The stiffness of the spring is 2100 N m^{-1}.

(ii) Let the mass of the heaviest object be M kg, so the maximum thrust is Mg N. Then Hooke's law for a compression of 15 mm gives

$$Mg = 2100 \times 0.015$$

$$\Rightarrow \quad M = 3.214...$$

The mass of the heaviest object that can be measured is 3.21 kg (to 3 s.f.)

> **Note**
> These scales would probably be calibrated to a maximum of 3 kg.

Strings and springs

Exercise 11.1

① In each of these diagrams in Figure 11.5 an object is suspended by a light elastic string. The top of the string is attached to a fixed ceiling. The object is in equilibrium.

In each diagram, information is provided about the mass of the object and two out of the natural length, l_0 m, the length l m and the extension x m.

In each case, find

(a) the tension in the string

(b) the stiffness of the string

(c) the modulus of elasticity of the string.

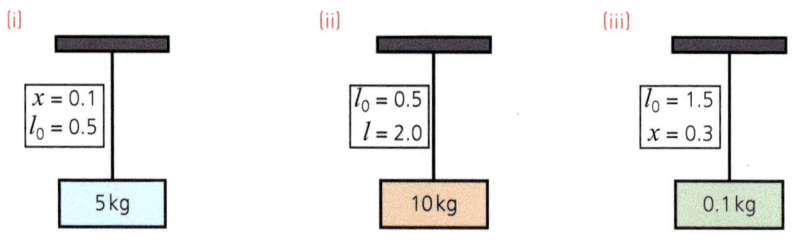

(i) $x = 0.1$, $l_0 = 0.5$, 5 kg

(ii) $l_0 = 0.5$, $l = 2.0$, 10 kg

(iii) $l_0 = 1.5$, $x = 0.3$, 0.1 kg

Figure 11.5

② In each of these diagrams in Figure 11.6 an object is suspended by a light elastic string. The top of the string is attached to a fixed ceiling. The object is in equilibrium.

In each diagram, information is provided about the tension in the string T N, the stiffness of the string k N m^{-1} and the length of the string l m.

In each case, find

(a) the mass of the object

(b) the natural length of the string

(c) the modulus of elasticity of the string.

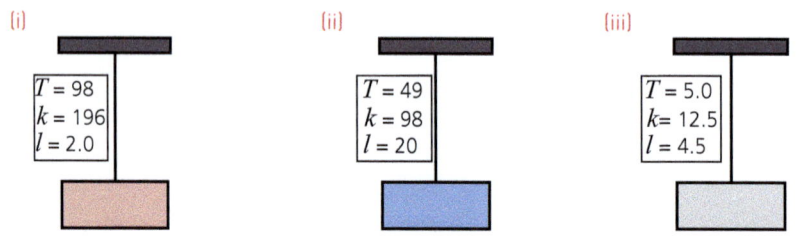

(i) $T = 98$, $k = 196$, $l = 2.0$

(ii) $T = 49$, $k = 98$, $l = 20$

(iii) $T = 5.0$, $k = 12.5$, $l = 4.5$

Figure 11.6

③ An elastic string has natural length 20 cm. The string is fixed at one end. When a force of 20 N is applied to the other end the string doubles in length.

(i) Find the modulus of elasticity.

(ii) Another elastic string also has natural length 20 cm. When a force of 20 N is applied to each end the string doubles in length.

Find the modulus of elasticity.

(iii) Explain the connection between the answers to parts (i) and (ii).

④ A light elastic spring of stiffness k is attached to a ceiling. A block of mass m kg hangs in equilibrium, attached to the other end of the spring.

(i) Draw a diagram showing the forces acting on the block.

The mass of the block is 0.25 kg and the extension of the spring is 0.4 m.

(ii) Find the value of k in S.I. units.

The natural length of the spring is 2 m.

(iii) Find the modulus of elasticity of the spring.

⑤ A light spring has stiffness $0.75\,\text{N}\,\text{m}^{-1}$. One end is attached to a ceiling, the other to a particle of weight $0.03\,\text{N}$ which hangs in equilibrium below the ceiling. In this situation, the length of the spring is 49 cm.

(i) Find the tension in the spring.

(ii) Find the extension of the spring.

(iii) Find the natural length of the spring.

The particle is removed and replaced with one of weight w N. When this hangs in equilibrium the spring has length 60 cm.

(iv) What is the value of w?

⑥ An object of mass 0.5 kg is attached to an elastic string and causes an extension of 8 cm when the system hangs vertically in equilibrium.

(i) What is the tension in the string?

(ii) What is the stiffness of the string?

(iii) What is the mass of an object which causes an extension of 10 cm?

The modulus of elasticity of the string is 73.5 N.

(iv) What is the natural length of the string?

⑦ In this question take the value of g to be $10\,\text{m}\,\text{s}^{-2}$. Figure 11.7 shows a spring of natural length 60 cm which is being compressed under the weight of a block of mass m kg. Smooth supports constrain the block to move only in the vertical direction.

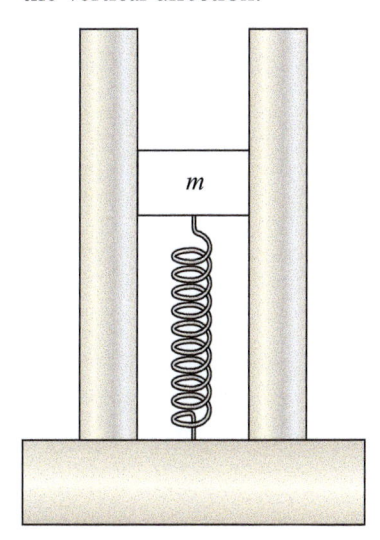

Figure 11.7

The modulus of elasticity of the spring is 180 N. The system is in equilibrium and the length of the spring is 50 cm. Find

(i) the thrust in the spring

(ii) the value of m

(iii) the stiffness of the spring.

More blocks are piled on.

(iv) Describe the situation when there are seven blocks in total, all identical to the first one.

⑧ An open coiled spring has natural length 30 cm and modulus of elasticity 80 N. The spring is fully compressed when its length is 15 cm.

If the spring is extended to twice its natural length it passes its elastic limit and can no longer return to its natural length.

Find the limits of the applied force for which Hooke's law may be used as a model for this spring.

2 Using Hooke's law with more than one spring or string

Hooke's law allows you to investigate situations involving two or more springs or strings in various configurations.

Example 11.3

A particle of mass 0.4 kg is attached to the midpoint of a light elastic string of natural length 1 m and modulus of elasticity λ N. The string is then stretched between a point A at the top of a doorway and a point B which is on the floor 2 m vertically below A.

(i) Find, in terms of λ, the extensions of the two parts of the string.

(ii) Calculate their values in the case when $\lambda = 9.8$.

(iii) Find the minimum value of λ that will ensure that the lower half of the string is not slack.

Solution

For a question like this, it is helpful to draw two diagrams, one showing the relevant natural lengths and extensions, and the other showing the forces acting on the particle.

Since the force of gravity acts downwards on the particle, its equilibrium position will be below the midpoint of AB. This is also shown in Figure 11.8.

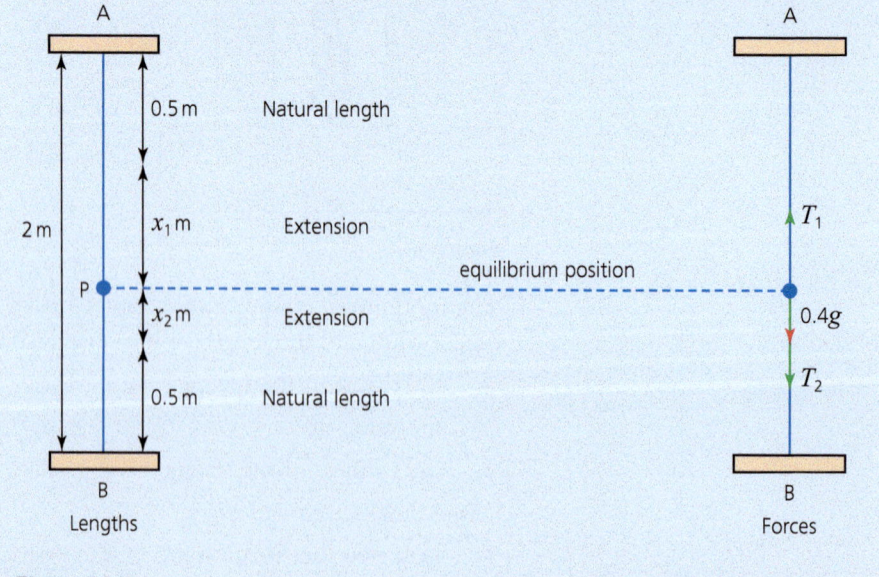

Figure 11.8

(i) The particle is in equilibrium, so the resultant vertical force acting on it is zero.

Therefore $\quad T_1 = T_2 + 0.4g \quad$ ①

Hooke's law can be applied to each part of the string.

For AP: $\quad T_1 = \dfrac{\lambda}{0.5} x_1 \quad$ ②

For BP: $\quad T_2 = \dfrac{\lambda}{0.5} x_2 \quad$ ③

Substituting these expressions in equation ① gives

$$\dfrac{\lambda}{0.5} x_1 = \dfrac{\lambda}{0.5} x_2 + 0.4g$$

$$\Rightarrow \lambda(x_1 - x_2) = 0.5 \times 0.4g$$

$$\Rightarrow x_1 - x_2 = 0.2 \dfrac{g}{\lambda} \quad ④$$

But from the first diagram it can be seen that

$$x_1 + x_2 = 1 \quad ⑤$$

Adding ④ and ⑤ gives

$$2x_1 = 1 + 0.2 \dfrac{g}{\lambda}$$

$$\Rightarrow x_1 = 0.5 + 0.1 \dfrac{g}{\lambda}$$

Similarly subtracting ④ from ⑤ gives

$$x_2 = 0.5 - 0.1 \dfrac{g}{\lambda} \quad ⑥$$

(ii) Since $\lambda = 9.8$, the extensions are 0.6 m and 0.4 m.

(iii) The lower part of the string will not become slack providing $x_2 > 0$. It follows from equation ⑥ that

$$0.5 - 0.1 \dfrac{g}{\lambda} > 0$$

$$\Rightarrow 0.5 > 0.1 \dfrac{g}{\lambda}$$

$$\Rightarrow \lambda > 0.2g$$

The minimum value of λ for which the lower part of the string is not slack is 1.96 N, and in this case BP has zero tension.

Using Hooke's law with more than one spring or string

> **Historical note**
>
> If you search for Robert Hooke (1635–1703) on the internet, you will find that he was a man of many parts. He was one of a talented group of polymaths (which included his rival Newton) who have had an enormous impact on scientific thought and practice. Among other things, he designed and built Robert Boyle's air pump, discovered the red spot on Jupiter and invented the balanced spring mechanism for watches. His work on microscopy led to his becoming the father of microbiology and he was the first to use the term 'cell' with respect to living things. Hooke worked closely with his friend Sir Christopher Wren in the rebuilding of the City of London after the great fire, and was responsible for the realisation of many of his designs including the Royal Greenwich Observatory. Both Hooke and Wren were astronomers and architects and they designed the Monument to the fire with a trapdoor at the top and a laboratory in the basement so that it could be used as an enormous 62 m telescope. Hooke, the great practical man, also used the column for experiments on air pressure and pendulums.

Exercise 11.2

① Figure 11.9 shows a uniform plank of weight 120 N symmetrically suspended in equilibrium by two identical elastic strings, each of natural length 0.8 m and modulus of elasticity 1200 N.

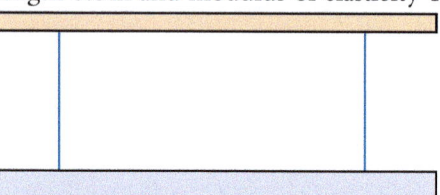

Figure 11.9

Find

(i) the tension in each string

(ii) the extension of each string.

The two strings are replaced by a single string, also of natural length 0.8 m, attached to the middle of the plank. The plank is in the same position.

(iii) Find the modulus of elasticity of this string and comment on its relationship to that of the original strings.

② The manufacturer of a sports car specifies the coil spring for the front suspension as a spring of 10 coils with a natural length 0.3 m and a compression 0.1 m when under a load of 4000 N.

(i) Calculate the modulus of elasticity of the spring.

(ii) If the spring were cut into two equal parts, what would be the stiffness of each part?

The weight of a car is 8000 N and half of this weight is taken by two such 10-coil front springs so that each bears a load of 2000 N.

(iii) Find the compression of each spring.

(iv) Two people each of weight 800 N get into the front of the car. How much further are the springs compressed? (Assume that their weight is carried equally by the front springs.)

③ The coach of an impoverished rugby club decides to construct a scrummaging machine as illustrated in Figure 11.10. It is to consist of a vertical board, supported in horizontal runners at the top and bottom of each end. The board is held away from the wall by springs, as shown, and the players push the board with their shoulders, against the thrust of the springs.

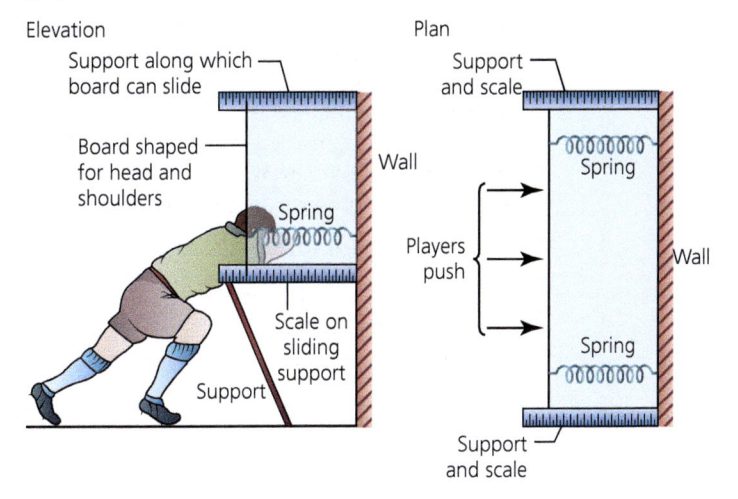

Figure 11.10

The coach has one spring of length 1.4 m and stiffness 5000 N m^{-1}, which he cuts into two pieces of equal length.

(i) Find the modulus of elasticity of the original spring.

(ii) Find the modulus of elasticity and the stiffness of each of the half-length springs.

(iii) On one occasion, the coach observes that the players compress the springs by 20 cm. What total force do they produce in the forward direction?

④ Figure 11.11 shows the rear view of a load of weight 300 N in the back of a pickup truck of width 2 m.

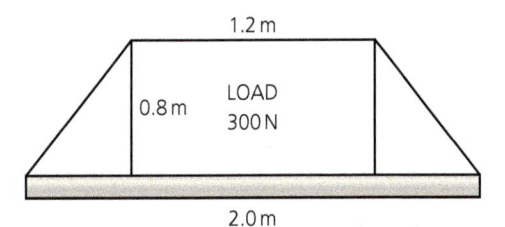

Figure 11.11

The load is 1.2 m wide, 0.8 m high and is situated centrally on the truck. The coefficient of friction between the load and the truck is 0.4. The load is held down by an elastic rope of natural length 2 m and modulus of elasticity 400 N which may be assumed to pass smoothly over the corners and across the top of the load. The rope is secured at the edges of the truck platform.

Find

(i) the tension in the rope

(ii) the normal reaction of the truck on the load

(iii) the percentage by which the maximum possible frictional force is increased by using the rope

Using Hooke's law with more than one spring or string

(iv) the shortest stopping distance for which the load does not slide, given that the truck is travelling at $30\,\text{m}\,\text{s}^{-1}$ initially. (Assume constant deceleration and use 10 for g.)

⑤ Two springs of stiffness k_1 and k_2 are connected in series as shown in Figure 11.12 and a force F is applied to each end.

Figure 11.12

(i) Write down the tension in each spring and find expressions for their extensions in terms of F, k_1 and k_2.

(ii) If these two springs are equivalent to one spring of stiffness k show that
$$\frac{1}{k} = \frac{1}{k_1} + \frac{1}{k_2}$$

The two springs (which are of the same length) are now connected in parallel, and held so that their extensions are equal as shown in Figure 11.13.

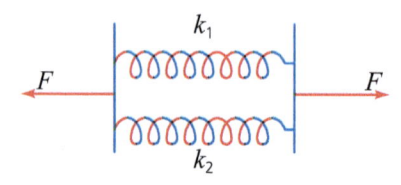

Figure 11.13

(iii) Show that they are now equivalent to a spring with stiffness $k_1 + k_2$.

⑥ Figure 11.14 diagram shows two light springs, AP and BP, connected at P. The ends A and B are secured firmly and the system is in equilibrium.

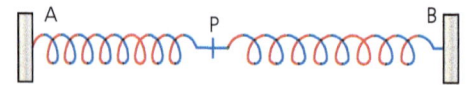

Figure 11.14

The spring AP has natural length 1 m and modulus of elasticity 16 N.
The spring BP has natural length 1.2 m and modulus of elasticity 30 N.
The distance AB is 2.5 m and the extension of the string AP is x m.

(i) Write down an expression, in terms of x, for the extension of the spring BP.
(ii) Find expressions, in terms of x, for the tensions in both springs.
(iii) Find the value of x.

⑦ Figure 11.15 shows two light springs, CQ and DQ, connected to a particle, Q, of weight 20 N. The ends C and D are secured firmly and the system is in equilibrium, lying in a vertical line.

The spring CQ has natural length 0.8 m and modulus of elasticity 16 N; DQ has natural length 1.2 m and modulus of elasticity 36 N. The distance CD is 3 m and QD is h m.

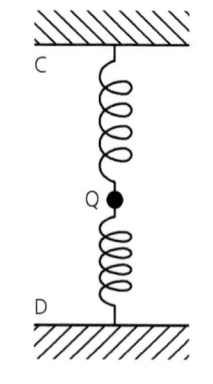

Figure 11.15

(i) Write down expressions, in terms of h, for the extensions of the two springs.

(ii) Find expressions, in terms of h, for the tensions in the two springs.

(iii) Use these results to find the value of h.

(iv) Find the forces the system exerts at C and at D.

⑧ Figure 11.16 shows a block of wood of mass m lying on a plane inclined at an angle α to the horizontal. The block is attached to a fixed peg by means of a light elastic string of natural length l_0 and modulus of elasticity λ; the string lies parallel to the line of greatest slope. The block is in equilibrium.

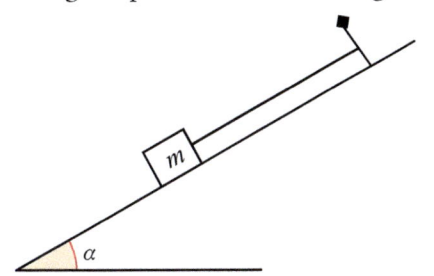

Figure 11.16

Find the extension of the string in the following cases.

(i) The plane is smooth.

(ii) The coefficient of friction between the plane and the block is μ ($\mu \neq 0$) and the block is about to slide (a) up the plane (b) down the plane.

⑨ In this question take g to be $10\,\mathrm{m\,s^{-2}}$. A baby bouncer consists of a light, inextensible harness attached to a spring. It is suspended in a doorway on the end of a chain so that the baby's feet just touch the floor. The baby can then use its feet to bounce up and down. A harness, with a spring of natural length 20 cm, is set up for Emily (who has mass 10 kg). Before Emily is put into the harness (i.e. when the spring is not extended) the bottom of the harness is 17 cm from the ground. When she sits in the harness with her feet off the ground, the bottom of the harness is 15 cm above the ground.

(i) Find the modulus of elasticity of the spring.

Figure 11.17

Using Hooke's law with more than one spring or string

The baby bouncer is also used by Charlotte and its height is not adjusted for her. Charlotte's mass is 12 kg (the limit recommended for the bouncer).

(ii) What is the extension of the spring when Charlotte sits in the bouncer with her feet off the ground?

(iii) Find an expression for the reaction R N, between Charlotte's feet and the ground in terms of the height, h cm, of the harness above the ground, assuming her to be in equilibrium at the time.

10. A strong elastic band of natural length 1 m and of modulus of elasticity 12 N is stretched round two pegs P and Q which are in a horizontal line a distance 1 m apart. A bag of mass 1.5 kg is hooked onto the band at H and hangs in equilibrium so that PH and QH make angles of θ with the horizontal. Make the modelling assumptions that the elastic band is light and runs smoothly over the pegs.

(i) Use Hooke's law to show that the tension in the band is $12\sec\theta$.

(ii) Find the depth of the hook below the horizontal line PQ.

(iii) Is the modelling in this question realistic?

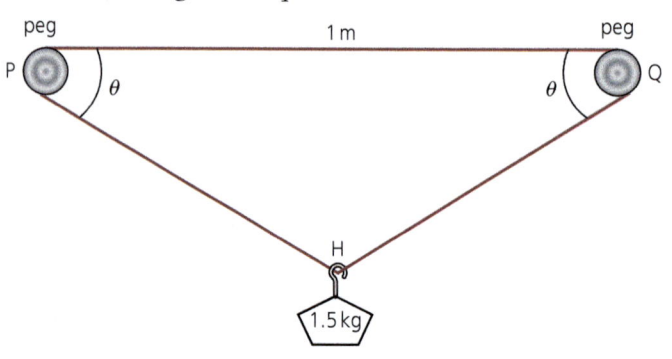

Figure 11.18

11. A light spring AB has natural length 0.8 m and modulus of elasticity 200 N. The end A is fixed and a small ball is attached at B. The ball hangs in equilibrium below A.

(i) Given that the length of the spring is 1 m, calculate the mass of the ball.

(ii) If, instead, the mass of the ball is 2 kg, calculate the length of the spring.

The end A of the spring is now fixed to a vertical wall and the end B is fixed to the midpoint of a light rod CD, of length 1.2 m, as shown in Figure 11.19. The end C of the rod is freely hinged to the wall vertically below A and a small ball of mass m kg is attached to the end D of the rod. The rod rests in equilibrium perpendicular to the spring and at an angle of 60° to the upward vertical.

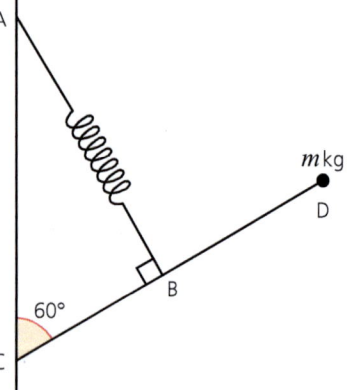

(iii) Show that the extension of the spring is 0.239 m (correct to 3 significant figures) and hence calculate the tension in the spring.

Figure 11.19

(iv) Calculate m.

The end A is now attached to a different point on the wall. In this position the rod rests horizontally in equilibrium and angle ABC = θ.

(v) Show that $3\tan\theta - 4\sin\theta = 1.37$ correct to 3 significant figures.

⑫ Many cafeterias have a device for stacking plates where, for any number of plates in the stack, the top of the top plate is always at the counter level, as shown in the diagram on the left of Figure 11.20. This is achieved by standing the plates on a metal base which is supported by a number of springs which hang vertically as, shown in the diagram on the right. The base is shaped so that when there are no plates on the stack, the top of the base is level with the counter.

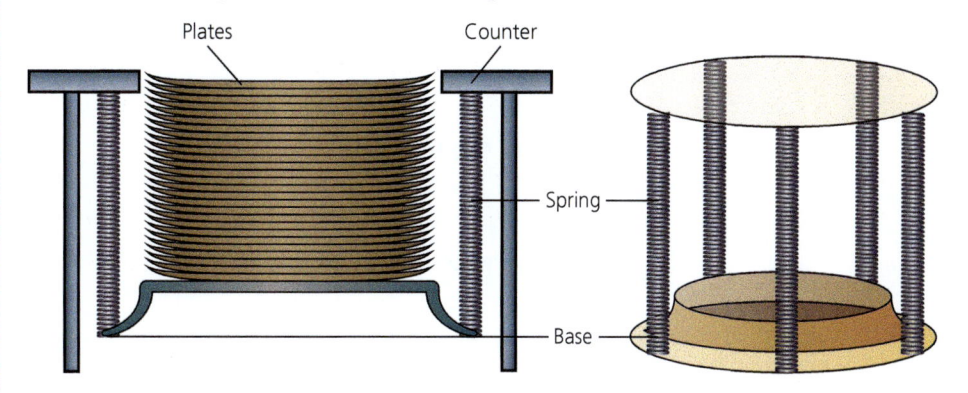

Figure 11.20

The situation may be modelled by assuming that each plate has a mass of 0.1 kg and raises the vertical height of the stack by 1.5 cm when placed on another plate (or the base). The springs have a natural length of 10 cm and a modulus of 0.8 N. The springs may be assumed to be light and resistances to motion due to friction may be neglected.

(i) Suppose that n springs are attached.

  (a) Show that the extension in each spring when a mass m kg is supported by the system is given by $\frac{mg}{8n}$ m.

  (b) What is the further extension of each spring when one plate is added to the stack?

(ii) Show that nine springs are required if the addition of each plate allows the top of the plate to be as near to the counter level as possible but to be above, not below, the counter level.

(iii) Assuming that nine springs are used, approximately how many plates would be above the counter level if there were 40 plates in the stack?

The system can be adjusted so that the top of the plate is at counter level by reducing the natural length of the springs.

(iv) When eight springs are used, what should be the natural length of each spring, correct to three decimal places? [MEI]

⑬ A light elastic string, of natural length l_0, is hung at one end from a fixed point. When a particle of mass m is hung from the other end the string extends a distance d. Show that the modulus of elasticity of the string is $\frac{mgl_0}{d}$.

The particle is removed and attached to the midpoint of the string. The ends of the string are now tied to two points A and B, where B is vertically below A and AB $> l_0$. In the equilibrium position, the lower part of the string remains taut. Show that the displacement of the particle from the midpoint of AB is $\frac{d}{4}$.

14) Blocks A and B are attached to opposite ends of a light elastic string of natural length 2 m and modulus of elasticity 6 N. A is at rest on a rough horizontal table. The string passes over a small smooth pulley P at the edge of the table, with the part AP of the string horizontal and of length 1.2 m. The frictional force acting on A is 1.5 N and the system is in equilibrium. Find the distance PB.

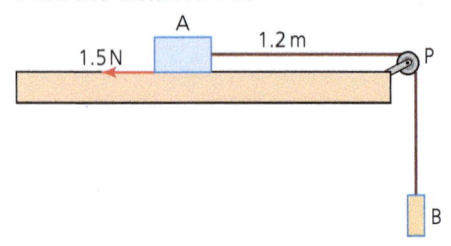

Figure 11.21

3 Work and energy

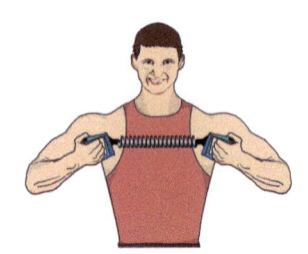

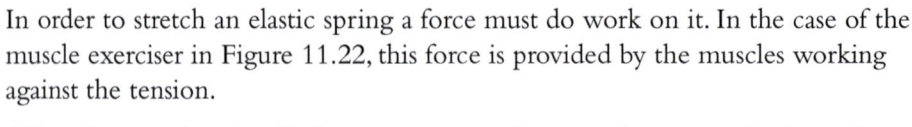

In order to stretch an elastic spring a force must do work on it. In the case of the muscle exerciser in Figure 11.22, this force is provided by the muscles working against the tension.

When the exerciser is pulled at constant speed, at any given time the force F applied at each end is equal to the tension in the spring; consequently, it changes as the spring stretches.

Figure 11.22

Suppose that one end of the spring is stationary and the extension is x, as in Figure 11.23.

By Hooke's law, the tension is given by

$$T = kx \text{ and so } F = kx$$

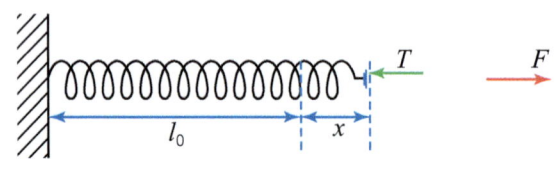

Figure 11.23

The work done by a *constant* force F in moving a distance d in its own direction is given by Fd. To find the work done by a variable force, the process has to be considered in small stages. Now imagine that the force extends the string a small distance δx. The work done is given by $F\delta x = kx\delta x$.

The work done in stretching the spring many small distances is

$$\Sigma F\delta x = \Sigma kx\delta x$$

In the limit as $\delta x \to 0$, the work done is

$$\int F dx = \int kx dx$$

$$= \frac{1}{2}kx^2 + c$$

When the extension $x = 0$, the work done is zero, so $c = 0$.

The total work done in stretching the spring an extension x from its natural length l_0 is therefore given by:

$$\frac{1}{2}kx^2 \text{ or } \frac{1}{2}\frac{\lambda}{l_0}x^2$$

The result is the same for the work done in compressing a spring.

Elastic potential energy

The tensions and thrusts in perfectly elastic springs and strings are conservative forces, since any work done against them can be recovered in the form of kinetic energy. A catapult and a jack-in-a-box use this property.

The work done in stretching or compressing a string or spring can therefore be regarded as potential energy. It is known as **elastic potential energy**.

The elastic potential energy stored in a spring which is stretched or compressed by an amount x is given by

$$\frac{1}{2}kx^2 \text{ or } \frac{1}{2}\frac{\lambda}{l_0}x^2$$

Figure 11.24

> **Note**
> Notice that this is different from gravitational potential energy. Potential energy is energy which is available to be converted.

Example 11.4

An elastic rope of natural length 0.6 m is extended to a length of 0.8 m. The modulus of elasticity of the rope is 25 N. Find

(i) the elastic potential energy in the rope

(ii) the further energy required to stretch it to a length of 1.65 m over a car roof-rack

> **Note**
> In Example 11.4, the string is stretched so that its extension changes from x_1 to x_2. The work required to do this is:
> $\frac{1}{2}kx_2^2 - \frac{1}{2}kx_1^2 = \frac{1}{2}k(x_2^2 - x_1^2)$
> or $\frac{1}{2}\frac{\lambda}{l_0}(x_2^2 - x_1^2)$
> You can see by using algebra that this expression is *not* the same as $\frac{1}{2}k(x_2 - x_1)^2$, so it is *not* possible to use the extra extension $(x_2 - x_1)$ directly in the energy expression to calculate the extra energy stored in the string.

Solution

(i) The extension of the elastic is $(0.8 - 0.6) = 0.2$ m.

The energy stored in the rope is $\frac{1}{2}\frac{\lambda}{l_0}x^2$

$$= \frac{25}{2 \times 0.6} 0.2^2$$

$$= 0.83 \text{ J (to 2 dp)}$$

(ii) The extension of the elastic rope is now $1.65 - 0.6 = 1.05$ m

The elastic energy stored in the rope is $\frac{25}{2 \times 0.6} 1.05^2$

$$= 22.97 \text{ J}$$

The extra energy required to stretch the rope is 22.14 J (correct to 2 d.p.).

Work and energy

Example 11.5

A catapult has prongs which are 16 cm apart and the elastic string is 20 cm long. A marble of mass 70 g is placed in the centre of the elastic string and pulled back so that the string is just taut. The marble is then pulled back a further 9 cm and the force required to keep it in this position is 60 N. Find

(i) the stretched length of the string

(ii) the tension in the string and its stiffness

(iii) the elastic potential energy stored in the string and the speed of the marble when the string regains its natural length, assuming they remain in contact.

Solution

> A and B are the ends of the elastic string and M_1 and M_2 are the two positions of the marble (before and after the string is stretched). D is the midpoint of AB.

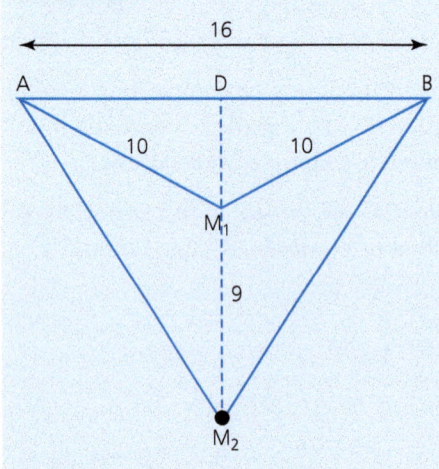

Figure 11.25

> **Note**
> You need to make these modelling assumptions.
> - There is no elasticity in the frame of the catapult.
> - The motion takes place in a horizontal plane.
> - Air resistance is negligible.

(i) Using Pythagoras' theorem in triangle DBM_1 gives
$$DM_1 = \sqrt{10^2 - 8^2} = 6 \text{ cm}.$$
So
$$DM_2 = 9 + 6 = 15 \text{ cm}.$$
Using Pythagoras' theorem in triangle DBM_2 gives
$$BM_2 = \sqrt{15^2 + 8^2} = 17 \text{ cm}$$
The stretched length of the string is $2 \times 17 = 34$ cm.

(ii) Take the tension in the string to be T N.

Resolving parallel to M_2D:

$2T \cos \alpha = 60$

Now $\cos \alpha = \dfrac{DM_2}{BM_2} = \dfrac{0.15}{0.17}$

So $T = \dfrac{60 \times 0.17}{2 \times 0.15} = 34$

The extension of the string is $(0.34 - 0.2) = 0.14$ m.

By Hooke's law the stiffness k is given by $k = \dfrac{T}{x}$

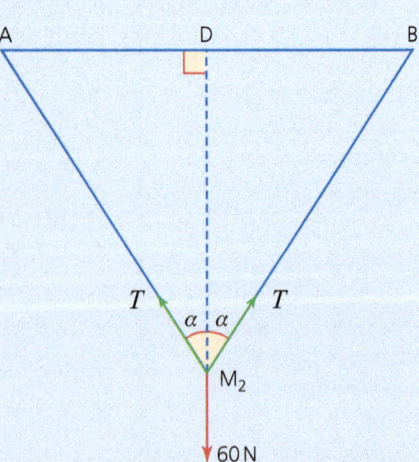

Figure 11.26

$$k = \frac{34}{0.14} = 242.85\ldots$$

The stiffness of the string is $240\,\text{N m}^{-1}$ (to 2 s.f.)

(iii) The elastic potential energy stored in the string is

$$\tfrac{1}{2}kx^2 = \tfrac{1}{2} \times 242.85\ldots \times 0.14^2 = 2.38\,\text{J}$$

By the principle of conservation of energy, this is equal to the kinetic energy given to the marble. The mass of the marble is $0.07\,\text{kg}$, so

$$\tfrac{1}{2} \times 0.07 v^2 = 2.38$$

$$\Rightarrow v = 8.246\ldots$$

The speed of the marble is $8.25\,\text{m s}^{-1}$.

Exercise 11.3

① An open coiled spring has natural length $0.3\,\text{m}$ and stiffness $20\,\text{N m}^{-1}$. Find the elastic potential energy in the spring when:
  (i) it is extended by $0.1\,\text{m}$
  (ii) it is compressed by $0.01\,\text{m}$
  (iii) its length is $0.5\,\text{m}$
  (iv) its length is $0.3\,\text{m}$.

② A spring has natural length $0.4\,\text{m}$ and modulus of elasticity $20\,\text{N}$. Find the elastic energy stored in the spring when:
  (i) it is extended by $0.4\,\text{m}$
  (ii) it is compressed by $0.1\,\text{m}$
  (iii) its length is $0.2\,\text{m}$
  (iv) its length is $0.45\,\text{m}$.

③ A pinball machine fires small balls of mass $50\,\text{g}$ by means of a spring and a light plunger. The spring and the ball move in a horizontal plane. The spring has stiffness $600\,\text{N m}^{-1}$ and is compressed by $5\,\text{cm}$ to fire a ball.

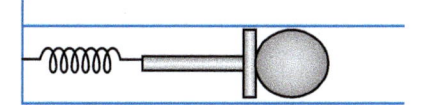

Figure 11.27

  (i) Find the energy stored in the spring immediately before the ball is fired.
  (ii) Find the speed of the ball when it is fired.

④ A catapult is made from elastic string with modulus of elasticity $5\,\text{N}$. The string is attached to two prongs which are $15\,\text{cm}$ apart, and is just taut. A pebble of mass $40\,\text{g}$ is placed in the centre of the string and is pulled back $4\,\text{cm}$ and then released in a horizontal direction.

  (i) Calculate the work done in stretching the string.
  (ii) Calculate the speed of the pebble on leaving the catapult.

Figure 11.28

Work and energy

⑤ A simple mathematical model of a railway buffer consists of a horizontal open coiled spring attached to a fixed point. The stiffness of the spring is $10^5\,\mathrm{N\,m^{-1}}$ and its natural length is 2 m.

The buffer is designed to stop a railway truck before the spring is compressed to half its natural length, otherwise the truck will be damaged.

Figure 11.29

(i) Find the elastic energy stored in the spring when it is half its natural length.

(ii) Find the maximum speed at which a truck of mass 2 tonnes can approach the buffer safely. Neglect any other reasons for loss of energy of the truck.

A truck of mass 2 tonnes approaches the buffer at $5\,\mathrm{m\,s^{-1}}$.

(iii) Calculate the minimum length of the spring during the subsequent period of contact.

(iv) Find the thrust in the spring and the acceleration of the truck when the spring is at its minimum length.

(v) What happens next?

⑥ Two identical springs are attached to a sphere of mass 0.5 kg that rests on a smooth horizontal surface, as shown. The other ends of the springs are attached to fixed points A and B.

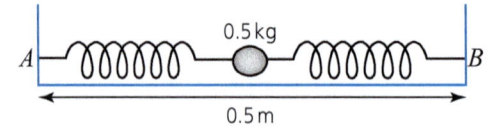

Figure 11.30

The springs each have modulus of elasticity 7.5 N and natural length 25 cm. The sphere is at rest at the midpoint when it is projected with speed $2\,\mathrm{m\,s^{-1}}$ along the line of the springs towards B. Calculate the length of each spring when the sphere first comes to rest.

⑦ Two light springs are joined and stretched between two fixed points A and C which are 2 m apart, as shown in Figure 11.31. The spring AB has natural length 0.5 m and modulus of elasticity 10 N. The spring BC has natural length 0.6 m and modulus of elasticity 6 N. The system is in equilibrium.

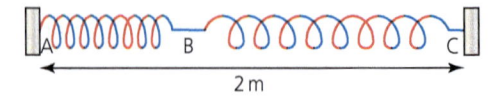

Figure 11.31

(i) Explain why the tensions in the two springs are the same.

(ii) Find the distance AB and the tension in each spring.

(iii) How much work must be done to stretch the springs from their natural length to connect them as described above?

A small object of mass 0.012 kg is attached at B and is supported on a smooth horizontal table. A, B and C lie in a straight horizontal line and the mass is released from rest at the midpoint of AC.

(iv) What is the speed of the mass when it passes through the equilibrium position of the system? [MEI]

⑧

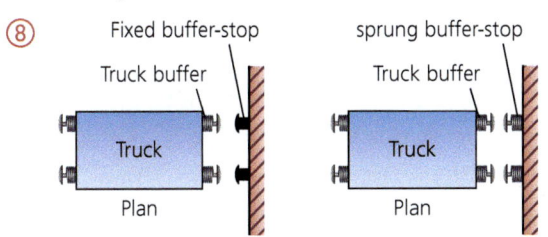

Figure 11.32

A railway truck of mass 4.5 tonnes, travelling with a speed of $0.5\,\text{m s}^{-1}$, collides with a *fixed* buffer-stop, as indicated in the diagram on the left of Figure 11.32.

The truck itself has, at each end, two buffers of negligible mass, each of which may be modelled as a spring of stiffness $25\,000\,\text{Nm}^{-1}$. The truck comes momentarily to rest with the buffers compressed by a distance x cm and you may neglect the work done against any forces other than those in the buffers.

(i) Calculate the kinetic energy of the truck immediately before the impact.

(ii) Calculate the value of x.

The truck's buffers are designed to be compressed by 24 cm.

(iii) Calculate the greatest speed of the truck if it can be brought momentarily to rest by compression of the buffers.

On another occasion the same truck is travelling at $0.8\,\text{m s}^{-1}$ when it collides with a *sprung* buffer-stop, as indicated in the diagram on the right of Figure 11.32. The sprung buffer-stop has two buffers, each of which makes contact with a buffer on the truck. Each buffer on the buffer-stop has negligible mass and may be modelled by a spring of stiffness $20\,000\,\text{N m}^{-1}$. The truck is brought momentarily to rest when its buffers are compressed by a distance x_1 m and those of the stop by a distance x_2 m. You may assume that the forces of compression in each spring are equal in magnitude when the truck comes momentarily to rest.

(iv) Write down two equations involving x_1 and x_2 and hence determine their values.

⑨ A light elastic band is made from a piece of elastic of total natural length $2a$ (i.e. it is of length a when lying naturally).

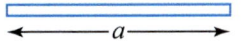

Figure 11.33

The band is hung vertically over a small, smooth peg. When a mass m is attached to the bottom of the band its length is trebled.

(i) Show that the modulus of elasticity is $\frac{mg}{4}$.

The band is now stretched over two small, smooth pegs a distance $2a$ apart in a horizontal line. The mass m is fixed to the centre of the lower strand of the band and gently lowered to a position in which the mass is a distance $2a$ below the line of the pegs, as shown in Figure 11.34.

(ii) Calculate the extension in the band.

(iii) Show that the mass hangs in equilibrium in this position.

(iv) How much energy is given to the band while the mass is being lowered?

(v) Why is your answer to part (iv) not equal to the potential energy lost by the mass on being lowered? [MEI]

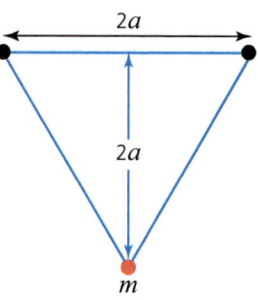

Figure 11.34

⑩ The end A of a light elastic string AB is fixed to a smooth horizontal table. A small bead of mass 0.05 kg is attached to the end B. Also attached to the end B is another light elastic string BC. The end C is fixed to a point on the table so that the strings lie in a horizontal straight line with the bead resting in equilibrium on the table and with AC equal to 2.3 metres as shown in Figure 11.35.

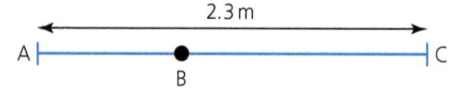

Figure 11.35

The string AB has natural length 0.4 m and modulus of elasticity 4 N. The string BC has natural length 0.5 m and modulus of elasticity 2 N.

(i) The extension in AB is x_1 m and the extension in BC is x_2 m. Show that $5x_1 = 2x_2$ and calculate x_1 and x_2.

The bead is held at A and released.

(ii) Determine whether the string BC goes slack.

(iii) Calculate the maximum extension of the string AB. [MEI]

4 Vertical motion involving elastic forces

There are two common approaches to the analysis of motion involving elastic strings and springs: using energy and using calculus. Both are covered in this section in the context of vertical motion.

Using energy

Example 11.6

A particle of mass m is attached to one end, A, of a light elastic string with natural length l_0 and stiffness k. The other end of the string is attached to a fixed point O. The particle is released from O.

Initially it falls freely with the string slack but after some time it reaches a point P and the string becomes taut and exerts an upward force on the particle. At P, the particle has velocity u downwards. Air resistance is negligible.

(i) Draw a diagram illustrating the situation.

(ii) Find an expression for u at the instant when the string becomes taut.

(iii) Write down the energy equation of the system at a time when the extension of the string is x m and its velocity vertically downwards is v.

(iv) Obtain an equation for the value of x when the particle is at its lowest point.

Solution

> **Note**
> Notice that no units are given in this example. In such cases, you can assume that a consistent set of units is being applied to all the quantities.

(i)

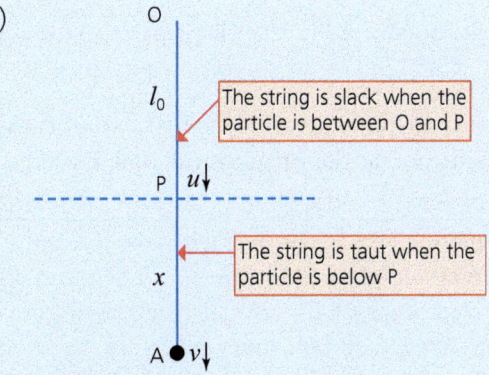

```
        O
        |
     l₀ |
        |       The string is slack when the
        ↙       particle is between O and P
      P | u↓
    - - - - - - - - - -
        |
        |       The string is taut when the
      x |←      particle is below P
        |
      A ● v↓
```

Figure 11.36

(ii) Between O and P the particle loses gravitational potential energy mgl_0 and gains kinetic energy $\frac{1}{2}mu^2$.

Using the law of conservation of energy, $\frac{1}{2}mu^2 = mgl_0$

$\Rightarrow u = \sqrt{2gl_0}$

(iii) When the particle has travelled a distance x m below P:

Gravitational potential energy lost $= mgx$

Elastic potential energy stored in the string $= \frac{1}{2}kx^2$

Kinetic energy gained $= \frac{1}{2}mv^2 - \frac{1}{2}mu^2$

Using conservation of energy:

$\frac{1}{2}mv^2 - \frac{1}{2}mu^2 + \frac{1}{2}kx^2 = mgx$

(iv) At the lowest point, the particle is stationary so $v = 0$

$\frac{1}{2}kx^2 - mgx - \frac{1}{2}mu^2 = 0$

and since $\frac{1}{2}mu^2 = mgl_0$, this equation can be written as

$\frac{1}{2}kx^2 - mgx - mgl_0 = 0$

> **Note**
> Notice that this is a quadratic equation and so will have two roots. One value is at the bottom of the particle's motion. The other would be at the top, but by then the string will have gone slack and so the model used in this example would no longer apply.

Vertical motion involving elastic forces

Using calculus

You can sometimes acquire more detailed information about the motion of an object by using calculus. The starting point is Newton's second law. This involves the acceleration of the body and there are three ways in which acceleration can be written.

- $\frac{dv}{dt}$ relates the velocity to the time taken.
- $v\frac{dv}{ds}$ relates the velocity to the distance travelled. (It is often written as $v\frac{dv}{dx}$.)
- $\frac{d^2x}{dt^2}$ gives rise to a second-order differential equation involving derivatives of x. It is not covered in this chapter but its use for simple harmonic motion is explained in the next chapter on page 321.

The next example involves the first two of these forms. It involves exactly the same situation as the previous example but the approaches are different.

Example 11.7

A particle of mass m is attached to one end, A, of a light elastic string with natural length l_0 and stiffness k. The other end of the string is attached to a fixed point O. The particle is released from O. Initially it falls freely with the string slack but, after some time, it reaches a point P and the string becomes taut and exerts an upward force on the particle. At P, the particle has velocity u downwards. Air resistance is negligible.

(i) Write down the equation of motion for the particle when the string is taut using $v\frac{dv}{dx}$ for the acceleration.

(ii) Solve this differential equation to find v in terms of x and interpret the solution.

(iii) Write the equation of motion for the particle when the string is taut using $\frac{dv}{dt}$ for the acceleration and comment on whether this is useful.

Solution

(i) Figure 11.37 shows the forces on the particle.

The equation of motion is $mg - kx = ma$

or

$$v\frac{dv}{dx} = g - \frac{k}{m}x$$

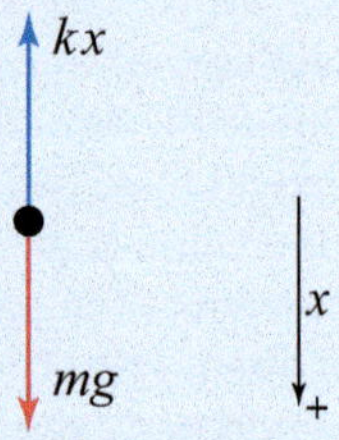

Figure 11.37

(ii) Separating variables gives $\int v\,dv = \int \left(g - \frac{k}{m}x\right)dx$

and so

$$\frac{1}{2}v^2 = gx - \frac{k}{2m}x^2 + c$$

When $x = 0$, $v = u$, so $c = \frac{1}{2}u^2$

> These are the boundary conditions. In this case, they are also the initial conditions and the solution is: $\frac{1}{2}v^2 = gx - \frac{k}{2m}x^2 + \frac{1}{2}u^2$.

You can interpret this two in ways.

It gives an equation for v in terms of x, $v = \pm\sqrt{u^2 + 2gx - \frac{k}{m}x^2}$ or $v = \pm\sqrt{2g(l_0 + x) - \frac{k}{m}x^2}$

> Replacing u^2 by $2gl_0$

With a little rearrangement, it becomes the energy equation
$\frac{1}{2}mv^2 - \frac{1}{2}mu^2 + \frac{1}{2}kx^2 = mgx$

(iii) The equation of motion can also be written as $\frac{dv}{dt} = g - \frac{k}{m}x$.

This is not a useful form as it involves 3 variables, v, t and x, and so you cannot solve the differential equation.

ACTIVITY 11.1

The bungee jump

Figure 11.38

You may have noticed that the situation in the last two examples could be used to match the bungee jump described at the start of this chapter.

Typical parameters for a mobile crane bungee jump of the type usually done in Britain are:

Height of jump station: 55 m
Bottom safety space: 5 m
Static line length: 5 m (non-elastic straps etc.)
Unstretched elastic rope length: 12 m
Stiffness: 80 N m^{-1}

(i) Use these figures to decide on the right length of rope for a jumper. Does it depend on the person's mass?

(ii) Calculate the maximum deceleration of a jumper.

Vertical motion involving elastic forces

Exercise 11.4

1. A particle of mass 0.2 kg is attached to one end of a light elastic spring of stiffness 10 N m^{-1}. The system hangs vertically and the particle is released from rest when the spring is at its natural length. The particle comes to rest when it has fallen a distance h m.
   (i) Write down an expression in terms of h for the energy stored in the spring when the particle comes to rest at its lowest point.
   (ii) Write down an expression in terms of h for the gravitational potential energy lost by the particle when it comes to rest at its lowest point.
   (iii) Find the value of h.

2. A particle of mass m is attached to one end of a light vertical spring of natural length l_0 and modulus of elasticity $2mg$. The particle is released from rest when the spring is at its natural length. Find, in terms of l_0, the maximum length of the spring in the subsequent motion.

3. A block of mass m is placed on a smooth plane inclined at 30° to the horizontal. The block is attached to the top of the plane by a spring of natural length l_0 and modulus of elasticity λ. The system is released from rest with the spring at its natural length. Find an expression for the maximum length of the spring in the subsequent motion.

4. A particle of mass 0.1 kg is attached to one end of a spring of natural length 0.3 m and modulus of elasticity 20 N. The other end is attached to a fixed point and the system hangs vertically. The particle is released from rest when the length of the spring is 0.2 m. In the subsequent motion the extension of the spring is denoted by x m.
   (i) Show that $0.05\dot{x}^2 + \dfrac{10}{0.3}(x^2 - 0.1^2) - 0.98(x + 0.1) = 0$
   (ii) Find the maximum value of x.

5. A small apple of mass 0.1 kg is attached to one end of an elastic string of natural length 25 cm and modulus of elasticity 5 N. David is asleep under a tree and Sam fixes the free end of the string to the branch of the tree just above David's head. Sam releases the apple level with the branch and it just touches David's head in the subsequent motion. How high above his head is the branch?

6. A block of mass 0.5 kg lies on a light scale pan which is supported on a vertical spring of natural length 0.4 m and modulus of elasticity 40 N. Initially the spring is at its natural length and the block is moving downwards with a speed of 2 m s^{-1}. Gravitational potential energy is measured relative to the initial position and g should be taken to be 10 m s^{-2}.
   (i) Find the initial mechanical energy of the system.
   (ii) Show that the speed v m s^{-1} of the block when the compression of the spring is x m is given by $v = 2\sqrt{1 + 5x - 50x^2}$.
   (iii) Find the minimum length of the spring during the oscillations.

7. A scale pan of mass 0.5 kg is suspended from a fixed point by a spring of stiffness 500 N m^{-1} and natural length 10 cm.
   (i) Calculate the length of the spring when the scale pan is in equilibrium.
   (ii) A bag of sugar of mass 1 kg is gently placed on the pan and the system is released from rest. Find the maximum length of the spring in the subsequent motion.

⑧ A bungee jump is carried out by a person of mass m kg using an elastic rope which can be taken to obey Hooke's law. The supervisor ensures that in any jump the total length of the rope will never exceed the limit of four times its original length. Prove that the tension in the rope is at most $\frac{8}{3} mg$ N.

⑨ A particle of mass m is attached to one end of a light elastic string with natural length l_0 and modulus of elasticity λ. The other end of the string is attached to a fixed point O. The particle is released from O. Air resistance is negligible.

(i) Show that, at the instant when the string first becomes taut, the speed, u, of the particle is given by $u = \sqrt{2gl_0}$.

(ii) Write down the equation of motion of the particle once the string has become taut, using a to represent its acceleration and x the extension of the string.

(iii) Now write the equation of motion as a differential equation using $v\frac{dv}{dx}$ for the acceleration, where v is the velocity of the particle in the downwards direction.

(iv) Solve this differential equation and so write v in terms of x, g, m and l_0.

(v) At a certain instant, T, the velocity of the particle is given by $v = -\sqrt{2gl_0}$.

Find the value of x at this time and interpret your answer.

(vi) Write down a differential equation for $\frac{dv}{dt}$ immediately after the instant T. Solve your differential equation and state for how long your solution is valid.

⑩ A conical pendulum consists of a bob of mass m attached to an inextensible string of length l. The bob describes a circle of radius r with angular speed ω, and the string makes an angle θ with the vertical, as shown in Figure 11.39.

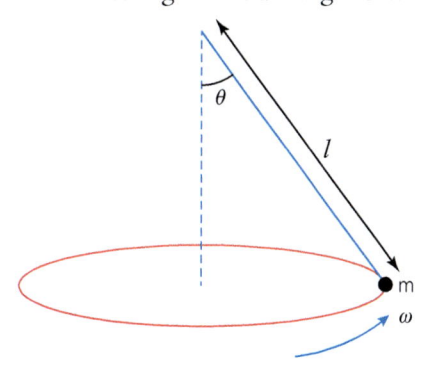

Figure 11.39

(i) Find an expression for θ in terms of ω, l and g.

The string is replaced with an elastic string of stiffness k and natural length l_0.

(ii) Find an expression for the new value of θ in terms of ω, m, g, l_0 and k.

⑪ A light, elastic string has natural length 0.5 m and modulus of elasticity 49 N. The end A is attached to a point on a ceiling. A small object of mass 3 kg is attached to the end B of the string and hangs in equilibrium.

(i) Calculate the length AB.

A second string, identical to the first one, is now attached to the object at B and to a point C on the floor, 2.5 m vertically below the point A.

Vertical motion involving elastic forces

The system is in equilibrium with B a distance x m below A, as shown in Figure 11.40.

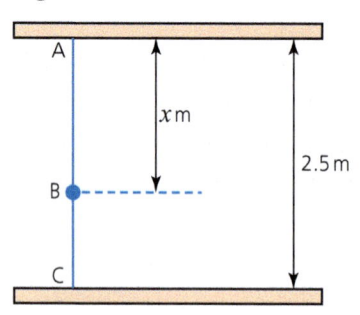

Figure 11.40

(ii) Find the tension in each of the strings in terms of x and hence show that $x = 1.4$.

(iii) Calculate the total elastic potential energy in the strings when the object hangs in equilibrium.

The object is now pulled down 0.1 m from its equilibrium position and released from rest.

(iv) Calculate the speed of the object when it passes through the equilibrium position. Any resistances to motion may be neglected. [MEI]

⑫ A light elastic string AB has stiffness k and natural length l_0.

The end A of the string is fixed to a vertical wall, and the end B to a block of mass M which is supported by a smooth horizontal plane. To the other side of the block is attached an inelastic light string which passes over a smooth pulley and is then tied to a particle of mass m at C which hangs freely at all times. The block is initially held against the wall and then is moved gently towards the pulley until it is in equilibrium. The elastic string and the part of the other string between the block and the pulley are horizontal, as shown in Figure 11.41.

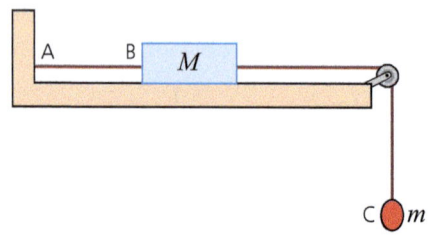

Figure 11.41

Find expressions for the following in terms of some or all of m, g, k and l_0.

(i) The extension in the elastic string.

(ii) The potential energy lost by the hanging mass as the system is moved to its equilibrium position.

(iii) The energy stored in the elastic string.

(iv) Compare your answers to part (ii) and (iii). Why is energy not conserved?

(v) If the string supporting the hanging mass breaks when the system is in equilibrium, show that the block will hit the wall with a speed v given by $v^2 = \dfrac{m^2 g^2}{Mk}$. Find also an expression for the acceleration of the block immediately after the string breaks.

(vi) Show that the quantities v^2 and $\dfrac{m^2 g^2}{Mk}$ have the same dimensions. [MEI]

⑬ A man unloading 25 kg sacks drops each one 2 m, from rest, onto a light horizontal springboard which breaks the fall. The spring supporting the board is initially 50 cm long and compresses down to a minimum length of 15 cm under the impact of each falling sack, which is then removed by another man.

Assuming that there is no energy loss on impact,

(i) show that the potential energy lost by the sack when it reaches its lowest point is about 576 J

(ii) show that the stiffness of the spring is 9400 N m^{-1}

(iii) find the maximum deceleration experienced by the falling sack. [MEI]

⑭ A light elastic string has one end fastened to a fixed point O and it hangs freely with a particle of mass m attached to the other end. In equilibrium, the length of the string is $\frac{5l}{3}$ where l is the natural length of the string. If the particle is raised to the point O and allowed to fall, show that the greatest length of string subsequently is $3l$. Find also the speed of the particle when it is passing through the equilibrium position.

⑮ A light elastic string of natural length 3.6 m and modulus of elasticity λ N has its ends attached to two points A and B, where AB = 3.6 m and AB is horizontal. A particle P of mass 0.5 kg is attached to the midpoint of the string. P rests in equilibrium at a distance of 0.75 m below the line AB, as shown in Figure 11.42.

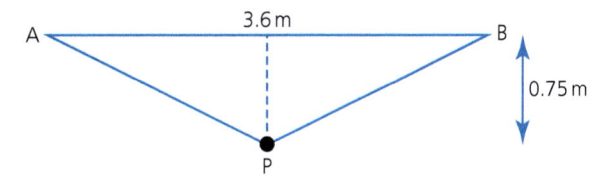

Figure 11.42

(i) Show that $\lambda = 76.44$ N.

The particle is pulled downwards from its equilibrium position until the total length of the elastic string is 6 m. The particle is released from rest.

(ii) Find the speed of P when it passes the line AB.

KEY POINTS

1 **Hooke's law**

The tension T in an elastic string or spring and its extension x are related by
$$T = kx \text{ or } T = \frac{\lambda}{l_0} x$$
where k is the stiffness, λ is the modulus of elasticity and l_0 is the natural length of the string or spring.

2 When a spring is compressed, x is negative and the tension becomes a thrust.

3 **Elastic potential energy**

The elastic potential energy (E.P.E.) stored in a stretched spring or string, or in a compressed spring, is given by
$$\text{E.P.E.} = \tfrac{1}{2} kx^2 \text{ or } \text{E.P.E.} = \tfrac{1}{2} \frac{\lambda}{l_0} x^2$$

Vertical motion involving elastic forces

4 The tension or thrust in an elastic string or spring is a conservative force and so the elastic potential energy is recoverable.

5 When no frictional or other dissipative forces are involved, elastic potential energy can be used with kinetic energy and gravitational potential energy to form equations using the principle of conservation of energy.

LEARNING OUTCOMES

When you have completed this chapter, you should be able to
- understand the language associated with elasticity
- apply Hooke's law to strings and springs
- calculate stiffness and modulus of elasticity
- find the tension in a string or spring and the thrust in a spring
- find the equilibrium position of a system involving strings or springs
- calculate the energy stored in a string or spring
- use energy to model a system involving elastic strings or springs including determining extreme positions
- understand when Hooke's law is not applicable
- form and work with differential equations for motion under forces from elastic strings or springs.

12 Modelling oscillations

Backwards and forwards half her length; With a short uneasy motion

Samuel Taylor Coleridge,
The Rime of the Ancient Mariner

What do the guitar, the clock and water ripples have in common?

They all involve **oscillations** or **vibrations** of particles or bodies.

- In the guitar, the strings vibrate in a controllable way, and the instrument transmits them as sound waves (vibrations of air molecules).
- In the clock, the pendulum oscillates in the familiar swinging pattern, and this regular motion is used to operate the clock mechanism.
- Ripples are created when the surface of water is disturbed. The fluid particles vibrate up and down in a regular wave pattern. The same pattern is visible in ocean waves, or in the wake of boats.

1 Oscillating motion

The remarkable thing about all these vibrations, and many others that occur in natural and man-made systems, is that they are essentially of the same form. The vibrations don't go on for ever, but, over a reasonable interval, you can plot the displacement of a vibrating particle against time for any of these systems and you will obtain a sine wave.

The graph in Figure 12.1 shows the displacement of an oscillating particle against time.

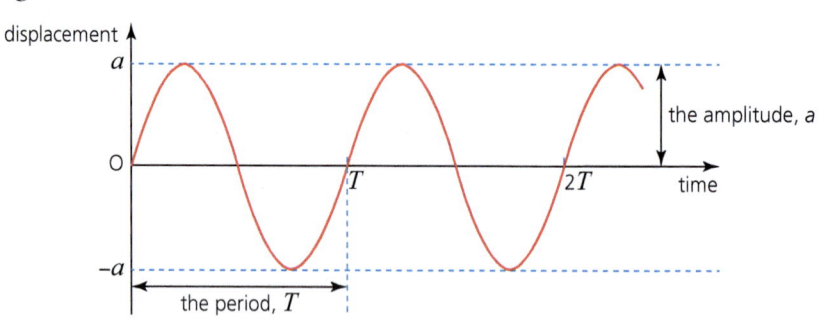

Figure 12.1

From the graph, you can see a number of important features of such motion.

- The particle oscillates about a central position, O.
- The particle moves between two points with displacements $+a$ and $-a$. The distance a is called the **amplitude** of the motion.
- The motion repeats itself in a cyclic fashion. The number of cycles per unit time (usually per second) is called the frequency, and is usually denoted by the Greek letter v.
- The motion repeats itself after a time T. The time interval T is called the period: it is the time for one complete cycle of the motion.

The frequency and period are reciprocals. For example, a period of $\frac{1}{10}$ of a second corresponds to a frequency of 10 cycles per second.

Usually the **period** is used when describing relatively slow mechanical oscillations and the **frequency** for faster oscillations or vibrations.

The S.I. unit for frequency is *hertz* (Hz). One hertz is one cycle per second. The unit is named after Heinrich Rudolph Hertz (1857–94) who was the first person to produce electromagnetic waves artificially. You may be familiar with the use of the megahertz as a measure of the frequency of radio waves. A radio station which is broadcasting on 99.1 megahertz is producing electromagnetic waves with a frequency of 99 100 000 cycles per second.

Historical note

Pythagoras (c.572–497 BC) studied the pitch of notes produced by stretched strings in the first recorded acoustic experiments. He showed that recognisable musical intervals are produced by segments of a stretched string when their lengths are in a simple numerical ratio.

In May 1939, shortly before the outbreak of the second world war, an international conference in London unanimously agreed to adopt a frequency of 440 cycles per second for the note 'A' in the treble clef. There are then standard relationships between this and the frequencies of other notes. For many years, before electronic music-making devices became readily available, an 'A' of this frequency was broadcast regularly on the radio for the use of musicians.

Using energy: a physical model of an oscillating system

> **Discussion point**
> How can this be done so that the only horizontal force is the force in the spring?

A particle P, of mass m kg is attached to a light, perfectly elastic spring which has stiffness $k\,\mathrm{N\,m^{-1}}$. The other end, E, of the spring is attached to a fixed point and P moves horizontally.

The spring is at its natural length when P is at the fixed point O. The particle is pulled to a point A where OA = a m and released.

> **Discussion point**
> What happens to P as it moves from A to B? Then what happens?

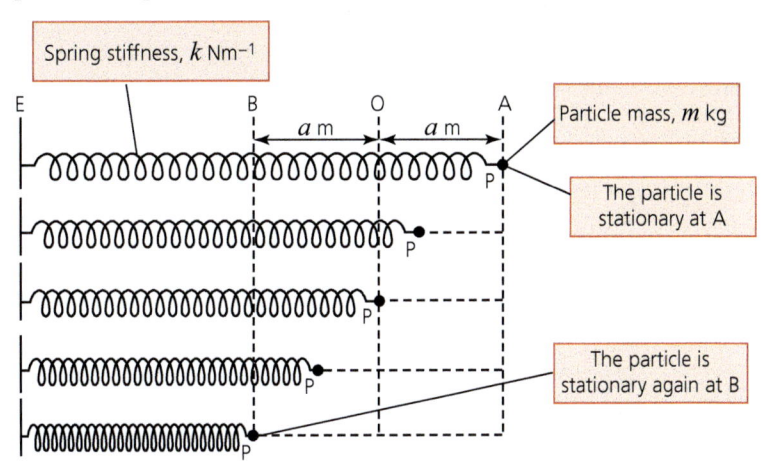

Figure 12.2

> **Discussion point**
> If you could fix a pen at P and let it draw on a strip of paper moving at a steady rate perpendicular to EA (down the page), what would be the result?

Now think about energy. At A, the spring has elastic energy $\frac{1}{2}ka^2$ and the particle has zero kinetic energy. The particle first comes to rest again at B so the elastic energy at B must also be $\frac{1}{2}ka^2$; the distance from O to B is a m. This is the amplitude of the motion.

When the extension of the spring is x m and P has speed $v\,\mathrm{m\,s^{-1}}$, the total energy is $\frac{1}{2}mv^2 + \frac{1}{2}kx^2$ so the principle of conservation of energy gives

$$\tfrac{1}{2}mv^2 + \tfrac{1}{2}kx^2 = \tfrac{1}{2}ka^2$$

$$\Rightarrow \quad v^2 = \frac{k}{m}\left(a^2 - x^2\right)$$

> **Discussion point**
> What is the speed at O? What is the maximum speed?

This gives the speed of the particle in any position, even when x is negative, providing Hooke's law still holds.

Using calculus: a mathematical model for simple harmonic motion

At the instant when the particle, P, is x m to the right of O, the forces acting on it are as shown in Figure 12.3.

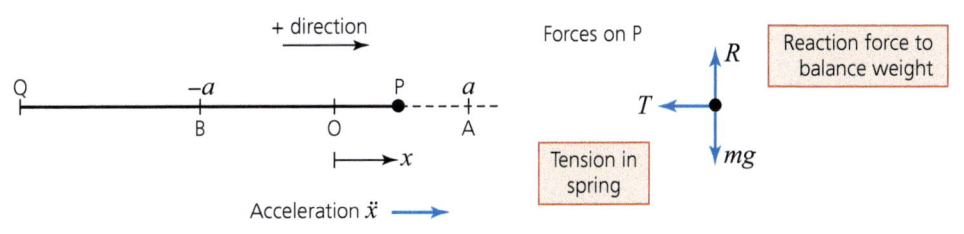

Figure 12.3

Oscillating motion

> **Discussion point**
> What is the effect of the minus sign in this equation?

The horizontal equation of motion is $-T = m\ddot{x}$

By Hooke's law, $T = kx$ so
$$-kx = m\ddot{x}$$
$$\ddot{x} = -\frac{k}{m}x \quad \text{①}$$

or
$$\frac{d^2x}{dt^2} = -\frac{k}{m}x$$

In the equation ①, k and m are both positive constants so $\frac{k}{m}$ can be written as one positive constant. By convention this is denoted by ω^2 so the equation may be written as

> *Writing it as a square ensures that it is always positive*

$$\ddot{x} = -\omega^2 x \quad \text{②}$$

> **Hint**
> ω is the lower case Greek letter omega; it is a long o so it sounds like 'oh'.

The equation for the velocity that you found in the last section can then be written as
$$v^2 = \omega^2(a^2 - x^2) \quad \text{or} \quad \dot{x}^2 = \omega^2(a^2 - x^2) \quad \text{③}$$

To derive equation ③ from the differential equation ②, start by rewriting the acceleration $\ddot{x}$ in the form $v\frac{dv}{dx}$.

> *Remember you can write acceleration as $\frac{dv}{dt}$ and then use the chain rule $\frac{dv}{dt} = \frac{dv}{dx} \times \frac{dx}{dt} = \frac{dv}{dx} \times v = v\frac{dv}{dx}$*

So equation ② becomes $v\frac{dv}{dx} = -\omega^2 x$

Separating the variables gives
$$\int v\, dv = -\int \omega^2 x\, dx$$
$$\Rightarrow \quad \frac{v^2}{2} = -\frac{\omega^2 x^2}{2} + C$$

Using the initial condition that $v = 0$ when $x = a$ gives
$$0 = -\frac{\omega^2 a^2}{2} + C$$

> **Discussion point**
> What is v when $x = a$, $-a$ and 0?

$$\Rightarrow \quad C = \frac{\omega^2 a^2}{2}$$
$$\Rightarrow \quad v^2 = \omega^2(a^2 - x^2)$$

There are many other similar systems which produce an equation of the same form as equation ②. Because the same equation of motion applies to all of them, they all have the same type of oscillating motion called *simple harmonic motion* (SHM).

Simple harmonic motion is defined by the equation $\ddot{x} = -\omega^2 x$. Remember that, in this equation, $\ddot{x}$ means acceleration and x means the displacement from the centre. It may be stated in words as follows.

> The acceleration is proportional to the magnitude of the displacement from the centre point of the motion and is directed towards the centre point.

The two equations $v^2 = \omega^2(a^2 - x^2)$ and $\ddot{x} = -\omega^2 x$ tell you a lot about the motion.

From the first equation you can see that:
- the motion is symmetrical about the point O where $x = 0$
- x must always lie between $-a$ and a, otherwise v^2 would be negative

- at the extreme points, when $x = \pm a$, the velocity is zero
- the maximum speed is when $x = 0$ and $v = \pm a\omega$.

This is when the particle passes through O

The second equation tells you that:

- $\ddot{x}$ is always directed towards O, so the same must be true of the resultant force
- $\ddot{x}$ and hence the resultant force are zero when $x = 0$, so O is the equilibrium position
- $\ddot{x}$ has a maximum magnitude of $\omega^2 a$ when $x = \pm a$.

These results for $\ddot{x}$ and v in terms of x are shown in Figure 12.4.

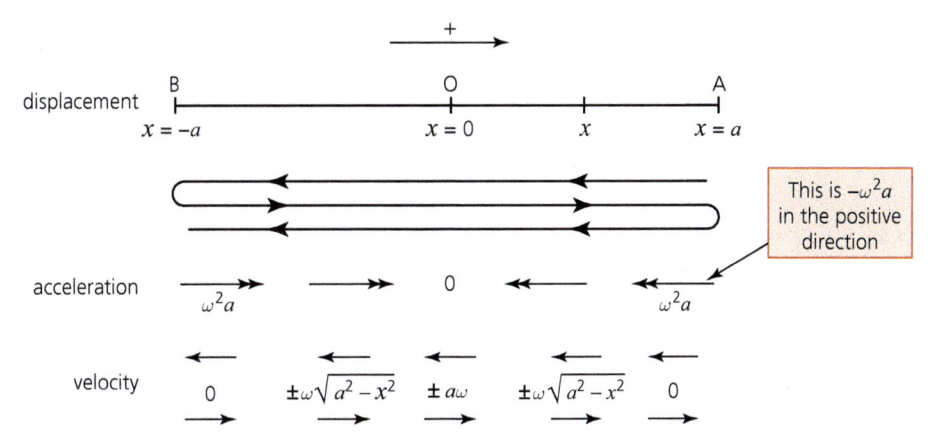

Figure 12.4

The frequency of the motion depends on the value of ω. In the next section, you will see how to write x, v and $\ddot{x}$ in terms of time. In the meantime, you can use the result

$$\omega = 2\pi \times \text{frequency}$$

Example 12.1

When a violin string is playing an 'A' with frequency 880 Hz, a particle on the string oscillates with amplitude of 0.5 mm.

(i) Calculate the time taken for one complete oscillation.

(ii) Express ω in terms of π and write down the equation of motion.

(iii) Find the maximum speed of the particle and its maximum acceleration.

(iv) Find the acceleration and velocity when the particle is 0.25 mm from its central position.

Solution

(i) The particle does 880 oscillations per second, so the time for one oscillation is $\frac{1}{880} = 0.001 1\dot{3}\dot{6}$ s. This is the period of the motion.

(ii) $\omega = 2\pi \times \text{frequency} = 1760\pi$

The equation of motion is $\ddot{x} = -\omega^2 x$

$\Rightarrow \quad \ddot{x} = -(1760\pi)^2 x$

Oscillating motion

(iii) You can use the equation with mm as long as your units are consistent.

Maximum speed $\quad a\omega = 0.5 \times 1760\pi \, \text{mm s}^{-1}$

$\qquad\qquad\qquad\qquad = 2764.60... \, \text{mm s}^{-1}$

$\qquad\qquad\qquad\qquad = 2.76 \, \text{m s}^{-1} \, (3 \text{ s.f.})$

Maximum acceleration $\quad a\omega^2 = 0.5 \times (1760\pi)^2 \, \text{mm s}^{-2}$

$\qquad\qquad\qquad\qquad = 1.528 ... \times 10^7 \, \text{mm s}^{-2}$

$\qquad\qquad\qquad\qquad = 15\,300 \, \text{m s}^{-2} \, (3 \text{ s.f.})$

(iv) When $x = 0.25$,

$$\ddot{x} = -(1760\pi)^2 \times 0.25 \, \text{mm s}^{-2}$$

$\Rightarrow \quad$ acceleration $= -7640 \, \text{m s}^{-2} \, (3 \text{ s.f.})$

The velocity is given by

$$v^2 = \omega^2 (0.5^2 - x^2)$$

$\Rightarrow \quad$ velocity $= \pm 1760\pi \sqrt{0.25 - 0.0625} \, \text{mm s}^{-1}$

$\qquad\qquad\quad = \pm 2.39 \, \text{m s}^{-1} \, (3 \text{ s.f.})$ ← The particle can be travelling in either direction.

When $x = -0.25$

$$\ddot{x} = +(1760\pi)^2 \times 0.25 \, \text{mm s}^{-2}$$

$\Rightarrow \quad$ acceleration $= +7640 \, \text{m s}^{-2}$

The velocity is $\pm 2.39 \, \text{m s}^{-1}$, as before.

Exercise 12.1

In all these questions assume that time is measured in seconds.

① Write down the equation of motion in the following cases of simple harmonic motion. Calculate

(i) the velocity and magnitude of the acceleration at the centre of the motion

(ii) the velocity and magnitude of the acceleration at the ends of the motion

(iii) the speed when x is half the amplitude.

(a) $\omega = 3$, amplitude $= 2 \, \text{cm}$

(b) $\omega = 10$, amplitude $= 0.1 \, \text{m}$

(c) $\omega = \pi$, amplitude $= a \, \text{m}$.

② A particle is moving with SHM with $\omega = 2$. Initially it is 10 cm from the centre of the motion and moving in the positive direction with a speed of $6 \, \text{cm s}^{-1}$. Write down the equation of motion and calculate

(i) the amplitude

(ii) the acceleration at the ends of the motion

(iii) the speed at the centre

(iv) the speed when it is 5 cm from the centre

(v) the distance from the centre when the speed is half its maximum.

③ Musical notes which are an octave apart have frequencies in the ratio 1 : 2. The note A above middle C has a frequency of 440 Hz. On a full size keyboard there are 4 As below it and 3 above it (the range on the keyboard is just over 7 octaves)

(i) Work out the values of ω corresponding to the frequencies of these seven As.

(ii) Find the maximum speed of points on piano strings which are vibrating with amplitude 1 mm to produce the highest and lowest of these notes.

④ A loudspeaker cone sounding a pure note of frequency 2000 Hz is modelled by SHM of amplitude 2 mm.

(i) Calculate ω and the maximum speed of the cone.

(ii) Write down the equation of motion and calculate the maximum acceleration.

⑤ A particle of dust lands at a point A on a surface which is vibrating vertically with SHM centre O and $\omega = 20$. The particle cannot stay in contact with the surface when the downwards acceleration is greater than g. How far (in cm) is the particle from O when this happens? Can you be certain whether it is above or below O?

⑥ A piston in an engine oscillates with a period of 0.03 s and an amplitude of 0.35 m. Modelling the oscillations as SHM,

(i) draw a sketch graph to illustrate the oscillations

(ii) calculate the frequency of the motion and hence find ω

(iii) calculate the maximum speed of the piston.

⑦ Air sickness might be caused by the rhythmic vibrations of an aircraft. It has been observed that about 50% of the passengers of an aircraft suffer air sickness when it bounces up and down with a frequency of about 0.3 Hz and a maximum acceleration of $4\,\text{m s}^{-2}$. Assuming SHM, find

(i) the value of ω and hence the amplitude of the motion

(ii) the greatest vertical speed during this motion.

⑧ A jig-saw operates at 3000 strokes per minute with the tip of the blade moving 17 mm from the top to the bottom of the stroke. (One stroke is a complete cycle.) Assuming that the motion is simple harmonic, find

(i) the maximum speed of the blade

(ii) the maximum acceleration of the blade

(iii) the speed of the blade when it is 6 mm from the central position.

⑨ The waveforms of two musical notes, P and Q, are shown below.

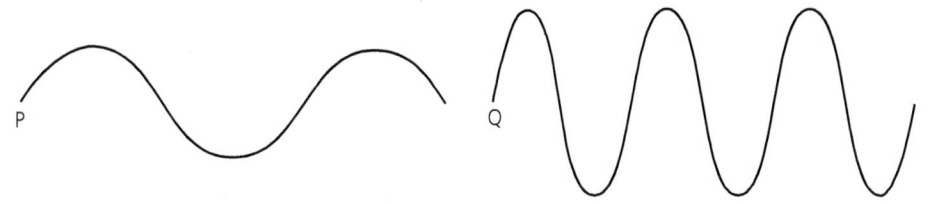

Figure 12.5

Which of the following statements are true?
(i) P is lower than Q.
(ii) P is louder than Q.
(iii) The frequency of P is twice that of Q.
(iv) The period of P is twice that of Q.
(v) The amplitude of Q is larger than that of P.

⑩ A particle is oscillating with SHM.
Find expressions in terms of a and ω for
(i) its speed when it is a distance $\frac{1}{4}a$ from the centre
(ii) its distance from the centre when its speed is half its maximum speed.

2 Simple harmonic motion as a function of time

> **Note**
> Remember that all the angles must be in radians when you use calculus.

The text on page 307 shows you how to integrate the SHM equation so that you can write x, $\dot{x}$ and $\ddot{x}$ in terms of the time, but you can also demonstrate how the SHM equation can be satisfied by certain trigonometrical functions as in the next example.

Example 12.2

(i) Show that $x = 10 \sin 3t$ satisfies the simple harmonic motion equation $\ddot{x} = -9x$.

(ii) Sketch the graph of $x = 10 \sin 3t$ and deduce the amplitude, period and frequency of this motion.

(iii) Verify that $\dot{x}^2 = v^2 = \omega^2 \left(a^2 - x^2\right)$.

(iv) Show that $x = 25 \sin 3t$ also satisfies $\ddot{x} = -9x$ and comment on this result.

Solution

(i) $x = 10 \sin 3t$

Differentiating with respect to t to find the velocity and acceleration:

$v = \dot{x} = 30 \cos 3t$ ①

and $\ddot{x} = -90 \sin 3t$

$\ddot{x} = -9x$

This is the SHM equation given in the question.

(ii) The graph of the function is shown below.

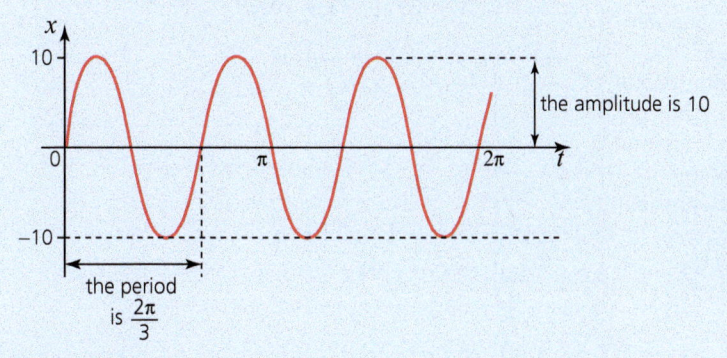

Figure 12.6

The graph shows that the value of x always lies between -10 and 10, so the amplitude of the motion is 10 units.

Each cycle repeats in the time $\frac{2\pi}{3}$ so the period of oscillations, denoted by T, is $\frac{2\pi}{3}$. The frequency is $\frac{1}{T} = \frac{3}{2\pi}$.

(iii) From ①

$$\dot{x}^2 = 900 \cos^2 3t$$
$$= 900(1 - \sin^2 3t)$$
$$= 9(100 - 100 \sin^2 3t)$$
$$= \omega^2(a^2 - x^2)$$

(iv) Differentiating the function $x = 25 \sin 3t$ twice gives
$$\dot{x} = 75 \cos 3t$$
$$\ddot{x} = -225 \sin 3t = -9(25 \sin 3t)$$
$$\Rightarrow \qquad \ddot{x} = -9x \quad \text{as required}$$

This shows that the amplitude of the oscillation is not determined by the differential equation. In this case, it can be 10 or 25, or indeed any other value.

A general form for SHM

Any motion given by an equation of the form $x = a \sin \omega t$ (where a and ω are positive constants) has a similar displacement–time graph and represents SHM with amplitude a.

Differentiating this equation gives
$$v = \dot{x} = a\omega \cos \omega t$$
and $$\ddot{x} = -a\omega^2 \sin \omega t = -\omega^2 x.$$

Figure 12.7 shows how the graphs for x, $\dot{x}$ and $\ddot{x}$ are related.

The period is shown in Figure 12.7, but it can also be found from the equations for x, $\dot{x}$ and $\ddot{x}$. Since $\sin(\omega t + 2\pi) = \sin \omega t$ and $\cos(\omega t + 2\pi) = \cos \omega t$, the values of x, $\dot{x}$ and $\ddot{x}$ remain unchanged when ωt is increased by 2π. This is the smallest increment for which this is true. Also $(\omega t + 2\pi) = \omega\left(t + \frac{2\pi}{\omega}\right)$, so, whenever you start measuring, all aspects of the motion will be the same after a period of time $T = \frac{2\pi}{\omega}$.

Simple harmonic motion as a function of time

> **Discussion point**
> Show that the equation $x = a\cos\omega t$ also satisfies the definition of SHM. Draw sketches of the graphs of $x = a\sin\omega t$ and $x = a\cos\omega t$ and compare the properties of the motions represented by them.

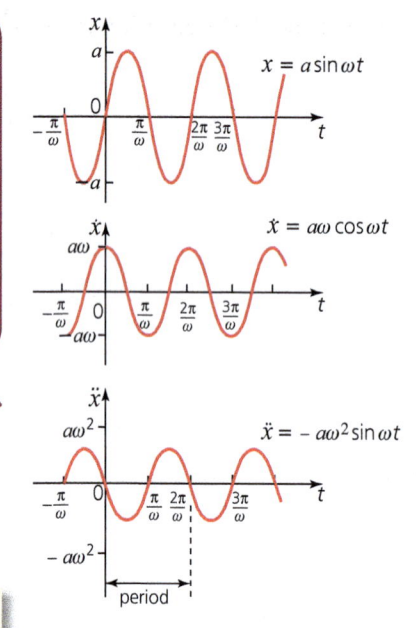

Figure 12.7

In general, $x = a\sin\omega t$ represents SHM with the following properties.

- The amplitude is a (>0).
- The period T is $\dfrac{2\pi}{\omega}$.
- The frequency $f = \dfrac{1}{T} = \dfrac{\omega}{2\pi}$.
- $x = 0$ when $t = 0$.

> **Note**
> In these mathematical models, ωt is an angle; ω is sometimes called the *angular frequency*. It is important to note that, when the model is applied to an oscillating system, ω is a constant which depends on the properties of the system, such as the stiffness of a spring or the length of a pendulum: ω rarely involves a physical angle and, in particular, ω is *not* the angular velocity of the pendulum.

Phase difference

For $x = a\cos\omega t$, $x = a$ when $t = 0$. Its graph $x = a\cos\omega t$ is a translation of the graph $x = a\sin\omega t$ along the t axis by a displacement of $-\dfrac{\pi}{2}$ (or $\dfrac{3\pi}{2}$ or $\dfrac{7\pi}{2}$ etc.). Both equations describe SHM but their oscillations are at a different stage in the cycle when $t = 0$.

They are said to have a **phase difference** of $-\dfrac{\pi}{2}$ (or $\dfrac{3\pi}{2}$ etc.).

Relationships between acceleration, velocity and displacement

Provided t is measured from an instant when the particle is at the centre and moving in the positive direction. SHM is described by the following equations.

> When the velocity is written in terms of t, it is helpful to denote it by $\dot{x}$ to stress the fact that it is the derivative of x with respect to t.

Displacement: $\qquad x = a\sin\omega t$ ①

Velocity: $\qquad v = \dot{x} = a\omega\cos\omega t$ ②

Acceleration: $\qquad \ddot{x} = -a\omega^2\sin\omega t$ ③

It can be seen from equations ① and ③ that

$$\ddot{x} = -\omega^2 x \qquad ④$$

Squaring equation ② gives

$$v^2 = \dot{x}^2 = a^2\omega^2\cos^2\omega t$$
$$= \omega^2(a^2 - a^2\sin^2\omega t).$$

Therefore $\qquad v^2 = \omega^2(a^2 - x^2)$ ⑤

> **Discussion point**
> You have already shown that $x = a\cos\omega t$ satisfies the equation of motion for SHM. Now show that $\dot{x}$ satisfies the equation $\dot{x}^2 = \omega^2(a^2 - x^2)$.

You have already seen that the SHM equation $\ddot{x} = -\omega^2 x$ is equivalent to $v^2 = \omega^2(a^2 - x^2)$.

This is the same as the differential equation $\dfrac{dx}{dt} = \pm \omega \sqrt{a^2 - x^2}$.

You can solve this differential equation using the separation of variables method

$$\int \dfrac{1}{\pm\sqrt{a^2 - x^2}}\, dx = \int \omega\, dt.$$

The integrals on the left-hand side have well-known standard results.

$$\int \dfrac{1}{\sqrt{a^2 - x^2}}\, dx = \arcsin\left(\dfrac{x}{a}\right) \text{ and } \int \dfrac{1}{-\sqrt{a^2 - x^2}}\, dx = \arccos\left(\dfrac{x}{a}\right).$$

So the solution of the differential equation is

either $x = a \sin(\omega t + \varepsilon_1)$ or $x = a \cos(\omega t + \varepsilon_2)$.

These are very important results.

> **Note**
> These two forms are equivalent to each other because the constants of integration, written here as ε_1 and ε_2, are arbitrary.

Example 12.3

In a harbour the cycle of tides can be modelled as SHM with a period of 12 hours 30 minutes. On a certain day, high water is 10 m above low water.

(i) Sketch a graph of the height x m of the water above (or below) the mean level against t, the time in hours since the water was at mean level and rising.

(ii) Find a suitable expression to model x in terms of t.

(iii) Determine for how long the water was more than 6 m above the low water mark.

(iv) Find the rate at which the tide is rising or falling when the water is 6 m above the low water mark.

(v) Find the maximum rate at which the tide rises.

Solution

(i)

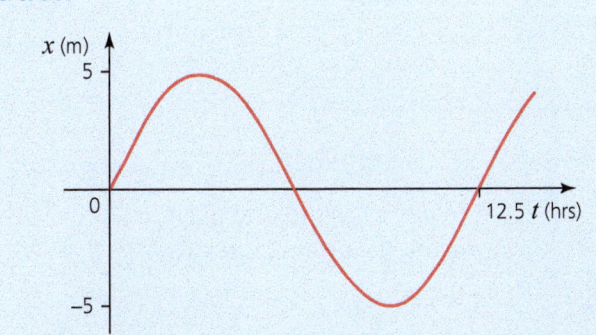

Figure 12.8

(ii) First find ω and a.

The period of the tide $T = 12.5$ hours.

$$\omega = \dfrac{2\pi}{T} = 0.503$$

Since T is in hours, ω is in radians per hour

From the graph in part (i), the amplitude of the oscillation is 5 m, so $a = 5$.

Simple harmonic motion as a function of time

Since the water has risen x m in t hours after it was at the mean level, a suitable equation is

$$x = a \sin \omega t$$
$$x = 5 \sin (0.503t)$$

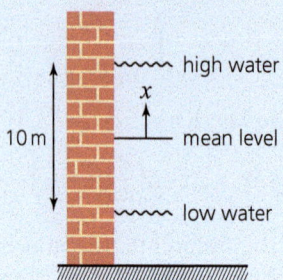

Figure 12.9

(iii) The tide is 6 m above low water when $x \geq 1$ and $x = 1$ when

$$5 \sin (0.503t) = 1$$
$$\Rightarrow \quad \sin (0.503t) = 0.2 = \sin (0.201)$$

The first two values of t satisfying this equation are t_1 and t_2, where

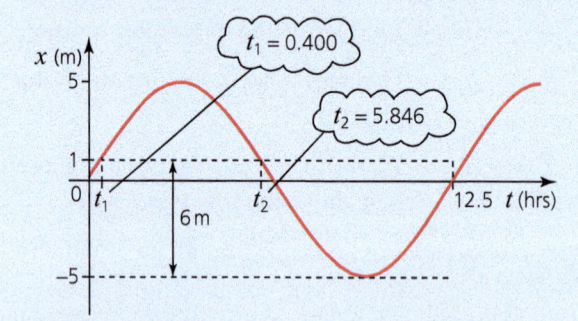

$$0.503 t_1 = 0.201 \quad \Rightarrow \quad t_1 = 0.400$$
and $\quad 0.503 t_2 = \pi - 0.201 \quad \Rightarrow \quad t_2 = 5.846$

Figure 12.10

The water is 6 m above its lowest level for $(t_2 - t_1)$ hours i.e. about $5\frac{1}{2}$ hours.

(iv) The water is 6 m above its lowest level when $x = 1$. The velocity of the oscillation at this point is given by

$$v^2 = \omega^2(a^2 - x^2)$$
$$\Rightarrow \quad v = \pm 0.503\sqrt{25 - 1}$$
$$= \pm 2.46$$

The rate of rise or fall is 2.46 m per hour, or about 4 cm per minute.

(v) Since $v^2 = \omega^2(a^2 - x^2)$, the maximum value of v is $a\omega$ when $x = 0$.

The water is rising fastest at the centre of its motion and the rate at which it is rising is

$$a\omega = 0.503 \times 5$$
$$= 2.515 \text{ m per hour} = 4.2 \text{ cm per minute.}$$

> Remember that the time, t, is in hours.

> **Note**
> A tidal range of 10 m is large, but is realistic for several places around the British coastline. The rate at which the water is rising, 4.2 cm per minute, does not sound high, but if you think about how fast the water would approach your deck chair up a typical beach (with a gradient of say 3°) you will see that it is quite dramatic.

Exercise 12.2

① Figure 12.11 illustrates the SHM of a particle.

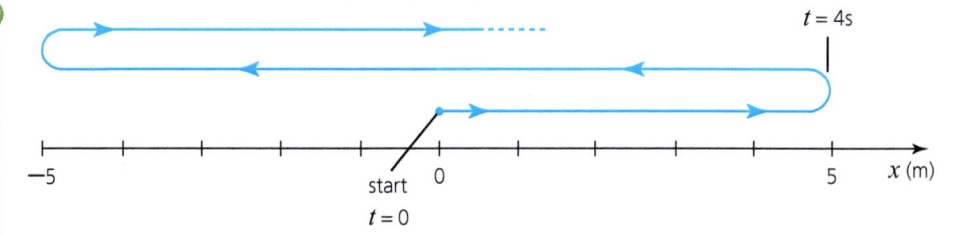

Figure 12.11

(i) Write down the amplitude of the SHM.

(ii) Write down the period.

(iii) The motion can be described by the equation
$$x = a \sin \omega t$$
Write down the values of a and ω.

(iv) Find
  (a) the displacement
  (b) the velocity
  (c) the acceleration of the particle when $t = 0$.

② A particle is performing SHM with five complete cycles per second. At a particular instant it is stationary. It travels 16 cm before it is next stationary.

(i) Write down the period and amplitude of the motion.

(ii) Its motion can be described by the equation $x = a \cos \omega t$. Write down the values of a and ω.

(iii) Use differentiation to find an expression for $\dot{x}$ in terms of t and calculate x and $\dot{x}$ when $t = 0$.

(iv) Find the position and velocity after 0.05 s. In what direction is the particle moving?

③ (i) For SHM with period 2 s and amplitude 2.5 cm, sketch graphs of
  (a) displacement (from the central position) against time
  (b) velocity against time
  (c) acceleration against time.

Line the three graphs up vertically and use the same scale for time in all three.

(ii) All three quantities (displacement, velocity and acceleration) have zero, maximum positive and maximum negative values. Look at your graphs and state which of these events occur at the same time.

④ A particle is performing SHM with period 12 s and amplitude 2 m. The motion can be described by the equation $x = a \sin \omega t$.

(i) Write down the values of a and ω.

(ii) What distance does the particle travel in the first minute?

(iii) What is its maximum speed?

(iv) Use differentiation to find an expression for the velocity at time t s.

(v) How long after leaving the centre does it take to reach half its maximum speed?

Simple harmonic motion as a function of time

⑤ A particle is performing SHM described by the equation
$$x = a \sin \omega t$$
Its maximum speed is $10\,\mathrm{cm\,s^{-1}}$ and its period is $\frac{\pi}{2}$s. Lengths are in cm.
  (i) Find the values of ω and a.
  (ii) Differentiate to find an expression for the velocity $\dot{x}$ and show that $\dot{x}$ is first zero when t is one quarter of the period.
  (iii) Find the velocity after
    (a) 0.2 s
    (b) 1 s.
    In which direction is the particle travelling in each case?
  (iv) How far does the particle travel after leaving the central position in
    (a) 0.2 s
    (b) 1 s.

⑥ A particle describes SHM with period 12 s and amplitude 10 cm. Initially, $x = 0$.
  (i) Sketch the graph of x against t.
  (ii) Find ω in terms of π and write down a suitable equation for x in terms of t.
  (iii) Find the displacement when $t = 1, 2, 3$.
  (iv) Find the distances travelled during the first, second and third seconds of the motion and explain why they are not equal.
  (v) Give an example of two 1-second intervals during which the particle does travel equal distances.

⑦ A particle oscillates with SHM, period 8 s and amplitude 10 cm. Time, t, is measured in seconds from the instant that the particle has the greatest positive displacement. Lengths are in cm.
  (i) Find ω in terms of π and write down a suitable equation for x in terms of t.
  (ii) Differentiate your equation to find an expression for the velocity and calculate the velocity when $t = 0, 1, 2$. Describe the direction of motion in each case.
  (iii) Explain why the speed does not change by equal amounts in equal intervals of time.

⑧ A particle describes SHM with period 24 s and amplitude 20 cm. Its motion can be described by the equation $x = a \sin \omega t$. Lengths are in cm.
  (i) Write down the values of a and ω and obtain an equation for $\dot{x}$ at time t s.
  (ii) Find x and $\dot{x}$ when
    (a) $t = 0$
    (b) $t = 2$.
  (iii) Draw a diagram to illustrate the motion in the first 6 s.
  (iv) Find the two smallest values of t for which $x = 10$ and the values of $\dot{x}$ at each of these times.

⑨ A particle describes SHM with period 24 s and amplitude 20 cm. Its motion can be described by the equation $x = a \cos \omega t$.
  (i) Write down the values of a and ω and obtain an equation for $\dot{x}$ at time t.

(ii) Find x and $\dot{x}$ when
  (a) $t = 0$
  (b) $t = 2$.

(iii) Draw a diagram to illustrate the motion in the first 6 s.

(iv) Find the two smallest values of t for which $x = -10\sqrt{3}$ and the values of $\dot{x}$ at each of these times.

⑩

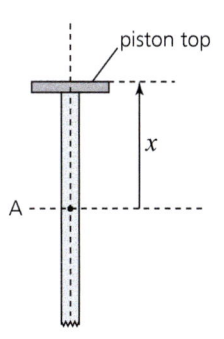

Figure 12.12

The top of a piston has a motion which is modelled as simple harmonic with a period of 0.1 s and an amplitude of 0.2 m about a mean position A.

(i) Show that x, the displacement of the top of the piston from A after t s, is given by the equation $x = 0.2 \sin 20\pi t$, given that $x = 0$ when $t = 0$.

Where appropriate, your answers to the following questions should be expressed in terms of π.

(ii) What is the greatest piston speed?

(iii) What is the greatest magnitude of the acceleration of the piston?

(iv) For what fraction of the period is $x > 0.1$? [MEI]

⑪ A small hook moves in a vertical line with displacement y m relative to a fixed point O. The positive sense of y is upwards and the motion of the hook is simple harmonic given by $\ddot{y} = -3 - 2t$, where the time t is in seconds.

(i) State the amplitude and the period of the simple harmonic motion.

(ii) Find the maximum speed of the hook.

(iii) Find the acceleration of the hook as a function of y.

Figure 12.13

A light, inextensible string is hung from the hook with a small mass at the lower end. The system starts to move at time $t = 0$.

(iv) How far does the mass move before the string first becomes slack?

(v) At what time does the string first become slack? [MEI]

Alternative forms of the equation for SHM

⑫ The motion of a particle is described by the equation $x = 4 + 3 \sin \pi t$.
  (i) Sketch the graph of the motion and write down its period and amplitude.
  (ii) Where is the centre of the oscillations?
  (iii) Given that $y = x - 4$, show that $\ddot{y} = -\pi^2 y$.
  (iv) Find an expression for the acceleration of the particle at time t.
  (v) Describe the motion given by $x = h + a \sin \omega t$.

⑬ After a boat passes, a duck floating on a river bobs up and down for a short time with SHM period 1 s and amplitude 15 cm. When there is no disturbance, the depth of the water under the duck is 0.5 m.
  (i) What are the greatest and least depths during the motion?
  (ii) Assuming that the water rises initially, write down an expression for the depth t seconds after the motion starts.
  (iii) Calculate the first time that the depth is
    (a) 0.55 m
    (b) 0.4 m.

⑭ At a certain location, in a year of 365 days, the latest sunrise is at 8.05 am on 1 January and the earliest is at 3.45 am on 1 July. Sunrise times over a year are to be modelled by a simple harmonic variation of time about a mean time.
  (i) Determine the mean time in minutes after midnight.
  (ii) Find the amplitude of the sunrise variation in minutes.
  (iii) Sketch a graph of sunrise times for a year against day of the year measured from 1 January as day 1.
  (iv) Write down the angular frequency ω of this variation.
  (v) Derive an expression for the time of sunrise in minutes after midnight in terms of the day, D, of the year.
  (vi) Use the result in part (v) to find the time of sunrise in hours and minutes (am) at the end of April (day 120 of the year). [MEI]

3 Alternative forms of the equation for SHM

In the previous section, you saw that $x = a \sin \omega t$ and $x = a \cos \omega t$ are solutions of the SHM differential equation $\ddot{x} = -\omega^2 x$. In this section, you are introduced to a number of alternative forms of the solution, in each case showing that they satisfy the SHM differential equation.

The forms $x = a \sin(\omega t + \varepsilon)$ and $x = a \cos(\omega t + \varepsilon)$

Since the graph of $x = a \sin \omega t$ passes through the origin, it represents SHM in which the particle is at the centre of its oscillation at time zero. Similarly, $x = a \cos \omega t$ represents SHM in which the particle is initially at maximum positive displacement.

There will be times when you need to write an expression for SHM which starts at some other point in the cycle, and this is done by introducing a phase shift of an angle ε (the Greek letter 'epsilon'). This is equivalent to a phase shift in the time of $\dfrac{\varepsilon}{\omega}$ since

$$\omega t + \varepsilon = \omega\left(t + \dfrac{\varepsilon}{\omega}\right).$$

When $t = \dfrac{\varepsilon}{\omega}$, $x = a \sin \omega t$

When $t = 0$, $x = a \sin \varepsilon$

$x = a \sin \omega t$

$x = a \sin(\omega t + \varepsilon)$

$t = \dfrac{\varepsilon}{\omega}$

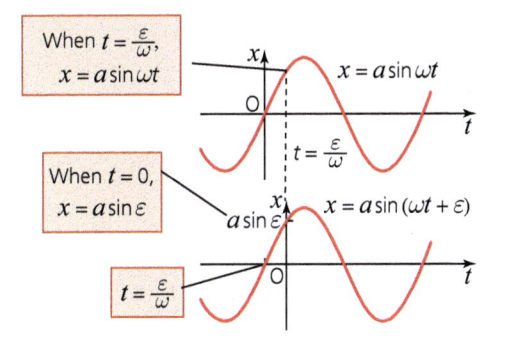

Figure 12.14

The equation $x = a \sin \omega t$ then becomes $x = a \sin(\omega t + \varepsilon)$, and the effect of this on the graph is shown in Figure 12.14. The effect on $x = a \cos \omega t$ is similar.

Example 12.4

The functions f and g are given by

f: $x = a \sin(\omega t + \varepsilon)$ and g: $x = a \cos(\omega t + \varepsilon)$

where ε (epsilon) is a positive constant.

For each of these functions:

(i) differentiate it with respect to time to find v (or $\dot{x}$) and show that

$v^2 = \omega^2 (a^2 - x^2)$

(ii) differentiate v with respect to time to find $\ddot{x}$ and show that $\ddot{x} = -\omega^2 x$.

Solution

(i) For f:

$x = a \sin(\omega t + \varepsilon)$

$\Rightarrow \quad v = \dot{x} = a\omega \cos(\omega t + \varepsilon)$ ①

Therefore $v^2 = a^2 \omega^2 \cos^2(\omega t + \varepsilon)$

$= \omega^2 [a^2 - a^2 \sin^2(\omega + \varepsilon)]$

$\Rightarrow \quad v^2 = \omega^2 (a^2 - x^2)$

Similarly, for g:

$x = a \cos(\omega t + \varepsilon)$

$\Rightarrow \quad v = \dot{x} = -a\omega \sin(\omega t + \varepsilon)$ ②

Therefore $v^2 = a^2 \omega^2 \sin^2(\omega t + \varepsilon)$

Alternative forms of the equation for SHM

$$= \omega^2 [a^2 - a^2 \cos^2(\omega + \varepsilon)]$$
$$\Rightarrow v^2 = \omega^2(a^2 - x^2)$$

(ii) Differentiating equation ① gives

$$\ddot{x} = -a\omega^2 \sin(\omega t + \varepsilon)$$
$$\Rightarrow \ddot{x} = -\omega^2 x$$

Similarly differentiating ② gives

$$\ddot{x} = -a\omega^2 \cos(\omega t + \varepsilon)$$
$$\Rightarrow \ddot{x} = -\omega^2 x$$

> These results show that the functions f and g represent SHM.

The form $x = A \cos \omega t + B \sin \omega t$

The function $x = A \cos \omega t + B \sin \omega t$ represents the sum of two SHMs, $A \cos \omega t$ and $B \sin \omega t$. These have the same period $\left(\dfrac{2\pi}{\omega}\right)$ and frequency, but different amplitudes (A and B).

They are a quarter of a cycle out of phase because

$$\sin \omega t = \cos\left(\omega t - \frac{\pi}{2}\right) = \cos \omega \left(t - \frac{\pi}{2\omega}\right).$$

What is the effect of adding two SHMs in this way?

By differentiating twice with respect to time, you can show that the function obeys the SHM equation $\ddot{x} = -\omega^2 x$.

$$x = A \cos \omega t + B \sin \omega t$$
$$\dot{x} = -A\omega \sin \omega t + B\omega \cos \omega t$$
$$\ddot{x} = -A\omega^2 \cos \omega t - B\omega^2 \sin \omega t$$

This expression for $\ddot{x}$ may be written as

$$\ddot{x} = -\omega^2 (A \cos \omega t + B \sin \omega t)$$

and so $\ddot{x} = -\omega^2 x$.

This proves that $x = A \cos \omega t + B \sin \omega t$ represents SHM with period $\dfrac{2\pi}{\omega}$.

The following steps show that this form is equivalent to $x = a \sin(\omega t + \varepsilon)$.

The function $x = A \cos \omega t + B \sin \omega t$ is rewritten as

$$x = \sqrt{A^2 + B^2}\left(\frac{A}{\sqrt{A^2 + B^2}} \cos \omega t + \frac{B}{\sqrt{A^2 + B^2}} \sin \omega t\right)$$

In the right-angled triangle shown in Figure 12.15, for the case when A and B are both positive

$$\sin \varepsilon = \frac{A}{\sqrt{A^2 + B^2}} \text{ and } \cos \varepsilon = \frac{B}{\sqrt{A^2 + B^2}}.$$

The hypotenuse is $\sqrt{A^2 + B^2} = a$.

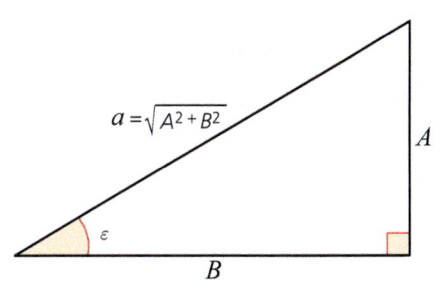

Figure 12.15

Using these results gives

$$x = a(\sin\varepsilon \cos\omega t + \cos\varepsilon \sin\omega t).$$

Using the compound angle formula $\sin(\theta+\phi) = \sin\theta\cos\phi + \cos\theta\sin\phi$, this can be written

$$x = a\sin(\varepsilon + \omega t) = a\sin(\omega t + \varepsilon)$$

Thus the SHM $x = A\cos\omega t + B\sin\omega t$ is equivalent to the SHM $x = a\sin(\omega t + \varepsilon)$, where the amplitude a is $\sqrt{A^2 + B^2}$, and the phase angle ε is given by

$$\sin\varepsilon = \frac{A}{\sqrt{A^2+B^2}} \text{ and } \cos\varepsilon = \frac{B}{\sqrt{A^2+B^2}}.$$

This is also equivalent to a cosine form, since for any angle α

$$\sin\alpha = \cos\left(\alpha - \frac{\pi}{2}\right)$$

and so x can be written as

$$x = a\cos\left(\omega t + \varepsilon - \frac{\pi}{2}\right)$$
$$= a\cos(\omega t + \varepsilon') \text{ where } \varepsilon' = \varepsilon - \frac{\pi}{2}.$$

(If ε is an acute angle, ε' is negative.)

The effect of adding together two SHMs of the same period is to create a single SHM, also with the same period but with greater amplitude. This is shown in Figure 12.16 for $x = 3\cos t$ and $x = 4\sin t$.

> **Discussion point**
>
> When you hear several musical instruments play notes of the same pitch, the vibrations which reach your ears are a combination of oscillations of different amplitudes. In addition, these may have been set in motion at different stages in the cycle and so be out of phase.
>
> How is it possible for the music to sound pleasant?

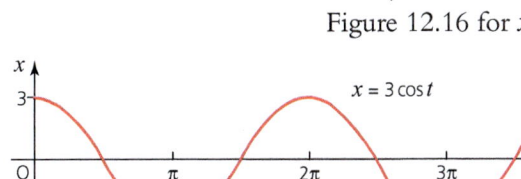

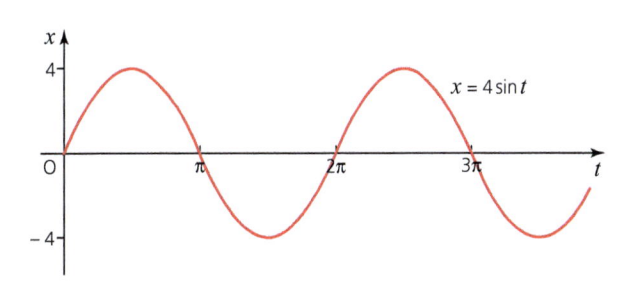

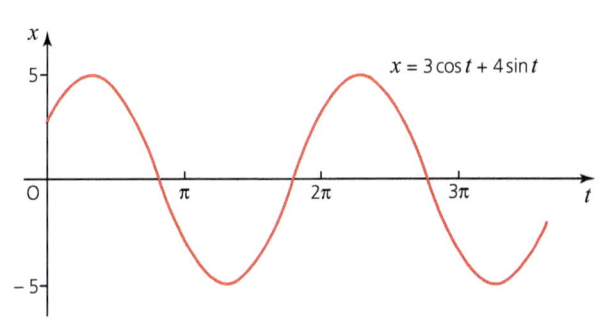

Figure 12.16

Alternative forms of the equation for SHM

The form $x = x_0 + a \sin \omega t$

Although the equation $x = x_0 + a \sin \omega t$ does not satisfy the SHM equation $\ddot{x} = -\omega^2 x$, it does represent SHM about the fixed point x_0 as you can see from Figure 12.17.

You may find it helpful to think of this motion in terms of a new variable, z, representing the displacement from the central position. This is given by

$$z = x - x_0$$
$$= a \sin \omega t.$$

The variable z does satisfy the SHM equation $\ddot{z} = -\omega^2 z$ and all the standard SHM results also hold for z.

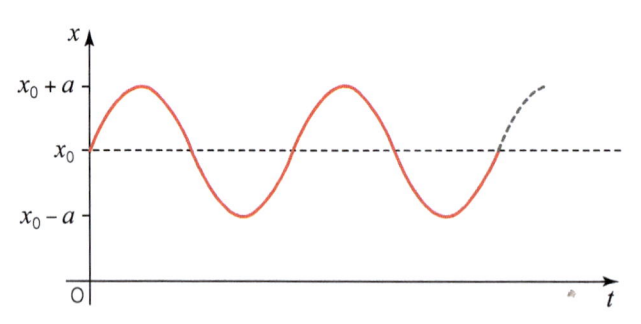

Figure 12.17

Choosing the most appropriate function to model a particular oscillation

You have seen that any particular example of SHM can be described using at least one of a variety of functions.

SHM about $x = 0$ with period $\frac{2\pi}{\omega}$, amplitude a	SHM about $x = x_0$ with period $\frac{2\pi}{\omega}$, amplitude a
$x = a \sin(\omega t + \varepsilon)$	$x = x_0 + a \sin(\omega t + \varepsilon)$
$x = a \cos(\omega t + \varepsilon)$	$x = x_0 + a \cos(\omega t + \varepsilon)$
$x = A \cos \omega t + B \sin \omega t$ where $\sqrt{A^2 + B^2} = a$	$x = x_0 + A \cos \omega t + B \sin \omega t$ where $\sqrt{A^2 + B^2} = a$

The constants a, A, B and α are determined by the *initial conditions*, that is, the speed, direction and displacement at time zero.

You will find it helpful to sketch the graph of the oscillation. This will show you the initial conditions and help you to choose the most appropriate form.

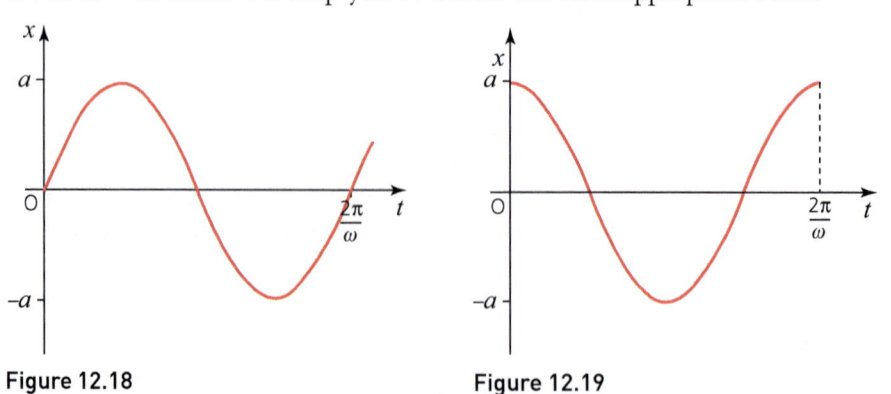

Figure 12.18

Figure 12.19

In the case when $t = 0$, $x = 0$ and $\dot{x} > 0$, the most appropriate form is $x = a\sin\omega t$.

In the case when $t = 0$, $x = a$ and $\dot{x} = 0$, the most appropriate form is $x = a\cos\omega t$.

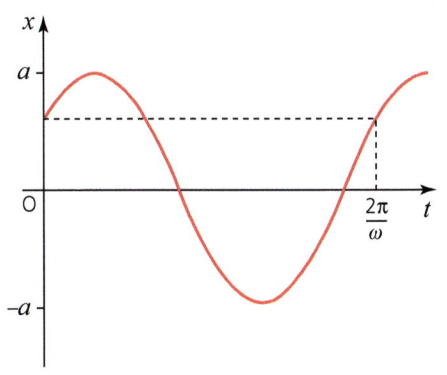

Figure 12.20

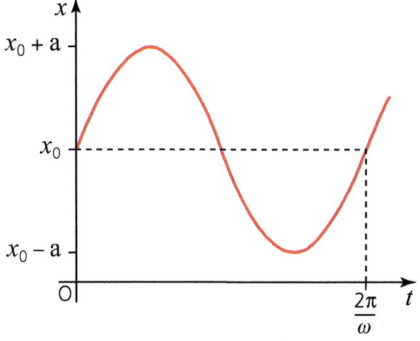

Figure 12.21

When the oscillation starts somewhere between the centre and an extreme, i.e. neither $x = 0$ nor $\dot{x} = 0$ when $t = 0$, the most appropriate form will be either

$$x = a\sin(\omega t + \varepsilon)$$

or $\quad x = a\cos(\omega t + \varepsilon)$

or $\quad x = A\cos\omega t + B\sin\omega t$

When the centre of the oscillations is not at the origin but at a point x_0, the appropriate equation will be one of those above but with x_0 added on. In this case

$$x = x_0 + a\sin\omega t$$

Discussion point

The graphs below show cases where the initial conditions are different from those covered above. What are the most appropriate forms to model these oscillations?

(i)

(ii)

(iii)

(iv)

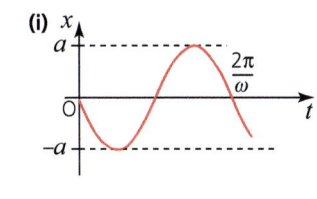

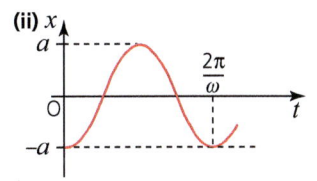

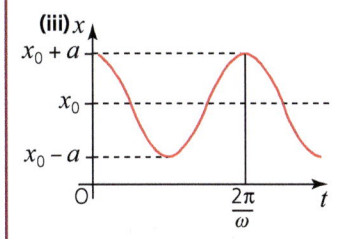

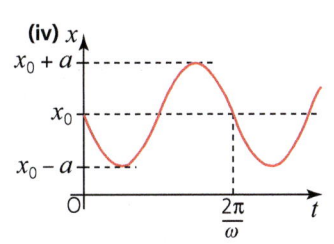

Figure 12.22

Example 12.5

A particle is moving with SHM of period π. Initially it is 10 cm from the centre of the motion and moving in the positive direction with a speed of 6 cm s^{-1}. Find an equation to describe the motion.

Alternative forms of the equation for SHM

Solution

The information given is shown in Figure 12.23.

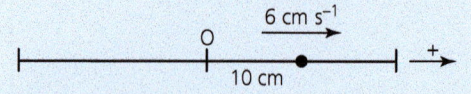

Figure 12.23

The initial speed is positive, so an appropriate equation is
$x = a\sin(\omega t + \varepsilon)$,
and you need to find the values of a, ω and ε.

Finding ω

Since the period of the motion is π,

$$\frac{2\pi}{\omega} = \pi \implies \omega = 2$$

Finding a

Using $\quad v^2 = \omega^2(a^2 - x^2)$

$$6^2 = 2^2(a^2 - 10^2)$$

$$\implies a = \sqrt{109}$$

Finding ε

Substituting $t = 0$ in $x = a\sin(\omega t + \varepsilon)$ gives

$$10 = \sqrt{109}\sin\varepsilon$$

$$\implies \varepsilon = 1.28 \text{ rad (see Note)}.$$

So the equation for the motion is

$$x = \sqrt{109}\sin(2t + 1.28)$$

> **Note**
>
> When finding ε you must be careful that you have selected the correct root of the equation.
>
> In this case, at $t = 0$, the particle has positive displacement and positive velocity (it is on its way out and not on its way back), so $t = 0$ corresponds to an angle between 0 and $\frac{\pi}{2}$. The next root of the equation $10 = \sqrt{109}\sin\varepsilon$ is $(\pi - 1.28)$. This lies between $\frac{\pi}{2}$ and π and would be the correct value if the particle were on its way back, with displacement +10 and velocity −6.

SHM as the projection of circular motion

There is a close relationship between circular motion at constant speed and SHM. This can be illustrated by rotating a bob on the end of a string in a horizontal circle with constant angular velocity, and thus forming a conical pendulum. If this is done between the light of an overhead projector and the wall, the shadow of the bob on the wall will perform SHM. (For true SHM the rays of light should be parallel and an approximation to this can be achieved if the pendulum is close to the wall and the overhead projector is as far away as possible.)

Assuming the rays of light are parallel, Figure 12.24 shows the position, C, of the bob and its shadow, P, at a particular instant. As the bob moves round the circle from A to B, the shadow moves along the straight line from L to N and back again.

> MP = OQ = $a \cos\theta$

> The projection of uniform circular motion onto a straight line, illustrated here, is the only case where ω actually does represent a physical angular velocity.

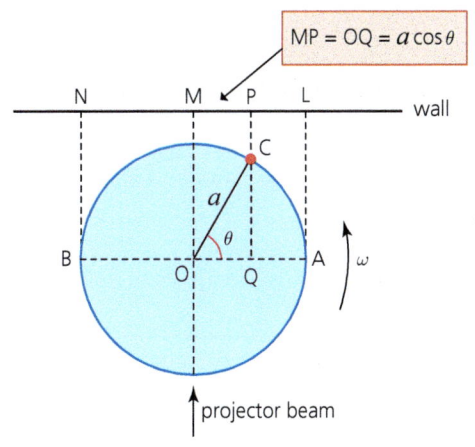

Figure 12.24

Assuming that $t = 0$ when the bob is at A, the angle θ is given by ωt, where ω is the angular speed of the bob. Thus

MP = OQ = $a\cos\omega t$.

This is one of the standard forms of SHM.

Example 12.6

An astronomer observes a faint object close to a star. Continued observations show the object apparently moving in a straight line through the star, as shown in Figure 12.25.

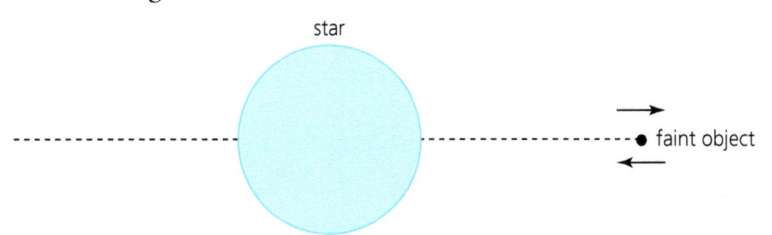

Figure 12.25

The astronomer is able to estimate the apparent distance of the object from the centre of the star and records this at 30-day intervals, resulting in the following table.

Day, t	0	30	60	90	120
Distance (10^{11} m), x	1.0	1.5	1.9	2.0	1.9

The astronomer thinks that the object is a planet moving around the star in a circular orbit and that she is observing it from a point in the plane of the orbit. She decides to model the apparent distance from the centre by the SHM equation

$x = 2\sin(\omega t + \varepsilon)$

(i) Use the values of x for $t = 0$ and $t = 90$ to find values for the constants ω and ε and verify that the other values of x are consistent with this model.

(ii) Assuming that the model is correct, find

(a) the radius of the orbit

(b) the speed of the planet

(c) the number of Earth days the planet takes to go round the star.

[MEI]

Alternative forms of the equation for SHM

Solution

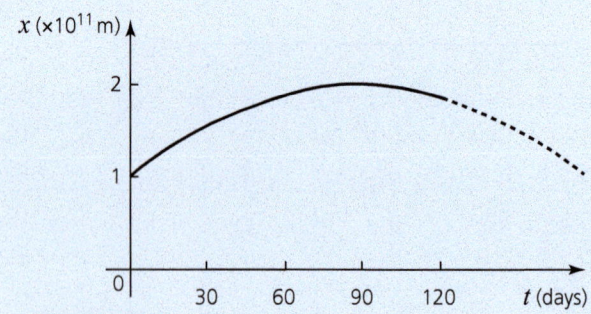

Figure 12.26

(i) Using $x = 2\sin(\omega t + \varepsilon)$:

When $t = 0$, $x = 1$

$\Rightarrow 1 = 2\sin\varepsilon$

$\Rightarrow \varepsilon = \dfrac{\pi}{6}$

> The equation $\sin\varepsilon = \dfrac{1}{2}$ has other roots (e.g. $\dfrac{5\pi}{6}$), but the graph shows that $\dfrac{\pi}{6}$ is the one you want.

When $t = 90$, $x = 2$

$\Rightarrow 2 = 2\sin\left(90\omega + \dfrac{\pi}{6}\right)$

$\Rightarrow \sin\left(90\omega + \dfrac{\pi}{6}\right) = 1$

$\Rightarrow 90\omega + \dfrac{\pi}{6} = \dfrac{\pi}{2}$

$\Rightarrow \omega = \dfrac{\pi}{270}$

So the model is $x = 2\sin\left(\dfrac{\pi t}{270} + \dfrac{\pi}{6}\right)$

For the other values of t:

t	Observed displacement	Model's prediction
30	1.5	$2\sin\left(\dfrac{\pi}{9} + \dfrac{\pi}{6}\right) = 1.53$
60	1.9	$2\sin\left(\dfrac{2\pi}{9} + \dfrac{\pi}{6}\right) = 1.88$
120	1.9	$2\sin\left(\dfrac{4\pi}{9} + \dfrac{\pi}{6}\right) = 1.88$

This shows that the model is a very good predictor of the actual position of the object.

(ii) (a) The radius of the orbit is the amplitude a of the motion:

$$\text{radius} = 2 \times 10^{11}\,\text{m}$$

(b) The speed of the planet is

$$a\omega = 2 \times 10^{11} \times \dfrac{\pi}{270} = 2.3 \times 10^{9}\,\text{m s}^{-1}$$

(c) The total time for one orbit is the period of the SHM i.e. $\dfrac{2\pi}{\omega}$.

$$\text{Number of days} = 2\pi \div \dfrac{\pi}{270}$$

$$= 540 \text{ days.}$$

Solving SHM equations as second-order linear differential equations

The SHM equation $\ddot{x} = -\omega^2 x$ is an example of a second-order differential equation with constant coefficients. So is the equation $\ddot{x} = -\omega^2(x - x_0)$ for SHM about a point other than the origin.

These two equations can be written as $\ddot{x} + \omega^2 x = 0$ and $\ddot{x} + \omega^2 x = \omega^2 x_0$.

The first step is to find the complementary function. The right-hand side is replaced by 0 (if it isn't zero already). In both cases, this gives the equation $\ddot{x} + \omega^2 x = 0$.

Then a solution of the form $x = ae^{\lambda t}$ is sought. Differentiating this twice with respect to t gives $\ddot{x} = a\lambda^2 e^{\lambda t}$ and substituting in the equation gives $a\lambda^2 e^{\lambda t} + a\omega^2 e^{\lambda t} = 0$.

This simplifies to $\lambda^2 + \omega^2 = 0$. ◄ *This is called the auxiliary equation*

The roots of this equation are $\lambda = \pm\omega i$, which give rise to the complementary function $x = Pe^{i\omega t} + Qe^{-i\omega t}$, where P and Q are arbitrary constants.

Since $e^{i\theta} = \cos\theta + i\sin\theta$ and $e^{-i\theta} = \cos\theta - i\sin\theta$, the complementary function may also be written as

$x = A\cos\omega t + B\sin\omega t$ ◄ *Notice that this is a 2nd order differential equation so you would expect 2 arbitrary constants. A and B are related to P and Q by $A = P + Q$ and $B = P - Q$*

where A and B are also arbitrary constants.

The next step is to find a particular integral. This is any solution of the original full equation.

In the case of $\ddot{x} + \omega^2 x = 0$, the particular integral is $x = 0$.

In the case of $\ddot{x} + \omega^2 x = \omega^2 x_0$, it is $x = x_0$.

Then, the general solution is the sum of the complementary function and the particular integral.

In the case of $\ddot{x} + \omega^2 x = 0$, the general solution is $x = A\cos\omega t + B\sin\omega t$.

In the case of $\ddot{x} + \omega^2 x = \omega^2 x_0$, it is $x = A\cos\omega t + B\sin\omega t + x_0$.

The constants A and B are dependent on the initial conditions. If, for example, the initial conditions for the equation $\ddot{x} + \omega^2 x = 0$ are that when $t = 0$, $x = a$ and $\dot{x} = 0$,

substituting $t = 0$ and $x = a$ in $x = A\cos\omega t + B\sin\omega t$ gives $A = a$, and

substituting $t = 0$ in $\dot{x} = -\omega A\sin\omega t + \omega B\cos\omega t$ gives $B = 0$.

So the particular solution in this case is $x = a\cos\omega t$, a familiar form of SHM.

> **Historical note**
>
> In 1822, Jean-Baptiste Joseph Fourier (1768–1830) showed that any function of t can be written as a sum of sines of multiples of t and this is now called a Fourier series. It follows that any vibration which can be written as a function of t can be reproduced by adding simple harmonic vibrations. He discovered this theorem while working on the flow of heat. He established the partial differential equation governing heat diffusion and solved it by using infinite series of trigonometric functions.

Alternative forms of the equation for SHM

Exercise 12.3

1. (i) Sketch graphs of the following functions.
   - (a) $x = 3\cos t$
   - (b) $x = 3\cos 2t$
   - (c) $x = 3\cos t + 4\sin t$
   - (d) $x = 5\cos\left(0.2t + \frac{\pi}{4}\right)$

   (ii) In each case, write down the amplitude, period and frequency of the oscillations.

2. Find a suitable simple harmonic model, giving x (in m) in terms of t (in s), for each of the following.
   - (i) Period = 3 s, and initially $\dot{x} = 0$ and $x = 5$.
   - (ii) Period = 2 s, amplitude = 6 m and initially $x = 0$.
   - (iii) Period = 5 s, amplitude = 4 m, and initially $x = 2$.
   - (iv) Period = 4 s, and initially $x = 1.5$ and $\dot{x} = 6$.

3. The displacement of a particle along a straight line at time t is given by
   $$x = 4\cos\left(\frac{\pi t}{12} + \frac{\pi}{6}\right)$$

   (i) Sketch the displacement–time curve.

   (ii) Is it possible to describe x by the equation
   $$x = p\sin\omega t + q\cos\omega t?$$
   If so, find the values of p and q.

4. The displacements of a particle along a straight line at different times are given in the table below.

t	0	1	2	3	4	5	6	7	8	9
x	3.54	5	3.54	0	-3.54	-5	-3.54	0	3.54	5

   (i) These data may be modelled using the SHM equation
   $$x = a\cos(\omega t - \varepsilon).$$
   Find the values of a, ω and ε.

   (ii) An alternative equation is $x = a\sin(\omega t + \delta)$. Find the value of δ.

   (iii) A third equation to describe the data is
   $$x = b\sin\omega t + b\cos\omega t.$$
   Find the value of b and show that this form of the equation does indeed describe the data.

5. A particle is executing SHM. Its position, y (in m), at time t (in s) is given in the table below.

t	2	4	6	8	10	12	14	16
y	8	5.4	5.4	8	10.6	10.6	8	5.4

   (i) Draw the graph y of against t and write down the central value of y for the motion.

   The motion may be described by the equation
   $$y = y_0 + a\cos(\omega t + \varepsilon).$$

   (ii) Use the information in the table to determine the values of ω, ε and a.

⑥ A SHM is described by the equation
$$x = 2\cos\tfrac{\pi}{4}t + \sqrt{5}\sin\tfrac{\pi}{4}t$$
(i) Plot the graph of x against t for $0 \leq t \leq 20$.

The motion may be described by an equation of the form
$$x = a\sin(\omega_1 t + \varepsilon).$$
(ii) Determine the values of a, ω_1 and ε.

Another way of describing the motion is given by the equation
$$x = b\cos(\omega_2 t + \delta).$$
(iii) State which of b, ω_2 and δ are equal, respectively, to a, ω_1 and ε.

(iv) State the values of b, ω_2 and δ.

⑦ As a result of storms in different places, two swell wave patterns, both running in the same direction, occur at the same time over a stretch of open sea. Their heights above the mean sea level can be modelled as follows.

Wave pattern A: $h_A = 1.5\sin\tfrac{\pi}{15}t$ (t is in s, h is in m).

Wave pattern B: $h_B = 2\cos\tfrac{\pi}{15}t$.

(i) Plot the two wave patterns on the same piece of graph paper taking values of t from 0 to 45 at 5 s intervals.

(ii) The overall height of the water, h, is given by
$$h = h_A + h_B.$$
Plot the values of h for $0 \leq t \leq 45$ on the same graph that you used for h_A and h_B.

(iii) Show algebraically that the effect of the two wave patterns is that of a single wave pattern described by
$$h = a\sin(\omega t + \varepsilon)$$
and state the values of a, ω and ε.

⑧ The centre of the London Eye observation wheel is approximately 70 m above the ground (about as high as Big Ben, which is on the opposite side of the Thames). The wheel's diameter is 135 m and it takes 30 minutes to make one revolution. Assuming that it turns continuously at a steady speed, find the angular velocity of the wheel.

Figure 12.27

(i) Write down a suitable equation for the height above the ground of a passenger t minutes after boarding at the lowest level.

(ii) Estimate for how long during a flight of one revolution passengers are higher than the highest point on the Houses of Parliament (102 m).

Alternative forms of the equation for SHM

⑨ Data on sunspots show that their number in any year, N, follows an 11-year cycle. An appropriate model gives N as $N = N_0 + a\cos\omega T$, where T is the number of years $(0, 1, 2, 3, \ldots)$ since the year in which there was last a maximum. A maximum of 150 occurred in 1948 and the subsequent minimum was 20.

  (i) Determine the appropriate values of N_0, a and ω from the given information.

  (ii) Estimate the number of sunspots in 1950 and 1955.

⑩ The height, h m, of water above the bottom of a harbour varies with the tide.

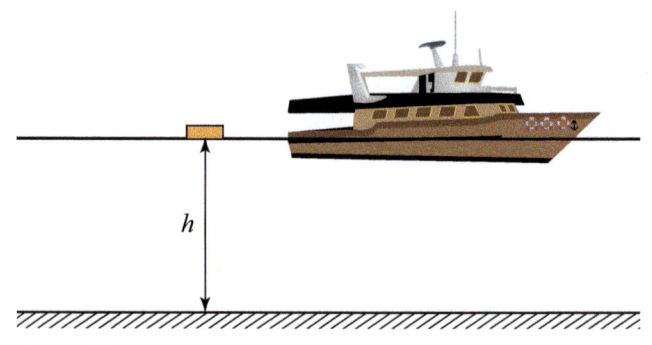

Figure 12.28

The vertical motion of a piece of wood floating on the surface may be modelled by the equation
$$h = h_0 + a\sin(\omega t + \varepsilon)$$
where t is the time in hours since midnight.

  (i) Describe the vertical motion of the piece of wood in terms of h_0, a and ω.

The heights at certain times on one day are given in the table below.

t (hours)	2	5	8	11	12
h (metres)	10	6	2	6	8

  (ii) Find the values of h_0, a, ω and ε.

  (iii) What are the vertical speed and acceleration of the piece of wood when $t = 8.6$?

  (iv) What is the greatest speed at which the water level rises?

⑪ The positions of the points B, B', A, A' and O are shown on Figure 12.29.

Figure 12.29

A particle is released from rest at the point B at time $t = 0$ and moves with simple harmonic motion, centre O, with period $\frac{2\pi}{\omega}$.

  (i) Write down an expression for the displacement x from O of the particle at time t.

  (ii) Write down an expression for the speed v of the particle as it passes the point A and show that $b = \sqrt{a^2 + \frac{v^2}{\omega^2}}$.

(iii) Show that the time taken by the particle to travel directly from A to A' is given by $\frac{1}{\omega}\left[\pi - 2\arccos\left(\frac{a}{b}\right)\right]$.

A second particle is released from rest at the point A at time $t = 0$. It moves with simple harmonic motion, centre O, with period $\frac{2\pi}{\omega}$.

(iv) How much longer does this particle take to travel from A to A'?

A machine component is subject to a variable force which causes it to move with simple harmonic motion. When released from rest at point A, it travels 0.4 m before coming momentarily to rest after 0.1 s. It is desired to shorten the time of motion of the component over the 0.4 m and this is to be achieved by giving the component an initial speed of $2\,\text{m s}^{-1}$.

(v) Assuming that the same law of force applies to the new motion, calculate the time saved.

⑫ The motion of the fore and hind wings of a locust can be modelled approximately using the ideas of oscillation. The motion of the forewings is modelled by

$$\alpha = 1.5 + 0.5\sin(1.05t - 0.005)$$

where α is the angle between the forewing and the vertical, and t is measured in hundredths of a second.

(i) Find the period and amplitude of the motion.

The hindwings initially make an angle of 1.5 rad to the vertical, and then they oscillate with period 0.06 s and amplitude 1.5 rad.

(ii) Construct a model of the form

$$\beta = \beta_0 + a\sin(kt)$$

for the motion of the hindwings.

⑬ A piston performs simple harmonic motion with amplitude 0.1 m about a point O.

The displacement from O is denoted by x metres and the time by t seconds. In a test, the piston is first observed at $t = 0$ when $x = 0.05$ and it is moving *towards* O.

(i) Sketch a graph of x against t for one complete oscillation starting at $t = 0$.

An expression for x in the form of $x = a\sin(\omega t + \varepsilon)$ is sought, where a, ω and ε are positive constants.

(ii) Write down the value of a and find the value of ε.

The piston passes through O after 0.025 seconds.

(iii) Calculate ω and the period of the motion.

(iv) Calculate the acceleration of the piston when it is first observed. [MEI]

⑭ A particle moves along a straight line through an origin. Its displacement, x metres, is given by the differential equation $\ddot{x} = -9(x - 8)$. The time, t, is measured in seconds.

(i) Find the general solution of the differential equation.

Initially, the particle is stationary and $x = 2$.

(ii) Find the particular solution subject to these initial conditions.

(iii) Describe the motion in words, relating it to your answer to part (ii).

(iv) Find the displacement, velocity and acceleration of the particle when $t = 8$.

4 Oscillating mechanical systems

There are very many mechanical systems which can be modelled using SHM. Two of these are the spring-mass oscillator and the simple pendulum. The motion of the simple pendulum approximates to SHM for small angles, as you will see in the next section.

The simple pendulum

A simple pendulum consists of a bob suspended on the end of a light inelastic string, as illustrated by the apparatus in Figure 12.30.

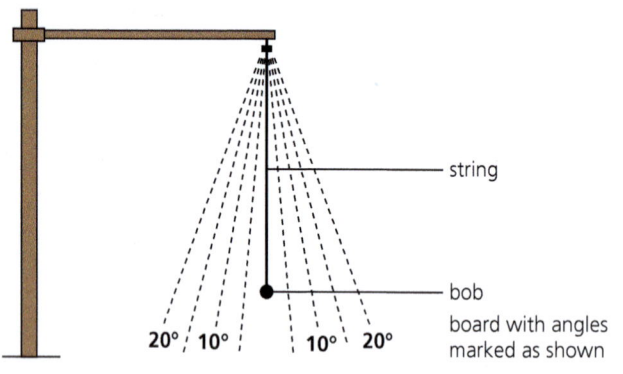

Figure 12.30

EXPERIMENT

Set up the apparatus as shown, making sure that the board is as close as possible to the pendulum without touching it. Use the apparatus to investigate whether the period of small oscillations depends on
- the mass of the bob, m
- the length of the string, l
- the amplitude of the swing
- the starting point in the cycle at angle α to the vertical.

In order to construct a mathematical model for the motion of a simple pendulum, take a general position some time t after it has been set in motion, when the string makes an angle θ with the vertical.

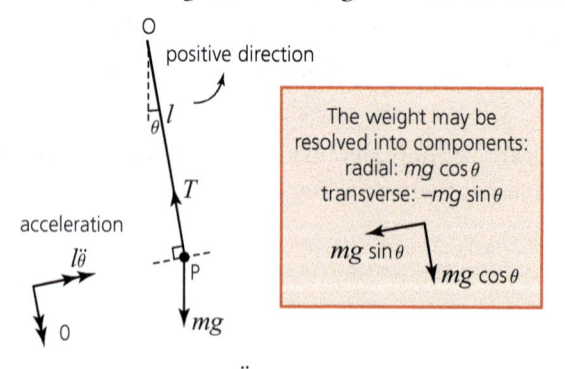

The weight may be resolved into components:
radial: $mg \cos\theta$
transverse: $-mg \sin\theta$

Figure 12.31

The forces acting on the bob are the tension in the string and the force of gravity mg, as shown in Figure 12.31. It swings through a small arc of a circle of radius l.

There is no motion in the radial direction. In the transverse direction, the acceleration, $l\ddot{\theta}$, is given by

$$-mg\sin\theta = ml\ddot{\theta}$$ ← This is Newton's second law

$$\Rightarrow \quad \ddot{\theta} = -\frac{g}{l}\sin\theta$$

When the angle is measured in radians, $\sin\theta \approx \theta$ for small angles (up to about 0.3 rad for accuracy correct to 2 d.p.). In this case

$$\ddot{\theta} = -\frac{g}{l}\theta$$

This is the standard equation for SHM, $\ddot{x} = -\omega^2 x$, with x replaced by θ and ω^2 replaced by $\frac{g}{l}$.

A pendulum is usually set in motion by pulling the bob to one side, say to an angle α, and then releasing from rest. If this is the case, $\theta = \alpha$ and $\dot{\theta} = 0$ when $t = 0$.

The appropriate form of the SHM equation is

$$\theta = \alpha\cos\sqrt{\frac{g}{l}}t$$ ← $\theta = \alpha$ and $\dot{\theta} = 0$ when $t = 0$

The period is given by

$$T = \frac{2\pi}{\omega} = 2\pi\sqrt{\frac{l}{g}}$$

Notice that this equation is dimensionally consistent. The LHS has dimensions T. The dimensions of the RHS are $\sqrt{\frac{L}{LT^{-2}}} = T$

There are several points to note:

- The SHM involves the angular displacement, θ, rather than the linear displacement of the bob.
- SHM is a good model for small values of θ, but the approximation becomes less good with increasing θ.
- The mass of the bob is not present in the SHM equation, so its value does not affect the motion.
- The amplitude is specified only by the initial conditions.
- The period $2\pi\sqrt{\frac{l}{g}}$ is not affected by the amplitude of the motion or the mass of the bob. It depends only on g and the length of the string.
- It is important not to confuse the angular velocity, $\dot{\theta}$ of the pendulum with ω, the angular frequency of the SHM.

Example 12.7

A simple pendulum consists of a mass hanging on the end of a light inextensible string.

The angle θ radians between the string and the vertical satisfies the differential equation

$$\ddot{\theta} = -\frac{g}{l}\theta$$

(i) Find the length of the pendulum for which the period for small oscillations is 2s.

The pendulum is released when the string makes an angle of 0.2 rad with the vertical.

Oscillating mechanical systems

(ii) Find an equation for θ in terms of t.

(iii) Find the times when the pendulum is in the equilibrium position.

(iv) Find also the time taken for the pendulum to move from the equilibrium position to an angle halfway to the end of the oscillation.

Solution

(i) The equation of motion, $\ddot{\theta} = -\frac{g}{l}\theta$, is the SHM differential equation with $\omega^2 = \frac{g}{l}$. All the standard results for SHM apply.

The period is 2s, so $\frac{2\pi}{\omega} = 2 \Rightarrow \omega = \pi$.

Therefore $\pi^2 = \frac{g}{l}$

$$\Rightarrow \quad l = \frac{g}{\pi^2} = \frac{9.8}{(3.14\ldots)^2} = 0.992\ldots$$

The length of the pendulum is 0.993 m or about 1 m.

(ii) The pendulum is released when $\theta = 0.2$ ($\theta = 0.2$ when $t = 0$). The most appropriate function to use to model the motion is

$\theta = 0.2\cos\omega t$

You have already seen that $\omega = \pi$

Therefore $\theta = 0.2\cos\pi t$

(iii) The pendulum is in the equilibrium position when $\theta = 0$, i.e. when
$0.2\cos\pi t = 0$

$\Rightarrow \quad \cos\pi t = 0$

$\Rightarrow \quad \pi t = \frac{\pi}{2}, \frac{3\pi}{2}, \frac{5\pi}{2}, \ldots$

$\quad t = \frac{1}{2}, \frac{3}{2}, \frac{5}{2}, \ldots$

(iv) The pendulum is first at the equilibrium position, $\theta = 0$, when $t = 0.5$.

It is halfway to the end of the oscillation when $\theta = -0.1$.

The value of t when $\theta = -0.1$ is given by

$0.2\cos\pi t = -0.1$

$\Rightarrow \quad \pi t = \frac{2\pi}{3}$ $\cos\frac{2\pi}{3} = -0.5$

$\Rightarrow \quad t = \frac{2}{3}$

The time taken from the centre to the halfway angle is $\frac{2}{3} - \frac{1}{2} = \frac{1}{6}$ s.

The graph illustrates the first two swings of the pendulum.

> The time interval required = $\frac{2}{3} - \frac{1}{2}$

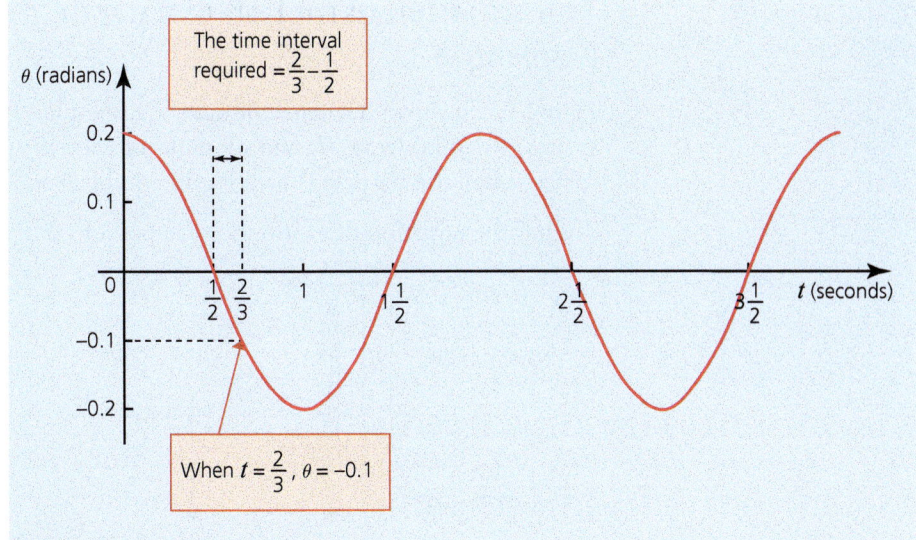

When $t = \frac{2}{3}$, $\theta = -0.1$

Figure 12.32

> **Note**
> Notice that the time taken to travel from the centre halfway to the end is one third of and not half of the time taken to travel to the end. This is because, for SHM, the velocity is greater near the centre of the motion than near the ends.

EXPERIMENT

The spring–mass oscillator

Set up a spring–mass oscillator consisting of a weight suspended by a spring, as shown in Figure 12.33.

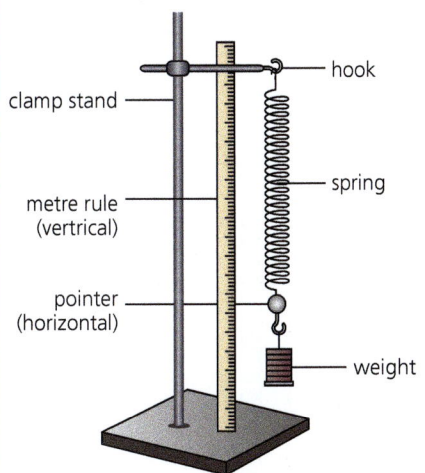

Figure 12.33

Use the apparatus to investigate whether the period of small oscillations depends on

(i) the mass of the weight
(ii) the modulus of elasticity of the spring
(iii) the natural length of the spring
(iv) the amplitude of the oscillation.

Oscillating mechanical systems

The equation of motion of a particle suspended from a spring

Figure 12.34 shows a particle of mass m suspended from a perfectly elastic, light spring of natural length l_0, and modulus of elasticity λ. The extension of the spring when the particle is hanging in equilibrium is e.

To find the equation of motion for the particle, start by finding an equation for e.

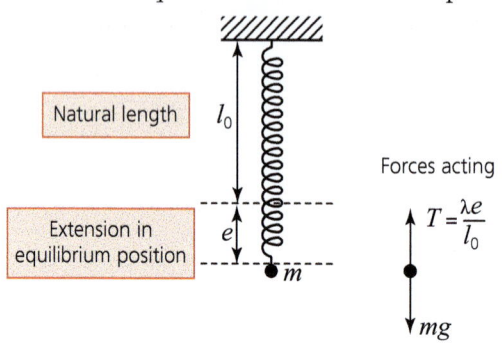

Figure 12.34

The tension T in the spring is given by $T = \dfrac{\lambda e}{l_0}$ and this is equal to the weight of the particle, mg. Thus

$$\frac{\lambda e}{l_0} = mg \quad \text{①}$$

Now look at the situation when the spring has an extension x in the downwards direction from the equilibrium position, as in Figure 12.35. The total extension is now $e + x$.

The particle is not in equilibrium, and its acceleration in the downwards direction is denoted by $\ddot{x}$.

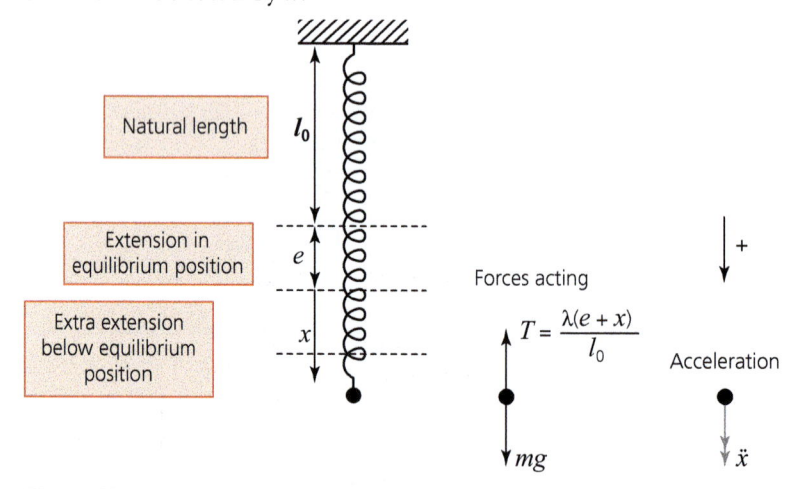

Figure 12.35

There are two forces acting on the particle: the tension in the spring, $\dfrac{\lambda(e+x)}{l_0}$, and its weight, mg.

By Newton's second law

$$m\ddot{x} = mg - \frac{\lambda(e+x)}{l_0}$$

$$= mg - \frac{\lambda e}{l_0} - \frac{\lambda x}{l_0}.$$

But from ① $\quad \dfrac{\lambda e}{l_0} = mg$

so $\quad\quad\quad m\ddot{x} = mg - mg - \dfrac{\lambda x}{l_0}$

giving the differential equation

$$\ddot{x} = -\dfrac{\lambda}{ml_0}x.$$

This is the standard equation for SHM with

$$\omega^2 = \dfrac{\lambda}{ml_0}.$$

Its period is $\dfrac{2\pi}{\omega} = 2\pi\sqrt{\dfrac{ml_0}{\lambda}}$.

If k is the stiffness of the spring, $k = \dfrac{\lambda}{l_0}$ and so this becomes $2\pi\sqrt{\dfrac{m}{k}}$.

This means that the period of the oscillation depends only on the mass and the stiffness of the spring.

Note that this model is good only as long as Hooke's law holds, but, provided this is so, the motion is an example of true SHM, unlike that of the simple pendulum which only approximates to SHM.

Example 12.8

A particle of mass 200 g is attached to a light spring of natural length 40 cm and stiffness 50 N m^{-1}. The particle is allowed to hang vertically in equilibrium.

(i) Find the extension of the spring in this position.

The spring is now pulled down 3 cm and released from rest.

(ii) Find the length of the spring as a function of time.

Solution

(i) Figure 12.36 shows the relevant lengths, and the forces acting on the particle in equilibrium. The extension of the spring is x_0 m.

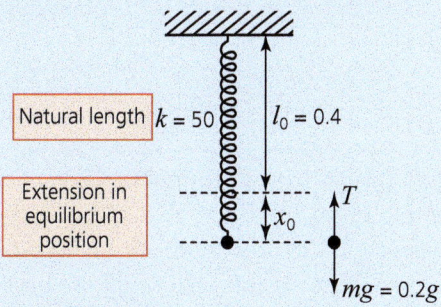

Figure 12.36

By Hooke's law, $T = kx_0 = 50x_0$

Since the particle is in equilibrium,

$$T = 0.2g$$
$$\Rightarrow 50x_0 = 0.2g$$

The extension is 0.0392 m $= 3.92$ cm.

(ii) Let x m be the displacement from the equilibrium position in the downwards direction.

Oscillating mechanical systems

Figure 12.37

The extension of the spring is then $x + x_0$

By Hooke's law, $T = 50(x + x_0)$

Applying Newton's second law in the downwards direction,

$$0.2g - 50(x + x_0) = 0.2\ddot{x}$$
$$\Rightarrow 0.2g - 50x - 50x_0 = 0.2\ddot{x}$$

However, as found in part (i), $0.2g = 50x_0$

and so the equation may be simplified to

$$0.2\ddot{x} = -50x$$

$$\ddot{x} = -250x$$

This is the SHM equation with $\omega^2 = 250$, and so $\omega = \sqrt{250}$.

Since the particle starts at the end of the oscillation with $x = 0.03$, the appropriate equation is of the form $x = a\cos\omega t$, with $a = 0.03$ and $\omega = \sqrt{250}$.

So at time t, $\quad x = 0.03\cos\sqrt{250}\,t$

and the total length is $0.4 + 0.0392 + 0.03\cos\sqrt{250}\,t$

$$= 0.4392 + 0.03\cos\sqrt{250}\,t$$

Discussion point
Would the period of the oscillations in the above example be the same on the Moon?

Example 12.9

Two springs have the same modulus of elasticity of 30 N, but are of natural length 0.4 m and 0.6 m. An object of mass 0.5 kg is attached to one end of each spring and the other ends are attached to two points which are 1.2 m apart on a smooth horizontal table. Find the period of small oscillations of this system.

Solution

The extensions in the springs are e_1 m and e_2 m and the tension, T N is the same on both sides.

Hint
The first step is to find the equilibrium position of the object. Figure 12.38 shows the relevant lengths and the horizontal forces acting when the object is in equilibrium.

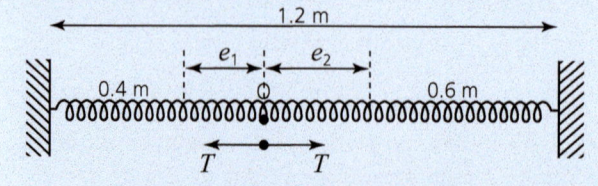

Figure 12.38

> **Hint**
> The vertical forces acting on the object, its weight and the normal reaction of the table, have no effect on the motion: they balance each other.

Hooke's law applied to each spring gives
$$T = \frac{30}{0.4} \times e_1 = 75e_1$$
and
$$T = \frac{30}{0.6} \times e_2 = 50e_2$$
$\Rightarrow \quad 75e_1 = 50e_2$
$\Rightarrow \quad e_2 = 1.5e_1$

The total length is 1.2 m, so
$$e_1 + e_2 = 0.2$$
$$2.5\, e_1 = 0.2$$

Hence $e_1 = 0.08$ and $e_2 = 0.12$

The next step is to find the equation of motion, so it is necessary to consider a general position for the object, and this is given by the displacement x m from the equilibrium position. The direction towards the right is taken to be positive.

The tensions in the springs are now different.

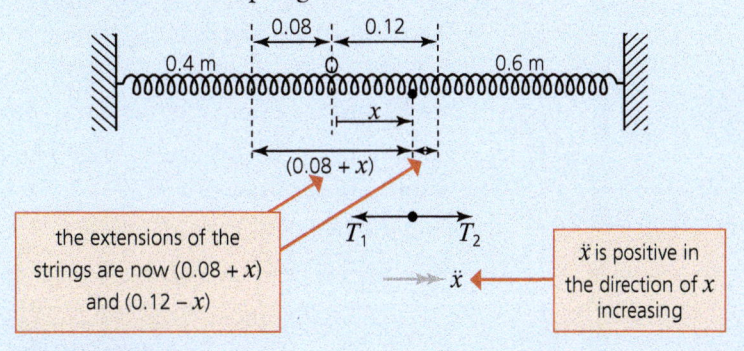

the extensions of the strings are now $(0.08 + x)$ and $(0.12 - x)$

$\ddot{x}$ is positive in the direction of x increasing

Figure 12.39

Hooke's law gives
$$T_1 = \frac{30}{0.4}(0.08 + x) = 75(0.08 + x)$$
$$T_2 = \frac{30}{0.6}(0.12 - x) = 50(0.12 - x)$$

Newton's second law can now be applied giving
$$T_2 - T_1 = m\ddot{x}$$
$\Rightarrow \quad 50(0.12 - x) - 75(0.08 + x) = 0.5\ddot{x}$
$\Rightarrow \quad -125x = 0.5\ddot{x}$
$\Rightarrow \quad \ddot{x} = -250x$

This is the equation of motion for SHM with $\omega = \sqrt{250}$.

The period is $\frac{2\pi}{\omega}$ or 0.40 s (to 2 d.p.).

Oscillating mechanical systems

Exercise 12.4

① A simple pendulum has length 0.5 m and a bob of mass 0.3 kg
  (i) Draw a diagram to show the forces acting on the bob when the string makes an angle of θ rad with the vertical. Show also the radial and transverse components of the acceleration of the bob.
  (ii) Write down the equation of motion of the bob in the transverse direction.
  (iii) State the conditions required for this motion to approximate to SHM.
  (iv) Write down the SHM equation and state the period.
  (v) Was it necessary to be told the mass of the bob?

② A simple pendulum of length 3 m has a bob of mass 0.2 kg. It is hanging vertically when it is set in motion by a single, sharp sideways blow to the bob which causes the pendulum to oscillate with an angular amplitude of 5°.
  (i) State the amplitude in radians.
  (ii) Calculate the approximate period of the pendulum.
  (iii) The motion of the pendulum can be modelled by $\theta = a\sin(\omega t + \varepsilon)$
  Write down the values of a, ω and ε.
  (iv) Calculate the maximum speed of the pendulum bob according to this model and the impulse of the blow applied to the bob.

③ A pendulum has a bob of mass 0.25 kg. The period of the pendulum is 2 s. The amplitude of its swing is 3°.
  (i) Find the length of the pendulum.
  (ii) State the effect (if any) on the period of the pendulum of
    (a) making the mass of the bob 0.75 kg
    (b) doubling the length of the pendulum
    (c) halving the amplitude of its swing
    (d) moving it to the Moon where the acceleration due to gravity is one sixth of that on Earth.

④ A pendulum consists of a stone of mass 0.2 kg, attached to a light inelastic string of length 4 m.
  (i) Formulate the equation of motion of the stone, stating any assumptions involved.
  (ii) Calculate the period of small oscillations.

⑤

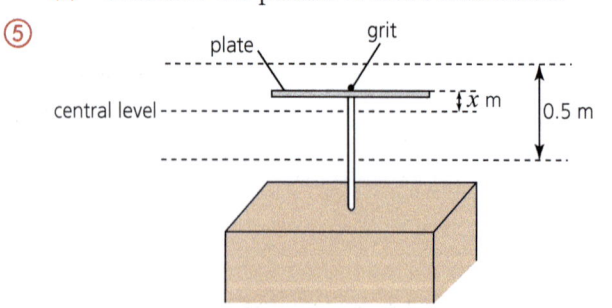

Figure 12.40

A thin horizontal plate is being driven by a mechanism so that its vertical motion is simple harmonic. It moves through two complete oscillations per second and the distance from the lowest to the highest point of the motion is 0.5 m. At the instant from which time is measured, the plate is moving upwards through the centre of its motion. At a time t s later, the plate is x m above this central level, as shown in Figure 12.40.

(i) Show that the acceleration, $\ddot{x}$, of the plate is given by
$$\ddot{x} = -16\pi^2 x.$$

(ii) Find an expression for x at time t.

(iii) Find an expression for v^2 in terms of x, where $v\,\text{m s}^{-1}$ is the speed of the plate.

When the plate is at its lowest point, it picks up a small piece of grit of mass m kg.

(iv) Draw a diagram showing the forces acting on the piece of grit while it is in contact with the plate, and derive the equation of motion for the piece of grit. Explain why the grit leaves the plate when $\ddot{x} = -g$.

(v) How far does the piece of grit travel while in contact with the plate? What is its speed when it leaves the plate?

(vi) For how long is the piece of grit in contact with the plate? [MEI]

⑥ A loaded test tube of total mass m floats in water and is in equilibrium when a length l is submerged as shown. The upward force exerted by the water on the tube is F.

(i) Why is F equal to mg in the equilibrium position?

(ii) Given that F is directly proportional to the submerged length, find the constant of proportionality in terms of l, m and g.

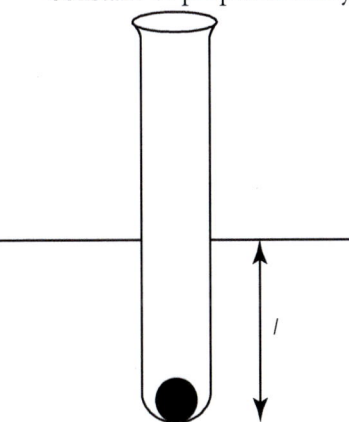

Figure 12.41

The test tube is now pushed down a small amount and released.

(iii) Find F when the bottom of the tube is a distance x below its equilibrium position, and use Newton's second law to write down the equation of motion of the test tube. Show that it will oscillate with SHM with period
$$T = 2\pi\sqrt{\frac{l}{g}}.$$

⑦ A small block of mass 2 kg is attached to a fixed point by a spring of stiffness 10 N m^{-1} and natural length 0.5 m. The block moves in a straight line on a smooth horizontal table. The block is held in a position such that the spring is stretched 0.2 m, and is then released. At time t s later the extension of the spring is x m.

Oscillating mechanical systems

(i) Show that the equation of motion is given by $\ddot{x}+5x=0$.

(ii) State the initial conditions for the motion in terms of x and t.

(iii) Show that the expression $x = 0.2\cos\sqrt{5}t$ satisfies both parts (i) and (ii).

(iv) State the frequency and amplitude of the block's oscillations.

(v) Find the greatest speed of the block.

⑧ A particle moving with simple harmonic motion performs 10 complete oscillations per minute and its speed when 20 cm from the centre of oscillation is $\frac{3}{5}$ of its maximum speed. Find the amplitude, the maximum acceleration and the speed when it is 15 cm from the centre.

⑨ Two identical springs of natural length 20 cm and stiffness 60 N m⁻¹ are attached to a block of mass 200 g and length 5 cm which lies on a smooth table. The other ends of the springs are attached to fixed points 45 cm apart and the springs and the block lie along a straight line, as shown in Figure 12.42.

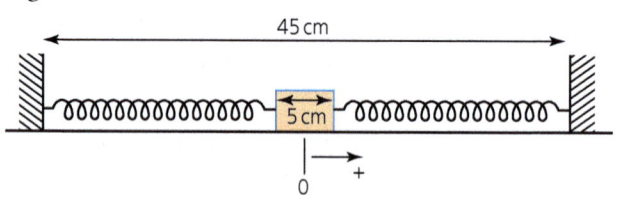

Figure 12.42

(i) Show that in the equilibrium position there is no tension in either spring.

The block is displaced 2 cm in the negative direction and released. At time t s later, its displacement is x cm.

(ii) Write down the equation of motion of the block.

(iii) Write in terms of x and t, the initial conditions of the motion.

(iv) Write down an expression for the displacement x at any time during the subsequent motion.

(v) State the frequency of the block's oscillations.

(vi) Find the greatest speed and the greatest acceleration of the block.

⑩ A particle P, of mass m is placed on a smooth, horizontal track and is attached by two springs to fixed points on the track. The spring AP has natural length $3l$ and modulus of elasticity λ. The spring BP has natural length $2l$ and modulus of elasticity 2λ. The points A and B are a distance $6l$ apart.

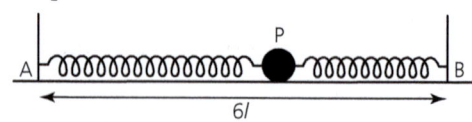

Figure 12.43

(i) Find the distance of the equilibrium position from A.

(ii) Find the tensions in the two springs when the particle is in equilibrium.

When the particle is stationary at the equilibrium position, it is given an impulse μ in the direction AB. Its subsequent displacement from the equilibrium position is given by x at time t.

(iii) Write down the equation of motion of the particle and its initial conditions.

(iv) Write down expressions for the amplitude and frequency of the subsequent oscillations.

(v) Find an expression for x in terms of t.

⑪ A particle moving with simple harmonic motion in a straight line has a speed of $6\,\text{m}\,\text{s}^{-1}$ when $4\,\text{m}$ from the centre of oscillation and $8\,\text{m}\,\text{s}^{-1}$ when $3\,\text{m}$ from the centre. Find the amplitude and the shortest time taken by the particle to move from an extreme position to a point halfway to the centre.

⑫ A block of mass $750\,\text{g}$ hangs vertically, attached to a light elastic string of natural length $50\,\text{cm}$ and modulus of elasticity $150\,\text{N}$. The other end of the string is attached to a ceiling.

(i) Taking g to be $10\,\text{m}\,\text{s}^{-2}$, find the extension of the string in the equilibrium position.

The block is then pulled down a further distance.

(ii) What is the tension in the string when the block is $x\,\text{m}$ below the equilibrium position?

(iii) Show that when the block is allowed to move, its motion is governed by the equation $\ddot{x} = -400x$.

The block is released from a position $2\,\text{cm}$ below the equilibrium position.

(iv) Find an expression for the displacement $x\,\text{cm}$, $t\,\text{s}$ after the block's release.

(v) On another occasion, the block is pulled down $3\,\text{cm}$ below the equilibrium position. Explain why, in this case, the subsequent motion is not simple harmonic.

⑬ Zeb, who should be modelled as a particle of mass $m\,\text{kg}$, sits on a bouncy toy which behaves like a vertical elastic spring of stiffness $k\,\text{N}\,\text{m}^{-1}$.

(i) The spring is compressed by x_0 metres when Zeb sits still in the equilibrium position, E. Show that
$$kx_0 = mg.$$

Zeb sets the toy moving so that it performs simple harmonic oscillations.

(ii) Draw diagrams similar to those in Figure 12.37 showing relevant lengths, forces and Zeb's acceleration when he is $x\,\text{m}$ below E. Include the natural length, l, of the spring. Write down Zeb's equation of motion.

(iii) Obtain the equation for the simple harmonic motion.

(iv) What is the maximum amplitude if Zeb stays fully in contact with the toy?

⑭ A particle of mass $0.02\,\text{kg}$ is performing SHM with centre O, period $6\,\text{s}$ and amplitude $2\,\text{m}$.

(i) Find, correct to 2 significant figures in each case,

(a) the maximum speed V of the particle

(b) the distance of the particle from O when its speed is $0.9V$

(c) the magnitude of the force acting on the particle when it is $1\,\text{m}$ from O.

(ii) Show also that the power exerted by the force on the particle is a periodic function of time and state the period.

Oscillating mechanical systems

15. A block of mass m is supported by two elastic strings of natural length l_0 and modulus of elasticity λ.

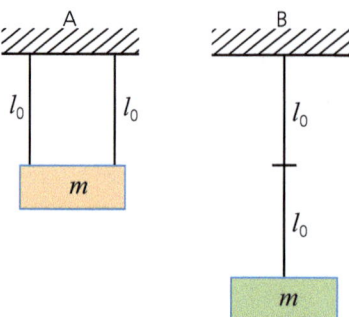

Figure 12.44

For each of the configurations A and B, find

(i) the equilibrium position

(ii) the equation of motion when the block is displaced from the equilibrium position

(iii) the period of oscillations, assumed small enough for the motion to be simple harmonic, when the block is displaced.

16. One end of a light, perfectly elastic string of natural length 4 m is suspended from a point O. A small object of mass 10 kg attached to the other end of the string hangs in equilibrium at a point E, which is 5 m vertically below O.

(i) Calculate the stiffness of the string.

The object is dropped from a point D in the line OE and first comes momentarily to rest when it is 2 m below E. Air resistance may be neglected.

(ii) Show that, while the string is taut, the motion of the object corresponds to simple harmonic motion about E. Express the simple harmonic motion in the form $x = A\cos\omega t$, where x is the displacement of the object below E and t is the time in seconds after the object reaches its lowest point.

When the object rises from its lowest point, its motion initially corresponds to simple harmonic motion and when the string becomes slack it moves freely under gravity.

(iii) What period of time elapses between the object being at the lowest point of the motion and the string becoming slack?

(iv) What is the speed of the object when the string first becomes slack?

(v) What period of time elapses between the object being at the lowest point of its motion in two consecutive oscillations? [MEI]

KEY POINTS

1 Motion for which $\ddot{x} = -\omega^2 x$ is simple harmonic.
2 The graph in Figure 12.45 illustrates the amplitude and period of simple harmonic motion.

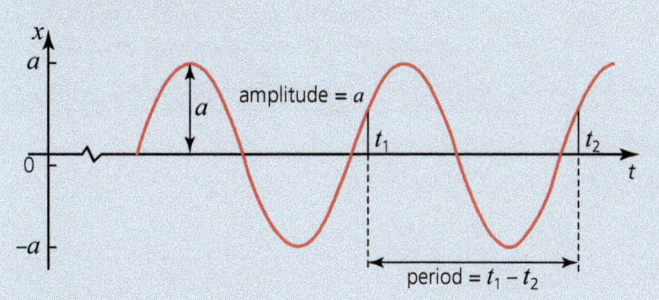

Figure 12.45

3 The speed at displacement x is given by $v^2 = \omega^2(a^2 - x^2)$
4 The period is $T = \dfrac{2\pi}{\omega}$
5 The frequency is $f = \dfrac{1}{T} = \dfrac{\omega}{2\pi}$
6 Different ways of expressing SHM

Initial conditions	Displacement x	Velocity $v = \dot{x}$	Acceleration $\ddot{x}$
$x = 0$ and $\dot{x} > 0$	$a \sin \omega t$	$a\omega \cos \omega t$	$-a\omega^2 \sin \omega t$
$x = a$ and $\dot{x} = 0$	$a \cos \omega t$	$-a\omega \sin \omega t$	$-a\omega^2 \cos \omega t$
Otherwise (i)	$a \cos(\omega t + \varepsilon)$	$-a\omega \sin(\omega t + \varepsilon)$	$-a\omega^2 \cos(\omega t + \varepsilon)$
or (ii)	$a \sin(\omega t + \varepsilon)$	$a\omega \cos(\omega t + \varepsilon)$	$-a\omega^2 \sin(\omega t + \varepsilon)$
or (iii) where $a = \sqrt{A^2 + B^2}$	$A \cos \omega t + B \sin \omega t$	$-A\omega \sin \omega t + B\omega \cos \omega t$	$-\omega^2(A\cos \omega t + B \sin \omega t)$

For all these functions, $x = 0$ in the position of equilibrium. If x takes another value, x_0, in the equilibrium position, then $\ddot{x} = -\omega^2(x - x_0)$ and x_0 must be added to functions in the displacement column.

LEARNING OUTCOMES

When you have finished this chapter, you should be able to
▶ recognise situations which may be modelled by simple harmonic motion (SHM)
▶ recognise the standard form of the equation of motion of SHM
▶ recognise and formulate the SHM equation expressed in non-standard forms and transform it into the standard form by means of substitution
▶ solve the equation for SHM, $\ddot{x} = -\omega^2 x$, and relate the solution to the context
▶ recognise the solution of the SHM equation in the forms $A\sin(\omega t + \varepsilon)$ or $A\cos(\omega t + \varepsilon)$ and be able to interpret these forms

Oscillating mechanical systems

- recognise other forms of the solution of the SHM equation, and be able to relate the various forms to each other
- select a form of the solution of the SHM equation appropriate to the context and initial or boundary conditions
- verify solutions of the SHM equation
- apply standard results for SHM in context
- analyse motion under the action of springs or strings as examples of SHM
- analyse the motion of a simple pendulum.

13 Centre of mass 2

Thou comest in such a questionable shape.
Hamlet, *William Shakespeare*

What do the shapes of the objects have in common? For each one, suggest a way of finding its volume.

How would you find the volume of:

➜ an egg?
➜ a table tennis ball?
➜ the moon?

1 Calculating volumes

One way of finding the volume of an irregular shape is to immerse it in water and measure the apparent increase in the volume of the water. This method is satisfactory for finding the volume of something small and dense like an egg, but you would find it difficult to use for a table tennis ball, and it would be impossible to find the volume of the moon in this way.

You will be familiar with the formula $V = \frac{4}{3}\pi r^3$ for the volume of a sphere. The methods you meet in this chapter will enable you to prove this formula, and to calculate the volumes and the positions of the centre of mass of other solid shapes with *rotational symmetry* like those illustrated above.

Volumes of revolution

If a set square (without a hole) is rotated through 360° about one of its shorter sides, its face will sweep out a solid cone, (Figure 13.1(a)). A 60° set square will sweep out different cones depending on the side chosen. In the same way, a semicircular protractor will sweep out a sphere if it is rotated completely about its diameter as shown in Figure 13.1 (b).

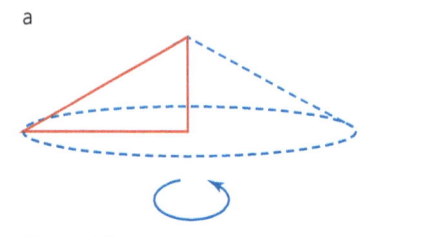

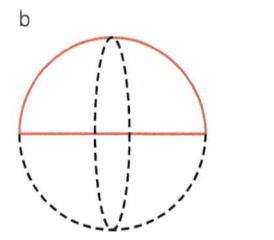

Figure 13.1

The cone and sphere are examples of **solids of revolution**. If any region of a plane is rotated completely about an axis in the plane, it will form a solid of revolution and any solid body with rotational symmetry can be formed in this way.

Imagine that such a solid is cut into thin slices perpendicular to the axis of rotation, just as a salami is sliced to make a pizza topping (Figure 13.2). Each slice will approximate to a thin disc, but the discs will vary in radius. The volume of the solid can be found by adding the volumes of these discs and then finding the limit of the volume as their thickness approaches zero. When thin discs are used to find a volume they are called elementary discs. (Similarly, when thin strips are used to find an area they are called elementary strips.)

> **Note**
> Thin slices are approximately cylindrical.

Figure 13.2

This is essentially the same procedure as that developed for finding the area under a curve, and so, as then, integration is required.

Volumes of revolution about the x-axis

Look at the solid formed by the rotation about the x-axis of the region under the graph of $y = f(x)$ between the values $x = a$ and $x = b$, as shown in Figure 13.3. (You should always start by drawing diagrams when finding areas and volumes.)

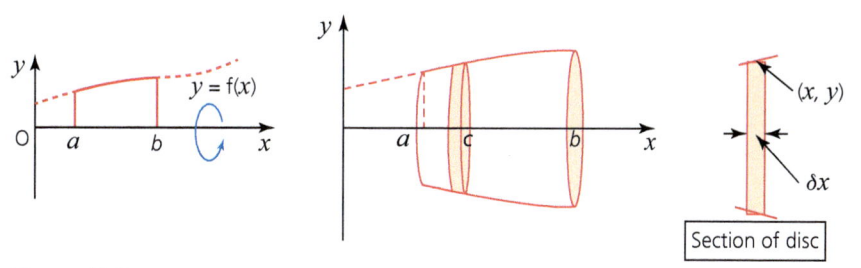

Figure 13.3

The volume of the solid of revolution (which is usually called the volume of revolution) can be found by imagining that it can be sliced into thin discs.

Each disc is a thin cylinder of radius y and thickness δx, so its volume is given by

$$\delta V = \pi y^2 \delta x$$

The volume of the solid is the limit of the sum of all these elementary volumes as $\delta x \to 0$ i.e. the limit as $\delta x \to 0$ of

$$\sum_{\substack{x=a \\ \text{Over all} \\ \text{discs}}} \delta V = \sum_{x=a}^{x=b} \pi y^2 \delta x$$

> In the limit as $\delta x \to 0$, the discs become infinitesimally thin and there are infinitely many of them.

The limiting values of sums such as these are integrals so

$$V = \int_a^b \pi y^2 \, dx$$

In this new situation, δx is written as dx and Σ is replaced by the integral symbol, $\int$ (an elongated letter S).

The limits are a and b because x takes values from a to b.

It is essential to realise that this integral is written in terms of dx and so it cannot be evaluated unless the function y is also written in terms of x. For this reason the integral is sometimes written as

$$V = \int_a^b \pi [f(x)]^2 \, dx$$

Calculating volumes

Example 13.1

Find the volume of revolution formed when the region between the curve $y = x^2 + 2$, the x-axis and the lines $x = 1$ and $x = 3$ is rotated completely about the x-axis.

Solution

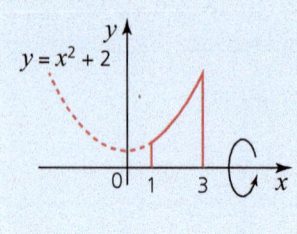

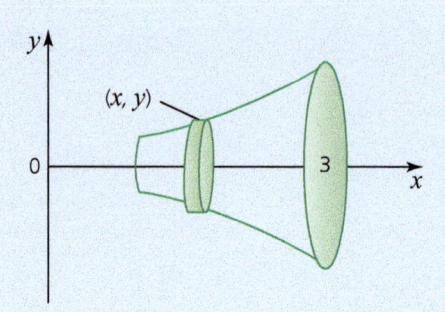

Figure 13.4

The volume is:

$$V = \int_a^b \pi [f(x)]^2 \, dx$$

$$= \int_1^3 \pi (x^2 + 2)^2 \, dx$$

$$= \int_1^3 \pi (x^4 + 4x^2 + 4) \, dx$$

$$= \left[\pi \left(\frac{1}{5} x^5 + \frac{4}{3} x^3 + 4x \right) \right]_1^3$$

$$= \pi \left[\left(\frac{3^5}{5} + 36 + 12 \right) - \left(\frac{1}{5} + \frac{4}{3} + 4 \right) \right]$$

The volume is $\frac{1366\pi}{15}$ cubic units or 286 cubic units correct to 3 significant figures.

> **Note**
>
> Unless a decimal answer is required, it is common practice to leave π in the answer, which is then exact.

Example 13.2

Find the volume of a spherical ball of radius 2 cm.

Solution

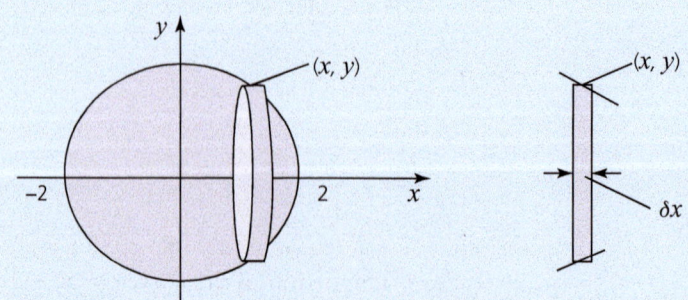

Figure 13.5

The volume of the sphere is found by using

$$V = \int_a^b \pi y^2 \, dx$$

with limits $a = -2$ and $b = 2$.

Since $x^2 + y^2 = 4$, $y^2 = 4 - x^2$, and the integral may be written as

$$V = \int_{-2}^{2} \pi(4 - x^2) \, dx$$

The constant π can be taken outside the integral so

$$V = \pi \left[4x - \frac{x^3}{3} \right]_{-2}^{2}$$

$$= \pi \left[\left(8 - \frac{8}{3}\right) - \left(-8 + \frac{8}{3}\right) \right]$$

$$= \frac{32\pi}{3} = 33.51\ldots$$

The volume of a spherical ball with radius 2 cm is 33.5 cm³ correct to 3 significant figures.

> The equation of a circle radius 2 centre (0, 0) is $x^2 + y^2 = 4$.

> Notice that this is the same answer as you get from substituting $r = 2$ in the formula for the volume of a sphere, $V = \frac{4}{3}\pi r^3$.

The volume of a sphere

The formula for the volume of a sphere of radius r can be found by following the same argument but using a circle of radius r rather than one of radius 2 cm. Its equation is $x^2 + y^2 = r^2$ and the limits of integration are $-r$ and r.

$$V = \int \pi y^2 \, dx$$

$$= \int_{-r}^{r} \pi(r^2 - x^2) \, dx$$

Therefore:

$$V = \pi \left[r^2 x - \frac{x^3}{3} \right]_{-r}^{r}$$

$$= \pi \left[\left(r^3 - \frac{r^3}{3}\right) - \left(-r^3 - \frac{-r^3}{3}\right) \right]$$

$$\Rightarrow V = \frac{4}{3}\pi r^3$$

Volumes of revolution about the y-axis

In Example 13.1, a region under the curve $y = x^2 + 2$ was rotated about the x-axis. If the same portion of the curve $y = x^2 + 2$ were to be used to form a region which could be rotated about the y-axis, a very different solid would be

Calculating volumes

obtained from that in Example 13.1. The region required would be that which lies between the curve and the y-axis and the limits $y = 3$ and $y = 11$, as shown in Figure 13.6.

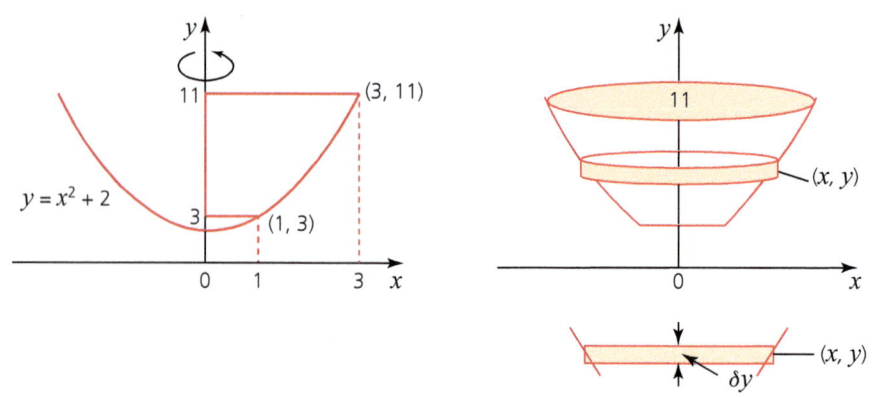

Figure 13.6

An elementary disc has an approximate volume $\delta V = \pi x^2 \delta y$ and the volume of revolution about the y-axis is given by

$$V = \int \pi x^2 \, dy$$

This time, it is necessary to write x^2 in terms of y. In this case, $x^2 = y - 2$ and so the final integral becomes

$$V = \int_{3}^{11} \pi (y - 2) \, dy$$

$$V = \left[\pi \left(\frac{y^2}{2} - 2y \right) \right]_{3}^{11}$$

$$\Rightarrow V = \pi \left[\left(\frac{11^2}{2} - 22 \right) - \left(\frac{3^2}{2} - 6 \right) \right] = 40\pi$$

The volume is 40π cubic units.

Exercise 13.1

① In each part of this question, a region is defined in terms of the lines which form its boundaries.

(a) Draw a sketch of the region.
(b) Find the volume of the solid obtained by rotating it through 360° about the x-axis.

(i) $y = 2x$, the x-axis and the lines $x = 1$ and $x = 3$.
(ii) $y = \sqrt{x}$, the x-axis and the line $x = 4$.
(iii) $y = 2x + 1$, the x-axis and the lines $x = 1$ and $x = 5$.
(iv) $y = \frac{1}{x}$, the x-axis and the lines $x = 1$ and $x = 3$.
(v) $y = 3e^x$, the x-axis, the y-axis and the line $x = 1.5$.
(vi) $y = \cos x$ (for $0 \leq x \leq \frac{\pi}{2}$), the x-axis and the y-axis.

Hint

$\cos^2 x = \frac{1}{2}(1 + \cos 2x)$

② In each part of the question, a region is defined in terms of the lines which form its boundaries.

  (a) Draw a sketch of the region.
  (b) Find the volume of the solid obtained by rotating it through 360° about the y axis.

   (i) $y = x^3$, the y-axis and the line $y = 8$.
   (ii) $y = 2x - 1$, the y-axis and the line $y = 5$.
   (iii) $x^2 + y^2 = 9$, the y-axis and the lines $y = 1$ and $y = 3$.

③ The triangle OAB shown in Figure 13.7 is rotated about the x-axis to form a solid cone.

  (i) Find the equation of the line OB.
  (ii) Hence show that the volume of a cone with radius r and height h is $\frac{1}{3}\pi r^2 h$.

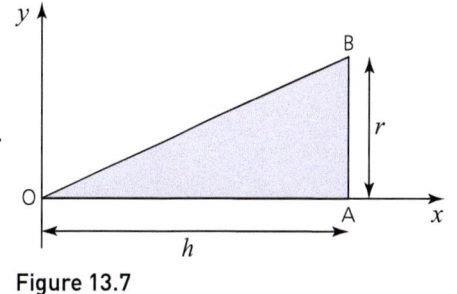

Figure 13.7

④ Find the volume generated when the area enclosed by the x-axis and the curve $y = x^2 - 4$ is rotated through 360° about the x-axis.

⑤ (i) Sketch the graph of $x^2 + y^2 = 36$.
  (ii) A hemispherical bowl of internal radius 6 cm is filled with water to a depth of 4 cm. Find the volume of water in litres (1 litre = 1000 cm³).

⑥ Figure 13.8 shows the ellipse $\frac{x^2}{a^2} + \frac{y^2}{b^2} = 1$, where $a > b$.

The region under this curve and above the x-axis is rotated through 360° about the x-axis to form an ellipsoid.

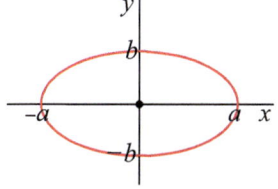

  (i) Draw a diagram to illustrate the solid formed.

Figure 13.8

  (ii) Show that the volume of this solid is $\frac{4}{3}\pi b^2 a$.

A mathematical model of an egg is that one end is a half ellipsoid of length a and greatest radius b and the other end is a hemisphere of radius b.

  (iii) Find the volume of the egg in terms of a and b.

⑦ (i) Draw a diagram to illustrate the solid formed when the ellipse $\frac{x^2}{a^2} + \frac{y^2}{b^2} = 1$ $(a > b)$ is rotated about the y-axis.

Figure 13.9 shows the elliptical galaxy M87. This galaxy is estimated to have a maximum diameter of 10 000 light years.

  (ii) Estimate its volume in m³. (You will need to take measurements from the photograph. The speed of light is approximately 3×10^8 m s⁻¹.)

Figure 13.9

Calculating volumes

⑧ The area bounded by the curve $y^2 = 8x$ and the lines $x = 0$ and $y = 4$ is rotated through 360° about the y-axis. Show that the volume of the solid obtained is $\dfrac{16\pi}{5}$ and find the volume of the solid obtained by rotating the same region about the x-axis.

⑨ Find the volume generated when the region between the curve $y = 2x - x^2$ and the line $y = \dfrac{x}{2}$ is rotated through 360° about the x-axis.

⑩ Figure 13.10 shows the hyperbola $\dfrac{x^2}{a^2} - \dfrac{y^2}{b^2} = 1$.

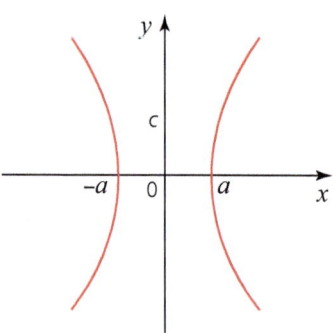

Figure 13.10

When it is rotated through 360° about the y-axis a hyperboloid is formed

(i) Show that the volume enclosed by this hyperboloid between $y = 0$ and $y = c$ is given by
$$V = \frac{\pi a^2 c}{3b^2}\left(3b^2 + c^2\right).$$

The cooling towers of power stations can be modelled as hyperboloids and the dimensions of one such tower are shown in Figure 13.11.

A = 51.3 m
B = 47.5 m
C = 24.5 m
D = 89.5 m
E = 85.5 m

Figure 13.11

(ii) Verify that the equation $\dfrac{x^2}{560} - \dfrac{y^2}{3600} = 1$ is a suitable mathematical model for the curve which is rotated to form the hyperboloid.

(iii) Use the formula above to find the volume occupied by the cooling tower, and show that the six towers of the power station occupy over 1.9 million cubic metres of space.

⑪ Figure 13.12 shows the ellipse $\dfrac{x^2}{a^2} + \dfrac{y^2}{b^2} = 1$.

When it is rotated through 360° about the y-axis an ellipsoid is formed.

(i) Show that the volume enclosed by this ellipsoid between $y = -c$ and $y = b$ is given by $V = \dfrac{\pi a^2}{3b^2}[2b^3 + c(3b^2 - c^2)]$.

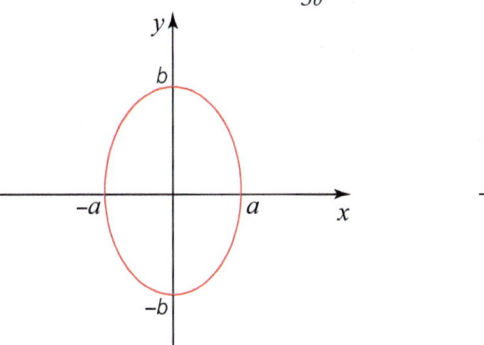

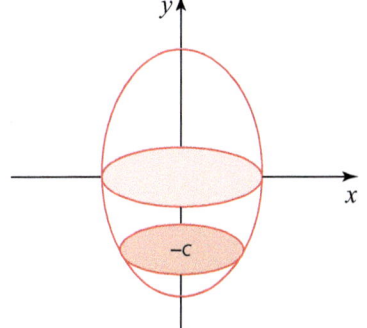

Figure 13.12

The London skyscraper the Gherkin can be modelled as an ellipsoid and the dimensions of this building are shown Figure 13.13.

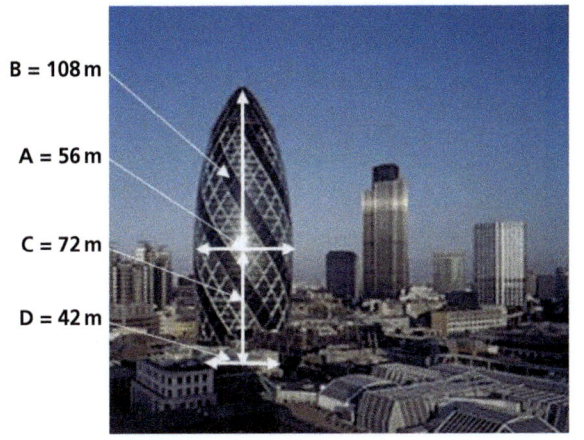

B = 108 m
A = 56 m
C = 72 m
D = 42 m

Figure 13.13

(ii) Verify that the equation $\dfrac{x^2}{28^2} + \dfrac{y^2}{108^2} = 1$ is a suitable mathematical model for the curve which is rotated to form the ellipsoid.

(iii) Use the formula above to find the volume occupied by the building.

⑫ A mathematical model for the curved surface of a measuring jug is obtained by rotating the part of the curve $y = 0.003x^4$ between $y = 1$ and $y = 10$ through 360° about the y-axis. It has a flat base. The units are centimetres.

(i) Sketch the jug.

(ii) Find the values of y for which marks must be placed on the side of the jug to indicate volumes of

(a) 100 ml (b) 0.5 l (c) 1 l.

⑬ The circle $x^2 + (y + 1)^2 = 5$ meets the x-axis at the points A and B.

The minor arc AB is rotated about the x-axis to form a solid of revolution which can be used to model a rugby ball.

(i) Find the coordinates of A and B and show that
$$y^2 = 6 - x^2 - 2\sqrt{5 - x^2}.$$

(ii) Hence calculate the volume of the solid of revolution.

(iii) A similar rugby ball is 30 cm long. Find its volume.

Centres of mass

2 Centres of mass

The position of the centre of mass of a solid of revolution will affect its stability and the way it will roll. Some toys are designed so that they can never be knocked over. Many birds that live on cliffs lay pointed eggs which roll round in circles so that they do not fall over the cliff edge. The position of the centre of mass is also important in the design of some sporting equipment.

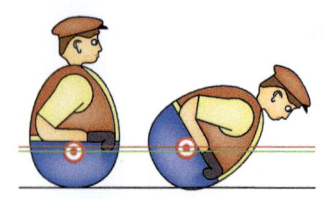

Figure 13.14

Using integration to find centres of mass

The calculus methods you have been using to determine the volumes of solids of revolution can be extended to find their centres of mass (assuming they are of uniform density).

Notice that, by symmetry, the centre of mass of a solid of revolution must lie on its axis, so provided you choose either the x-axis or the y-axis to be the axis of symmetry, there is only one coordinate to determine. For a solid of revolution about the x-axis, divide it into thin discs as before. An elementary disc situated at the point (x, y) on the curve, has a centre of mass at the point $(x, 0)$ on the x-axis, as shown in Figure 13.15.

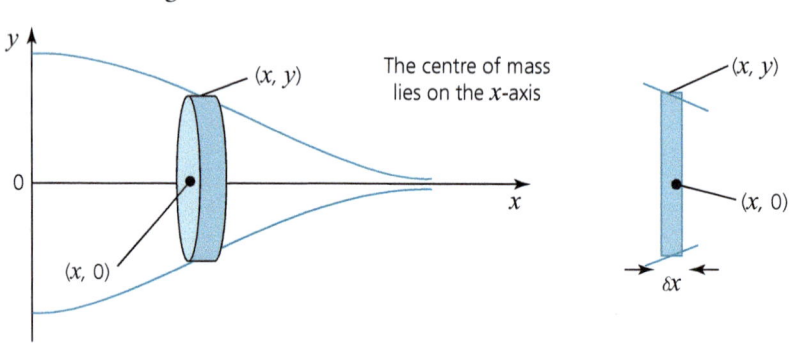

Figure 13.15

The volume of this disc is $\quad \delta V = \pi y^2 \delta x$

and so its mass is $\quad \delta M = \rho \pi y^2 \delta x$

where ρ is the density.

The sum of such discs forms a solid which approaches the original as $\delta x \to 0$ and the discs become thinner. Both the mass and the position of the centre of mass are known for each disc, so you can use the result from Chapter 7. For a composite body, the position, $\bar{x}$, of the centre of mass is given by

moment of whole mass at centre of mass = sum of moments of individual masses

$$M\bar{x} = \sum m_i x_i$$

In this case, $\left(\sum_{\text{All discs}} \delta M \right) \bar{x} = \sum_{\text{All discs}} (\delta M x)$

Substituting the expression for δM obtained above gives

$$\left(\sum \rho \pi y^2 \delta x\right)\bar{x} = \sum \rho \pi y^2 x \delta x$$

In the limit as $\delta x \to 0$ these sums may be represented by integrals and so

$$\left(\int \rho \pi y^2 \, dx\right)\bar{x} = \int \rho \pi y^2 x \, dx$$

Assuming that ρ is uniform, you can divide through by $\rho\pi$ to give

$$\left(\int y^2 \, dx\right)\bar{x} = \int y^2 x \, dx \quad \text{or} \quad \bar{x} = \frac{\int y^2 x \, dx}{\int y^2 \, dx}$$

This result is valid for any solid of revolution of *uniform density* which is formed by rotation about the x-axis.

It may also be written as

$$V\bar{x} = \int \pi y^2 x \, dx$$

where V is the volume of the solid.

In the next example, the centre of mass of a solid hemisphere is found using the above result.

Example 13.3

Find the centre of mass of a solid hemisphere of radius r.

> **Note**
>
> With the hemisphere oriented as in Figure 13.16, the point (x, y) lies on the curve $x^2 + y^2 = r^2$ and the limits for the integration are $x = 0$ and $x = r$.

> **Note**
>
> You also know that the volume, V, is $\frac{2}{3}\pi r^3$ but the equations will look simpler if this is substituted later.

Solution

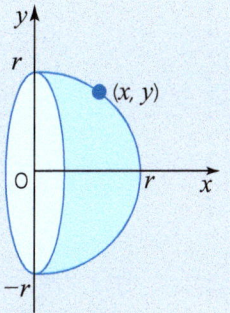

$$V\bar{x} = \int_0^r \pi y^2 x \, dx$$

Substituting $y^2 = r^2 - x^2$ gives

$$V\bar{x} = \int_0^r \pi(r^2 - x^2)x \, dx$$

$$= \int_0^r \pi(r^2 x - x^3) \, dx$$

$$= \pi \left[\frac{r^2 x^2}{2} - \frac{x^4}{4}\right]_0^r$$

So
$$V\bar{x} = \frac{1}{4}\pi r^4$$

Substituting for V gives
$$\frac{2}{3}\pi r^3 \bar{x} = \frac{1}{4}\pi r^4$$

$$\Rightarrow \quad \bar{x} = \frac{3}{8}r$$

The centre of mass of a solid hemisphere is $\frac{3}{8}r$ from the centre of its base.

Figure 13.16

Centres of mass

Example 13.4

Find the position of the centre of mass of the solid of revolution formed when the region between the curve $y = 2e^x$, the lines $x = 0$ and $x = 2$, and the x-axis is rotated through $360°$ about the x-axis.

Solution

Figure 13.17 show the region and the solid obtained.

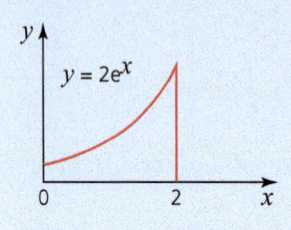

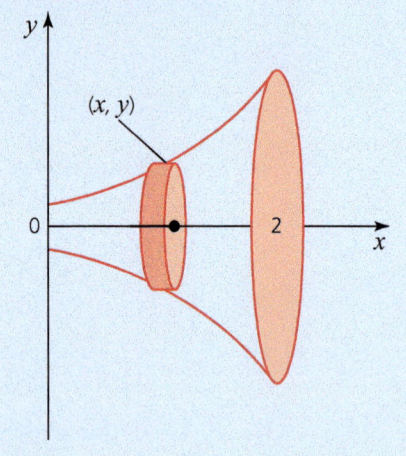

Figure 13.17

The volume V, of the solid is given by

$$V = \int \pi y^2 \, dx$$

$$= \pi \int_0^2 (2e^x)^2 \, dx$$

$$V = 4\pi \int_0^2 e^{2x} \, dx$$

$$= 4\pi \left[\frac{e^{2x}}{2}\right]_0^2$$

$$= 2\pi(e^4 - 1)$$

By symmetry, the y coordinate of the centre of mass is 0. The x coordinate is given by $\bar{x}$ in

$$V\bar{x} = \int \pi y^2 x \, dx$$

$$= \pi \int_0^2 (2e^x)^2 x \, dx$$

Therefore: $V\bar{x} = 4\pi \int_0^2 x e^{2x} \, dx$ ①

This integral requires the technique of integration by parts, expressed by the general formula

$$\int_a^b u \frac{dv}{dx} dx = [uv]_a^b - \int_a^b v \frac{du}{dx} dx$$

To find $\int xe^{2x} dx$

let $u = x \Rightarrow \frac{du}{dx} = 1,$

and let $\frac{dv}{dx} = e^{2x} \Rightarrow v = \frac{e^{2x}}{2}.$

The limits are $a = 0$ and $b = 2$.

Substituting these in the general formula, you obtain

$$\int_0^2 xe^{2x} dx = \left[x \frac{e^{2x}}{2} \right]_0^2 - \int_0^2 \frac{e^{2x}}{2} \times 1 \times dx$$

$$= \left[\frac{1}{2} xe^{2x} \right]_0^2 - \left[\frac{1}{4} e^{2x} \right]_0^2$$

$$= \left(e^4 - 0 \right) - \left(\frac{1}{4} e^4 - \frac{1}{4} \right)$$

$$= \frac{1}{4}\left(3e^4 + 1\right)$$

Substituting this and $V = 2\pi(e^4 - 1)$ in ①

$$V\bar{x} = 4\pi \int_0^2 xe^{2x} dx$$

gives $2\pi\left(e^4 - 1\right)\bar{x} = 4\pi \times \frac{1}{4}\left(3e^4 + 1\right)$

$$\bar{x} = \frac{\left(3e^4 + 1\right)}{2\left(e^4 - 1\right)}$$

$$= 1.54 \text{(correct to 2 d.p.)}.$$

The centre of mass is at $(1.54, 0)$. ← Look at the diagram and check that this seems a reasonable answer

Note

If the answer is required in decimal form, it is best to substitute the numerical value of constants such as e and π later rather than sooner. Notice that π cancels in this example.

Centres of mass

Centres of mass of composite bodies

Once the positions of the centres of mass of standard solids have been found, it is possible to use these results to find the positions of the centres of mass of composite bodies. Some useful results are summarised in the following table.

Diagram	Body	Volume	Height of c.o.m. above base
	Solid sphere, radius r	$\frac{4}{3}\pi r^3$	r (above lower point)
	Solid hemisphere radius r	$\frac{2}{3}\pi r^3$	$\frac{3}{8}r$
	Solid cone, height h, radius r	$\frac{1}{3}\pi r^2 h$	$\frac{1}{4}h$

You may also find it helpful to know the position of the centre of mass for some shells (hollow bodies with negligible wall thickness), and these are given below.

Diagram	Body	Curved Surface area	Height of c.o.m. above base
	Hollow hemisphere, radius r	$2\pi r^2$	$\frac{1}{2}r$
	Hollow cone, height h radius r	$\pi r l$ $\left(l = \sqrt{r^2 + h^2}\right)$	$\frac{1}{3}h$

Example 13.5

(i) Find the position of the centre of mass of a uniform hemispherical bowl of thickness 1 cm and inside radius 9 cm.

(ii) A light handle AB of length 18 cm is attached to a point A on the rim of the bowl in such a way that the line AB passes through the centre of the hemisphere. What angle does AB make with the vertical when the bowl is hung from the end B?

Solution

(i) Think of the bowl as a solid hemisphere of radius 10 cm from which another solid hemisphere of radius 9 cm has been removed. Then the original 10 cm hemisphere can be treated as a composite body, consisting of the bowl and the 9 cm hemisphere.

You can put all the information in a table.

	The 10 cm hemisphere =	the bowl +	the 9 cm hemisphere
Mass	$\frac{2}{3}\pi\rho \times 10^3$	$\frac{2}{3}\pi\rho(10^3 - 9^3)$	$\frac{2}{3}\pi\rho \times 9^3$
Distance from O to c.o.m	$\frac{3}{8} \times 10$	$\bar{x}$	$\frac{3}{8} \times 9$

Taking moments gives:

$$\left(\frac{2}{3}\pi\rho \times 10^3\right) \times \left(\frac{3}{8} \times 10\right) = \left(\frac{2}{3}\pi\rho(10^3 - 9^3)\times \bar{x}\right) + \left(\frac{2}{3}\pi\rho \times 9^3\right) \times \left(\frac{3}{8} \times 9\right)$$

This can be simplified by dividing through by $\frac{2}{3}\rho\pi$ to give

$$\frac{3}{8} \times 10^4 = (10^3 - 9^3)\bar{x} + \frac{3}{8} \times 9^4$$

$$\bar{x} = \frac{3(10^4 - 9^4)}{8(10^3 - 9^3)}$$

$$= 4.76 \text{ (to 3 s.f.)}$$

Hint
To save time, you could rotate your page to look at the first diagram in Figure 13.18 with BG vertical instead of drawing this.

(ii) The handle is light so the position of the centre of mass, G, is unchanged when it is attached. For equilibrium G must be vertically below B and the angle required is the angle ABG = α.

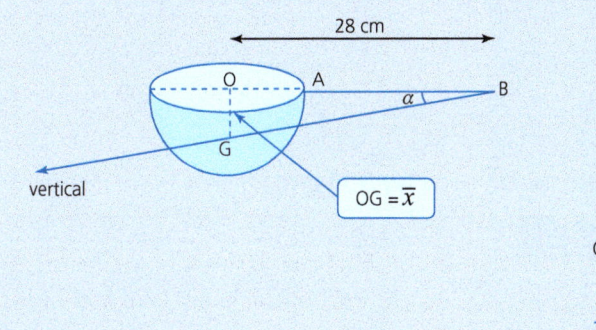

Figure 13.18

Centres of mass

From the diagram

$$\tan \alpha = \frac{OG}{OB} = \frac{\bar{x}}{28}$$

$$\Rightarrow \quad \alpha = 9.65°$$

The angle between AB and the vertical is about 10°.

> **Note**
>
> An alternative, but equivalent method for finding $\bar{x}$ is to regard the bowl as the sum of a solid hemisphere of radius 10 cm and a solid hemisphere of radius 9 cm which has negative mass. In this case, the moments equation would be written as
>
> $$\frac{2}{3}\pi\rho(10^3 - 9^3)\bar{x} = \left(\frac{2}{3}\pi\rho \times 10^3\right) \times \left(\frac{3}{8} \times 10\right) + \left(-\frac{2}{3}\pi\rho \times 9^3\right) \times \left(\frac{3}{8} \times 9\right)$$

Example 13.6

A traffic cone is modelled as a hollow cone of height 45 cm standing on a heavy cylindrical disc of radius 20 cm and height 5 cm. The mass of the disc is twice that of the cone.

(i) Find the position of the centre of mass of the traffic cone.

(ii) What is the angle of the steepest slope on which it can be placed without toppling?

Solution

(i) You can put the information in a table.

	Cone	Disc	Together
Mass	m	$2m$	$3m$
Height of c.o.m above O in cm	$\frac{1}{3} \times 45 + 5$	$\frac{1}{2} \times 5$	$\bar{y}$

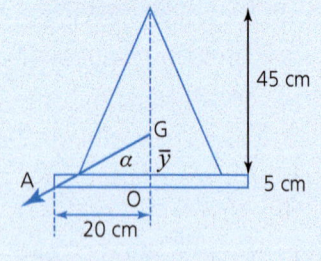

Figure 13.19

Then $\quad 20m + 5m = 3m\bar{y}$

$$\Rightarrow \quad \bar{y} = \frac{25}{3}$$

(ii) The cone begins to topple when the line GA is vertical.

Then $\tan \alpha = \dfrac{20}{\bar{y}} = \dfrac{20 \times 3}{25} = 2.4$

$\alpha = 67.4°$

The steepest slope is 67.4° to the horizontal.

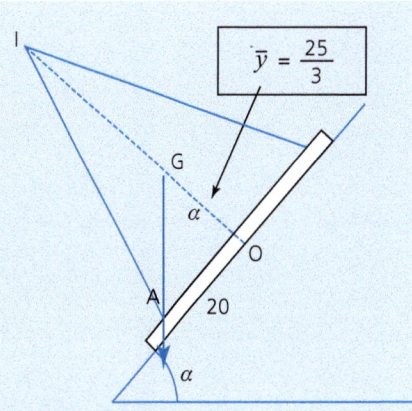

Figure 13.20

Exercise 13.2

1. In Exercise 13.1 question 1, you found the volumes of several solids of revolution produced by rotating certain regions through 360° about the x-axis. These regions are described again below and the volumes of the resulting solids of revolution are given. In each case:

   (a) draw a diagram of each solid showing an elementary disc at the point (x,y) on the curve

   (b) determine the position of its centre of mass by equating $V\bar{x}$ to a suitable integral.

   (i) $y = 2x$, the x-axis and the lines $x = 1$ and $= 3$ $\left(V = \dfrac{104\pi}{3} \right)$.

   (ii) $y = \sqrt{x}$, the x-axis and the line $x = 4$ $(V = 8\pi)$.

   (iii) $y = 2x + 1$, the x-axis and the lines $x = 1$ and $x = 5$ $\left(V = \dfrac{652\pi}{3} \right)$.

   (iv) $y = \dfrac{1}{x}$ the x-axis and the lines $x = 1$ and $x = 3$ $\left(V = \dfrac{2\pi}{3} \right)$.

   (v) $y = 3e^x$, the x-axis, the y-axis and the line $x = 1.5$ $\left(V = \dfrac{9\pi}{2}(e^3 - 1) \right)$.

   (vi) $y = \cos x$ (from $x = 0$ to $\dfrac{\pi}{2}$), the x-axis and the y-axis $\left(V = \dfrac{\pi^2}{4} \right)$.

2. In Exercise 13.1 question 2, you found the volumes of several solids of revolution produced by rotating certain regions through 360° about the y-axis. These are described again below and their volumes are given. In each case:

   (a) draw a diagram of each solid showing an elementary disc at the point (x,y) on the curve

   (b) determine the position of its centre of mass by equating $V\bar{y}$ to a suitable integral.

   (i) $y = x^3$, the y-axis and the line $y = 8$ $\left(V = \dfrac{96\pi}{5} \right)$.

   (ii) $y = 2x - 1$, the y-axis and the line $y = 5$ $(V = 18\pi)$.

   (iii) $x^2 + y^2 = 9$, the y-axis and the lines $y = 1$ and $y = 3$ $\left(V = \dfrac{28\pi}{3} \right)$.

Centres of mass

③ (i) Sketch the curve $y = x^2(2 - x)$.

(ii) Find the volume of the solid formed when the closed region between the curve and the x-axis is rotated about this axis.

(iii) Find the position of the centre of mass of this solid.

④ (i) Sketch the curve $y^2 = 4x$ (i.e. $y = \pm 2\sqrt{x}$) and shade the region between the curve, the x-axis and the lines $x = 1$ and $x = 4$.

(ii) Find the volume and the position of the centre of mass of the solid generated when the shaded region is rotated completely about the x-axis.

(iii) The region between the same portion of the curve and the y-axis is to be rotated through 360° about the y-axis. Find

(a) appropriate limits for y

(b) the volume of revolution so formed

(c) the position of the centre of mass of this new solid of revolution.

⑤ Water fills a light hemispherical bowl of radius 12 cm to a depth of 6 cm. Find the height of the centre of mass of the water above the base of the bowl.

⑥ (i) Sketch the ellipse $\dfrac{x^2}{9} + \dfrac{y^2}{4} = 1$ and shade the region lying between the curve and the axes for positive values of x and y.

(ii) Find the volume and centre of mass of the solid obtained by rotating the shaded region through 360° about the x-axis.

⑦ A toy clown is modelled by a solid cone of radius r and height h, attached to a solid hemisphere of radius r and centre O, as shown in Figure 13.21.

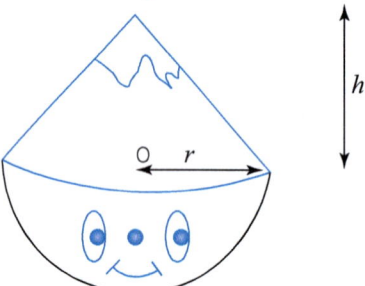

Figure 13.21

(i) Copy and complete the following table using the results above.

	Clown	Cone	Hemisphere
Mass			
Distance of c.o.m. above O	$\bar{y}$		

(ii) Write down an equation for finding $\bar{y}$. (Divide by any common factors.)

(iii) In the case when the centre of mass is at the centre of the hemisphere, use your equation to find the ratio of h to r.

(iv) In the case when the ratio of h to r is less than that obtained in part (iii), what position will the toy assume when placed with a point on the hemisphere in contact with the ground?

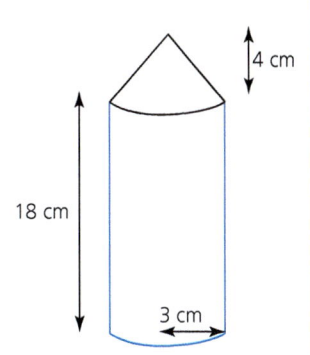

⑧ Figure 13.22 shows a container consisting of a hollow cylinder of radius 3 cm and height 18 cm with a circular base, centre O, topped by a hollow cone of the same radius and height 4 cm. The container is made of thin, uniform material. The origin O is at the centre of the base.

(i) Copy and complete the following table.

	Whole container	Cylinder base	Cylinder walls	Cone
Mass				
Distance of c.o.m. above O	$\bar{y}$			

(ii) Find the height of the centre of mass of the container above the base.

(iii) The container is placed with its circular base on a flat surface in a boat and is prevented from slipping. The boat keels over so that the surface makes an angle α to the horizontal.

Find the value of α at which the empty container will just topple over.

(iv) If the container is filled with liquid to the top of the cylinder, is it more or less likely to topple over than when it is empty? Give a reason for your answer.

⑨ The part of the curve with equation $y = (4-x)\sqrt{x}$ between $x = 0$ and $x = 4$ is denoted by C. A solid S is formed by rotating the region of the plane bounded by C and the x-axis through 2π rad about the x-axis. The lengths are measured in centimetres.

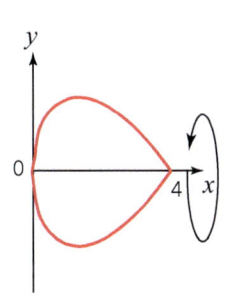

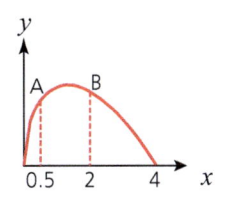

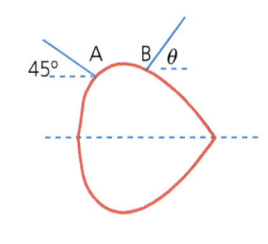

Figure 13.23

(i) Calculate the volume of S. (You may leave π in your answer.)

(ii) Calculate the position of the centre of mass of S.

The points A and B on the curve C have x coordinates 0.5 and 2, respectively, as shown in the middle diagram of Figure 13.23.

In preparation for a test in a wind tunnel, the solid S is suspended with its axis of symmetry horizontal by strings attached to the points A and B, as in the diagram on the right. The string attached to the point A is inclined at 45° to the horizontal.

(iii) Calculate the angle θ that the string attached to the point B makes with the horizontal. [MEI]

⑩ The shape of the bowl of a wine glass is produced by rotating the part of the curve $y = kx^2$ which lies between the origin and the line $y = h$ through 360° about the y-axis.

(i) Draw a diagram of the bowl and, by integration, find the volume of the solid of revolution contained within it.

Centres of mass

(ii) Show that the centre of mass of this solid is at the point $\left(0, \frac{2}{3}h\right)$ and hence write down its distance below the top of the glass. (Notice that this is independent of the value of k.)

(iii) The bowl of the glass can be modelled as a solid block of depth 9 cm with another similar block of depth 8.8 cm scooped out. Show that the centre of mass of the bowl is 4.45 cm below the rim.

(iv) The complete wine glass can be modelled by a circular base of negligible thickness and radius 3 cm, a cylindrical stem of height 8 cm and the bowl (as above) of depth 9 cm. The masses of these three parts are in the ratio 1 : 1 : 2. Find the distance of the centre of mass of the whole glass from the circular base.

(v) If the glass is carried on a tray, what is the maximum angle to the horizontal that the tray can be held without the glass toppling over. You may assume that the glass does not slide.

⑪ The region in the x, y plane between the lines $x = h$, $y = 0$ and $y = kx$, shown in the diagram on the left of Figure 13.24, is rotated through 360° about the x-axis to form a right circular cone C.

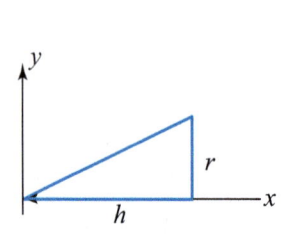

Figure 13.24

(i) Use calculus to prove that the volume of the cone C is $\frac{1}{3}\pi r^2 h$ and that the coordinates of the centre of mass are $\left(\frac{3h}{4}, 0\right)$.

A hollow cone B is formed by removing from C a similar smaller cone. The smaller cone removed has base radius kr and height kh, where $0 < k < 1$. This is shown in the diagram on the right with the cone B now standing upright with the centre of its base at the origin.

(ii) Show that the coordinates of the centre of mass of the hollow cone B are $\left(0, \dfrac{h(1-k^4)}{4(1-k^3)}\right)$.

For a cone of small thickness, k is close to 1 and so may be written as $k = 1 - \varepsilon$, where ε is small.

(iii) Show that $k^3 = 1 - 3\varepsilon$ when ε is very small, and find a similar expression for k^4 in terms of ε.

(iv) Hence show that for a hollow cone made of uniform material of negligible thickness, the centre of mass is one third of the way from the centre of the base to the vertex.

[MEI]

3 Centres of mass of plane regions

> **ACTIVITY 13.1**
> Find the position of the centre of mass of a semicircular protractor by suspending it from one corner. In what ratio does it divide the axis of symmetry? In Chapter 7 you found the centres of mass of some plane shapes made up from rectangles. In this section, that work is taken further to include shapes with curved edges, like the protractor in the Activity you have just done.

Vocabulary

- A thin plane surface, like a protractor, is called a **lamina** (plural laminae).
- The laminae considered in this chapter are all **uniform**; that is, they have the same mass per unit area, throughout. The letter σ (sigma) is often used to denote this area density.
- The **centroid** of a plane region is the centre of mass of a lamina of the same shape and negligible thickness.

Calculus methods for determining the centre of mass of a lamina

When a lamina or plane region is bounded by curves for which equations are known, you can use calculus methods to find the position of its centre of mass.

When a lamina occupies a region between a curve and x-axis, as shown in Figure 13.25, it can be divided into elementary strips of width δx and height y. One such strip, situated at the point (x, y) on the curve is shown. The dot indicates its centre of mass. The mass per unit area of the lamina is denoted by σ.

The height of the strip is y and its width is δx, so its mass δM is $\sigma y \delta x$.

The coordinates of the centre of mass of the strip are $\left(x, \frac{y}{2}\right)$ so $\bar{x}$ can be found using

$$(\Sigma \delta M)\bar{x} = \Sigma(\delta M \times x)$$

Substituting $\delta M = \sigma y \delta x$ in

$$(\Sigma \delta M)\bar{x} = \Sigma(\delta M x)$$

gives

$$(\Sigma \sigma y \delta x)\bar{x} = \Sigma(\sigma y \delta x \times x)$$

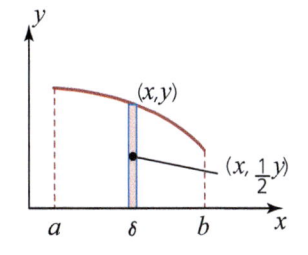

Figure 13.25

Centres of mass of plane regions

If the material is uniform, the mass per unit area is constant and so the equation can be divided through by σ. In that case,

$$(\Sigma \, y\delta x)\bar{x} = \Sigma(yx\delta x)$$

and in the limit as $\delta x \to 0$

$$\left(\int_a^b y \, dx\right)\bar{x} = \int_a^b xy \, dx \quad \text{①}$$

Notice that the first integral gives the area of the lamina.

You can find $\bar{y}$ in a similar way. Using the y coordinate, $\frac{y}{2}$, of the centre of the strip and dividing by σ as before

$$(\Sigma \, y\delta x)\bar{y} = \Sigma\left(y\delta x \times \frac{y}{2}\right)$$

In the limit as $\delta x \to 0$ this becomes

$$\left(\int_a^b y \, dx\right)\bar{y} = \int_a^b \frac{y^2}{2} \, dx \quad \text{②}$$

The equations ① and ② can be combined to give the coordinates of the centre of mass of the lamina in the form of a position vector:

$$A\begin{pmatrix} \bar{x} \\ \bar{y} \end{pmatrix} = \begin{pmatrix} \int_a^b xy \, dx \\ \int_a^b \frac{y^2}{2} \, dx \end{pmatrix}$$

where A is the total area of the lamina or $\int_a^b y \, dx$.

Example 13.7

Find the position of the centre of mass of a uniform semicircular lamina of radius r.

Solution

Figure 13.26 shows the lamina.

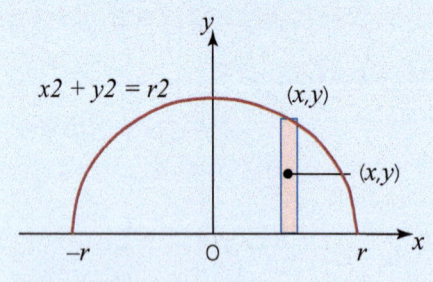

Figure 13.26

By symmetry, $\bar{x} = 0$.

To find $\bar{y}$, use $A\bar{y} = \int_a^b \frac{y^2}{2} \, dx$.

In this case, $A = \frac{1}{2}\pi r^2$ (because the lamina is a semicircle), and the limits are $-r$ and $+r$.

Since the equation of the curve is $x^2 + y^2 = r^2$, you can write y^2 as $r^2 - x^2$. This gives

$$\frac{1}{2}\pi r^2 \bar{y} = \int_{-r}^{r} \frac{1}{2}(r^2 - x^2)\,dx$$

$$= \frac{1}{2}\left[r^2 x - \frac{x^3}{3}\right]_{-r}^{r}$$

$$\Rightarrow \frac{1}{2}\pi r^2 \bar{y} = \frac{1}{2}\left\{\left(r^3 - \frac{r^3}{3}\right) - \left(-r^3 - \frac{(-r)^3}{3}\right)\right\}$$

$$= \frac{2}{3}r^3$$

$$\Rightarrow \bar{y} = \frac{4r}{3\pi}$$

This is the distance of the centre of mass of the semicircular lamina from its centre.

It is roughly 0.4 times the radius. How does this compare with your own measurements in the Activity on page 361?

Example 13.8

Find the coordinates of the centroid of the region between the curve $y = 4 - x^2$ and the positive x- and y-axes.

Solution

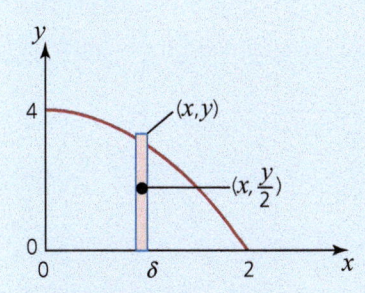

Figure 13.27

It is best to find the area, A, first. In this case,

$$A = \int y\,dx$$

$$= \int_0^2 (4 - x^2)\,dx$$

$$= \left[4x - \frac{x^3}{3}\right]_0^2$$

$$= \left(8 - \frac{8}{3}\right) - 0$$

$$= \frac{16}{3}$$

Centres of mass of plane regions

Then use $A\begin{pmatrix} \bar{x} \\ \bar{y} \end{pmatrix} = \begin{pmatrix} \int_0^2 xy\,dx \\ \int_0^2 \frac{y^2}{2}\,dx \end{pmatrix}$ to give

$$A\bar{x} = \int_0^2 (4-x^2)x\,dx \qquad A\bar{y} = \int_0^2 \frac{(4-x^2)^2}{2}\,dx$$

$$= \int_0^2 (4x - x^3)\,dx \qquad = \int_0^2 \frac{16 - 8x^2 + x^4}{2}\,dx$$

$$= \left[\frac{4x^2}{2} - \frac{x^4}{4}\right]_0^2 \qquad = \frac{1}{2}\left[16x - \frac{8x^3}{3} + \frac{x^5}{5}\right]_0^2$$

$$= 4 \qquad\qquad\qquad = \frac{128}{15}$$

Substituting $A = \frac{16}{3}$ gives

$$\bar{x} = 4 \times \frac{3}{16} \qquad\qquad \bar{y} = \frac{128}{15} \times \frac{3}{16}$$

$$\bar{x} = \frac{3}{4} = 0.75 \qquad\qquad \bar{y} = \frac{8}{5} = 1.6$$

The coordinates of the centroid are (0.75, 1.6).

Using strips parallel to the x-axis

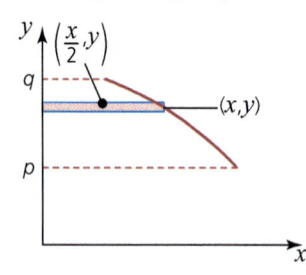

Figure 13.28

Sometimes it is necessary (or easier) to divide the region into strips parallel to the x-axis, as shown in Figure 13.28. The area A is then $\int_p^q x\,dy$ and

$$A\begin{pmatrix} \bar{x} \\ \bar{y} \end{pmatrix} = \begin{pmatrix} \int_p^q \frac{x^2}{2}\,dy \\ \int_p^q yx\,dy \end{pmatrix}$$

> **Note**
> In this case, the x in each integral should be written in terms of y. When there is a choice between methods, choose the one that gives the easier integral to evaluate.

Exercise 13.3

① The regions (A) to (D) below are all symmetrical about one axis and are defined in terms of the lines and curves which form their boundaries. For each region:

(i) Draw a sketch of the region and, using symmetry, write down one coordinate of the centroid G.

(ii) Show on your diagram an elementary strip parallel to the y-axis situated at the point (x, y) on the curve and mark a dot at its centre. Show the coordinates of this dot on your diagram.

(iii) Write down the area of the strip in terms of x and δx.

(iv) Use $A\bar{x} = \int xy\, dx$ or $A\bar{y} = \int \frac{y^2}{2}\, dx$, as appropriate, to find the other coordinate of G.

   (a) The curve $y = 4 - x^2$ and the x-axis.

   (b) The curves $y = e^x$ and $y = -e^x$, the y-axis and the line $x = 1$.

   (c) The curve $y^2 = 4x$ (i.e. $y = \pm 2\sqrt{x}$) and the line $x = 4$. (Take care over the length of the strip.)

   (d) The curve $y = \sin x$ between $x = 0, x = \pi$ and the x-axis.

② In Figure 13.29, OAB is a uniform right-angled triangular lamina. OA = 6 cm and OB = 12 cm.

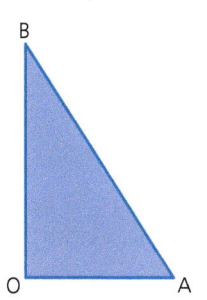

Figure 13.29

(i) Write down the area of the triangle.

(ii) Using OA as the x-axis and OB as the y-axis, find the equation of the line AB.

(iii) Find, by integration, the coordinates $(\bar{x}, \bar{y})$ of the centre of mass, G, of the triangle and verify that $\bar{x} = \frac{1}{3}OA$ and $\bar{y} = \frac{1}{3}OB$.

③ Find the centroid of the region shown in Figure 13.30. It is bounded by the curve $y = \frac{1}{x}$, the x-axis and the lines $x = \frac{1}{2}$ and $x = 2$.

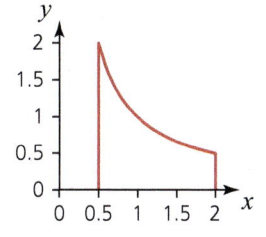

Figure 13.30

④ (i) Sketch the curve $y = x^2(3 - x)$.

(ii) Find the coordinates of the centroid of the region between this curve and the x-axis. (Note that this region is not symmetrical.)

Centres of mass of plane regions

⑤ (i) Draw a diagram showing the region R bounded by the curve $y^2 = 4x$ and the line $x = 4$. Mark on your diagram a strip parallel to the x-axis, passing through a general point (x, y) on the curve.

(ii) Write down the area of the strip and the x coordinate of its centroid.

(iii) Find, by integrating with respect to y, the centre of mass of the region R.

⑥ Find the coordinates of the centre of mass of each of the following uniform laminae.

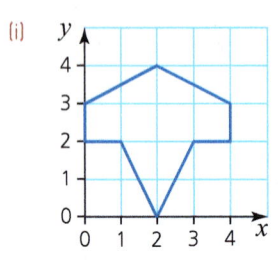

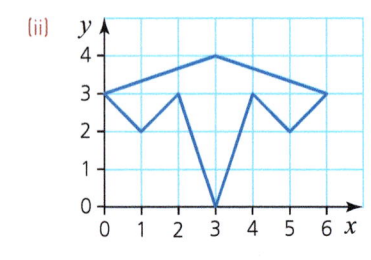

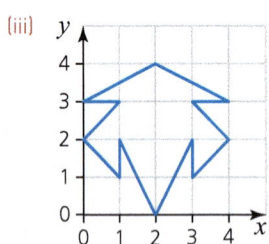

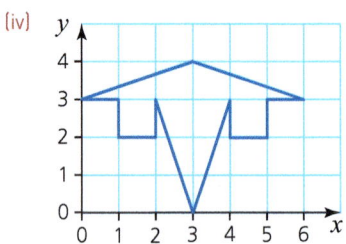

(i)

(ii)

(iii)

(iv)

⑦ (i) The vertices of a uniform triangular lamina OAB are $(0, 0)$, $(a, 0)$ and $(0, b)$.

Write down the coordinates of its centre of mass.

Figure 13.31 shows another triangular lamina, PQR. It is divided into elementary strips parallel to QR, as shown.

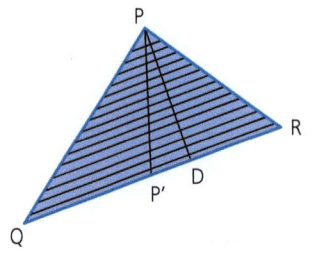

Figure 13.31

(ii) Explain why the centre of mass, G, of PQR lies on the median PP'.

(iii) PQR is made up of two right-angled triangles, PDQ and PDR.

Draw a diagram showing the positions of the centres of mass of PDQ and PDR. Hence show that PG and GP' are in the ratio 2:1.

In questions 8–10 you can use the result for the position of the centre of mass of a semicircle found in Example 13.7. It is at a distance $\frac{4r}{3\pi}$ from the centre.

⑧

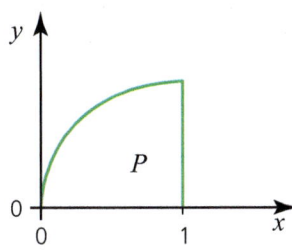

Figure 13.32

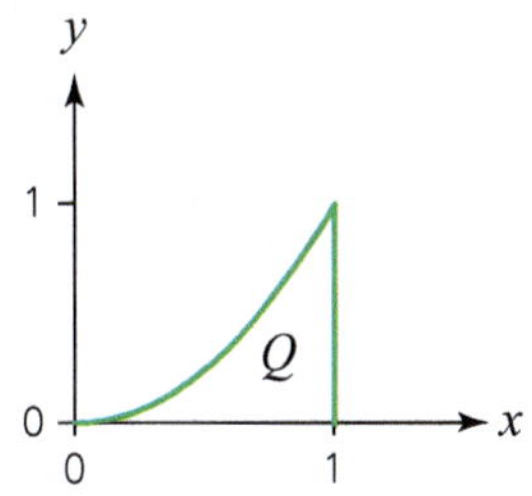

Figure 13.33

(i) The region P of a uniform lamina satisfies the inequalities $(x-1)^2 + y^2 \leq 1$, $0 \leq x \leq 1$, and $y \geq 0$ (i.e. P is a quadrant of a circle of radius 1 and centre $(1, 0)$, as shown in Figure 13.32). Find $\bar{y}$ for P and hence show that the coordinates of the centre of mass of P are $\left(\dfrac{3\pi-4}{3\pi}, \dfrac{4}{3\pi}\right)$.

(ii) The region Q of a uniform lamina satisfies the inequalities $y \leq x^2$, $0 \leq x \leq 1$ and $y \geq 0$, as shown in Figure 13.33. Find the coordinates of the centre of mass of Q.

The uniform lamina R is obtained by taking the region P defined above and then removing the region Q, as shown in Figure 13.34.

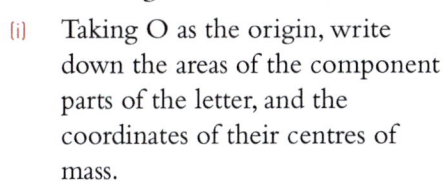

(iii) Find the coordinates of the centre of mass of R, referred to the axes shown in Figure 13.34, giving your answers to three decimal places. [MEI]

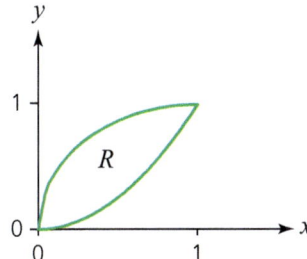

⑨ A letter P is made up from a rectangle and a semicircle with a smaller semicircle cut out as shown in Figure 13.35.

(i) Taking O as the origin, write down the areas of the component parts of the letter, and the coordinates of their centres of mass.

(ii) Find the coordinates of the centre of mass of the letter.

(iii) What angle will AO make with the vertical if the letter is hung from the corner A?

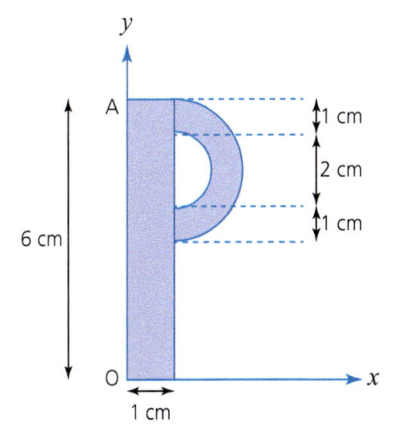

Figure 13.34

Figure 13.35

Centres of mass of plane regions

⑩ (i) Draw a diagram to show the circle $x^2 + y^2 = 4$ and the line $x = 1$.

(ii) Show that the area of the minor segment of the circle $x^2 + y^2 = 4$ which is cut off by the line $x = 1$ is
$$A = \frac{4\pi}{3} - \sqrt{3}$$

(iii) Find the x coordinate of the centre of mass of this segment by finding a suitable integral between the limits 1 and 2.

(iv) A crescent is formed by removing a segment of this shape from a semicircle of radius $\sqrt{3}$ units. Find the position of the centre of mass of this crescent.

(v) Find the angle between the diameter of the semicircle and the vertical when the crescent is hung from one end of this diameter.

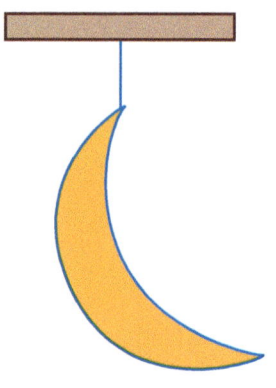

⑪ (i) Find the position of the centre of mass of the region A defined by the inequalities $x^2 - 1 \leq y \leq 1 - x^2$, $0 \leq x \leq 1$.

Figure 13.36

(ii) Find the position of the centre of mass of the region B defined by the inequalities $0.25x^2 - 1 \leq y \leq 1 - 0.25x^2$, $0 \leq x \leq 2$.

A pendant C is made up from a uniform lamina in such a way that region A is removed from region B as shown in Figure 13.37.

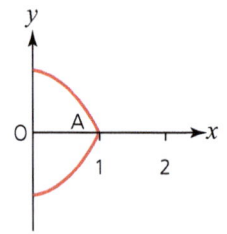

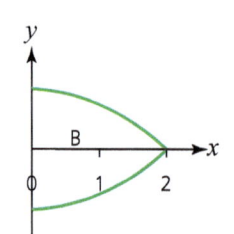

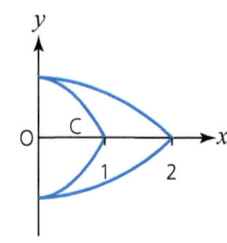

Figure 13.37

(iii) Find the position of the centre of mass of the pendant.

(iv) The pendant is suspended from a vertical string attached to the point Y with coordinates (0, 1). Find the angle that OY makes with the vertical.

⑫ (i) Show that the centre of mass of a uniform lamina in the form of a semicircle of radius a is at a distance $\frac{4a}{3\pi}$ from the straight edge.

(ii) A uniform lamina is in the form of an isosceles triangle OBC, in which OB = OC and BC = $2a$, with a semicircle of radius a on the side BC. If AO = $h (> a)$ and the centre of mass of this lamina is at G, find OG in terms of a and h.

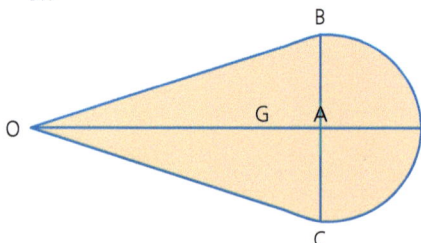

Figure 13.38

(iii) If G coincides with A, show that $\frac{h}{a} = \sqrt{2}$.

⑬ Find the coordinates of the centre of mass of the area enclosed between the curve $y = \sqrt{x^3}$ and the straight line $y = 2x$.

⑭ Find the coordinates of the centre of mass of the uniform lamina made from the region between the curves $y = 4 - x^2$ and $y = x^2$ and the y-axis.

⑮ The region between the curve $y = 4 - x^2$ and the curves $y = 2x - x^2$ and $y = -2x - x^2$ is shown in Figure 13.39.

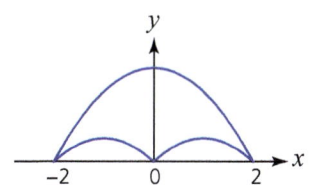

Figure 13.39

Find the position of the centre of mass of the region.

⑯ Figure 13.40 is composed of a semicircle of radius R from which two semicircles of radius r are removed and a semicircle of radius $R - 2r$ is added.

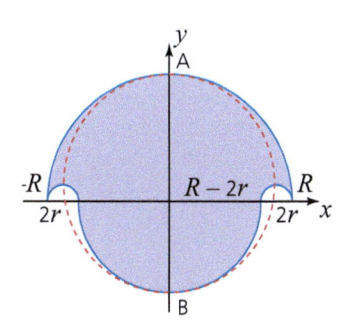

Figure 13.40

(i) Show that the area of the shape is the same as that of a circle centred at $(0, r)$ and of radius $R - r$.

(ii) Find the position of the centre of mass of the shape.

> **Note**
> Archimedes proved in his *Book of Lemmas* that this figure, which he called *salinon* (salt cellar), has an area equal to the circle with AB as diameter.

⑰ (i) Find the area and centre of mass of each of the seven pieces constituting this tangram square in Figure 13.41.

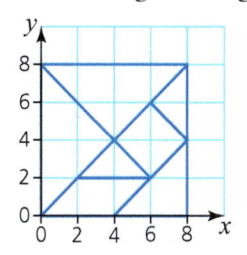

Figure 13.41

(ii) Find the centre of mass of the following shapes made up of the seven pieces shown in (i).

(a)

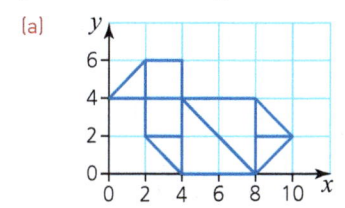

Figure 13.42

Centres of mass of plane regions

(b)

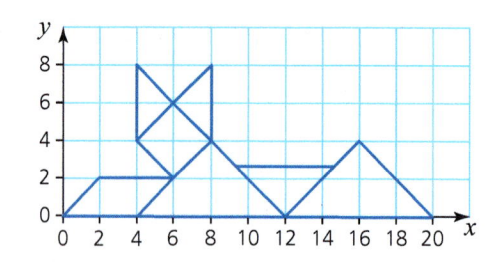

Figure 13.43

> **Historical note**
>
> Archimedes of Syracuse (287 BC–212 BC) was an ancient Greek mathematician. He anticipated modern calculus and analysis by applying concepts of infinitesimals and the method of exhaustion to derive and rigorously prove a range of geometrical theorems. He was able to apply mathematics to physical phenomena, and thus founded hydrostatics and statics, including an explanation of the principle of the lever. He is credited with designing innovative machines such as the screw pump, compound pulleys and defensive war machines to protect his native Syracuse from invasion.

KEY POINTS

Volumes of revolution

1 About the x-axis:

$$V = \int_a^b \pi y^2 \, dx$$

   About the y-axis:

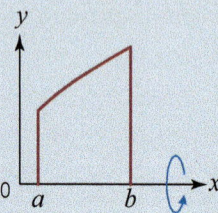

$$V = \int_p^q \pi x^2 \, dy$$

Figure 13.44

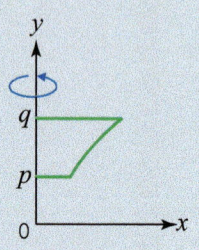

Figure 13.45

Centres of mass of uniform bodies

2 For a volume of revolution

   About the x-axis:

$$\left(\int_a^b \pi y^2 \, dx \right) \bar{x} = \int_a^b \pi x y^2 \, dx$$

   and $\bar{y} = 0$

   About the y-axis:

   $\bar{x} = 0$ and

$$\left(\int_p^q \pi x^2 \, dy \right) \bar{y} = \int_p^q \pi y x^2 \, dy$$

3   For a uniform plane lamina, area A, as shown in Figures 13.46 and 13.47

$$A = \int_a^b y\,dx \qquad\qquad A = \int_p^q x\,dy$$

$$A\begin{pmatrix}\overline{x}\\\overline{y}\end{pmatrix} = \begin{pmatrix}\int_a^b xy\,dx\\\int_a^b \dfrac{y^2}{2}\,dx\end{pmatrix} \qquad A\begin{pmatrix}\overline{x}\\\overline{y}\end{pmatrix} = \begin{pmatrix}\int_p^q \dfrac{x^2}{2}\,dy\\\int_p^q yx\,dy\end{pmatrix}$$

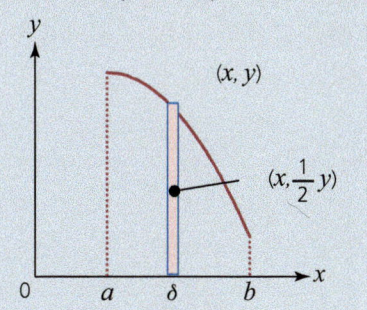

Figure 13.46

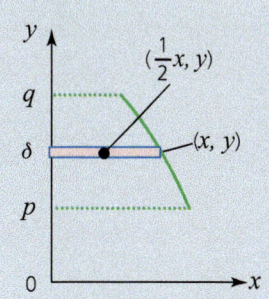

Figure 13.47

LEARNING OUTCOMES

When you have completed this chapter, you should be able to
- calculate the volume generated by rotating a plane region about an axis
- use calculus methods to calculate the centre of mass of a solid body formed by rotating a plane region about an axis
- find the centre of mass of a compound body, parts of which are solids of revolution
- use calculus methods to find the position of the centre of mass of a plane lamina
- find the position of the centre of mass of a compound shape made up of plane regions.

14 Oblique impact

Pray always for all the learned, the oblique, the delicate. Let them not be quite forgotten at the throne of God when the simple come into their kingdom.

Evelyn Waugh

Discussion point
In what direction should the white cue ball be struck for the blue ball to be potted? Is it possible to pot the red ball?

1 Impulse and momentum in more than one dimension

In Chapter 6 you met situations involving impact between objects moving along a straight line. This involved working with momentum and impulse. It is summed up by the equation

final momentum = initial momentum + impulse

In this chapter, these ideas are extended to motion in more than one direction.

Both impulse and momentum are vectors. The impulse of a force is in the direction of the force and the momentum of a moving object is in the direction of its velocity. So the equation above can be represented as the vector diagram in Figure 14.1.

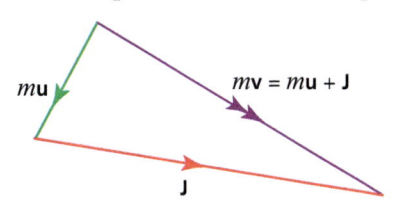

Figure 14.1

Written in symbols, the equation is

$$m\mathbf{v} = m\mathbf{u} + \mathbf{J}$$

The quantities $\mathbf{u}$ and $\mathbf{v}$ can usually be measured but $\mathbf{J}$ cannot and has to be inferred, using the impulse-momentum equation in the form

$$\mathbf{J} = m\mathbf{v} - m\mathbf{u}$$

Figure 14.2 shows how this applies to a ball which changes direction when it is hit by a bat.

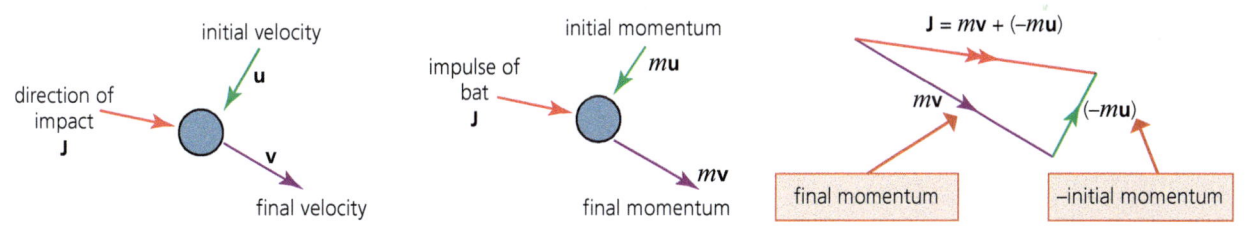

Figure 14.2

Example 14.1

In a game of snooker, the white cue ball of mass $0.2\,\text{kg}$ is hit towards a stationary red ball at $0.8\,\text{m}\,\text{s}^{-1}$. The balls are smooth and have the same mass and radius. After the collision the cue ball is moving at $0.6\,\text{m}\,\text{s}^{-1}$ having been deflected through $30°$.

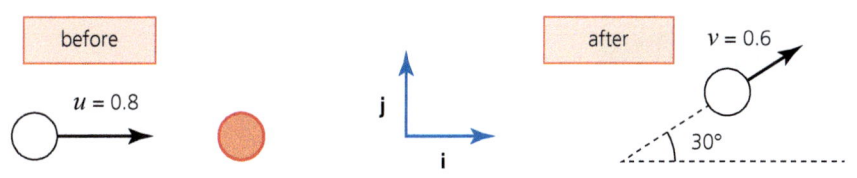

Figure 14.3

Find the impulse on the cue ball and show this in a vector diagram.

Impulse and momentum in more than one dimension

Solution

In terms of unit vectors **i** and **j** the velocities of the ball before and after the collision are given by:

$$\mathbf{u} = 0.8\mathbf{i}$$
$$\mathbf{v} = 0.6\cos 30°\,\mathbf{i} + 0.6\sin 30°\,\mathbf{j}$$

Then, using the impulse–momentum equation:

$$\mathbf{J} = m\mathbf{v} - m\mathbf{u}$$
$$= 0.2(0.6\cos 30°\,\mathbf{i} + 0.6\sin 30°\,\mathbf{j}) - 0.2(0.8\mathbf{i})$$
$$= -0.056\mathbf{i} + 0.06\mathbf{j}$$

Magnitude of impulse:
$$= \sqrt{0.056^2 + 0.06^2}$$
$$= 0.082$$

Direction of impulse:

$$\tan\alpha = \frac{0.06}{0.056}$$
$$\alpha = 47°$$
$$\theta = 133°$$

The impulse has magnitude 0.082 N s at an angle of 133° to the initial motion of the ball.

Figure 14.4

This is shown in the vector diagram, Figure 14.5. Note that the impulse–momentum equation shows the direction of the impulsive force acting on the cue ball.

> **Discussion point**
> What happens to the red ball?

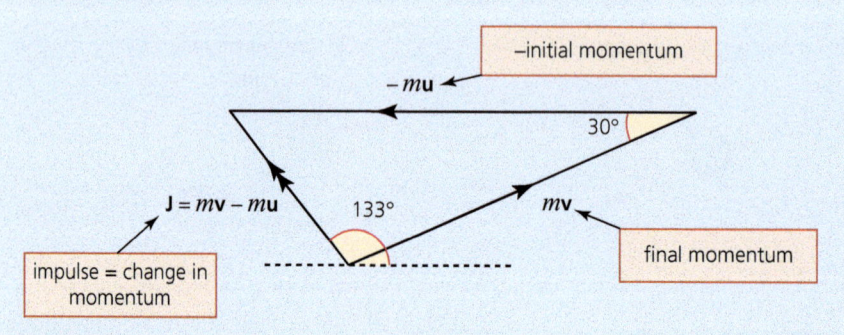

Figure 14.5

Example 14.2

A hockey ball of mass 0.15 kg is moving at $4\,\text{m s}^{-1}$ parallel to the side of a pitch when it is struck by a blow from a hockey stick that exerts an impulse of 4 N s at an angle of 120° to its direction of motion. Find the final velocity of the ball.

Solution

The Figure 14.6 shows the motion of the ball.

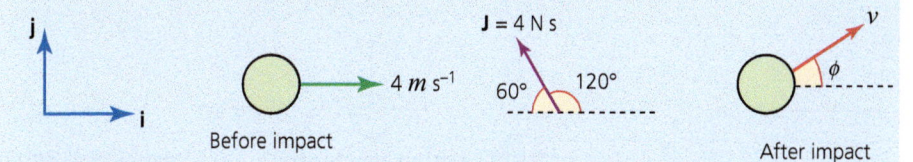

Figure 14.6

In terms of unit vectors **i** and **j**:

$$\mathbf{u} = 4\mathbf{i}$$

and

$$\mathbf{J} = -4\cos 60°\,\mathbf{i} + 4\sin 60°\,\mathbf{j}$$
$$= -2\mathbf{i} + 3.46\mathbf{j}$$

Using

$$\mathbf{J} = m\mathbf{v} - m\mathbf{u}$$
$$-2\mathbf{i} + 3.46\mathbf{j} = 0.15\mathbf{v} - 0.15 \times 4\mathbf{i}$$
$$\Rightarrow \quad 0.15\mathbf{v} = -2\mathbf{i} + 0.6\mathbf{i} + 3.46\mathbf{j}$$
$$\Rightarrow \quad 0.15\mathbf{v} = -1.4\mathbf{i} + 3.46\mathbf{j}$$
$$\Rightarrow \quad \mathbf{v} = -9.33\mathbf{i} + 23.1\mathbf{j}$$
$$V = \sqrt{9.33^2 + 23.1^2} = 24.9\,\text{m s}^{-1}$$
$$\tan\theta = \frac{23.1}{9.33} \Rightarrow \theta = 68°$$
$$\phi = 180° - 68°$$
$$= 112°$$

Figure 14.7

After the blow, the ball has a velocity of magnitude $24.9\,\text{m s}^{-1}$ at an angle of $112°$ to the original direction of motion.

Oblique impact of a sphere on a plane

When an object hits a smooth plane there can be no impulse parallel to the plane so the component of momentum and hence velocity, is unchanged in this direction. Perpendicular to the plane, the momentum is changed but Newton's law of impact still applies.

Figure 14.8 show the components of the velocity of a ball immediately before and after it hits a smooth plane with coefficient of restitution e.

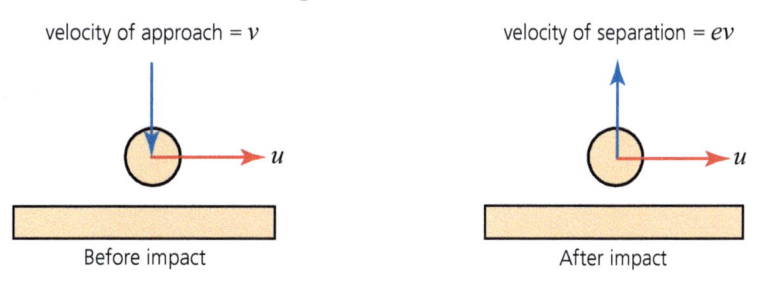

Figure 14.8

Impulse and momentum in more than one dimension

When the ball is travelling with speed U at an angle α to the plane, the components of the final velocity are $U\cos\alpha$ parallel to the plane and $eU\sin\alpha$, perpendicular to the plane.

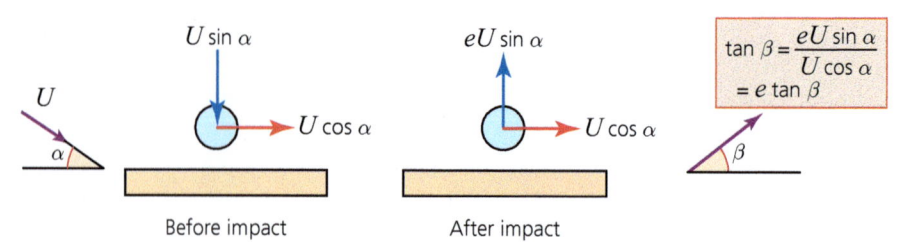

$$\tan\beta = \frac{eU\sin\alpha}{U\cos\alpha} = e\tan\beta$$

Figure 14.9

The **impulse** on the ball is equal to final momentum − initial momentum. This is perpendicular to the plane because there is no change in momentum parallel to the plane.

In Figure 14.8 the impulse is

$$mev - m(-v) = (1+e)mv \text{ upwards.}$$

In Figure 14.9 the impulse is

$$meU\sin\alpha - m(-U\sin\alpha) = (1+e)mU\sin\alpha \text{ upwards.}$$

Whenever an impact takes place, energy is likely to be lost. In the cases illustrated in Figure 14.9, the **loss in kinetic energy** is

$$\tfrac{1}{2}m(u^2+v^2) - \tfrac{1}{2}m(u^2+e^2v^2) = \tfrac{1}{2}m(1-e^2)v^2$$

or

$$\tfrac{1}{2}m(1-e^2)U^2\sin^2\alpha$$

> **Discussion point**
> What happens to the ball when $e = 0$ and $e = 1$?

Example 14.3

A ball of mass 0.2 kg moving at $12\,\text{m s}^{-1}$ hits a smooth horizontal plane at an angle of $75°$ to the horizontal. The coefficient of restitution is 0.5. Find

(i) the impulse on the ball

(ii) the impulse on the plane

(iii) the kinetic energy lost by the ball.

Solution

(i) Figure 14.10 shows the velocities before and after impact.

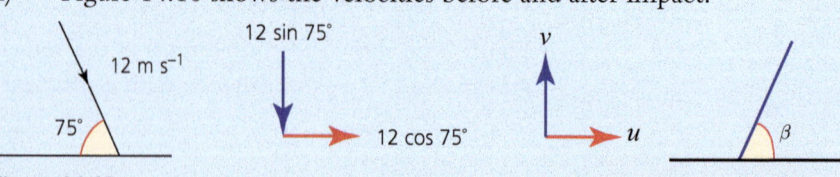

Figure 14.10

Parallel to the plane: $u = 12\cos 75°$ ◄ No change in velocity parallel to the plane.

Perpendicular to the plane: $v = 0.5 \times 12\sin 75°$ ◄ Using Newton's law of impact with $e = 0.5$.

$\qquad\qquad\qquad\qquad\quad = 6\sin 75°$

The impulse on the ball = final momentum − initial momentum

$$\mathbf{J} = 0.2 \begin{pmatrix} 12\cos 75° \\ 6\sin 75° \end{pmatrix} - 0.2 \begin{pmatrix} 12\cos 75° \\ -12\sin 75° \end{pmatrix}$$

> Using directions **i** and **j** as shown.

$$= \begin{pmatrix} 0 \\ 3.6\sin 75° \end{pmatrix}$$

The impulse on the ball is $3.6\sin 75°$ **j**, that is, $3.48\,\text{Ns}$ perpendicular to the plane and upwards in the **j** direction.

(ii) By Newton's third law, the impulse on the plane is equal and opposite to the impulse on the ball. It is $3.48\,\text{Ns}$ perpendicular to the plane in the direction of $-\mathbf{j}$.

(iii) The initial kinetic energy $= \frac{1}{2} \times 0.2 \times 12^2 = 14.4\,\text{J}$

Final kinetic energy $= \frac{1}{2} \times 0.2 \times \left[(12\cos 75°)^2 + (6\sin 75°)^2\right]$
$= 4.32\,\text{J}$

Loss in kinetic energy $= 14.4 - 4.32 = 10.1\,\text{J}$ (3 s.f.)

Example 14.4

A ball moving with speed $10\,\text{m s}^{-1}$ hits a smooth horizontal plane at an angle of $60°$ to the horizontal. The coefficient of restitution between the ball and the surface is $\frac{1}{3}$. The ball rebounds with speed v at an angle β with the surface.

(i) Find v.

(ii) Find β.

Solution

(i)

Figure 14.11

Before impact / After impact

> Using $\sin 60° = \frac{\sqrt{3}}{2}$ and $\cos 60° = \frac{1}{2}$.

$$v = \sqrt{\left(\frac{5}{\sqrt{3}}\right)^2 + 5^2} = \sqrt{\frac{100}{3}} = 5.77\,\text{m s}^{-1}$$

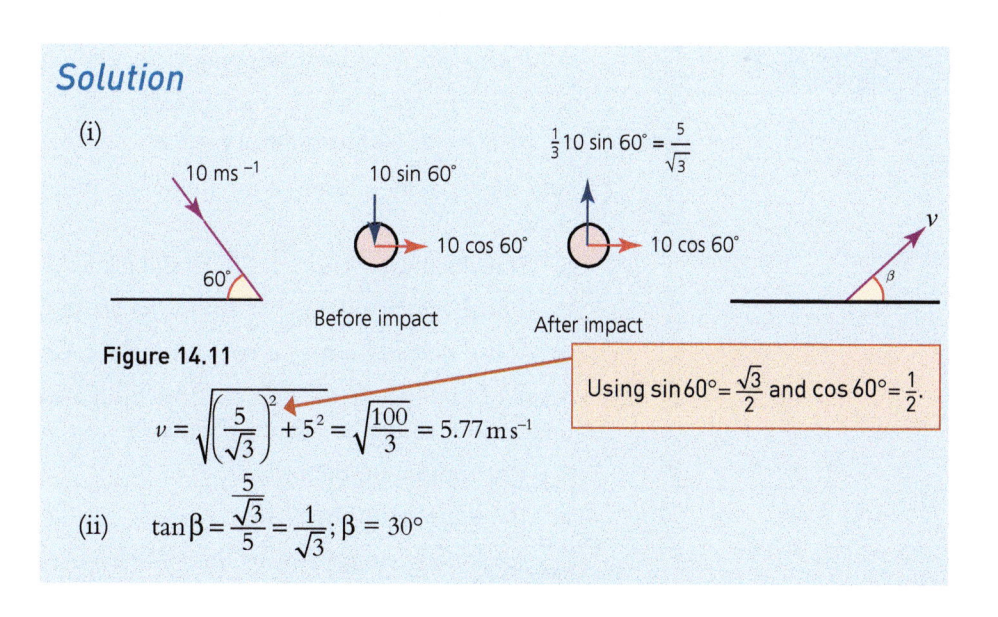

(ii) $\tan\beta = \dfrac{\frac{5}{\sqrt{3}}}{5} = \dfrac{1}{\sqrt{3}}; \beta = 30°$

Impulse and momentum in more than one dimension

Exercise 14.1

① A snooker ball of mass 0.08 kg is travelling with speed 3.5 m s^{-1} when it hits the cushion at an angle of 60°. After the impact the ball is travelling with speed 2 m s^{-1} at an angle of 30° to the cushion.

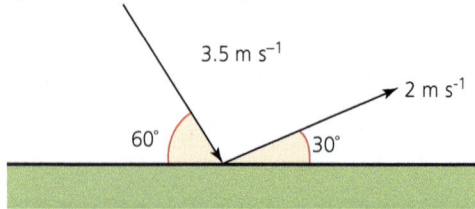

Figure 14.12

(i) Draw accurate scale diagrams to represent the following vectors:

the momentum of the ball before impact

the momentum of the ball after impact

the change in momentum of the ball during impact.

(ii) Use your answers to part (i) to **estimate** the magnitude and direction of the impulse acting on the ball.

(iii) Resolve the velocity of the ball before and after the impact into components parallel and perpendicular to the cushion.

(iv) Use your answers to part (iii) to **calculate** the impulse which acts on the ball during its impact with the cushion. Comment on your answers.

② A hockey ball of mass 0.15 kg is travelling with velocity $12\mathbf{i} - 8\mathbf{j}$ (in m s^{-1}), where the unit vectors $\mathbf{i}$ and $\mathbf{j}$ are in horizontal directions parallel and perpendicular to the length of the pitch, and the vector $\mathbf{k}$ is vertically upwards. The ball is hit by Jane with an impulse $-4.8\mathbf{i} + 1.2\mathbf{j}$.

(i) What is the velocity of the ball immediately after Jane has hit it?

The ball goes straight, without losing any speed, to Fatima in the opposite team who hits it without stopping it. Its velocity is now $14\mathbf{i} + 4\mathbf{j} + 3\mathbf{k}$.

(ii) What impulse does Fatima give the ball?

(iii) Which player hits the ball harder?

③ Find the velocity of each of the following after one impact with a smooth plane.

(i) Initial velocity 4 m s^{-1} at 20° to the plane. Coefficient of restitution 0.5.

(ii) Initial velocity 10 m s^{-1} at 40° to the plane. Coefficient of restitution 0.1.

(iii) Initial velocity u m s^{-1} at α° to the plane. Coefficient of restitution 0.8.

④ A ball of mass 0.1 kg moving at 10 m s^{-1} hits a smooth horizontal plane at an angle of 80° to the horizontal. The coefficient of restitution is 0.6. Find

(i) the impulse on the ball

(ii) the impulse on the plane

(iii) the kinetic energy lost by the particle.

⑤ A particle of mass 0.05 kg moving at 8 m s⁻¹ hits a smooth horizontal plane at an angle of 45° to the horizontal. The coefficient of restitution is 0.6. Find

    (i) the impulse on the particle

    (ii) the impulse on the plane

    (iii) the kinetic energy lost by the particle.

⑥ A ball of mass m kg moving at u m s⁻¹ hits a smooth horizontal plane at an angle of $\alpha°$ to the horizontal. The coefficient of restitution is 0.

    (i) Find the impulse on the ball.

    (ii) Show that the kinetic energy lost is $\frac{1}{2}mu^2\sin^2\alpha$.

⑦ Show that the kinetic energy lost by a particle of mass m kg which hits a smooth plane when it is moving with velocity u m s⁻¹ at an angle of $\alpha°$ to the plane is $\frac{1}{2}mu^2(1-e^2)\sin^2\alpha$, where e is the coefficient of restitution.

⑧ A ball is hit from level ground with initial components of velocity u_x m s⁻¹ horizontally and u_y vertically. Assume the ball is a particle and ignore air resistance.

    (i) Show that its horizontal range is $R = \dfrac{2u_x u_y}{g}$.

The ball bounces on the ground with coefficient of restitution 0.6.

    (ii) How much further does it travel horizontally before the next bounce?

    (iii) Find an expression for the horizontal range after the nth bounce.

    (iv) By considering the sum of a geometric series, calculate the total horizontal distance travelled up to the sixth bounce.

⑨ A small marble is projected horizontally over the edge of a table 0.8 m high at a speed of 2.5 m s⁻¹ and bounces on smooth horizontal ground with coefficient of restitution 0.7.

Calculate

    (i) the components of the velocity of the marble just before it hits the ground

    (ii) its horizontal distance from the edge of the table when it first hits the ground

    (iii) the horizontal distance travelled between the first and second bounces

    (iv) the horizontal distance travelled between the nth and $(n + 1)$th bounces

    (v) the number of bounces before the distance between bounces is less than 20 cm.

⑩ A smooth snooker ball moving at 2 m s⁻¹ hits a cushion at an angle of 30° to the cushion.

The ball then rebounds and hits a second cushion which is perpendicular to the first. The coefficient of restitution for both impacts is 0.8.

    (i) Find the direction of motion after each impact.

    (ii) Find the magnitude of the velocity after the second impact.

    (iii) Repeat parts (i) and (ii) for a ball moving at u m s⁻¹ which hits the first cushion at an angle α. Assume that the coefficient of restitution is e. Hence show that the direction of a ball is always reversed after hitting two perpendicular cushions and state the factor by which its speed is reduced.

Impulse and momentum in more than one dimension

⑪ A standard table tennis table is 1.52 m wide and 2.75 m long. It is divided across the middle by a net 15.25 cm high. A ball is served horizontally at 6 m s⁻¹, without spin, from a point 0.3 m above the level of the smooth table. It hits the table at A and then rebounds and passes over the net to hit it again at B. The coefficient of restitution is 0.8.

Figure 14.13

(i) Calculate the length AB.

The ball just passes over the net at a point C.

(ii) Calculate the two possible horizontal distances between B and C.

(iii) Given that B is in fact a point on the shorter edge of the table, find at what angle to the net the ball is served.

⑫ Two circular discs slide on a smooth horizontal surface. Disc A has mass 6 kg and disc B has mass 14 kg and both are initially at rest. A force of 12 N acts on disc A for 4 seconds and this disc then collides directly with disc B. The coefficient of restitution between the two discs is 0.25.

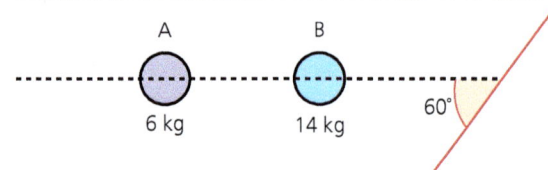

Figure 14.14

(i) Calculate the velocity of disc A before the collision.

(ii) Show that, after the collision, disc B has speed 3 m s⁻¹ and find the new speed of disc A.

(iii) Calculate the impulse on disc A in this collision.

Disc B now collides with a smooth surface at 60° to the line of its motion, as shown in Figure 14.14. The speed of the disc after the collision is 1.6 m s⁻¹.

(iv) Calculate the coefficient of restitution between the disc and the plane.

⑬ A ball of mass 0.5 kg falls from a height of 62.5 cm onto a plane inclined at 60° to the horizontal.

The coefficient of restitution between the ball and the plane is $\frac{4}{7}$.

(i) Find the speed of the ball immediately before striking the plane.

(ii) Find the magnitude and direction of the velocity of the ball after impact.

(iii) Find the loss in kinetic energy of the ball due to the collision.

⑭ A ball is projected horizontally from a table top of height h with speed u. The coefficient of restitution between the ball and the ground is e.

(i) Find an expression for the time during which the ball is moving.

(ii) Find the total horizontal distance travelled.

⑮ A ball falls vertically and strikes a fixed plane inclined at an angle θ ($\theta < 45°$) to the horizontal. The coefficient of restitution is $\frac{7}{25}$ and the ball rebounds horizontally.

(i) Show that $\tan\theta = \frac{1}{5}\sqrt{7}$.

(ii) Show that the fraction of kinetic energy lost in the collision is $\frac{18}{25}$.

⑯ The wind blowing against a sail can be modelled as a series of particles hitting the smooth sail at an angle of 30° and with zero coefficient of restitution. The wind blows at $20\,\text{m s}^{-1}$ and the density of the air is $1.4\,\text{kg m}^{-3}$. Calculate

(i) the mass of air hitting one square metre of sail each second

(ii) the impulse of this air on the sail and hence the force acting on a $2\,\text{m}^2$ sail.

2 Oblique impact of smooth elastic spheres

Two smooth spheres A of mass m_A and B of mass m_B collide. Immediately before impact the velocity of A is u at an angle α with the line of centres of the spheres, and the velocity of B is v at an angle β with the line of centres.

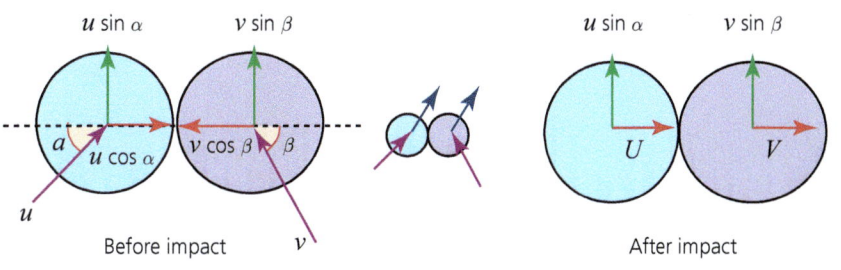

Figure 14.15

When analysing an impact like this you need to consider the components of the motion in two directions: perpendicular to the line of centres and along the line of centres.

Motion perpendicular to the line of centres

There is no impulse between the spheres in the direction of their common tangent at the point of contact and the momentum of each sphere in this direction is unchanged by the impact.

Hence, the component velocities after the collision in this direction are $u\sin\alpha$ for A and $v\sin\beta$ for B.

Oblique impact of smooth elastic spheres

Motion along the line of centres

Calling the components of the velocities in the direction of the line of centres U and V, conservation of momentum gives:

$$m_A u \cos\alpha - m_B v \cos\beta = m_A U + m_B V$$

The coefficient of restitution is e so that Newton's law of impact gives:

$$e(u\cos\alpha + v\cos\beta) = V - U$$

Speed of approach. — left side. *Speed of separation.* — right side.

These two simultaneous equations are sufficient to determine U and V.

Once U and V are known, the velocities of A and B after the collision can be written in vector form as:

$$\mathbf{v}_A = U\mathbf{i} + u\sin\alpha\,\mathbf{j} \quad \text{and} \quad \mathbf{v}_B = V\mathbf{i} + v\sin\beta\,\mathbf{j}$$

where the directions along and perpendicular to the line of centres are denoted by $\mathbf{i}$ and $\mathbf{j}$.

Example 14.5

In a game of snooker, the cue ball moving with speed $2\,\text{m}\,\text{s}^{-1}$ strikes a stationary red ball. The cue ball is moving at an angle of $60°$ to the line of centres of the two balls. Both balls are smooth and have the same radius and mass m. The coefficient of restitution between the balls is $\frac{1}{2}$.

Find the velocities of the two balls after impact.

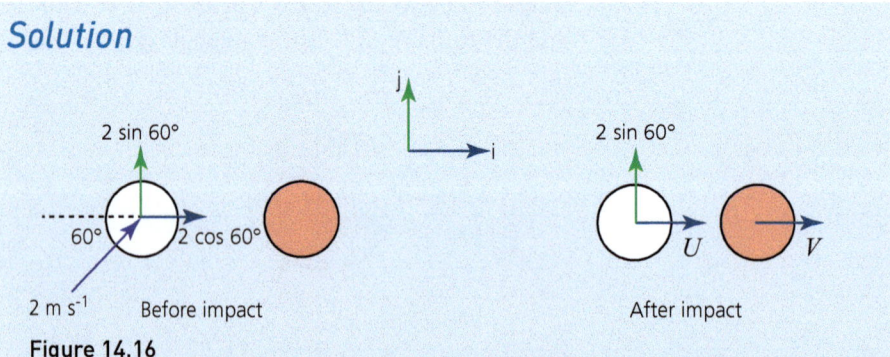

Solution

Figure 14.16

Let the component velocities in the direction of the line of centres be U for the cue ball and V for the red ball.

Conservation of momentum in the direction of the line of centres:

$$m \times 2\cos 60° = mU + mV$$

$$1 = U + V \quad \text{(A)}$$

Divide by m and use $\cos 60° = 0.5$.

Newton's law of impact:

$$e \times 2\cos 60° = V - U$$

Speed of approach. / *Speed of separation.*

$$\tfrac{1}{2} = V - U \quad \text{(B)}$$

(A) + (B) $\quad \tfrac{3}{2} = 2V \Rightarrow V = \tfrac{3}{4}$

(A) − (B) $\quad \tfrac{1}{2} = 2U \Rightarrow U = \tfrac{1}{4}$

The velocity of the red ball is $\frac{3}{4}\mathbf{i}$ and the velocity of the white ball is $\frac{1}{4}\mathbf{i} + 2\sin 60°\mathbf{j} = \frac{1}{4}\mathbf{i} + \sqrt{3}\mathbf{j}$.

The red ball moves with speed $0.75\,\text{m s}^{-1}$ along the line of centres. The cue ball moves with speed $1.75\,\text{m s}^{-1}$ at 82° to the line of centres.

$$\sqrt{\left(\frac{1}{4}\right)^2 + 3} = \sqrt{\frac{49}{16}} = \frac{7}{4}$$

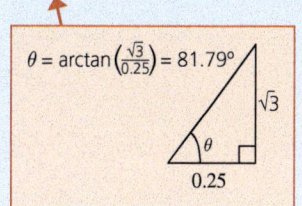

$\theta = \arctan\left(\frac{\sqrt{3}}{0.25}\right) = 81.79°$

Example 14.6

A smooth sphere A of mass $2m$, moving with speed $4\,\text{m s}^{-1}$ collides with a smooth sphere B of mass m moving with speed $2\,\text{m s}^{-1}$. The velocity of A immediately before impact makes an angle of 45° to the line of centres. The velocity of B immediately before impact is at 90° to the line of centres. The coefficient of restitution between the two balls is 0.6.

(i) Draw a diagram showing the situation before and after the collision.

(ii) Calculate the velocities of the two spheres after impact.

(iii) Calculate the loss of kinetic energy sustained by the system during the impact.

Solution

(i) The velocities of the two spheres are shown as well as their components along and perpendicular to the line of centres.

The components perpendicular to the line of centres ($4\sin 45° = 2\sqrt{2}$ for A and 2 for B) are not affected by the collision.

The components along the line of centres are taken to be V_A and V_B.

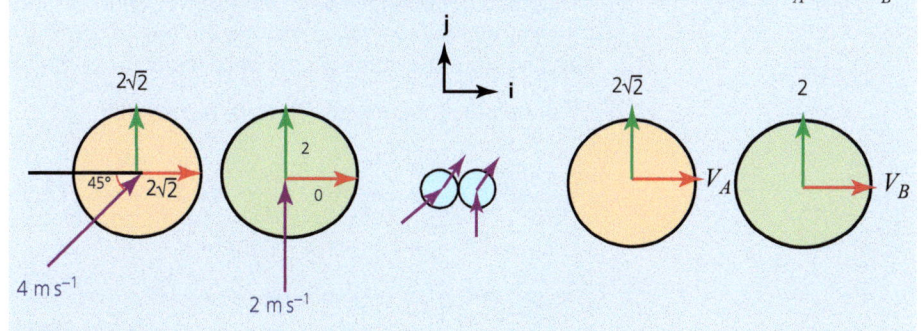

Figure 14.17

Conservation of momentum along line of centres:

(ii) $2m \times 4\cos 45° = 2mV_A + mV_B$

Using $\cos 45° = \frac{\sqrt{2}}{2}$ and dividing by m.

$4\sqrt{2} = 2V_A + V_B$ (A)

Oblique impact of smooth elastic spheres

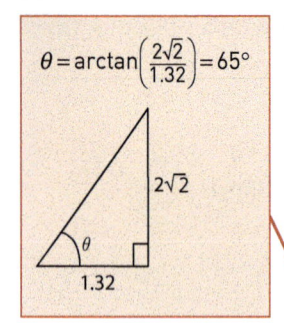

$\theta = \arctan\left(\frac{2\sqrt{2}}{1.32}\right) = 65°$

[triangle diagram with sides $2\sqrt{2}$, 1.32, and angle θ]

Newton's law of impact:

$e \times 4\cos 45° = V_B - V_A \qquad 2\sqrt{2}e = V_B - V_A \qquad$ (B)

(A) − (B): $(4 - 2e)\sqrt{2} = 3V_A \qquad V_A = \frac{\sqrt{2}}{3}(4 - 2e)$

$V_A = \frac{2.8\sqrt{2}}{3} = 1.319\ldots$

$4 - 2e = 4 - 2 \times 0.6$

(A) + 2(B): $4(1+e)\sqrt{2} = 3V_B$

$V_B = \frac{4\sqrt{2}}{3}(1+e)$

$4(1+e) = 4(1 + 0.6)$

$V_B = \frac{6.4\sqrt{2}}{3} = 3.016\ldots$

$\sqrt{1.32^2 + (2\sqrt{2})^2} = \sqrt{1.32^2 + 8} = 3.12$

Velocity of A after impact: $1.32\mathbf{i} + 2\sqrt{2}\mathbf{j}$

A moves with speed $3.12\,\text{m s}^{-1}$ at an angle of 65° to the line of centres.

Velocity of B after impact: $3.02\mathbf{i} + 2\mathbf{j}$

B moves with speed $3.62\,\text{m s}^{-1}$ at an angle of 33.5° to the line of centres.

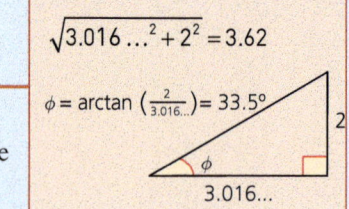

$\sqrt{3.016\ldots^2 + 2^2} = 3.62$

$\phi = \arctan\left(\frac{2}{3.016\ldots}\right) = 33.5°$

[triangle diagram with sides $3.016\ldots$, 2, and angle ϕ]

(iii) The kinetic energy of the system before the collision is equal to:

$\frac{1}{2} \times 2m \times 4^2 + \frac{1}{2} \times m \times 2^2 = 18m$

The kinetic energy of the system after the collision is equal to:

$\frac{1}{2} \times 2m \times 3.12^2 + \frac{1}{2} \times m \times 3.62^2 = 16.29m$

The loss in kinetic energy is:

$18m - 16.29m = 1.71m$

> **Note**
>
> This result could have been obtained by consideration of the contribution from the components of velocity along the line of centres only as there is no change arising from the components perpendicular to the line of centres:
>
> K.E. before: $\frac{1}{2} \times 2m \times (2\sqrt{2})^2 + \frac{1}{2} \times m \times 0 = 8m$
>
> K.E. after: $\frac{1}{2} \times 2m \times \left(\frac{2.8\sqrt{2}}{3}\right)^2 + \frac{1}{2} \times m \times \left(\frac{6.4\sqrt{2}}{3}\right)^2 = 6.293m$
>
> Loss in K.E. $8m - 6.293m = 1.706m$

Exercise 14.2

In questions 1–6, a smooth sphere A of mass m_A collides with a smooth sphere B of mass m_B and equal radius, as shown in Figure 14.18.

The coefficient of restitution between the spheres is e.

Immediately before the collision, A is moving with speed u_A at an angle α with the line of centres and B is moving with speed u_B at an angle β with the line of centres.

Immediately after impact, A is moving with speed v_A at an angle α_A with the line of centres and B is moving with speed v_B at an angle β_B with the line of centres.

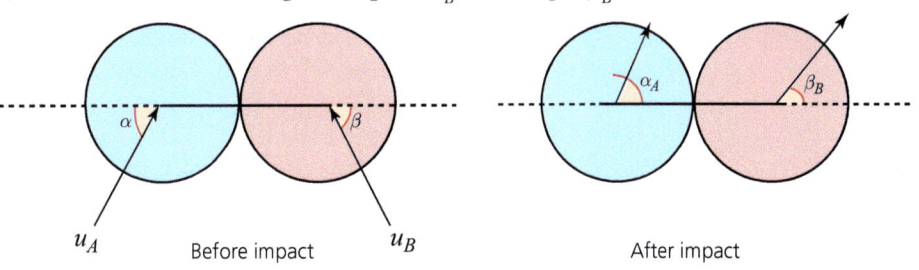

Figure 14.18

① $m_A = 4\,\text{kg}, m_B = 2\,\text{kg}, u_A = 2\,\text{m s}^{-1}, u_B = 4\,\text{m s}^{-1}, \alpha = \beta = 45°, e = 0.5$.
Calculate v_A, v_B, α_A and β_B.

② $m_A = m_B = m, \alpha = 60°, u_A = u, u_B = 0, e = 0.6$.
Calculate v_A, v_B, α_A and β_B.

③ $m_A = m_B = m, u_A = u_B = u, \alpha = 0°, \beta = 90°, e = 0.5$.
Calculate v_A, v_B, α_A and β_B.

④ $m_A = m_B = m, u_A = u_B = u, \alpha = 60°, \beta = 60°, e = 0.5$.
Calculate v_A, v_B, α_A and β_B.

⑤ $m_A = m, m_B = 5m, u_A = u, u_B = 0, \alpha = 60°, \alpha_A = 90°$.
Calculate e.

⑥ $m_A = m_B = m, u_B = 0, \alpha = 45°, e = \frac{2}{3}$.
Calculate α_A.

⑦ Two identical smooth balls of mass m are moving with equal speed u in opposite directions. The balls collide obliquely, so that the line of centres between the balls is at 30° to the direction of motion. Show that the loss in kinetic energy due to the impact is 75% of what it would be if the impact were direct.

⑧ A smooth sphere A of mass $2m$ moving with speed $2u$ collides with a smooth sphere B of mass m moving with speed u.

At the moment of impact, A is moving at 60° to the line of centres and B is moving at 90° to the line of centres.

The coefficient of restitution between the spheres is 0.5.

(i) Find the component of velocity along the line of centres after impact for each sphere.

(ii) Find the velocities of the spheres after impact.

(iii) Find the loss in kinetic energy for the system.

⑨ In this question all the discs are circular and have the same radius.

(i) A disc of mass m is sliding across a table when it collides with a stationary disc with the same mass. After the collision, the directions of motion of the two discs are at right angles.

Oblique impact of smooth elastic spheres

Prove that the collision is perfectly elastic.

(ii) On another occasion the disc of mass m collides with a stationary disc of mass km, where $k > 1$, and the directions of their subsequent motion are at right angles. The coefficient of restitution is e.

Prove that $e = \dfrac{1}{k}$.

(iii) State a modelling assumption required for parts (i) and (ii).

⑩ Figure 14.19 illustrates a collision between two smooth spheres of equal mass m. Initially they are moving along parallel lines but in opposite directions. At impact the acute angle between their line of centres and the directions of their original movement is α. The coefficient of restitution in the collision is e. Before the impact both spheres have speed u.

Before impact · On impact · After impact

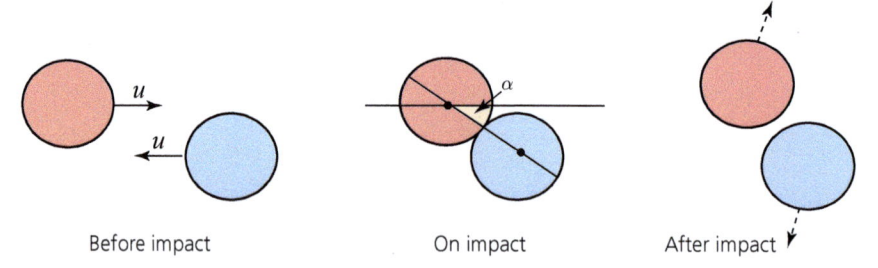

Figure 14.19

(i) Show that the loss of kinetic energy in the collision is $mu^2 \cos^2\alpha(1 - e^2)$.

(ii) Show that, in the case when $\alpha = 30°$ and $e = \dfrac{1}{3}$, the direction of motion of each of the spheres after impact is at right angles to its direction before impact.

⑪ Two uniform circular discs with the same radius, A of mass 1 kg and B of mass 5.25 kg, slide on a smooth horizontal surface and collide obliquely with smooth contact.

Figure 14.20 gives information about the velocities of the discs just before and just after the collision.

- The line XY passes through the centres of the discs at the moment of collision.
- The components parallel and perpendicular to XY of the velocities of A are shown.
- Before the collision B is at rest, and after it is moving at $2\,\text{m s}^{-1}$ in the direction XY.

just before collision · at collision · just after collision

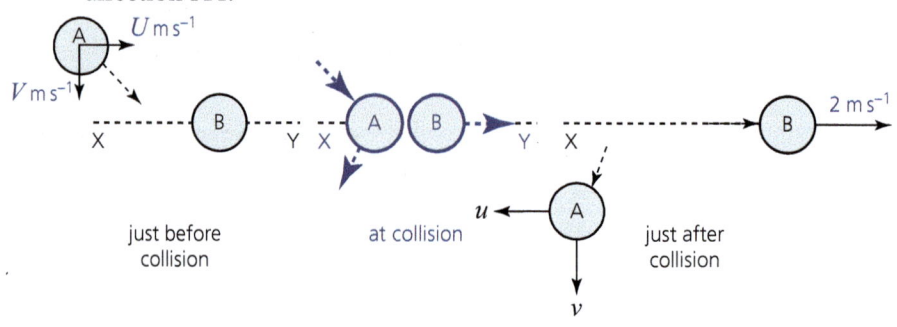

Figure 14.20

The coefficient of restitution between the two discs is $\frac{2}{3}$.

(i) Find the values of U and u.

(ii) What information in the question tells you that $v = V$?

The speed of disc A before the collision is $8.5\,\text{m}\,\text{s}^{-1}$.

(iii) Find the speed of disc A after the collision.

⑫ Figure 14.21 shows a white snooker ball with centre W and a red one with centre R. The straight line through W and R passes through the centre, C, of one of the pockets. WR = 100 cm and RC = 40 cm.

Apart from their colour the balls are identical. Their diameter is 5.25 cm.

A model for this snooker table is that a ball will go into the pocket if the line of approach of its centre passes within 2.5 cm of the centre of the pocket

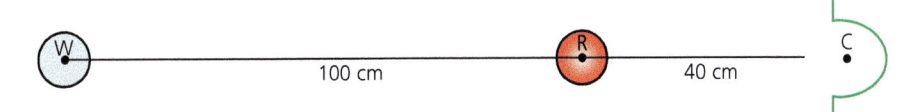

Figure 14.21

(i) A player tries to hit the white ball exactly along the straight line WRC so that the red ball will go into the pocket. Instead, however, he hits the ball at an angle α to the required line.

What happens to the red ball in the cases when (a) $\alpha = 0.5°$ (b) $\alpha = 0.15°$.

Figure 14.22 shows a different situation. There are two red balls with centres, R_1 and R_2, on the line WC. $R_1R_2 = 20\,\text{cm}$ and $R_2C = 20\,\text{cm}$.

Figure 14.22

The player hits the white ball into the first red ball, which then hits the second red ball. If the shot is successful the second red ball goes into the pocket. A shot like this is called a 'plant'.

The player hits the white ball at an angle α to the line WC.

(ii) Show that, if $\alpha = 0.15°$, the shot is not successful.

(iii) Find, to 2 significant figures, the smallest value of α for which the shot is unsuccessful.

(iv) Explain why the plant is not a popular shot with serious snooker players.

Oblique impact of smooth elastic spheres

KEY POINTS

1 Collision between a sphere and a fixed plane

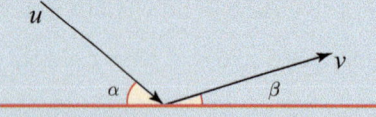

Figure 14.23

Component of velocity parallel to surface remains unchanged [$v \cos \beta = u \cos \alpha$]
Component of velocity perpendicular to surface: [$v \sin \beta = -eu \sin \alpha$]
Loss in kinetic energy: $\frac{1}{2} mu^2 \sin^2 \alpha (1 - e^2)$

2 Oblique impact between smooth spheres

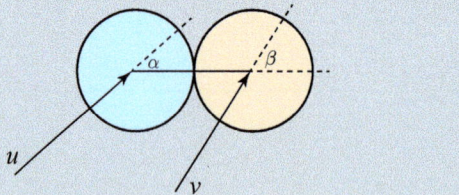

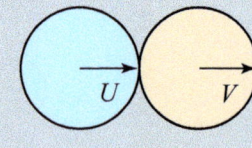

Figure 14.24

Perpendicular to line of centres
$u \sin \alpha$ and $v \sin \beta$ remain unchanged by the collision.

Along line of centres
Conservation of momentum:
$$m_A u \cos \alpha + m_B v \cos \beta = m_A U + m_B V \quad \text{①}$$

Newton's law of impact:
$$V - U = e(u \cos \alpha - v \cos \beta) \quad \text{②}$$

Equations ① and ② can be solved to find U and V.

LEARNING OUTCOMES

When you have completed this chapter, you should

➤ understand the term oblique impact and the assumptions made when modelling oblique impact

➤ know the meaning of Newton's experimental law and of the coefficient of restitution when applied to an oblique impact

➤ be able to solve problems involving impact between an object and a fixed smooth plane by considering components of motion parallel and perpendicular to the line of impulse

➤ be able to solve problems involving impact between two spheres by considering components of motion in directions parallel and perpendicular to the line of centres

➤ be able to calculate the loss of kinetic energy in an oblique impact.

PRACTICE QUESTIONS: SET 2

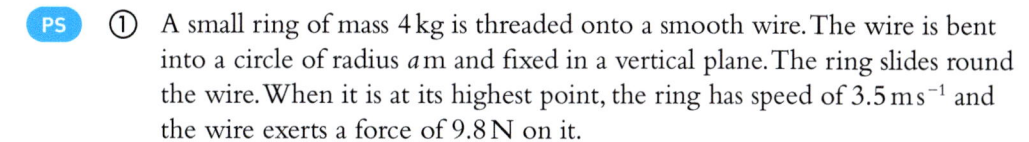

1. A small ring of mass 4 kg is threaded onto a smooth wire. The wire is bent into a circle of radius a m and fixed in a vertical plane. The ring slides round the wire. When it is at its highest point, the ring has speed of $3.5\,\text{m s}^{-1}$ and the wire exerts a force of 9.8 N on it.

   (i) Determine the possible values of a. [4 marks]

   (ii) What is the largest possible speed of the ring? Give your answer correct to 3 significant figures. [3 marks]

2. A smooth plane is inclined at 30° to the horizontal. A small ball has velocity $U\,\text{m s}^{-1}$ at 45° to the plane when it hits the plane at a point P. The ball bounces from the plane with a coefficient of restitution of $\dfrac{1}{\sqrt{3}}$. The ball next hits the plane at a point Q which is a distance 15 m down the plane from P. This information is shown in Figure 1.

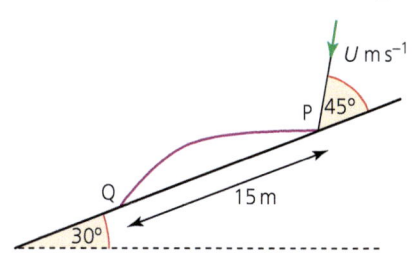

   Figure 1

   (i) Prove that the ball is travelling horizontally immediately after it bounces at P. [3 marks]

   (ii) Show that the ball has a speed of $10.5\,\text{m s}^{-1}$ immediately after it bounces at P. [4 marks]

   (iii) Find U. [3 marks]

3. Newton's law of universal gravitation states that the magnitude of the force F_P of attraction between point masses m_1 and m_2 a distance d apart is given by

   $$F_P = \frac{Gm_1m_2}{d^2}$$

   where G is the universal gravitational constant.

   (i) Find the dimensions of G. [2 marks]

   The magnitude of the force of attraction, F_i, between a particle of mass m and the Earth for a particle **inside** the earth and a distance r from its centre may be modelled by

   $$F_i = \tfrac{4}{3}\pi\rho\, Gmr$$

   where ρ is the average density of the Earth.

   (ii) Show that this expression is dimensionally consistent. [2 marks]

Practice Questions: Set 2

The magnitude of the force of attraction between a particle of mass m and the Earth for a particle **on or outside** the earth and a distance r from its centre may be modelled by assuming that the Earth may be treated as a particle at its centre.

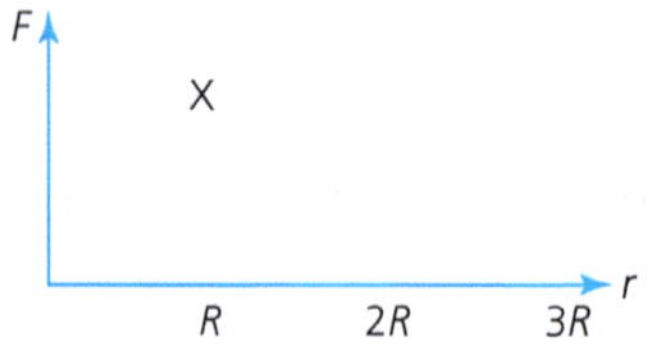

(iii) Copy Figure 2 and sketch on it a graph of the magnitude, F, of the force of attraction between the Earth and a particle where $0 \leq r \leq 3R$, where R is the radius of the Earth. The value of F when $r = R$ has been marked with a cross. [2 marks]

Figure 2

A straight tube is inside the Earth on a diameter of the Earth. The inside of the tube is smooth and the air has been removed so that a particle of mass m can slide in the tube without any resistance to its motion.

A particle P is released from rest inside the tube with P level with the Earth's surface.

(iv) Using the expression for F_i above, with the positive direction of r taken to be away from the centre of the Earth, find the equation of motion of P in terms of r, G and ρ and hence show that this motion is simple harmonic. [3 marks]

Suppose that the tube runs along the whole of a diameter of the Earth.

(v) You are given that, in S.I. units, G is 6.67×10^{-11} and ρ is 5500.

Show that after releasing P from surface level, it would return to its starting position after about 80 minutes. [3 marks]

④ A region of the plane between the line $x = \frac{a}{2}$ and the circle $x^2 + y^2 = a^2$ is shown shaded in Figure 3. The uniform solid S is formed by rotating this shaded region through 2π radians about the x-axis.

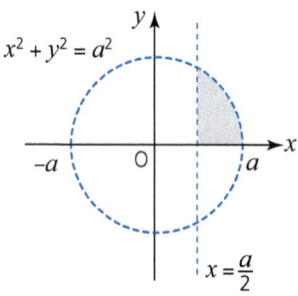

Figure 3

(i) Show that the centre of mass of S is at a distance $\frac{7a}{40}$ from the centre of its plane face. [6 marks]

S has mass M. A uniform thin rod of length l with density $\frac{27M}{40a}$ per unit length is attached to S at Q, the centre of its plane face; the rod is perpendicular to this face and lies on a z-axis with origin Q. S with the rod forms the object T shown in a side view in Figure 4 on the left.

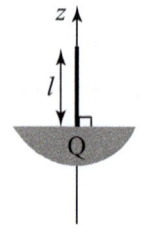

Figure 4

(ii) Show that the centre of mass of T is at the point on the z-axis where
$$z = \frac{27l^2 - 14a^2}{2(40a + 27l)}.$$
[4 marks]

When $l = 2a$, the centre of mass of T is at the point G.

(iii) The object S is part of a sphere. Show that G is at the centre of that sphere. [1 mark]

Figure 4 on the right shows T placed on a horizontal plane with the rod not quite vertical. B is the point of contact of T with the plane.

(iv) Why does the normal to the plane at B pass through G?

T is released from rest.

State with a reason what will happen if $l < 2a$. [2 marks]

PS M ⑤ In this question take $g = 10$.

One end of a light elastic string with modulus 50 N is fixed to a point A. The other end is attached to a small object of weight 80 N.

The object is dropped from rest at A and falls vertically a distance of 10 m before coming instantaneously to rest.

(i) Find the maximum speed of the object as it falls. [10 marks]

(ii) State a modelling assumption you have made in addition to the information given in this question. [1 mark]

PS T ⑥ Figure 5 shows the path of a particle P moving in the Cartesian plane with origin O, drawn with graph-drawing software.

The position of P at time t s is $\mathbf{r} = (2t^3 - 3t^2 + 2)\mathbf{i} + (t-1)^2\mathbf{j}$, where $\mathbf{i}$ and $\mathbf{j}$ are unit vectors in the directions Ox and Oy and $-1 \leq t \leq 2$.

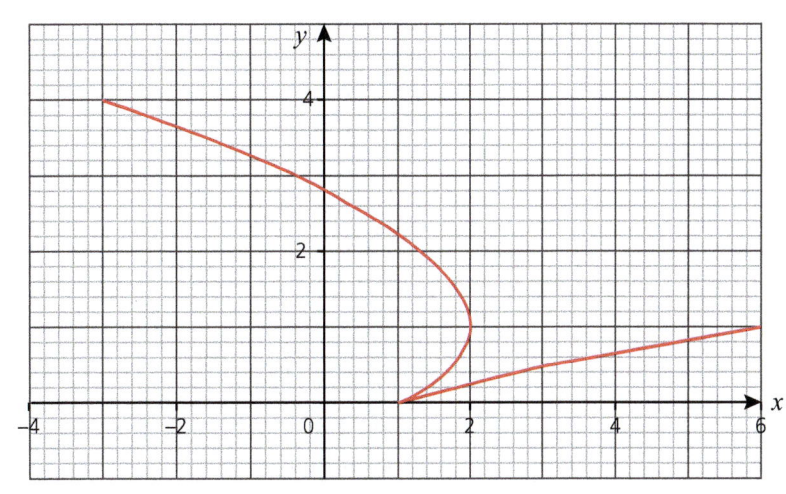

Figure 5

(i) Determine the time(s), if any, when P is instantaneously at rest. [3 marks]

(ii) Sketch a copy of the path of P and indicate the points where $t = -1, 0, 1$ and 2 and the direction of travel.

Describe briefly the motion of P about the time when $t = 0$.

Describe briefly the motion of P about the time when $t = 1$. [4 marks]

Answers

Chapter 1

Discussion point page 1
Mostly it will be vertically downwards and after some initial acceleration the velocity will be fairly constant. If there is a wind blowing the velocity will also have a horizontal component motion.

Exercise 1.1
1. (i) $-100, 900$ (ii) $1, 9$
2. (a) (i) $20, 10$ (ii) -10
   (iii) 50 m
   (iv) $-6\,\text{ms}^{-1}, 6\,\text{ms}^{-1}$ for $0 \leq t \leq 5$; $0\,\text{ms}^{-1}$, $0\,\text{ms}^{-1}$ for $5 \leq t \leq 7$; $6\tfrac{2}{3}, 6\tfrac{2}{3}\,\text{ms}^{-1}$ for $7 \leq t \leq 10$
   (v) $-1\,\text{ms}^{-1}$
   (vi) $5\,\text{ms}^{-1}$
   (b) (i) $0, 20$ m
   (ii) 20 m (iii) 60 m
   (iv) $5\,\text{ms}^{-1}, 5\,\text{ms}^{-1}$ for $0 \leq t \leq 2$; $-5\,\text{ms}^{-1}$, $5\,\text{ms}^{-1}$ for $2 \leq t \leq 6$; $5\,\text{ms}^{-1}, 5\,\text{ms}^{-1}$ for $6 \leq t \leq 12$
   (v) $1\tfrac{2}{3}\,\text{ms}^{-1}$
   (vi) $5\,\text{ms}^{-1}$
3. (i) 1 and $3\tfrac{2}{3}$, (ii) $t = 2\tfrac{1}{3}$,
   (iii) $37\tfrac{2}{3}$
4. (i) [graph of x vs t, parabola from 0 to 2.5]
   (ii) 2 m (iii) -1.25 m
   (iv) 1.2 s; 9.2 m
   (v) 15.65 m
5. (i) 1.9583 h
   (ii) $51.06\,\text{km h}^{-1}$
   (iii) $0\,\text{km h}^{-1}$
6. 500 s
7. $6.81\,\text{ms}^{-1}$
8. (i) 200 m (ii) 30 s
   (iii) 150 m
9. (i) 7.5 mph
   (ii) 10.91 mph
10. (i) $20\,\text{ms}^{-1}, 0\,\text{ms}^{-1}$
    (ii) [velocity-time graph, peaks at 40]
    (iii) 1200 m
11. (i) [velocity-time graph, peaks at 6]
    (ii) 24 m (iii) $1\,\text{ms}^{-2}$
    (iv) $3\,\text{ms}^{-1}$
12. (i) [velocity-time graph, trapezoid]
    (ii) 4800 m
13. (i) 500 m, 1500 m, 1500 m, -500 m (ii) 4000 m
    (iii) 180 s
14. $8.96\,\text{ms}^{-1}$
15. 110 s
16. (i) $\tfrac{5}{54}\,\text{ms}^{-2}$ (ii) $\tfrac{5}{18}\,\text{ms}^{-2}$
    (iii) $\tfrac{50}{3}\,\text{ms}^{-1}$

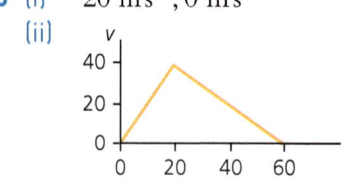

Exercise 1.2
1. (i) $10\,\text{ms}^{-1}$ (ii) -4 m
   (iii) $5.66\,\text{ms}^{-1}$ (iv) -24 m
   (v) $15\,\text{ms}^{-1}$
2. $2\,\text{ms}^{-2}$; 225 m
3. 122.5 m
4. 4.146 s after the first ball is thrown; $-20.63\,\text{ms}^{-1}$; $-15.83\,\text{ms}^{-1}$
5. (i) $5\,\text{ms}^{-2}$ (ii) $10\,\text{ms}^{-1}$
   (iii) 11 s (iv) $9.0\dot{9}\,\text{ms}^{-1}$
6. (i) 40 m (ii) 20.4 m
7. (i) Janet (ii) 5.62 m
   (iii) 0.70 s
8. 60 s; 1500 m
9. $356.6\,\text{ms}^{-1}$
10. (i) $16\tfrac{2}{3}\,\text{ms}^{-1}$ (ii) $\tfrac{5}{18}\,\text{ms}^{-2}$
    (iii) $50\,\text{ms}^{-1}$
11. $19.6\,\text{ms}^{-1}$; 19.6 m
12. 4.12 m
13. Sprinter
14. (i) 45 s (ii) $0.1234...\,\text{ms}^{-2}$
    (iii) 31.24 m
15. (i) [velocity-time graph, trapezoid reaching 30]
    (ii) 4500 m (iii) $\tfrac{5}{9}\,\text{ms}^{-2}$
    (iv) 360 m
16. (ii) $18\,\text{ms}^{-1}$ (iii) 6.125 m

Exercise 1.3
1. (a) (i) $4 - 2t$ (ii) $2; 4$
   (iii) $2; 6$
   (b) (i) $10t - 3t^2$
   (ii) $0; 0$
   (iii) 0 and $\tfrac{10}{3}; \tfrac{500}{27}$
   (c) (i) $4t^3 - 2t$ (ii) $2; 0$
   (iii) 0 and $\pm\tfrac{1}{\sqrt{2}}; \tfrac{13}{8}$
2. $76\,\text{ms}^{-1}, 42\,\text{ms}^{-2}$
3. (i) $s = 2.5t^2 - 2t + 3$
   (ii) $s = t^3 + 2t^2 - 1$
4. (i) $v = 6t^2 - 8t + 3$;
   $s = 2t^3 - 4t^2 + 3t + 5$
   (ii) $v = \tfrac{1}{6}t^3 - \tfrac{1}{10}t^2 + t - \tfrac{1}{15}$
   $s = \tfrac{1}{24}t^4 - \tfrac{1}{30}t^3 + \tfrac{1}{2}t^2 - \tfrac{1}{15}t + \tfrac{7}{120}$
5. 38 m
6. (i) $t = 1: v = 0\,\text{ms}^{-1}$, $a = -2\,\text{ms}^{-2}$; $t = 2$: $v = 1\,\text{ms}^{-1}, a = 4\,\text{ms}^{-2}$
   (ii) $t = 1: 0$ m; $t = \tfrac{5}{3} : \tfrac{4}{27}$ m
   (iii) $10\,\text{ms}^{-2}$
7. 16 m
8. (i) $0\,\text{ms}^{-2}, 10\,\text{ms}^{-1}$
   (ii) $13.\dot{3}$ m (iii) $10.\dot{6}$ s

9 (i) 10 m (ii) $36 + 6t - 6t^2$
   (iii) $-2, 3; -34$ m, $+91$ m
   (iv) 98 m (v) 3 times
10 (i) 0 s, 2 s (ii) 3 s
   (iii) $\frac{27}{4}$ m (iv) 4 s
11 (i) 0 s, 6 s (ii) 32 m s^{-1}
   (iii) 108 m
12 (i) $-24 + 18t - 3t^2$; 2 s, 4 s
   (ii) -2 m, 2 m (iii) 28 m
13 $v = 18\cos 3t - 24\sin 3t$
   $a = -54\sin 3t - 72\cos 3t$
14 (i) 10 m s^{-1} for both
   (ii) $13\frac{1}{3}$ m for A, 10 m for B
   (iii) $10\frac{2}{3}$ s for A, 11 s for B
   (iv) A wins by $\frac{1}{3}$ s and $3\frac{1}{3}$ m
15 John finishes in 2 h 54 m 45 s,
   Euan finishes in 2 h 55 m 9 s;
   John by 24 s or 34 m.

Chapter 2

Exercise 2.1

1 (i) $6.\dot{6}$ m s^{-2} (ii) 10 000 m s^{-2}
  (iii) 0.1 m s^{-2}
2 16 000 N
3 (i) 2 m s^{-2}, 4 s (ii) 960 N
4 (i) 61.5 N (ii) 36.5 N
  (iii) 49 N (iv) 36.5 N
5 (i) $3\frac{4}{15}$ m s^{-2}, $65\frac{1}{3}$ N
  (ii) 1.4 m s^{-1} (iii) 0.1 m
6 (i) [diagram: blocks C (4g), A (10g), B (6g) with forces T_1, T_2, R]
  (ii) $T_2 - T_1 = 10a$
      $6g - T_2 = 6a$
      $T_1 - 4g = 4a$
  (iii) 0.98 m s^{-2}, 43.1 N, 52.9 N
7 (i) [diagram: Trailer 300 N ← , T → ; Truck 250 N ← , T ← , 2500 N →]
  (ii) 1.22 m s^{-2} (iii) 726.6 N
8 (ii) 4100 N (iii) -0.1 m s^{-2}
  (iv) 100 N
9 (i) [diagram: A (2g) with T; B (0.5g) with R_1; C (g) with R_1, R_2]
  (ii) A: $2g - T = 2a$
       B: $R_1 - 0.5g = 0.5a$
       C: $R_2 - R_1 - g = a$
  (iii) 1.4 m s^{-2}; 16.8 N; 5.6 N, 16.8 N
10 (i) [diagram: A (5g) with T_1, R; B (g) with T_1, T_2; C (2g) with T_2]
   (ii) A: $5a = T_1$; B: $a = g + T_2 - T_1$; C: $2a = 2g - T_2$
   (iii) 3.675 m s^{-2}, $T_1 = 18.375$ N, $T_2 = 12.25$ N

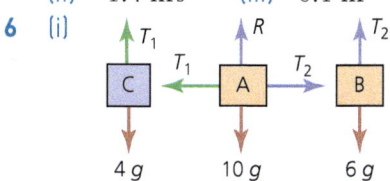

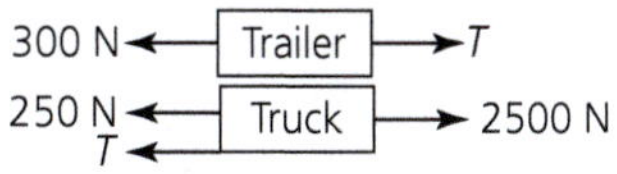

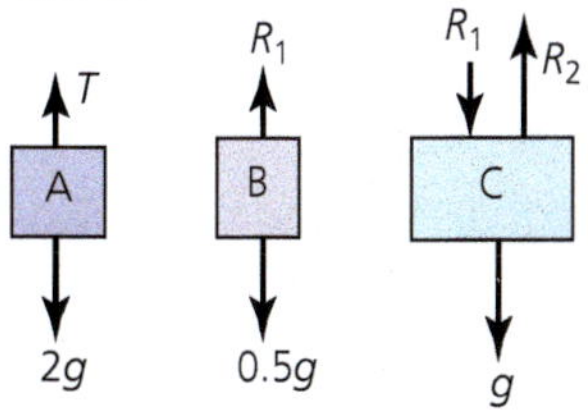

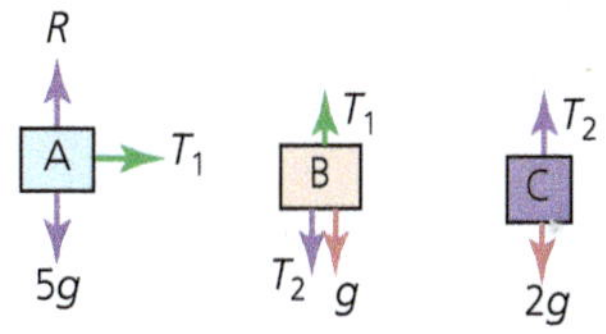

Exercise 2.2

1 (i) $9\mathbf{i} - 3\mathbf{j}$ (ii) $4\mathbf{i} - 2\mathbf{j}$
  (iii) $-7\mathbf{i} + 2\mathbf{j}$ (iv) $4\mathbf{i} - 6\mathbf{j}$
  (v) $-3\mathbf{i} + 11\mathbf{j}$ (vi) $-13\mathbf{i} + 9\mathbf{j}$
2 (i) $\mathbf{i} + 2\mathbf{j}, 5\mathbf{i} + \mathbf{j}, 7\mathbf{i} + 8\mathbf{j}$
  (ii) $\overrightarrow{AB} = 4\mathbf{i} - \mathbf{j}$
      $\overrightarrow{BC} = 2\mathbf{i} + 7\mathbf{j}$
      $\overrightarrow{CA} = -6\mathbf{i} - 6\mathbf{j}$ 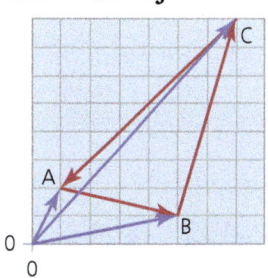
      [diagram: triangle ABC on grid]
3 $9\mathbf{i} - 10\mathbf{j}$
4 (i) 13, $-22.6°$ (ii) 25, 73.7°
  (iii) 1.41, 135° (iv) 5, 53.1°
  (v) 3.61, $-56.3°$
  (vi) 2.24, $-116.6°$
5 (i) $5.64\mathbf{i} + 2.05\mathbf{j}$
  (ii) $-5.36\mathbf{i} + 4.50\mathbf{j}$
  (iii) $1.93\mathbf{i} - 2.30\mathbf{j}$
  (iv) $-1.45\mathbf{i} - 2.51\mathbf{j}$
6 (i) $\frac{5}{13}\mathbf{i} + \frac{12}{13}\mathbf{j}$ (ii) $15\mathbf{i} + 36\mathbf{j}$
7 $8\mathbf{i} - 1.8\mathbf{j}$
8 (i) $2.30\mathbf{i} + 1.93\mathbf{j}$;
      $-0.92\mathbf{i} + 2.54\mathbf{j}$;
      $-2.42\mathbf{i} - 1.4\mathbf{j}$;
      $1.7\mathbf{i} - 2.94\mathbf{j}$;
      $\mathbf{R} = 0.66\mathbf{i} + 0.13\mathbf{j}$
  (ii) $1.35\mathbf{i} + 2.34\mathbf{j}; -2\mathbf{i}$;
       $-0.35\mathbf{i} - 1.97\mathbf{j}$;
       $2.68\mathbf{i} - 1.55\mathbf{j}$;
       $\mathbf{R} = 1.68\mathbf{i} - 1.18\mathbf{j}$
9 [diagram: vectors A, B, C, D on axes]
  (i) $\begin{pmatrix} 4 \\ 5 \end{pmatrix}$ (ii) $\begin{pmatrix} -2 \\ 7 \end{pmatrix}$
  (iii) $\begin{pmatrix} 6 \\ -2 \end{pmatrix}$ (iv) $\begin{pmatrix} -6 \\ 2 \end{pmatrix}$
10 (i) $\mathbf{a} = a\mathbf{i}$;
       $\mathbf{b} = -b\cos\theta\,\mathbf{i} + b\sin\theta\,\mathbf{j}$
   (ii) $\mathbf{a} + \mathbf{b} = (a - b\cos\theta)\mathbf{i} + b\sin\theta\,\mathbf{j}$; $|\mathbf{a} + \mathbf{b}|^2$
       $= (a - b\cos\theta)^2 + (b\cos\theta)^2$
   (iii) $c^2 = a^2 + b^2 - 2ab\cos\theta$

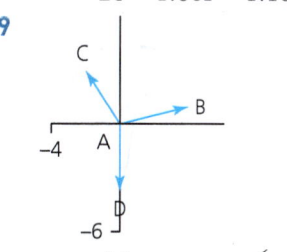

Discussion point page 44

Draw a vertical line to represent the weight, $10g = 98$ N. Then add the line of the force T_2 at 40° to the horizontal (note the length of the vector is unknown), and then the line of the force T_1 at 20° to the horizontal (70° to the vertical). C is the point at which these lines meet.

Discussion point page 45

The angles in the triangle are $180° - \alpha, 180° - \beta$ and $180° - \gamma$. The sine rule holds. Using $\sin(180° - \alpha) = \sin\alpha$, $\sin(180° - \beta) = \sin\beta$ and $\sin(180° - \gamma) = \sin\gamma$ results in Lami's theorem.

Exercise 2.3

1 (i) -49 N, -78 N
  (ii) 1 N, 2 N
  (iii) -1 N, -2 N
2 (i) [diagram: block on incline with R, F, 2g]
  (ii) 15.0 N (iii) 12.6 N

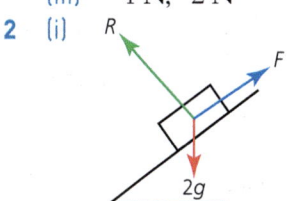

3   5.83 N, 31°
4   (i)   98 N
    (ii) [diagram: block with R up, 30 N at angle, F left, 10g down]
    (iii) 70.8 N; 12.7 N
5   15 N
6   (i)   [diagram: block with R up, 60 N at angle θ, 35 N left, 10g down]
    (ii) 54.3°   (iii) 49.3 N
7   20 N, 16.9 N
8   (i)   [diagram: inclined block with R, T, 10g]
    (ii) 50.7 N, 71.7 N
9   (i)   [diagram: circle with 10 N, R, 20 N, F, 3g]
    (ii) 7.15 N
    (iii) 11.90 N left
10 (ii) 42.6**i** + 82.5**j**; 92.8 N at 62.7° to the horizontal.
    (iii) 32.6 N, −94.4°
11 (i)   5000 cos 15° + T cos 25° along *l*; 5000 sin 15° − T sin 25° perpendicular to *l*.
    (ii) 3062 N   (iii) 7605 N
12 (i)   [diagram: ball on slope with R, F, 60g, 20°]
    (ii) (−60g sin 20° + F) and (−60g cos 20° + R)
    (iii) 552.5 N, 201.1 N
    (iv) 402.2 N

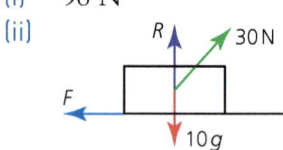

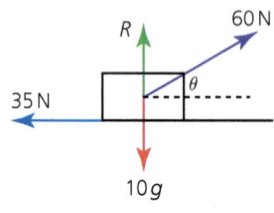

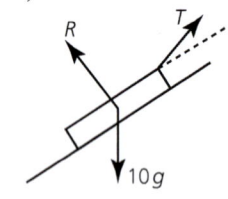

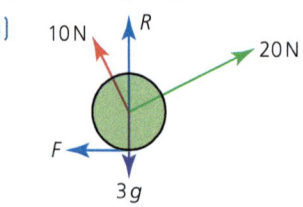

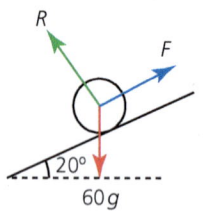

13 (i)   [diagram: block on slope with R, T, F, 10g]
    (ii) T − F − 10g sin 30° and R − 10g cos 30°
    (iii) 19.6 N   (iv) 3 kg
14 T_{AB} = 196 N in tension,
    T_{AC} = 261.$\dot{3}$ N in tension,
    T_{AD} = 326.$\dot{6}$ N in compression
15 (i)   T sin 65° = 735 − R
    (ii) 810.98 N, 82.75 kg
    (iii) 342.7 N
16 (i)   525 N   (ii) 13.1°, 517.5 N

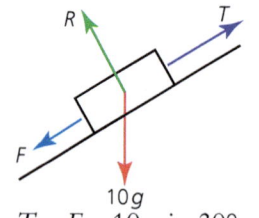

Discussion point page 51
It is much easier to choose to resolve in directions which ensure that one component of at least one unknown force is zero.

Discussion point page 51
Start with AB and BC. Then draw a line in the right direction for CD and another perpendicular line through A. These lines meet at D.

Discussion point page 52
(i)   The sledge accelerates up the hill.
(ii) The sledge is stationary or moving with constant speed. (Forces in equilibrium).
(iii) The acceleration is downhill.

Exercise 2.4
1   [diagram: vectors 6 N, 5 N, 10 N, 3 N, F]
    (iii) **F** = 3**i** + 5**j**, F = 5.83 N at 59° to the horizontal.

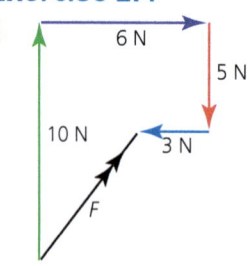

2   [diagram: vectors 5 N, 4 N at 40°, 8 N, F]
    (iii) **F** = 7.83**i** − 4.79**j**, F = 9.18 N, 31.4° below horizontal.
3   [diagram: triangle with 2 N, 2 N, 2√2 N]
    (iii) **F** = 0
4   [diagram: parallelogram 2 N, 5 N, 5 N, 2 N]
    (iii) **F** = 0
5   [diagram: 10 N, 30 N, 25 N, 20 N, F]
    (iii) **F** = 0.34**i** + 0.23**j**, F = 0.41 N at 34° to the slope.
6   [diagram: 8 N, 4 N, 4 N, 6 N, F, θ]
    (iii) **F** = 7.14**i** − 7.26**j**, F = 10.2 N, θ = −45.5°.
7   42.9 N, bearing of 300°
8   (i)   7.73**i** + 20.67**j**
    (ii) 22.1 N at 69.5° to the horizontal
    (iii) **a** = 5.15**i** + 13.78**j**
9   (i)   6 N at 30° to the horizontal.
    (ii) 3.6 m s^{-1}; 5.4 m from O.
10 7.81 N, 26.3°
11 P = 10 N, Q = 17.3 N
12 $Q = P\sqrt{\frac{5}{2}}$, 142°

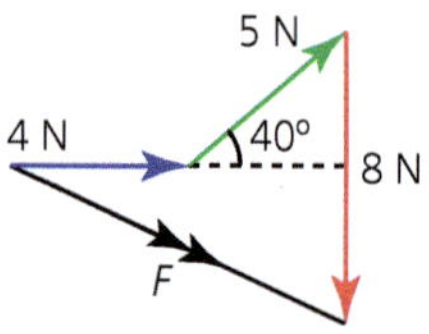

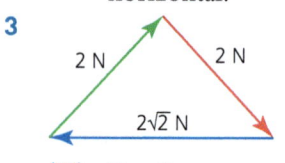

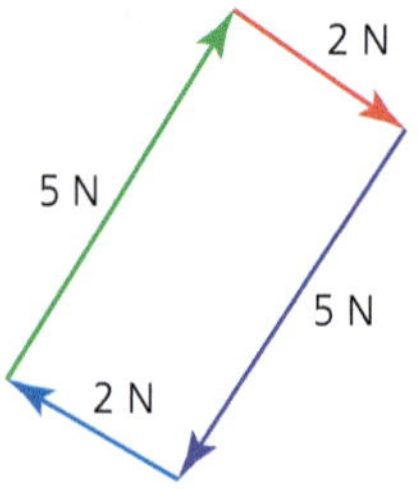

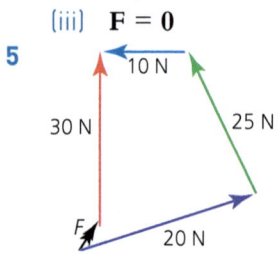

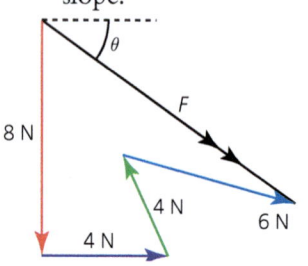

Chapter 3

Discussion point page 58
Assumptions: Cars are treated as particles, frictional force with the road is uniform, road is horizontal, use linear motion with constant deceleration.

Discussion point page 59
A downward slope would extend the skid so u is an overestimate; opposite for upward slope. A smaller final speed would indicate a lower u while a higher final speed would indicate a higher u for the same length of skid. Treating the car and driver as a particle means discounting the effects of air resistance. In reality this would reduce the skid making u an underestimate.

Discussion point page 60
The brakes don't lock. Friction acts between the brake pads and the wheels.

Discussion point page 60
Forwards when pedalling, backwards when freewheeling.

Exercise 3.1
1. (i) 0.082 (ii) 0.020

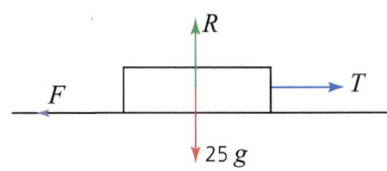

2. 0.245
3. 0.068
4. 0.68
5. (a) $a = 2.156 \text{ ms}^{-2}$; $T = 61.15$ N; $F = 35.3$ N
   (b) $a = 0.22 \text{ ms}^{-2}$; $T = 4.79$ N; $F = 3.92$ N
   (c) $a = 0 \text{ ms}^{-2}$; $T_1 = 58.8$ N; $T_2 = 39.2$ N; $F = 19.6$ N
   (d) $a = 0.065\dot{3} \text{ ms}^{-2}$; $T_1 = 78.9$ N; $F = 17.6$ N; $T_2 = 97.3$ N;
6. 0.60
7. (i) 0.8 ms^{-2} (ii) 0.04 N (iii) 0.082 (iv) 40 m
8. (i) 7.35 ms^{-2} (ii) 17.66 ms^{-1} (iii) 59.9 m
9. (i) 34.3 N (ii) 35.2 N
10. (i) 5 ms^{-2}
    (ii) 4.29 N; 44.4 N; 0.097
    (iii) 3.28 ms^{-2}; 8.10 ms^{-1}
11. (i) 0.194 (ii) 4.84 ms^{-2}
    (iii) 9.84 ms^{-1}
    (iv) 9.84 ms^{-1}
12. (i) 0.408 ms^{-2} (ii) 2.21 s
    (iii) 0.48 ms^{-1}
13. $151 \text{ N} < T < 1341 \text{ N}$
14. (i) $T = \dfrac{100}{\cos\alpha + 0.5\sin\alpha}$
    (ii) 26.6°, 89.4 N
15. (i) 148.4 N (ii) 5.88 N

Chapter 4

Discussion point page 73
The pliers consist of two first class levers: the forces applied tighten the grip on the nut. An extra force at right angles to the previous forces are then applied to tighten the nut.

The adjustable wrench consists of one first class lever. This fits the nut head exactly so that all the force produced is used to tighten the nut.

Discussion point page 79
The sails produce forces at right angles to the mast and so produce a moment on the mast about its base. The tensions in the stays have components perpendicular to the mast acting at its top. The moment of these components helps to balance that of the force from the sails and so makes it less likely that the mast will break.

Exercise 4.1
1. (i) −10 Nm (ii) +25.2 Nm
   (iii) −0.945 Nm
   (iv) −11.73 Nm
2. (i) +0.48 Nm
   (ii) +2.88 Nm
   (iii) +6.2 Nm (iv) 0 Nm
3. (i) $33\tfrac{1}{3}$ N; $16\tfrac{2}{3}$ N
   (ii) 35 N; 55 N
   (iii) 35 N; 75 N
4. 5.36 m
5. $\tfrac{1}{6}$ m from fulcrum on the lighter child's side.
6. $0.37 < x < 1.63$
7. (i) [diagram with T_1, T_2 and 50 N]
   (ii) $T_1 = 16\tfrac{2}{3}$ N; $T_2 = 33\tfrac{1}{3}$ N
8. (i) $R_X = 61.2\dot{4}$ N; $R_Y = 66.7\dot{5}$ N
   (ii) 14.06 kg
9. (i) 280 kg (ii) 28 kg
10. $X = 8$ N; $Y = 12$ N
11. The resultant has magnitude 2 N, is pointing downwards, and its line of action is 7.5 m to the right of A.
12. (i) $\tfrac{1}{4}g(25 + 5m_1 - m_2)$
    (ii) $m_1 = 4\tfrac{1}{6}$ kg; $m_2 = 5\tfrac{5}{6}$ kg

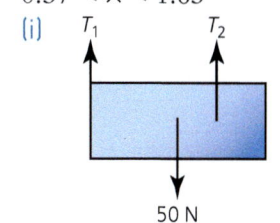

Discussion point page 85
There are two answers. Either it doesn't matter because if the force is downwards it will be negative upwards, or, and better, taking moments about A at the right-hand end shows it must be upwards to counteract the moment of the weight.

Discussion point page 86
No, the rod is symmetrical about its centre so the forces must cancel each other out exactly.

Exercise 4.2
1. (i) 6 Nm
   (ii) −10.72 Nm
   (iii) 22.98 Nm (iv) 0
   (v) −4.24 Nm
   (vi) 4.24 Nm
2. David and Hannah (by radius × 0.027 Nm).

3. (i) 5915.5 kg
   (ii) 4531.5 sec θ kg
4. (i) 42.4 N (ii) 27.7 N
   (iii) 30.1 N
5. (i) $T \cos 30° = 0.866T$; $T \sin 30° = 0.5T$
   (iii) 30 Nm
   (v) $R_H = 8.04$ N, $R_V = 15.36$ N
   (vi) (a) 33.69° (b) 3.23 m
   (vii) $T = \frac{30}{3.23} = 9.28$ N
6. (i) 1405.26 N
   (ii) 638 N, 1611 N
   (iii) $1611 \times 3 = 1405 \sin 55° \times 4.2$
   (iv) (a) The jib stays put
   (b) The jib will rotate in an anticlockwise direction
7. (i) [diagram: B, R_1, R_2, 60°, A, F_2, 50g]
   (ii) 0 Nm (iii) 141.5 N
   (iv) 141.5 N; $\mu \geq 0.29$
   (v) $141.5 \times 6 \sin 60° + 490 \times 3 \cos 60° - 490 \times 6 \cos 60° = 0$
8. (i) [diagram: S, l, R, 20g, α, F]
   (ii) (a) 56.6 N, 56.6 N, 196 N
   (b) 98 N, 98 N, 196 N
   (iii) (a) 0.29 (b) 0.5
9. (i) [diagram: F, 40°, A, Y, 10°, C, B, X, T, 35°]
   (ii) 162 N (iii) 61.7 N
10. (i) $8000 + 10000 \sin 45° - 3000 - 14000 \sin 60° = -53.3$ N
    $10\,000 \cos 45° - 14\,000 \cos 60° = 71.1$ N
    $\sqrt{(53)^2 + 71.1^2} = 88.8$ N < 100 N
    (ii) 1 600 000 Nm
    (iii) 529 N, 529 N
11. (i) [diagram: S, 1.4 m, 1.4 m, 12g, R, 60°, F]
    (ii) 25.5 N, 102.9 N
    (iii) 0.514 (iv) 2.25 m
12. (i) [diagram: YN, 1.5 m, 1 m, 1.5 m, 1 m, RN, A, B, 1000 N, 1500 N, 1000 N]
    (ii) 3596 N (iii) 3497 N at 28.15° above the horizontal
13. (i) MX = 0.2 m, XC = 0.8 m
    (ii) arctan(0.05) = 2.86°
    (iii) 1456.5 N, 1664.6 N
14. $\tan \theta = \frac{1}{2} \tan \varnothing$
15. (ii) $\mu \geq 0.328$

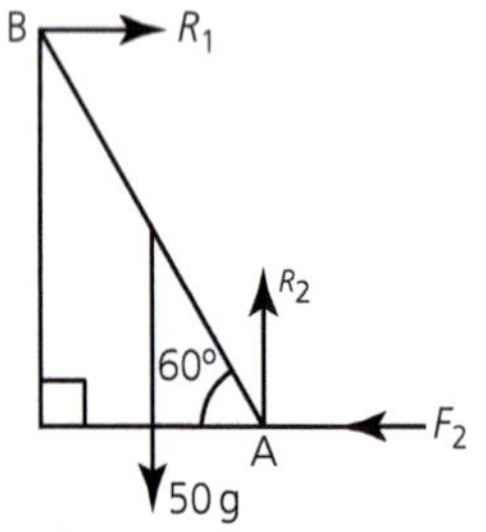

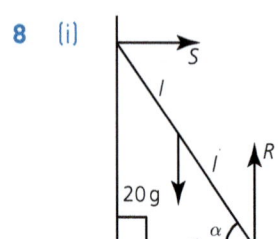

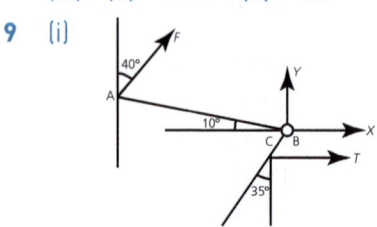

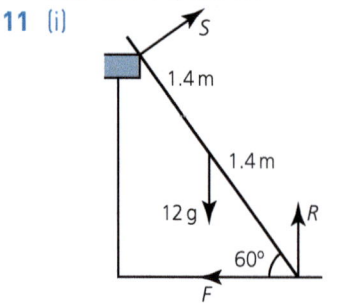

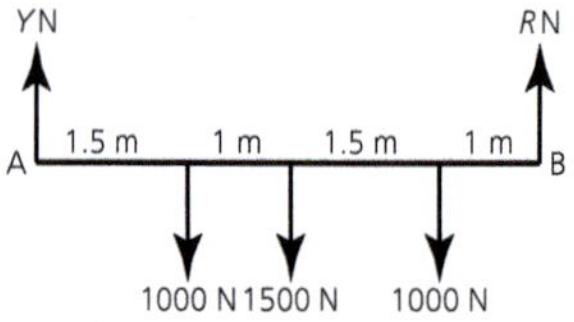

Discussion point page 93
It is likely to topple. Toppling depends on the relative mass of upstairs and downstairs passengers.

Discussion point page 93
In the first case it slides, in the second case it topples. The bus is similar to the second case.

Discussion point page 94
There is a resultant moment about the edge E.

Discussion point page 96
Yes when $\mu = 0.5$ and $\alpha = 26.6°$.

Exercise 4.3
1. (i) 27.44 N (ii) 34.3 N
   (iii) slide
2. (i) 19.6μ (ii) 5.88 N
   (iii) $\mu < 0.3$ (iv) $\mu > 0.3$
3. (i) 14.0° (ii) 18.4°
   (iii) sliding
4. It slides
5. (a) (i) 22.51 N
       (ii) 21.96 N
       (iii) topples
   (b) (i) 22.76 N
       (ii) 25.90 N (iii) slides 63.4°, 22.36 N
6. (i) (a) 50 by 20
       (b) 20 by 10
   (ii) The shortest side is perpendicular to the plane of the slope for maximum likelihood of sliding.
   (iii) (a) $\mu < 0.2$ (b) $\mu > 5$
7. (ii) $F = \mu(150 - P \cos \theta)$ and $F = P \sin \theta$
   (iii) Vertically upwards on edge AB (v) $\mu < \tan \theta$
8. (i) It stays put.
   (ii) It topples.
9. $T \times \frac{4}{5}l = T \times \frac{3}{5}l + W \times \frac{l}{2}$
   $\Rightarrow T = 2.5W$

Chapter 5

Discussion point page 100
Water is captured when the tide is high and allowed to flow away when the tide is low. The flowing water turns turbines, which generate electricity. So the gravitational potential energy of the water is converted into electrical energy. Thus the tidal wave is the source of the energy. The tidal wave is caused by the gravitational pull of the Moon on the Earth's surface and so the energy originates from the Earth–Moon system, resulting in the Moon getting very slightly further away from the Earth with every tide.

Exercise 5.1

1. (i) 2500 J (ii) 40 000 J
   (iii) 5.6×10^9 J
   (iv) 3.7×10^{28} J (v) 10^{-25} J
2. (i) 1000 J (ii) 1070 J
   (iii) 930 J (iv) None
3. (i) 4320 J (ii) 4320 J
   (iii) 144 N
   (iv) $a = 144 \div 60 = 2.4$
   $v = \sqrt{2 \times 2.4 \times 30} = 12$
4. (i) 540 000 J, No
   (ii) 3600 N (iii) No
5. (i) 500 000 J (ii) 6667 N
6. (i) (a) 5250 J
       (b) −13 750 J
   (ii) (a) 495 250 J
        (b) 476 250 J
7. (i) 64 J (ii) dissipated
   (iii) 64 J (iv) 400 N
   (v) 89.4 m s^{-1}
8. (i) 314 600 J (ii) 8279 N
   (iii) Dissipated as heat and sound.
   (iv) Some of the work is dissipated as heat.
9. 18.6 m s^{-1}
10. (i) 240 N (ii) 5.5 m
    (iii) 1320 J
    (iv) 0.5 m s^{-2}, 270 N, 270 J
    (v) 960 J, 90 J

Discussion point page 113

More work cycling into the wind, less if at an angle, minimum if the wind is behind.

Exercise 5.2

1. (i) 9.8 J (ii) 94.5 J
   (iii) −58.8 J (iv) −58.9 J
2. (i) −27.44 J (ii) 54.88 J
   (iii) −11.76 J
3. 17.64 J
4. 23 284.8 J
5. (i) (a) 1504 J (b) 280 J
   (ii) (a) 15.65 m s^{-1}
        (b) 16.15 m s^{-1}
6. (i) 2122 J (ii) The same
7. (i) (a) 1701 J
       (b) 8.69 m s^{-1}
   (ii) (a) Unaltered
        (b) Decreased
8. (i) 1750 J
   (ii) 1750 J, 8.37 m s^{-1}
   (iii) 50°
   (iv) It is always perpendicular to the motion.
9. (i) 153 743 J (ii) 20 000 J
   (iii) The car is not raised by 200 m but by 200 sin 5°.
   (iv) 137 743 J
10. (i) 156.8 J
    (ii) $1.96(80 − x)$
        $= 156.8 − 9.6t^2$
    (iii) $0 \leq t \leq 4.04$
    (iv) 10 m s^{-1} (v) 90 J
11. (i) 34 300 J, 21 875 J
    (ii) 248.5 N (iii) 5061 N
12. (i) 9.8 m s^{-1}
    (ii) $1.47(10t − 4.9t^2)$,
        $0 \leq t \leq 2.04$
    (iii) 5.10 m, 10**i**
    (iv) 10**i** + 10**j**, 14.14 m s^{-1}, 15 J
    (v) No air resistance; No.
13. (i) 109.16 m s^{-1}
    (ii) 114.6 N
    (iii) The heavier (relatively less affected by resistance).
14. (i) 12 J, 8.7612 J
    (ii) 3.24 J (iii) 0.217 N
    (iv) 14.05 m s^{-1}
15. (i) 591.6 J (ii) 758 700 J
16. (i) 960 J (ii) 2352 J
    (iii) 2392 J (iv) 16.9°

Exercise 5.3

1. (i) 308.7 J (ii) 37 044 J
   (iii) 10.29 W
2. (i) 2352 J (ii) 1176 W
   (iii) 1881.6 W; 0 W; 2822.4 W
3. (i) 31 752 J (ii) 16 200 J
   (iii) 15 98.4 J (iv) 1332 N
   (v) Power of the winch = 1598.4 J
4. (i) 703 N
   (ii) The mass of the car.
5. 576 N
6. 245 kW
7. (i) 560 W (ii) 168 000 J
8. (i) $2 \neq \tfrac{1}{2}(0+3) \times 1.5$
   (ii) 0.241 W
9. (i) 20 m s^{-1}
   (ii) 0.0125 m s^{-2}
   (iii) 25 m s^{-1}
10. (i) 1.6×10^7 W
    (ii) 0.0025 m s^{-2}
    (iii) 5.7 m s^{-1}
11. (i) 16 (ii) 320 N
    (iii) 6400 W
    (iv) (a) 1.98 m s^{-2}
        (b) 1.12 m s^{-2}
12. (i) 9800 N, 9746.3 N
    (ii) 3024.4 N
    (iii) 50.406 kW
    (iv) 95.2 km h^{-1}
13. (i) 61 263 J (ii) 510.5 W
    (iii) 46.9 s
    (iv) $\dfrac{0.64^2}{2 \times 5.87} = 0.035$ m
14. (i) 2000 N (ii) 2609 N
    (iii) 32 s; 15 584 W
15. (i) 33.3 m s^{-1}
    (ii) 18.35 m s^{-1}
    (iii) 0.78 m s^{-2}
16. (i) 1.1 m s^{-2} (ii) 750 m

Chapter 6

Discussion point page 127

$t = 0.1 \Rightarrow 20 = −10 + 0.1a$
$\Rightarrow a = 300 \Rightarrow F = 0.06 \times 300 = 18$ N
$t = 0.015 \Rightarrow a = 30 \div 0.015$
$= 2000 \Rightarrow F = 0.06 \times 2000 = 120$ N.

Average means it stays the same over the time period.

Discussion point page 127

Cricket ball: momentum is 6 Ns; kinetic energy is 120 J.

Train: momentum is 200 Ns; kinetic energy is 1 J.

Exercise 6.1

1. (i) 500 Ns
   (ii) 20 000 Ns
   (iii) 2.8×10^8 Ns
   (iv) 2×10^{-22} Ns
2. (i) 18 200 Ns
   (ii) 0.002 25 Ns
   (iii) 3 Ns
   (iv) 10 Ns
3. (i) 15 N
   (ii) 20 m

(iii) 20 m s^{-1}
(iv) 300 J. Work = K.E. gain
(v) 30 Ns, impulse = mom. gain

4 (i) $0.2v - 0.2 \times 5$
   $= 20 \times 0.1 \Rightarrow v = 15\,\text{m s}^{-1}$
 (ii) $v = 5 + \left(\dfrac{20}{0.2}\right) \times 0.1\,\text{m s}^{-1}$
   $= 15$
 (iii) They give the same answer.

5 (i) 1.2 Ns upwards
 (ii) 2 s
 (iii) 0
 (iv) 1.2 Ns

6 (i) 2.125 Ns
 (ii) (a) 21.25 N
      (b) 42.5 N
 (iii) Smaller impulse on hands as it increases the time taken for the ball to stop.

7 (i) 11 800 Ns
 (ii) 99 000 N
 (iii) $11g\,\text{m s}^{-1}$
 (iv) Lower deceleration

8 (i) 5.42 m s^{-1}
 (ii) 108.4 Ns
 (iii) 108.4 Ns
 (iv) 542 N

9 (i) +30 000 Ns
 (ii) −15 000 Ns
 (iii) −45 000 Ns
 (iv) The impulse
 (v) 450 000 N

10 (i) 12 800 Ns
 (ii) 5.12 m s^{-1}

Discussion point page 133
Between impact and separation car travels 0.625 m, van travels 0.125 m.

Exercise 6.2
1 195.45 m s^{-1}
2 (i) 2 m s^{-1}
 (ii) 1.5 m s^{-1}
3 (i) 25.6 m s^{-1}
 (ii) 4444 Ns forward
 (iii) 4444 Ns backwards
4 (i) $1\tfrac{2}{3}$ m s^{-1}
 (ii) 1670 Ns forward on car, backwards on lorry.
5 (i) 0.623 m s^{-1}
 (ii) 9.97 Ns
 (iii) 997 N
6 (i) 4990 m s^{-1}
 (ii) 5000.001 m s^{-1}
7 (i) 3 m s^{-1}
 (ii) Impulse 1500 Ns is too great.
8 (i) 0
 (ii) M: −0.75 m s^{-1}, A: 1.05 m s^{-1}
 (iii) M: −52.5 Ns, A: +52.5 Ns
 (iv) 0
9 (i) 49 000 J
 (ii) 7 m s^{-1}
 (iii) 4 m s^{-1}
 (iv) 42.9%
10 (i) 10 m s^{-1}
 (ii) 24 000 Ns
 (iii) 24 000 Ns
 (iv) 966 000 N
 (v) 0.5 m
11 (i) 1 m s^{-1}
 (ii) 9 m s^{-1}
 (iii) 21 m s^{-1}
 (iv) 33 m s^{-1}
12 (i) 0.196 m s^{-1}
 (ii) 0.385 m s^{-1}
 (iv)

graph of v vs n: points rising and leveling off near $v = 10$

 (v) Faster, ball has negative momentum.
13 (i) $\tfrac{2}{3}$ m s^{-1}
 (iii) true

Discussion point page 138
Tennis ball will rebound higher than the cricket ball.
Heights of second bounces will be lower than those of first bounces.

Exercise 6.3
1 (i) $\tfrac{2}{3}$
 (ii) 1.44 m s^{-1}
 (iii) $\tfrac{3}{4}$
 (iv) 3.2 m s^{-1}
2 (i) 0.3
 (ii) 0
 (iii) 0.95
 (iv) 1
3 (i) 0.8
 (ii) 1.62 Ns
 (iii) 2.43 J
4 (i) 4.43 m s^{-1}
 (ii) 3.98 m s^{-1}
 (iii) 0.9
 (iv) 0.149 J
 (v) 0.149 J
 (vi) 0.656 m
5 (a) (ii) 2.5 m s^{-1}, 3.5 m s^{-1}
      (iii) 3.75 J
 (b) (ii) −0.5 m s^{-1}; 2.5 m s^{-1}
      (iii) 33.75 J
 (c) (ii) 1.2 m s^{-1}; 1.2 m s^{-1}
      (iii) 4.8 J
 (d) (ii) −1 m s^{-1}; 2 m s^{-1}
      (iii) 0 J
 (e) (ii) −0.5 m s^{-1}; 1 m s^{-1}
      (iii) 2.25 J
 (f) (ii) 2 m s^{-1}; 4 m s^{-1}
      (iii) 96 J
6 (i) 1 m s^{-1}
 (ii) 0.2
 (iii) 450 Ns
 (iv) 900 J
7 (i) 19.8 m s^{-1}
 (ii) 0.76
 (iii) 1740 Ns
 (iv) 4175 J
 (v) a low one
8 (i)

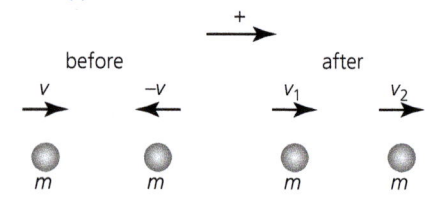

before / after diagram: masses m moving with velocities v and $-v$ before; v_1 and v_2 after

 (ii) $-ev, ev$
 (iv) Kinetic energy cannot be gained during a collision.

9 $\dfrac{13}{32}, \dfrac{15}{32}, \dfrac{9}{8}$

10 $-\dfrac{47}{16}, \dfrac{7}{16}$

11 (i)

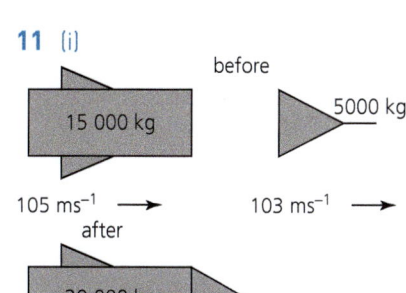

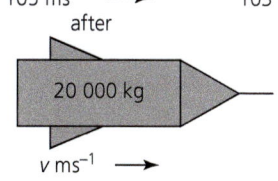

before: 15 000 kg at 105 ms⁻¹, 5000 kg at 103 ms⁻¹
after: 20 000 kg at v ms⁻¹

- (ii) 104.5 m s⁻¹
- (iii) 2 m s⁻¹ forwards
- (iv) 18.73 kg

12 (i) 180 N s

- (ii) The only forces acting are due to the impact. These are *internal* to the pair of particles but *external* to each separate particle.
- (iii) $\frac{2}{9}$
- (iv) $m = 24$; 120 N s in opposite direction to A's original motion.
- (v) 8 kg; it would go backwards.

13 (i)

before: A 2 kg at u ms⁻¹, B 3 kg at 0 ms⁻¹
after: A at v_A ms⁻¹, B at v_B ms⁻¹

- (ii) $2u = 2v_A + 3v_B$; $eu = v_B - v_A$; $v_B = \frac{2}{5}u(1+e)$
- (iii) $e > \frac{2}{3}$
- (iv) $e = \frac{5}{6}$; $\frac{11}{60}u^2$ J

14 (i) $\sqrt{\frac{2h}{g}}, \sqrt{2gh}$

- (ii) $e^2 h$
- (iii) he^{2n}
- (iv) $\sqrt{\left(\frac{2h}{g}\right)}(1+2e)$, $\left(\sqrt{\frac{2h}{g}}\right)(1 + 2e + \ldots + 2e^{n-1})$

- (vi) $\frac{h(1+e^2)}{(1-e^2)}$

16 $v_A = \frac{1}{2}(1-e)u$;

$v_B = \frac{1}{4}(1-e^2)u$;

$v_C = \frac{1}{4}(1+e)^2 u$

Chapter 7

Discussion point page 147

Yes, centre of mass vertically below P.

Discussion point page 149

$4 \times 1\frac{2}{15} + 5 \times \frac{2}{15} = 6 \times \frac{13}{15}$

Exercise 7.1

1 (i) 0.2 m
 (ii) 0
 (iii) −0.72 m
 (iv) 1.19 m
 (v) +0.275 m
 (vi) 0.36 m
 (vii) −0.92 m
 (viii) 0.47 m
2 2.18 m from 20 kg child
3 4.2 cm
4 4680 km
5 0.92 m
6 3.33 mm from centre
7 2.95 cm
8 1.99 kg
9 42 kg
10 $\frac{m_2 l}{(m_1 + m_2)}$ from m_1 end
11 (i) 3.35 m, tips over
 (ii) 4.55 tonnes
 (iii) $L(l-d) < Md + C(a+d)$, $C(a-d) < Md$
 (iv) $\frac{2Mad}{(l-d)(a-d)}$

Exercise 7.2

1 (i) (2.3, −0.3)
 (ii) (0, 1.75)
 (iii) $\left(\frac{1}{24}, \frac{1}{6}\right)$
 (iv) (−2.7, −1.5)
2 $(5, 6\frac{1}{3})$
3 (i) (20, 60)
 (ii) (30, 65)
 (iii) (30, 60)
4 23 cm
5 (i) (3, 2)
 (ii) $\left(1\frac{1}{6}, 1\frac{1}{6}\right)$
 (iii) (1.6, 1.6)
6 (i) (1.5, −1.5)
 (ii) (1.5, −2.05)
7 (i) 0.2 cm below O
 (ii) 9.1°
8 24.4°
9 (i) (0.5a, 1.2a)
 (ii) 3.9°
 (iii) $2m$
10 8.78 cm from the base on the axis of symmetry.
11 (i) (28, 60)
 (ii) (52, 60)
 (iv) 40 cm
12 (i) (a) (10, 2.5)
  (b) (12.5, 5)
  (c) (15, 7.5)
  (d) (17.5, 10)
  (e) (20, 12.5)
 (ii) 5
 (iii) $(9 + n, 2.5n)$, 11
 (iv) 102.5 cm
13 (i) 2.25
 (ii) 0.56 m; not feasible as it would not stay within the shape.
 (iii) 0.40, $\left(\frac{1}{2}, 1\frac{1}{2}\right)$
15 $\left(-1, \frac{4}{\pi}\right)$
16 (i) (a) $\left(\frac{4m+M}{8m+4M}\right)h$
  (b) $\frac{h}{2}\left(\frac{M\alpha^2 + m}{M\alpha + m}\right)$

Chapter 8

Discussion point page 168

e.g. Cube: $V = x^3$, $[V] = L^3$

Cone: $V = \frac{1}{3}\pi r^2 h$, $[V] = L^3$

Sphere: $V = \frac{4}{3}\pi r^3$, $[V] = L^3$

Activity 8.1 page 170

Quantity	Formula	Dimensions	S.I. unit
Area	$l \times w$	L^2	m^2
Volume	$l \times w \times h$	L^3	m^3
Speed	$\frac{d}{t}$	LT^{-1}	ms^{-1}
Acceleration	$\frac{v}{t}$	LT^{-2}	ms^{-2}
g	acceleration	LT^{-2}	ms^{-2}
Force (= mass × acceleration)	$F = ma$	MLT^{-2}	N, newton
Weight	mg	MLT^{-2}	N, newton
Kinetic energy	$\frac{1}{2}mv^2$	ML^2T^{-2}	J, joule
Gravitational potential energy	mgh	ML^2T^{-2}	J, joule
Work	Fs	ML^2T^{-2}	J, joule
Power	Fv	ML^2T^{-3}	W, watt
Impulse	Ft	MLT^{-1}	Ns
Momentum	mv	MLT^{-1}	Ns
Pressure (= force/area)	force/area	$ML^{-1}T^{-2}$	Nm^{-2}
Density	mass/volume	ML^{-3}	kgm^{-3}
Moment	Fd	ML^2T^{-2}	Nm
Angle	$\theta = s/r$	dimensionless	radian
Gravitational constant (G)	$F = \frac{Gm_1m_2}{d^2}$	$M^{-1}L^3T^{-2}$	Nm^2kg^{-2}
Coefficient of friction	$F = \mu R$	dimensionless	–
Coefficient of restitution	v separation/v approach	dimensionless	–

Exercise 8.1

1. (i) All L^2T^{-2}; consistent
   (ii) All L; consistent
   (iii) All MLT^{-2}; consistent
   (iv) L.H.S. MLT^{-2}, R.H.S. ML^2T^{-2}; inconsistent
   (v) L.H.S. ML^2T^{-2}, R.H.S. MLT^{-1}; inconsistent
   (vi) All MLT^{-2}; consistent
   (vii) L.H.S. ML^2T^{-2}, R.H.S. MLT^{-2}; inconsistent
   (viii) All ML^2T^{-2}; consistent
   (ix) L.H.S. ML^2T^{-3}, R.H.S. L^2T^{-3}; inconsistent

2. (i) $[v] = LT^{-1}$, $[h] = L$, $[\rho] = ML^{-3}$, $[g] = LT^{-2}$
   (ii) $\alpha = \frac{1}{2}$, $\beta = 0$, $\gamma = \frac{1}{2}$, $v = k\sqrt{hg}$
   (iii) Deep water
   (iv) No difference

3. (i) $t = kd^\alpha g^\beta$
   (ii) $\alpha = \frac{1}{2}$, $\beta = -\frac{1}{2}$, $t = k\sqrt{\dfrac{d}{g}}$
   (iii) $k = 150$
   (iv) 36.7 s

4. (ii) $T = k\sqrt{\dfrac{a}{g}}$
   (iii) $k = 7.70$

5. (i) $e = \dfrac{\text{velocity}}{\text{velocity}}$
   (ii) $\alpha = 2$, $\beta = 0$, $\gamma = -1$, $h = \dfrac{kv^2}{g}$
   (iii) h is independent of m so both bounce to the same height
   (iv) because e is dimensionless and is included in k
   (v) $h = \dfrac{e^2 v^2}{2g}$
   (vi) $k = \dfrac{e^2}{2}$ is dimensionless

6. (ii) $x + y = 3$
   (iii) $R = 6.72 \times 10^6 \times \dfrac{r^4}{a}$
   (iv) 0.213 m^3 s^{-1}

7. (i) $V = \dfrac{kmg}{r\eta}$
   (ii) $m = \dfrac{4}{3}\pi r^3 \rho$
   (iii) $V = \dfrac{k_1 r^2 \rho g}{\eta}$
   (iv) 0.113 cm

8. (i) π is the circumference of a circle divided by its diameter; dimensionless.
   (ii) $M^{-1}L^3T^{-2}$
   (iii) 1.54×10^9
   (iv) π (dimensionless) is independent of units, G (not dimensionless) is dependent on its units

9. (i) $M^{-1}L^3T^{-2}$
   (ii) 1.002
   (iii) $0.0123 M_E$, $0.273 R_E$, $0.165 g_E$
   (iv) $0.107 M_E$, $0.533 R_E$, $0.379 g_E$

10. (ii) $ML^{-1}T^{-2}$, ML^{-3}
    (iii) $\alpha = -1$, $\beta = \frac{1}{2}$, $\gamma = -\frac{1}{2}$; by experiment or analysis
    (iv) 1.2
    (v) much greater; $A \propto \rho c^2$ and $c_{water} \gg c_{air}$, $\rho_{water} \gg \rho_{air}$

11. (i) $M^{-1}L^3T^{-2}$
    (ii) $t = k\sqrt{\dfrac{r_0^3}{Gm}}$
    (iii) Yes
    (iv) $t = \dfrac{k_1}{\sqrt{G\rho_0}}$

12. (i) $f = \dfrac{k}{l}\sqrt{\dfrac{T}{m}}$
    (ii) $f = \dfrac{1}{2l}\sqrt{\dfrac{T}{m}}$
    (iii) 316.2 cycles s^{-1}

13. (iii) MT^{-1}
    (iv) Dimensionless
    (v) $\varepsilon = \dfrac{kcu}{mg}$, $R = R_M\left(1 - \dfrac{kcu}{mg}\right)$

14. (i) $T^2 L^{-3}$
    (ii) 2.98×10^{-19}
    (iii)

Mercury	0.241
Venus	0.615
Earth	1
Mars	1.874
Jupiter	11.9
Saturn	29.5
Uranus	84.1
Neptune	165

Practice questions: Set 1 (page 181)

1. [Fuel consumption in litre per 100 km] $= \dfrac{L^3}{L} = L^2$
   Need to express in m^2.
   1 litre per 100 km is 10^{-8} m^2

2. (i) PCLM (2); NEL (2);
   $v_A = \dfrac{U}{3}(2-e)$,
   $v_B = \dfrac{2U}{3}(1+e)$
   (ii) PCLM with coalescence giving
   $v_D = \dfrac{U}{6}(2+2e-3k)$
   (iii) Need
   $\dfrac{U}{3}(2-e) > \dfrac{U}{6}(2+2e-3k)$
   so ... $k > \dfrac{2}{3}(2e-1)$.
   (iv) Either: linear momentum is conserved through the whole of the process of obtaining E. Or: Equate initial and final momentum so
   $2mU - mkU = 4mv_E$
   so v_E is independent of e.
   Put $k = \dfrac{4}{9}$ to give
   $v_E = \dfrac{7U}{18}$ \hfill (1) [4]
   That the final answer is independent of e comes neatly from considering initial and final momenta but the other method gets full marks.

3. (i) Use of $P = Fv$
   $F - 1200 \times 9.8 \times 0.1 - 250 = 1200 \times 0.7$
   (so $F = 2266$)
   $P = 33\,990$ so about 34 kW.
   (ii) $0 - \dfrac{1}{2} \times 1200 \times 12^2$
   $= -\begin{pmatrix} 1200 \times 9.8 \times 0.1 \\ + 1200 \times 9.8 \times 0.4 \\ \times \cos(\sin^{-1}(0.1)) \end{pmatrix}$
   $d - 1500$

86 400 − 1500 = $d \times 5856.42...$ so $d = 14.496...$ so 14.5 m (3 s.f.)

(iii) Coulomb's law applies; slope is uniformly steep; slope is uniformly rough; slides in a straight line; …

4 (i) Moment A $5\sin\alpha \times T - 2.5W\cos\alpha = 0$ so $T = \dfrac{\cos\alpha}{2\sin\alpha}W$
$T = F; R = W; F = \mu R$
so $\mu = \dfrac{\cos\alpha}{2\sin\alpha} = \dfrac{1}{2\tan\alpha}$.

(ii) Doesn't say on the point of slipping so $F \le \mu R$.

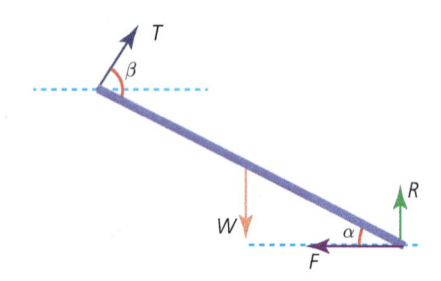

Values of $\sin\beta$, $\cos\alpha$ etc
$T\sin\beta + R - W = 0$;
$F = T\sin\alpha$;
$5T - 2.5W\cos\alpha = 0$
$\mu \ge \dfrac{12}{41}$ (0.2926…)

5 (i) Let distance of C.o.m from A be X m.
$(4 \times 4.5 + 6 \times 1.5)$
$X = 18 \times 2 + 9 \times 7$ so
$X = \dfrac{99}{27} = \dfrac{11}{3}$

(ii) $54\begin{pmatrix}\bar{x}\\\bar{y}\end{pmatrix} = 27\begin{pmatrix}\tfrac{11}{3} - 5\\0\end{pmatrix}$
$+ 27\begin{pmatrix}0\\\tfrac{11}{3}\end{pmatrix}; \begin{pmatrix}\bar{x}\\\bar{y}\end{pmatrix} = \begin{pmatrix}-\tfrac{2}{3}\\\tfrac{11}{6}\end{pmatrix}$

$\tan\alpha = \dfrac{\tfrac{2}{3}}{\left(10 - \tfrac{11}{6}\right)}$
$= \dfrac{2}{3} \times \dfrac{6}{49} = \dfrac{4}{49}$

(iii) so $\alpha = 4.6668...°$

6 (i) Tension in the string is mg when system in equilibrium.
c.w. moment is $0.25g \times 1.6\sin(\theta)$; a.c moment is $mg \times 2\sin(\phi)$.

(ii) 1.35 rad

(iii) The a.c. moment is greater than the c.w. moment so the system will move a.c.

(iv) One or more assumptions are not correct. Most likely there is friction at the hinge or on the string passing over the pulley.

Chapter 9

Exercise 9.1

1 $12.65\ \text{m s}^{-1}$
2 $6.32\ \text{m s}^{-1}$; bearing 072°
3 $\begin{pmatrix}12t\\0\\10\end{pmatrix}; \begin{pmatrix}12mt\\0\\10m\end{pmatrix}$
4 $\begin{pmatrix}\tfrac{5}{4}t^3 + 2t\\\tfrac{1}{2}t^3 + 1\\\tfrac{3}{4}t^2 + 5t + 3\end{pmatrix}$
5 (i) $-0.1\mathbf{i} + 0.2\mathbf{j}$, $5\mathbf{i} + 3\mathbf{j}$;
  (ii) $6\tfrac{2}{3}$ s, $6.13\ \text{m s}^{-1}$;
  (iii) 39.6 m, 51.8°
6 15.26°
7 (i) $\begin{pmatrix}8\\-6\\4\end{pmatrix}, \begin{pmatrix}4\\-3\\2\end{pmatrix}$;

  (ii) $\begin{pmatrix}-30\\15\\10\end{pmatrix}$;
  (iii) 5 s
8 $13\ \text{m s}^{-2}$; bearing = 247°
9 (i) $\mathbf{v} = 2t^2\mathbf{i} + (6t - t^2)\mathbf{j}$;
  $\mathbf{r} = \tfrac{2}{3}t^3\mathbf{i} + \left(3t^2 - \tfrac{1}{3}t^3\right)\mathbf{j}$
  (ii) 2 s, $11.31\ \text{m s}^{-1}$
  (iii) 10.75 m, 29.7°
10 (i) $4.33\mathbf{i} - 2.5\mathbf{j}$
   (ii) $\mathbf{v} = 14.33\mathbf{i} + 2.5\mathbf{j}$;
   $\mathbf{r} = 76.67\mathbf{i} - 8.33\mathbf{j}$
11 (i) 73.5 m, 045°
   (ii) $\begin{pmatrix}20\\30t - 3t^2\end{pmatrix}$ cannot be 0 as $v_x = 20$ for all t.
   (iii) 5 s
   (iv) $77.6\ \text{m s}^{-1}$
12 (ii) $3\mathbf{i} + 6\mathbf{k}$
   (iii) 6.71 m
   (iv) 63.4°
13 (i) $3\ \text{m s}^{-2}$
   (iii) $(1.2t + 0.9t^2)\mathbf{i} + (1.6t + 1.2t^2)\mathbf{j}$
   (iv) $58.5\mathbf{i} + 63\mathbf{j}$
14 (i) $\mathbf{v} = -2\lambda t\sin\lambda t^2\mathbf{i} + 2\lambda t\cos\lambda t^2\mathbf{j} + 2\lambda t\mathbf{k}$;
   $\mathbf{a} = (-2\lambda\sin\lambda t^2 - (2\lambda t)^2\cos\lambda t^2)\mathbf{i} + (2\lambda\cos\lambda t^2 - (2\lambda t)^2\sin\lambda t^2)\mathbf{j} + 2\lambda\mathbf{k}$
   (iii) $4m\lambda^2 t^2$
   (iv) $4m\lambda$

Exercise 9.2

1 (i) $y = 2.4x - 0.2x^2$
  (ii) $x = \dfrac{y^2}{32}$
  (iii) $y = \dfrac{1}{16}(-5x^2 - 18x + 23)$
  (iv) $y = 4 - \dfrac{x}{5}$

(v) $x = \left(\frac{y-1}{5}\right) + \sqrt[3]{\frac{y-1}{5}}$

(vi) $y = (\ln x)^2$

(vii) $y = \frac{10}{x}$

2 (i) [graph: curve from 0 rising to about 4 then falling, x from 0 to 30]

(ii) [graph: curve rising to about 30 then falling, x from 0 to 30]

(iii) [graph: figure-eight/lemniscate shape, x and y from −5 to 5]

3 (a) (i) $\mathbf{r} = 4t\mathbf{i} + (3t - 5t^2)\mathbf{j}$

(ii) $y = \frac{3}{4}x - \frac{5}{16}x^2$

(b) (i) $\mathbf{r} = 3t\mathbf{i} + \left(3t^2 - \frac{1}{3}t^3\right)\mathbf{j}$

(ii) $y = \frac{1}{3}x^2 - \frac{1}{81}x^3$

4 (i) $\left(2t + \frac{1}{2}t^2\right)\mathbf{i} + \left(5t - t^2\right)\mathbf{j}$

(ii) [graph: curve rising to 4 then falling, x from 0 to 20]

(iii) $a = 2.236$

5 (i) $\begin{pmatrix} 30 - 2t \\ -10t \end{pmatrix}$

(ii) $\begin{pmatrix} 30t - t^2 \\ 80 - 5t^2 \end{pmatrix}$

(iii) [graph: curve from (0,80) down to about (100,0)]

6 (i) $\begin{pmatrix} 10 \\ 3t - 6t^2 + 20 \end{pmatrix}$

(ii) $\begin{pmatrix} 10t \\ 1.5t^2 - 2t^3 + 20t \end{pmatrix}$

(iii) $y = 2x + 0.015x^2 - 0.002x^3$

(iv) [graph: curve rising to about 40 then falling, x from 0 to 30]

7 (i) A circle centre (0, 0) radius 3 m

(ii) $\mathbf{v} = \begin{pmatrix} -3\sin t \\ 3\cos t \end{pmatrix}$, $\mathbf{a} = \begin{pmatrix} -3\cos t \\ -3\sin t \end{pmatrix}$

(iii) Speed = 3 ms^{-1}, Magnitude of acceleration = 3 ms^{-2}

8 (i) Circle centre (1, −1); radius 2 m

(ii) $\mathbf{v} = \begin{pmatrix} -6\sin 3t \\ 6\cos 3t \end{pmatrix}$, $\mathbf{a} = \begin{pmatrix} -18\cos 3t \\ -18\sin 3t \end{pmatrix}$

(iii) $\omega = 3$, $\mathbf{c} = \begin{pmatrix} -1 \\ 1 \end{pmatrix}$

9 $(x-2)^2 + (y-4)^2 = 1$

10 (i) $y = 1 - 2x^2$. It cuts the x-axis at $\left(\pm\frac{1}{\sqrt{2}}, 0\right)$ and the y-axis at (0, 1).

(ii) 2π

(iii) $\frac{\pi}{2}, \frac{3\pi}{2}$

(iv) It starts at the top, moves to the right until it reaches the point (1, −1) where it stops momentarily and then retraces its path back to the top. Then it does the same on the left reaching the point (−1, −1) stopping momentarily then returning to the top having completed one cycle when $t = 2\pi$. To show this using software you need to slow it down by using very small steps. It is also helpful to split the motion up into several parts; otherwise it is not clear when it is retracing the same path.

(v) 0.78

Exercise 9.3

1 (i) $\begin{pmatrix} 21 \\ 28 \end{pmatrix}$

(ii) $\mathbf{v} = \begin{pmatrix} 21 \\ 28 \end{pmatrix} - \begin{pmatrix} 0 \\ 9.8 \end{pmatrix}t$,

$\mathbf{r} = \begin{pmatrix} 21 \\ 28 \end{pmatrix}t - \frac{1}{2}\begin{pmatrix} 0 \\ 9.8 \end{pmatrix}t^2$

(iii) 40 m

(iv) 120 m

2 Greatest height of the stone is 3.265... m < 4 m. The stone reaches the house at height 0.975 m and 0.8 < 0.975 < 2.0 so it hits the window.

3 (i) $x = 10t$, $y = 10\sqrt{3}t - 4.9t^2$

(iii) 35.3 m

(iv) The ball passes below the bird.

4 (i) 35 ms^{-1} at angle arctan 2 = 63.4° to the horizontal

(ii) (A) and (B) Both 100 m

5 (i) and (ii) The dimensions of all three terms are shown to be L.

6 (ii) $\sin 2\alpha$ has maximum value of 1 when $2\alpha = 90°$ and so $\alpha = 45°$. The maximum range is $\frac{u^2}{g}$.

7 (i) 44.0 ms^{-1} at 63.0° to the horizontal

(ii) 77.8°

8 (i) $x = ut\cos\alpha$; $y = ut\sin\alpha - \frac{1}{2}gt^2$

(iii) 35.77° and 61.35°

(iv) 87.11 m and 77.28 m.

9 (ii) 33.7°

(iii) 6.52 m s^{-1}

10 (i) Conjecture: that two particles projected from the same place with the same initial speed and angles of projection α and β will land in the same place if $\alpha + \beta = 90°$

(ii) Difference in flight time is $\frac{2u}{g}(\cos\alpha - \sin\alpha)$ where α is the smaller angle.

11 (i) $y = x\tan\alpha - \frac{x^2}{250}(\tan^2\alpha + 1)$

(iii) 80 500 m^2

12 Conditions $p_2 = q_2$, $p_3 = q_3$,
$p_1 > q_1$, $\dfrac{2p_3}{g} > \dfrac{a}{p_1 - q_1}$
Height $\dfrac{ap_3}{(p_1 - q_1)} - \dfrac{ga^2}{2(p_1 - q_1)^2}$

Exercise 9.4

1 (i) $\mathbf{a} = -g\sin\theta\mathbf{i} - g\cos\theta\mathbf{j}$,
$\mathbf{u} = u\cos\alpha\mathbf{i} + u\sin\alpha\mathbf{j}$

(ii) $\mathbf{v} = (u\cos\alpha - gt\sin\theta)\mathbf{i}$
$+ (u\sin\alpha - gt\cos\theta)\mathbf{j}$
$\mathbf{r} = (ut\cos\alpha - \tfrac{1}{2}gt^2\sin\theta)\mathbf{i}$
$+ (ut\sin\alpha - \tfrac{1}{2}gt^2\cos\theta)\mathbf{j}$

(iii) When $\theta = 0$ the slope is not a slope but a horizontal plane. The expression for R is that for the range of a projectile across a horizontal plane.

2 2.36 s, 27.21 m

3 9.15 m

4 $v_X = \dfrac{25}{\sqrt{3}}$, $v_Y = -25 \Rightarrow \tan\theta = \sqrt{3}$

5 (a) 19.9 m, (b) 74.3 m

6 (i) 13.9°
(ii) It lands at O

7 (i) 40.9° (ii) 90°
(iii) 61.25 m
(iv) It will not go any further up the plane.

9 (ii) $\dfrac{2V^2}{g}\sin\beta(1 + \tan^2\beta)$;
(iii) $2\tan\beta$

10 (i) $\dfrac{2u}{g\cos\theta}$
(ii) $\dfrac{2u^2\sin\theta}{g\cos^2\theta}$
(iii) $\tfrac{1}{2}\cot\theta$

11 (i) $y = \dfrac{u^2}{2g} - \dfrac{gx^2}{2u^2}$
(ii) $y = mx$
(iii) $m = \tfrac{3}{4}$, $\theta = 36.9°$

12 (ii) $\dfrac{dR}{d\alpha} = \dfrac{2u^2}{g\cos^2\theta}\cos(2\alpha + \theta) = 0$ when $2\alpha + \theta = 90°$
(iii) $2\alpha + \theta = 90° \Rightarrow \alpha = \tfrac{1}{2}(90° - \theta)$
(iv) $R = \dfrac{u^2}{g\cos^2\theta}[\sin(2\alpha + \theta) - \sin\theta] \Rightarrow$
$R_m = \dfrac{u^2}{g\cos^2\theta}[1 - \sin\theta] = \dfrac{u^2}{g(1 + \sin\theta)}$

Exercise 9.5

1 (i) $\dfrac{dv}{dt} = 5t + 1$; $12\,\text{ms}^{-1}$

(ii) $v\dfrac{dv}{dx} = \dfrac{2}{5+x}$; $2\sqrt{\ln 2}\,\text{ms}^{-1}$

(iii) $v\dfrac{dv}{dx} = \dfrac{2}{(1+x)^2}$; $\sqrt{2}\,\text{ms}^{-1}$

(iv) $\dfrac{dv}{dt} = 9 - v^2$; $\tfrac{1}{6}\ln(2)\,\text{s}$

(v) $v\dfrac{dv}{dx} = v^2 + 1$; $\tfrac{1}{2}\ln 2\,\text{m}$

(vi) $\dfrac{dv}{dt} = v^2 + 1$; $\dfrac{\pi}{4}$

(vii) $v\dfrac{dv}{dx} = \dfrac{2}{(2+x)^3}$; $0.53\,\text{ms}^{-1}$

(viii) $\dfrac{dv}{dt} = 2\sin 3t$; $\tfrac{2}{3}\,\text{ms}^{-1}$

2 (i) $\begin{pmatrix} 10 - 2t \\ 20 - 10t \end{pmatrix}$; $\begin{pmatrix} 10t - t^2 \\ 20t - 5t^2 \end{pmatrix}$

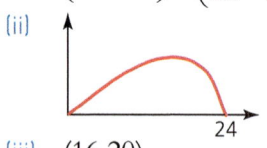

(ii) [graph]

(iii) (16, 20)

3 (ii) $69e^{-0.2t} - 49$
(iii) $345(1 - e^{-0.2t}) - 49t$
(iv) 16.1 m

4 (ii) 3.93 m

5 (i) $\begin{pmatrix} 15e^{-0.5t} \\ 40e^{-0.5t} - 20 \end{pmatrix}$

(ii) $\begin{pmatrix} 30(1 - e^{-0.5t}) \\ 80(1 - e^{-0.5t}) - 20t \end{pmatrix}$

(iii) $y = \tfrac{8}{3}x + 40\ln\left(1 - \dfrac{x}{30}\right)$

(iv) [graph]

6 (ii) $2040(1 - e^{-0.005t})$
(iii) 126.4 m

7 (ii) $v = 16\left(1 - e^{-\tfrac{1}{8}t}\right)$
(iii) 47.1 m

8 (i) 2.4 m
(ii) $\begin{pmatrix} \dfrac{4}{4t+1} \\ 3 - 10t \end{pmatrix}$

(iii) $\begin{pmatrix} \ln(4t+1) \\ 3t - 5t^2 \end{pmatrix}$

(iv) $y = \tfrac{1}{16}(1 - e^x)(5e^x - 17)$

(v) 1.22 m

9 (ii) $\dfrac{2U^{1.5}}{3k}$

10 (i) 1.002 s
(ii) 7.98 m
(iii) $v = 8(1 - e^{-1.25t})$
(iv) $x = 8t - 6.4(1 - e^{-1.25t})$

11 (ii) [ellipse graph, x from −5 to 5, y from −4 to 4]

(iii) $\dfrac{x^2}{16} + \dfrac{y^2}{9} = 1$

12 (i) $a = 2x(x^2 - 4)$; 2.625 N
(ii) $2\left(\dfrac{1 - e^{-4t}}{1 + e^{-4t}}\right)$
(iii) 2 m

13 (A) (i) $k = \dfrac{3mu^2}{8s}$
(ii) $[k] = \text{MLT}^{-2}$
(iii) The probe never leaves the gas cloud.
(iv) $\dfrac{4s}{3}$

(B) (i) $k = \dfrac{mu}{2s}$
(ii) $[k] = \text{MT}^{-1}$
(iii) The probe never leaves the gas cloud.
(iv) $2s$

(C) (i) $k = \dfrac{m\ln 2}{s}$
(ii) $[k] = \text{ML}^{-1}$
(iii) $\dfrac{u}{8}$
(iv) $3s$

Chapter 10

Discussion point page 226
Forces which pull them towards the centre of the circle.
Gravity pulls it in.
It moves off at a tangent. No.

Exercise 10.1
1. (i) 8.2 rad s^{-1}
   (ii) 4.7 rad s^{-1}
   (iii) 3.5 rad s^{-1}
2. 2865 rpm
3. (i) (a) 0.033 rpm
      (b) 0.0035 rad s^{-1}
   (ii) 0.24 m s^{-1}
4. 32.5 rad s^{-1}
5. (i) 50 rad s^{-1}
   (ii) 150 rad s^{-1}
6. (i) 3820 rpm
   (ii) 2080 rpm
7. (i) 1.99×10^{-7} rad s^{-1}
   (ii) 7.27×10^{-5} rad s^{-1}
   (iii) 465 m s^{-1}
   (iv) About 290 m s^{-1} at latitude 51.5°
8. 2.29:1
9. (i) 61.7 J
   (ii) Points on a large object would travel with different speeds.
10. (i) big: 0.126 m s^{-1}, small: 0.00140 m s^{-1}
    (ii) 90:1 the radius is also involved.
11. (i) 4.91 m
    (ii) 12.3 m s^{-1}
12. (i) $v = 2\cos t\mathbf{i} - 2\sin t\mathbf{j} - \frac{1}{2}\mathbf{k}$
    (ii) $|v| = \sqrt{4.25} = 2.06$ m s^{-1}
    (iii) $\mathbf{a} = -2\sin t\mathbf{i} - 2\cos t\mathbf{j}$; magnitude 2 m s^{-2} horizontally towards the vertical axis.

Activity 10.1 page 236
When you turn fast enough, the coin flies off the card. When the card is tilted it stays put at higher angular speeds.

Discussion point page 237
The answer is described in the text that follows.

Discussion point page 239
1. Resolve perpendicular to the slope:
   $R - mg\cos\alpha = m\dfrac{v^2}{r}\sin\alpha$. Then parallel to the slope. No slipping down if
   $mg\sin\alpha - F = m\dfrac{v^2}{r}\cos\alpha$, and $F < \mu R$. No slipping up if $mg\sin\alpha + F = m\dfrac{v^2}{r}\cos\alpha$, and $F < \mu R$.
   Substitute for F and R and rearrange.
2. The bend is safe at 30 mph. In general, bends are safer for large r. As long as $\mu > \tan\alpha$, there is no lower limit for v and then α can be increased in order to increase the upper limit.

Exercise 10.2
1. (i) Neither, both have $\omega = 0.75$ rad s^{-1}.
   (ii) No because they have the same angular speed.
   (iii) 13.5 m s^{-2}, 11.25 m s^{-2}
   (iv) Towards the centre for circular motion
2. (i) (a) Neither slips
       (b) B slips, A doesn't
       (c) Both slip
   (ii) A slips first, radius matters, mass doesn't matter.
3. (i) Accelerates because direction changes.
   (ii) 11.25 m s^{-2}
   (iii) 2250 N
   (iv) No, outside wheels go faster so force is greater.
4. (i) T for fixed seats.
   (ii) F, as $v = r\omega$ so speed depends on r.
   (iii) F, as $a = r\omega^2$ so acceleration depends on r.
5. (i) (a) 0.5 rad s^{-1}
       (b) 1 m s^{-2}
       (c) 60 N towards centre
   (ii) skater is a particle
6. B has greater force because greater acceleration.
7. (i) (a) $\dfrac{(2 \times 10^7)}{\sqrt{r}}$ (3 s.f.)
       (b) $\pi r^{\frac{3}{2}} \times 10^{-7}$ s
   (ii) $T^2 = \pi^2 \times 10^{-14} r^3$
   (iii) 4.23×10^7 m
8. (i) 263 N
   (ii) The weight of the sphere is very small compared with the tension of the cord.
   (iii) 23 m s^{-1}
9. (i) 5.71×10^{-3} m s^{-2}
   (ii) 1.77×10^{30} kg
   (iii) Any planet in this orbit would have the same period whatever its mass.
10. (i) Vertical force required to balance weight.
    (ii) 12.57 rad s^{-1}

(iii) 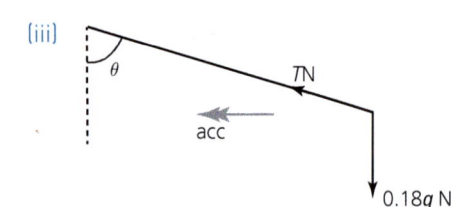 [diagram: angle θ, T N, acc, 0.18g N]

(iv) $T\sin\theta = mr\omega^2 = 0.18 \times 0.8\sin\theta \times 12.57^2$;
$T\cos\theta = mg = 1.764$
in second column in Q10:

(v) $\arccos\left(\dfrac{1.764}{0.18 \times 0.8 \times 12.57^2}\right) = 85.55\ldots°$

(vi) 22.8 N

11 (i) 44 mph (19.8 m s^{-1})
   (ii) 4 mph (1.98 m s^{-1}) faster

12 (i) 6272 N
   (a) The car is about to skid on a bend.
   (b) The car is accelerating or braking and is about to skid.
   (ii) 69 mph (30.7 m s^{-1})
   (iii) 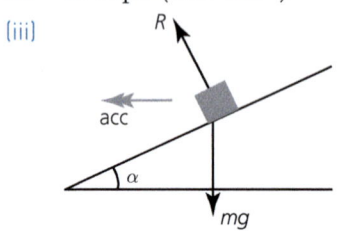 [diagram: R, acc, α, mg]

(iv) $R\sin\alpha = \dfrac{mv^2}{r}$, $R\cos\alpha = mg$

(vi) 10.8° or 0.189 rad

13 (i) $\dfrac{\pi}{30}$ rad s^{-1}
   (ii) $\dfrac{\pi}{3}$ m s^{-1}
   (iii) No transverse acceleration.
   (iv) $40g\cos\theta - R\cos\phi = \dfrac{4}{9}\pi^2$
   (v) 388.1, 30.3°

14 (i) $M = 0.6m$
   (ii) 5.72 rad s^{-1}

15 (ii) 2.8 m s^{-1}
   (iii) 1.35 s

16 (ii) $6T_1 + 8T_2 = 30$; $T_1 = 0.57$ N $T_2 = 3.32$ N

Exercise 10.3

1 (i) 0.02 rad s^{-2}
  (ii) 900 rad

2 (i) 6.28 rad s^{-2}
  (ii) 4 revs

3 (i) 4 rad s^{-1}
  (ii) 0.0005 rad s^{-2}
  (iii) 16 000 rad
  (iv) 32 000 m

4 9.42 m s^{-1}

5 (i) area = total angle turned through 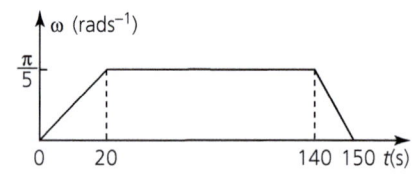
  [graph: ω (rad s^{-1}) vs t(s), rising from 0 to π/5 at t=20, constant until t=140, falling to 0 at t=150]
  (ii) 84.82 rad, 254 m
  (iii) 1.18 m s^{-2} 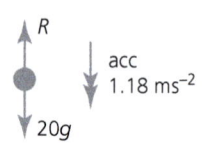
  [diagram: R upward, acc 1.18 m s^{-2} downward, 20g downward]
  (iv) 0.03 π m s^{-2} vertically upwards and 0.03 π^2 m s^{-2} horizontally towards the centre.

Discussion point page 253
No, see text that follows.

Activity 10.2 page 253
If the string breaks the object will fly off at a tangent to the circle. If a rod were used rather than a string, the motion would be the same for 1 and 2. For 3, when a string is used, the object leaves the circle and falls in a parabola. On a rod, it swings back as a pendulum.

Discussion point page 255
$T = mr\omega^2 - mg\cos\alpha$, but $R = mg\cos\beta - mr\omega^2$ so $T > 0$ if ω is sufficiently large and $R > 0$ if ω is sufficiently small.

Discussion point page 257
(i) and (iv)

Exercise 10.4

1 (i) A: 4 m s^{-2} B: 40 m s^{-2}
  (ii) (a) A yes, B No
       (b) A no, B yes
       (c) A no, B yes
       (d) A yes, B yes

2 (A) (i) 22.2m J
      (ii) Complete revolutions; 4.98 m s^{-1}
      (iii) (a) 73.8m N towards O
            (b) 15m N towards O
  (B) (i) 18m J
      (ii) Stops; 1.84 m
      (iii) (a) 18m N towards O
            (b) 9m N away from O
  (C) (i) 4.74m J

- (ii) Stops, 0.48 m
- (iii) (a) $6.49m$ N away from O
  - (b) $9.49m$ N away from O

3 (ii) $2mg$

4 (ii) $R = \dfrac{mv^2}{a} + mg\cos\theta$

$v^2 = u^2 - 2ga(1-\cos\theta) = ga(1+2\cos\theta)$
$\Rightarrow R = mg(1+3\cos\theta)$

5 (i) $0.186mg$ J
- (iv) 0.598 m
- (v) No, it leaves the track.

6 (ii) $3mg$

7 (i) $0.8g$ J, 6.35 m s^{-1}
- (ii) $\sqrt{9+1.6g(1-\cos\theta)}$
- (iii) (a) 0.725 N
  - (b) 30.125 N
- (iv)

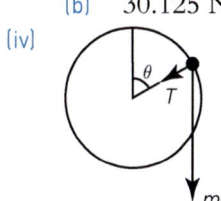

$T = 15.43 - 14.7\cos\theta,$
$g\sin\theta$

8 (i) 82 m s^{-1}, 53 m s^{-1}
- (ii) 67.2 m s^{-2}, 28.6 m s^{-2}
- (iii)

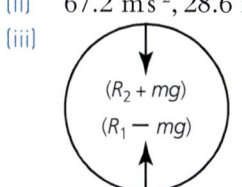

$R_1 = 5393$ N, $R_2 = 1316$ N

- (iv) He would fail to complete the loop.
- (v) 138 m

9 (i) 15 cm
- (ii) 3.45 rad s^{-1}
- (iii) 1.9 rad s^{-2}
- (iv) Girl lets go before reaching the vertical.

10 (i) Almost zero speed at the top of the loop; not sufficient.
- (ii) 20 m
- (iii) It stops below the centre and returns to C; 8 m.

11 (i) 12 m s^{-1}, 27 mph
- (ii) Traffic used to travel more slowly.
- (iii) Increase the radius by making the approaches less steep.

12 (i) K.E. $= \frac{1}{2} \times 200 \times 21^2$
$= 44\,100$
The energy equation including K.E. and P.E. gives
$200g \times 20 + \frac{1}{2} \times 200v^2$
$= 44\,100$
$v = 7$ m s^{-1}
- (ii) Radial acceleration = 4.9 m s^{-2};
$R = -980$ N
Force from track is up so could not operate.
- (iii) 14.7 m s^{-2}; 8.49 m s^{-2}
$\arctan\left(\dfrac{\frac{\sqrt{3}}{2}g}{14.7}\right) = 30°$

13 (i) $v^2 = gl(2\cos\theta - 1)$
- (iii) $2mg$ when $\theta = 0$
- (iv) Perpendicular to AB
- (v) 0.32 rad

Chapter 11

Discussion point page 267

Use energy considerations. See the investigation at the end of this chapter.

Exercise 11.1

1 (i) 49 N, 490 N m^{-1}, 245 N
- (ii) 98 N, 65.$\dot{3}$ N m^{-1}, 32.$\dot{6}$ N
- (iii) 0.98 N, 3.26 N m^{-1}, 4.9 N

2 (i) 10 kg, 1.5 m, 294 N
- (ii) 5 kg, 19.5 m, 1911 N
- (iii) 0.51 kg, 4.1 m, 51.25 N

3 (i) 20 N
- (ii) 20 N
- (iii) Tensions required to double the length is the same. There is a 20 N force at the fixed end in the part (i).

4 (i)

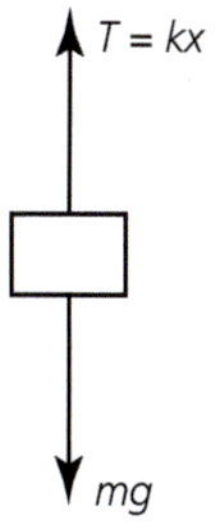

- (ii) 6.125 N m^{-1}
- (iii) 12.25 N

5 (i) 0.03 N
- (ii) 0.04 m
- (iii) 0.45 m
- (iv) 0.1125

6 (i) 4.9 N
- (ii) 61.25 N m^{-1}
- (iii) 0.625 kg
- (iv) 1.2 m

7 (i) 30 N
- (ii) 3
- (iii) 300 N m^{-1}
- (iv) Spring becomes fully compressed with fewer than seven blocks.

8 -40 N $<$ force $<$ 80 N

Exercise 11.2

1 (i) 60 N
- (ii) 0.04 m
- (iii) 2400 N; could be two strings together (side by side).

2 (i) 12 000 N
- (ii) 80 000 N m^{-1}
- (iii) 0.05 m
- (iv) 0.02 m

3 (i) 7000 N
- (ii) 7000 N, 10 000 N m^{-1}
- (iii) 4000 N

4 (i) 198 N
- (ii) 654 N
- (iii) 118%
- (iv) 51.6 m

5 (i) $T = F$ for each spring, $\dfrac{F}{k_1}, \dfrac{F}{k_2}$

6 (i) $(0.3 - x)$ m
- (ii) $16x$ N, $25(0.3 - x)$ N
- (iii) 0.183

7 (i) $2.2 - h$ m, $h - 1.2$ m
- (ii) $44 - 20h$ N, $30h - 36$ N
- (iii) 1.2 m
- (iv) 20 N, 0 N

8. (i) $\dfrac{l_0}{\lambda} mg \sin\alpha$

   (ii) (a) $\dfrac{l_0}{\lambda} mg(\mu\cos\alpha + \sin\alpha)$

   (b) $\dfrac{l_0}{\lambda} mg(\sin\alpha - \mu\cos\alpha)$

9. (i) 1000 N
   (ii) 0.024 m
   (iii) $R = 5000h - 730$

10. (i) 0.306 m
    (iii) An elastic string is unlikely to pass smoothly over a peg.

11. (i) 5.1 kg
    (ii) 0.8784 m
    (iii) 59.8 N
    (iv) 3.52 kg

12. (i) (b) $\dfrac{g}{80n}$ m
    (iii) 4
    (iv) 0.098 m

13. $\dfrac{\lambda d}{l_0} = mg \Rightarrow \lambda = \dfrac{mgl_0}{d}$

    $x_1 =$ extension of top half;
    $x_2 =$ extension of bottom half
    $\Rightarrow$ displacement $= \dfrac{1}{2}(x_1 - x_2)$

    Equilibrium: $\dfrac{2\lambda}{l_0}x_1 = \dfrac{2\lambda}{l_0}x_2 + mg$

    $\Rightarrow x_1 = x_2 + \dfrac{1}{2}d$

    $\Rightarrow$ displacement $= \dfrac{1}{4}d$

14. 1.3 m

Exercise 11.3

1. (i) 0.1 J
   (ii) 0.001 J
   (iii) 0.4 J
   (iv) 0 J

2. (i) 4 J
   (ii) 0.25 J
   (iii) 1 J
   (iv) 0.0625 J

3. (i) 0.75 J
   (ii) 5.48 m s^{-1}

4. (i) 0.006 67 J
   (ii) 0.577 m s^{-1}

5. (i) 5×10^4 J
   (ii) 7.07 m s^{-1}
   (iii) 1.29 m
   (iv) 7.07×10^4 N, 35.4 m s^{-2}

   (v) Truck moves back along the rail at 5 m s^{-1} if other forces ignored.

6. 0.433 m, 0.067 m

7. (i) B is in equilibrium.
   (ii) 0.8 m, 6 N
   (iii) 2.7 J
   (iv) 10 m s^{-1}

8. (i) 562.5 J
   (ii) 0.15
   (iii) 0.8 m s^{-1}
   (iv) $1440 = 25\,000 x_1^2 + 20\,000 x_2^2$, $5x_1 = 4x_2$, $x_1 = 0.16$, $x_2 = 0.2$

9. (ii) $2\sqrt{5}a$
   (iv) mga
   (v) P.E. lost $= 7mga$. Energy is not conserved because the mass is lowered by some external force.

10. (i) 0.4, 1
    (ii) It does not go slack.
    (iii) 1.125 m

Activity 11.1 page 291

For a 90 kg person, the maximum extension is 33.2 m for a rope 12 m long giving rise to a deceleration of 19.7 m s^{-2}.
For a 60 kg person the maximum extension is 27.1 m for a rope 18 m long giving rise to a deceleration of 26.3 m s^{-2}.

Exercise 11.4

1. (i) $5h^2$ J
   (ii) $0.2\,gh$ J
   (iii) 0.392

2. $2l_0$

3. $l_0\left(1 + \dfrac{mg}{\lambda}\right)$

4. (ii) 0.1294

5. 0.463 m

6. (i) 1 J
   (iii) 0.2 m

7. (i) 0.1098 m
   (ii) 0.149 m

8. Conservation of energy:
   $\dfrac{1}{2}\left(\dfrac{\lambda}{l_0}\right)(3l_0)^2 = mg \times 4l_0$

   $\Rightarrow \lambda = \dfrac{8}{9}mg$

   Maximum tension:
   $T = \dfrac{\lambda}{l_0} \times 3l_0 = \dfrac{8}{3}mg$

9. (ii) $ma = mg - \dfrac{\lambda}{l_0}x$
   (iii) $v\dfrac{dv}{dx} = g - \dfrac{\lambda}{ml_0}x$
   (iv) $v = \sqrt{2gl_0 + 2gx - \dfrac{\lambda}{ml_0}x^2}$
   (v) $x = 0$. The string is about to become slack with the particle going upwards.
   (vi) $m\dfrac{dv}{dt} = mg$;
   $v = g(t - T) - \sqrt{2gl_0}$,
   for $T < t < T + \sqrt{\dfrac{2l_0}{g}}$

10. (i) $\arccos\left(\dfrac{g}{\omega^2 l}\right)$
    (ii) $\arccos\left(\dfrac{g(k - m\omega^2)}{\omega^2 l_0 k}\right)$

11. (i) 0.8 m
    (ii) $98(x - 0.5)$ N, $98(2 - x)$ N
    (iii) 57.3 J
    (iv) 0.81 m s^{-1}

12. (i) $\dfrac{1}{2}\dfrac{mg}{k}$
    (ii) $mg\left(l_0 + \dfrac{mg}{k}\right)$
    (iii) $\dfrac{1}{2}\dfrac{m^2 g^2}{k}$
    (iv) (ii) > (iii), external work done to move block.
    (v) $\dfrac{mg}{M}$

13. (iii) -122 m s^{-2}

14. $\sqrt{\dfrac{8}{3}gl}$

15. (ii) 14.06 m s^{-1}

Chapter 12

Discussion point page 299
The spring and particle could move along a smooth horizontal groove.

Discussion point page 299
The particle is pulled in towards O by the tension in the spring.

When it has passed O it is pushed back again by the thrust in the spring. It oscillates backwards and forwards about O.

Discussion point page 299
A sine wave starting at the top of its cycle.

Discussion point page 299
$a\sqrt{\dfrac{k}{m}}$ is its speed at O and this is its maximum speed.

Discussion point page 300
The acceleration is always directed towards O. When P is moving towards O it speeds up and when it is moving away from O it slows down.

Discussion point page 300
$0, 0, \pm a\omega$.

Exercise 12.1
1. (a) $\ddot{x} = -9x$
    (i) ± 6 cm s^{-1}, 0
    (ii) $0, 18$ cm s^{-2}
    (iii) 5.2 cm s^{-1}
   (b) $\ddot{x} = -100x$
    (i) ± 1 m s^{-1}, 0
    (ii) $0, 10$ m s^{-2}
    (iii) 0.87 m s^{-1}
   (c) $\ddot{x} = -\pi^2 x$
    (i) $\pm a\pi$ m s^{-1}, 0
    (ii) $0, a\pi^2$ m s^{-2}
    (iii) $\dfrac{\sqrt{3}}{2} a\pi$ m s^{-1}
2. (i) 10.4 cm
   (ii) ± 41.8 cm s^{-2}
   (iii) 20.9 cm s^{-1}
   (iv) 18.3 cm s^{-1}
   (v) 9.04 cm
3. (i) $55\pi, 110\pi, 220\pi, 440\pi$, below; $1760\pi, 3520\pi, 7040\pi$, above
   (ii) 22.1 m s^{-1}, 0.173 m s^{-1}
4. (i) $4000\pi, 25.1$ m s^{-1}
   (ii) $\ddot{x} = -16\,000\,000\,\pi^2 x$, $316\,000$ m s^{-2}
5. 2.45 cm above O

6. (i) [graph: x vs t, amplitude 0.35, period 0.03]
   (ii) 33.3 Hz, 209
   (iii) 73.3 m s^{-1}
7. (i) $1.885, 1.13$ m
   (ii) 2.12 m s^{-1}
8. (i) 2.67 m s^{-1}
   (ii) 839 m s^{-2}
   (iii) 1.89 m s^{-1}
9. (i), (iv) and (v) are true
10. (i) $\dfrac{\sqrt{15}}{4} a\omega$
    (iii) $\dfrac{\sqrt{3}}{2} a$

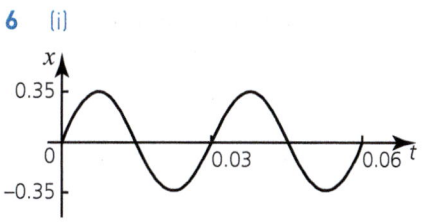

Discussion point page 306
$x = a\cos\omega t, \dot{x} = -a\omega\sin\omega t, \ddot{x} = -a\omega^2\cos\omega t = -\omega^2 x$

[graphs of $x = a\sin\omega t$ and $x = a\cos\omega t$]

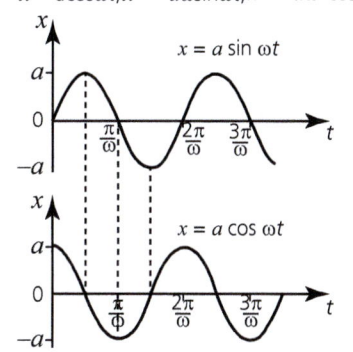

They have the same amplitude and period but start at different points in the cycle

Discussion point page 306
$\dot{x} = -a\omega\sin\omega t$ then square as in the text with $\sin\omega t$ and $\cos\omega t$ interchanged.

Exercise 12.2
1. (i) 5 m
   (ii) 16 s
   (iii) $5, \dfrac{\pi}{8}$
   (iv) (a) 0
        (b) 1.96 m s^{-1}
        (c) 0
2. (i) 0.2 s, 0.08 m
   (ii) $0.08, 10\pi$
   (iii) $-0.8\pi\sin 10\pi t, 0.08, 0$
   (iv) $0, -2.51$ m s^{-1}, negative direction.

3. (i)
   (a) [graph: x (cm), amplitude 2.5]
   (b) [graph: $\dot{x}$ (cm s^{-1}), amplitude 2.5π]
   (c) [graph: $\ddot{x}$ (cm s^{-2}), amplitude $2.5\pi^2$]

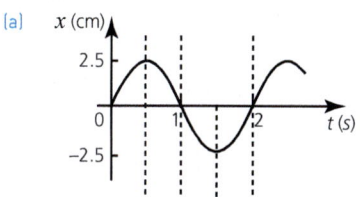

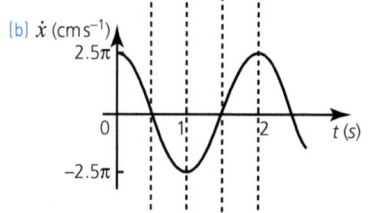

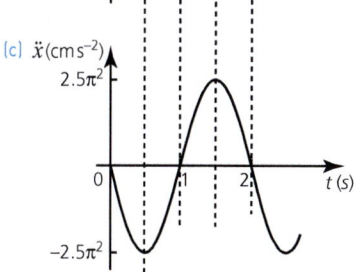

   (iii) x and $\ddot{x} = 0$ when $\dot{x}$ has maximum positive and maximum negative values; x has a maximum positive and $\ddot{x}$ has a maximum negative or vice versa when $\dot{x} = 0$.

4. (i) $2, \dfrac{\pi}{6}$
   (ii) 40 m
   (iii) 1.05 m s^{-1}
   (iv) $\dfrac{\pi}{3}\cos\dfrac{\pi}{6}t$
   (v) 2 s
5. (i) $4, 2.5$
   (ii) $10\cos 4t$
   (iii) (a) 6.97 cm s^{-1}, positive
        (b) -6.54 cm s^{-1}, negative
   (iv) (a) 1.79 cm
        (b) 6.89 cm
6. (i) [graph: x (cm), amplitude 10]
   (ii) $\dfrac{\pi}{6}, x = 10\sin\dfrac{\pi}{6}t$
   (iii) $5, 5\sqrt{3}, 10$ cm
   (iv) $5, 3.66, 1.34$ cm; speed is decreasing.

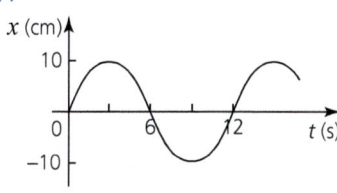

(v) e.g. 3rd and 4th seconds, when it covers the same 'ground' or when its positions are symmetrical about the centre.

7 (i) $\frac{\pi}{4}$, $x = 10\cos\frac{\pi}{4}t$

(ii) $\dot{x} = -\frac{5\pi}{2}\sin\frac{\pi}{4}t$, 0, -5.55 cm s^{-1}, -7.85 cm s^{-1}; both negative, x decreasing

(iii) the acceleration is not constant

8 (i) 20, $\frac{\pi}{12}$, $\dot{x} = \frac{5\pi}{3}\cos\frac{\pi}{12}t$

(ii) (a) 0, $\frac{5\pi}{3}$

(b) 10, $\frac{5\pi\sqrt{3}}{6}$

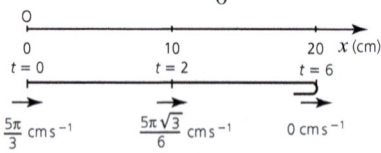

(iv) 2, 10, $\frac{5\pi\sqrt{3}}{6}$, $-\frac{5\pi\sqrt{3}}{6}$

9 (i) 20, $\frac{\pi}{12}$, $\dot{x} = -\frac{5\pi}{3}\sin\frac{\pi}{12}t$

(ii) (a) 20, 0

(b) $10\sqrt{3}$, $-\frac{5\pi}{6}$

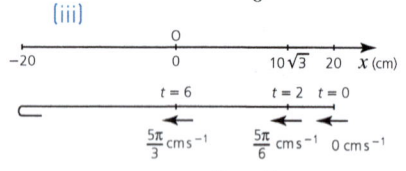

(iii)

(iv) 10, 14, $-\frac{5}{6}\pi$, $\frac{5}{6}\pi$

10 (ii) 4π m s^{-1}

(iii) $80\pi^2$ m s^{-2}

(iv) $\frac{1}{3}$

11 (i) 3 m, π s

(ii) 6 m s^{-1}

(iii) $\ddot{y} = -4y$

(iv) 5.45 m (the string is slack when the downward force necessary for SHM is greater than mg)

(v) 1.26 s

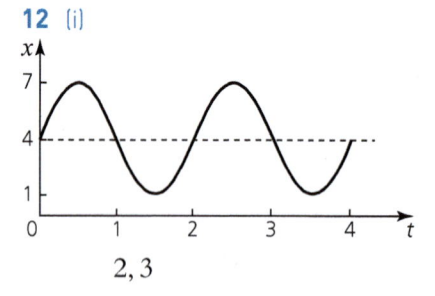

12 (i)

(ii) $x = 4$

(iv) $-3\pi^2\sin\pi t$

(v) SHM; centre, $x = h$; amplitude, a; period, $\frac{2\pi}{\omega}$

13 (i) 0.65 m, 0.35 m

(ii) $x = 0.5 + 0.15\sin 2\pi t$ (m)

(iii) (a) 0.05 s

(b) 0.62 s

14 (i) 355 minutes

(ii) 130 minutes

(iii)

(iv) $\frac{2\pi}{365}$ rad per day (approx.)

(v) $355 + 130\cos\left(\frac{2\pi(D-1)}{365}\right)$

(vi) 4.55 am

Discussion point page 315

All oscillations with the same frequency can be added to form a single oscillation with that frequency.

Discussion point page 317

(i) $x = a\sin(\omega t - \pi)$ or $-a\sin\omega t$

(ii) $x = a\sin\left(\omega t - \frac{\pi}{2}\right)$ or $-a\cos\omega t$

(iii) $x = x_0 + a\cos\omega t$

(iv) $x = x_0 - a\sin\omega t$

Exercise 12.3

1 (i) (a)

(b)

(c)

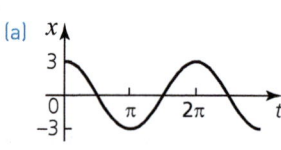

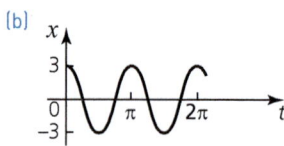

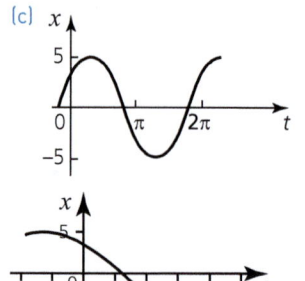

(ii) (a) $a = 3$, $T = 2\pi$, $f = \frac{1}{2\pi}$

(b) $a = 3$, $T = \pi$, $f = \frac{1}{\pi}$

(c) $a = 5$, $T = 2\pi$, $f = \frac{1}{2\pi}$

(d) $a = 5$, $T = 10\pi$, $f = \frac{1}{10\pi}$

2 (i) $x = 5\cos\left(\frac{2\pi t}{3}\right)$

(ii) $x = 6\sin\pi t$

(iii) $x = 4\sin\left(\frac{2\pi t}{5} + \frac{\pi}{6}\right)$

(iv) $x = 1.5\cos\frac{\pi t}{2} + \frac{12}{\pi}\sin\frac{\pi t}{2}$

3 (i)

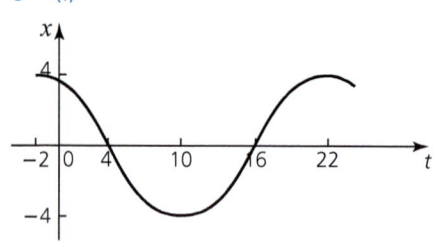

(ii) yes, $p = -2$, $q = 2\sqrt{3}$

4 (i) $a = 5$, $\omega = \frac{\pi}{4}$, $\varepsilon = \frac{\pi}{4}$

(ii) $\delta = \frac{\pi}{4}$

(iii) $b = 3.54$

5 (i) [graph]

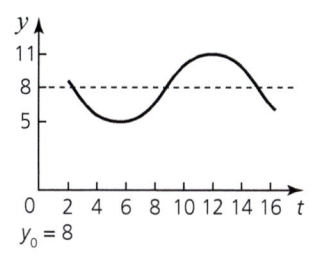

(ii) $\omega = \frac{\pi}{6}, \varepsilon = \frac{\pi}{6}, a = 3$

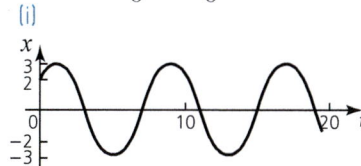

6 (i) [graph]

(ii) $a = 3, \omega_1 = \frac{\pi}{4}, \varepsilon = 0.73$

(iii) $a = b, \omega_1 = \omega_2$

(iv) $b = 3, \omega_2 = \frac{\pi}{4}$, $\delta = \varepsilon - \frac{\pi}{2} = -0.84$

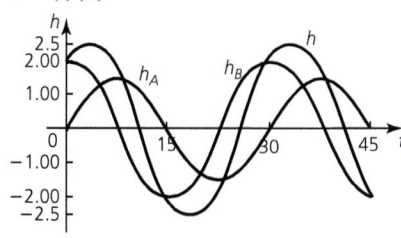

7 (i) (ii) [graph]

(iii) $a = 2.5, \omega = \frac{\pi}{15}, \varepsilon = 0.927$

8 $\frac{\pi}{15}$ rad min^{-1}

(i) $y = 70 - 67.5\cos\frac{\pi t}{15}$

(ii) 10.3 minutes

9 (i) $85, 65, \frac{2\pi}{11}$

(ii) 112, 42

10 (i) SHM; mean h_0; amplitude, a; period, $\frac{2\pi}{\omega}$

(ii) $6, 4, \frac{\pi}{6}, \frac{\pi}{6}$

(iii) 0.647 m h^{-1}, 1.043 m h^{-2}

(iv) 2.094 m h^{-1}

11 (i) $x = b\cos\omega t$

(ii) $v^2 = \omega^2(b^2 - a^2)$

(iv) $\frac{2}{\omega}\arccos\left(\frac{a}{b}\right)$

(v) 0.02 s

12 (i) 0.0598 s, 0.5

(ii) $\beta = 1.5 + 1.5\sin\left(\frac{\pi}{3}t\right)$

13 (i) [graph]

(ii) $0.1, \frac{5\pi}{6}$

(iii) $\frac{20\pi}{3}, 0.3$

(iv) -21.9 m s^{-2}

14 (i) $x = A\sin 3t + B\cos 3t + 8$

(ii) $x = 8 - 6\cos 3t$

(iii) Oscillating about 8 with period $\frac{2\pi}{3}$ and amplitude b

(iv) 5.45 m, -16.30 m s^{-1}, 22.91 m s^{-2}

Discussion point page 332
Yes, g cancels.

Exercise 12.4

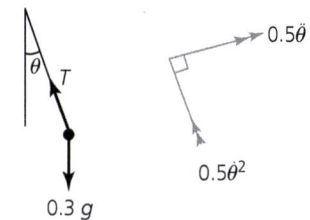

1 (i) [diagram]

(ii) $0.15\ddot{\theta} = -0.3g\sin\theta$

(iii) θ small so that $\sin\theta \approx \theta$

(iv) $\ddot{\theta} = -2g\theta$; 1.42 s

(v) No

2 (i) 0.0873 rad

(ii) 3.48 s

(iii) $a = 0.0873, \omega = 1.807, \varepsilon = 0$

(iv) 0.473 m s^{-1}, 0.095 Ns

3 (i) 0.993 m

(ii) (a) None
   (b) Multiplies by $\sqrt{2}$
   (c) None
   (d) Multiplies by $\sqrt{6}$

4 (i) $\ddot{\theta} = -\frac{g}{4}\theta$; stone is a particle, no air resistance, θ is small.

(ii) 4.01 s

5 (i) $x = 0.25\sin 4\pi t$

(iii) $v^2 = \pi^2(1 - 16x^2)$

(iv) [diagram: R up, mg down]

$R - mg = m\ddot{x}$

The contact force, R, must be ≥ 0.

(v) 0.312 m, 3.04 m s^{-1}

(vi) 0.145 s

6 (i) buoyancy = weight, $k = \frac{mg}{l}$

(ii) $F = \frac{mg}{l}(x+l), \ddot{x} = -\frac{g}{l}x$

7 (ii) $x = 0.2, \dot{x} = 0$ when $t = 0$

(iv) $a = 0.2, f = 0.356$

(v) 0.447 m s^{-1}

8 0.25 m, 0.27 m s^{-2}, 0.21 m s^{-1}

9 (ii) $\ddot{x} = -600x$

(iii) $t = 0, x = -0.02$

(iv) $x = 0.02\cos\left(\sqrt{600}t + \pi\right)$

(v) 3.90 Hz

(vi) 0.49 m s^{-1}, 12 m s^{-2}

10 (i) $\frac{15l}{4}$

(ii) $\frac{\lambda}{4}$

(iii) $\ddot{x} = -\frac{4\lambda}{3lm}x$

Initial conditions: $x = 0, v = \frac{\mu}{m}$

(iv) $a = \mu\sqrt{\frac{3l}{4\lambda m}}, f = \sqrt{\frac{\lambda}{3lm}} \times \frac{1}{\pi}$

(v) $x = \mu\sqrt{\frac{3l}{4\lambda m}}\sin\left(\sqrt{\frac{4\lambda}{3lm}}t\right)$

11 5 m, $\frac{\pi}{6}$ s

12 (i) 0.025 m

(ii) $7.5 + 300x$ N

(iv) $x = 0.02\cos(20t)$

(v) 3 cm > 0.025 m so string is not in tension throughout.

13 (ii) [diagram: spring with x_0, l, E, Thrust T, mg, $\ddot{x}$; $mg - T = m\ddot{x}$]

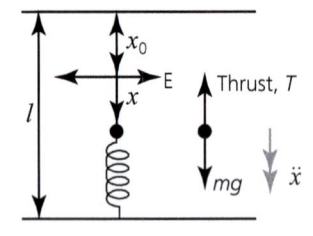

(iii) $\ddot{x} = -\dfrac{k}{m}x$

(iv) $\dfrac{mg}{k}$

14 (i) (a) $2.1\ \text{m s}^{-1}$
    (b) 0.87 m
    (c) 0.022 N
(ii) 3 s

15 (i) $l_0 + \dfrac{mgl_0}{2\lambda}$ below the ceiling, $2l_0 + \dfrac{2mgl_0}{\lambda}$ below the ceiling.

(ii) $\ddot{x} = \dfrac{-2\lambda x}{ml_0},\ \ddot{x} = -\dfrac{\lambda x}{2ml_0}$

(iii) $\pi\sqrt{\dfrac{2ml_0}{\lambda}},\ 2\pi\sqrt{\dfrac{2ml_0}{\lambda}}$

16 (i) $10g\ \text{Nm}^{-1}$
(ii) $x = 2\cos\sqrt{g}\,t$
(iii) 0.669 s
(iv) $5.42\ \text{m s}^{-1}$
(v) 2.4 s

Chapter 13

Exercise 13.1

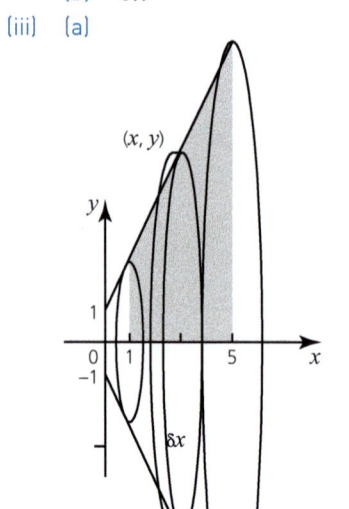

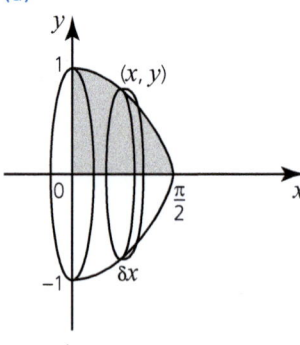

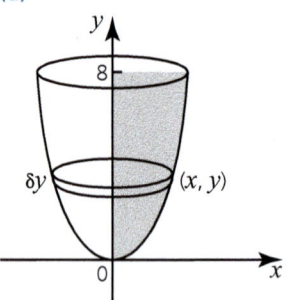

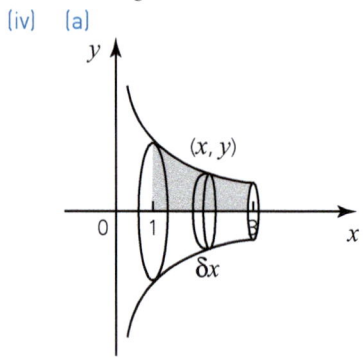

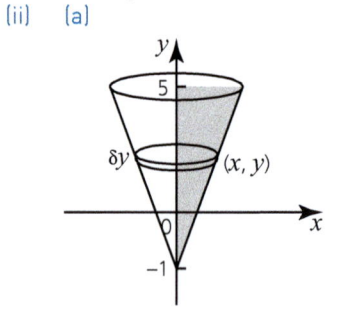

1 (i) (a) [diagram]
   (b) $\dfrac{104}{3}\pi$
(ii) (a) [diagram]
    (b) 8π
(iii) (a) [diagram]
    (b) $\dfrac{652}{3}\pi$
(iv) (a) [diagram]
    (b) $\dfrac{2}{3}\pi$
(v) (a) [diagram]
    (b) $\dfrac{9}{2}\pi(e^3-1)$
(vi) (a) [diagram]
    (b) $\dfrac{1}{4}\pi^2$

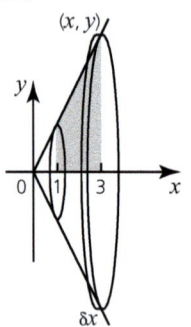

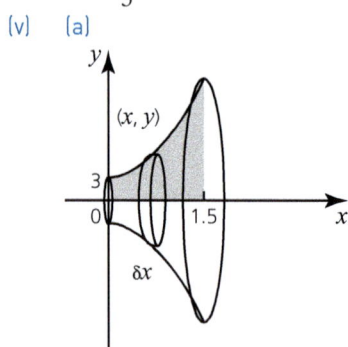

2 (i) (a) [diagram]
    (b) $\dfrac{96}{5}\pi$
(ii) (a) [diagram]
    (b) 18π
(iii) (a) [diagram]
    (b) $\dfrac{28}{3}\pi$

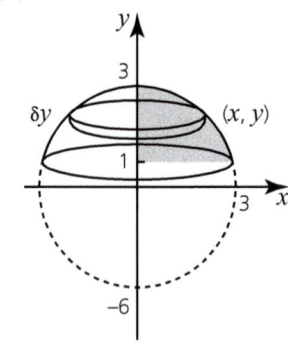

3 (i) $y = \dfrac{rx}{h}$
(ii) $0.235\ l$

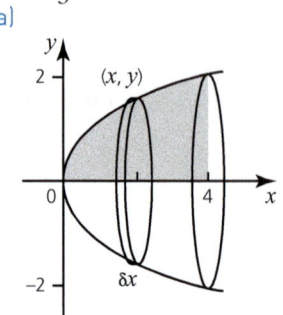

4 $34\dfrac{1}{3}\pi$

5 (i) [graph: circle radius 6 centered at origin]

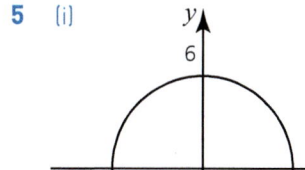

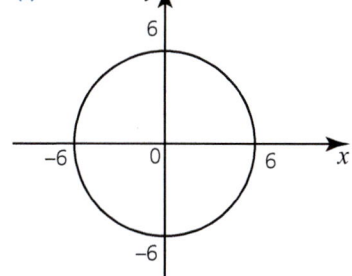

   (ii) 0.235 1

6 (i) [diagram: ellipsoid with vertical disc cross-section]

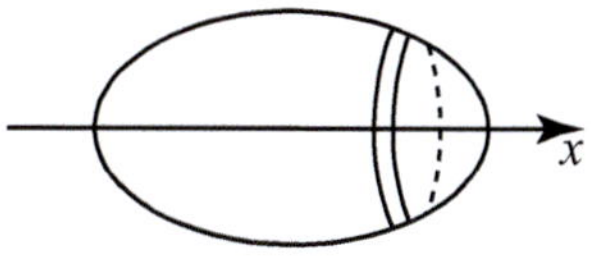

   (iii) $\frac{2}{3}\pi b^2(a+b)$

7 (i) [diagram: sphere with radius a horizontal and b vertical, with a band/cap]

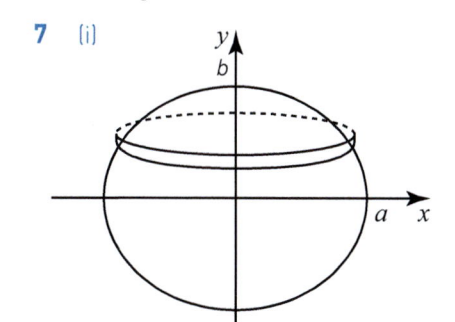

   (ii) $a \approx 4.73 \times 10^{19}$;
       $b \approx 4.26 \times 10^{19}$;
       $V \approx 4 \times 10^{59}\,\text{m}^3$

8   16π

9   $34\tfrac{1}{3}$

10 (iii) 101.775π

11 (iii) $3.2 \times 10^5\,\text{m}^3$

12 (i) [diagram: bowl-shaped surface, heights 1 and 10]

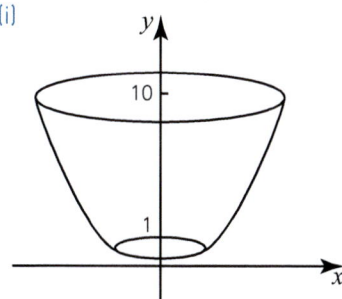

   (ii) (a) 2.36 (b) 5.83
       (c) 9.03

13 (i) A(−2, 0) B(2, 0)
    (ii) 11.29
    (iii) 4765 cm³ = 4.765 l

Exercise 13.2

1 (a) For sketches see Exercise 13.1 Question 1.
  (b) (i) (2.31, 0)
      (ii) (2.67, 0)
      (iii) (3.70, 0)
      (iv) (1.65, 0)
      (v) (1.08, 0)
      (vi) (0.47, 0)

2 (a) For sketches see Exercise 13.1 Question 2.
  (b) (i) (0, 5)
      (ii) (0, 3.5)
      (iii) (0, 1.71)

3 (i) [graph: curve through origin with local max near x=2]

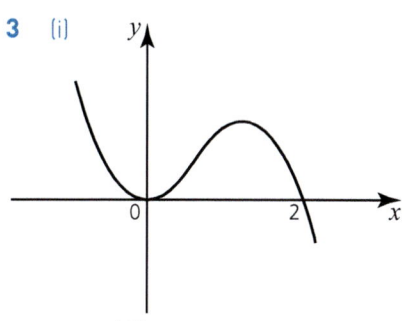

   (ii) $\dfrac{128}{105}\pi$
   (iii) (1.25, 0)

4 (i) [graph: sideways parabola with shaded region between x=1 and x=4, y up to 4]

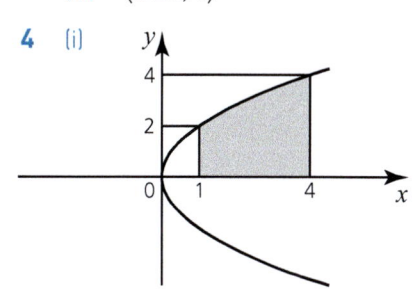

   (ii) $V = 30\pi$; (2.8, 0)
   (iii) (a) 2, 4
       (b) $\dfrac{62}{5}\pi$
       (c) (0, 3.39)

5 3.9 cm

6 (i) [graph: ellipse, semi-axes 3 and 2, shaded first quadrant]

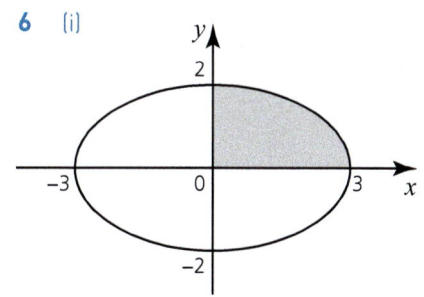

   (ii) $V = 8\pi$; (1.125, 0)

7 (i)

	Clown	Cone	Hemisphere
Mass	$\frac{1}{3}\pi r^2 \rho(2r+h)$	$\frac{1}{3}\pi r^2 h \rho$	$\frac{2}{3}\pi r^3 \rho$
Distance of c.o.m. above O	y	$\frac{1}{4}h$	$-\frac{3}{8}r$

(ii) $\left(\frac{2}{3}r + \frac{1}{3}h\right)\bar{y} = \frac{1}{3}h \times \frac{1}{4}h - \frac{2}{3}r \times \frac{3}{8}r$

(iii) $\sqrt{3} : 1$

(iv) Upright

8 (i) Using σ as mass per unit area

	Whole container	Cylinder base	Cylinder walls	Cone
Mass	$132\pi\sigma$	$9\pi\sigma$	$108\pi\sigma$	$15\pi\sigma$
Distance of c.o.m. above O	y	0	9	$19\frac{1}{3}$

(ii) 9.56 cm

(iii) 17.42°

(iv) The centre of mass will be lower so it is less likely to topple.

9 (i) $\frac{64}{3}\pi$

(ii) (1.6, 0)

(iii) 74.6°

10 (i) $V = \frac{\pi h^2}{2k}$

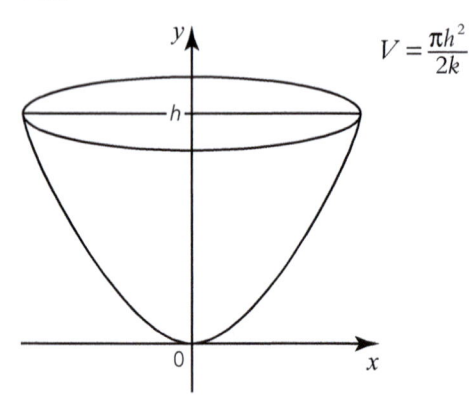

(ii) $\frac{1}{3}h$

(iii)

	Solid block	Glass	Part removed
Mass	$\frac{9^2\pi}{2k}\rho$	$\frac{\pi}{2k}(9^2 - 8.8^2)\rho$	$\frac{8.8^2\pi}{2k}\rho$
Distance of c.o.m. below rim	$\frac{1}{3} \times 9$	d	$\frac{1}{3} \times 8.8$

(iv) 7.3 cm

(v) 22.4°

11 (iii) $1 - 4\varepsilon$

Activity 13.1 Page 361

About 8 : 11; see Example 13.7.

Exercise 13.3

1 (a) (i) $\bar{x} = 0$

(ii)

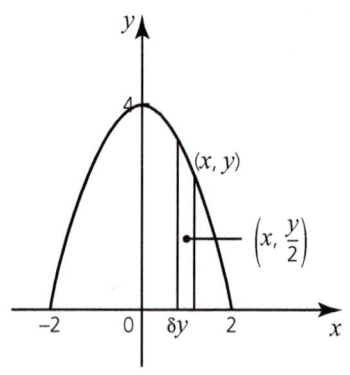

(iii) $(4 - x^2)\delta x$

(iv) (0, 1.6)

(b) (i) $\bar{y} = 0$

(ii)

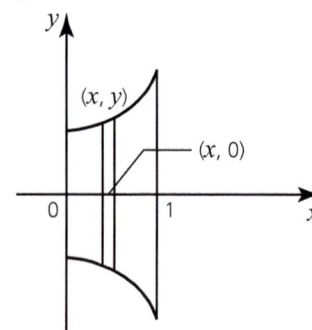

(iii) $2e^x \delta x$

(iv) (0.58, 0)

(c) (i) $\bar{y} = 0$

(ii)

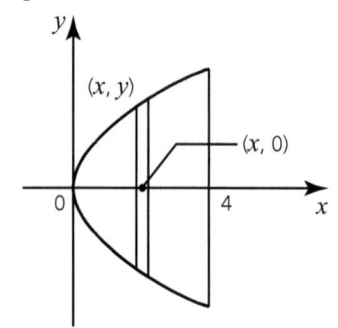

(iii) $4\sqrt{x}\,\delta x$

(iv) (2.4, 0)

(d) (i) $\bar{x} = \frac{\pi}{2}$

(ii)

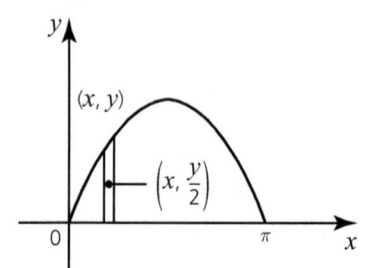

(iii) $\sin x \, \delta x$

(iv) $\left(\frac{\pi}{2}, \frac{\pi}{8}\right)$

2 (i) 36 cm²
  (ii) $y = -2x + 12$
  (iii) (2, 4)

3 $\left(\frac{3}{4}\ln 2, \frac{3}{8}\ln 2\right)$

4 (i)

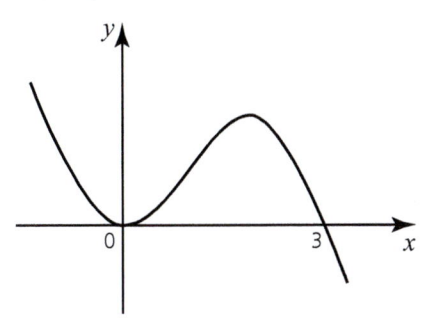

  (ii) (1.8, 1.54)

5 (i)

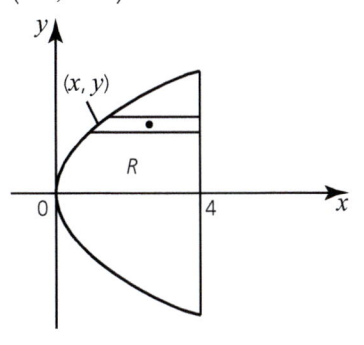

  (ii) $(4-x)\delta y, \frac{4+x}{2}$
  (iii) (2.4, 0)

6 (i) $\left(2, 2\frac{5}{12}\right)$
  (ii) $\left(3, 2\frac{2}{3}\right)$
  (iii) $\left(2, 2\frac{7}{24}\right)$
  (iv) $\left(3, 2\frac{5}{8}\right)$

7 (i) (1.08, 0.95)
  (ii) Centre of each strip is on PP'
  (iii) G_1 and G_2 are both $\frac{1}{3}$ PD from QR so G_1G_2 is parallel to QR. G lies on G_1G_2 and PH:HD = 2:1 so GP:GP' = 2:1.

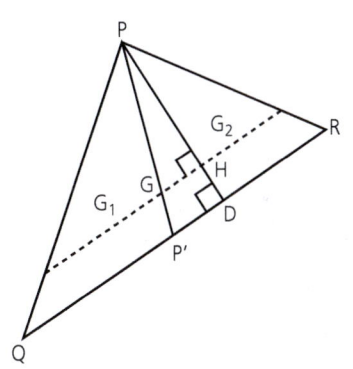

8 (ii) (0.75, 0.3)

  (iii) (0.447, 0.516)

9 (i) outer semicircle: $2\pi, \left(1+\frac{8}{3\pi}, 4\right)$
  inner semicircle: $\frac{\pi}{2}, \left(1+\frac{4}{3\pi}, 4\right)$
  rectangle: 6, (0.5, 3)
  (ii) (1.16, 3.44)
  (iii) 18.63°

10 (i)

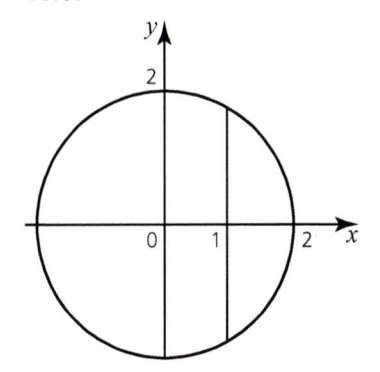

  (iii) 1.41
  (iv) 1.09 from centre
  (v) 32.2°

11 (i) $\left(\frac{3}{8}, 0\right)$
  (ii) $\left(\frac{3}{4}, 0\right)$
  (iii) $\left(\frac{9}{8}, 0\right)$
  (iv) 48.4°

12 (ii) $\dfrac{3\pi ah + 4(a^2 + h^2)}{3(2h+\pi a)}$

13 $\left(\frac{40}{21}, \frac{10}{3}\right)$

14 $\left(\frac{3}{8}\sqrt{2}, 2\right)$

15 (0, 2)

16 (ii) $\left(0, \frac{4r}{\pi}\right)$

17 (i) $16, \left(\frac{4}{3}, 4\right); 16, \left(4, \frac{20}{3}\right); 8, (6, 4); 8, (3, 1);$
  $8, \left(\frac{20}{3}, \frac{4}{3}\right); 4, \left(\frac{22}{3}, 16\right); 4, \left(4, \frac{8}{3}\right)$
  (ii) (a) $\left(5\frac{1}{8}, 2\frac{5}{8}\right)$
    (b) (9.375, 2.227…)

Chapter 14

Discussion point page 372

The cue ball should be struck in such a direction that when it reaches the blue ball, the line joining the centres of the balls is in the direction of the hole.

The red ball cannot be potted from this position as the black ball is in the way. It would be possible for the cue ball to hit the black ball so that it then sends the red ball into the hole, but this is not allowed in snooker.

Discussion point page 374
The red ball was initially stationary so its final momentum is equal to the impulse it has received. This is equal in magnitude but opposite in direction to the impulse **J** acting on the white ball. So its direction is 47° from the **i** direction.

Discussion point page 376
When $e = 0$, the ball does not rebound and moves only along the plane. All the kinetic energy from the motion perpendicular to the plane is lost. When $e = 1$, the collision is perfectly elastic and there is no loss in kinetic energy.

Exercise 14.1
1. (i) [diagram: triangle with sides $-m\mathbf{u}$, $m\mathbf{v} - m\mathbf{u}$, $m\mathbf{v}$]
   (ii) 0.32 Ns at 85° to the horizontal
   (iii) $\begin{pmatrix}1.75\\-3.03\end{pmatrix}$ $\begin{pmatrix}1.73\\1\end{pmatrix}$
   (iv) $\mathbf{J} = 0.08\begin{pmatrix}-0.02\\4.03\end{pmatrix}$
2. (i) $-20\mathbf{i}$
   (ii) $5.1\mathbf{i} + 0.6\mathbf{j} + 0.45\mathbf{k}$
   (iii) Fatima
3. (i) $\begin{pmatrix}3.76\\0.68\end{pmatrix}$ (ii) $\begin{pmatrix}7.66\\0.64\end{pmatrix}$ (iii) $\begin{pmatrix}u\cos\alpha\\0.8u\sin\alpha\end{pmatrix}$
4. (i) 1.58 Ns in **j** direction;
   (ii) 1.58 Ns in −**j** direction;
   (iii) 3.10 J
5. (i) 0.45 Ns in **j** direction
   (ii) 0.45 Ns in −**j** direction
   (iii) 0.512 J
6. (i) $mu\sin\alpha$ Ns
   (ii) $\frac{1}{2}mu^2 - \frac{1}{2}mu^2\cos^2\alpha = \frac{1}{2}mu^2\sin^2\alpha$
7. $\frac{1}{2}mu^2 - \frac{1}{2}mu^2\cos^2\alpha - \frac{1}{2}mu^2e^2\sin^2\alpha$
   $= \frac{1}{2}mu^2(1-e^2)\sin^2\alpha$
8. (i) Time of flight $= \dfrac{2u_y}{g}$; range $= \dfrac{2u_x u_y}{g}$
   (ii) 0.6 R
   (iii) $0.6^n \times R$ (iv) 2.38R
9. (i) $\begin{pmatrix}2.5\\-0.4\end{pmatrix}$
   (ii) 1.01 m (iii) 1.41 m
   (iv) 2.02×0.7^n (v) 7
10. (i) at 24.8° to cushion after first impact; at 60° to cushion after second impact
    (ii) 1.6 m s^{-1}
    (iii) at β to cushion with $\tan\beta = e\tan\alpha$, at $90° - \alpha$ to second cushion, speed is reduced by e^2.
11. (i) 2.38 m
    (ii) 0.65 m; 1.73 m
    (iii) 53°
12. (i) 8 m s^{-1} (ii) 1 m s^{-1}
    (iii) −42 Ns (iv) 0.214
13. (i) 3.5 m s^{-1} (ii) 3.19 m s^{-1} at 18.3° to the plane
    (iii) 0.52 J
14. (i) $\sqrt{\dfrac{2h}{g}}\left(\dfrac{1+e}{1-e}\right)$ (ii) $\sqrt{\dfrac{2h}{g}}\left(\dfrac{1+e}{1-e}\right)u$
15. (i) $\tan\theta = \dfrac{eu\cos\theta}{u\sin\theta} \Rightarrow \tan^2\theta = e = \dfrac{7}{25}$
    (ii) $(1-e^2)\cos^2\theta = \left[1 - \left(\dfrac{7}{25}\right)^2\right]\left(\dfrac{1}{1+\frac{7}{25}}\right) = \dfrac{18}{25}$
16. (i) 14 kg (ii) 280 N

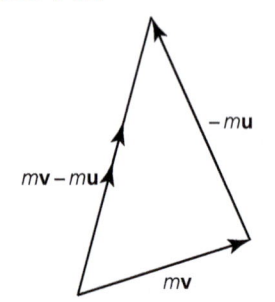

Exercise 14.2
1. 1.58 m s^{-1}, 3.16 m s^{-1}; 116.6°, 63.4°
2. $1.23u$, $0.4u$, 85°, 0°
3. $\frac{1}{4}u$, $\frac{5}{4}u$, 0°, 53°
4. $0.90u$, $0.90u$, 106.1°, 73.9°
5. 0.2
6. 80.5°
7. Loss in K.E. for direct impact $= mu^2(1-e^2)$
   Loss in K.E. in oblique impact $= \frac{3}{4}mu^2(1-e^2)$
8. (i) $\frac{1}{2}u$; u
   (ii) A: $1.80u$ at 74°; B: $u\sqrt{2}$ at 45°
   (iii) $\frac{1}{4}mu^2$
9. (i) [diagram: before and after collision of two balls, with u at angle α before, and $u\sin\alpha$, V after]
   Conservation of momentum $mu\cos\alpha = mV$

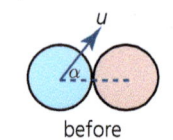

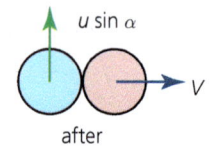

Newton's law of impact:
$V = eu\cos\alpha \Rightarrow e = 1$

(ii) Conservation of momentum:
$mu\cos\alpha = kmV$
Newton's law of impact:
$V = eu\cos\alpha \Rightarrow ke = 1$

(iii) The contact between the two discs is smooth.

10 (i) $2 \times [\frac{1}{2}mu^2(1-e^2)\cos^2\alpha]$

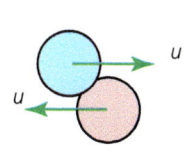

(ii)

before — u, u
after — $u/\sqrt{3}$, $u/\sqrt{3}$

11 (i) $U = 7.5$, $u = 3$
(ii) The contact is smooth.
(iii) $5\,\text{m s}^{-1}$

12 (i) (A) It is 6.38 cm off line and so does not go into the pocket.
(B) It is 1.89 cm off line and so goes into the pocket.
(ii) It is 2.69 cm off line and so does not go into the pocket.
(iii) $0.14°$ (to 2 sf)
(iv) A higher level of accuracy is required than is the case for a shot with a single impact. Any error in the original direction is increased in the second impact.

Practice questions: Set 2 (page 389)

1 (i) Two cases: $4g \pm 9.8 = \frac{4 \times 3.5^2}{a}$ giving $a = 1$ or $\frac{5}{3}$.

(ii) Must be at the bottom with the larger a.
Using conservation of energy, $v^2 = \frac{931}{12}$ so $v = 8.81\,\text{m s}^{-1}$ (3 s. f.)

2 (i) The ball hits the plane at 45°.
Let V be the speed immediately after the bounce and β the angle with the plane.
$V\cos\beta = U\cos 45°$ and $V\sin\beta = \frac{1}{\sqrt{3}}\sin 45°$
$\tan\beta = \frac{1}{\sqrt{3}}\tan 45° = \frac{1}{\sqrt{3}}$

So $\beta = 30°$ and so after the first bounce the ball leaves the plane horizontally.

(ii) After the bounce $Vt = 15\cos 30°$ and $\frac{1}{2}gt^2 = 15\sin 30°$

so $\frac{1}{2}g\left(\frac{15\cos 30°}{V}\right)^2 = 15\sin 30°$ and so $V = 10.5$

(iii) At P, conserving LM parallel to the plane gives $V\cos 30° = U\cos 45°$ (o.e.)
so $\frac{\sqrt{3}}{2}V = \frac{1}{\sqrt{2}}U$ and so $U = \sqrt{\frac{3}{2}}V$ (o.e.)
Working backwards, $U = 10.5\sqrt{\frac{3}{2}}$ (12.85…).

3 (i) $MLT^{-2} = [G] \times \frac{M \times M}{L^2}$ so $[G] = M^{-1}L^3T^{-2}$

(ii) [density] $= ML^{-3}$
LHS: MLT^{-2}
RHS: $(ML^{-3})(M^{-1}L^3T^{-2}) \times M \times L$
$= M^{1-1+1} \times L^{-3+3+1} \times T^{-2} = MLT^{-2}$

(iii) Straight line from origin to value at R then inverse square decay.

(iv) Newton's second law away from the centre of the Earth: $m\ddot{r} = -\frac{4}{3}\pi\rho Gmr$
so $\ddot{r} = -\frac{4}{3}\pi\rho Gr$ which is of the form $\ddot{r} = -\omega^2 r$ and so is SHM

(v) Period is $\frac{2\pi}{\omega}$ and
$\omega = \sqrt{\frac{4}{3}\pi \times 6.67 \times 10^{-11} \times 5500}$
so period is ≈ 5070 seconds (as units in SI). This is about $84 \approx 80$ minutes

4 (i) $V = \int_{a/2}^{a}(\pi y^2)dx = \pi\int_{a/2}^{a}(a^2-x^2)dx = \frac{5a^3\pi}{24}$

$\rho V\bar{x} = \rho\int_{a/2}^{a}(\pi xy^2)dx = \rho\pi\int_{a/2}^{a}(a^2 x - x^3)dx = \frac{9a^4\pi\rho}{64}$

so $\bar{x} = \frac{27a}{40}$. This is $\frac{27a}{40} - \frac{a}{2} = \frac{7a}{40}$ from the plane face.

(ii) $\left(M + \frac{27M}{40a}l\right)\bar{y} = -M \times \frac{7a}{40} + \frac{27M}{40a} \times \frac{l^2}{2}$ so
$\bar{y} = \frac{27l^2 - 14a^2}{2(40a + 27l)}$.

(iii) $l = 2a$ gives $\bar{y} = \frac{a}{2}$

(iv) When $l = 2a$ the shape will balance as the weight and normal reaction both go through G. If $l > 2a$, the c.o.m. will be nearer the top of the rod and so will have a moment about the point of contact and the shape will fall over.

5 (i) Maximum speed is when the object has zero acceleration.
Need first to find natural length, a.

Conservation of energy from top to bottom gives

$80 \times 10 = \frac{1}{2a} \times 50 \times (10-a)^2$ so

$32a = (10-a)^2$ and $a^2 - 52a + 100 = 0$.

This gives $a = 2$ or $a = 50$. Hence $a = 2$ in this scenario.

For zero acceleration tension in string equals weight of object so if this happens when extension is e, $80 = \frac{50}{2}e$ so $e = \frac{16}{5}$.

Conservation of energy from top to this extension gives

$80 \times \left(2 + \frac{16}{5}\right) = \frac{1}{2} \times \frac{80}{10} \times v^2 + \frac{1}{2} \times \frac{50}{2} \times \left(\frac{16}{5}\right)^2$

This gives $v^2 = 72$ and $v = 6\sqrt{2}$.

(ii) Elastic string obeys Hooke's law; Negligible air resistance; other answers possible

6 (i) $\mathbf{v} = (6t^2 - 6t)\mathbf{i} + 2(t-1)\mathbf{j}$; $\mathbf{v} = \mathbf{0}$ only when $t = 1$ as both components must be zero.

(ii) $(-3, 4)$, $(2, 1)$, $(1, 0)$, $(6, 1)$; arrows
Travelling in negative y direction but goes from positive x to negative x directions through instantaneous zero speed in x-direction at $t = 0$, [the point $(2, 1)$]
Comes instantaneously to rest at a cusp or equivalent.

Index

A

acceleration 2
  circular motion 230, 245–7, 264–5
  constant acceleration formulae 11–15, 190–2
  dimensional analysis 167
  magnitude of 188
  in more than one dimension 188–90
  relationship to position and velocity 223–4
  simple harmonic motion equation 306–8, 312–16
acceleration, variable 17–21
  dependent on position 218–20
  dependent on velocity 214–17
acceleration due to gravity 13–14, 199
acceleration–time graphs 3, 6
air resistance 214–15, 218
amplitude 298
angle of friction (λ) 65
angle of projection 202–3
angular frequency (ω) 306
angular speed (ω) 227–8
Archimedes of Syracuse 369
area, dimensional analysis 167
average speed 5
average velocity 5

B

banked tracks 236–40
bounding parabolas 203–4
braking force 28, 30
bungee jumping 267–8, 291
buoyancy force 29

C

centre of mass 148
  of composite bodies 150–1, 354–7
  of cones, spheres and hemispheres 354
  determination by integration 350–3
  key points 165, 370
  of one-dimensional bodies 148–50
  of plane regions 361–4
  of a triangle 157
  of two- and three-dimensional bodies 153–9, 350–7
centripetal force 232
centroid of a plane region 361
centroid of a triangle 157
circular motion
  angular speed 227–8
  banked tracks 236–40
  breakdown of 254–8
  conical pendulum 233–6
  with constant acceleration 245–7
  with constant speed 231
  forces required 232–3
  investigation of 253
  key points 265–6
  notation 227
  relationship to simple harmonic motion 318–20
  velocity and acceleration 230, 264–5
  vertical 248–53
coefficient of friction (μ) 59
coefficient of restitution (e) 139
collisions 131–5
  bodies moving in the same straight line 139–41
  elastic and inelastic 139
  impact with a fixed surface 139
  Newton's law of impact 138–41
  oblique impact of a sphere on a plane 375–7
  oblique impact of smooth elastic spheres 381–4
components of a vector 35–6
compression of springs 268
cones, centre of mass 158, 354
conical pendulums 233–6
conservation of mechanical energy 104–5, 110
conservation of momentum 131–5
conservative forces 104
constant acceleration formulae 11–15, 190–2
Coulomb, Charles Augustin de 65
  laws of friction 59
counterweights 70
couples 73–4

D

deceleration (retardation) 3
differential equations 215–20, 224
  second-order 321
  dimensional analysis 167–9
  finding the form of a relationship 172–4
  key points 180
dimensional consistency 171–2
dimensionless quantities 169
dimensions, method of 174
displacement 2, 187
  finding from velocity 19–21
  oscillating motion 298
  simple harmonic motion equation 306–8, 312–16
  from a velocity–time graph 5–6
dissipative forces 104
distance travelled 2
  in more than one dimension 187
  from a speed–time graph 5
distance–time graphs 4
driving force 28, 105–6

E

elastic potential energy 283–5
  key points 295
elasticity 268
  Hooke's law 269–71, 274–5
energy 101–2
  conservation of mechanical energy 104–5, 110
  elastic potential energy 283–5
  gravitational potential energy 109–12
  key points 125
  work-energy principle 102–3
equation of motion 29–31
equilibrium 42–6
  and moments 74–6
  sliding and toppling 93–6
explosions 135
extension of springs and strings 268
  Hooke's law 269–71, 274–5
  work and energy 282–5

F

falling objects 13–14
forces 26–8
  at an angle to the direction of motion 113
  and circular motion 232–3
  couples 73–4
  dimensional analysis 167
  dissipative and conservative 104
  driving and resistance 105–6
  equilibrium 42–6
  frictional 59–65
  impulse 127–9
  key points 56
  resolving into components 38–9
  resultant forces 34–5, 39–40, 50–4, 77–8
  sliding and toppling 93–6
  triangle of 42–4
  see also moments
Fourier, Jean-Baptiste Joseph 321
frequency (ν) 298
friction
  key points 69
  model for 59
  modelling with 60–5
  skid mark interpretation 58–60
  sliding and toppling 93–6
friction, coefficient of (μ) 59
frictional force (frictional contact force) 27, 110–11
  and travel around bends 238–40

G

graphs of motion 2–4
gravitational potential energy 109–12

gravity 26
  acceleration due to 13–14, 199

H

hemispheres, centre of mass 158–9, 354
hertz (Hz) 298
hinges 74–5
Hooke, Robert 276
Hooke's law 269–71
  key points 295
  with more than one spring or string 274–5

I

impact
  Newton's law of 138–41
  see also collisions
impact, oblique
  of smooth elastic spheres 381–4
  of a sphere on a plane 375–7
impact problems 132–5
impulse 127–9
  key points 146
  in more than one dimension 373–5
  oblique impact of a sphere on a plane 375–7
impulse–momentum equation 129
inclined planes, projectile motion on 207–12

J

Joule, James 113

k

kinetic energy 101–2
  work-energy principle 102–3

L

laminae, centre of mass 159, 361–4, 370
Lami's theorem 45
levers 77–8

M

magnitude of a vector 37–8
magnitude of acceleration 2
mechanical energy, conservation of 104–5, 110
method of dimensions 174
modelling terms 26
modulus of elasticity (λ) 270
moments 71–3
  and centre of mass 148–9
  conventions and units 73
  couples 73–4
  equilibrium 74–6
  of forces acting at an angle 83–6
  investigation of 82–3
  key points 99
  levers 77–8

momentum 101
  conservation of 131–5
  and impulse 127–9, 146
  in more than one dimension 373–5
motion
  equation of 29–31
  Newton's laws 28–9
  relationships between descriptive variables 223–4
  two-dimensional 113–14
motion, circular
  angular speed 227–8
  banked tracks 236–40
  breakdown of 254–8
  conical pendulums 233–6
  with constant acceleration 245–7
  with constant speed 231
  equation of 29–31
  forces required 232
  investigation of 253
  key points 265–6
  notation 227
  relationship to simple harmonic motion 318–20
  velocity and acceleration 230, 264–5
  vertical 248–53
motion, vertical
  circular 248–53
  involving elastic forces 288–91
motion in more than one dimension 113–14
  constant acceleration formulae 190–2
  equation of a path 195–7
  key points 223–4
  notation and vocabulary 186–90
  path of a projectile 199–204, 207–12
motion in one dimension 2–3
  average speed and average velocity 4–5
  constant acceleration formulae 11–15
  finding displacement from velocity 19–21
  finding distances and displacements 5–8
  finding velocity from acceleration 19–20
  key points 23–4
  notation and units 3
motion under variable acceleration 17–21
  acceleration dependent on position 218–20
  acceleration dependent on velocity 214–17
musical notes 298

N

natural length, strings and springs 268
newton (N) 172
Newton, Isaac 29
  law of impact 138–41
  laws of motion 28–9
normal reaction (normal contact force) 27
notation 3

O

oblique impact
  key points 388
  of smooth elastic spheres 381–4
  of a sphere on a plane 375–7
oscillating mechanical systems
  simple pendulum 326–9
  spring-mass oscillator 329–33
oscillating motion 297–8, 301–2
  mathematical model 299–301
  phase difference 306
  physical model 299
  see also simple harmonic motion

P

parameters 196
path, equation of 195–7
pendulums
  conical 233–6
  simple 326–9
period of oscillating motion 298
phase difference 306
position 2, 186
  acceleration dependent on 218–20
  relationship to velocity and acceleration 223–4
position vectors 36
  in more than one dimension 186, 188
position–time graphs 2, 4, 7–8
potential energy 101
  elastic 283–5, 295
  gravitational 109–12
power 118–21
  key points 125
projectile motion 199–201
  angle of projection 202–3
  bounding parabolas 203–4
  key points 224
  on a uniform slope 207–12
pyramids, centre of mass 158
Pythagoras 298

R

resistive force 28, 30, 105–6
restitution, coefficient of (e) 139
resultant forces 34–5, 39–40, 50–4, 77–8
rigid body model 72
rough surfaces 60

S

scalars 2
semicircular lamina, centre of mass 159
S.I. units 3
simple harmonic motion (SHM) 300–1
  choosing the most appropriate function 316–18
  as a function of time 304–5
  general form 305–6
  key points 339

Index

relationship to circular motion 318–20
simple pendulum 326–9
spring-mass oscillator 329–33
simple harmonic motion equations 306–8
  alternative forms 312–16
  solution as second-order differential equations 321
skid mark interpretation 58–60
sliding 59, 93–6
smooth surfaces 60
solids of revolution 324
speed 2, 223
  angular 227–8
  average 5
  changing units of 5
  dimensional analysis 168
  in more than one dimension 187, 188–90
speed–time graphs 4, 7
spheres
  centre of mass 354
  oblique impact of 381–4
  oblique impact with a plane 375–7
  volume of 344–5
spring-mass oscillator 329–33
springs and strings
  bungee jumping 267–8, 291
  Hooke's law 269–71, 274–5
  investigation of 269
  key points 295
  vertical motion 288–91
  work and energy 282–5
stiffness of a spring 270, 271
strings and springs 268
suvat equations 12

T

tension 26–7, 31
  in springs and strings 268, 270
terminal velocity 173
thrust 26–7
  of springs and strings 268, 270
toppling 93–6
trajectories
  equation of 195–7
  path of a projectile 199–204
triangle of forces 42–4
triangles, centre of mass 157

U

unit vectors 38
units 3, 173–4
  changes of 170
  of moments 73
  of speed 5

V

vectors 2
  addition of 34
  components of 35–6
  direction of 37–8
  magnitude of 37–8, 191
  notation and representation 34
  position vectors 36, 186
  resultant forces 34–5, 39–40, 50–4
  scalar product of 191
  between two points 36–7
  unit vectors 38
velocity 2
velocity, acceleration dependent on 214–17
  average 5
  circular motion 230, 264–5
  finding from acceleration 19–20
  in more than one dimension 187, 188
  relationship to position and acceleration 223–4
  simple harmonic motion equation 306–8, 312–16
  variable 17–19
velocity–time graphs 2, 4, 6
vertical circles, motion in 248–53, 255–8, 266
vertical motion involving elastic forces 288–91
volume, dimensional analysis 168
volume of a sphere 344–5
volumes of revolution 342–3
  about the x-axis 343–5
  about the y-axis 345–6
  key points 370

W

watt (W) 118
Watt, James 120
weight 26
work 101–2, 104–6
  forces at an angle to the direction of motion 113
  key points 125
  stretching springs 282–3
work-energy principle 102–3

Y

Young's modulus (E) 270